American Foreign Policy Since World War II

American Foreign Policy Since World War II

SEVENTEENTH EDITION

STEVEN W. HOOK
Kent State University

JOHN SPANIER
University of Florida

CQ PRESS

A DIVISION OF CONGRESSIONAL QUARTERLY INC.
WASHINGTON, D.C.

CQ Press
1255 22nd St., NW, Suite 400
Washington, DC 20037

Phone: 202-729-1900; toll-free, 1-866-427-7737 (1-866-4CQ-PRESS)

Web: www.cqpress.com

Cover design: Auburn Associates, Inc., Baltimore, Maryland
Interior and map design: Kachergis Book Design, Pittsboro, North Carolina
Map on page 336: Laris Karklis; maps on pages 155, 267, 353: International Mapping Associates
Composition: Judy Myers

♾ The paper used in this publication exceeds the requirements of the American National Standard for Information Sciences—Permanence of Paper for Printed Library Materials, ANSI Z39.48-1992.

Printed and bound in the United States of America

10 09 08 07 06 1 2 3 4 5

Library of Congress Cataloging-in-Publication Data

Hook, Steven W.
American foreign policy since World War II / Steven W. Hook, John Spanier.—17th ed.
p. cm.
Includes bibliographical references and index.
ISBN 1-933116-71-4 (alk. paper)
1. United States—Foreign relations—1945–1989. 2. United States—Foreign relations—1989– . I. Spanier, John W. II. Title.
E744.H646 2007
327.73009'045—dc22

2006020516

To our students, near and far

Contents

Maps, Tables, Figures, and Boxes

Maps

Tables

Figures

Boxes

Preface

More than five years after the terrorist attacks of September 11, 2001, the United States remains engaged in an open-ended "war on terrorism" with no foreseeable endpoint. American troops are involved in protracted state-building missions in Iraq and Afghanistan, where more than 2,500 U.S. troops have died and more than 20,000 have been wounded. The nation's military spending, more than $1 trillion collectively in 2005 and 2006, has surpassed that of the rest of the world combined. As the only world power that has divided the globe into regional military commands, the United States has literally left no territory beyond its sphere of influence. Yet in waging this unconventional war, the nation remains insecure as political leaders openly anticipate another attack on the homeland.

Perhaps this insecurity is the inevitable burden of being the world's lone superpower, whose predominance naturally provokes resentment from weaker states. Also, perhaps, the precarious nature of America's world power owes much to the character of its own government and society. The very openness and fragmentation of American government increases the nation's vulnerability to an invisible and stateless enemy. Unfamiliarity with foreign peoples, a by-product of the nation's geographic insulation, characterizes U.S. civil society as well, leading policy makers to misread ethnic and cultural dynamics overseas and to underestimate the depths of mass attitudes that are hostile toward the West. No less important, as the world's foremost trading state, the United States is identified with the dark side of globalization as well as its blessings.

Amid all these tensions, American leaders will face monumental choices in the days and years to come. How should they respond to the many military, economic, and political challenges facing the United States? What options should they consider in pursuing national interests in the volatile, rapidly changing world around them? Will they adapt to a new form of warfare—low-intensity and long-term *asymmetric* conflict—that runs counter to the nation's tradition of large-scale conventional war followed by a return to peaceful "normalcy"? And how effectively can American leaders convert the lessons of their historical experience into foreign policies that reflect their proclaimed values? These are the central questions to be explored in this new edition of *American Foreign Policy Since World War II.*

In keeping with previous editions, our focus in this volume is on the *conduct* of American foreign policy rather than its *formulation*, the focal point of most textbooks. Detailed knowledge of the policy-making process, including legal and institutional restraints and standard operating procedures, is clearly essential for all students of foreign policy. Yet only by exploring America's past actions in the global arena and only by searching for historical precedents and patterns can students fully grasp the dilemmas facing the United States today. Through this process of historical reflection, students become better equipped to evaluate the performance of current leaders and to weigh the prospects of Washington's attempts to confront Iraqi insurgents, ease unrest in Latin America, reduce extreme poverty in Africa, and meet the challenges to American primacy being posed by China, Russia, and members of the European Union.

This search for historical lessons is a perpetual one that is notoriously elusive and fraught with conflicting judgments. Ignoring such lessons, however, tempts far greater perils. "When the past no longer illuminates the future, the spirit walks in darkness," observed Alexis de Tocqueville, the French political theorist and author of *Democracy in America*. The Spanish-born American philosopher George Santayana put it a bit differently: "A country without memory is a country of madmen." Such insights inspired and sustain this volume's inquiry into American foreign policy, which was first published in 1961 and raised similar questions during the height of the Cold War.

A National Style Evolving

As described in the pages that follow, the United States has long approached world politics with a peculiar national style that reflects the inescapable demands posed by the interstate system along with the nation's geographical position and abundant natural resources. Historical analysis reveals how American foreign policy has been further shaped by long-standing cultural values and their impact on the nation's identity and definitions of friends and enemies. Political culture, a "historically transmitted pattern of meanings," is commonly expressed through popular conceptions of national identity.[1] Public policies, both foreign and domestic, are natural outgrowths of these collective attitudes and beliefs.[2]

Underlying American foreign policy is the tension between the anarchic and conflict-prone international system and the normative values

1. Clifford Geertz, *The Interpretation of Cultures: Selected Essays* (New York: Basic Books, 1973), 89.

2. Charles Lockhart, *The Roots of American Exceptionalism: Institutions, Culture, and Policies* (New York: Palgrave Macmillan, 2003).

widely held by Americans on individual liberty, representative government, free markets, and national self-determination. Driven by these values, American foreign policy evolved into a moral campaign aimed not simply at protecting the nation's interests but also at saving the self-destructive interstate system from itself. The two goals were commonly regarded as inseparable: a more democratic world, it was assumed, would be more peaceful, and only in such a world would the United States be truly secure. This moralistic approach was epitomized by Ronald Reagan's depiction of the Soviet Union as an "evil empire" in the 1980s. The 2001 terrorist attacks reinforced the nation's tendency to view world politics as a clash between good and evil.

America's peculiar approach to foreign policy is also expressed in alternating impulses by national leaders to detach the United States from global diplomacy and to remake the world in America's image. Detachment in this context is not synonymous with *isolation,* a term that means complete noninvolvement with the outside world and is frequently (and erroneously) used to define early American foreign policy. Rather, detachment refers to a pervasive sense that the United States should be actively engaged in global commerce but have "as little political connection as possible" with other countries—the stance recommended by President George Washington in his Farewell Address. Today, such detachment takes several forms, including the government's penchant for unilateral action and selective regard for intergovernmental agreements and organizations. Across civil society, this sense of detachment is reflected in primary school systems that neglect world history and geography, in public misperceptions of global issues, and in a commercial news media that has reduced coverage of global issues even as the United States has assumed unprecedented stature across the globe.

For all of its historic consistency, the Bush Doctrine's call in September 2002 for extended American primacy marked a radical shift in one vital respect. After World War II, the United States reassured its allies and neutral states by embedding its overwhelming power in a "constitutional" world order.[3] But by the 1990s, many in Washington were convinced that the key features of this order—international organizations, laws, and agreements—were increasingly posing a threat to U.S. sovereignty. The solution chosen by the second Bush administration was to spurn these arrangements and go it alone or with ad hoc "coalitions of the willing." In place of the constitutional order, the United States would create a hegemonic order based on the nation's values but ultimately sustained by its vast military power. Through different means, then, the

3. For an elaboration, see G. John Ikenberry, *After Victory: Institutions, Strategic Restraint, and the Rebuilding of Order after Major Wars* (Princeton, N.J.: Princeton University Press, 2001).

desired end remained: a stable world of democratic states busily engaged in economic, not military, competition. Such a world order, if realized, would represent the fulfillment of America's self-appointed mission.

Despite its position of global predominance, the United States faces a variety of challenges today. Military superiority has not allowed the U.S. government to impose its will, and political system, on highly resistant Afghan and Iraqi societies. Nor has military superiority led to the capitulation of al Qaeda or to the renouncement by Islamic religious leaders of continued anti-American terrorist attacks. Elections in the Palestinian territories, far from elevating moderate leaders to power, were won instead by Hamas, a terrorist group sworn to the destruction of Israel, an American ally. The war on terrorism, combined with sweeping tax cuts and the enormous domestic costs associated with Hurricane Katrina, has produced massive U.S. budget deficits and foreign borrowing. Other economic problems confront the United States as well, including a chronic trade deficit and the loss of manufacturing jobs to developing countries. Meanwhile, spiraling oil prices have eroded the spending power of American consumers while revealing the consequences of U.S. dependence on foreign energy sources.

Most disabling is the erosion of the nation's moral authority, a primary asset during its ascension as a great power. While justified as a legitimate act of self-defense, the preventive U.S. invasion of Iraq in 2003 ruptured the post–World War II constitutional world order. The failure to find weapons of mass destruction further undermined the mission's legitimacy, as did the subsequent abuse of Iraqi detainees at Abu Ghraib prison and the reports of civilian massacres in Iraq and Afghanistan. Building democracy in Iraq, the adopted war rationale that aligned with America's sense of moral mission, bogged down in the midst of a burgeoning insurgency. Democratizing efforts were not helped by the fact that the U.S. government had largely absented itself from diplomatic circles in other areas of world politics.

Taken together, these problems will demand thoughtful and creative responses by American foreign policy makers. Most fundamentally, the United States must recognize its own limitations, not measured as economic output or military spending, but in terms of the values that have always guided the nation. As political scientist Samuel Huntington observed long ago, the central elements of the "American Creed"—liberty, equality, individualism, democracy, and the rule of law—are difficult to reconcile in a complex modern state, let alone one that has attained global primacy. When leaders fail to live up to these values, periods of "creedal passion" follow that are characterized by public cynicism, bitter political conflict, and strenuous efforts by reformers to "return to first principles." Such passions erupted in the Vietnam era, when "Americans embarked on crusades against the CIA, the FBI, defense spending, the use of military force abroad, the military-industrial complex, and the imperial Presidency, attempting to expose, weaken, dismantle, or abolish the institutions that protected their liberal society against foreign threats."[4]

The similarities to the current period are inescapable as the actions of U.S. leaders have exposed again what some observers see as a gap between the nation's principles and practices. Although the government's assertion of power is costly at home and abroad, some comfort can be drawn from recent returns to first principles. Constitutional checks have fostered restraint and accountability in some cases. The Supreme Court asserted the rights of unlawful combatants, for example, and Congress conducted thorough and often damning inquiries into the causes of the September 11 attacks, intelligence failures prior to the Iraq invasion, and the lack of improvements in homeland security. Recent opinion surveys have registered widespread public disfavor with unilateral military interventionism and broad public support for America's return to the international community.[5] Finally, individuals have retained their capacity to shape policy debates. Although Cindy Sheehan, whose son was killed in Iraq, was not able to alter the course of Bush's war strategy by holding a vigil outside his ranch in 2005, her actions rallied other citizens to make their voices heard.

Still, the United States has not yet experienced an antiwar movement comparable to that of the Vietnam era. Reports of domestic spying, secret overseas prisons, and a mounting death toll in Iraq and Afghanistan have yet to spark large-scale public protests. Rather than issues of war and peace, the nation's attention early in 2006 focused on two *intermestic* issues: illegal immigration, primarily across the Mexican border, and gasoline prices at more than $3 a gallon. Both issues figured more prominently in the year's congressional campaigns than the war on terrorism, and in most races domestic rather than foreign policy issues dominated political debates and press coverage. All of this may seem unusual for the world's preponderant power, but such patterns of behavior are entirely consistent with the American style of foreign policy.

4. Samuel Huntington, *American Politics: The Promise of Disharmony* (Cambridge, Mass.: Harvard University Press, 1981), 238.

5. Overseas opinion surveys are generally more critical of the United States and reveal growing disfavor with the attitudes and lifestyles of American citizens. See Andrew Kohut and Bruce Stokes, *America against the World: How We Are Different and Why We Are Disliked* (New York: Times Books, 2006). Also see Julia E. Sweig, *Friendly Fire: Losing Friends and Making Enemies in the Anti-American Century* (New York: Public Affairs, 2006).

This Edition's Outline and Refinements

Several steps have been taken to make this edition of *American Foreign Policy Since World War II* more useful. After the first chapter introduces the book's analytic framework, Chapters 2–8 examine the Cold War from President Harry S. Truman's adoption of the containment doctrine through the Soviet Union's collapse in 1991. The final six chapters are devoted to the years following the Cold War. Chapters 9–11 review the first decade of this period, during which widespread optimism about the "new world order" gave way to renewed struggles overseas and debates at home about the American grand strategy. Chapter 12 recounts the terrorist attacks of September 2001 and the adoption of the Bush Doctrine. The U.S.-led wars in Afghanistan and Iraq are detailed in Chapter 13, and the final chapter examines other unresolved foreign policy problems, including the imminent nuclear breakout of North Korea and Iran and economic upheavals from East Asia to South America. The book concludes with an examination of various international orders that have existed throughout American history and an assessment of the hegemonic order the United States seeks to create in the twenty-first century.

Our narrative is complemented by features designed to engage our readers and ensure comprehensive coverage. Throughout the text, readers are introduced to important figures at home and abroad who exerted extraordinary "impact and influence" during each period described. Graphics scattered within the chapters highlight important national and global trends. The first of the two appendixes identifies the most influential foreign policy makers in U.S. administrations since World War II, and the second provides a chronology of important developments in world politics throughout the period under study. A detailed bibliography is also featured at the end of the book, with an emphasis on recent books that elaborate on the problems and debates covered in the text. A list of Web sites of interest to students of foreign policy follows.

All these features are designed to stimulate informed, critical thinking during this epochal period in American history. The immense potential of the United States to transform the world beyond its shores was recognized during its infancy. Georg W. Hegel (1770–1831), the German philosopher, described the United States of the early nineteenth century as "the land of the future, where, in the ages that lie before us, the burden of the World's History shall reveal itself." This vision of the nation's historic potential has now been realized, and the decisions made in Washington reverberate daily in all societies. With the stakes for global security never higher, informed scrutiny of American foreign policy, past and present, is itself a vital national interest.

Acknowledgments

Preparing this new edition amid the profound and rapidly changing developments in American foreign policy posed a tremendous challenge to all involved. First, we wish to express our gratitude to the external reviewers who provided invaluable guidance throughout the editions of this text. For this edition, we owe great thanks to Vicki Clarke of Northern Illinois University; Robert Hager of California State University, Dominquez Hills; and Richard Nolan of the University of Florida. As in the past, we are grateful to the entire editorial and production team at CQ Press. Brenda Carter and Charisse Kiino again demonstrated their enduring commitment to this project by providing the resources and expertise necessary to maintain its quality. Freelancer Sabra Bissette Ledent edited the manuscript skillfully, Talia Greenberg managed the book's composition and graphic presentation with great care, and Anne Stewart did a superb job on the photo research. We are also indebted to our research assistants, particularly Xiaoyu Pu and Gabriella Paar-Jakli. As always, the most helpful guidance for this new edition came from the students who have read and used the book and freely shared their impressions about its strengths and weaknesses. We hope to continue this tradition by inviting responses to the new edition via shook@kent.edu.

American Foreign Policy
Since World War II

CHAPTER ONE

The American Approach to Foreign Policy

With his left hand on the bible, President George W. Bush takes the oath of office that begins his second term as president in January 2005. A born-again Christian, Bush frequently invoked biblical phrases and images to support his far-reaching goals in American foreign policy.

President George W. Bush strode across a makeshift stage just before noon on January 20, 2005, to take the oath of office for his second term. The newly reelected president stood beside his wife, Laura, on that cold morning and scanned the sea of government officials, foreign dignitaries, and more than 100,000 citizens assembled on the grounds of the U.S. Capitol. After taking the oath, Bush addressed the crowd along with millions of television viewers. He did not take long to make his point:

> The survival of liberty in our land increasingly depends on the success of liberty in other lands. The best hope for peace in our world is the expansion of freedom in all the world. . . . Advancing these ideals is the mission that created our Nation. It is the honorable achievement of our fathers. Now it is the urgent requirement of our nation's security, and the calling of our

> time. So it is the policy of the United States to seek and support the growth of democratic movements and institutions in every nation and culture, with the ultimate goal of ending tyranny in our world.[1]

Such soaring rhetoric is not uncommon to presidential inaugurations, and not unusual for Bush, who frequently casts American foreign policy in biblical terms. But this time around the ambitious tone of his speech contrasted sharply with deepening troubles for the United States overseas and growing anxieties at home. In early 2005, the United States remained mired in wars in Afghanistan and Iraq with no end of military involvement in sight. Meanwhile, Osama bin Laden, the mastermind of the September 2001 terrorist attacks on New York City's World Trade Center and the Pentagon in Washington, remained at large. Further complicating matters, the White House was forced into tense negotiations with North Korea and Iran, two members of Bush's "axis of evil" that seemed bent on becoming nuclear powers.

The state of the Union only worsened as Bush's second term progressed. In August 2005, Hurricane Katrina ravaged the Gulf Coast and crippled the city of New Orleans. American motorists then took a hit financially as gasoline prices soared to more than $3 a gallon, in part because of damaged refineries in the Gulf of Mexico. The federal government, already running a budget deficit of more than $400 billion, now faced the additional costs of relief and reconstruction. The nation's trade deficit also reached record levels, and in many cities the steady loss of manufacturing jobs produced a growing underclass with nowhere to turn. Further setting the nation on edge, in December members of a bipartisan commission on the September 11 attacks released a follow-up report that found the United States little more prepared for terrorist attacks than it was four years earlier.[2]

All these problems tarnished the stature of the United States as the world's predominant power. Not so long ago, in 1991, the nation had emerged victorious after nearly a half-century of waging the Cold War with the Soviet Union. For many, the outcome of the conflict affirmed not only America's predominance in world politics, but also the superiority of its political and economic system. The combination of individual liberty and free enterprise proved far more effective in meeting societal needs than Moscow's one-party government and state-owned industries. Having crushed the fascist regimes in Germany and Japan in

1. White House, "President Bush Sworn-In to Second Term," January 20, 2005, http://www.whitehouse.gov/news/releases/2005/01/print/20050120-1.html (accessed February 10, 2006).

2. 9/11 Public Discourse Project, "Final Report on 9/11 Commission Recommendations," December 5, 2005, http://www.9-11pdp.org (accessed April 6, 2006). The report included "grades" on thirty-nine measures of improved security, which, when averaged along a four-point academic scale, came to a 1.75, or C+.

World War II and facing no imminent threats from the other great powers, the American model seemed to resolve once and for all the timeless debates about what constituted the superior means of organizing states and societies. As one scholar declared, "What we may be witnessing is not just the end of the Cold War, or the passing of a particular period of history, but the end of history as such; that is, the end point of mankind's ideological evolution and the universalization of Western liberal democracy as the final form of human government."[3] Francis Fukuyama's triumphant statement was accepted as conventional wisdom by many Americans, who conceived of the "new world order" as the United States *writ large.* Their perceptions were reinforced by news of rapid democratic and market reforms in the post-Soviet states, of peaceful transitions of power in Latin America, and of dynamic, export-led economic growth in East Asia. No, the "American Century" did not begin in 1941 as *Time* magazine publisher Henry Luce had proclaimed. Its moment came a half-century later, on Christmas Day 1991, when the Soviet flag finally came down in Red Square.

As in the aftermath of World Wars I and II, however, winning the peace proved difficult for the United States. Smoldering ethnic and religious conflicts reignited in many regions, and humanitarian disasters in "failed states" prompted the deployment of American troops and United Nations (UN) peacekeepers. At home, political leaders could not agree on a defense strategy to replace communist containment, the doctrine that had linked all administrations from Harry S. Truman to George H. W. Bush. Unable to reach consensus, Washington went in every direction at once. President Bill Clinton declared the "enlargement" of democratic rule his priority and pledged to "engage" friends, foes, and a wide range of international institutions. Meanwhile, Congress froze U.S. dues payments to the UN, slashed foreign aid, and blocked a variety of international agreements. The United States intervened in Somalia, Haiti, and the former Yugoslavia, but not in Rwanda and Burundi, sites of the most horrific outbreaks of genocide since World War II. Nor did the United States take action to prevent the Arab leaders of Sudan from slaughtering their black citizens in the southern region.

For its part, the general public showed little interest in foreign affairs. Most Americans knew little about the civil wars and regional conflicts overseas. And when they supported military intervention, they had zero tolerance for American casualties. Repeated terrorist attacks during the 1990s on U.S. targets, including the World Trade Center in February 1993, did not arouse much public concern or provoke strong countermeasures. Domestic controversies, including the marital infidelities of

3. Francis Fukuyama, "The End of History?" *National Interest* (summer 1989): 4.

President Clinton, dominated press coverage and preoccupied the White House and Congress. The terrorist threat, it seemed, could be put off for another day. The United States could stand up to any other world power, let alone a motley crew of terrorists.[4]

The haphazard course of American foreign policy in the Clinton years perplexed foreign governments, which looked to the United States to exercise the global leadership it had assumed after World War II and maintained after the Cold War. Instead, political leaders bickered over the nation's future course. While the president preached the gospel of global engagement, most members of Congress turned away from the "constitutional" world order that their predecessors helped to create in the postwar era.[5] By century's end, the United States was the "lonely superpower . . . with one or a few partners, opposing most of the rest of the world's states and peoples." [6] The estrangement of the United States intensified after Bush took office in January 2001. The president rejected the Kyoto Protocol on Climate Change, renounced the Antiballistic Missile (ABM) Treaty with Russia, and shunned the International Criminal Court (ICC). Bush's defiant approach to foreign affairs was most clearly demonstrated in March 2003 when, alleging Saddam Hussein's weapons stockpiles and links to Islamic terrorism, he ordered an invasion of Iraq without support from the UN or most U.S. allies. The diplomatic isolation of the United States continued in Bush's second term. As of 2006, only two countries had not ratified the UN Convention on the Rights of the Child: the United States and the "failed state" of Somalia, whose government was barely equipped to conduct routine diplomacy.

Bush was not the first president to resist multilateral commitments. Indeed, in the eighteenth and nineteenth centuries American leaders consistently adopted a go-it-alone foreign policy.[7] Of particular concern at the nation's founding were the monarchies and feudal societies of Europe that were engaged in unending spasms of political violence. "Europe has a set of primary interests which to us have none or a very remote relation. Hence she must be engaged in frequent controversies, the causes of which are essentially foreign to our concerns," President George Washington observed in his 1796 Farewell Address. "Our detached and distant situa-

4. When asked to identify the biggest foreign policy problems facing the United States in 1999, respondents in a national survey most often replied, "Don't know." John E. Rielly, ed., *American Public Opinion and U.S. Foreign Policy 1999* (Chicago: Council on Foreign Relations, 1999), 11.

5. G. John Ikenberry, *After Victory: Institutions, Strategic Restraint, and the Rebuilding of Order after Major Wars* (Ithaca, N.Y.: Cornell University Press, 2001).

6. Samuel Huntington, "The Lonely Superpower," *Foreign Affairs* 78 (March–April 1999): 41.

7. John Lewis Gaddis, *Surprise, Security, and the American Experience* (Cambridge, Mass.: Harvard University Press, 2004).

tion invites and enables us to pursue a different course." Washington's successors followed his advice, expanding westward without assistance and avoiding peacetime military alliances for more than 150 years.

Bush was also not alone in favoring a more muscular approach to the world at the dawn of the twenty-first century. His top aides believed the United States should exploit its hard-won primacy by remaking the world in America's image, by force if necessary. Both the containment and détente policies of the Cold War, and Bill Clinton's engagement policy in the 1990s, were dismissed as too passive by the neoconservatives, or the "Vulcans," as some called them.[8] Bush, with little foreign policy experience before entering office, found the Vulcans' dogmatic approach compatible with his own worldview, which was shaped by his experience as a born-again Christian. The Bush Doctrine, which took form after the September 11 attacks, was based on the indefinite extension of American primacy. "Our forces will be strong enough to dissuade potential adversaries from pursuing a military build-up in hopes of surpassing, or equaling, the power of the United States," Bush declared in 2002.[9] The United States would form ad hoc coalitions of states rather than depend on the UN and other intergovernmental organizations to pursue its goals. And the United States would strike first, or *preemptively,* to thwart attacks on the United States or its allies.

Anti-American sentiments, voiced even in the friendly capitals of Europe, were put aside in the immediate aftermath of the September 11 attacks by al Qaeda terrorists. Al Qaeda, led by Osama bin Laden, espoused a radical brand of Islamic militarism that threatened all industrialized nations. But goodwill toward the United States quickly dissipated as Bush's counter-offensive shifted from eliminating al Qaeda's training camps, along with the extremist Taliban government, in Afghanistan to invading Iraq and overthrowing Saddam Hussein. A December 2002 survey found that the United States lost public support in nineteen of twenty-seven countries surveyed since 2000.[10] In a variety of subsequent polls taken overseas, most respondents identified the United States as the primary threat to world peace.[11] By the time Bush

8. See James Mann, *Rise of the Vulcans: The History of Bush's War Cabinet* (New York: Viking, 2004); and Stefan Halper and Jonathan Clarke, *America Alone: The Neo-Conservatives and the Global Order* (New York: Cambridge University Press, 2004).

9. George W. Bush, "The National Security Strategy of the United States of America," September 2002, http://www.whitehouse.gov/nsc/nss.html (accessed February 10, 2006).

10. Pew Research Center for the People and the Press, "What the World Thinks in 2002," December 4, 2002, http://people-press.org/reports/display.php3?ReportID=165 (accessed February 10, 2006).

11. Glenn Kessler and Mike Allen, "Bush Faces Increasingly Poor Image Overseas," *Washington Post,* February 24, 2003, A1; Pew Research Center, *Trends 2005* (Washington, D.C.: Pew Research Center, 2005), chap. 7, http://pewresearch.org/reports/?ReportID=6 (accessed April 6, 2006).

delivered his second inaugural address in 2005, a majority of citizens in sixteen of twenty-one countries surveyed found his reelection to be "negative for peace and security in the world." [12]

All these developments raise profound questions about the present status and future course of American foreign policy. Is the United States, with all of its wealth and firepower, truly secure today? How should the nation manage the global primacy it has long identified as its destiny? Should the nation go it alone in world politics or embrace the international community? More generally, should the U.S. government be primarily concerned with advancing national interests or with seeking solutions to global problems? Should the United States act as global policeman, or, in the skeptical words of Secretary of State John Quincy Adams, should the United States "go abroad in search of monsters to destroy"?

Learning from Experience

Coming to terms with these questions begins with the proposition that American citizens and their leaders, like those in other countries, have a unique perspective of the world beyond their national borders. Many factors affect how governments conduct foreign policy, including the pressures imposed by the international system, the demands of civil society, and the structure of political institutions. Taking into account such factors, along with shared historical experiences, each government adopts a distinctive approach to world politics. National "styles" of foreign policy vary considerably, but all governments exhibit distinctive patterns of behavior as they strive to make sense of developments around them in the turbulent, often threatening interstate system.[13]

Because for most of its existence the United States detached itself politically and militarily from the European powers, its national style was molded by its domestic experiences and cultural traditions more than that of other major powers. Such detachment permitted the United States to consolidate its system of government, develop an advanced market economy, and expand its territory across North America. Yet the nation found this detachment impossible to sustain once it emerged as a great power early in the twentieth century and played a decisive role in the two world wars. Still, Americans felt largely insulated from the perils of the "outside world," a sentiment that persisted into the new millennium.

This book explores how America's national style has influenced its conduct of foreign policy—that is, how the ambivalent attitude of many

12. BBC World Service, "Global Poll Slams Bush Leadership," January 19, 2005, http://news.bbc.co.uk/1/hi/world/americas/4185205.stm (accessed February 10, 2006).

13. Robert Dallek, *The American Style of Foreign Policy: Cultural Politics and Foreign Affairs* (New York: Oxford University Press, 1989).

Americans (a sort of love-hate relationship with the outside world) reflects historical patterns established long before the United States became a global superpower. The early chapters examine how America's approach to foreign affairs contributed to its victory over the Soviet Union in the Cold War. Later chapters consider the U.S. government's efforts to consolidate the nation's predominant world role after the Cold War and to adapt to the more complex international system of the twenty-first century. Of particular concern in the final chapters is the U.S. response to the terrorist attacks of September 2001, whose consequences will be felt for generations to come. The study concludes by addressing other challenges facing the United States and considering the impact of recent American actions on the nation's future and that of the global balance of power.

The Volatile State System

American foreign policy since World War II is largely the story of the tension between the interstate system and the nation's political culture. Both the monumental achievements of the United States and its failures can be attributed to this uneasy relationship. In the anarchic nation-state system that came into place a century before America's independence, each state must ultimately depend on itself for its preservation and safety. Heads of state in such a system tend to regard their counterparts as potential competitors, and it does not take much for one state to arouse another's suspicions and to stimulate reciprocal images of hostility. This turbulent global context, however, has historically been alien to many Americans, who have felt free of overseas pressures and secure in their own system of government and civil society. Although such aloofness was possible during the nation's formative years, it proved more difficult to sustain after the United States emerged as a major world power in the twentieth century. Still, American foreign policy continued to reflect the cultural attitudes and beliefs that prevailed earlier. The experience of the United States today can be traced in large measure to these persistent cultural influences.

The Shifting Balance of Power

In view of this "security dilemma" and in the absence of a world government, a balance of power among the strongest states is required to maintain peace. During the nineteenth century, the United States was able to enjoy an unprecedented degree of security because a balance of power, created at the Congress of Vienna in 1815, existed on the European continent and was effectively maintained by Britain together with

Austria, France, and Russia. The Concert of Europe, devised to implement the decisions of the Congress of Vienna, imposed a rare degree of stability on Europe. It also allowed the United States to fulfill President Washington's pledge to avoid "permanent alliances."

That balance was shattered, however, by Germany's unification in 1871 and the subsequent demise of several European empires, which forced the United States to play a pivotal role as a great power. The growing strength of Germany hastened the decline of Britain's power. With the collapse of czarist Russia in 1917 and the transfer of almost two million German soldiers from the Russian to the western front, a German victory in World War I became a distinct possibility. The United States would then have faced a Germany astride an entire continent, dominating European Russia and, in alliance with Austria-Hungary and perhaps the Ottoman Empire, extending German influence into the Balkans and the Middle East. It was at that point that Germany's unrestricted submarine warfare, which included attacks on American shipping, led to a U.S. declaration of war. With America's entry into the conflict, the Allies were able to contain and ultimately crush Germany's imperial ambitions.

After its victory, the United States retreated into its hemispheric shell, but only after a failed attempt by President Woodrow Wilson to make the world "safe for democracy." In his famous Fourteen Points speech delivered in January 1918, Wilson called for all countries to reduce arms, end colonialism, refrain from secret diplomacy, respect freedom of the seas, and take other steps to establish trust and goodwill. In addition, Wilson proposed that a League of Nations be established to prevent future wars through a system of collective security. Under this system, member countries would agree to defend any nation that had been invaded. Given such a deterrent, foreign aggression would presumably never be contemplated. The son of a Presbyterian minister, Wilson was so convinced of the righteousness of his cause that he personally represented the United States at the Paris Peace Conference. Almost singlehandedly, Wilson persuaded European leaders to sign the Treaty of Versailles, which ended the war, and to join the League of Nations. Upon returning from France, Wilson proclaimed victory and declared that "America is the hope of the world."

In seeking to transform world politics, however, Wilson forgot about American politics, particularly the role of Congress in ratifying treaties. Senate leaders felt snubbed by Wilson, who had excluded them from the peace conference. More important, they questioned whether the League would undermine the nation's sovereignty by forcing the United States to deploy troops overseas even when its own vital interests were not at stake. The Senate therefore rejected the treaty, and the United States never joined the League.

IMPACT AND INFLUENCE

WOODROW WILSON

The American style of foreign policy was personified nearly a century ago by President Woodrow Wilson (left). Wilson, the son of a Presbyterian minister, often described world politics as a struggle between good and evil. The United States, he believed, had a moral responsibility not merely to promote its own self-interests, but also to free the interstate system from its anarchic structure and warlike tendencies.

Shown here with French president Raymond Poincare, Wilson led the United States and its allies to victory in World War I, and then chaired the U.S. commission at the Paris Peace Conference in 1919. He proposed "Fourteen Points" to reform world politics, including global disarmament, decolonization, freedom of the seas, and the abolition of secret diplomacy. Wilson also called for an "association of nations" to maintain order through a system of collective security. More than sixty foreign governments approved his plan and created the League of Nations. But Wilson, who won the Nobel Peace Prize for his efforts, could not persuade leading members of the Senate to ratify the Treaty of Versailles, and the United States never joined the League of Nations.

Although the postwar U.S. economy rivaled that of all Europe, the U.S. government refused to define for the nation a political and military role consistent with its economic power. The United States was decisive in Germany's defeat, but its leaders wanted nothing to do with great-power politics. To the contrary, the United States sought again to abolish war, this time through the 1928 Kellogg-Briand Pact, in which sixty-two countries renounced war as "an instrument of national policy." Then, as Adolf Hitler consolidated his power in Germany in the 1930s and as Benito Mussolini, the Italian dictator, moved into Africa, Congress passed two Neutrality Acts that prevented an assertive American response.

The United States began to play a role in international politics again only when the balance of power in Europe was upset once more by the eruption of World War II in 1939 and the German defeat of France in 1940. With America again facing the possibility of Britain's defeat and the control of Eurasia by Germany and its allies, President Franklin D. Roosevelt undertook several measures to help Britain withstand any Nazi assault. He sent fifty old destroyers to defend the English Channel and established a "lend-lease" program to provide munitions, food, and other material support. This commitment to Britain was necessary even though Roosevelt's actions increased the risk of war with Germany. By the time Japan bombed Pearl Harbor in December 1941, a second and even bloodier world war was inevitable. Its outcome would determine the balance of power for the rest of the century.

MAINTAINING HEMISPHERIC SECURITY

Before the world wars, the United States did not maintain a global military or diplomatic presence. The nation was secure in the Western Hemisphere, which during the century after the American Revolution had witnessed the dismantling of European colonial control. The United States, along with Japan, had joined the ranks of the great powers through a combination of economic expansion and regional military competition. But while Japan, lacking many vital natural resources, began the twentieth century as a "predator" state, the United States was largely satisfied, both with its ample domestic resources and its lack of foreseeable threats across its borders. Maintaining that security, while effectively distancing the United States from the disputes of the other great powers, had served the nation well.

In any assessment of U.S. actions during the world wars, two points deserve emphasis. First, the defense of the United States has always involved more than physical security. The German threat during World War I was not one of immediate invasion, nor was an invasion the primary threat even after the defeat of France early in World War II. Rather, the United States twice forsook its "splendid isolation" because American *society* was threatened. If Germany controlled Eurasia, the United States would have to mobilize its resources fully and be on constant alert for attack. To maintain its hemispheric security, it would have to transform itself into a "garrison state"—a disciplined, militarized society that would sacrifice democracy in the name of security and individual liberty in the name of self-defense.

The second point deserving emphasis is that despite the U.S. concern with security in Europe, the timing of its interventions in 1917 and 1941 was not in each instance a rational decision made in Washington. It was Berlin's decision in 1917 to launch submarine warfare that brought the United States into the war, and it was Tokyo's decision in 1941 to attack the U.S. fleet at anchor in Hawaii that led to the American declaration of war against Japan. Without Hitler's reckless 1941 declaration of war against the United States—a country he held in great contempt—U.S. power would have been directed only against Japan, and Germany, the far stronger power, would have faced only Britain and Russia. Thus but for German and Japanese mistakes, the United States might *not* have entered the two world wars, even though the balances of power in Europe and Asia were transformed and American security in the Western Hemisphere was in jeopardy. The United States, in this respect, was saved from itself by its enemies.

Great powers usually do not leave decisions about their security to their adversaries. The strategy of the major states in the state system is—or should be—to oppose any state that seeks predominance, because such predominance would constitute a grave threat to their own security. That the United States twice failed to act according to the logic dictated by the balance of power largely stemmed from its own particular national style.

The American Sense of Destiny

The style reflected in the American response to war in Europe and later to the Cold War was the product of domestic experience. With nonthreatening neighbors to the north and south and open seas to the east and west, the United States could take its security for granted. Free from external threats, it could focus on its own economic and political development. The ability of the United States to maintain its detachment from great-power politics for such a long time cannot be attributed *only* to the nation's distance from Europe or to Europe's preoccupation with industrialization and class conflict at home and colonialism abroad. The nature of democracy has to be considered as well. The United States saw itself as more than just the world's "first new nation." [14] It also was the world's first constitutional democracy and, as such, the first country whose government was designed to make its leaders politically accountable to the public at large.

14. Seymour Martin Lipset, *The First New Nation: The United States in Historical and Comparative Perspective* (New York: Basic Books, 1963).

Democratic theory posits that people are potentially rational and moral, which means that they can settle their differences by reasoned deliberation and moral exhortation. Americans believed that peace—the result of harmony among people—was a natural or normal condition, whereas conflict was a deviation caused primarily by wicked leaders whose morality and reason had been corrupted. "Power politics," the defining element of Old World statecraft, was an instrument used by selfish and autocratic rulers for whom war was a grand game. They could remain in their palatial homes and suffer none of war's hardships. These fell upon the ordinary people, who had to leave their families to fight, endure the higher taxes to pay for the war, and possibly see their homes and families destroyed. The conclusion was clear: undemocratic states were inherently warlike and evil; democratic nations, in which the people controlled and regularly changed their leaders, were peaceful and moral.

The American experience seemed to support this conclusion: the United States was a democracy, its economy was growing steadily, and it generally was at peace with foreign powers. Furthermore, peace seemed to be the normal state of affairs. It was logical, then, that democracy and peaceful behavior should be thought synonymous. Americans rarely wondered whether democracy was responsible for the peace they enjoyed, or whether it was the product of other forces. The frequent wars in Europe appeared to provide the answer: European politics was power politics, reflecting the feudal origins of European regimes. To quarantine itself from Europe's hierarchical social structures and violent conflicts, hemispheric detachment was the morally correct policy. "Repudiation of Europe," novelist John Dos Passos once said, "is, after all, America's main excuse for being."

From the beginning, Americans professed a strong belief in what they considered to be their destiny—to spread *by example* freedom and social justice and to lead humankind away from its wicked ways to the New Jerusalem on earth. Early settlers considered it their providential mission to inspire other societies to follow their lead, and the massive wave of immigration of the late nineteenth century reinforced this sense of destiny. The United States, then, would voluntarily reject power politics as unfit for its domestic or foreign policy. The Monroe Doctrine, proclaimed in 1823, first stressed this ideological difference between the New World and the Old World. President James Monroe declared that the American political system was "essentially different" from that of Europe. In this spirit Monroe warned, "We should consider any attempt on [Europeans'] part to extend their system to any portion of this hemisphere as dangerous to our peace and safety." [15]

15. Quoted in Armin Rappaport, ed., *Sources in American Diplomacy* (New York: Macmillan, 1966), 53. For a recent assessment, see Gaddis Smith, *The Last Years of the Monroe Doctrine, 1945–1993* (New York: Hill and Wang, 1994).

This view also allowed the United States to behave hypocritically by acting like other nations in its continental expansion while casting its motives in the noblest of terms. It would not be the last time the United States would invoke such a double standard, proclaiming a moral position loftier than that of other great powers, then behaving in much the same way. In advocating U.S. military expansion into Mexico in 1845, for example, journalist John O'Sullivan argued that it is "the right of our manifest destiny to overspread and to possess the whole of the continent which Providence has given us for the development of the great experiment of Liberty and federated self-government entrusted to us. Its floor shall be a hemisphere—its roof the firmament of the star-studded heavens, and its congregation a Union of many Republics, compromising hundreds of happy millions . . . governed by God's natural and moral law of equality." [16]

By drawing the distinction between the New and Old Worlds, by warning Europeans to keep their hands off the Western Hemisphere, and by depicting themselves as agents of providence, Americans were in effect opening the way for U.S. primacy on a worldwide basis. This primacy would not take the form of an *empire,* or the assumption of sovereign authority over distant territories. Instead, the United States would expand its informal sphere of influence, or *hegemony,* from its base in the Western Hemisphere to the international system as a whole. Such an extension of power by any other state would be highly distressing. But in the hands of the United States, whose democratic values were presumed to be universal, hegemony seemed natural and beneficial to all nations.

THE DEPRECIATION OF POWER POLITICS

The American perception of an international harmony of interests contrasted sharply with the state system's emphasis on the inevitability of conflict and differences of interests among states. As noted, Americans traditionally regarded conflict as an abnormal condition, whereas the rest of the state system perceived harmony to be an illusion. The United States, long isolated from Europe and therefore not socialized by the state system, did not accept the reality and permanence of conflicts among its members. Indeed, differences between nation-states were considered unnatural. But when they did occur, they were attributed to wicked leaders (who could be eliminated), authoritarian political systems (which could be reformed), or misunderstandings (which could be resolved if the adversaries approached each other with sincerity and

16. Quoted in Howard Jones, *The Course of American Diplomacy: From the Revolution to the Present,* 2d ed. (Chicago: Dorsey Press, 1988), 143.

empathy). Once these obstacles were removed, peace, harmony, and goodwill would reign supreme.

The association of peace with democracy was not the only reason for the American depreciation of power politics in the eighteenth and nineteenth centuries. The European countries were, by and large, three-class societies. In addition to a middle class, they contained in their bodies politic an aristocracy, devoted either to keeping itself in power or to recapturing power and returning to the glorious days of a feudal past, and a proletariat, born out of the urbanization and industrialization of the nineteenth century. Because it felt it did not receive a fair share of the national income, the proletariat became a revolutionary class. By contrast, America was, as French political observer Alexis de Tocqueville observed in 1835, "born free" as an egalitarian, democratic society. "As a result one finds a vast multitude of people with roughly the same ideas about religion, history, science, political economy, legislation, and government." [17]

This widespread agreement on the fundamental values of American society and Europe's intense class struggles reinforced the American misunderstanding of the nature and functions of power on the international scene. Dissatisfied groups never developed a revolutionary ideology because the growing prosperity spread to them before they could translate their grievances against the capitalist system into political action. African Americans were an important exception. They never shared this wealth or political power; in fact, the "peculiar institution" of slavery so defied America's democratic values that it thrust the country into civil war. Otherwise, the United States was politically secure, socially cohesive, and economically prosperous. It resolved most of its political differences peacefully, and its people could believe in an evolutionary, democratic, economically prosperous historical process. Revolution and radicalism were condemned from this perspective.

Private enterprise and economic development further reinforced this disregard for power politics.

John Locke, the British political theorist who inspired the American founders, believed the role of the state should be to promote "life, liberty, and the pursuit of property." The best government, Thomas Jefferson declared, was the government that governed least. Arbitrary political interference with the economic laws of the market only upset the results—widespread prosperity and public welfare—these laws were intended to produce. The United States, therefore, would not isolate itself from the outside world in a commercial sense. To the contrary, economic expansion based on foreign trade was a central element of early

17. Alexis de Tocqueville, *Democracy in America* (New York: Harper and Row, 1966), 56.

American foreign policy. The key was ensuring that no political strings were attached. As Washington proclaimed in his Farewell Address, "The great rule of conduct for us, in regard to foreign Nations is, in extending our commercial relations, to have with them as little Political connection as possible."

This simple dichotomy between economics and politics came naturally to Americans, for whom the benefits of economic freedom were as "self-evident" as the truths stated in the Declaration of Independence. Abundant natural resources, free enterprise, and supportive government policies would enable the American people to become the "people of plenty." [18] Because Americans viewed the power of the state as threatening, they struggled to restrict this power. It was with this purpose in mind that the drafters of the U.S. Constitution divided authority between the states and the federal government and, within the latter, among the executive, legislative, and judicial branches. The principles of federalism and separation of powers were deliberately designed to limit the power of the central government. Domestic conflicts would be resolved by the individual citizen's own economic actions in society.

It was hardly surprising that in these circumstances the solution to international problems in America's first century was considered a matter of economics—not politics. Economics was identified with social harmony and the welfare of all peoples; politics was equated with conflict, war, and death. Just as the "good society" was to be the product of free competition, so the peaceful international society would be created by free trade. Trade depended on mutual prosperity; by contrast, war impoverished and destroyed and created ill will among nations. Commerce, which benefited all the participating states, created a vested interest in peace; war was economically unprofitable and therefore obsolete. Free trade and peace, in short, were one and the same cause.[19]

FOREIGN POLICY AS MORAL MISSION

Americans' perception of their nation as *exceptional,* or qualitatively different than others, is based not on a common ethnic identity, language, or religion, but on widely shared beliefs about individual liberties, limited government, and vigorous civil society. Such principles form a "civil religion" in the United States that defines the relationship between state and society and provides the basis for American nationalism.

18. David M. Potter, *People of Plenty: Economic Abundance and the American Character* (Chicago: University of Chicago Press, 1954).

19. These ideas were most thoroughly developed at the time by Scottish economist Adam Smith in his 1776 book *The Wealth of Nations* (New York: Oxford University Press, 1976).

Because Americans have commonly viewed themselves as part of an exceptional society, their attitude toward government has been animated historically by a sense of moral mission. John Winthrop, the Puritan defector from the Church of England and first governor of Massachusetts, declared New England in 1630 to be a "city upon a hill, the eyes of all people are upon us." The European settlers of North America, he proclaimed, would establish a haven of piety, solidarity, and just government far from the corrupted halls of religion and government in the Old World. "If we shall deal falsely with our God in this work we have undertaken," Winthrop warned, "we shall shame the faces of many of God's worthy servants, and cause their prayers to be turned into curses upon us till we be consumed out of the good land whither we are going." [20]

References to religious values and symbols have since been common in the discourse of American politics and foreign policy. To Thomas Jefferson, Americans were "the chosen people of God, if ever He had a chosen people, whose breasts He has made His peculiar deposit for substantial and genuine virtue." [21] In the midst of the Spanish-American War, President William McKinley claimed that he received divine guidance to "educate the Filipinos, and uplift and civilize them, and by God's grace do the very best we could by them, as our fellow-men for whom Christ also died." [22] To Ronald Reagan during the revived Cold War of the 1980s, "There is sin and evil in the world, and we're enjoined by Scripture and the Lord Jesus to oppose it with all our might." [23]

This sense of divine mission extends to American citizens as well. A 1998 survey of the citizens of forty-three countries found that Americans ranked first in believing in a "personal God," in following "absolute guidelines about what is good and evil," and in assigning religion a "very important" role in their lives.[24] Such views, in turn, shape the foreign policy views of American citizens. In a 2004 survey, nearly three-fourths of respondents believed "following moral principles" should be a top foreign policy priority (see Table 1-1).[25]

20. Quoted in Walter A. McDougal, *Promised Land, Crusader State* (Boston: Houghton Mifflin, 1997), 37–38.

21. Robert W. Tucker and David C. Hendrickson, *Imperial Temptations: The New World Order and America's Purpose* (New York: Council on Foreign Relations, 1992), 30.

22. McDougal. *Promised Land, Crusader State,* 112.

23. Remarks made to the National Association of Evangelicals, March 8, 1983, and reported in Strobe Talbott, ed., *The Russians and Reagan* (New York: Vintage Books, 1984), 113.

24. Pew Research Center for the People and the Press, "Foreign Policy Attitudes Now Driven by 9/11 and Iraq," August 18, 2004, http://people-press.org/reports/display.php3?ReportID=222 (accessed February 10, 2006); Ronald Inglehart, Miguel Basanez, and Alejandro Moreno, *Human Values and Beliefs: A Cross Cultural Sourcebook* (Ann Arbor: University of Michigan Press, 1998).

25. Religious beliefs are so closely tied to foreign policy opinions that a "divine divide"

TABLE 1-1 **American Foreign Policy Priorities: American Public Opinion, 2004**

	Percent who believe ___ should be "top priority" in American foreign policy
Following moral principles	72
Being cautious	66
Being decisive	62
Being practical	58
Being compassionate	54
Being flexible	40
Following religious principles	33
Being idealistic	25
Being forceful	23

Source: Pew Research Center for the People and the Press, "Foreign Policy Attitudes Now Driven by 9/11 and Iraq" (August 18, 2004), 23.

Although more pronounced in recent years, these religious attitudes have long influenced American foreign policy. Frequently, their impact is even profound, especially with regard to the use of military force. The immoral enemy who threatens the integrity, if not the existence, of the nation's democratic principles has to be destroyed. American power, then, has to be "righteous" power; only by exercising it fully can Americans ensure salvation. Thus the world wars of the early twentieth century became profound moral as well as geopolitical challenges. Making the world "safe for democracy"—Woodrow Wilson's stated objective during World War I—was to be achieved by democratizing the populace of the offending nation—in this case, Germany—and making its new rulers responsible to the people they governed, thereby converting the menacing regime into a peaceful democratic state and banishing power politics for all time. Once that aim was achieved, the United States could again withdraw into itself, secure in the knowledge that American works had again proved to be "good works."

For similar reasons, American leaders divorced force from diplomacy during the nation's early years. In peacetime, diplomacy was supposed to preserve the harmony among states. Although Americans regarded

has appeared in recent surveys. Ironically, the most conservative religious denominations, including evangelical Christians, are the most inclined to favor the unilateral assertion of U.S. military force. See Daniel Yankelovich, "Poll Positions," *Foreign Affairs* 84 (September–October 2005): 2–16; and James L. Guth, John C. Green, Lyman A. Kellstedt, and Corwin E. Smidt, "Faith and Foreign Policy: A View from the Pews," *Review of Faith and International Affairs* 3 (fall 2004): 3–9.

diplomacy as a rational process for straightening out misunderstandings between nations, they also were extremely suspicious of it. Diplomacy, in their view, required bargaining and compromise among states that would lead inevitably to the sacrifice of the nation's moral purity. For this reason, the U.S. government refused to create a large, permanent diplomatic corps until long after the nation's arrival as a great power. As for the use of military force, early American leaders feared that a standing army would ultimately threaten the central government and the liberty of private citizens. When military muscle was required, the Department of War would be called on to mobilize a largely reserve force, which would be disbanded after the conflict.

This pattern has been the one observed historically in American foreign policy: a pendulum-like swing "back and forth between the extremes of an indiscriminate detachment from great-power politics and an equally indiscriminate internationalism or globalism."[26] Woodrow Wilson's frustrations over the League of Nations most clearly illustrate this schizophrenic approach, as the U.S. government veered from its attempt to save the world toward an equally determined effort to escape from it. According to Harvard professor Stanley Hoffmann, "Both extremes have in common the intention to avoid the contamination of unhealthy foreign troubles."[27]

Since the Cold War, both impulses have been evident at once. President Clinton's engagement policy coincided with Congress's backlash against UN peacekeeping and foreign aid. His successor's quest to make the Middle East safe for democracy accompanied his retreat from a variety of global agreements. Even when the United States is "engaged," its interests are protected through special treatment: veto power in the UN Security Council, weighted voting in the World Bank, command of North Atlantic Treaty Organization (NATO) forces, and exemptions from key provisions of the Chemical Weapons Convention and the International Criminal Court treaty.[28] The war on terrorism naturally lends itself to the belief that America again faces a climactic showdown between good and evil, and that all measures must be used to see that justice prevails. Compromise is not possible, nor can one submit to the delays and constraints posed by international law and organizations. Even the concerns of presumed allies must be disregarded if they stand in the way of the exercise of righteous power.

26. Hans J. Morgenthau, *A New Foreign Policy for the United States* (New York: Praeger, 1969), 15.

27. Stanley Hoffmann, *Gulliver's Troubles, or the Setting of American Foreign Policy* (New York: McGraw-Hill, 1968), 98.

28. For a more detailed review of these "hegemonic prerogatives," see David Skidmore, "Understanding the Unilateralist Turn in U.S. Foreign Policy," *Foreign Policy Analysis* 1 (July 2005): 207–228.

Although Americans traditionally regard their values as universal and their government's actions on the world stage as inspired by "special providence," they frequently disagree about the appropriate *means* for achieving foreign policy goals.[29] The first and more modest path—leading by example—would encourage citizens to focus on domestic development, restrain Washington from reckless foreign adventures, and prevent the rise of a strong, expensive, and potentially oppressive military establishment. The second path—proactively intervening overseas and acting as the world's policeman—would accelerate the historical trend toward global freedom and vindicate the nation's moral mission.

"Examplarists" followed George Washington's call for detachment in the nation's first century, whereas the "vindicationists" such as Woodrow Wilson have generally prevailed since the United States became a great power.[30] When President George W. Bush took office in 2001, he embraced the nation's earlier tradition. "I think the United States must be humble," Bush said in a presidential debate in October 2000. "We must be proud and confident of our values, but humble in how we treat nations that are figuring out how to chart their own course." But the events of September 11, 2001, represented the "perfect vindicationist storm." It combined an unprecedented degree of American military power, a direct attack on the United States by "nonbelievers," and a surge of religious fundamentalism among American citizens.[31] Bush, instantly converted to the cause of vindicating the forceful export of American values, never looked back.

Self-Doubts, Revisionism, and Social Construction

One of the most telling characteristics of America's national style in conducting foreign policy has been the scrutiny and criticism applied during and after every major war to the reasons for the country's participation in the struggle. Antiwar activists organize demonstrations and encourage resistance; former government officials challenge the country's behavior on the op-ed pages; and scholars "revise" the historical record to rebut the conventional wisdom. In a typical recent critique, diplomatic historians Fred Anderson and Andrew Cayton concluded that American forces throughout history "have fought less to

29. Walter Russell Mead, *Special Providence: American Foreign Policy and How It Changed the World* (New York: Knopf, 2003).

30. H. W. Brands, *What America Owes the World: The Struggle for the Soul of Foreign Policy* (New York: Cambridge University Press, 1998).

31. Jonathan Monten, "The Roots of the Bush Doctrine: Power, Nationalism, and U.S. Democracy Promotion in U.S. Strategy," *International Security* 29 (spring 2005): 140.

preserve liberty than to extend the power of the United States *in the name of* liberty."[32]

During the twentieth century, the revisionist histories featured two common themes. First, with the exception of the two world wars, the conflicts in which the United States became entangled did not in fact threaten its security interests. America's entry in the regional and civil wars of the past century was unnecessary or immoral or both. The enemy identified as the *provocateur* actually did not represent a direct threat to American security at all. To the contrary, the threat came from within.

Second, the United States became involved in conflicts because its leaders were seduced by propagandists who aroused and manipulated public opinion, by military officials with bureaucratic motives, and, above all else, by bankers and industrialists—the "merchants of death" of the 1930s, the "military-industrial complex" of the 1960s—whose economic interests benefited from the struggle. William Appleman Williams, the foremost proponent of this view, contended in 1959 that the United States was driven to global expansion and foreign conflicts by the threat of economic stagnation and the fear of social upheaval at home.[33] Similarly, Joyce and Gabriel Kolko argued in 1972 that American foreign policy after World War II was driven "not by the containment of communism, but rather more directly the extension and expansion of American capitalism."[34]

These critics challenged the traditional view that the United States had broader interests in these military conflicts, including the promotion of democratic values and human rights. Critical historians also challenged the notion that the pursuit of economic gain served as an acceptable objective for the United States and its citizens because it reduced rather than increased the nation's appetite for war. Economic expansion, they argued, far from serving as a worthy objective, risked corrupting America's very soul, because it diverted attention and resources from reform at home to military preparation and war. This viewpoint, originally maintained by a small group of critics, became widespread as the United States intervened repeatedly in regional conflicts during the Cold War.

Inspired by the revisionist historians of the Cold War, a new generation of political scientists contends that concepts such as sovereignty,

32. Fred Anderson and Andrew Cayton, *The Dominion of War: Empire and Liberty in North America, 1500–2000* (New York: Viking, 2005), emphasis in original.

33. William Appleman Williams, *The Tragedy of American Diplomacy* (New York: Harper and Row, 1959). For a related critique of early American foreign policy, see Walter LaFeber, *The New Empire: An Interpretation of American Expansion, 1860–1898* (Ithaca, N.Y.: Cornell University Press, 1963).

34. Joyce Kolko and Gabriel Kolko, *The Limits of Power: The World and United States Foreign Policy, 1945–1954* (New York: Harper and Row, 1972), 480.

anarchy, and "Third World" (see Chapter 4) are "socially constructed" by government leaders and are therefore not a legitimate basis for diplomatic relations.[35] In dominating the discourse of American foreign policy, constructivists argue, American leaders have routinely glorified the nation's values, vilified adversaries, and exaggerated overseas threats in order to preserve America's dominant position in the world. The news media served as an accomplice in this effort by the U.S. government to manipulate public opinion. The Cold War, David Campbell observed, "was both a struggle which exceeded the military threat of the Soviet Union, and a struggle into which any number of potential candidates—regardless of their strategic capacity to be a threat—were slotted as a threat." [36]

The bitter domestic debates over America's intentions and conduct in the three global conflicts of the twentieth century were revealing, particularly given the favorable outcome of each for the United States. Such divisions continued after the conflicts of the post–Cold War era. Thomas McCormick argued that "short-term concerns over the American and global economies" led the United States to war with Iraq in 1991.[37] Efforts by the United States in 1993 to bring order to Somalia and later in that decade to stop ethnic cleansing in Yugoslavia provoked charges at home of neo-imperialism. Even the attacks of September 11 provided an opportunity for self-criticism. Noam Chomsky, a prominent critic of America's world role, predicted that the war against terrorism would be difficult to win because the United States was itself "a leading terrorist state." [38]

The second war in Iraq, launched in 2003, has especially provoked criticism, because the Bush administration's stated rationale—removing Saddam Hussein's weapons of mass destruction—proved erroneous. President Bush's shift toward democratic state building in Iraq, a mission that draws on America's traditional values and sense of identity, fueled charges that American leaders were acting hypocritically by supporting military dictators (in Pakistan) and repressive monarchs (in Saudi Arabia), by violating the human rights of war prisoners, and even by secretly spying on Americans at home. To those who argued the war was "all about oil," sufficient evidence was found in President Bush's and Vice President Dick Cheney's past association with the oil industry.

35. See Alexander Wendt, "Anarchy Is What States Make of It: The Social Construction of Power Politics," *International Organization* 46 (spring 1992): 395–424.

36. David Campbell, *Writing Security: United States Foreign Policy and the Politics of Identity* (Minneapolis: University of Minnesota Press, 1992), 34.

37. Thomas McCormick, *America's Half-Century: United States Foreign Policy in the Cold War and After,* 2d ed. (Baltimore: Johns Hopkins University Press, 1995), 248.

38. Noam Chomsky, *9-11* (New York: Seven Stories Press, 2001), 16.

In summary, today the United States faces the world with attitudes and behavior patterns formed by its long and ambivalent relationship with foreign powers. The Cold War dominated world politics for nearly half a century, with profound implications for the domestic and foreign policies of nearly every other country. The country's erratic behavior since that conflict, its antagonism toward international institutions, and its call for a world order based on American primacy have equally profound implications for the new century. The United States today faces no direct challenge from another world power, and the Bush administration's "unilateral turn" has yet to produce anti-American alliances or other measures to counter the nation's predominance.[39] Still, U.S. actions provoke opposition and resentment from many foreign governments and societies, and these tensions are unlikely to dissipate in the foreseeable future. America's love-hate relationship with the world beyond its shores is an enduring reality that must be understood. The chapters that follow will explore both the Cold War experience and the subsequent conduct of the United States in the context of this enduring style of foreign policy.

39. Keir A. Leiber and Gerard Alexander, "Waiting for Balancing: Why the World Is Not Pushing Back," *International Security* 30 (summer 2005): 109–139.

CHAPTER TWO

From World War to Cold War

President Franklin Roosevelt (center) confers with Soviet leader Joseph Stalin (left) and British prime minister Winston Churchill (right) in Teheran in November 1943. The three leaders, who had joined forces to defeat Germany, would meet again in Yalta in February 1945 to discuss military strategy and the structure of the postwar world.

After World War II, the United States remained prosperous, politically stable, and militarily strong. By contrast, the European landmass from France to Russia lay in ruin. In East Asia, Japan and its short-lived empire were devastated; China was immersed in civil war. For the second time in three decades, the United States had been drawn into world war and had triumphed. It had attained a "preponderance of power" after seeing its influence expand steadily from continental to regional to global scale.[1] For those who were convinced that America

1. See Melvyn P. Leffler, *A Preponderance of Power: National Security, the Truman Administration, and the Cold War* (Stanford, Calif.: Stanford University Press, 1992).

was bound to achieve its "manifest destiny," the moment of truth seemed to have arrived.

But even before the embers of World War II had cooled, the sparks of a new conflict illuminated the future of American foreign policy. Allies in the struggles against the Axis powers, the United States and the Soviet Union confronted one another with rival political systems and conflicts of interest throughout the world. Signs of this coming schism were largely ignored as the final battles of World War II were waged in central Europe and East Asia.[2]

Such neglect was reflected in a U.S. War Department memorandum written before a wartime conference between British Prime Minister Winston Churchill and President Franklin Roosevelt. The report concluded that the Soviet Union would be the dominant power in Eurasia for the foreseeable future: "With Germany crushed, there is no power in Europe to oppose her [the Soviet Union's] tremendous military forces. . . . The conclusions from the foregoing are obvious. Since Russia is the decisive factor in the war, she must be given every assistance, and every effort must be made to obtain her friendship. Likewise, since without question she will dominate Europe on the defeat of the Axis, it is even more essential to develop and maintain the most friendly relations with Russia."[3]

The importance of this assessment lies less in its prediction of the Soviet Union's postwar position, which was fairly obvious, than in its statement of American expectations about future U.S.-Soviet relations. Military leaders apparently accepted without any major misgivings the prospect of the Soviet Union as the new dominant power in Europe; they did not imagine that it might replace Nazi Germany as a grave threat to the European and global balance of power. Although twice in the twentieth century the United States had been propelled into Europe's wars at exactly those moments when Germany became so powerful that it almost destroyed this balance, the lessons of history—specifically, the impact of any nation's domination of Europe on American security—had not yet been absorbed. Roosevelt and the U.S. government did not attempt to reestablish a balance of power in Europe to safeguard the United States; they expected this security to stem from mutual U.S.-Soviet goodwill, unsupported by considerations of power. This reliance on goodwill and mutual esteem was to prove foolish at best—and potentially fatal at worst.

2. For an elaboration of this critical "hinge" period from several perspectives, see Arnold A. Offner and Theodore A. Wilson, eds., *Victory in Europe, 1945: From World War to Cold War* (Lawrence: University of Kansas Press, 2000).

3. Quoted in Robert E. Sherwood, *Roosevelt and Hopkins, An Intimate History,* vol. 2 (New York: Bantam Books, 1950), 363–364.

American Wartime Illusions

Postwar expectations of an "era of good feelings" between the Soviet Union and the United States epitomized the idealistic nature of American foreign policy, which perceived war as a disruption of the normal harmony among nations. Once the war was finished, this thinking presumed, natural harmony would be restored and the struggle for power would end. In Washington, government leaders celebrated the triumph of America's moral vision and its rejection of old-style power politics. As World War II wound down, Secretary of State Cordell Hull anticipated the day in which "there will no longer be need for spheres of influence, for alliances, for balance of power, or any other of the special arrangements through which, in the unhappy past, the nations strove to safeguard their security or to promote their interests." [4]

Such optimism about future U.S.-Soviet relations made it necessary to explain away continuing signs of Soviet distrust, particularly during World War II when the Allies delayed opening up a western front against Germany. When the front was postponed from 1942 to 1943 to 1944, Soviet leader Joseph Stalin rejected Allied explanations that they were not yet properly equipped for such an enormous undertaking. Stalin especially denounced Churchill for refusing to intervene until the Germans were so weakened that Allied forces would not have to suffer massive losses.

It is no wonder, then, that the Soviets adopted their own interpretation of American and British behavior. From the Marxist viewpoint, the Allies were doing exactly what a rational observer would expect: postponing the second front until the Soviet Union and Germany, the communist and fascist superpowers in Europe, respectively, had exhausted each other. Then the United States and Britain could land in France, march into Germany without heavy losses, and dictate the peace to both countries. The Western delay was seen in Moscow as a deliberate attempt by the world's leading capitalist powers to destroy their two major ideological opponents at one and the same time.

For their part, American leaders found a ready explanation for the Soviets' suspicions. Roosevelt placed Soviet distrust squarely in the context of the West's previous anti-Sovietism: the Allied intervention in Russia at the end of World War I aimed at overthrowing the Soviet regime and, after the failure of that attempt, the establishment of a *cordon sanitaire* in eastern Europe to keep Soviet influence from spreading; the West's rejection of Soviet offers in the mid- to late 1930s to build an alliance against Adolf Hitler; and, especially, the effects of the Munich

4. Quoted in Herbert Feis, *Churchill, Roosevelt, Stalin: The War They Waged and the Peace They Sought* (Princeton, N.J.: Princeton University Press, 1957), 238.

agreement of 1938, when Britain and France stood by while the Nazi dictator destroyed Czechoslovakia, opening his gateway to the East. These efforts by the West to weaken and ultimately destroy the Soviet Union, as well as its attempts to turn Hitler's threat away from Western Europe and toward Russia, were considered the primary reasons for Soviet hostility. To overcome this attitude, American leaders thought they had only to demonstrate good intentions.

Roosevelt's efforts to gain this cooperation focused on Stalin. In that respect, Roosevelt's instincts were correct: if he could gain Stalin's trust, postwar U.S.-Soviet cooperation would be possible. But in another respect, his instincts were poor. Roosevelt's political experience was in the domestic arena. He had dealt successfully with all sorts of politicians and had managed to resolve differences by finding compromise solutions. As a result, he had great confidence in his ability to win Stalin's favor. He would talk to Stalin as "one politician to another." In short, Roosevelt saw Stalin as a Russian version of himself—a fellow politician who could be won over by a mixture of concessions and goodwill. It did not occur to Roosevelt that all of his considerable skill and charm might not suffice. At home, these qualities were enough, because he and his opponents agreed on ultimate goals; differences were largely over the means to achieve them. But the differences between the United States and the Soviet Union were over the ends, the kind of world each expected to see when the war was over.

In February 1945 at the Yalta Conference of the Big Three—Roosevelt, Stalin, and Churchill—Roosevelt and his advisers believed they had firmly established amicable and lasting relations with the Soviet Union. Stalin had made concessions on a number of vital issues and had pledged cooperation in the future. In the Declaration of Liberated Europe, he promised to support self-government and allow free elections in eastern Europe. He also responded to the wishes of the American military and promised to enter the war against Japan after Hitler was finally subdued. And Stalin, to whom Roosevelt often referred in congenial terms, repeatedly expressed his hope for fifty years of peace and great-power cooperation.

Upon his return from Yalta, Roosevelt told Congress and the American people that his recent conference with Stalin and Churchill "ought to spell the end of the system of unilateral action, the exclusive alliances, the spheres of influence, the balances of power, and all the other expedients that have been tried for centuries—and have always failed." Instead: "We propose to substitute for all these, a universal organization in which all peace-loving nations will fully have a chance to join." [5]

5. Quoted in James MacGregor Burns, *Roosevelt, The Soldier of Freedom* (New York: Harcourt Brace Jovanovich, 1970), 582.

The new era of goodwill was to be embodied in the United Nations (UN), the embodiment of democracy working on a global scale. Through the UN, power politics would be replaced by reliance on sound universal principles and cooperation. Roosevelt hosted the UN's organizing conference, held in San Francisco even as the final battles of World War II were being waged early in 1945. Under the plan approved by fifty governments at the conference, the UN's General Assembly would provide a forum for all countries to meet and discuss their concerns. The most pressing and immediate problems would come before the UN Security Council, comprised of fifteen countries. While ten of these seats would rotate among all UN members, the United States and four other great powers, including Britain, China, France, and the Soviet Union, would have permanent seats and be able to veto proposed actions they opposed. These measures were a bow to realism that was lacking in Woodrow Wilson's League of Nations, and assured passage of the UN Charter and construction of the UN headquarters in New York City.[6]

The State Department had been even more emphatic about the subordination of power politics to universal moral principles. Its Subcommittee on Territorial Problems pointed out that "the vital interests of the United States lay in following a 'diplomacy of principle'—of moral disinterestedness instead of power politics." No comment could have summed up more aptly the American habit of viewing international politics in terms of abstract moral principles rather than in terms of clashes of interest and power.

The Russo-Soviet Approach to Foreign Policy

In Chapter 1 it was argued that, before World War II, American foreign policy was shaped by a cultural tradition that reflected the nation's detachment from the great powers of Europe and its pursuit of regional security in the Western hemisphere. It is thus useful to contrast the American tradition with that of its Cold War rival, the Soviet Union, whose leaders also inherited a distinct style of foreign policy, the product of centuries of fractious coexistence with a diverse and often-menacing external environment. These leaders then integrated the lessons of Russian history with the maxims of Marxist-Leninist ideology to fashion an assertive and confrontational approach to postwar foreign

6. For an elaboration on the UN's founding, structures, and current status, see Thomas G. Weiss, David P. Forsythe, and Roger A. Coate, *The United States and Changing World Politics*, 4th ed. (Boulder, Colo.: Westview Press, 2004).

affairs. The emergence of the Soviet Union as a global superpower, and the American response to this shift in the balance of power, would dominate world politics for nearly half a century.

THE RUSSIAN BACKGROUND

Understanding the source of the Russo-Soviet "style" of foreign policy begins by simply analyzing a globe. Unlike the United States and other maritime powers, Russia was not blessed by geography. Unprotected by natural barriers such as oceans or mountains, its people were vulnerable to invasions from several directions. And the enormous size of its territory rendered internal cohesion, communication, and transportation very difficult—a situation exacerbated by the diverse ethnic backgrounds, languages, and religious identities of the Russian people.

During the thirteenth and fourteenth centuries, Mongols from the East ruled Russia. By the 1460s, their domination had been repelled, and a Russian state had emerged with Muscovy (Moscow) as its capital. In more modern times, Napoleon Bonaparte's armies invaded and captured Moscow in 1812; British and French armies landed in the Crimea in 1854–1856, capturing several cities in bloody battles; and Japan attacked and claimed territories in eastern Russia in 1904–1905. Germany invaded Russia twice during the twentieth century. Its first attack prompted the final collapse of the Russian monarchy, civil war, and the rise of the communists to power, and its second cost the Soviet Union millions of lives and untold destruction of property.

Historically, then, Russia could not take its security for granted or give priority to domestic affairs. In these circumstances, power became centralized in whichever political body, under both the czars and the communist leaders, firmly held the far-flung regions together. Such efforts, however, required large standing military forces, and much of the Russian population was mobilized in their service. Indeed, the Russian armed forces were consistently larger than those of the other European great powers, a fact not lost on political leaders in Warsaw, Budapest, Paris, and London.

This militarization of Russian society, purportedly for defensive purposes, also carried with it the potential for outward aggression. To the historian Richard Pipes, Russia no more became the world's largest territorial state by repelling repeated invasions than a man becomes rich by being robbed.[7] The same lack of natural frontiers that failed to protect

7. Richard Pipes, as quoted by Zbigniew Brzezinski, *Game Plan: A Geostrategic Framework for the Conduct of the U.S.-Soviet Contest* (Boston: Atlantic Monthly Press, 1986), 19–20.

Russia from invasion also allowed its power to extend outward from its frontiers. Indeed, sustained territorial expansion has been called the "Russian way." According to President Jimmy Carter's national security adviser, Zbigniew Brzezinski, any list of aggressions against Russia in the last two centuries would be dwarfed by Russian expansionist moves against its neighbors.[8]

Whether Russian motives were defensive or offensive, the result was a pattern of expansion. To the degree that Russian rulers feared attacks, they pushed outward to keep the enemy as far away as possible. Territorial extension became a partial substitute for the lack of wide rivers or mountains that might have afforded a degree of natural protection. Individual rulers' ambitions, such as Peter the Great's determination to have access to the sea, also resulted in territorial conquest and defeat of the power blocking that aim (in this case, Sweden). Even before the communist revolutionaries, or Bolsheviks, seized power and established a one-party state, authoritarianism, militarism, and expansionism characterized Russian government. The basic "rules" of power politics—the emphasis on national interests, distrust of other states, expectation of conflict, self-reliance, and the possession of sufficient power, especially military power—were deeply ingrained in Russia's leaders.

THE SOVIET INGREDIENT

These attitudes were modified and strengthened by the outlook of the new regime after 1917. Russian political culture was fused with Marxist ideology and adapted to Russian circumstances by Vladimir Lenin, the founder and first premier of the Soviet Union. His all-encompassing *weltanschauung* (worldview) did not dictate action in specific situations. Instead, Lenin's perspective provided the new regime with a broad framework for understanding and relating to the outside world.

To Lenin and his fellow Bolsheviks, history centered around the class struggle between, on the one hand, the rich and privileged who owned the means of production and, on the other hand, the greater numbers of propertyless citizens who worked for them. Why were most human beings poor, illiterate, and unhealthy? Why did states fight wars? The answer was that a small minority of capitalists, monopolizing the industrialized world's wealth and power, exploited the men and women who worked in their factories to maximize profits. To keep wages down, they kept food prices low, with the result that agricultural labor also lived in

8. Zbigniew Brzezinski, "The Soviet Union: The Aims, Problems, and Challenges to the West," in *The Conduct of East-West Relations in the 1980s*, Adelphi Paper No. 189, Part I (London: International Institute for Strategic Studies, 1984).

destitution. Domestically as well as internationally, wars were one product of the ongoing search by these capitalists for profits.

The predictable result was the conflict waged over dividing up the non-European colonial world. For Lenin, global imperialism represented the "highest stage of capitalism." As he summed up his argument in 1917: "Imperialism is capitalism in that stage of development in which the dominance of monopolies and finance capital has established itself; in which the export of capital has acquired pronounced importance; in which the division of the world among the international trusts has begun; in which the division of all territories of the globe among the great capitalist powers has been completed." [9]

In this respect, Lenin viewed World War I as a climactic showdown among capitalist empires, a fight for the spoils of the developing world now that their own frontiers were settled. Like a shark, the capitalist economy could not be still. Capitalists had to expand their firms and markets constantly lest they be swallowed up in the competition for economic markets. If human beings were ever to live in freedom and enjoy a decent standard of living in peace and fraternity with other countries, Lenin concluded, capitalism would have to be replaced by communism.

As Lenin was aware, the application of Marxism to Russia suffered from one glaring deficiency. In Karl Marx's dialectic view, communism stemmed directly from the failures of capitalism. Thus a communist society must first experience industrialization, urbanization, and the enlistment of its working classes into an organized "proletariat," none of which occurred in Russia to the extent necessary to spark revolution. Lenin attempted to resolve this problem by centralizing power in a "vanguard" of enlightened Marxists, who would bring communism to the Russian people without first exposing them to the contradictions and inequalities of capitalism. Once firmly in place within the Kremlin, this vanguard would then disseminate Lenin's ideological vision through a pervasive propaganda campaign.

Soviet leaders believed the state system, increasingly composed of capitalist states with close economic ties, was a very hostile environment. They rejected the latter's professions of goodwill and peaceful intentions and committed their country to the "inevitable and irreconcilable struggle" against these states. They fostered a strong emphasis on self-reliance and an equally intense concern with Soviet power. Tactically, they were convinced that when an enemy made concessions in negotiations or became more accommodating, it was not because the enemy wanted a friendlier relationship but because it was *compelled* to

9. Vladimir I. Lenin, *Imperialism: The Highest Stage of Capitalism* (New York: International Publishers, 1939), 89.

do so by the Soviet Union's growing strength, a viewpoint that led to a self-sustaining rationale for ever more military power.

Russian history stood as a warning to Soviet leaders that peace was but preparation for the next war. Their ideological perceptions strengthened the view that peace was but a continuation of the last war by other means. The Soviet worldview, in short, reinforced the historically repetitious cycles that had resulted in further expansion of Soviet power. Even if insecurity, rather than any historical mission, drove this expansion, the result for neighboring states remained the same—they were vulnerable. They were perceived as inherent threats to Soviet interests, and they represented possible additions to the Soviet Union's own frontiers. Such a drive to achieve absolute security in a system in which no state could achieve that aim short of total domination left other states insecure and contributed to the volatility of the international system throughout the Cold War.

The contrast between American culture and national style, which emphasized peace as normal and conflict as abnormal, and that of the Soviet Union, which stressed the pervasiveness of war, could not have been more striking. Both societies felt a sense of historical mission, yet their principles, goals, and tactics were worlds apart. These clashing approaches to foreign policy were to confront one another as the Soviet and Western armies, led by the United States, advanced from the opposite sides of Europe.

Soviet Expansion after World War II

The American dream of postwar peace and Big Three cooperation was shattered when the Red Army, having finally halted the Nazi armies and decisively defeated the Germans at Stalingrad in late 1942, slowly began to drive the enemy out of the Soviet Union and then pursue the retreating Germans to Berlin. The Soviet Union, which in 1940 had annexed the three Baltic states (Latvia, Lithuania, and Estonia) after signing the Molotov-Ribbentrop Pact, thus expanded into eastern and central Europe and began to impose its control on Poland, Hungary, Bulgaria, Romania, and Albania even before the end of the war.[10] (Yugoslavia was by then under the communist control of Marshal Josip Tito, the Yugoslav partisan leader who had fought bravely against the German occupation, and Czechoslovakia was under the threat of the Red Army.)

10. The August 1939 pact, named after the foreign ministers of the Soviet Union and Germany, respectively, called for mutual nonaggression and the division of regional territories into spheres of influence. Nazi Germany violated the agreement in June 1941 by invading the Soviet Union.

SOVIET EXPANSION IN EUROPE, 1939–1948

In each of the nations of Eastern Europe occupied by their troops, the Soviets unilaterally established pro-Soviet coalition governments. The key posts in these regimes—the ministry of the interior, which usually controlled the police, and the ministry of defense, which controlled the army—were in the hands of the communists. With these decisive levers of power in their grasp, the Soviets found it an easy matter to extend their domination and subvert the independence of these countries. As the war drew to a close, it became clear that the words of the Yalta Declaration, in which the Soviets had pledged to allow free elections and democratic governments in Eastern Europe, meant something quite different to the Soviets than to the Americans. For the Soviet Union, control of Eastern Europe, and especially Poland, was essential, because this area was a vital link in its security belt. After suffering two German invasions in less than thirty years, it was perhaps inevitable that the Soviet Union would try to establish "friendly" governments throughout the area. To the Soviets, democratic governments meant communist regimes, and free elections meant elections free from parties not favorable to the communists. The peace treaties with the former German satellite states (Hungary, Bulgaria, Romania), which were painfully negotiated by the victors in a series of foreign ministers' conferences during 1945 and 1946, could not loosen the tightening Soviet grip on what were by now Soviet satellite states.

In terms of the state system, the Soviet behavior was understandable. Each state had to act as its own guardian against potential adversaries in a system characterized by conflict among states and a sense of insecurity and fear on the part of its members. As the alliance against the common enemy came to an end, the Soviet Union predictably would strengthen itself against the power most likely to be its new opponent. As czarist Russia, with a long history of invasions from the east and the west, it had learned the basic rules of the international game through bitter experience. As the Soviet Union, its sense of peril and mistrust had been intensified by an ideology that posited capitalist states as implacable enemies. In the war, it had suffered over twenty million casualties, soldiers and civilians. Thus the establishment of noncommunist regimes in Eastern Europe was unacceptable, and the American insistence on free elections was seen as an attempt to push the Soviet Union out of Europe.

U.S.-SOVIET DIFFERENCES

The question of elections vividly illustrated the differences between the United States and the Soviet Union. During the war, Roosevelt worried that Soviet and U.S. interests might clash in the period of flux after Germany's defeat. He therefore single-mindedly pursued a policy of friendship toward the Soviet Union. Roosevelt, however, did not view free elections in Eastern Europe in terms of the creation of a new anti-Soviet belt. For him, free elections and a friendly attitude between East and West were quite compatible.

The model he had in mind was Czechoslovakia. As the only democracy in that area, Czechoslovakia had maintained close ties with the West since its birth after World War I. But because France and Britain had failed to defend Czechoslovakia at Munich in 1938 and betrayed it by appeasing Hitler, it also had become friendly with the Soviet Union. After 1945, Czechoslovakia, like the other East European states, knew that it lay in the Soviet sphere of influence and that its security depended on getting along with, not irritating, its powerful neighbor. Thus Czech leaders expressed amicable feelings for the Soviet Union and signed a security treaty with Moscow. Later, in one of the rare free elections the Soviets allowed in Eastern Europe, the Communist Party received the largest vote of any party and therefore the key posts in the government.

During World War II, the heroic Soviet war effort and sacrifices had created a reservoir of goodwill in the West. Had the Soviets acted with greater restraint after the war and accepted states that, regardless of their governments' composition, would have adjusted to their Soviet neighbor, Stalin could have had the security he was seeking. But Stalin did not trust Roosevelt. No matter how personable the president was, no matter how sincere his statements of goodwill and postwar friendship were, Stalin saw him as the leader of a capitalist nation. As a "tool of Wall Street," Roosevelt could not be sincere in his peaceful professions.

Churchill, concerned about Stalin's behavior in Eastern Europe, urged the United States to send forces to capture the symbolically important German capital of Berlin and to advance U.S. troops as far east as possible, including farther into Czechoslovakia. He also suggested that, until Stalin observed his agreements in Eastern Europe, U.S. forces not pull back to their agreed-upon occupation zones in Germany and the United States not shift the bulk of its military power from Europe to the Far East for the final offensive against Japan. Roosevelt rejected all of these suggestions. He had assured Stalin that all American troops would be withdrawn within two years after the war. Why then should Stalin worry about U.S. opposition to his efforts to control Eastern Europe? The Soviet leader exercised caution when he encountered opposition, but he ignored diplomatic notes of protest. Carefully waiting to see what the United States would do, Stalin allowed free elections in Czechoslovakia and Hungary, the two states closest to American power. But continued U.S. and British verbal warnings, unsupported by action, did not impress the Soviet leader.

Consequently, Hungary's freedom was soon squashed by the Soviets.[11] Then in 1948 the Czech government was overthrown by the Soviets in a coup d'état, even though the Communist Party had the largest plurality. Contrary to Roosevelt's expectations, not even a communist-controlled coalition government was acceptable to Stalin. Indeed, as the Soviet satellization of Eastern Europe was to show, the failure of the United States was not the failure of efforts to accommodate Soviet interests in the region; it was the failure to resist Stalin earlier. The Soviet leader's conception of Soviet security left little, if any, security for his neighbors. Those limits had to be defined by the United States.

THE SOVIET PUSH TO THE SOUTH

Just as in the two world wars when Britain had led the effort to contain Germany, London—not Washington—took the first step toward opposing the Soviet Union after 1945. Indeed, the United States at first tried to play the role of mediator between the Soviet Union and Britain. Only when British power proved to be insufficient did the United States take over the task of balancing Soviet power. America's initiative, discussed in greater detail later in this chapter, evolved gradually over 1946–1947 and was precipitated by Stalin's attempt to consolidate his power beyond Eastern Europe. The Soviets began moving even before the smoke from World War II cleared. Turkey, Greece, and Iran were the first to feel their pressure. If Soviet behavior in Eastern Europe could be explained in defensive terms, this was less true for the area south of the Soviet Union, the line from Turkey to India. Long before Stalin, the czars sought access to the Mediterranean via the Dardanelles Strait. Simultaneously, they tried to expand southward to establish a warm-water port and to bring Soviet power closer to the Middle East and the Persian Gulf.

The Soviet Union first sought to gain influence in Turkey. Indeed, the Soviets had begun to do so as early as June 1945 when they made several demands: the cession of several Turkish districts lying on the Turkish-Soviet frontier, a revision of the Montreux Convention governing the Dardanelles Strait in favor of a joint Soviet-Turkish administration, the severance of Turkey's ties with Britain and the conclusion of a treaty with the Soviet Union similar to those the Soviet Union had concluded with its Balkan satellites, and finally, an opportunity to lease bases in the Dardanelles for Soviet naval and land forces to be used for "joint defense." The United States sent a naval task force into the Mediterranean immediately after the Soviets issued these demands. Twelve days

11. For elaboration, see Charles Gati, *Hungary and the Soviet Bloc* (Durham, N.C.: Duke University Press, 1986).

later, the United States formally replied to the Soviets by rejecting their demand to share responsibility for the defense of the straits with Turkey. Britain sent a similar reply.

In Greece, communist pressure was exerted on the government through widespread guerrilla warfare, which began in the fall of 1946. Civil war in Greece was nothing new. During World War II, communist and anticommunist guerrillas had spent much of their energy battling each other instead of the Germans. When the British landed in Greece and the Germans withdrew, the communists attempted to take over Athens. Only after several weeks of bitter street fighting and the landing of British reinforcements was the communist control of Athens dislodged; a truce was signed in January 1945. Just over a year later, the Greeks held a general election in which right-wing forces captured the majority of votes. In August 1946, the communist forces renewed the war in the north, where the Soviet satellites in Eastern Europe could keep the guerrillas well supplied.

Meanwhile, the Soviet Union intensified pressure on Iran by refusing to withdraw its troops from that country. The troops had been there since late 1941, when the Soviet Union and Britain had invaded Iran to forestall increased Nazi influence and to use the nation as a corridor through which the West could ship military aid to the Soviet Union. The Soviets had occupied northern Iran, the British the central and southern sections. When the British withdrew, the Soviets sought to convert Iran into a Soviet satellite. The Iranian prime minister's offer of oil concessions to get the Soviets to withdraw was rebuffed. Moscow's goal was nothing less than detaching the northern area of Azerbaijan and then by various means pressuring Iran into servile status. The U.S. government was once more confronted with the need to support Britain. After the United States and Britain delivered firm statements that they would use force to defend Iran, Stalin finally relented.

Although U.S. efforts in these areas were largely effective, actions taken by President Harry Truman, Roosevelt's successor, were merely swift reactions to immediate crises; they were not the product of an overall American strategy. Such a coherent strategy came only after a reassessment of Soviet foreign policy that placed the Soviet Union's actions in Eastern Europe and beyond in historical perspective.

The Strategy of Containment

Eighteen months passed before the United States undertook that review—from the surrender of Japan on September 2, 1945, until the announcement of the Truman Doctrine on March 12, 1947. Perhaps such a reevaluation could not have been made any more quickly. Public opinion in a democratic country does not normally shift drastically overnight. It would have been too much to expect Americans to suddenly abandon their friendly attitude toward the Soviet Union, inspired largely by the images of Soviet wartime bravery and endurance and by hopes for peaceful postwar cooperation. Moreover, war-weary citizens of the United States wished to be left alone to occupy themselves once more with domestic affairs.

Military leaders, including Secretary of War Robert Patterson, Army Chief of Staff George Marshall, and Secretary of the Navy James Forrestal, urged Truman to reduce the armed forces gradually in order to safeguard the enhanced strategic position of the United States. But the president and Congress, sensing the national desire for detachment from foreign concerns, ordered the "most rapid demobilization in the history of the world." [12] Total active-duty troop levels fell from more than 12 million in 1945 to less than 1.5 million in 1948 (see Figure 2-1). This reduction in military strength, a symptom of America's psychological demobilization, no doubt encouraged the Soviet Union's intransigence in Europe and its attempts to extend its influence elsewhere. Even with the steep reductions in military personnel, the United States continued to possess the largest navy in the world and a nuclear monopoly. But after U.S. commitments to occupied territories were taken into account, "the United States lacked the ground forces required to intervene in anything greater than a minor conflict." [13]

When Soviet expansion finally led to a reevaluation of American policy, three strategic positions became clear. At one extreme stood that old realist Winston Churchill, who had long counseled against the withdrawal of American troops from Europe. He insisted that the presence of British and American troops would force the Soviet Union to live up to its Yalta obligations to allow free elections in Eastern Europe and to withdraw the Red Army from eastern Germany. After the United States rejected his plea, Churchill took his case directly to the American public in a March 1946 speech at Fulton, Missouri: "From Stettin in the Baltic to Trieste in the Adriatic, an iron curtain has descended across the continent. Behind that line lie all the capitals of the ancient states of Central and Eastern Europe. Warsaw, Berlin, Prague, Vienna, Budapest, Belgrade, Bucharest, and Sofia, all the famous cities and populations around them lie in the Soviet sphere and all are subject in one form or another, not only to Soviet influence but to a very high and increasing measure of control from Moscow." [14]

12. Stephen E. Ambrose, *Rise to Globalism: American Foreign Policy since 1938*, 5th rev. ed. (New York: Penguin, 1988), 79.

13. Robert A. Pollard, *Economic Security and the Origins of the Cold War, 1945–1950* (New York: Columbia University Press, 1985).

14. The entire speech can be found in Thomas G. Paterson, ed., *The Origins of the Cold War*, 2d ed. (Lexington, Mass.: D. C. Heath, 1974), 11–17.

FIGURE 2-1 American Demobilization after World War II

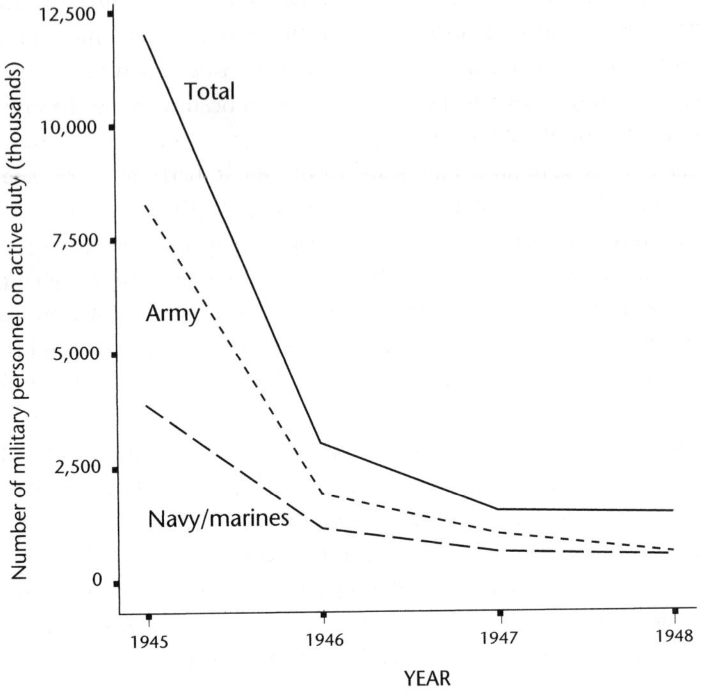

Source: U.S. Bureau of the Census, *Historical Statistics of the United States, Colonial Times to 1970,* No. 2 (Washington, D.C.: Government Printing Office, 1975), 1141.

Churchill did not believe that the Soviets wanted war: "What they desire is the fruits of war and the indefinite expansion of their power and doctrines." And the only thing lying between the Soviets and their desires was the opposing power of the British Commonwealth and the United States. In short, Churchill was saying bluntly that the Cold War had begun, and that Americans must recognize this fact and give up their dreams of Big Three unity in the United Nations.

At the other extreme stood Secretary of Commerce Henry A. Wallace, who felt it was precisely the kind of aggressive attitude expressed by Churchill that was to blame for Soviet hostility. The United States and Britain, he said, had no more business in Eastern Europe than the Soviet Union had in Latin America; for each, the respective area was vital for national security. Western interference in nations bordering the Soviet Union was bound to arouse Soviet suspicion. "We may not like what Russia does in Eastern Europe," said Wallace. "Her type of land reform, industrial expropriation, and suspension of basic liberties offend the great majority of the people of the United States. But whether we like it or not, the Russians will try to socialize their sphere of influence just as we try to democratize our sphere of influence." The tough attitude demanded by Churchill and other "reactionaries" at home and abroad was precisely the wrong policy; it would only increase international tension. "The tougher we get, the tougher the Russians will get," Wallace pointed out.[15] Only mutual trust would allow the United States and the Soviet Union to live together peacefully, and such trust could not be created by an unfriendly American attitude and policy.

The American government and public wavered between these two positions and tentatively adopted a third strategy. The administration recognized that Big Three cooperation had ended. The U.S. government, then, would make no further concessions to lend the appearance of cooperation with the Soviet Union. It had tried to gain Soviet amity through cooperation and unilateral defense cutbacks; now it was up to Soviet leaders to demonstrate a constructive approach toward the United States as well. Paper agreements, written in such general terms that they hid divergent purposes, were regarded as having little value. Something more was needed: Soviet words would have to be matched by deeds. Thus the United States would seek neither to roll back communism nor to maintain cordial relations with Moscow. The American secretary of state, James Byrnes, called this third strategy the "policy of firmness and patience." American steadfastness presumably would wear the Soviets down and moderate their conduct.

GEORGE KENNAN AND THE NEW GRAND STRATEGY

George F. Kennan, the U.S. State Department's foremost expert on the Soviet Union, presented in 1946 the basis of what was to be a new American policy that recognized the hostile character of the Soviet regime. In a detailed telegram sent from the U.S. embassy in Moscow, Kennan analyzed the communist outlook on world affairs.[16] In the minds of the Soviet leaders, he said, the Soviet Union had no community of interest with the capitalist states; to the contrary, they saw their relationship with the Western powers as one of innate antagonism. Moreover, communist ideology had taught them that it was their duty to eventually overthrow

15. Henry Wallace, "The Way to Peace," September 12, 1946, http://www.lib.uiowa.edu/spec-coll/MSC/ToMsc200/MsC177/index. speechesby1946.htm (accessed April 6, 2006).

16. This "long telegram" was later reprinted in the famous "X article" entitled "The Sources of Soviet Conduct," which appeared in the July 1947 issue of *Foreign Affairs*. It is also reproduced in George F. Kennan, *American Diplomacy, 1900–1950* (Chicago: University of Chicago Press, 1951), 107–128.

the political forces in the outside hostile world, and "the powerful hands of Russian history and tradition" sustained them in this feeling.[17]

According to Kennan, this Soviet hostility would continue until the capitalist world had been destroyed. From this antagonism flowed many of the elements the West found "disturbing in the Kremlin's conduct of foreign policy: the secretiveness, the lack of frankness, the duplicity, the war suspiciousness, and the basic unfriendliness of purpose." He explained that "these characteristics of the Soviet policy, like the postulates from which they flow, are basic to the *internal* nature of Soviet power, and will be with us . . . until the nature of Soviet power is changed." [18] Until that moment, he said, Soviet strategy and objectives would remain the same.

The U.S.-Soviet struggle would thus be a long one, but Kennan stressed that Soviet hostility did not mean the Soviets would embark on a do-or-die program to overthrow capitalism by a fixed date. Given their sense of historical inevitability, they had no timetable for conquest. In a brilliant passage, Kennan outlined the Soviet concept of the struggle:

> The Kremlin is under no ideological compulsion to accomplish its purposes in a hurry. Like the Church, it is dealing in ideological concepts which are of a long-term validity, and it can afford to be patient. It has no right to risk the existing achievements of the revolution for the sake of vain baubles of the future. The very teachings of Lenin himself require great caution and flexibility in the pursuit of communist purposes. Again, these precepts are fortified by the lessons of Russian history: of centuries of obscure battles between nomadic forces over the stretches of a vast unfortified plain. Here caution, circumspection, flexibility, and deception are the valuable qualities. . . . The main thing is that there should always be pressure, increasing constant pressure, toward the desired goal. There is no trace of any feeling in Soviet psychology that the goal must be reached at any given time.[19]

How could the United States counter such a policy? Kennan's answer was that American policy would have to be one of "long-term, patient, but firm and vigilant containment." He viewed containment as a test of American democracy to conduct an intelligent, long-range foreign policy *and* simultaneously contribute to changes within the Soviet Union that ultimately would bring about a moderation of its revolutionary aims. The United States, he emphasized in a passage that was to take on great meaning four decades later,

> has it in its power to increase enormously the strains under which Soviet policy must operate, to force upon the Kremlin a far greater degree of moderation and circumspection than it has had to observe in recent years, and

17. Kennan, *American Diplomacy,* 111–112.
18. Ibid., 115, emphasis added.
19. Ibid., 118.

IMPACT AND INFLUENCE

GEORGE KENNAN

The euphoria surrounding the end of World War II quickly gave way in the United States to concerns about the emerging Cold War. The U.S. government turned to George Kennan, a State Department officer based in the Soviet Union during and after World War II, to devise an appropriate response to the Soviet challenge in central Europe. U.S. presidents would follow Kennan's "containment" strategy, described in this chapter, until the collapse of the Soviet Union in 1991.

Although Kennan profoundly influenced American foreign policy after World War II, he spent most of the postwar era out of government. In 1950, he joined Princeton University's Institute for Advanced Study, from where he continued to inform the foreign policy debate, often deflecting criticism that his containment policy had led directly to U.S. interventions in Korea, Vietnam, and Latin America. Defending his record, Kennan charged that American leaders had strayed from the strategy he proposed. More generally, he criticized the "legalistic-moralistic" approach to American foreign policy and claimed it had prevented the nation from focusing on its national interests in the late twentieth century. In this respect, Kennan is considered one of the key postwar realists whose views ran counter to the American style of foreign policy.

in this way to promote tendencies which must eventually find their outlet in either the breakup or the gradual mellowing of Soviet power. For no mystical, messianic movement—and particularly not that of the Kremlin—can face frustration indefinitely without eventually adjusting itself in one way or another to the logic of that state of affairs.[20]

20. Ibid., 127–128.

And why was the United States so favorably positioned for a long-term struggle with the Soviet Union? The reason, Kennan argued, was that industry was the key ingredient of power and the United States controlled most of the centers of industry. There were five such centers in the world: the United States, Britain, West Germany, Japan, and the Soviet Union. The United States and its allies constituted four of these centers, the Soviet Union just one. Containment meant confining the Soviet Union to that one. The question, Kennan said, was not whether the United States had sufficient power to contain the Soviet Union, but whether it had the patience and wisdom to do so.[21]

ALTERNATIVES TO CONTAINMENT

Kennan's containment strategy was generally well received in Washington, whose leaders then embarked on the complex task of translating its generalities into specific initiatives. These would entail new strategies for the military services, a greater emphasis on economic statecraft and foreign assistance, and an ongoing effort to enlist foreign countries into bilateral and multilateral alliance networks (see Chapter 3). But in adopting containment, the Truman administration implicitly rejected two other courses of action that had substantial support.

The first was a retreat into the traditional pattern of U.S. isolation from European diplomacy. This alternative was rejected when, on the afternoon of February 21, 1947, the first secretary of the British embassy in Washington visited the State Department and handed American officials two notes from His Majesty's government. One concerned Greece, the other Turkey, but in effect they said the same thing: Britain could no longer meet its traditional responsibilities to those two countries. Because both countries were on the verge of collapse, the meaning of the British notes was clear: a Soviet breakthrough could be prevented only by an American commitment to stopping it.

February 21 was a turning point for the West. Britain, the only remaining power in Western Europe, was acknowledging its exhaustion. It had fought Philip II of Spain, Louis XIV and Napoleon Bonaparte of France, Kaiser Wilhelm II and Adolf Hitler of Germany. It had long preserved the balance of power that had protected the United States, but its ability to protect that balance had declined steadily in the twentieth century and twice it had needed American help. Each time, however, Britain

21. For a recent profile of Kennan, who died in March 2005, see T. Christopher Jesperson, ed., *Interviews with George Kennan* (Jackson: University of Mississippi Press, 2002). For a retrospective analysis of Kennan's impact on American foreign policy, see Richard L. Russell, *George F. Kennan's Strategic Thought: The Making of an American Political Realist* (Westport, Conn.: Praeger, 1999).

had fought the longer battle; the United States had entered the wars only when it was clear that Germany and its allies were too strong for Britain and that America would have to help safeguard its own security.

The second course rejected in adopting the strategy of containment was a preventive war. The United States had an atomic monopoly until late 1949. In 1950 the United States had fifty bombs plus the means to deliver them, while the Soviet Union had only tested an atomic device. For a short time, then, the United States possessed the opportunity to establish a *Pax Americana,* or world empire. But exploitation of this atomic monopoly was never seriously considered. Quite apart from the relatively small size of the stockpile, the launch of an atomic Pearl Harbor on the Soviet Union was contrary to American tradition and universal standards of morality. Indeed, after Hiroshima the conviction grew that atomic weapons were too horrible to use and that in a future war there would be no winners.

The bomb, then, signaled a significant change: historically the principal task of military armaments had been to win wars; from now on their main purpose would be to *deter* them. Atomic weapons could have no other rationale. Conflicts between great powers—between Athens and Sparta for the control of ancient Greece, between Rome and Carthage for control of the Mediterranean, or, in more modern times, between Germany and England for control of Europe—had been settled on the battlefield. Such a solution, however, was no longer feasible; the United States now had to conduct a *protracted conflict* alien to its style. The term frequently given to this conflict—Cold War—was apt indeed. *War* signified that the U.S.-Soviet rivalry was serious; *Cold* referred to the fact that nuclear weapons were so utterly destructive that war, even with conventional weapons, could not be waged.

Even though communist containment was adopted as the linchpin of U.S. strategy, it drew criticism from many quarters. Some felt it did not go far enough, that it failed to exploit U.S. military and economic supremacy and provided the Soviets with the initiative to set the time and place of superpower confrontations.[22] Others felt it went too far. By codifying the U.S.-Soviet conflict, it cemented a pervasive U.S. role in Europe and beyond and ensured a prolonged and dangerous global competition. Located as it was between the two extremes, however, the containment alternative attracted support among moderates both in the United States and abroad. Future leaders would modify the strategy, but they would adhere to its broader objectives with unusual consistency. It thus heralded an auspicious new era in U.S. foreign policy, perhaps best

22. For a prominent critique, see Walter Lippmann, *The Cold War: A Study in U.S. Foreign Policy* (New York: Harper, 1947).

reflected in the title of Secretary of State Dean Acheson's memoir, *Present at the Creation.* To Acheson, the late 1940s "saw the entry of our nation, already one of the superpowers, into the near chaos of a war-torn and disintegrating world society. To the responsibilities and needs of that time the nation summoned an imaginative effort unique in history and even greater than that made in the preceding years of fighting. All who served in those years had an opportunity to give more than a sample of their best." [23]

The Cold War that followed was characterized by long-term hostility and by a mutual determination to avoid a cataclysmic military showdown. As it took over Britain's role as the keeper of the balance of power, the United States had to learn power politics. But in protecting itself, it also had to learn how to manage a protracted conflict in peacetime, a new experience and one at odds with its historical ways of dealing with foreign enemies and the international system.

THE GEOPOLITICS OF CONTAINING MOSCOW

The United States would play in the Cold War a role similar to that played traditionally by Britain: primarily a naval power, the United States would contain the outward thrust of a land power from the Eurasian "heartland." After World War I, a British geographer, Halford J. Mackinder, interested in the relationship of geographic position to international politics (referred to as *geopolitics*), stated the axiom "Who rules East Europe commands the Heartland [Eurasia]; Who rules the Heartland commands the World-Island [Eurasia and Africa, which, on the map, look like a centrally located island]; Who rules the World-Island commands the World." [24] A generation later, an American geopolitician, Nicholas Spykman, coined a reply to Mackinder: "Who controls the Rimland [the peripheral areas around Eurasia] controls Eurasia; who rules Eurasia controls the destinies of the world." [25] Although these axioms may be too simplistic—and there is some danger in accepting geography as too deterministic a factor in explaining the behavior of states—they explain rather well the essence of the British-German and the U.S.-Soviet conflicts.

Indeed, before World War I, before the German threat received Britain's primary attention, *czarist* Russia—then incorporating Finland,

23. Dean Acheson, *Present at the Creation: My Years in the State Department* (New York: Norton, 1969), 725.

24. Sir Halford J. Mackinder, *Democratic Ideals and Reality: A Study in the Politics of Reconstruction* (New York: Henry Holt, 1919), 150.

25. Nicholas Spykman, *The Geography of the Peace* (New York: Harcourt, Brace, 1944). Also see Spykman, *America's Strategy in World Politics: The United States and the Balance of Power* (New York: Harcourt, Brace, 1944).

the three Baltic states, and Poland—had been London's concern. Russian power was spreading east to the Pacific, southeast toward the frontier of British India (today's Afghanistan and Pakistan), southeast from Siberia into Manchuria and into northern China, and southwest from the Caucasus to Turkey and Iran. British power along the rim running from Turkey to India guarded the perimeter around Russia. When Russia pushed into Korea toward Japan, Japan attacked and defeated Russia, thereby also limiting the spread of Russian influence in northern China. After that, Russia focused on the Balkans, where it came into conflict with Austria-Hungary, ally of the European continent's most powerful country, Germany. Germany became the great threat to British interests, and Britain twice went to war with Germany, which, in each conflict, invaded Russia. A victorious Germany would have controlled the heartland—indeed, in World War II victory would have conceivably given Germany control from the Atlantic to the Pacific—as well as the Middle East, the area linking Europe, Asia, and Africa.

After Germany's second defeat in 1945, the Russian threat reemerged. Already the heartland power, Soviet Russia extended its arm into the center of Europe, reclaimed its dominant position in northern China, and sought to exploit weaknesses along its southern border from Turkey to Pakistan. Thus one reason for the postwar conflict was *geopolitical:* Russian land power expanded but was halted by the countervailing power exerted by a maritime nation, the United States. These clashes occurred along the perimeter from Turkey to Iran and then in Western Europe.

The Soviet Union did not represent a direct threat to the security of the United States in the Western Hemisphere. But the Soviet army, even after substantial demobilization, remained a formidable force of 175 divisions and certainly one able to pressure Soviet neighbors to the south and in Europe and hold America's friends and potential allies hostage. That is why the governments of Iran, Turkey, Greece, and Western Europe feared a revival of American isolationism and sought U.S. countervailing support. To be sure, the small U.S. atomic arsenal could have wreaked great damage on Russian cities, but it could not have stopped the Soviet army from overrunning Western Europe.

In the balance that emerged after World War II, the United States greatly benefited from its productive economy, which had not been damaged by the war; from its atomic monopoly, although the number of bombs and bombers available to deliver them remained small in the first years after the war; and from the appeal of its democratic political system. The Soviet Union had the advantages of its powerful conventional forces; its geographical position at the center of Eurasia; and, at a time when democracy was still widely identified with the failed capitalism of the 1930s and the Soviet Union with its heroic resistance to the Nazis, its communist ideology. That ideology appealed to the working classes in nations such as France and Italy, as well as to the political movements that were seeking power in countries such as China. Thus American political leaders after 1945 did not conclude that the United States was a hegemonic power. To the contrary, they were anxious about a balance of power that appeared to them to be very precarious.

Declaring Cold War: The Truman Doctrine

On March 12, 1947, President Harry Truman went before a joint session of Congress to deliver one of the most important speeches in American history. After outlining the situation in Greece, he spelled out what would become known as the Truman Doctrine. The United States, he said, could survive only in a world in which freedom flourished. And it would not realize this objective unless it was

> willing to help free peoples to maintain their institutions and their national integrity against aggressive movements that seek to impose upon them totalitarian regimes. *This is no more than a frank recognition that totalitarian regimes imposed on free peoples, by direct or indirect aggression, undermine the foundations of international peace and hence the security of the United States. . . .*
>
> At the present moment in world history nearly every nation must choose between alternative ways of life. The choice is often not a free one. . . .
>
> I believe that we must assist free peoples to work out their own destinies in their own way.[26]

The president asked Congress to appropriate $400 million for economic aid and military supplies for Greece and Turkey and to authorize the dispatch of American personnel to assist with reconstruction and to provide their armies with appropriate instruction and training. And he implicitly offered U.S. assistance to other states with his open-ended appeal to "free peoples." One of his most critical tactical victories in winning approval for these measures was that over Michigan senator Arthur Vandenberg, a prominent Republican isolationist and chairman of the Senate Foreign Relations Committee. With Vandenberg's endorsement, Congress embraced the spirit and financial requirements of the Truman Doctrine.[27]

26. Emphasis added. The drama of this period and Truman's speech to Congress are still best captured in Joseph M. Jones, *The Fifteen Weeks* (New York: Viking Press, 1955), 17–23.

27. For recent elaborations on the Truman Doctrine, see Jan S. Prybyla, *The American Way of Peace: An Interpretation* (Columbia: University of Missouri Press, 2005), chap. 7; and Arnold A. Offner, *Another Such Victory: President Truman and the Cold War, 1945–1953* (Stanford, Calif.: Stanford University Press, 2002), chap. 8.

The United States thus initiated the policy of containment. The emerging clash between the postwar superpowers, anticipated by the Truman administration in the late 1940s, was evident in the hostile actions being taken on both sides. To many, the defining moment occurred on July 2, 1947, when the Russian delegation walked out of a meeting in Paris of Americans and other Western leaders to discuss the distribution of Marshall Plan aid (see Chapter 3). From then on, the two antagonists would not even put forward the appearance of great-power cooperation or *rapprochement.*

In this volatile atmosphere, Soviet behavior left the United States with little choice but to adopt a countervailing policy. During World War II, the United States had sought to overcome the Kremlin's suspicions of the West, to be sensitive to Soviet security concerns in eastern Europe, and to lay the foundation for postwar cooperation. At the end of the war, the principal concern of American policy makers was not to eliminate the Soviet Union, the self-proclaimed bastion of world revolution and enemy of Western capitalism, nor did they seek to push the Soviet Union out of eastern Europe. After all, American policy was not the product of a virulent and preexisting anticommunist ideology. Rather, it was animated by its desire to prevent a major nation from achieving dominance in Europe, an occurrence that twice in the twentieth century had led the United States into war.

In this respect, American military strategy toward Europe at the dawn of the Cold War was consistent with that in the early stages of the two world wars, which were fought, first, against a conservative monarchy in Germany, and then against the fascist states of Germany and Italy. In the Cold War, the adversary was the Soviet Union, a repressive communist regime. American strategy and subsequent action remained the same regardless of the opponent's ideology. This does not mean, however, that ideology was irrelevant to these conflicts. To the contrary, all these adversaries maintained systems of government and state-society relations that offended American democratic ideals and seemed threatening to those ideals. Thus the fascist and "godless" communist regimes, located at both ends of the ideological spectrum, also inflamed the moral passions of the American government and provided a further rationale for Cold War. The strategy fit neatly into the traditional American dichotomy of seeing the world as either good or evil, thereby arousing the nation for yet another moral crusade.

The contrasting nature of U.S. and Soviet conduct after World War II reinforced these normative tensions. The Soviet Union, which already had annexed the Baltic states, imposed communist regimes on its neighbors and stationed Soviet forces there to ensure the loyalty of these states. In fact, none of these governments could have survived without the presence of Soviet troops. By contrast, Iran, Turkey, and Greece invited American assistance because they feared Soviet pressure and intimidation. Soviet expansion meant their loss of independence; American assistance was designed to preserve it. All shared the U.S. perception of the Soviet Union as a threat to their political independence and territorial integrity and urged Washington to redress the post-1945 imbalance. Their concern was not U.S. expansion and hegemony, but abandonment.

The Truman Doctrine in its immediate application was intended to be specific and limited, not global. American policy makers were well aware that the United States, although a great power, was not omnipotent; national priorities had to be decided carefully and power applied discriminately. American responses, then, would depend both on where the external challenges occurred and on how Washington defined the relation of such challenges to the nation's security. Containment was to be implemented only where the Soviet state appeared to be expanding its power. The priority given to balance of power considerations was evident from the very beginning.

Despite the democratic values expressed in the Truman Doctrine, it was first applied to Greece and Turkey, neither of which was democratic. Their strategic locations were considered more important than the character of their governments. In Western Europe, however, America's strategic and power considerations were compatible with its democratic values; containment of the Soviet Union could be equated with the defense of democracy. The United States thus confronted a classic dilemma: protecting strategically located but undemocratic nations such as Iran, Turkey, and Greece might make the containment of Soviet power possible, but it also risked America's reputation and weakened the credibility of its policy. Yet alignment only with democratic states, of which there were all too few, might make U.S. implementation of its containment policy impossible. The purity of the cause might be preserved, but the security of democracy would be weakened. This dilemma was to plague U.S. policy throughout the Cold War, and the same dilemma persists today in the war against terrorism.

In summary, the emerging bipolar state system and the character and behavior of the Soviet Union were fundamental factors precipitating the Cold War. What, if any, was America's contribution to the onset of the Cold War? Perhaps at the time the United States could not have done more than simply protest the Soviet satellization of Eastern Europe. It was true that the American people, like the British, admired the heroic efforts of the Red Army in stopping and driving back the Nazi forces. Moreover, the staggering Soviet losses, compared with the relatively light losses of the Allies, were recognized in the West. In these circumstances, the hope for good postwar relations with the Soviet Union was understandable.

These optimistic projections, however, were quickly dispelled by events in Eastern Europe. As the United States proceeded with its withdrawal and military demobilization, Soviet leaders made it clear that their control over the region would be firm and anything but temporary. Thus the threatened states bordering the Soviet bloc, which were greatly weakened by the war, looked to Washington to exert countervailing power. The United States finally took the necessary measures to oppose Stalin and draw the lines beyond which Soviet expansion would not be tolerated. Stalin, incapable of defining the limits of his ambitions, now found that the United States would do it for him.

CHAPTER THREE

Containment: From Theory to Practice

Members of the U.S. Army's Second Infantry Division search for communist-held positions during the Korean War. The conflict, which erupted in 1950, represented a direct challenge to the containment doctrine adopted by the United States in the late 1940s.

Twenty-one years separated the two world wars, providing their combatants with time to recover from their losses, restore some semblance of domestic order, redefine their national interests, and prepare for future challenges. But that was not true after World War II. Even before the conflict was over, both the Soviet Union and the Western allies were posturing for spheres of influence in central Europe. And it was only six months after the Japanese surrender that Winston Churchill gloomily proclaimed that an "iron curtain" had descended across central Europe, defining the battle lines of the next global confrontation. If there was an "interwar" period in this case, it was hardly perceptible.

Fortunately for the United States, the late 1940s were among the most imaginative years in U.S. diplomatic history. With the guidance of an unusually cohesive team of advisers, President Harry Truman transformed the nation's foreign policy so the United States could compete indefinitely as a political, economic, and military superpower. The "wise men" of the Truman administration established the basis of the Western strategy that ultimately prevailed in the Cold War.[1]

America's political leaders generally agreed that George Kennan's containment strategy was the most sensible response to Soviet expansionism in the aftermath of World War II (see Chapter 2). A retreat into isolation was not possible, particularly because U.S. withdrawal in the 1920s only provided encouragement to German and Japanese expansionists. Nor was it feasible to attempt to destroy the Soviet Union through a preemptive military strike. Representing a middle ground, the goal of containment seemed most consistent with the country's means.

The global scope of the challenge guaranteed that implementing containment would be a monumental task. The obstacles were especially great given the traditional American penchant for withdrawal and isolation from great-power politics in peacetime. Further hampering the United States was the lack of an institutional basis for dealing with a worldwide threat that was not likely to disappear or be defeated militarily within a few years. The U.S. government had maintained a permanent Foreign Service only since the end of World War I, and a standing army always had been viewed with great apprehension. But as this chapter describes, America's leaders overcame these obstacles and created a web of national security structures, bilateral ties, and multilateral organizations that put Kennan's theory of communist containment into practice.

These arrangements served American foreign policy interests that extended beyond the struggle against communism. The central role of the United States in creating and managing the postwar order gave American leaders added leverage with their European allies along with developing countries from East Asia to Africa and Latin America. Indeed, the enduring value of this order would be evident decades later as the web of domestic and global institutions established in the late 1940s remained intact long after the Cold War. But for those in power at the time, the immediate concern was resisting the threat posed by the Soviet Union.

In its first step, the Truman administration sought to revive its war-ravaged allies in Western Europe, which, from Washington's point of view, urgently needed to form a united front against Moscow. Such a task would be impossible, however, if the historic internal rivalries among the European states were allowed to persist. The United States thus encouraged close cooperation among the European governments in rebuilding their economies, settling their political disputes, and pro-

1. Walter Isaacson and Evan Thomas, *The Wise Men: Six Friends and the World They Made* (New York: Simon and Schuster, 1986).

tecting the region from external aggression. Such cooperation would be supported not only rhetorically but also financially by the United States, which covered much of the costs of Western Europe's recovery.

But the United States could not stop with Europe. To contain communism, it also would have to become actively engaged elsewhere. In the late 1940s and early 1950s, the Asian perimeter of the Soviet Union and China became the second target of U.S. containment. In contrast to Western Europe, many Asian states had only recently emerged from colonialism and their nationalistic and anti-Western feelings were very strong. The collapse of Nationalist China and the establishment of a communist Chinese government on the mainland in 1949 particularly weakened the U.S. position in Asia. The United States suddenly confronted two militarily powerful communist states, one (the Soviet Union) covering the largest landmass in the world, the other (China) governing the world's largest population.

New Economic and Military Structures

Unlike the situation confronting other great powers, U.S. military strength was greater *after* World War II than before, accentuated by the country's undiminished industrial capacity, its monopoly on nuclear weapons, and its global deployment of troops. The U.S. economy had been strengthened by the war on an absolute basis and relative to those of its competitors, which were devastated physically and faced years of reconstruction. The United States accounted for more than one-quarter of global output even after the recovery of its economic competitors, giving it unprecedented wealth to match its military muscle (see Figure 3-1).

Developing a globalist foreign policy required more than a grand strategy, no matter how widely supported that strategy was. An essential first step for the United States was to convert its vast resources into the brick and mortar of political institutions. In addition to leading the effort to create the United Nations, American officials focused on two areas. First, they created an international economic system to support commerce among the capitalist states. Second, they rebuilt the country's military structures and created an elaborate web of alliances. Taken together, these reforms established the institutional blueprint that remained in place throughout the Cold War and has endured in its aftermath.

The Bretton Woods System

Long before World War II ended, Western governments agreed that a new framework was needed to manage global economic relations. They recognized that trade restrictions, subsidies for national industries, and other forms of mercantilism had contributed to the Great Depression of

FIGURE 3-1 Distribution of World Economy, 1950 (gross domestic product, in billions of 1990 US$)

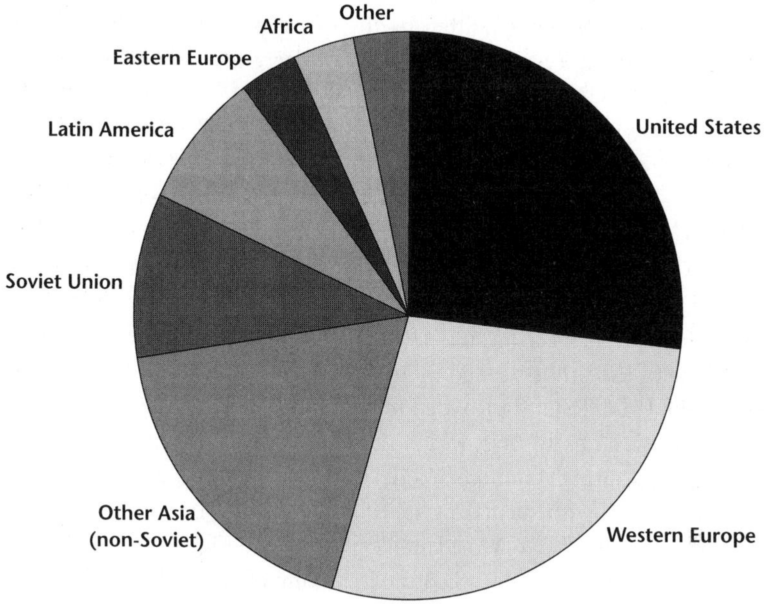

Source: Angus Maddison, *The World Economy: A Millennial Perspective* (Paris: Organisation for Economic Co-operation and Development, 2001), 261.

the 1930s, which, in turn, had aroused nationalist passions and led to the birth of Nazi Germany. It was widely believed that a "liberal international economic order," based on open markets and economic cooperation and leading to the recuperation of the European industrial states, could prevent a recurrence of this pattern.[2] The market-based economic order also would reduce the appeal of communism by creating prosperous capitalist societies. But the latter goal was secondary to the former. Even before the Cold War, America's leaders had agreed that the country's economic prosperity, and global stability in general, depended on an integrated global economy that encouraged trade and investments across national borders.[3]

2. An influential argument at the time was made by theorist Nicholas Spykman in *America's Strategy in the World* (New York: Harcourt, Brace, 1942).

3. See Robert L. Pollard, *Economic Security and the Origins of the Cold War, 1945–1950* (New York: Columbia University Press, 1985).

American officials welcomed the opportunity to replicate the U.S. economic model on an international scale. Along with European leaders, they devised a plan for international economic, fiscal, and monetary cooperation to be underwritten by the vast economic resources of the United States. In 1944 representatives of forty-four countries met at Bretton Woods, New Hampshire, to approve this plan, which already had been devised by American and British officials. The Bretton Woods system played a critical role in hastening the recovery of the industrialized states. Along the way, the new system strengthened the market economies against their communist rivals.

The Bretton Woods accords created two institutions to promote economic growth among the market economies.[4] First, the International Bank for Reconstruction and Development (IBRD), or World Bank, would lend the funds needed by member states to rebuild their industries. The United States provided much of the World Bank's funding in the institution's early days, which the bank then lent to member states on generous terms. As the recipients of World Bank funding recovered, which they did with surprising speed in the late 1940s and 1950s, they, in turn, contributed to World Bank programs designed to speed economic growth in developing countries, many of which were becoming free of colonial rule. Second, the International Monetary Fund (IMF) would govern currency exchanges and provide credits for member states facing short-term currency crises. To receive these credits, recipients were required to enact IMF provisions for government taxing and spending and for adopting "responsible" monetary policies. Members were thus prevented from simply printing more money to cover their deficits, a practice that had led to rampant inflation and the collapse of central banks in many countries during the 1930s. The major economic powers tried, but failed, to create a third institution that would govern international trade. The International Trade Organization (ITO), proposed in the 1948 Havana Charter, called for sweeping controls over global commerce, including foreign investment, employment policies, and prices for commodities. But several governments, including the United States, felt the ITO went too far and would violate their economic sovereignty as well as the principles of free enterprise. Instead, the United States joined twenty-two other countries in approving the General Agreement on Tariffs and Trade (GATT), which established rules for "nondiscrimination" in world markets. Subsequent GATT

4. For a comprehensive historical review, see Harold James, *International Monetary Cooperation since Bretton Woods* (New York: Oxford University Press, 1996).

negotiations would further restrict the ability of states to violate the rules of free trade.[5]

The Bretton Woods system laid the foundation for a more integrated world economy. The stability of the market economies was maintained by a system of fixed currency exchange rates based on the U.S. dollar, which was based on the value of U.S. gold reserves at $35 an ounce.[6] The dollar thus became a world currency that provided reassurance to financial markets and a simple framework for trade and foreign investment. Once they had benefited from the Bretton Woods reforms, the Marshall Plan (described later in this chapter), and other assistance programs from Washington, U.S. allies in Western Europe and Japan were able to rebound quickly from World War II and enjoy unprecedented economic growth. Meanwhile, the Soviet Union continued to isolate itself, along with its client states in Eastern Europe, from the market-based global economy, a move that had ominous implications for the outcome of the Cold War.

THE NATIONAL SECURITY ACT

As the Cold War set in, President Harry Truman received strong congressional support to reshape the nation's military structures so they would be able to meet the demands of containing communism. Under the National Security Act of 1947, the formerly separate Departments of the Army and Navy were brought together in the new Department of Defense (DOD), a successor to the Department of War. Now the United States would have a *permanent* military establishment based on the general principle of national defense rather than war fighting. As part of the reorganization, the air force, a third branch of the military formerly controlled by the army, became an independent service. It soon overshadowed the two older services because its principal task was to organize the growing U.S. nuclear arsenal.

In addition, the act created the Central Intelligence Agency (CIA), an offspring of the Office of Strategic Services (OSS), which had gathered foreign intelligence and conducted spy operations during World War II. The OSS, widely considered a "rogue" operation that undertook secret missions around the world with little oversight, was disbanded immediately after the war. A larger intelligence operation than OSS, the CIA quickly became an essential, albeit controversial, part of America's

5. These GATT rounds ultimately led to the creation of the World Trade Organization in 1995 (see Chapter 9). For details on the domestic politics of GATT in the United States, see I. M. Destler, *American Trade Politics*, 4th ed. (Washington, D.C.: Institute for International Economics, 2005), chap. 2.

6. The United States held about 75 percent of the world's gold reserves at the time, amounting to about $25 billion.

containment effort. The agency was essential because it collected and analyzed information that became the basis of American foreign policy. It was controversial because it, in the tradition of the OSS, often carried out "dirty tricks" overseas and sought to subvert governments believed hostile to the United States.

Finally, the act established the National Security Council (NSC) to help the president coordinate foreign policy. Located in the White House, the NSC was composed of the president (its chair), the vice president, and the secretaries of state and defense. The head of the Joint Chiefs of Staff and the CIA director also often attended NSC meetings, along with other government officials whose advice the president sought. A small NSC staff was created to provide information to these leaders, and the national security adviser, a new position, was to serve as a "gatekeeper" and close confidant of the president. Through the NSC, the president gained greater control over U.S. foreign policy, in part by reining in departments such as State and Defense, whose leaders were widely suspected of being captives to their respective bureaucracies. And, no less important, the NSC became the primary crisis management agency for the president, a function that took on increasing urgency in the nuclear age.[7]

The concentration of foreign policy powers within the executive branch and the creation of a large, permanent military force ran counter to the nation's traditional style of foreign policy. As noted earlier, the founders had deliberately constrained presidential powers and avoided standing armies in order to prevent the United States from behaving recklessly in foreign affairs. Thomas Jefferson and other early leaders further feared the creation of a "garrison state" and a "warrior class" that could someday threaten individual liberties.[8] Although their worst fears were not realized, the heightened presidential control over security policy was widely accepted as the price of world power.

Reviving the Western European Allies

Europe's collapse after World War II raised anew a fundamental question that had bedeviled U.S. leaders since the nation's founding: was Euro-

7. See John Prados, *Keeper of the Keys: A History of the National Security Council from Truman to Bush* (New York: Morrow, 1991). For more recent analyses, see David J. Rothkopf, *Running the World: The Inside Story of the National Security Council and the Architects of American Power* (New York: Public Affairs, 2005); and Karl F. Inderfurth and Loch K. Johnson, eds., *Fateful Decisions: Inside the National Security Council* (New York: Oxford University Press, 2004).

8. For an elaboration, see Aaron L. Friedberg, *In the Shadow of the Garrison State: America's Anti-Statism and Its Cold War Grand Strategy* (Princeton, N.J.: Princeton University Press, 2000).

pean stability vital to U.S. security? America's interventions in the two world wars suggested the answer was obvious. But both times the United States had been drawn into the conflicts only after prolonged periods of hesitation and by threats of German domination of the continent. At the end of each conflict, the United States had tried to detach itself politically from Europe, the almost pathological instinct of Americans dating back more than two centuries. After the Second World War, however, the United States was forced, for the first time, to establish an *ongoing*, multifaceted relationship with Western Europe because, in the precarious postwar order, America alone had the resources to take the initiative.

Europe's vital importance became especially clear in the emerging bipolar world. The region ranked second only to the United States in its collective economic power—in industry, productivity, skilled workers, scientists, and engineers. Moreover, trading networks and cultural ties between the United States and Western Europe were long-standing and strong. And, not least, Western Europe represented a "buffer zone" between the two superpowers and thus occupied a crucial strategic position in the emerging Cold War. Because of Western Europe's enormous potential and its geographic position, its stability was inseparable from U.S. security.

The war in Europe had devastated the economies of all its countries, winners and losers alike. Britain's state of postwar exhaustion, largely economic in nature, was symptomatic of the situation throughout Europe. An island nation, Britain traditionally depended on international trade for its livelihood. But the war had crippled its merchant marine industry and destroyed many of its factories. Meanwhile, postwar conditions in Germany also were dreadful. The war had penetrated its heartland, and few cities or towns had escaped Allied bombing, street fighting, or willful destruction by the Nazis as they retreated. Millions of people had no food or shelter. Three-quarters of the factories still standing in the American and British zones of occupation were closed. By January 1947, production had fallen to 31 percent of the 1936 level.

The French, more than all others, were not in the mood to rebuild their huge, troublesome neighbor. The French economy had been damaged badly during the war, and by 1947 its iron and steel production reached only half of its prewar total. Unable to import coal from the other European states, French manufacturing industries were unable to produce sufficient goods to meet demand. Meanwhile, the urban population was short of food, and the government had to spend scarce resources to buy food from abroad. The harsh winter of 1946–1947 only intensified these problems.

This situation was made to order for the large, well-organized French Communist Party. One-quarter of France's electorate—practically the entire working class—voted for the communists just after the war. In Italy, one-third of the electorate cast their lot with the party. The reason was simple: French and Italian capitalism had alienated voters. Workers voted communist to protest a system they felt had long mistreated them. Unlike workers in Britain and the United States, they had suffered all the hardships of capitalism while enjoying few of its benefits, such as good wages and social opportunities. As a result, the communist parties in France and Italy enjoyed a powerful position in regional politics and trade unions.

These difficult conditions forced American officials to respond immediately. It was obvious they could not limit their actions to a single area such as economic development, military defense, or political reform. Their response must be comprehensive, including all these areas, and dedicated to preserving Western Europe as the front-line of Cold War defense.

THE MARSHALL PLAN

With Western Europe on the verge of not only economic ruin but also political and social upheaval, the region's weary governments were forced into dependence on the United States. Most of the items needed for reconstruction and economic vitality—wheat, cotton, sulfur, sugar, machinery, trucks, and coal—could be obtained in sufficient quantities only from American suppliers. But short of food and fuel, with its cities and factories destroyed, Europe could not earn the dollars to pay for these products. Moreover, the United States was so well supplied with everything that it did not have to buy much from abroad. The result was a dollar gap, a term that denoted Europe's dependence on the United States for recovery.

Because the United States could not permit the Soviet Union to extend its influence beyond the iron curtain, U.S. policy makers had to find a way to help Western Europe recover. The prescribed cure was a massive injection of dollars. Secretary of State George Marshall, stressing the economic cooperation required by the United States, called on the European states to devise a plan for their common needs and common recovery. The United States would furnish the funds through the European Recovery Program (later known as the Marshall Plan), but the Europeans had to assume the initiative and do the planning. The result was the Organization for European Economic Cooperation (OEEC), which estimated the cost of Europe's recovery over a four-year period to be $33 billion. President Truman asked Congress for $17 billion, but lawmakers cut the sum to $13 billion. The amount actually spent between 1948 and the end of 1951, when the program ended, was just over $12 billion. Britain, France, and West Germany received more than half of this amount.

The original offer by the United States was deliberately extended to *all* European countries, including the Soviet Union and the nations of Eastern Europe. If the United States had invited only the nations of Western Europe, it would have placed itself in a politically disadvantageous position in which it would have been blamed for the division of Europe and the intensification of the Cold War. Actually, had the Soviets participated, Congress probably would not have supported the Marshall Plan for two reasons: first, the costs would have risen astronomically because of the very heavy damage suffered by the Soviet Union during the war, and, second, hostility toward Moscow was growing stronger each day. The risk had to be accepted, however. It had to be the Soviets who, by their rejection of Marshall Plan aid, would be responsible for the division of Europe. Fortunately, Stalin failed to call the Americans' bluff. He refused the offer of assistance and ordered his clients in Eastern Europe to do likewise.[9]

Was the Marshall Plan a success? The results tell their own story. By 1950 Europe already was exceeding its prewar production by 25 percent; two years later this figure was 200 percent higher. British exports were doing well, French inflation was slowing, and German production had reached its 1936 peak. The dollar gap had been reduced from $12 billion to $2 billion. Europe's cities were being rebuilt and its factories were busy, its stores restocked, and its farmers productive. The Marshall Plan was a huge success, and at a cost that represented only a tiny fraction of the U.S. national income over the same four-year period. The Europeans themselves, of course, were primarily responsible for their achievements, but such a rapid turnaround would not have been possible without the Marshall Plan, which Winston Churchill called "the most unsordid act in history."

ROOTS OF THE EUROPEAN UNION

In making American aid to Western Europe conditional on economic cooperation among the European states, the United States clearly was holding itself up as a model. The Economic Cooperation Act of 1948 called specifically for the creation of an integrated European market—in much the same way the fifty American states were organized economically. America, it stated, was "mindful of the advantage which the United States has enjoyed through the existence of a large-scale domestic market with no internal trade barriers and [believed] that similar advantages can accrue to

9. In place of the Marshall Plan, the Soviet Union created the Council for Mutual Economic Assistance (CMEA) to provide economic assistance to the Eastern European governments. The actual aid extended by Moscow, however, was modest compared with that of the Marshall Plan.

the countries of Europe." In official American opinion, economic integration was essential for Europe's recovery and for long-range prosperity.

Renewed fears of Germany's rising strength further stimulated efforts toward European integration. The specter of a fully revived Germany struck fear into most of its neighbors. The French, with their memories of the Franco-Prussian War (1870–1871) and both world wars, were particularly alarmed by the prospect. Germany's recovery, stimulated by America's response to the Cold War, posed a serious problem for Germany's partners: how could they hold Germany in check when it was potentially the strongest nation in Europe outside of the Soviet Union?

The failure of the traditional balance-of-power strategy, in which a weaker power seeks to balance against a stronger one, led France to seek a new way to exert some control over Germany's growing power. French leaders found an imaginative means in European integration. Through the creation of a *supranational* community to which Germany and other European states would transfer certain sovereign rights, German power could be controlled. Instead of serving national purposes, Germany's strength would serve Europe's collective purposes while its government regained some measure of regional credibility.

France made a bold move in the direction of a united Europe in May 1950, when Foreign Minister Robert Schuman proposed the formation of the European Coal and Steel Community (ECSC) composed of "Little Europe" (France, West Germany, Italy, and the "Benelux" countries of Belgium, the Netherlands, and Luxembourg). The aim of the Schuman Plan was to interweave German and French heavy industry to such an extent that it would be impossible to separate them. Germany never again would be able to use its coal and steel industries for nationalistic and militaristic purposes. War between Germany and France would become not only unthinkable but also impossible.

In addition, French leaders eagerly anticipated a united Europe that would be independent of American pressure. Acting alone, France was too weak to pursue an active role in a world dominated by the two superpowers. Even in the Western coalition, the most influential European nation was not France but Britain. With Germany's recovery, its role in regional affairs would likely expand. By itself, France would remain dependent on its American protector, powerless to affect major Western policy decisions. A united Europe, with Franco-German unity at its core, was France's alternative to remaining subservient to the United States.

As the benefits of pooling heavy industry became clear, European leaders expected that other sectors of the economy would follow suit, possibly leading to political integration and the creation of a "United

States of Europe." [10] They took a momentous step in this direction in 1957 when the six governments of "Little Europe" established the European Economic Community (EEC), more commonly known as the Common Market. Its objective was to join the countries together in an economic union. Members of the EEC agreed to eliminate the tariffs and quota systems that hampered trade among them and to abolish restrictions on the regional movement of goods, services, labor, and capital. In addition, they created a variety of governing bodies, including a European Parliament, to pave the way toward political unification.

Not surprisingly, the Soviet Union voiced strong opposition to the Common Market. A thriving Western Europe, economically prosperous and politically stable, not only would prove a powerful barrier to Soviet expansion, but also might threaten the status quo in Eastern Europe. The Western European societies were a magnetic attraction for Soviet clients, especially when the gaps in living standards between the two blocs became evident. After Stalin's protests fell on deaf ears in the West, the Soviet leader redoubled his efforts to isolate Eastern Europeans and subject them entirely to Moscow's control.

MILITARY REARMAMENT AND THE NATO ALLIANCE

Soon after the Marshall Plan was launched, it became clear that economic measures alone would not adequately counter Soviet expansion. In February 1948, the Soviets engineered a coup d'état in Prague, and—ten years after the Munich agreement and Adolf Hitler's subsequent seizure of that betrayed nation—Czechoslovakia disappeared behind the iron curtain. A few months later, in June, the Soviets challenged the postwar division of Germany that had left West Germany occupied by the Western powers, East Germany in Soviet hands, and the city of Berlin similarly divided. The challenge took the form of a Soviet blockade of West Berlin in an effort to dislodge the occupying Allied powers. It is not surprising that Western Europeans were alarmed by these overt acts of Soviet hostility. It suddenly became clear that a second prerequisite for Europe's continued economic recovery, along with regional integration, was military security.

The Europeans already had taken modest steps in this direction. In March 1947, France and Britain had signed the Treaty of Dunkirk to provide for their mutual defense against a threat to their security. A year later, Britain, France, the Netherlands, Belgium, and Luxembourg signed the Brussels Pact for their collective self-defense. Its members expected the

10. For an early elaboration of this "functionalist" approach to regional integration, see David Mitrany, *A Working Peace System* (Chicago: Quadrangle Books, 1966). Also see Ernst Haas, *The Uniting of Europe: Political, Social, and Economic Forces, 1950–1957* (Stanford, Calif.: Stanford University Press, 1958).

system of collective defense, officially proclaimed the Western European Union, to attract American military support. They were not disappointed. In April 1949, these countries—along with the United States, Canada, Denmark, Iceland, Italy, Norway, and Portugal—created the North Atlantic Treaty Organization (NATO). The NATO treaty called for "continuous and effective self-help and mutual aid" among its signatories; an invasion of one "shall be considered an attack against them all." Former isolationist Arthur Vandenberg, chair of the Senate Foreign Relations Committee, hailed the agreement as "the most important step in American foreign policy since the promulgation of the Monroe Doctrine."

The creation of NATO set a precedent for the United States. Long wary of "entangling alliances," especially with the European powers, the United States committed itself to an alliance in peacetime. It would not allow another gap in the balance of power, nor would it allow itself to become drawn into a war after it had begun. It would commit itself indefinitely to preserving the European balance. From Washington's perspective, NATO would serve two vital functions. First, in countering the Soviet threat the alliance would enhance the *collective defense* of its members against Soviet provocations. Second, by subordinating their military forces to the U.S.-led alliance the Western European governments would defuse their internal rivalries, which had sparked both world wars. This function of regional *collective security*, though rarely emphasized by European and American leaders, played a vital role in their calculations.[11] When West Germany joined NATO in May 1955, the alliance's role in dampening internal tensions became even greater.

Like the Marshall Plan, the birth of NATO provoked the Soviet Union to respond in kind. Just after West Germany's entry into NATO, the Soviets established the Warsaw Treaty Organization, comprising the Soviet Union and its seven satellite states in Eastern Europe: Albania, Bulgaria, Czechoslovakia, East Germany, Hungary, Poland, and Romania. The Warsaw Pact, as it became known, was modeled on NATO, although the Soviet satellites played a relatively minor role in managing the alliance. Indeed, Eastern Europeans had little choice in the matter given that their governments were controlled by Moscow.

The creation and expansion of NATO were closely linked to the future of Germany, which bordered on the Soviet bloc. Germany had held the key to the European balance of power since at least 1870 when Prussia defeated France, Europe's preeminent land power, and established a united Germany. And Germany continued in that role even after

11. This dual purpose helps to explain NATO's persistence today, long after the collapse of its proclaimed adversary. See Steven W. Hook and Richard Robyn, "Regional Collective Security in Europe: Past Patterns and Future Prospects," *European Security* 8 (autumn 1999): 82–100.

its defeat in 1945. Given this crucial role, it was inevitable that the Soviet Union and the United States would clash over the future of Germany. As noted, Soviet troops occupied the eastern part of Germany, and the Allies controlled the western region. Late in the war, the leaders of the Soviet Union, Britain, France, and the United States had established a four-power Allied Control Commission to administer postwar Germany as a single unit. The occupying powers would, under the plan, control separate zones until a reformed German state could be created. But in practice this task proved impossible; the Allied and Soviet powers pursued very different goals in the occupied zones.

This stalemate produced the division of Germany along Cold War lines. The Allies, which had merged their territories, sought to create an independent, democratic, and economically viable West Germany based in Bonn. Meanwhile, the Soviet Union consolidated its hold over East Germany and installed a pro-Soviet government that would become part of the communist bloc in Eastern Europe. The Allies, which had decided to assist rather than punish their former enemy, benefited most from this arrangement. West Germany contained the great majority of Germany's population and the heart of its industrial power. East Germany possessed far fewer resources, and what little of value it retained after World War II was hauled away in boxcars to the Soviet Union.

RECURRING CONFLICTS OVER BERLIN

The Soviets reacted to the creation of a potentially strong West Germany by blockading West Berlin in 1948. Berlin, like Germany, was supposed to be administered by the four occupying powers, but the growing Cold War had divided the city just as it had Germany. Lying deep in East German territory, surrounded by Soviet divisions, the western half of the city was a vulnerable spot in which the Soviets could apply pressure on the Western powers. But the issue at stake was more than the Western presence in Berlin: it was Germany itself. Berlin, as the old capital of Germany, was the symbol of the ongoing conflict between the Soviet Union and Germany. Furthermore, if the Allies could be forced out of Berlin, German confidence in the United States would be undermined.

The Soviet attempt to drive the United States out of Western Europe left Washington with little choice but to defend its position in West Berlin. To that end, President Truman launched a continuous airlift of supplies to Berlin instead of attempting to puncture the blockade on the ground, which might have sparked armed conflict between the superpowers. The Soviets waited to see if the Western powers could take care of West Berlin's 2.5 million citizens indefinitely. It would require a minimum of 4,000 tons of food and fuel daily—an enormous amount of tonnage to ship in by air. But after 324 days the Soviets were convinced that the Americans and British were more than equal to the task. Although the total supplies did not immediately reach the 4,000-ton target, Western planes, landing at three-minute intervals, eventually flew in as much as 13,000 tons daily, or 60 percent more than the 8,000 tons previously sent in each day by ground transport. Faced with this colossal Allied achievement, the Soviets called off the blockade in May 1949.

The U.S. determination to hold Western Europe and not allow further Soviet expansion had been demonstrated. The West Germans saw clearly that they could count on America to protect them. The United States had laid the basis for Germany's economic recovery through Marshall Plan funds. In NATO, West Germany would be given the sense of military security required for its economic reconstruction and political rehabilitation. Later attempts by the Soviet Union to evict the Western allies from Berlin only strengthened West Germany's resolve and its stature within NATO. Indeed, West Berlin itself was able to hamper Soviet control of East Germany by serving as a conduit for the thousands of young, skilled professionals who left East Germany through West Berlin in the 1950s. Joseph Stalin's successor, Nikita Khrushchev, was left with an almost impossible task. His attempted reforms, designed to soften the hard edges of Stalinism, only encouraged dissent and threats to Soviet control over Eastern Europe. The stability of the Soviet position depended basically on destroying the freedom of West Berlin. Thus Khrushchev continued to pursue this objective, even issuing an ultimatum to the Allies in 1958 to end the four-power occupation of the city in six months. His threats, however, fell on deaf ears. Finally, in 1961, Khrushchev ordered the construction of a wall through Berlin to separate the eastern and western parts of the city and eliminate the escape hatch for East Germans. The Berlin Wall became the most vivid symbol of the protracted Cold War in Europe.

Overall, America's postwar strategy in Western Europe during the early phases of the Cold War accomplished its many objectives. The Truman Doctrine discouraged Soviet meddling in the domestic politics of America's allies. The Bretton Woods accords and Marshall Plan set Western Europe on the path to economic recovery, democracy, and social stability. Through NATO, the United States established a formidable military presence that further enhanced European security. Most of all, by drawing a clear line between the American and Soviet spheres of influence, the United States demonstrated that it was in Europe to stay.

Confronting Revolution in East Asia

Whereas Europe held strategic priority in the U.S. defense strategy of the early Cold War years, Asia was of secondary interest, as it always had been. In fact, the United States found Western Europe so vital to American security that it vowed that any Soviet move into the region would provoke an all-out clash with the United States and NATO. Moreover, it explicitly delivered this promise to Soviet leaders throughout this period. By contrast, no single area in Asia was thought to be worth the cost of total war. The region was too distant, its economies too peripheral to Western interests, and its political and social systems too distinct from those in the West.

Yet as the United States undertook efforts to revive Western Europe, it also began to recognize that, to contain communism, it would have to channel its economic resources and combat forces to other parts of the world, including the Asian perimeter of the Soviet Union and China. But whereas pressure on Europe united the Western powers, developments in Asia divided Europe and the United States by producing a split over the character and nature of the new Chinese regime and the degree to which it threatened Western interests. In Washington, upheavals in Asia inspired a prolonged and heated debate between "Asia firsters" and those seeking to limit U.S. containment efforts to Western Europe. Events would propel the United States into action on both fronts.

The collapse in 1949 of Nationalist China, on whom the United States was counting in the emerging Cold War, led to the establishment of the People's Republic of China (PRC) under the leadership of communist Mao Zedong. The communists' victory was quickly followed by China's annexation of neighboring Tibet, a treaty of friendship between China and the Soviet Union, and the invasion of South Korea by communist North Korea. The logic of George Kennan's containment strategy would be put to the test far from the iron curtain, as would the leadership of the United States in the emerging anticommunist coalition. American resolve required more than words. Concrete action was essential to sustain containment on a global scale.

THE CHINESE REVOLUTION

During World War II, the United States had two goals in the Pacific: to defeat Japan and to help sustain the government of China so it could play a leading role in protecting the postwar peace in East Asia.[12] At a meeting in Cairo in 1943, President Franklin Roosevelt and British prime minister Winston Churchill promised Chinese premier Chiang Kai-shek that all Chinese territories conquered by Japan would be returned after the war. In typically American fashion, Roosevelt thought

12. See Herbert Feis, *The China Tangle: The American Effort in China from Pearl Harbor to the Marshall Mission* (New York: Atheneum, 1967).

IMPACT AND INFLUENCE

MAO ZEDONG

Today's People's Republic of China (PRC), one of the world's major superpowers, still stands in the shadow of its founding father, Mao Zedong. Born in 1893, Mao had childhood memories of the Chinese government struggling to break free from foreign interference at the turn of the century. After receiving a modern education, Mao struck out as a social reformer, organizing peasant and industrial unions in the 1920s. He then moved into the countryside and established rural "soviets," or revolutionary groups bent on creating a communist system. In the 1930s, Mao's attention shifted to military struggle and civil war, and, as chairman of the breakaway Soviet Republic of China, he led the "long march" in 1934 and 1935 of antigovernment revolutionaries across the country. During World War II, he led his armies against two enemies at once: the Japanese occupying forces and those of China's Nationalist regime, led by Chiang Kai-shek.

As the first leader of the PRC in 1949, Mao soon amassed unrivaled control over the world's largest population. At the age of fifty-six, he placed himself at the center of government and society, forcing all citizens to adopt the Chinese Communist Party's "mass line." After several years, Mao briefly softened his rigid posture, declaring in 1956 that Beijing would "let a hundred flowers bloom, let all the schools of thought contend." But he quickly reversed this move toward liberal reform after watching anticommunist rebels nearly topple the Soviet Union's client state in Hungary. He announced that dissent would not be tolerated in China, and that he personally would distinguish between "flagrant flowers and poisonous weeds." Mao then ruled China ruthlessly for the rest of his life, through such societal upheavals as the "Great Leap Forward" and the Cultural Revolution. His death in 1976 left the Communist Party still firmly in control, but it also left the Chinese economy paralyzed by more than a quarter-century of central planning and social engineering that left tens of millions of citizens dead or dislocated. Mao's break with the Soviet Union in the 1960s, and his opening of diplomatic relations with the United States in 1972, made him less threatening to the United States in his final years in power.

that the mere pronouncement of China as a great power could actually convert it into one: one need only believe strongly enough in the desirability of an event for it to happen. But American faith without a viable Chinese government was not enough to accomplish the task. In their desire to create stability in East Asia based on a U.S.-Sino alliance, the Roosevelt and Truman administrations ignored the depth of hostilities between the ruling Chinese Nationalists and communists, who at the time were engaged in a protracted civil war.

Already in control of large segments of China before World War II, the communists had extended their sphere during the war. Meanwhile, the pro-American Nationalist regime was losing popular support and disintegrating. Chiang's failure to satisfy the peasants, the vast majority of China's population, as well as rampant corruption among government officials, paralyzed his efforts to gain control of the country. A government whose principal supporters were the landlords was unlikely to carry out the reforms the peasants sought. As Chiang continued to lose popularity, he turned to repressive measures to hold his position. The resulting police and military crackdowns further alienated the people, ensuring a communist victory in the civil war. Recognizing his defeat, Chiang withdrew to Taiwan (then called Formosa), an island lying one hundred miles off China's coast. In the fall of 1949, the leader of the communist forces, Mao Zedong, proclaimed victory and established the People's Republic of China.

In Washington, policy makers debated the question of whether the United States could have prevented the PRC's victory. The answer was "perhaps"—*if* American officers had taken over the command of the Nationalist armies; *if* the United States had been willing to commit large-scale land, air, and sea forces; and *if* the United States had been willing to commit even more financial aid than the some $2 billion it had contributed since its victory over Japan. But these conditions could not have been met. America's rapid demobilization had left it with too few forces either to supply the officers needed to direct the Nationalist forces or to intervene in China. The United States had only a modest standing army at home, even after the signing of the National Security Act. Nor were the American people in any mood to rearm and remobilize in the late 1940s. There was little enough sentiment in favor of "rescuing" Eastern Europe from Soviet domination—far less for fighting a war in China.

Looking beyond the communist victory in China, American officials were optimistic. Secretary of State Dean Acheson expressed his belief that, despite the common ideological points of view of the Chinese and Soviet regimes, they eventually would clash. Acheson predicted that Russia's traditional appetite for a sphere of influence in Manchuria and northern China would arouse Chinese nationalism. Thus Acheson warned the Truman administration and Congress that the United States "should not deflect from the Russians to ourselves the righteous anger and hatred of the Chinese people." [13]

The implications of Acheson's point of view were clear. If the Chinese communists were genuinely concerned about the preservation of China's national interest, they would resist Soviet advances. Mao might become an independent communist leader like Yugoslavia's Marshal Josip Tito, who refused to join the Soviet bloc in Eastern Europe. But if Mao proved subservient to the Soviet Union, he would lose the support of the Chinese people. His regime would be identified with foreign rule because he would appear to serve the interests of another power, even a fellow communist regime. In the end, despite their ideological affinities Stalin and Mao distrusted one another and each viewed himself as the true leader of international communism. Even as the two leaders signed a treaty of friendship in 1950, their mutual antagonism was apparent. But before the U.S. divide-and-conquer strategy could be tested, war broke out in another part of East Asia. The conflict on the Korean peninsula created a bitter gulf between the United States and the PRC that lasted for a generation.

HOT WAR IN KOREA

Mounting concerns within the Truman administration led to the release in April 1950 of the report known as NSC-68, a dire warning by the National Security Council about communist expansion beyond Europe. "The issues that face us are momentous, involving the fulfillment or destruction not only of this Republic but of civilization itself," wrote Paul Nitze, the primary author of the government report.[14] The report was designed to gain congressional approval for a major increase in U.S. defense spending. More important, the authors of NSC-68 sought to alarm the general public, whose support would be required for the escalation of the Cold War advocated in the report.

Events in East Asia quickly affirmed NSC-68's call to arms. The invasion of South Korea by North Korea in June 1950 provoked a military response by the United States, under the aegis of the United Nations, and represented the first test of George Kennan's containment strategy. More broadly, the Korean War demonstrated that the Cold War would occasionally become "hot," thrusting the superpowers into active hostilities all along the containment frontier.

13. Dean Acheson, *Present at the Creation: My Years in the State Department* (New York: Norton, 1969), 356.

14. Quoted from the report in Ernest R. May, ed., *American Cold War Strategy: Interpreting NSC-68* (New York: Bedford, 1993), 26.

Korea had been a divided country since the end of World War II. Under the terms of the postwar settlement, the Soviets would disarm the Japanese above the thirty-eighth parallel and the United States would take on the task below, thereby dividing the country until a new government could be established. With the beginning of the Cold War, however, this division became permanent. All American attempts to negotiate an end to the division and establish a united Korea failed.[15] The United States had taken the problem to the United Nations in 1947, calling on it to sponsor free elections throughout the Korean peninsula. The Soviets, however, refused to allow elections in North Korea, which had been transformed into a dictatorship, and thus only the South Koreans cast ballots. After the elections, the United States recognized South Korea as the official republic and the government of Syngman Rhee as its legitimate representative.

Both the South and North Korean governments regarded themselves as the legitimate representatives of the Korean people, and each was dedicated to the reunification of the peninsula under its control. In that sense, the war that broke out when North Korea attacked South Korea on June 25, 1950, was a civil war between two regimes determined to eliminate each other. But it also was an international war because events in Korea after 1945 served as a microcosm of the Cold War rivalry. North Korea's invasion could not have occurred without Stalin's approval, which, according to evidence revealed later, was given in March 1949.[16]

The survival of South Korea became immediately identified with the security interests of the United States. North Korea's aggression altered the basis on which Korea's strategic significance had been originally calculated. If the principal purpose of containment was to prevent further Soviet expansion, American inaction in the face of such overt provocation would only encourage future aggressive acts. And if the United States stood by while South Korea fell, it would demonstrate to the world that the United States was either afraid of Soviet power or unconcerned about the safety of its allies. American guarantees to help preserve other nations' political independence would be regarded as valueless, leaving them with no alternative but to turn to neutralism for protection and to seek some form of accommodation with the Soviet Union.

At first, the United States tried to stem the North Korean advance using air and sea forces alone. But after a few days, Gen. Douglas

15. See William W. Stueck, *The Korean War: An International History* (Princeton, N.J.: Princeton University Press, 1995). Also see Bruce Cumings, *The Origins of the Korean War* (Princeton, N.J.: Princeton University Press, 1981).

16. See Kathryn Weathersby, "The Soviet Role in the Early Phase of the Korean War: New Documentary Evidence," *Journal of American–East Asian Relations* 2 (winter 1993): 425–458.

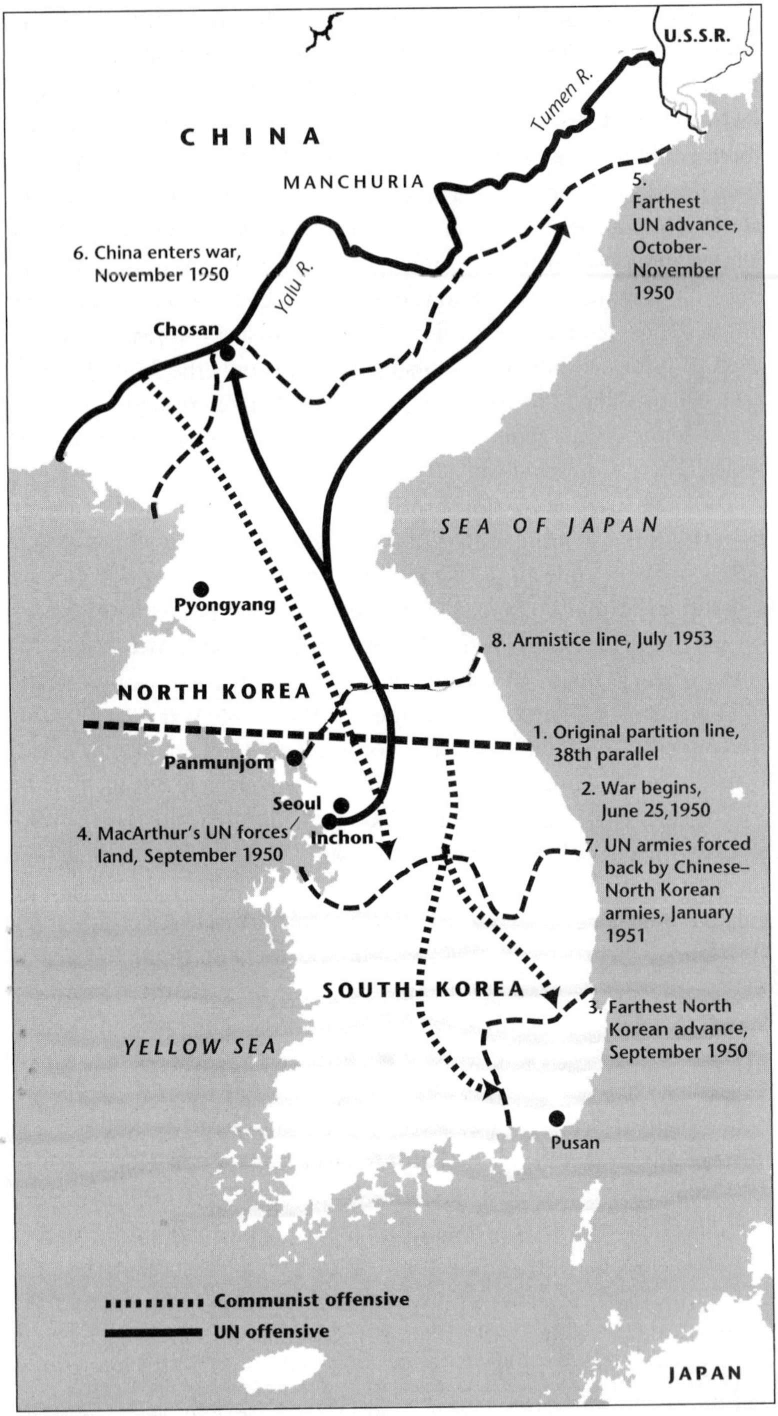

THE KOREAN WAR, 1950–1953

MacArthur, the U.S. military commander in the Far East, reported that Korea would be lost unless ground forces were deployed to halt the advancing enemy army. In response, Washington ordered its occupation troops from Japan to Korea to participate officially in a multinational United Nations peacekeeping force. The UN's involvement in the conflict suited the United States because one of the aims of American foreign policy was to associate its Cold War policies with the humanitarian values and peace-making functions of the United Nations. Although countries traditionally had justified their policies in moral terms, the United States had shown a marked propensity for doing so. American power had to be "righteous" power, used not for purposes of power politics and selfish national advantage but for the peace and welfare of all people. All this being said, the war in its execution was an American effort, not one controlled by the world body.

After initial setbacks, the war went well for the U.S.-led UN forces. On September 15 in a daring operation, MacArthur, now UN supreme commander, landed an army at the west coast port of Inchon, 150 miles behind North Korean lines. These forces then drove northward, trapping more than half the enemy army. The rest of the shattered communist army was in flight. On September 30, the UN forces reached the thirty-eighth parallel. The question confronting the United States was whether to cross it. The political aims of the war were compatible with the restoration of South Korea; they did not require a total war and the elimination of the North Korean government or the unconditional surrender of its troops. But the military situation favored the fulfillment of an American goal of several years' standing: the unification of the Korean peninsula. Thus the U.S. government shifted its emphasis from containing the expansion of Soviet power to the forceful elimination of a communist state. The result—North Korean retrenchment, Chinese intervention, and ultimate stalemate—was to teach the United States the foolishness of changing limited political goals in the middle of a war in response to battlefield successes.

The new objective of a militarily united Korea was sanctioned by a UN resolution on October 7. The Chinese viewed the resulting march to their border as threatening, just as Washington had felt threatened by North Korea's march southward toward Japan. So Beijing sent its armies into North Korea under the guise of "volunteers" and in late November launched a major offensive that drove the UN forces south of the thirty-eighth parallel. Throughout December 1950 and early January 1951, it was far from clear that UN troops could hold the peninsula, but they rallied and turned back the Chinese offensive. By March, they had once more advanced to the thirty-eighth parallel. The United States was again faced with the decision of whether to seek a militarily unified Korea or accept the status quo, a divided Korea.[17]

There was no doubt about what MacArthur, articulating the traditional American approach to war, wanted to do. War, he said, indicated that "you have exhausted all other potentialities of bringing the disagreements to an end," and, once engaged, "there is no alternative than to apply every available means to bring it to a swift end. War's very objective is victory—not prolonged indecision. In war there is no substitute for victory."[18] MacArthur recommended a naval blockade of the Chinese coast; air bombardment of China's industrial complex, communications network, supply depots, and troop assembly points; reinforcement of his forces with Chinese Nationalist troops; and "diversionary action possibly leading to counter-invasion" by Chiang Kai-shek against the mainland.

The Truman administration rejected MacArthur's proposals as too risky. It feared that bombing China and defeating the Soviet Union's principal ally would lead to another global war. The Sino-Soviet treaty bound the Soviet Union to come to the aid of China if it were attacked by Japan "or any other state which should unite with Japan" (an obvious reference to the United States). Soviet self-interest in the Far East and the need to maintain Soviet prestige in the communist sphere would make it difficult for the Soviet Union to ignore a direct attack on the Chinese mainland.

The truce talks begun in the summer of 1951 produced nothing but deadlock. The war was a drain on the United States and had to be ended. When Dwight D. Eisenhower took office in January 1953, he decided that if his efforts to gain an armistice failed, the United States would bomb Chinese bases and supply sources, blockade the mainland coast, and possibly use atomic weapons. It is doubtful, however, that the administration's threats were primarily responsible for the Chinese government's willingness to conclude the war in July. Other factors appeared more critical. Chief among these was Stalin's death in March. His successors called for "peaceful coexistence" with the West and tried to convince the noncommunist world that they wanted to relax international tensions. Agreement on an armistice would provide evidence of their goodwill. More important, the Soviets could not afford to risk an enlarged war at a time when they were engaged in a struggle among themselves to succeed Stalin.

The Korean War thus ended just where it had begun—at the thirty-eighth parallel—and on basically the same terms the Truman administra-

17. See Rosemary Foot, *A Substitute for Victory: The Politics of Peacemaking at the Korean Armistice Talks* (Ithaca, N.Y.: Cornell University Press, 1990).

18. Quoted in John Spanier, *The Truman-MacArthur Controversy and the Korean War* (Cambridge, Mass.: Belknap Press, 1959), 222.

tion had been unable to reach. As a result, the Korean partition became part of the global dividing line between the communist and noncommunist blocs. In August 1953, the United States signed a mutual security pact with South Korea designed to deter another attack from the north, a pact that remained in place throughout—and beyond—the Cold War.

The line of containment also was drawn in the Taiwan Strait, where U.S.-Sino relations had turned increasingly bitter after China's revolution and subsequent intervention in Korea. To Mao, Taiwan was an "outlaw province" that must be brought under Beijing's control; to American leaders, Taiwan was the legitimate seat of China's government. Eisenhower requested and received from Congress in January 1955 the authority to deploy American forces to protect Taiwan and "such related positions and territories" as the president judged necessary. As in Korea, the United States established its commitment to defend a line of containment in East Asia, this time a few miles off the PRC's coast. The struggle over Taiwan, with its attending provocations and frequent threats of war, defined the Cold War in East Asia in much the same way the Berlin Wall epitomized the conflict in Europe.

Domestic Pressures for a Global Crusade

The Chinese revolution and the Korean War dramatically altered American foreign policy less than a decade after its conception. Whereas U.S. policy had been limited to containing Soviet power in Western Europe and the Mediterranean, it now spilled over into a broader anticommunist crusade. Americans were shocked by the collapse in 1949 of Nationalist China, the establishment of a communist PRC, and the hot war in Korea. Suddenly, the security achieved by the containment policies in Europe—the Truman Doctrine, the Marshall Plan, the Berlin airlift, and NATO—seemed to have disintegrated. It appeared that the United States had stemmed communism in Europe only to see it achieve a breakthrough in Asia.

The resulting insecurity and anxiety were heightened by other developments. The first was the explosion in 1949 of the Soviet Union's first atomic bomb, which shattered the American monopoly on the weapon widely regarded as the principal deterrent against a Soviet attack. The second was the successful prosecution in early 1950 of Alger Hiss, a high-ranking U.S. government official during World War II, for perjury in connection with charges he had delivered classified U.S. documents to the Soviet government in the 1930s. The Hiss case was followed shortly by the confession of British scientist Klaus Fuchs that he had passed atomic secrets to the Soviets, apparently pointing to Soviet espionage in high places. The outbreak of the Korean War and communist China's subsequent intervention compounded America's sense of betrayal and anxiety.

At home, bipartisan support for U.S. policy in Asia was eroding. The conservative wing of the Republican Party had long been restless. In the past, these Republicans recognized, whenever the United States had been drawn into the international arena its actions had met with quick success. American forces had defeated the British, Mexicans, Spanish, Germans, and Japanese. And, unlike most other nations, the United States had never been invaded, defeated, or occupied. The nation's leaders had made many mistakes, but using the country's considerable resources and geographic advantages they had been able to rectify their missteps. America's history had witnessed only victories; the unbroken string of successes seemed to provide clear evidence of national omnipotence and "manifest destiny."

This unquestioned assumption suggested to Republicans the reason for America's failures: treason within its own government. If America was all-powerful, its setbacks must have been the result of its own policies. Ostensibly the reason China fell was that the "pro-communist" administrations of Franklin Roosevelt and Harry Truman had either deliberately or unwittingly "sold China down the river." This conspiracy charge, articulated by Republican senator Joseph R. McCarthy and supported by fellow Republicans Robert Taft and Richard Nixon (who became Eisenhower's vice president and later president), was simplicity itself. America's China policy had ended in communist control of the mainland; the administration leaders and the State Department were responsible for the formulation and execution of foreign policy; therefore, the government must be filled with communists and communist sympathizers who "tailored" American policy to advance the global aims of the Soviet Union. Low morale among the Chinese Nationalists, the Nationalist government's corruption and military ineptitude, and Chiang's repressive policies, which had alienated the population, had nothing to do with it. Nor did the communists' superior organization, direction, morale, and ability to identify with popular aspirations.

The State Department bore the brunt of this rhetorical onslaught; the attacks on its Foreign Service officers and regional directors and on Secretary of State Dean Acheson himself were incessant. But the accusations, usually carried in the press, were not directed only toward the State Department or government officials. Academics and others also were charged with being security risks or were accused of being "un-American." Many of the accused were fired, and others—especially stage actors and Hollywood figures—were blacklisted. Nationally, the political atmosphere during the 1950s bordered on hysteria.

The most significant result was the transformation of American foreign policy from a limited anti-Soviet orientation to a broader anticommunist crusade. The primary goal was now to prevent territorial expansion by any member of the Sino-Soviet bloc. All communist states were considered enemies, regardless of size, location, or status—that is, tied to Moscow as satellites or existing as nationalist communist states (Yugoslavia and communist China) pursuing their own interests, even in conflict with the Soviet Union. Distinctions between America's vital and secondary interests, the importance of concentrating on the main adversary and not getting bogged down and wasting resources on conflicts with secondary threats, and the ability to distinguish communist regimes that represented a threat to American interests from those that did not—all were lost in the crusading spirit.

Nuclear Strategy and the 'Balance of Terror'

Nuclear weapons played a key role in the globalized struggle against communism. The fear of nuclear annihilation by the United States was expected to discourage the Soviets and Chinese from crossing the line. In the early 1950s, Moscow had a very limited capability to reach the United States with nuclear weapons; Beijing had none. By contrast, the bomber forces controlled by the U.S. Strategic Air Command (SAC) were growing rapidly and could strike both communist powers from a variety of overseas bases.

In short, nuclear weapons were not so much designed to be used, but to serve the vital function of *deterrence* against communist attacks on the United States and its key allies. A U.S. promise to respond to communist expansion with "massive retaliation" against population centers as well as military installations would presumably make Soviet and Chinese leaders think twice. Nuclear weapons also made possible a reduction in overall military expenditures. In addition to his credentials as a war hero, President Eisenhower was a fiscal conservative, and he was impressed by the ability of nuclear weapons to give the United States "more bang for the buck." [19] For this and other reasons, Eisenhower assigned nuclear weapons a prominent role in his restructuring of U.S. security policy, labeled the "New Look." In the future, U.S. military forces would rely less on conventional forces—which cost a great deal to train, equip, and maintain—and more on nuclear firepower.

Above all, massive retaliation was consistent with America's style of foreign policy, a style that traditionally was based on a worldview of mutually exclusive conditions: war or peace, force or diplomacy, aggres-

19. Eisenhower's nuclear strategy faced strong resistance from the Pentagon, which claimed the president was trying to maintain American security "on the cheap." See Dale R. Herspring, *The Pentagon and the Presidency: Civil–Military Relations from FDR to George W. Bush* (Lawrence: University of Kansas Press, 2005), chap. 4.

sors or peace-loving states. Peace was normal; war was abnormal. Force was not necessary in the absence of conflict and hostilities; it was to be used only in wartime to destroy the source of war itself. Massive retaliation, then, fit this American approach completely. It was an all-or-nothing strategy that could not be used short of a Soviet attack on the United States or Western Europe. At the same time, American presidents consistently rejected preventive war, both at the time of the nation's atomic monopoly and later, during the 1950s and 1960s, the period of gradually declining strategic superiority. Deterrence was the American goal; nuclear weapons would be used only after the opponent had struck first. If the United States were attacked, however, it would punish and destroy the enemy in ways not conceivable until 1945.[20]

Atomic weapons, and the more destructive hydrogen weapons that soon followed, enabled the United States to pursue an old American dream in a new and perverse way. By making nuclear war too destructive to fight, by making the distinction between victor and vanquished in such a conflict meaningless, the deterrent strategy aimed at eliminating war itself. The old American dream had been sought in vain through Woodrow Wilson's quest to see that World War I would be the "war to end all wars," through international organizations, and through free trade and economic interdependence among nations. That dream could now be realized because war had become unthinkable: a balance of power would be punctuated by a "balance of terror."

This basic policy decision reflected Secretary of State John Foster Dulles's conviction that the only effective means of stopping an invasion was to give fair warning of what constituted aggression and to make clear that the punishment for an attack would far outweigh any possible military gains. Dulles believed the communists would not have invaded South Korea had they known their attack would be met with retaliatory air strikes on Moscow. It was the absence of such a warning that had led North Korea to act. The Eisenhower administration did not intend to repeat this mistake. It meant to draw the line so clearly that the enemy would have no doubt about the consequences of crossing the line. The expectation was that by going to the "brink of war," the United States would be able to deter future Koreas.[21]

In the recurring crises of the early Cold War period, American leaders learned three lessons that were essential to preserving the line around what was then still viewed as a cohesive Sino-Soviet bloc. The first lesson was that the advent of nuclear weapons left no alternative to peace.

20. See John Lewis Gaddis, *Strategies of Containment: A Critical Appraisal of Postwar American National Security Policy* (New York: Oxford University Press, 1982), chap. 5.

21. See Richard H. Immermann, *John Foster Dulles and the Diplomacy of the Cold War* (Princeton, N.J.: Princeton University Press, 1990).

However destructive, a conventional war distinguished winners from losers and, with time, both recovered from the human losses and the destruction of their cities and industries. But a nuclear war was likely to be suicidal; all participants would lose and no recovery would be possible. Total war, in short, had become irrational because the cost of war was disproportionate to any conceivable gains.

A second lesson of the nuclear arms race was that mutual deterrence was not automatic. Indeed, advancing technology might upset the stability of the deterrent balance. Simply possessing the bomb was insufficient; the key to a *stable* deterrent balance was an invulnerable retaliatory force. If country A's forces were vulnerable to attack by country B, A might be tempted to strike B preemptively rather than have its forces caught on the ground. In the late 1950s and early 1960s, the Soviets claimed they were mass-producing missiles that made American bombers vulnerable. If true, this claim would have meant that the credibility of U.S. deterrence had declined. Such developments affected the calculations of policy makers in Moscow and Washington whose adherence to the principle of "mutual assured destruction" (MAD) was essential to preventing a nuclear cataclysm.[22]

In this environment, the survival of U.S. nuclear forces became central not only to the nation's security, but also to that of its allies, which were protected by the "extended" deterrent of U.S. and NATO nuclear forces. In recognition of this situation, the Eisenhower administration sought to disperse the nation's nuclear forces in a "triad"—ground-based launchers, aircraft, and submarines—so that the weapons were less vulnerable to a surprise attack. The goal of protecting nuclear forces thus became as crucial as their production. Preserving deterrence was a continuing, never-ending task, not simply because some change in the balance might precipitate war, but because shifting strategic balances might affect the risks each side was willing to take.[23]

The third lesson revealed by the early Cold War crises was the extent to which military power, nuclear and conventional, would be used to protect "frontiers" across the globe. These frontiers were clear: along the inter-German border and through the middle of Berlin; at the thirty-eighth parallel in Korea; along the coast of China; and along the southern tier of Asian states from Turkey to Iran and Pakistan. Any attempt by communist forces to cross these frontiers, either openly by direct attack

22. The Soviet Union tested the world's first intercontinental ballistic missile (ICBM) in August 1957 and then launched the first man-made satellite, *Sputnik,* two months later. This development, in particular, shocked the United States and its allies; they had long taken their technical superiority for granted.

23. For an elaboration, see Lawrence Freedman, *Deterrence* (Cambridge, UK: Polity Press, 2004). Also see Freedman, *The Evolution of Nuclear Strategy* (New York: St. Martin's Press, 1989), 83–88.

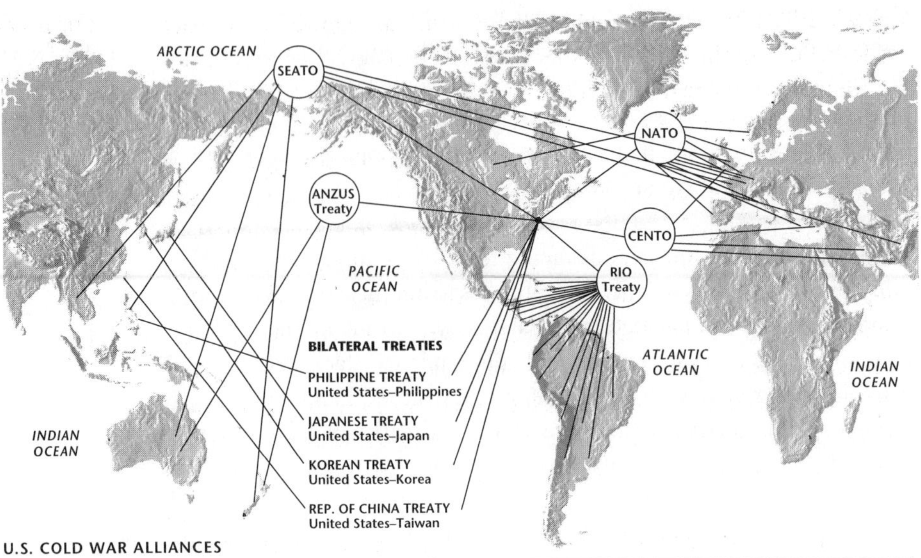

U.S. COLD WAR ALLIANCES

Rio Treaty (Organization of American States)

UNITED STATES	HAITI	PERU
CUBA	DOMINICAN REP.	BOLIVIA
HONDURAS	COSTA RICA	PARAGUAY
MEXICO	PANAMA	BRAZIL
GUATEMALA	VENEZUELA	CHILE
EL SALVADOR	ECUADOR	ARGENTINA
NICARAGUA	COLOMBIA	URUGUAY

North Atlantic Treaty Organization (NATO)

UNITED STATES	BELGIUM
CANADA	LUXEMBOURG
ICELAND	ITALY
NORWAY	PORTUGAL
UNITED KINGDOM	FRANCE
NETHERLANDS	GREECE
DENMARK	TURKEY
W. GERMANY	

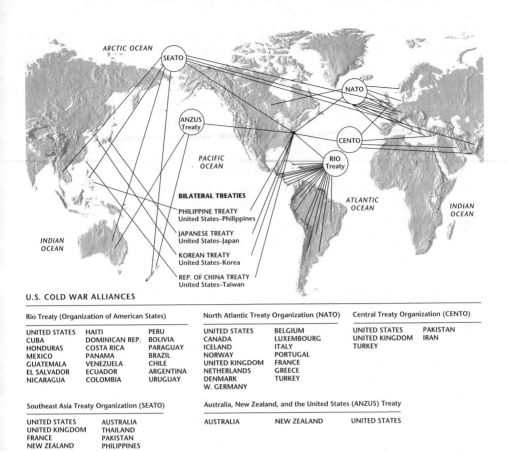

Central Treaty Organization (CENTO)

UNITED STATES	PAKISTAN
UNITED KINGDOM	IRAN
TURKEY	

Southeast Asia Treaty Organization (SEATO)

UNITED STATES	AUSTRALIA
UNITED KINGDOM	THAILAND
FRANCE	PAKISTAN
NEW ZEALAND	PHILIPPINES

Australia, New Zealand, and the United States (ANZUS) Treaty

AUSTRALIA	NEW ZEALAND	UNITED STATES

or covertly by guerrilla warfare, risked Western retaliation.[24] Conversely, the United States could not seriously entertain hopes of "rolling back" communist gains in Eastern Europe and elsewhere, despite the pledges frequently made by American leaders to do so.

Because the lines of containment drawn outside of Europe were extremely tenuous, revealed by North Korea's attack on South Korea, the U.S. government sought to clarify matters by creating a network of bilateral and multilateral alliances that would more explicitly define the containment belt. In doing so, American leaders departed even further from the nation's traditional aversion to "entangling alliances." In addition to NATO, the United States pledged in 1947 to defend the countries of the Western Hemisphere through the Inter-American Treaty of Reciprocal

24. American leaders secretly deployed nuclear weapons along much of this frontier during the peak of the Cold War, transporting the missiles far beyond Western Europe to frontline Asian states such as South Korea, Taiwan, and the Philippines. See Robert S. Norris et al., "Where They Were," *Bulletin of the Atomic Scientists* 55 (November–December 1999): 26–35.

Assistance. The Rio Treaty, as it became known, was followed a year later by the creation of the Organization of American States, in which twenty-one countries in the region extended their cooperation beyond collective security. In 1951 the United States joined Australia and New Zealand in creating the ANZUS alliance in the Pacific. Individual security guarantees also were extended to Japan, the Philippines, Taiwan, and South Korea as "pactomania" took hold among American military planners.

This process of alliance building, however, proved more difficult than originally expected. The Southeast Asia Treaty Organization (SEATO)—established in 1954 by the United States, Australia, Britain, France, New Zealand, the Philippines, Pakistan, and Thailand—and the Central Treaty Organization (CENTO)—established in 1959 by the United States, Britain, Iran, Pakistan, and Turkey—were alliances in areas where nationalist forces opposed them. As a result, the alliances had little popular support in those regions, even within member states. When these states sought to maintain the containment walls, they were often unable, despite American help, to mobilize popular support.

Indeed, the United States may have been better off had it not created what turned out to be poor replicas of NATO, which existed in a region where its people supported containment against clearly perceived potential external aggression. The less successful alliances were organized in developing regions where containment was widely perceived to be an attempt to preserve Western influence and prop up authoritarian regimes. America's containment strategy thus encountered greater difficulties as its geographic scope widened, a pattern that became painfully evident in the developing world during the 1960s and 1970s.

CHAPTER FOUR

Developing Countries in the Crossfire

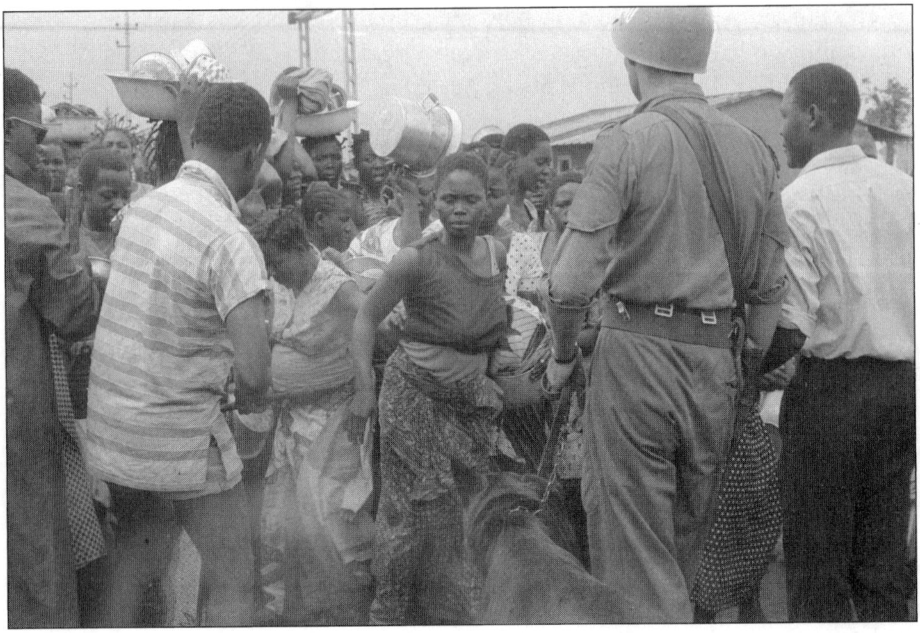

Congolese refugees wait in line for food from international relief organizations during the country's civil war in November 1961. The crisis in the former Belgian colony was typical of other conflicts during the Cold War, when East-West tensions between the United States and Soviet Union collided with efforts by dozens of developing countries to create stable governments after decades of colonial rule.

The globalized Cold War of the early 1950s elevated four areas of the world to major power centers: the United States, the Soviet Union, the People's Republic of China, and the nations of Western Europe. "In all four," one scholar observed at the time,

> productivity is on the increase, and the political system performs relatively well its integrating and decision-making functions. Despite major differences among them . . . these four areas are likely to be in a position to play major roles in political, economic, and cultural international affairs in the coming decade. In contrast, the Middle East, Southeast Asia, tropical Africa, and Latin America are apt to remain power vacuums during this period, owing to their lack of unity, political instability, economic stagnation, and cultural heterogeneity. It seems highly improbable that ten years from now

> any of the areas mentioned above will cease to be, respectively, a power center or a power vacuum.[1]

During the 1950s and 1960s, which witnessed the liberation of many European colonies in Africa and southern Asia, U.S. leaders became increasingly anxious about the unstable political and economic conditions that accompanied the birth of the new nation-states in the emerging "Third World."[2] The evolving membership of the United Nations (UN) confirmed the importance of these countries. In 1946 the United Nations had 55 members; in 1955, 76 members; in 1970, 127 members; and in 1980, 154 members. By 2000 UN membership stood at 189. With each increment of growth, the proportion of states located in developing regions increased (see Table 4-1). In the UN General Assembly, with its principle of one country–one vote, these member-states could—and would—dominate the agenda.

In the bipolar context of the Cold War the developing countries did not represent independent centers of power but rather objects of competition for the two superpowers, each seeking the support, if not the allegiance, of Third World leaders. During their early years of independence, however, most former colonies refused to align themselves politically or militarily with either superpower. Among their first collective efforts were the establishment of a "nonaligned movement" and the assertion of their independence from Washington and Moscow, efforts that in most cases proved futile.

Communist leaders saw decolonization as proof that the international capitalist order was disintegrating. The colonial powers such as Britain and France had maintained capitalist economies that, according to Marxist-Leninist theory, depended on captive overseas territories for raw materials and export markets (see Chapter 2). This theory found it equally significant that World War I and the Great Depression occurred only after capitalist states had exhausted their opportunities for colonial expansion. Peering through the lens of this perception of history, Soviet and Chinese leaders saw an opportunity to embrace and support the new states. Once made, their overtures were frequently well received and appealed to the understandable hostility within many developing countries toward their former colonial rulers.

From Washington's very different perspective, worries about the introduction of Soviet and Chinese communism into developing areas

1. Guy J. Pauker, "Southeast Asia as a Problem Area in the Next Decade," *World Politics* (April 1959): 325.

2. Although the term *Third World* obscures the regional diversity among developing countries, for political leaders and most scholars of the period the term served to differentiate these largely impoverished states from northern capitalist countries—the *First World*—and communist countries—the *Second World.*

TABLE 4-1 **Composition of UN Membership, 1950-1980**

	1950	1960	1970	1980
Total UN members	60	99	127	154
Less-developed countries (LDCs) in UN membership	40	67	96	121
LDCs percentage of UN membership	67%	69%	76%	79%

Source: United Nations, "Growth in United Nations Membership," http://www.un.org/Overview/growth.htm.

stemmed not from fears of conspiracy or military control but from the repressive model of development that communism offered. The Soviet Union held itself up as a model of a primitive feudal society that had been transformed into a modern industrial state in one generation. Overlooked, however, were the force, massive terror, and staggering human costs associated with that accomplishment. Joseph Stalin's forced collectivization of Soviet agriculture resulted in the death of more than ten million peasants (*kulaks*), either through the purges and mass murders of Stalin's opponents or through the crushing famine of the early 1930s.[3] The Soviet leader waged an undeclared war throughout the period against non-Russian minorities in the Soviet Union, particularly Muslims, and his security forces brutally suppressed leaders of the once-flourishing Christian churches. The inefficiencies, corruption, and social exhaustion produced by the central planners further pulled the Soviet Union into a political and economic spiral from which it never returned.

An even greater number of Chinese peasants died under Mao Zedong's reform efforts, particularly the "Great Leap Forward" initiated in 1958. In the years that followed, the Chinese leader forced the huge population of peasants into massive agricultural collectives and then ordered them to produce steel and manufactured goods as well as commodities. In the end, though, his grandiose experiment produced mainly chaos and a massive famine, bringing China's agricultural and industrial production to a crashing halt.[4] Then, in the mid-1960s, Mao launched a "Cultural Revolution" against his enemies and dispatched thousands of Red Guards to harass, torture, and kill those who strayed from his "mass line." Teachers, artisans, and intellectuals were the primary targets, but the crackdown included anyone who was suspected of having sympathy for, or any contact with, Western values. The social

3. See Robert Conquest, *The Great Terror: A Reassessment* (New York: Oxford University Press, 1990).

4. See Frederick C. Teiwes, *China's Road to Disaster: Mao, Central Politicians, and Provincial Leaders in the Unfolding of the Great Leap Forward, 1955–1959* (Armonk, N.Y.: M. E. Sharpe, 1999).

upheaval that resulted further isolated China from most foreign countries and produced a sullen, resentful popular mood that persisted long after Mao's death in 1976. An estimated seventy million Chinese citizens died from Mao's social engineering and executions of "counter-revolutionaries."[5] The casualties also included natives of Tibet, a formerly independent region in western China whose Buddhist customs and monasteries were destroyed in Mao's reign of terror.[6]

Despite these calamities and atrocities committed by the Soviet Union and China, U.S. leaders worried that the heads of poor countries might decide that the potential benefits of communism outweighed its social costs. Compounding their anxiety, the atrocities being committed under Stalin and Mao were generally unknown outside those closed societies; all that was conveyed publicly was the promise of mass liberation. In this context, U.S. policy makers believed that the economic model developing countries chose to adopt was critical to U.S. security and, more broadly, to an international environment safe for open societies and democratic values. Thus American offers to help new countries establish a basis for economic growth stemmed not just from a humanitarian concern for the countries' long-suffering populations, but also from recognition that progress toward prosperity and political stability would lessen the appeal of communism and prevent the global balance of power from shifting against the United States and its allies.

Obstacles to Political and Economic Development

In the colonial era, the Western powers, including the United States in the Philippines, had justified their imperial domination in terms of bringing the "backward" peoples of the earth the benefits of Western democracy, medical science, and technology. It was the "white man's burden," or duty, to educate the people so that one day they could govern themselves. The colonial powers apparently had taught their lesson well, but in a perverse way; they had ruled their colonies autocratically while proclaiming the virtues of democracy. The nationalist movements later used the same democratic ideals to challenge their rulers and ask them to practice what they preached. Indeed, many leaders of these movements, who often were educated in Europe or the United States, fought the colonial rulers by using the principles of democracy and national freedom they had learned. For them, these principles were incompatible with imperialism and compatible with wars of "national liberation."

5. Jung Chang and Jon Halliday. *Mao: The Unknown Story* (New York: Knopf, 2005), 83.
6. For an elaboration, see Mary Craig, *Tears of Blood: A Cry for Tibet* (New York: HarperCollins, 1992).

Once these countries became independent, they confronted a legacy of poverty, illiteracy, and disease. In the 1950s, for example, the annual per capita income of these states rarely reached $100, and life expectancies seldom exceeded fifty years. To remedy their distress, and to narrow the enormous gap between poor and rich nations, many new countries sought to transform their traditional agrarian societies into modern industrial states. This transformation also had great political significance, for it demanded that citizens transfer their allegiance from their local communities and the ethnic and religious groups that had held their loyalty to their new nations. The fact that the concept of national loyalty was largely unfamiliar to the citizens of the newly independent countries intensified the need to satisfy the popular "revolution of rising expectations." The fledgling states had to prove they could offer their people something not otherwise attainable. By achieving improved standards of living, their leaders would demonstrate that they deserved the popular support and allegiance they needed to survive and grow.

THE POPULATION EXPLOSION IN DEVELOPING COUNTRIES

In considering their prospects for economic development, leaders of the new countries realized their success depended on whether their economic growth would advance faster than their population growth. In 1830 the world population was one billion; by 1930 it had doubled to two billion, and by 1975—just forty-five years later—it had doubled again to four billion. In October 1999 the global population surpassed six billion. According to the best estimates, the world's population will grow to almost seven billion by 2010 and to more than eight billion by 2020. Just as developing countries represented a majority of nation-states by 1970, their share of the world's population also grew dramatically, so that in 2005 more than 80 percent of the world's population of 6.5 billion lived in the developing world.[7]

The concern among leaders of rich and poor countries alike in the 1950s and 1960s was that, despite the expected slowing of population growth rates sometime in the twenty-first century, developing countries would face the dilemma described by the Reverend Thomas Malthus two centuries ago. Simply put, Malthus predicted that growing poverty and human misery would result in countries where population growth exceeded economic growth. To Malthus, who also was an economist, this fate would be inevitable unless population growth was limited either by

7. Population Reference Bureau, *2005 World Population Data Sheet*, http://www.prb.org/datafind/datafinder6.htm (accessed March 9, 2006).

"positive checks" such as wars or epidemics, which result in high death rates, or by "preventive checks" such as family planning, which produce low birthrates.

In the West, birthrates did decline after 1850; with industrialization and the growth of cities came the spread of literacy and birth-control techniques. Indeed, the fate Malthus anticipated for the West did not materialize because preventive checks were adopted, with many industrialized states achieving zero population growth by the late twentieth century and some facing the prospect of *declining* populations. But developing states, in which improvements in health care raised life expectancies, did not reach a comparable level of economic development. Meanwhile, family planning programs confronted an array of obstacles and spread more slowly than expected. The poorer the populations were in developing countries, the higher their rates of population growth.[8]

In contrast to the developing countries, the West had made impressive economic progress after the Industrial Revolution of the late eighteenth century, despite a population increase. Improved harvesting techniques provided plentiful food, and industrial advances raised living standards to heights never before attained. As for feeding their people, the European states reaped the benefits of the industrial age and of their colonial empires, which provided them with outlets to relieve their population pressures. The developing countries, upon their independence, had no overseas territories to absorb their burgeoning populations.

Many of these countries were burdened not only with too many people but also with inadequate capital. Sufficient internal savings could not be squeezed out of people living at a subsistence level. As for earning capital through trade—particularly exports of primary products or raw materials—the developing countries discovered that such exports were unprofitable. Because their economies remained tied to those of their former colonial rulers and other industrialized states, their exports rose or declined with every fluctuation in Western prosperity. In any case, the United States and Western Europe protected their farmers from foreign competition despite their high-profile demands for "free trade" from other agricultural producers.

Foreign investment was another possible source of funding for economic development. In the first years after independence, however, private capital was in short supply for the kind of long-range investment

8. Whereas the population growth rates of industrialized countries averaged 0.2 percent in 1995, the growth rates of developing countries averaged nearly 2 percent, with many of the world's poorest countries in sub-Saharan Africa recording growth rates well over 3 percent. For an elaboration of this trend, see Richard J. Tobin, "Environment, Population, and the Developing World," in *Environmental Policy in the 1990s: Reform or Reaction?* ed. Norman J. Vig and Michael E. Kraft (Washington, D.C.: CQ Press, 1997), 321–344.

needed by the developing countries. Private American investments outside the United States consisted largely of those made by a small group of oil companies to build refineries and to develop oil fields in the Middle East and Latin America. Most investment capital stayed home because of the boom the American economy experienced for most of the Cold War period. This situation also characterized European investment, which was concentrated on rebuilding, modernizing, and expanding the continent's industrial base.

Because the leaders of some developing countries associated capitalism with colonialism, they refused foreign investment and greater involvement in global trade and capital markets. Even so, economic growth was the principal task of all developing countries. Their leaders soon realized, however, that such growth was not just an economic undertaking; it was a political, social, and cultural undertaking as well. Indeed, economic development was a revolutionary process frequently marked by political instability and violence rather than by evolutionary, peaceful change.

TENSIONS BETWEEN NATIONALISM AND STATE BUILDING

One reason for this instability was that, as noted earlier, most of the new states lacked administrative and political cohesion. Because their populations often had no common culture or language, ethnic and regional conflicts abounded. Citizens also had no natural loyalty to their newly created states, whose boundaries were frequently drawn crudely along colonial frontiers, and no tradition of cooperation was in place except on the one overriding issue of eliminating the colonial ruler. Once the struggle for independence ended, power tended to fragment. India, for example, split violently into Hindu and Islamic regions after independence, and the latter dissolved further into Pakistan and Bangladesh. The Belgian Congo fell apart when the Belgians withdrew (a situation described later in this chapter), and Biafra broke away from Nigeria, only to lose the subsequent civil war. Cyprus divided into Turkish and Greek factions, which resulted in partition and an endless United Nations peacekeeping presence.

Even where actual disintegration did not occur, religious, linguistic, and racial differences tended to tear apart the fabric of those states that lacked any history of unity. In 1972, for example, the Tutsi tribe in the African nation of Burundi slaughtered more than 100,000 Hutus, initiating a cycle of violence that reached a more horrifying scale in 1994, when half a million Tutsis were slain in Burundi and neighboring Rwanda. Sri Lanka, a large island lying just off the southeastern coast of India, was immersed in almost constant bloodshed between the Hindu

Tamils and Buddhist Sinhalese. On the thousands of islands that formed the newly independent country of Indonesia, the government's first order of business was conquering and pacifying the Timorese and other ethnic minorities trapped within Indonesia's vast political boundaries. Despite these crackdowns, the fragmented peoples of these regions remained more loyal to their ethnic and cultural identities than to the countries that now ruled them.

The absence of a strong sense of state identity was soon reflected in the way many of the leaders of the new countries built themselves up as symbols of nationhood. They did not find this essential task difficult, because, as leaders of the movements for independence, their prestige was usually high. Indeed, just as Louis XIV had proclaimed, "*L'état, c'est moi,*" they, too, *were* the state. Without their presence as its symbol, the nation would not hold together as a unit. One-party rule or military governments existed almost everywhere in the developing world. For example, in Africa, the world's last continent to be freed from colonialism, three-fourths of its 345 million people lived under single-party or military rule by 1970, ten years after independence.

Such regimes were highly repressive, but political leaders believed them to be justified and necessary. In their view, an American-style democracy would have led not just to a change of government but also to the disintegration of the state. Thus the alternatives facing these countries often were not democracy or dictatorship but statehood or disintegration. The dual pressures of consolidating power at home and resisting foreign domination "helped ensure that leaderships willing and able to build up centralized coercive and administrative organizations would come to the fore." [9]

Domestic debates in these countries quickly moved beyond "reform" to revolution because of the crucial and competing interests at stake. Yet the fundamental question remained: Who could, or should, control the emerging nation-states? The ruling elites committed to the preservation of the traditional order, or those who sought its abolition? Only one thing was certain: few leaders who possess the instruments of power yield their dominant position without a struggle.

Social unrest occurred even where economic development was under way, where national bonds had not disintegrated, and where a reform-minded elite was in control. This instability stemmed from a standard of living that, while improving, did not improve rapidly enough to create a satisfied population.[10] Historically, capital for investment was sought in

9. Theda Skocpol, *States and Social Revolutions: A Comparative Analysis of France, Russia, and China* (Cambridge: Cambridge University Press, 1979), 286.

10. See Ted Robert Gurr, *Why Men Rebel* (Princeton, N.J.: Princeton University Press, 1970).

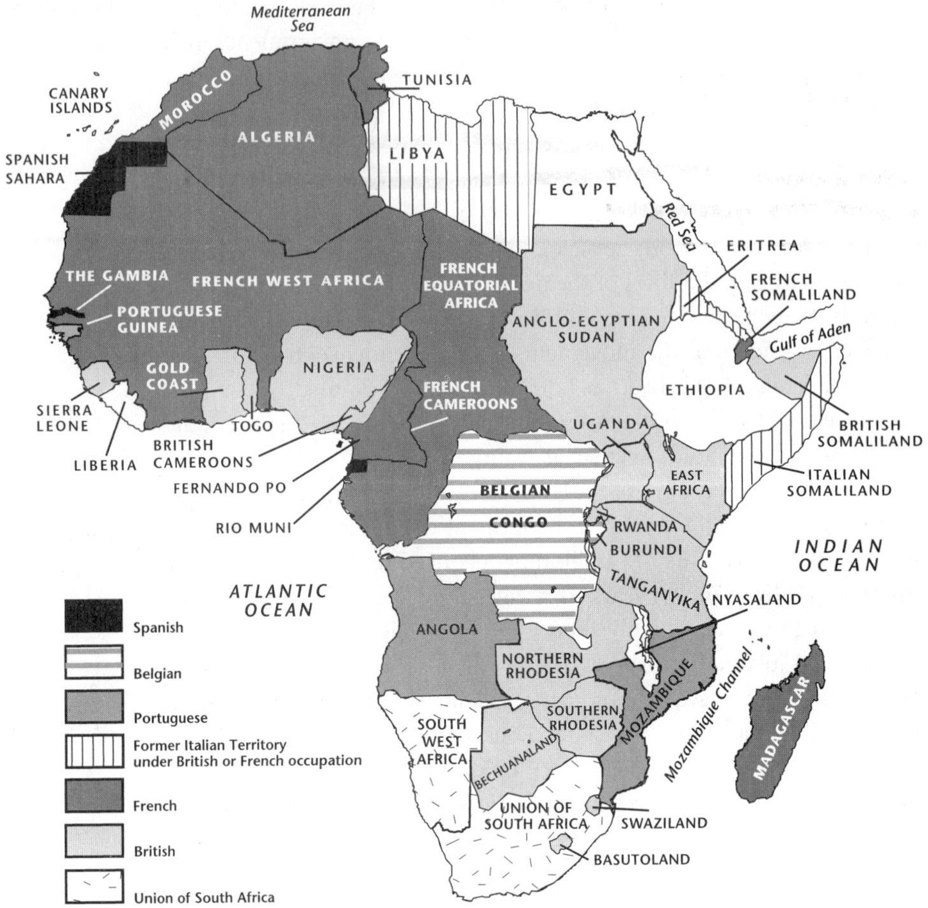

AFRICA IN 1945

many poorer countries by keeping wages low, which, in turn, allowed the reinvestment of the capital saved into further economic expansion. In the newly independent countries, higher wages and mass consumption were postponed in favor of "capital formation" and economic expansion. Thus, although living conditions may have improved slowly over time, they could not meet rising expectations.

Once the populations of developing countries realized that they no longer had to live in the poverty of the past, that change was possible, and that people could create a better life through their own efforts, their dissatisfaction grew. This gap between their expectations and achievements was particularly aggravating when the rulers lived in luxury.

AFRICA TODAY

Those living less comfortably became frustrated, and their frustration spawned social discontent and an increasingly hostile and radical mood. In many cases, their wrath was directed not only toward their governments, but also toward the United States and other industrialized countries that supported their leaders.

Clashing Models of Economic Development

Confronting an amalgam of political, social, and cultural changes, developing countries in the 1960s were uncertain they could climb what economist Robert L. Heilbroner termed the "great ascent."[11] In this context, the Soviet Union and China were willing to present themselves as models of development. To people suffering from chronic hunger and poverty, it may not have mattered that the Soviet Union had advanced economically by brutally squeezing the necessary sacrifices out of the people, or that Maoist China had modernized its system of agriculture at the cost of tens of millions of lives. "Command" economics would at least provide the organization and efficiency needed to extract from the masses the sacrifices and the discipline to hold a developing nation together, to speed up the pace of its cultural revolution while controlling social tensions produced by the early stages of development, and to depose ruthlessly the traditional ruling classes blocking progress.

To many in the developing countries, communism offered a disciplined means of bringing about rapid political, social, economic, and cultural change. Supposedly, the beneficiaries of this system were not the rulers (who themselves saw communism as a means of seizing power and legitimizing dictatorial rule), but the mass populations who had labored for centuries without receiving a significant share of the wealth they produced. Communism, either in the Soviet (Leninist) or Chinese (Maoist) form, thus promised an egalitarian form of economic growth with the benefits of development redistributed fairly among all segments of the population. The emphasis was to be on internal development and the detachment of the developing countries from a global market that, according to neo-Marxist thought, benefited the "core" Western capitalist states and perpetuated the dependency of "peripheral" developing countries.[12]

These arguments appealed to the leaders of many developing countries, who sought to create a "new international economic order" that would be less dependent on the wealthy industrialized states. In the United Nations, the developing countries formed the Group of 77 to serve as a catalyst for promoting their economic interests. Given their numerical superiority in the UN General Assembly, the developing countries expected to control the UN's agenda, dictate the structure and goals of UN agencies, and, through their strength in numbers, force the industrialized states to meet their demands.

11. Robert L. Heilbroner, *The Great Ascent: The Struggle for Economic Development in Our Time* (New York: Harper Torchbook, 1963).

12. Influential works during this period included Immanuel Wallerstein, *The Modern World-System: Capitalist Agriculture and the Origins of the European World-Economy in the Sixteenth Century* (New York: Academic Press, 1974); Gunner Myrdal, *Economic Theory and Underdeveloped Regions* (New York: Harper and Row, 1971); and Andre Gunder Frank, *Capitalism and Underdevelopment in Latin America: Historical Studies of Chile and Brazil* (New York: Monthly Review Press, 1969). For a more recent assessment, see Wallerstein, "The Inter-State Structure of the Modern World-System," in *International Theory: Positivism and Beyond*, ed. Steve Smith et al. (Cambridge: Cambridge University Press, 1996), 87–107.

But this would not be so easy. Many Western scholars and political leaders insisted that the economic development of developing countries would stem from their integration in, not their isolation from, the market-based economic order established by the Bretton Woods system. Although authoritarian rule might be necessary in the short term to ensure stability, economic growth would pave the way for political reform.[13] For these analysts, global markets were the engines for economic growth, and they rejected the claims of neo-Marxist critics that the governments of capitalist states were merely the puppets of business interests. To the contrary, they optimistically predicted that, with the assistance of industrialized states, the developing countries would evolve through predictable "stages of growth" into modern, industrial, democratic societies.[14]

To make this happen, the industrialized countries agreed to contribute a fixed share of their gross national product (GNP) for development aid. In 1969 the World Bank's Pearson Commission endorsed a minimum contribution of 1 percent of GNP, a figure that was lowered to 0.7 percent by the United Nations and widely accepted by the governments of industrialized states. Western aid was intended to close the gap between rich and poor states, modernize the new nations, satisfy their rising expectations, and create socially stable societies. This process, in turn, was expected to establish democratic governments and a more peaceful world by giving developing countries the means for sustained economic growth.

But, in practice, these aid flows benefited the donors as much as the recipients. After the eruption of the Korean War, most U.S. economic aid was, in fact, military aid, especially because "economic" aid could free up funds for military spending. Moreover, after the recovery of Western Europe, most U.S. aid was channeled to pro-U.S. regimes that were not among the world's poorest. These recipients included Pakistan, South Korea, South Vietnam, Turkey, and, in the 1980s and 1990s, Israel and Egypt. Meanwhile, Britain and France disbursed foreign aid primarily to their former colonies, prompting charges of "neocolonialism," while Japan offered large-scale aid only to its neighbors in East Asia so they could pay for Japanese exports. Wealthy countries that actually offered aid to countries based on objective measures of human need were few and far between. Sweden and Denmark, for example, became respected

13. See Samuel Huntington, *Political Order in Changing Societies* (New Haven, Conn.: Yale University Press, 1968). For a critique, see D. Michael Shafer, *Deadly Paradigms: The Failure of U.S. Counterinsurgency Policy* (Princeton, N.J.: Princeton University Press, 1988), chap. 3.

14. See W. W. Rostow, *Politics and the Stages of Growth* (New York: Cambridge University Press, 1971).

"aid citizens," but they provided far less development aid than the larger industrialized countries.[15]

The self-interests underlying the U.S. aid program were widely apparent in developing countries, and their leaders became increasingly cynical about the proclaimed U.S. effort to raise global living standards. U.S. policy toward the developing countries suffered from three other liabilities as well. The first liability was that American dollars were all too often offered with the explicit or implicit assumption that the recipients would associate themselves with U.S. Cold War policies. The United States was reluctant to aid countries that would not join its anticommunist crusade.

The second liability that hampered U.S. policy toward developing countries was its own racial discrimination, which flagrantly violated the nation's oft-proclaimed democratic principles of freedom and human dignity. Conditions began to change during the 1960s as African Americans heard the Reverend Martin Luther King Jr. articulate their aspirations for a life of greater dignity, and after President Lyndon B. Johnson signed the Civil Rights Act of 1964. But racial problems continued to haunt the United States overseas. In Rhodesia (now Zimbabwe), the minority white-controlled government used abhorrent methods to control and exploit black citizens. The United States, in spite of its proclaimed disapproval of these policies and in spite of a UN embargo, continued to import Rhodesian chrome for years. Moreover, American companies in South Africa, given a green light by the U.S. government, continued to support that country's system of *apartheid* (strict racial segregation and discrimination) until pressure from other countries, the UN, and human rights groups became overwhelming in the early 1990s.

Third, and most fundamental, America's poor understanding of class struggle hampered U.S. relations with many developing countries. "Born free" as a bourgeois democratic society, America had managed to avoid the kinds of domestic conflicts over basic values that the countries of Europe had experienced and that plagued many developing countries. The United States had not experienced a genuine social revolution at its birth, one that seeks to destroy the institutions and social fabric of the old society and create a new society with new institutions and social classes. Despite its self-proclaimed revolutionary character, the United States was, according to Sen. J. William Fulbright, chair of the Senate Foreign Relations Committee from 1959 to 1974, a nonrevolutionary, conservative country.[16] America, then, was not particularly sympathetic to revolu-

15. See Steven W. Hook, *National Interest and Foreign Aid* (Boulder, Colo.: Lynne Rienner, 1995).

16. J. William Fulbright, *The Arrogance of Power* (New York: Vintage Books, 1967), 72–73.

tions and tended to equate them with communism. Meanwhile, Washington's reaction to the communist threat was to support almost any regime, no matter how repressive, if it claimed to be anticommunist. As a result, the United States often allied itself with governments whose days were numbered—Chiang Kai-shek in China, Bao Dai in Indochina, and Ferdinand Marcos in the Philippines were but three of many examples.

This attitude was typical of America's self-righteousness and its inability to understand the deeper social struggles of the Third World. In its attempt to contain communism—that is, to preserve the global status quo—the United States became committed to the domestic, social, and political status quo in these regions. In trying to preserve freedom, the United States was paradoxically supporting ramshackle anticommunist autocracies that were unrepresentative of their peoples' aspirations. But this internal contradiction within the U.S. alliance system eventually had to resolve itself. American support for "traditional" regimes only bottled up the social and political resentment and ferment even more, thereby adding to the explosive forces that would burst forth during the Cold War and in its aftermath.

Regional Conflicts in Africa and the Middle East

From the 1950s through the 1970s, the domestic transformation of the developing countries had repercussions beyond their borders. The upheavals tended to disturb an international system largely defined by the frontiers drawn between the two superpowers' spheres of influence. When the internal difficulties of the developing countries spilled over into neighboring states, or when they resulted in political disintegration and civil war, they attracted the Soviet Union or the United States, leading to confrontation and, often, military conflict.

Sub-Saharan Africa proved especially vulnerable to such "failed states," as they became known in the 1990s. As noted earlier, decolonization led to the creation of dozens of countries whose boundaries were drawn, often arbitrarily, by the departing European powers. The region, meanwhile, experienced rapid population growth and urbanization. For example, the population of Lagos, Nigeria, grew from 250,000 to 500,000 between 1950 and 1960—a decade that also saw the population of Nairobi, Kenya, soar from 119,000 to 344,000.[17] Such rapid growth across sub-Saharan Africa placed increased demands on the new states for expanded utilities, roads, housing, and public services. Lacking

17. Paul Nugent, *Africa since Independence* (New York: Palgrave Macmillan, 2004), 65.

the resources to cover these expenses, African leaders often had no choice but to turn to Washington or Moscow for help.

Social instability and turmoil were further propelled by the intellectual and cultural changes that accompanied the transformation of a traditional, static, rural society into a modern, dynamic, urban-industrial state. Many of the old customary and religious values that had provided some measure of social stability simply collapsed. People became disoriented, torn from their age-old moorings for which they had not yet found a substitute. Their precolonial traditions had provided cultural meaning for their lives; robbed of this, they became isolated and insecure in a rapidly changing environment that they neither had made nor comprehended.

In the Middle East, for example, Iran experienced this kind of upheaval in the 1970s. Religious leaders opposed the repressive, American-backed shah, leading to his overthrow and the establishment of an Islamic theocracy in 1979 (see Chapter 6).[18] Precisely because economic development was associated with secular values, few in the West took seriously the possibility of the Ayatollah Ruhollah Khomeini's succession. The idea of a religious icon coming to power was so at odds with contemporary ideas of modernization that the likelihood of such an outcome was dismissed as preposterous. Yet for the poor and the powerless in a rapidly changing society where tradition and customs were being eroded, often by forces alien to the indigenous population, religion retained a strong attraction and comfort. Elsewhere in the Middle East, political violence plagued the newly created state of Israel and its Arab neighbors, providing additional fertile territory for intervention by the Cold War superpowers.

NATIONAL DISINTEGRATION AND CIVIL WAR IN THE CONGO

One of the more dramatic examples of the way the survival of a new state involved the superpowers occurred in 1960 when the Belgian Congo became independent. Almost immediately the Congo fell into disorder. First, the rich mining province of Katanga, which provided the copper and cobalt exports that were a major source of revenue for the Congo, split off into a separate state. Katanga's president had the support of the powerful Belgian mining interests, eager to protect their investments. Then the Congolese army began to revolt, because it resented the continued presence of its Belgian officers and wanted them

18. See Said Amir Arjomand, *The Turban for the Crown: The Islamic Revolution in Iran* (New York: Oxford University Press, 1988).

replaced with native leadership. In a wild spree, Congolese soldiers began to attack white women (including nuns) and children, which prompted the Belgian settlers to flee, as well as the experts the Belgians had expected to leave behind to help the Congolese in their early period of self-government. All public services then collapsed, because the Congo lacked an educated native elite.

When the Belgians flew in paratroopers to protect their nationals, Congolese premier Patrice Lumumba saw the move as a Belgian attempt to restore colonial rule, and he appealed to the United Nations to send forces to help him. It was at this point that the Cold War was injected into the Congo. The UN troops, with no forces from the great powers, did not compel the Belgians to evacuate their paratroopers, because UN Secretary-General Dag Hammarskjöld had ordered UN forces not to become involved in internal conflicts or in the contending political factions seeking to gain power over their rivals. This order, however, had the effect of reinforcing the divisions of the Congo. Lumumba turned against the United Nations, bitterly attacked the secretary-general, and accused Belgium and the Western powers, especially the United States, of conspiring against him. Finally, he asked the Soviet Union for help and received Soviet diplomatic backing, military supplies, and offers of troops, or "volunteers."

In early 1962, after all efforts to unify the Congo had failed, the United Nations reversed its original stand and adopted the policy of forcefully quashing the opposition. Although UN efforts took many months and cost lives, the country was "unified." Mobutu Sese Seko, who emerged as the Congo's leader for several decades and who renamed the country Zaire, was supported by the United States for his anticommunist policies. Mobutu received vast amounts of U.S. foreign aid, most of which he used to solidify his rule rather than feed his people. Along the way, he expropriated much of Zaire's mineral wealth for his own purposes, to the point that he became one of the world's richest men while his country slipped further into poverty.

Mobutu's actions, and the case of Zaire in general, symbolized the disarray that resulted when Cold War politics collided with Third World development. The experience had profound implications for the post–Cold War era as well, a period that witnessed Mobutu's ejection from power and the creation of a fragile new government. The overthrow of Mobutu in 1997 demonstrated how vulnerable such tyrants were to popular backlash once deprived of their Cold War patrons. After Mobutu's overthrow, the explosion of civil war in the newly renamed Republic of the Congo—a war that drew in most of the country's neighbors—revealed the true costs of stunted political development and manipulation by outside powers.

REGIONAL RIVALRIES: THE ARAB-ISRAELI WARS

Beyond the impoverished states of Africa, no area better exemplified how regional disputes became intertwined with the Cold War than the Middle East, where three sets of rivalries intersected: Arab-Israeli tensions, intra-Arab rivalry, and the superpower competition. Each tended to reinforce the other. The Arabs, especially Egypt and Syria, received weapons and political support from the Soviet Union; Israel received similar support from the United States. With all this help, then, the Arabs and Israelis were able to fight repeated wars.

Arab antagonism toward Israel stemmed from the Balfour Declaration of 1917, in which Britain pledged the establishment of a "national home" for the Jewish people in Palestine while promising Arabs that the rights of non-Jews would be protected. Zionists took this pledge as a promise to convert Palestine into a Jewish state; they considered Palestine, which became a British mandate after the disintegration of the Ottoman Empire during World War I, their ancient and traditional homeland. The Arabs, meanwhile, feared that a Jewish state would deprive them of what they also regarded to be their rightful homeland. In November 1947, the United Nations partitioned Palestine into two independent states, one Jewish and the other Arab, but the Arabs refused to accept this solution. On May 10, 1948, the armies of the Arab League (Egypt, Jordan, Lebanon, Saudi Arabia, and Syria) invaded the new state. In the ensuing war, the Israeli army defeated the larger Arab armies, and the state of Israel became a political fact of life.

The Arabs, however, still refused to recognize Israel. But Egypt, the leading Arab power, needed arms before reconfronting Israel. In September 1955, Egypt stunned the West by concluding an arms deal with Czechoslovakia, acting for the Soviet Union. Under this arrangement, Egypt received a large quantity of arms, including MIG-15 fighter planes and tanks. Egypt's leader, Col. Gamal Abdel Nasser, believed he then had the means to achieve a decisive military victory over Israel. In April 1956, Egypt tightened the ring around Israel by forming a joint command with Saudi Arabia, Syria, and Yemen. When the United States angered Nasser by retracting its offer to finance his pet project, the Aswan High Dam, Nasser vowed to nationalize the Suez Canal, which connected the Red Sea and the Mediterranean, and use the revenues collected from it to finance the dam. Arab nationalists were ecstatic, and Nasser's stature reached new heights.

In this overheated environment, Israel took the offensive and marched into Egypt, where it quickly defeated the Egyptian forces on the Sinai Peninsula. British and French forces, still seeking a presence in the region, intervened in Israel's behalf and sought control of the canal. Far from receiving an American endorsement, however, their action infuriated President Dwight Eisenhower, who saw the invasion of Egypt as a golden opportunity to win Arab friendship. U.S. support of Britain, France, and Israel would leave the Soviet Union as the sole champion of Arab aspirations, but by saving Nasser, the United States could align itself with Arab nationalism. The favorable global contrast—Washington opposing foreign intervention in the Middle East at a time when the Soviets were intervening in Hungary to suppress its aspiration for national self-determination—provided further incentive for the United States to rebuff its allies.[19] In fact, in the end America's opposition to the invasion proved decisive. In the face of worldwide condemnation of the invasion, the British, French, and Israeli governments withdrew their forces.

Yet, unfortunately for Eisenhower, the Soviet Union reaped the benefits of the Suez crisis. After it had become clear that the United States would not support the British and French invasion, Soviet leaders threatened "to crush the aggressor." The Soviet Union risked nothing by delivering these threats to exterminate Israel and attack Britain and France, yet it received most of the credit from the Arabs for saving Nasser. Recognizing this Soviet public relations coup, Eisenhower urged Congress to support a new commitment to resisting communism in the Middle East—and it did. In 1957 Congress passed a joint resolution, known as the Eisenhower Doctrine, that declared the preservation of the Middle Eastern states vital to U.S. security. The United States was prepared to use armed force to assist any state requesting U.S. help to counter military threats "from any country controlled by international Communism."

Ten years later, in 1967, intra-Arab rivalries, combined with domestic economic failure, led Nasser to reassert his leadership of Arab nationalism. The result was another war. The Syrians, who had joined Egypt in a United Arab Republic only to quit it when Nasser moved to dominate the union, now sought to displace him as the leader of pan-Arabism. They openly and repeatedly called for Israel's destruction and stepped up their raids into that country. After the Israelis retaliated, the Syrians claimed in May 1967 that the Israelis were assembling their forces for a full-scale invasion of Syria. Nasser saw in that threat an opportunity to regain his leadership of Arab nationalism. The Egyptian leader was confident that, after eleven years of receiving Soviet training and arms, his

19. In 1956, amid growing anti-Soviet protests and a Hungarian declaration of independence, Soviet troops launched a brutal three-day assault on Budapest, killing 25,000 Hungarians and imposing even tighter control over the country. The Eisenhower administration allowed the Soviet crackdown to stand, despite previous U.S. pledges to support the "liberation" of Eastern Europe.

forces could destroy Israel, which this time would be fighting by itself, without the aid of France and Britain.

In preparation for the confrontation, the Egyptian leader moved reinforcements into the Sinai Desert and then demanded and obtained the withdrawal of the UN peacekeeping forces. Egyptian and Israeli forces now confronted each other for the first time since 1956. In his most deliberate provocation of Israel, Nasser blockaded the Gulf of Aqaba, Israel's lifeline through which it received its oil and other goods. He then signed an alliance with Jordan. As a result of that bold move, Arab armies surrounded Israel: Syria to the north, Egypt to the south, and Jordan to the east. Their military strategy was designed to cut Israel in two at its narrow waist. All these actions were accompanied by increasingly shrill calls for a holy "war of liberation" and the extermination of all of Israel's inhabitants.

In these circumstances, war was inevitable, unless Israel was willing to accept a major political defeat—an unlikely prospect. The preservation of peace, which could be achieved primarily by Nasser's removal of the blockade, depended on the United States and the Soviet Union. Washington was caught in a dilemma. On the one hand, the United States had recognized Israel's right to send ships through the gulf after compelling Israel to withdraw from that area after its 1956 victory. On the other hand, America was becoming deeply involved in Vietnam (see Chapter 5) and was therefore reluctant to take on a second conflict. Furthermore, a key question for American policy makers was whether such a test would precipitate a clash with the Soviet Union, which had with great fanfare sent warships into the eastern Mediterranean, fully supported the Arabs in their aims, and continually denounced Israel as an aggressive tool of American imperialism.

For Moscow, the Arab-Israeli conflict had global implications. If Western influence could be expelled from the Middle East and if the Soviet Union could establish itself as the dominant power over that oil-rich region, Europe would be weakened and perhaps even neutralized. If the Gulf of Aqaba blockade succeeded, the Soviet Union would earn the Arabs' everlasting gratitude as the primary force behind Egypt's political victory. Moreover, an effective blockade would demonstrate the Soviet Union's ability to inhibit the American navy and would jeopardize future American commitments to Israel. In short, the Soviet Union had an opportunity to replace the West as the region's leading power.

But Moscow's ambitions were quickly frustrated in the region. Because Washington was unable to arrange a diplomatic solution, the Israelis attacked to seize the initiative in what had become an unavoidable clash. Routing the air forces of their Arab opponents in a brilliantly coordinated set of air strikes during the first hours of hostilities, they defeated the Egyptian army and reached the Suez Canal in three days—two days ahead of the record they set in 1956. Israeli forces also routed the Jordanian army, and then captured half of Jerusalem and the western bank of the river Jordan. Finally, they turned on the Syrian army and eliminated the bases on the Golan Heights from which Syria had been launching terrorist raids and shelling Israeli settlements. Nasser's dreams of an Arab empire, and the Soviet Union's hopes for regional hegemony, were quickly shattered. Meanwhile, the United States maintained its imposing presence throughout the Middle East.

U.S. Policy toward Latin America

Events in Latin America further illustrate how the Cold War, and American foreign policy in general, were propelled by events in the developing world. As U.S. leaders saw it, mass-based revolutions in Latin America created a foothold for communism in the Western Hemisphere and thus constituted a threat to the United States. They responded to the growing unrest in their "backyard" by intervening throughout the region, indirectly in most cases, but directly when a communist victory was seen as imminent.

Latin Americans shared two aspirations that were sweeping through developing areas in the decades following World War II: a better life for their masses and self-determination of their national destinies. Since the early 1800s, the United States had dominated its hemispheric neighbors, usually through alliances with the wealthy, land-owning governing class. Americans may have believed they were free of Europe's taint of colonialism, but Latin Americans disagreed. The Monroe Doctrine had turned the entire Western Hemisphere into a U.S. sphere of influence; the United States did not have to resort to direct colonial rule. Invested American capital spoke louder than guns, and the U.S. government did not have to give political orders when a nation was a "banana republic."

In contrast to their rhetorical calls for democratic rule, U.S. leaders actively supported military rulers throughout Latin America and exercised their self-appointed "international police powers" in the region.[20] The United States intervened frequently in Central America and the Caribbean early in the twentieth century to maintain "stability," a word that was synonymous with U.S. control. When American troops withdrew, they left behind hand-picked military leaders to protect U.S. economic and military interests. The Good Neighbor Policy launched by

20. This term was coined by President Theodore Roosevelt, whose 1905 "corollary" to the Monroe Doctrine legitimized the recurring series of U.S. interventions and occupations in Latin America and the Caribbean. For a critical view, see Walter LaFeber, *Inevitable Revolutions: The United States in Central America*, 3d ed. (New York: Norton, 1993).

UNITED STATES
BAHAMA ISLANDS
PUERTO RICO
CUBA
MEXICO
CAYMAN ISLANDS
DOMINICAN REPUBLIC
HAITI
BELIZE
JAMAICA
HONDURAS
NICARAGUA
GUATEMALA
EL SALVADOR
VENEZUELA
COSTA RICA
PANAMA
COLOMBIA
CENTRAL AMERICA AND THE CARIBBEAN

TRINIDAD & TOBAGO
ATLANTIC OCEAN
VENEZUELA
GUYANA
SURINAME
FRENCH GUIANA
COLOMBIA
ECUADOR
PERU
BRAZIL
BOLIVIA
PACIFIC OCEAN
PARAGUAY
CHILE
ARGENTINA
ATLANTIC OCEAN
URUGUAY
FALKLAND ISLANDS
SOUTH AMERICA
Cape Horn

President Franklin Roosevelt in 1933 was designed primarily to cement close relations with pro-American dictators, including Fulgencio Batista of Cuba, Rafael Trujillo of the Dominican Republic, and Anastasio Somoza of Nicaragua, all of whom enjoyed lavish state visits to Washington. Of Somoza, Roosevelt reportedly remarked, "He's a son of a bitch, but at least he's our son of a bitch." [21]

The U.S. attitude toward Latin America took on an even harder edge during the Cold War, when the perceived threat was no longer defined generally as internal unrest but very specifically as communist revolution. As in Africa and southern Asia, the vast majority of Latin Americans possessed little wealth and even less political power. Their plight strengthened the appeal of Marxist ideology, which not only sought to explain their difficulties but also promised the peasants a way out. Consequently, the long-standing U.S. interest in dominating Latin American affairs became even stronger. Through the Organization of American States (OAS), created in 1948, the United States effectively guaranteed the security of its neighbors throughout the hemisphere. In so doing, the U.S. government also guaranteed that communism would not take hold in the region without a fight.

No single event more epitomized this approach than the 1954 U.S. intervention in Guatemala, one of the poorest and most repressive states in Latin America. For decades, the country's large and productive agricultural plantations had been controlled by a small elite that maintained closer contacts with U.S. banks and corporations than with the landless *campesinos* who made up more than 90 percent of Guatemala's population. Thus it should have come as no surprise when democratic reforms in the country produced opposition leaders who sought to abolish this system.

The United States, though preoccupied with fighting World War II in 1944, viewed warily the spreading protests against Guatemala's dictator, Gen. Jorge Ubico. Outrage against Ubico's repressive rule led to his downfall in that year and his replacement by Juan José Arévalo, a popular schoolteacher and political activist who became the first democratically elected leader in Guatemala's history. Arévalo was successful at first in instituting reforms, but his supporters soon fragmented into several competing factions. As the Cold War settled in, the political climate in the country became more ideologically charged, and in the elections of 1950 a more radical leftist candidate, Jacobo Arbenz Guzmán, gained power and promised additional sweeping reforms.

21. Quoted in Peter H. Smith, *Democracy in Latin America: Political Change in Comparative Perspective* (New York: Oxford University Press, 2005), 111. Also see Smith, *Talons of the Eagle: Dynamics of U.S.-Latin American Relations,* 2d ed. (New York: Oxford University Press, 2000), chap. 3.

Arbenz, who received support from a growing Communist Party in Guatemala, attempted to take over many of the plantations and give the land, including 225,000 acres owned by the U.S.-based United Fruit Company, to the peasants. Fearing that such drastic "land reform" would provoke further uprisings elsewhere in Central America and threaten U.S. control of the Panama Canal, the Eisenhower administration supported a plan to overthrow Arbenz. In 1954 Arbenz provided the pretext needed by the United States—the importation of weapons from Czechoslovakia—and the Central Intelligence Agency (CIA) executed its military coup. Within days, Arbenz was removed from power, his reforms were abolished, the military regained control of the *campesinos*, and the United States reinforced its image as an enemy of revolution in Latin America.[22]

In the face of this widespread resentment, American leaders declared their intention to use foreign assistance to improve the living standards of Latin Americans. Their stated goal was to help the Latin American economies foster a self-sustaining rate of economic growth and develop conditions in which enterprises other than the extraction of raw materials or agriculture directed at single exportable crops would attract private capital. Because of projections of a rapid increase in Latin America's population, the efforts to achieve these goals became all the more urgent. To meet this challenge, President John F. Kennedy, soon after assuming office in 1961, established the Alliance for Progress. He pledged $20 billion of primarily public money over the next decade to Latin America, and, even more significant, he emphasized the need for social change. Through the Peace Corps and other innovations, Kennedy hoped to revitalize Franklin Roosevelt's aspiration to make the United States a "good neighbor" of Latin America. Kennedy realized that, in the absence of such an effort, the possibilities of economic development were slight and the prospects of additional communist insurgencies were strong.

Kennedy's Alliance for Progress, however, never lived up to the president's stated objectives. The political atmosphere throughout Latin America had become so polarized that any attempt by the United States to support moderates proved futile. And in the economic sphere, any discussion of reducing the disparity of wealth and creating a middle class was thwarted by the elites, who clung to their wealth and to their close ties to the military. On the home front, Kennedy was unable to gain support for his initiative; congressional leaders stubbornly identified reform with revolution, and revolution with communism. As a result,

22. For an elaboration, see Stephen Schlesinger and Stephen Kinzer, *Bitter Fruit: The Untold Story of the American Coup in Guatemala* (Garden City, N.Y.: Anchor Press, 1982).

the president was forced to maintain the status quo in Latin America, which, during the peak of the Cold War, meant a high level of economic distress, political repression, and social unrest.

Superpower Confrontation in Cuba

The intrusion of Cold War tensions into U.S. relations with Latin America was most sharply demonstrated in Cuba. Its revolutionary government dated from January 1, 1959, when armed rebels overthrew the U.S.-backed dictatorship of Fulgencio Batista. Among the rebels, Fidel Castro identified himself with democratic government and social and economic justice and gained widespread popularity among the Cuban people. This public support ensured the victory of his guerrilla army against the larger government forces. The Castro revolution was essentially a social revolution. Thus in its opening months, the new government moved to remedy the conditions of the people by instituting land reform and building low-cost housing, schools, and clinics. But some features of this social revolution were bound to clash with the interests of the United States.

Although the United States had been instrumental in freeing Cuba from Spain in the Spanish-American War at the turn of the century, in 1902 members of Congress engineered an amendment to the Cuban constitution, known as the Platt Amendment, which granted Americans the right to intervene at any time in Cuba to preserve Cuban independence, to protect life, property, and individual liberty, and to help the discharge of Cuba's treaty obligations. By 1934, when the amendment was repealed, the United States had intervened militarily in Cuba once (1906–1909) and had established a naval base at Guantànamo Bay. American capital controlled 80 percent of Cuba's utilities, 90 percent of its mines and cattle ranches, nearly all of its oil, and 40 percent of its sugar production (approximately 25 percent of the American market was reserved for Cuban sugar). Despite this special commercial link, it was not surprising that the Cuban revolution directed its long pent-up nationalism and social resentment against the "Yankee imperialism" that dominated Cuba's economy. America's support of the Batista dictatorship until the moment of its collapse intensified anti-American sentiment. "Cuba, si! Yanqui, no!" became the Castro regime's rallying cry, the ceremonial burning of the American flag its ritual, and the confiscation of American property its reward.

Swept along by this anti-American nationalistic feeling deliberately fostered by Castro to increase the popularity of his regime, Castro's government became increasingly identified with communism. If he was going to break with Washington, which, Castro assumed, would oppose

IMPACT AND INFLUENCE

FIDEL CASTRO

Both during and after the Cold War, no developing country leader played a more visible role in denouncing the United States than Fidel Castro. In 1959 the Cuban leader directed a successful revolution against the U.S.-backed regime of Gen. Fulgencio Batista. He then took control of Cuba's new communist government, the first of its kind in the Western Hemisphere, and became a close ally of the Soviet Union.

Castro, along with his brother Raul and Ernesto "Che" Guevara, hoped to make Cuba an inspiration for other revolutionary movements. An attorney before the revolution, Castro extended social services to all Cubans, including education and health care. His dictatorial rule, however, prompted many to flee the island for the United States, and the Cuban economy steadily deteriorated under communist control. But Castro remained popular as a symbol of defiance as the feud between the United States and Cuba continued into the twenty-first century.

his reforms, then he had to look to Moscow, its rival. By doing so, the Cuban leader betrayed the revolution's original democratic promises, and Cuba became a dictatorship. All political parties were abolished except for one—the Communist Party—and Castro became increasingly dependent on its organizational strength. He then quickly aligned Cuba with the Soviet Union, which supplied Cuba with vast amounts of arms and military advisers. Cuba's economy also became integrated into that of the communist bloc; 75 percent of the island's trade was with countries behind the iron curtain.

In January 1961, the United States cut off diplomatic relations with Cuba after a series of alleged provocations. If Castro at that point had attempted to seize the Guantànamo base, there would have been an excuse for open American intervention. Castro, however, was too shrewd to risk a seizure, but he also ruled out an accommodation with the United States. Above all else, Castro wanted to play a major role on the world stage—a role he could not achieve as the leader of either a pro-American or a neutral developing country of ten million people. He could do so only as a revolutionary leader who took on his giant neighbor as an enemy. But to stand against the United States he would need the support of the other giant, the Soviet Union. Thus Castro turned down friendly overtures from the United States after he took power: a new, sympathetic American ambassador was kept waiting for weeks before being allowed to present his credentials, and offers of foreign aid were rejected.[23]

THE BAY OF PIGS

As Cuban-Soviet relations tightened, American leaders began to plan secretly for Castro's overthrow. To this end, in April 1961 the new Kennedy administration launched an attempt by a small force of Cuban exiles—many of them former Castro associates who had become disillusioned by the dictator's increasingly tyrannical rule, communist sympathies, and alignment with the Soviet Union—to land in Cuba and attempt to overthrow Castro. The CIA, which had developed the plans for this operation and supervised their execution, assumed that once the exiles had gained a beachhead in the Bay of Pigs, some units of Castro's army and much of Cuba's population would welcome the invaders as liberators.

But the CIA's predictions proved wrong, and the operation was a dramatic and appalling failure. The United States bungled it by basing a major foreign policy move involving American prestige on the glib assumption that a feeble beachhead operation would result in a mass uprising of Cubans against their government. Kennedy's refusal to provide air cover for the amphibious attack, on the grounds that such support would reveal U.S. complicity in the invasion, testified to his ambivalence while ensuring the military failure. Rumors and press reports conveyed the impression of a major invasion, making the Cuban victory appear even more spectacular.

American prestige, already damaged by the Guatemala coup and other U.S. interventions in the developing world, sank to a new low. The administration had fallen victim to its own half-heartedness. Worse, the

23. The changing U.S. views of Castro and his policies during his first two years in power are chronicled in Peter D. Eicher, ed., *Emperor Dead and Other Historic American Diplomatic Dispatches* (Washington, D.C.: CQ Press, 1997), 442–448.

United States had defied its own proclaimed standards regarding the sanctity of borders. As Sen. J. William Fulbright warned Kennedy days before the invasion, "To give this activity even covert support is of a piece with the hypocrisy and cynicism for which the United States is constantly denouncing the Soviet Union." [24] The results of the unsuccessful invasion were predictable: greater domestic support for Castro, revival of Latin America's hostility toward "Yankee imperialism," blunting of Kennedy's initially successful attempts to identify the United States with anticolonialism, and U.S. allies' loss of confidence in America's leadership.

THE CUBAN MISSILE CRISIS

After the Bay of Pigs fiasco, Cuba was emboldened to act as a communist base from which the Soviet Union could threaten the United States and elicit support from other developing nations in the Western Hemisphere. With Castro's victory, the United States no longer held a monopoly of power in the Caribbean and Latin America, the stated intention of the Monroe Doctrine. The Bay of Pigs disaster also incited new Soviet provocations. In Moscow, where unfriendly regimes were not tolerated but crushed, Kennedy's prestige plummeted. In the view of Soviet leaders, if it had been in the interest of the United States to eliminate Castro, then U.S. military intervention should have followed the bungled attempt by the CIA. A "serious" power does not tolerate its enemies so near and does not act squeamishly. It does what it has to do, regardless of international opinion. Moreover, if Castro's elimination had not been important enough for the United States to risk criticism, then the intervention should not have been launched in the first place. But to do so and fail suggested weak nerves and a lack of foresight. Worse, it revealed fear of the Soviet Union. Why else would the United States not intervene with its own military forces in an area so close to home, as it had done many times in the past? Perhaps the Soviet Union should push a little further and see if Kennedy would tolerate a further extension of Soviet power.

And that is just what Soviet leaders did. In October 1962, a U-2 spy plane discovered, to the great surprise and consternation of American policy makers, that the Soviets were building launching sites for approximately seventy short- and intermediate-range ballistic missiles that could carry nuclear warheads. That Nikita Khrushchev, the Soviet leader, had dared to move his missiles so close to the United States and

24. Quoted in Stephen E. Ambrose, *Rise to Globalism: American Foreign Policy since 1938*, 5th ed. rev. (New York: Penguin, 1988).

that he apparently expected no reaction beyond diplomatic protests were dangerous signs. But American vacillation at the Bay of Pigs and afterward had convinced Khrushchev that the United States would not fight to protect its vital interests. Besides, Khrushchev thought Kennedy too young and inexperienced. Kennedy, the Soviet leader said, was "too liberal to fight."

Khrushchev had a great deal to gain. U.S. failure to respond to his move would prove to America's allies in the North Atlantic Treaty Organization (NATO) what they already feared: the United States had become vulnerable to attack and could no longer be relied upon to protect Europe. Moreover, inaction in the face of Soviet missiles so close to the American coast would validate Khrushchev's claim of a shift in the nuclear balance. Renewal of Soviet pressure on Berlin, together with the likelihood of an even more cautious American reaction than before to Soviet actions in Cuba, would reinforce this impression. Only this time the Soviets could deliver an ultimatum to get out of Berlin or else, and they were in an increasingly favorable position to exert their will.

But for once Khrushchev overplayed his hand. He pressured the United States in the wrong place, and Washington could not resist the challenge. If the stakes were high for the Soviet Union, they were even higher for the United States, and Kennedy felt that under no circumstances could he afford to lose. Indeed, because he had warned the Soviet leader against placing offensive missiles in Cuba, Kennedy had to compel their withdrawal to preserve his credibility. From the outset, however, the young president realized that the central issue was Soviet and allied perceptions of the balance of power.

In Washington, Kennedy met night and day with his political and military advisers. Some recommended a diplomatic compromise; others pushed for massive air strikes or even a full-scale invasion of Cuba. The first option was rejected because Kennedy knew that even the appearance of compromising with the Soviet Union would result in America's further loss of face and prestige in the international community. The second and third options were dismissed as too dangerous. Thus the president chose a fourth option and ordered a blockade of Cuba to prevent any further missile shipments. Kennedy also demanded the removal of the missiles already in place. American firmness and determination left Moscow little choice. For once the Soviets had to decide whether to fire the first shot—to break the American blockade of their missile-carrying ships—and risk a possible escalation of the conflict. Much to everyone's relief, the Kremlin backed down, called back its ships, and ordered deactivation of the missile sites. As Secretary of State Dean Rusk vividly described it, "We were eyeball to eyeball, and the other fellow just blinked."

Chapter Four

Reasons for the Soviet capitulation have been debated ever since the Cuban missile crisis.[25] But it is clear that military considerations were central to Soviet calculations. Khrushchev recognized that the United States had enormous conventional, especially naval, superiority in the Caribbean, and that it could have mounted an overwhelming invasion. In the absence of sufficient conventional forces to support his ally so far away, Khrushchev was left with only one choice—risk nuclear war, which he was ultimately unwilling to do because he correctly recognized U.S. strategic superiority.

The missile crisis was followed by years of relaxed tensions between the United States and the Soviet Union. But there were other important outcomes as well. First, Kennedy declared publicly that the United States would not invade Cuba. Thus, although America had prevailed in the showdown, the Soviet Union retained its outpost in the Caribbean. Second, Khrushchev received assurances from Kennedy that the United States would dismantle the nuclear missiles it had recently installed in Turkey. Although this concession was largely symbolic—the United States simply shifted its nuclear arsenal to submarines in the Mediterranean—it was viewed by Soviet leaders as a tactical gain. Third, Soviet leaders vowed they would never be humiliated again and pledged to increase their nuclear forces to U.S. levels, if not surpass them. In this sense, the setback in Cuba only strengthened their resolve.

Finally, and most fundamentally, the Cuban missile crisis once again demonstrated the crucial role played by developing countries during the Cold War, mainly by serving as remote "theaters" of the struggle between the United States and the Soviet Union. In these areas, communism often proved appealing to impoverished peoples, many of whom were responsive to Soviet claims that the United States was primarily to blame for their troubles. Castro, who had unsuccessfully urged the Soviet Union to launch a direct attack against the United States during the crisis, nonetheless maintained his hold on power and became an even more dynamic symbol of anticapitalist defiance throughout the developing world.

Castro's influence in Latin America was aptly demonstrated in 1965 by the U.S. intervention in the Dominican Republic. The impetus for this event was the overthrow in 1961 of Rafael Trujillo, who had ruled the country as a dictator for thirty-one years. After a brief period of political turmoil, Juan Bosch, a man of genuinely democratic convictions, was elected president. Seven months later, however, Bosch was overthrown by a military coup whose leaders announced they would reestablish a

25. See Graham T. Allison and Philip D. Zelikow, *Essence of Decision: Explaining the Cuban Missile Crisis*, 2d ed. (New York: Longman, 1999); and Raymond L. Garthoff, *Reflections on the Cuban Missile Crisis*, rev. ed. (Washington, D.C.: Brookings, 1989).

"rightist state." In April 1965, the pro-Bosch forces revolted against this right-wing military government. Communists were thought to be active in the movement against the junta, and Washington feared they would create a second Cuba in the hemisphere. But the rebels claimed their revolution was led by noncommunists who sought only a return to constitutional government. Before the evidence was clear that the revolution was in fact communist-run, President Lyndon Johnson ordered the U.S. military to intervene and restore order on American terms.

The Dominican crisis demonstrated how obsessed the architects of the floundering Alliance for Progress were with Castro, without whom there likely would have been no large-scale efforts to encourage economic and political reforms in Latin America.[26] The overt U.S. intervention—the first in fifty years in Latin America—therefore proved to be the death knell of the Alliance for Progress, which had sought to persuade the region's ruling elites to share their power and wealth if they wished to avoid revolutionary violence. Latin America's ruling classes could now relax because there was an alternative to reform: the United States would save them from the consequences of their folly in preserving unjust societies. Thus American policy south of the U.S. border, as in other areas of the world, continued to be dictated by the bipolar global struggle.

In Latin America, then, just as in Africa and the Middle East, the globalization of containment had profound consequences. As many critics of the policy feared, the United States gradually became immersed in civil wars and regional conflicts far from its shores, many of which were grounded less in communist subversion than in the masses' aspirations for the same political and economic freedoms enjoyed by most Americans. In escalating containment into a boundless anticommunist crusade, American leaders violated the democratic values they supposedly were promoting, and they turned their presumed beneficiaries—the mass populations of developing countries—against the United States. To make matters worse, interventions by the United States frequently backfired, leading to the establishment of new regimes that were openly hostile to Washington. But American leaders, bound by the logic of containment and fearful of losing ground to the communists anywhere on the planet, stayed loyal to the policy. Their strategy led to the calamitous U.S. intervention in Vietnam, where the faltering consensus in the United States favoring global containment was put to the ultimate test.

26. See Theodore Draper, *The Dominican Revolt: A Case Study in American Policy* (New York: Commentary, 1968).

CHAPTER FIVE

Vietnam and the Cost of Containment

American F-105 Thunderchief bombers attack a North Vietnamese military target in June 1966. The bombing campaign, which escalated in the late 1960s and early 1970s, only hardened the resistance of North Vietnam during the war.

The wreckage of World War II yielded to an international order in the late 1940s and 1950s that was increasingly split between two rival blocs. Through their allies and proxies, the United States and the Soviet Union confronted one another in every region of the world and, in a series of actions and reactions, established "frontiers" between their spheres of influence. Even regions of otherwise marginal concern became arenas for the superpowers.

During the early Cold War period, which was shaped by a bipolar balance of power, each superpower was sensitive to shifts in regional power balances lest such shifts upset the equilibrium and give the enemy the upper hand. A gain for either side was perceived as an equivalent loss for the other. The opponent's moves, even if alleged to be defensive, were typically viewed as offensive and threatening. Similarly, internal developments in distant countries received close scrutiny, because the allegiance of their governments toward either superpower might affect the global competition. The early Cold War thus consisted of efforts by the United States and the Soviet Union to guard their respective spheres of influence against encroachment, subversion, and defection.

The developing world, as described in Chapter 4, emerged in the 1950s and 1960s as a crucial battleground in this struggle. Decolonization produced a large number of new countries that, despite their best efforts to remain nonaligned, often fell into the U.S. or the Soviet blocs. In Korea, both superpowers claimed vital interests to be at stake, leading to the country's partition and a protracted "hot war." Elsewhere, efforts by developing countries to produce viable governments and improve living standards were hampered, if not prevented altogether, by the intrusion of the superpower rivalry.

One part of the developing world to take center stage in the Cold War was Southeast Asia, or Indochina, which had been a French colony since the 1860s. For nearly a century, Indochina served as a key part of France's colonial empire and provided France with vast quantities of rice, rubber, oil, tungsten, and tin. As a result, French officials were reluctant to grant independence to Indochina after World War II, even though Japanese forces had displaced the French presence earlier during the conflict. As the United States prepared the Philippines for independence in July 1946, and as the British followed suit in India, Burma (now Myanmar), and Ceylon, French leaders insisted on reimposing colonial rule over Indochina. Their decision, however, would prove disastrous not only for France but also for the United States, which could not resist the temptation to view the conflict in Indochina as a microcosm of the East-West struggle.

Americans generally knew little about the history, cultural traditions, or politics of Indochina, which was previously of minimal concern to Washington. But the turmoil in the region after France's return transformed Vietnam, a province of Indochina, into a "vital interest" to the U.S. government. Still, the region remained a mystery to most Americans. This ignorance extended to the U.S. military, which "lacked the time and opportunity to see and understand Vietnam as anything other than a hot, humid, dangerous, and often hostile place." [1]

France's Ejection from Vietnam

Although they refused to leave Indochina, the French offered political concessions to Vietnam, the heavily populated, resource-rich province of Indochina located on the South China Sea. France recognized the Democratic Republic of Vietnam as a "free state" within the newly formed French Union, which also included Laos and Cambodia. Under the agreement, the French would be allowed to maintain garrisons in Vietnam for five years in return for allowing the Vietnamese to determine their future in a plebiscite. But in less than a year, the Vietminh, as the Revolutionary League for the Independence of Vietnam was known, accused the French of violating the agreement, and open conflict erupted in 1946 between the two sides. The fighting soon escalated into the "first" Vietnam War, which lasted eight years.

The conflict was led on the Vietnamese side by Ho Chi Minh, the Vietnamese revolutionary who had organized the Vietminh (also called the Viet Cong) during World War II and who now sought to convert Vietnam from a colonial ward to a classless communist society.[2] Ho had embraced communism in the 1920s after his efforts to establish an independent and democratic state were rebuffed by Western leaders at the Paris Peace Conference that followed World War I. During the period of Japanese occupation, however, the popular leader had shifted the Vietminh's emphasis from communism to nationalism in order to gain independence for Vietnam. After the war, emboldened by Japan's defeat and inspired by the United Nations' pledge to end colonial rule, Ho had reason to believe his nation's time had finally come. For the second time in less than three decades, however, he was sorely disappointed by the lack of support among the Western powers. His decision to launch a full-scale rebellion quickly followed.

With Vietnam under siege, French leaders installed Emperor Bao Dai, who previously had ruled the coastal region on behalf of the French government, as Vietnam's new leader. The Vietminh then escalated their campaign for independence, declaring themselves the true representatives of the Vietnamese people. By contrast, Bao Dai, who spent much of his time on the French Riviera, was widely viewed as a French puppet

1. Robert E. Vadas, *Cultures in Conflict: The Vietnam War* (Westport, Conn.: Greenwood Press, 2002), 58. For a detailed account of American misperceptions about Vietnam, see Jeffrey Record, *The Wrong War: Why We Lost Vietnam* (Annapolis, Md.: Naval Institute Press, 1998).

2. See Stanley Karnow, *Vietnam: A History* (New York: Penguin, 1983), chap. 3.

who could not survive one day without French military aid. In the continuing civil war, Ho, like Mao Zedong in China, adopted a strategy of guerrilla warfare that depended on control of the countryside and support among the peasants. The French, who generally held the cities, were at a disadvantage from the beginning. In the absence of genuine independence, most Vietnamese identified themselves with the Vietminh and saw the French, quite accurately, as illegitimate rulers.

American public opinion was unsympathetic to France's attempt to reestablish its colonial control over Indochina. Three events, however, led to U.S. involvement in this conflict. The first was the defeat of Chiang Kai-shek in 1949 and the creation of the communist-led People's Republic of China (PRC). This development was a blow to France, because the PRC could now provide assistance to the Vietminh. The second event was the outbreak of the Korean War, a direct challenge to the U.S. containment strategy. The final development was the shift in American public opinion away from its narrow concern with European security and toward a much wider campaign of anticommunism. As a result, perceptions of the French role in Vietnam changed. Rather than colonialists trying to hold onto the vestiges of their decrepit colonial empire, the French were now fighters in the global crusade against communism.

In 1950 the United States began to provide France with economic and military aid for use in the conflict; by 1954 American taxpayers were funding about 75 percent of the costs of the war. The French position continued to deteriorate, however, especially after the Korean armistice was signed in August 1953. Despite American warnings against intervention, the PRC shifted its pressure from Korea to Indochina and increased its assistance to the Vietminh. As a result, Ho's position grew steadily stronger at the very time France was losing its already feeble grip on the countryside. On March 13, 1954, Vietminh forces launched an assault against the strategically vital French fortress at Dien Bien Phu. With the French position in northern Vietnam close to collapse, it became painfully clear that the French could not hold on without American intervention. What was the United States to do?

Dien Bien Phu was the moment of decision for the United States.[3] President Dwight Eisenhower had declared Indochina to be of strategic importance to American security and had cautioned China against direct or indirect intervention. But the Chinese had ignored these warnings, and the U.S. government had to "put up or shut up." When push came to shove, American leaders shut up; their threats turned to bluffs. The reason for U.S. inaction was clear: American public opinion might

3. For a comprehensive study of this battle, see Martin Windrow, *The Last Valley: Dien Bien Phu and the French Defeat in Vietnam* (London: Wiedenfeld and Nicolson, 2004).

have been strongly anticommunist, but the nation was tired of war. For that reason, Eisenhower had withdrawn from Korea, and now he was unwilling to involve the United States in another such conflict. Furthermore, the administration was cutting the size of the army as part of the "New Look" military reorganization, and the army chief of staff had counseled against intervention because of a lack of available troops.

With these factors in mind, the administration considered two courses of action. The first was to rescue the French by attacking the communist positions around Dien Bien Phu with air power, but this strategy was rejected because air strikes by themselves could not halt the Vietminh's ground advance. Air power had failed to stop the North Korean army during the opening days of that war, forcing the commitment of U.S. troops. The alternative course of action was to attack China with nuclear weapons. That would have been consistent with the administration's announced policy of massive retaliation. But the administration did not follow its own policy for one simple reason: it is one thing to deliver a threat of massive retaliation to an opponent and quite another to have the opponent believe it. The Soviets had not believed such threats in Korea, nor would the Chinese in Vietnam. Thus the possible use of nuclear weapons was discussed—and rejected—by the president and his advisers. Both communist powers correctly guessed that the United States would not risk a total war for anything less than an attack on the United States or Western Europe.

In the end, the French government decided to make the best of the situation by negotiating in Geneva, Switzerland, an end to the war. The French people, mired in a second war in Algeria during this period, were as weary of Vietnam as the American public had been of Korea. Under the Geneva agreement, the war ended with the "temporary" division of Vietnam at the seventeenth parallel. Two separate and interim governments were to be established during this transition period: a communist regime in the north and a noncommunist regime in the south. Elections were scheduled for July 1956 to bring about Vietnam's "unity and territorial integrity."

The 'Domino Theory' and U.S. Intervention

Because the Geneva agreement called for a general election to be held in 1956, the Vietminh expected the unpopular regime in South Vietnam to collapse.[4] Leaders in Hanoi, the North Vietnamese capital, assumed that

4. For an instructive collection of articles published by the *New York Times* during the early years of this conflict, see Mark Lawrence, ed., *The Vietnam War,* vol. 1 (Chicago: Fitzroy Dearborn, 2001).

most of the twelve million South Vietnamese would vote for Ho, who had led the nationalist struggle against the French. When those votes were added to the widespread support for Ho in the North, the country would likely be reunited under communist control.

But American leaders maintained a strong interest in preventing this outcome in Vietnam, which was now liberated from France. They believed the seventeenth parallel dividing North and South Vietnam represented one of many crucial boundaries between the "free world" and the communist bloc. Just as these leaders decided to defend South Korea when North Korea crossed the thirty-eighth parallel, so they now decided to rescue South Vietnam. The United States sought to prevent a communist takeover by supporting the new government of Ngo Dinh Diem, a staunch anticommunist. The Eisenhower administration provided Diem with massive economic and military aid to "stabilize" the situation in Vietnam, a strategy that guaranteed yet another armed struggle for the control of Vietnam. Like the war in Korea, the "second" Vietnam War would be fought at a great distance from the United States in a remote area that was little known to most Americans.

Distance, however, was only one of the problems the United States encountered. Vietnam was a divided society: North against South, Buddhists against Catholics, lowlanders against *montagnards,* and peasants against urban dwellers. Moreover, loyalties were primarily local, and hostility to the central government ran deep, because, as in most developing countries, the government historically had been that of the colonial power, represented at the local level by the tax collector and recruiting sergeant. Further complicating the matter, transportation and communication networks were primitive and industrial development nonexistent. South Vietnam had no established political institutions and a precarious economy.

Ho's popularity compelled the United States and the new South Vietnamese government to oppose and ultimately prevent the 1956 elections promised in the Geneva agreement. The United States wanted the seventeenth parallel to be accepted as the new frontier, and Diem, a fervent Catholic and anticommunist, wanted to stay in power no matter what the Geneva agreement said about elections. In the face of such strong opposition, Hanoi saw its chances for a peaceful takeover fade, and with them its restraint. In 1959 the North Vietnamese began the armed struggle to unify the country, and the second Vietnam War commenced.

Despite the many similarities between the Korean and Vietnamese conflicts, U.S. involvement in Vietnam began quite differently. The Korean War had begun with a clear-cut, aggressive attack that had aroused the American public and united the principal Western allies against a common threat. Korea also had been a conventional war in

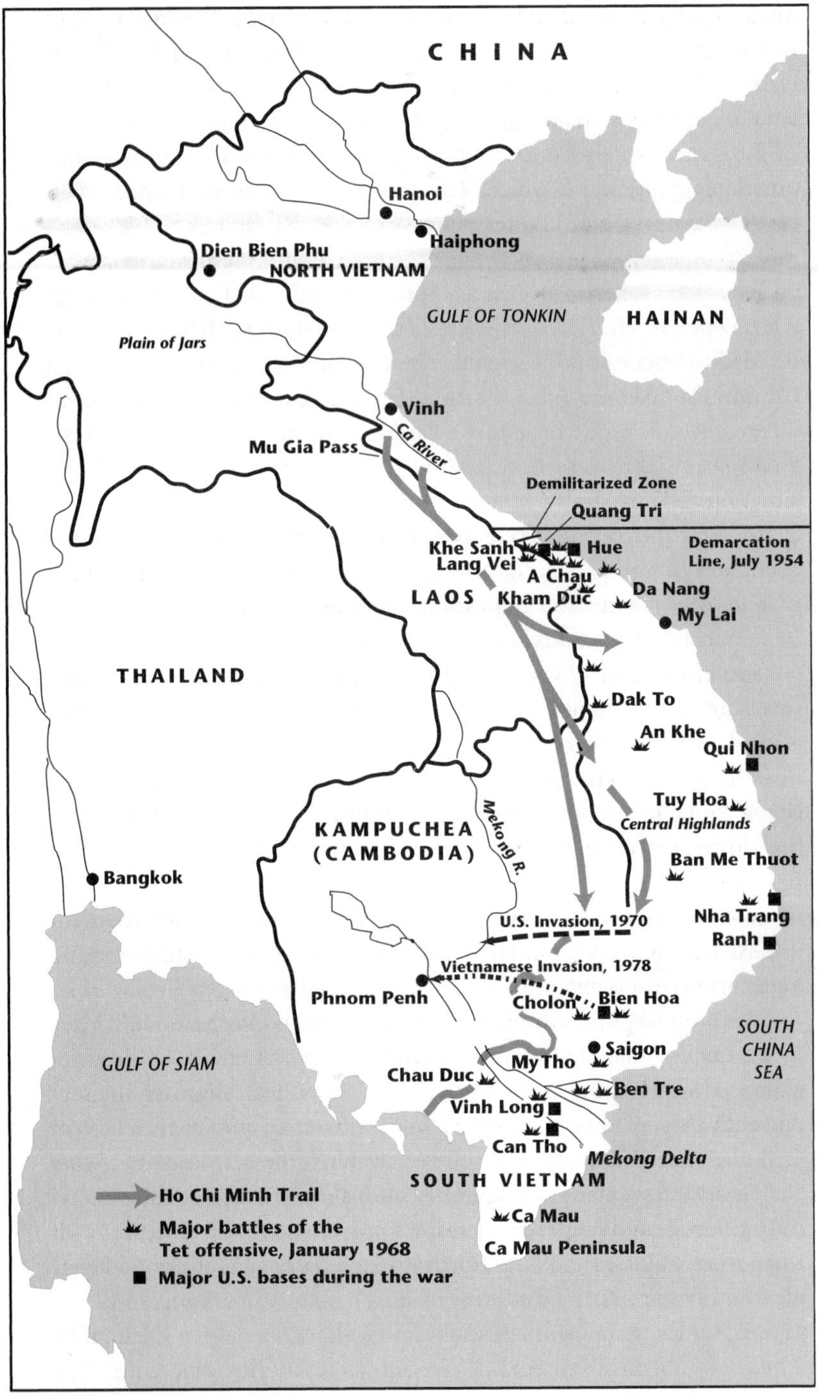
CHINA
Hanoi
Haiphong
Dien Bien Phu
NORTH VIETNAM
GULF OF TONKIN
HAINAN
Plain of Jars
Vinh
Ca River
Mu Gia Pass
Demilitarized Zone
Quang Tri
Khe Sanh
Hue
Demarcation Line, July 1954
Lang Vei
A Chau
Da Nang
LAOS
Kham Duc
My Lai
THAILAND
Dak To
An Khe
Qui Nhon
Tuy Hoa
Central Highlands
Mekong R.
KAMPUCHEA (CAMBODIA)
Ban Me Thuot
Bangkok
U.S. Invasion, 1970
Nha Trang
Ranh
Vietnamese Invasion, 1978
Phnom Penh
Cholon
Bien Hoa
SOUTH CHINA SEA
Saigon
GULF OF SIAM
My Tho
Chau Duc
Ben Tre
Vinh Long
Can Tho
Mekong Delta
SOUTH VIETNAM
Ho Chi Minh Trail
Major battles of the Tet offensive, January 1968
Major U.S. bases during the war
Ca Mau
Ca Mau Peninsula

THE VIETNAM WAR

which regular communist forces were checked by regular South Korean, American, and UN troops. By contrast, the French defeat at Dien Bien Phu in 1954 was a decisive moment in contemporary history because it demonstrated that guerrilla tactics could prevail against the larger and stronger army of a major power. An internal uprising of guerrillas was therefore a shrewder manner of "crossing" the seventeenth parallel. Diem's autocratic rule and his failure to enlist the support of his population—especially the peasantry—through political, social, and economic reforms helped to prepare the ground for a successful guerrilla campaign.

For the U.S. government, the Vietnam conflict represented a test of the nation's will, and the United States had to meet the challenge to maintain all frontiers. Until the noncommunist states in the region became more economically developed and possessed stable political systems and military defenses, the Asian balance seemed to depend on the United States. American leaders believed they could no more forgo the defense of the frontier in South Vietnam than in Korea. If either country fell, more communist victories would inevitably follow and the containment strategy would fail.

Given this logic, American leaders advanced a "domino theory" that sought to justify intervention in Vietnam. In their view, the political and psychological impact of a U.S. pullout would have repercussions elsewhere and ultimately upset the global balance of power. Specifically, Vietnam's collapse would provoke communist challenges throughout Indochina, across Burma, and into the Indian subcontinent. The Middle East would then feel the pressure, followed by the newly independent states of Africa. As Eisenhower stated, "You have a row of dominoes set up, you knock over the first one and what will happen to the last one is the certainty that it will go ever so quickly. So you could have a beginning of a disintegration that would have the most profound influences."[5]

The assumption underlying this viewpoint was that the Sino-Soviet bloc was united, despite increasing evidence to the contrary. Signs of discord between the Soviet Union and China were generally explained as tactical differences about how the "communist world" should wage its "war" against the United States. They were not seen as the fundamental conflicts of national interests between the two powers that Secretary of State Dean Acheson and others had predicted years before. If the Vietminh succeeded, Vietnam would be added to the Sino-Soviet bloc's column in the global power balance. Vietnam also would serve as proof for other revolutionary movements in Asia and elsewhere that the United States, despite its nuclear weapons and vast economic resources, could

5. Quoted in *New York Times,* April 8, 1954, 18.

be defeated. As for the nature of the warfare itself, Washington believed that the Vietminh's war against the South was similar to North Korea's aggression against South Korea, even if the Vietminh had not flagrantly crossed the dividing line. For U.S. military commanders, the struggle for Vietnam was just another variant of conventional warfare for which their soldiers and superior firepower were well prepared.

There was a double irony in this pattern of thinking. First, if the United States had sent diplomats to Beijing, they would have known that North Vietnam was not a puppet. Historically, China and Vietnam had been enemies, and in the early 1960s the last thing Mao wanted, with China in the midst of a domestic upheaval, was to risk a confrontation with the United States. Thus U.S. leaders, unaware of China's political climate or intentions—a lapse also true when China intervened earlier in Korea—once again paid a high price for its refusal to officially recognize the PRC. Second, if containment of China had been a key goal of the U.S. intervention, then the United States should have let South Vietnam fall. Ho was not just a communist, he was also a nationalist, and a nationalistic Vietnam would have proven a stronger barrier to any possible Chinese ambitions of hegemony in Southeast Asia than a noncommunist South Vietnam governed by a despotic, despised regime. But grasping these truths would have required close study of a distant and little-known part of the world, a burden that did not come naturally to American leaders who felt secure in their hemispheric comfort zone.

In truth, then, far from ensuring containment, the Vietnam War undermined containment. The beneficiary of this U.S. engagement was the Soviet Union, which gained an enormous advantage in the quest for global public opinion. Indeed, the key domino that fell was not South Vietnam, but the consensus within the U.S. and allied governments that had favored the containment strategy.

The Perils of Incrementalism

The massive U.S. intervention in Vietnam by President Lyndon Johnson was inevitable by 1965 because, beginning with the administration of Harry Truman, every president had deepened the involvement in Vietnam. Although Truman at first opposed France's postwar efforts to restore its colonial rule, he changed his position to overcome French resistance to the American plan for the revival of Germany, especially its rearmament. After the Korean War erupted, the French war in Indochina became part of the global struggle against communism. At the time of France's defeat at Dien Bien Phu in 1954, Eisenhower, even though deciding not to intervene militarily, did back the new government in South Vietnam, organized after France's defeat and withdrawal, with economic assistance and military training for its armed forces. But this training was in orthodox warfare, not in the unorthodox, or guerrilla, warfare that already had been observed in Vietnam. Besides, the Southeast Asia Treaty Organization (SEATO) was supposed to be the new state's security guarantee (see Chapter 4). President John Kennedy escalated the U.S. commitment in the early 1960s by sending in 16,500 military advisers to help the South Vietnamese army. Beginning in the spring of 1965, President Johnson transformed this commitment—and the conflict in general—by sending in a steadily growing U.S. troop presence that ultimately included more than 500,000 soldiers.

Particularly significant during these years of piecemeal commitments was that at no point did policy makers in Washington resolve some basic questions about Vietnam: Was it vital to American security interests and, if so, how vital? If it had been vital earlier, was it still so in the early 1960s? Could the situation in South Vietnam be saved militarily given the nature of the government in Saigon (the South Vietnamese capital) and its lack of popular support? If American forces were to be sent, then in what numbers? And how could they be used effectively in unorthodox warfare? What cost, if any, was South Vietnam "worth" to the United States?

Because incremental U.S. commitments were made whenever conditions in South Vietnam appeared ominous, these questions were never really debated at the highest levels of government. And if the reasons for America's involvement were not clear to its leaders, they were lost entirely on its citizens. But past American commitments foreclosed any meaningful debate except over how much force was needed to "save" South Vietnam. And once committed, American forces could not be withdrawn without widespread recognition that those forces had failed in their mission.

During the Kennedy years, military advisers managed to prevent South Vietnam's total collapse, but by 1965 Johnson—who after Kennedy's assassination in November 1963 had concentrated on passing a major domestic reform program and getting elected in his own right—could no longer operate on this basis and avoid the central question of what the United States ought to do. South Vietnam was rapidly crumbling under the weight of its corrupt and incompetent government. In the face of this reality, Johnson sent in 200,000 troops in 1965, deepening the U.S. involvement and turning an incremental policy into a long-term commitment. After years of neglect and procrastination and with the situation growing worse daily, Washington had neither the time nor the inclination to make a carefully calculated decision; when the crucial decision was made, it was made by Johnson, a new president, on the advice of the Kennedy staff and cabinet he had inherited. Long-range policy had become a prisoner of the earlier short-range decisions made to tackle crises.

Johnson's misfortune was that he could not procrastinate or make any more piecemeal moves. He was stuck with the choice of whether to escalate to prevent the defeat of the South Vietnamese army or to become, as he phrased it, the first president in U.S. history "to lose a war." Each president had done just enough to prevent this defeat. Johnson's escalation was the logical culmination of his predecessors' decisions. To make matters worse, Johnson could not count on substantial support from American allies even after launching his "More Flags" campaign in the summer of 1964. Despite Johnson's claims to the contrary, "neither friends nor foes around the world tended to see American credibility as being at stake in Vietnam."[6]

But perhaps even more important than foreign policy considerations in this escalation was American domestic politics. Originally, in 1947, anticommunism often was used as a means of arousing the public and mobilizing popular support for Cold War policies while the nation in fact pursued more limited aims. But once an administration had justified its policy in terms of an anticommunist crusade and had aroused the public by promising to stop communism, it opened itself to attacks by the opposition party if setbacks were encountered, even if they occurred for reasons beyond America's ability to prevent them. The ousted party could then exploit such foreign policy issues by accusing the party in power of appeasement, of having "lost" this or that country, and of being "soft on communism." These kinds of accusations made it difficult to recognize the People's Republic of China, to build bridges to Eastern Europe, to negotiate with the Soviet Union or Cuba, and especially to discriminate between areas of vital and secondary importance to U.S. security.

Democratic administrations were more deeply affected by this political rhetoric than Republican administrations. The Democrats, who were in power when Nationalist China collapsed, were accused of "treason," of "selling out" China, and they lost the 1952 presidential election as a result. The desire to avoid accusations of being soft on communism was one key reason Truman advanced northward across the thirty-eighth parallel in Korea before the 1950 midterm elections—and one reason he found it impossible to negotiate any settlement of the war that left Korea divided. Kennedy, who had campaigned on a tough anti-Castro platform, found it impossible to reject the Eisenhower-initiated plan to invade Cuba, although the new president had serious doubts about it. Even Eisenhower, a conservative Republican president and victorious

6. Frederik Logevall, "America Isolated: The Western Powers and the Escalation of War," in *America, the Vietnam War, and the World,* ed. Andreas W. Daum, Lloyd Gardner, and Wilfried Mausbach (New York: Cambridge University Press, 2003), 175.

general who had led the Allies to victory over Germany, and a man who hardly could be accused of disloyalty, had felt threatened enough by the right wing of the Republican Party that he did not pull the United States out of Vietnam in 1954. Instead, he kept America in Vietnam by supporting the new South Vietnamese government. The fear of accusations of being soft on communism also led the Kennedy and Johnson administrations to make their piecemeal commitments in Vietnam, lest the Democrats be charged with the "loss" of Indochina as well as China.

The Misconduct of Guerrilla Warfare

During its intervention in Southeast Asia, the United States virtually ignored the political structure of South Vietnam and thereby imperiled successful American prosecution of the war. As described earlier, for years the United States had supported Ngo Dinh Diem, the devout Catholic whose authoritarian rule and aloofness alienated most of the mainly Buddhist population. By the time the South Vietnamese military overthrew and murdered Diem in 1963 with Kennedy's knowledge and tacit blessing, the Vietminh already controlled much of South Vietnam; the social, political, and economic reforms needed to win the war had been neglected too long. That Diem's regime was so widely despised should have alerted future administrations; that Kennedy had said Diem had "gotten out of touch with the people" testified to the political bankruptcy in Saigon, as well as to the questionable wisdom of having the United States intervene militarily in the first place. Yet even with Diem gone, South Vietnam's government was unable to rally popular support for a vigorous prosecution of the war against the Vietminh.

Surprisingly, Saigon's succession of corrupt, reactionary, and repressive regimes never reminded U.S. policy makers of Chiang Kai-shek and his Nationalist government in postwar China. As it contemplated China's imminent collapse, the Truman administration had decided the country could not be saved, except perhaps—and it was only *perhaps*—by incurring enormous military and economic costs, which it felt the American public would not be willing to pay. In addition, these costs would have diverted the nation's resources and efforts from its area of primary interest, Europe, where American security was at stake. According to Secretary of State Dean Acheson, "Nothing that this country did or could have done within the *reasonable* limits of its capabilities" could have changed the result in the conflict between Mao Zedong and Chiang Kai-shek.[7] Likewise, the attempt at containment in South Vietnam was

7. U.S. Department of State, *United States Relations with China, with Special Reference to the Period 1944–1949* (Washington, D.C.: Government Printing Office, 1949), xvi (emphasis added).

risky in many respects. Truman's successors in Democratic administrations risked major domestic discontent. They also risked new questions about the fundamental assumptions of the foreign policy that had led to the war.

Certainly the possibility of achieving a quick victory over the Vietminh was remote, for guerrilla warfare is totally different from traditional warfare. The aim of a guerrilla war is to capture the government from within and do so by eroding the morale of the army and by undermining popular confidence in the government, thereby isolating it. To achieve this objective, guerrilla forces do not have to inflict a complete defeat on the government's forces or compel them to surrender unconditionally. Indeed, guerrillas do not even meet these forces openly until the final stage of the war, and then they do so only to apply the coup de grâce. A guerrilla war is, therefore, a protracted conflict in which the guerrillas use hit-and-run tactics and engage only those smaller and weaker government forces they can defeat. The government's only defense against this strategy is to deploy troops to guard every town, every village, and every bridge against possible attack. Unable to come to grips with the enemy and defeat it in battle, and suffering one small loss after another, the army becomes demoralized and its mood becomes defensive.

Although such tactics gradually weaken the military strength of an army, the guerrillas' main effort is directed at the civilian population. As the weaker side of the conflict, the guerrillas aim to wrest the allegiance of the population away from the government so that, without popular support, it simply collapses. The guerrillas do this in two ways. First, they gain control of the countryside where most of the people live, and, by winning battles with government forces, they demonstrate to the peasants that the government cannot protect them. The execution of village chiefs, who often are government representatives, is a common tactic used to drive this point home. Second, and even more important, the guerrillas exploit any existing popular grievances. Communist guerrillas do not usually receive support because they are communists; the populace supports them because it believes they will oust the unpopular government and install a new government that will meet the people's aspirations.

Indeed, according to Mao Zedong, guerrillas need the people "just as fish need water"; without popular support, guerrillas would not receive recruits, food, shelter, or information on the deployment of government forces. The guerrillas gain the support of the peasantry by successfully representing themselves as the liberators from colonialism or foreign rule, native despotic governments, economic deprivation, or social injustice. In this way, they isolate the government in its own country. Thus, unlike conventional warfare in which each army seeks the destruction of the other's military forces, guerrilla warfare is based on a strategy of mobilizing popular support. A government that has the allegiance of its population does not provide fertile soil for guerrillas; where social dissatisfaction exists, however, guerrillas find an opening.

This axiom is especially applicable when the combatants in such conflicts oppose foreign troops whom they believe wrongly occupy their territory and must be expelled. European powers, including the French in Vietnam, were the targets of such uprisings during the colonial period, and the United States was widely perceived as carrying on France's imperial ambitions. In such situations, guerrillas are able to exploit the existing deep reservoir of hostility toward the foreign armies, along with the tactical advantage of fighting in familiar surroundings. Together, these factors place the occupying forces on the defensive and lead to a high level of confidence and *esprit de corps* among guerrilla fighters. As one scholar observed, "The guerrilla's self image is not of a solitary fighter hiding among the people, but of a whole people mobilized for war, himself a loyal member, one among many. If you want to fight against us, the guerrillas say, you are going to have to fight civilians, for you are not at war with an army but with a nation. Therefore, you should not fight at all, and if you do, you are the barbarians, killing women and children." [8]

Guerrilla warfare is, therefore, not purely military; it also is political. Although the forces under attack must try to defeat the guerrillas in the field, their principal task is to tackle the political, social, and economic conditions that bred support for the guerrillas in the first place—that is, they must regain the "hearts and minds" of the populace. Counterguerrilla warfare, then, is an extremely difficult kind of war to wage—indeed, far more so than the traditional clash of armies—because the war cannot be won without extensive reforms. Yet these reforms have to be carried out in the midst of a war that is likely to last many years.

What all this means is that the United States, experienced only in conventional warfare, found guerrilla warfare hard to fight in Southeast Asia. Concerned primarily with social and political reforms, it ran counter to the traditional American military strategy. The length of the war also caused great frustration, because the U.S. government, under intense public pressure, had promised repeatedly that the war would end soon, that its leaders saw "light at the end of the tunnel." When this very different kind of warfare did not yield swift and successful results, U.S. troops faced the choice of either pulling out or seeking some shortcut to victory through military escalation.

8. Michael Walzer, *Just and Unjust Wars: A Moral Argument with Historical Illustrations* (New York: Basic Books, 1977), 180.

During the war in Vietnam, American policy makers misplaced their confidence in U.S. military prowess and its ability to change the guerrillas' "rules of the game." In 1965 the illusion of American omnipotence had not yet died. After all, the United States had successfully confronted the Soviet Union in Cuba and compelled it to back down. Could there really be much doubt that its well-trained generals, in command of armies equipped with the newest and latest weapons from America's industry and under the leadership of that most efficient Pentagon manager, Secretary of Defense Robert McNamara, would be able to beat a few thousand "peasants in black pajamas"? With its sizable forces and its superior mobility and firepower, why should the United States have any problem finding the enemy's troops and destroying them, thereby compelling that enemy to desist from taking over South Vietnam? Characteristically, then, the emphasis was strictly military.

To win against guerrilla warfare, U.S. forces would have had to secure villages and to stay in them to root out the Vietminh and show the villagers that Saigon did care about them. Instead, the military carried out massive search-and-destroy operations. And the guerrillas, even if driven away from the villages, returned after the helicopters left and continued to control the countryside. Because such large-scale operations could not be launched without preparation at the base camp and usually were preceded by air strikes and artillery bombardments of the area in which the troops would land, the Vietminh often disappeared and the whole operation ended in frustration.

American soldiers clearly did not understand the political nature of guerrilla warfare. They had been trained for conventional battle and to use maximum firepower to wear the enemy down in a war of attrition. The military was confident it could do this, because its helicopters provided superior mobility and modern technology gave it the necessary firepower. The measure of success became the daily body count of communist dead.

When the war was extended by air to the North, the purpose of the bombing clearly was not military, although the United States claimed its goal was to stem the flow of men and supplies going south. The aim of the attacks was political—to persuade North Vietnam to stop the war. By gradually extending these attacks northward, the United States was saying, in effect, that it would not withdraw and that the price Hanoi would have to pay for victory would be prohibitive.

But the bombing did not weaken Hanoi's will to prosecute the war, nor did it cut the flow of supplies sufficiently to hamper the fighting in

IMPACT AND INFLUENCE

ROBERT MCNAMARA

Robert McNamara, secretary of defense from 1961 to 1968, oversaw the American war effort in Vietnam. A former president of the Ford Motor Company, McNamara joined other "whiz kids" who sought to introduce modern analytical methods and technical innovations to the armed forces. Among his other initiatives, McNamara led the effort to shift U.S. nuclear strategy from the "massive retaliation" of the Eisenhower years to a strategy based on a "flexible response."

The pressures of the war in Vietnam, however, gradually consumed McNamara's energies. An early advocate of U.S. military involvement, he began to question the war effort and called for a negotiated settlement. When this proved impossible, McNamara left the Johnson administration in February 1968 to become president of the World Bank. During his thirteen-year tenure at that institution, the World Bank greatly increased its assistance to developing countries.

McNamara's 1995 memoir, In Retrospect: The Tragedy and Lessons of Vietnam, *detailed the many mistaken assumptions, political problems, and tactical errors that led to the U.S. defeat in Southeast Asia.*

the South or greatly reduce troop infiltration.[9] Hanoi's persistence, in turn, led to increased calls by the military and Washington for more air strikes and new targets. Those who advocated intensifying the air war did not acknowledge that air power alone could not win the war; instead, they insisted that it could if it were used with maximum efficiency. Air power, in short, came to be seen by some as an efficient, effective way of fighting the guerrillas, throttling their supply lines, breaking their morale, and finally compelling them to end the conflict at little cost in lives to the defender.[10]

9. Once again, important historical lessons were ignored. The sustained American attacks on Chinese supply lines in North Korea during the Korean War had shown that air power alone could not stop the flow of supplies to a fighting zone.

10. Secretary McNamara and his top aides confidently defended this strategy and predicted victory based on advanced computer models and cost-benefit calculations, most of which were proven wrong in the context of guerrilla warfare. See David Halberstam, *The Best and the Brightest* (New York: Random House, 1972).

This objective, however, remained unattainable. Moreover, the opposition was gaining strength. In South Vietnam, even the more stable military regime of Nguyen Van Thieu and Nguyen Cao Ky, which sought legitimation in the election of 1967, failed for years to implement a program of social and economic reform—that is, until 1970 when it adopted major land reform. It was particularly remiss in waiting so long to redistribute land from the usually absentee landlords to the peasants. Without such reforms, the Vietminh grew stronger. Militarily, every increase in American forces was met by the increased infiltration of both guerrillas and conventional troops from the North to the South. Nevertheless, the U.S. government issued optimistic battle reports and forecasts of victory on a regular basis.[11]

The 1968 Tet (Vietnamese New Year) offensive, launched on the last day of January, was the Johnson administration's Dien Bien Phu. Tet showed once and for all—and in full view of Americans, who saw it nightly on their televisions—that, despite the repeatedly optimistic predictions, the enemy had again been badly underestimated. The Vietminh launched a major countrywide offensive and attacked Saigon, Hué, and every other provincial capital; a Vietminh squad even penetrated the U.S. embassy compound, thereby scoring a significant symbolic victory. The fighting that followed, however, was bloody and the Vietminh were decimated. In fact, so many Vietminh were killed that the North Vietnamese army actually assumed the main burden of fighting the Americans. Nevertheless, the Vietminh had clearly demonstrated that neither an American army of half a million nor the far larger South Vietnamese army could ensure the security of urban dwellers—and the communists presumably already controlled much of the countryside.

THE POLITICAL BATTLEFIELD: THE UNITED STATES

In Vietnam, then, American power and its effectiveness in unorthodox warfare proved to be greatly exaggerated. Tactically, American forces had seized and retained the offensive, claiming the destruction of large numbers of enemy soldiers. But strategically the Vietminh had maintained the upper hand, and the Americans were on the defensive. For example, by using about 80 percent of their forces to find and destroy North Vietnamese troops in the relatively unpopulated central highlands and frontier regions, the Americans were unable to secure and protect the 90 percent of the South Vietnamese population living in the Mekong Delta and

11. For an elaboration, see H. R. McMaster, *Dereliction of Duty: Lyndon Johnson, Robert McNamara, the Joint Chiefs of Staff, and the Lies That Led to Vietnam* (New York: HarperCollins, 1997).

coastal plains. This strategy called into question not just America's protective capacity but also its wisdom.

As if this were not enough, a growing number of Americans believed the war to be morally ambiguous, if not downright immoral. There had never been a clear-cut transgression of the seventeenth parallel dividing North Vietnam and South Vietnam, which made the accusation that Hanoi was an aggressor less believable. The undemocratic Saigon government and its apparent lack of popularity gave credence to the view that the war was a rebellion against Saigon's repression and against the previous imposition of colonial rule.[12] The massive, sometimes indiscriminate use of American firepower, which led to the widespread destruction of civilian life; the creation of thousands of refugees; and, especially, the hostility of the peasants whose support was vital for military success—these things and more pricked the consciences of many Americans concerned about their nation's historical image as compassionate and humane.

Within the United States, the Tet offensive aroused antiwar feelings that had been growing throughout 1967 as the war continued, seemingly without end. President Johnson's initial support eroded on both the right and the left, with the right demanding an end to the war through escalation and the left seeking an end through de-escalation, if not withdrawal. The articulate opposition to the conflict expressed by various liberal and moderate Republican and Democratic senators, especially the chairman of the Senate Foreign Relations Committee, J. William Fulbright, lent respectability to the opposition also vocalized by many other politicians, professors, students, journalists, editorial writers, and television commentators. Indeed after Tet, Fulbright and his committee became an alternative source of interpretation and policy recommendations for the president.

Thus, although the Vietminh suffered heavy losses during the Tet fighting, the United States suffered a political defeat. The guerrilla strategy of psychologically exhausting the opponent had succeeded; the American strategy of physical attrition had failed. The U.S. military won many battles but lost the war as the American public grew tired of the struggle in Vietnam, which remained a mysterious and confusing place. Indeed, policy makers learned quickly that during such hostilities politics goes on as usual, with most domestic interest groups pursuing their specific sets of interests and preferences; butter is not automatically subordinated to guns. As the costs of a conflict rise in terms of lives, inflation, and taxes, public disaffection also grows. So, too, do antiwar demonstrations and parades. In the 1960s, some of these

12. In 1950 the South Korean government had a similar autocratic reputation, but the attack across the thirty-eighth parallel focused attention on North Korean ambitions and justified the American intervention. No one in the United States raised questions about defending a "corrupt dictatorship."

events spilled over into violent clashes with the police and supporters of the war.

The Vietnam War, then, played out on two battlefields. The first, in Vietnam, was bloody but inconclusive militarily.[13] The second, in the United States, was not bloody, but it was decisive politically.[14] As the war dragged on, the nation's will to continue it declined, unlike in the two world wars when the United States sensed that its security, if not its survival, was at stake. In a limited war, important issues may be at stake, but threats to survival may not be apparent. The guerrillas were well aware of the two battlefields and knew which one was more important. Gen. Vo Nguyen Giap, the North Vietnamese strategist who had overseen his country's victories against France and the United States, spoke of the impatience of democracies at war. He had surmised that a strategy in which the war never seemed to end, in which the minimum goal was simply not to lose, would eventually erode the opponents' will to continue. As the war dragged on and as the casualties and costs mounted, the democracies would throw in the towel. Their "home fronts" were where the "real battle" would be won.

For that reason, North Vietnam launched the Tet offensive just as the 1968 political primaries were about to begin in the United States against a background of widespread opposition to the war.[15] Giap's political calculation proved prophetic. The declining public support for the war—less than 40 percent by the November election—coincided with the war's steadily rising death toll, which surpassed thirty thousand by the end of the year (see Figure 5-1).

Disagreement over the war led two senators from the president's party, Eugene McCarthy and Robert F. Kennedy, to contest Johnson's renomination as the Democratic standard-bearer. Running as "peace candidates," they provided a rallying point for the growing numbers of Americans disenchanted with the war. But then in March 1968, at the end of the speech that laid the basis for the Paris peace talks, the president announced he would not run for a second term. Lyndon Johnson's tragedy was that he had come into office seeking a "Great Society" in America; instead, the war destroyed him. The changing American mood was evident in the 1968 presidential campaign. Vice President Hubert H. Humphrey, nominated by the Democrats in Chicago after bloody

13. For a defense of U.S. military strategy after the Tet offensive, see Lewis Sorley, *A Better War: The Unexamined Victories and Final Tragedy of America's Last Years in Vietnam* (New York: Harcourt, Brace, 1999).

14. For an elaboration of the domestic politics surrounding the American involvement in Vietnam, see Melvin Small, *At the Water's Edge: American Politics and the Vietnam War* (Chicago: Ivan R. Dee, 2005).

15. See Karnow, *Vietnam*, 558–566.

FIGURE 5-1 Vietnam War Trends, 1965–1971

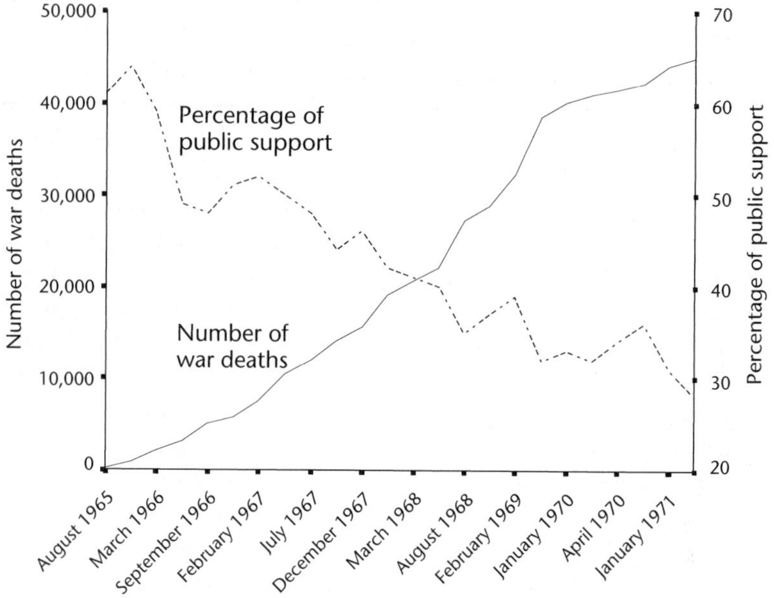

Source: Eric V. Larson, *Casualties and Consensus: The Historical Role of Casualties in Domestic Support for U.S. Military Operations* (Santa Monica: RAND, 1996), 111.

clashes between police and antiwar protestors (many of them McCarthy supporters) and bitter disagreement among the delegates over Vietnam, was mercilessly heckled during most of the campaign. As a member of the administration, he found it difficult to disavow the war; when he took his own "risk for peace," it was very late in the campaign.

In these circumstances of Democratic disunity, former vice president Richard Nixon, a career anticommunist and the Republican nominee, found it inexpedient to charge the Democrats with a "no win" policy; instead, he softened his views on the war. Indeed, in his speeches the menace abroad suddenly ran a poor second to the "moral decay" at home. Generally, both candidates fell over themselves in their eagerness to abandon both anticommunist slogans and the war, offering instead hopes for an "honorable" peace in Vietnam and for "law and order" at home. Halting communist aggression was abandoned as an issue; stopping further costly foreign adventures—"no more Vietnams"—became the new issue. In Vietnam, the only question was when to get out and on what terms.

Chapter Five

Disengagement from Vietnam

Before the United States could reshape its relationship with the Soviet Union and China—the opposing superpowers that represented legitimate security concerns to Americans—it had to unburden itself of the Vietnam War. Vietnam was a drain on U.S. resources and a political albatross for Nixon, who was reelected in 1972 and promised in January 1973 to bring "peace with honor" to the United States. But in their thinking about "acceptable" terms for withdrawal, Nixon and his national security adviser, Henry Kissinger, were heavily influenced by their perceptions of great-power relationships. One course open to Nixon, which would have brought him popular acclaim, was to pull all American forces immediately out of Vietnam on the grounds that the United States had fulfilled long enough its obligations to defend Saigon. But in the president's view, the central issue was maintaining American credibility abroad. "Peace with honor" became his slogan.

The Nixon administration was determined that it would not simply withdraw or accept any settlement that was tantamount to a defeat—namely, a coalition government in Saigon controlled by the communists. Nixon believed that it would not be feasible to establish a relaxation of tensions (détente) with the Soviet Union and China if America's prestige was tattered. Why should the Soviet Union, which was rapidly building up its strategic power, settle for parity and mutually acceptable peaceful coexistence if it sensed that America was weak and could be pushed around? Why should China tone down its revolutionary rhetoric and conduct a more traditional state-to-state diplomacy, and indeed move closer to the United States, if it could not count on American strength and determination to resist what Beijing saw as Soviet attempts at hegemony in Asia? In short, Nixon calculated that the country had to "hang tough" in Vietnam to normalize relations with the Soviet Union and China.

Nixon and Kissinger therefore devised a twofold strategy. First, American ground troops would be withdrawn gradually to reduce the costs of the war and make further hostilities tolerable for the "silent majority" of Americans, who, Nixon felt, were loyal, though fatigued, and would support him in an "honorable" ending of the war. He also hoped, however, that the continued involvement of some U.S. forces, especially in the air, would provide an incentive for Hanoi to negotiate an end to the war. This incentive presumably would be all the stronger if the president's strategy worked at home—that is, if Vietnam were removed as a principal issue in the 1972 presidential contest, thereby facilitating Nixon's reelection. Hanoi, then confronted with the prospect that the war could last at least four more years, would have a reason to settle the war diplomatically.

The second part of the president's strategy was the "Vietnamization" of the war. While American troops were being withdrawn, the South Vietnamese forces would receive the training and modern arms they needed to take over the ground fighting. This tactic would counter the pressure that had grown in Congress, on campuses, and elsewhere for faster U.S. troop withdrawals and for the abandonment of Saigon. But the danger inherent in the president's strategy was that the North Vietnamese would attack after American troops were withdrawn but before the South Vietnamese were ready to meet the enemy in battle.

In March 1970, Cambodia's Prince Norodom Sihanouk, who had long tolerated the communist troops and supply lines in his country, was overthrown by an anti-Vietnamese military regime that wanted communist troops out of Cambodia. When the communists moved toward the Cambodian capital to unseat the new government, Nixon decided to intervene and, without public knowledge, ordered air strikes deep into Cambodia. Once this intervention became known, it reignited domestic dissension. After Ohio National Guardsmen shot four Kent State University students to death on May 4 during an antiwar rally, campuses erupted nationwide and dozens of colleges and universities were completely shut down. Protesters then once again turned out for peaceful mass demonstrations in Washington and in other cities. The reaction to U.S. policy in Cambodia was not lost on the president; he knew it would be foolhardy to repeat such an action.

Unfortunately, South Vietnam's decrepit army remained the linchpin of the president's strategy. In the spring of 1972, after the withdrawal of U.S. troops from the battlefield, North Vietnam launched an unexpected, large-scale attack across the demilitarized zone between North Vietnam and South Vietnam. Again, the South Vietnamese army performed poorly. American air support staved off even worse losses, but the costs to Saigon were severe. With Vietnamization in danger, Nixon "re-Americanized" the war by ordering extensive bombing of the North and a blockade of North Vietnam's ports. Simultaneously, Nixon offered Hanoi the complete withdrawal of American forces from Vietnam within four months if all prisoners of war were returned and an internationally supervised cease-fire was established. But the North Vietnamese, suspicious of Nixon's intentions, rejected the offer.

The situation changed abruptly late in 1972. A month before the U.S. presidential election in November, Hanoi signaled its willingness to accept something less than a total victory. The terms of the agreement included a cease-fire that would halt all American bombing and bring about withdrawal of all U.S. forces within two months; separate future cease-fires were expected in Laos and Cambodia. Both sides would exchange prisoners of war. A series of mixed political commissions, composed of elements of the Vietminh, representatives of the Saigon government, and neutralists, would then be established to work out a new South Vietnamese political order, leading to a new constitution and the election of a new government.

The Nixon administration felt it had achieved an "honorable peace." The North Vietnamese, after having declared for years that the Thieu government would have to go as a precondition for a cease-fire, now accepted Thieu as the leader of the government faction. He remained in control of a sizable army and large police forces that he used in administering most of the countryside and all the urban centers, leaving only minor areas and a small percentage of the population under the control of the Vietminh and the approximately 145,000 North Vietnamese troops. The Thieu faction therefore seemed to have a good chance to compete politically and militarily with the communists after the fighting ended.

But Thieu stalled in agreeing to the tentative October 1972 settlement, because the United States had accepted the presence of North Vietnamese troops in areas of the South during the period of cease-fire. When Thieu stalled, so did the North Vietnamese; both sides appeared eager to strengthen their positions as the final stage of peace talks resumed in Paris. In response, Nixon ordered heavy bombing of the North, including civilian centers in Hanoi and Haiphong. The "Christmas bombings" of late 1972 continued for several days. But the president had to defend the bombardment against outcries from the public and Congress. He argued that it was necessary to demonstrate American resolve against North Vietnam in the crucial final days of conflict.

The end of the Vietnam War arrived in January 1973 when the North Vietnamese returned to the negotiating table and both sides signed a cease-fire agreement at the Hotel Majestic in Paris. Twelve nations, including the United States, the Soviet Union, and China, formally approved the treaty in March. In Washington, the Nixon administration could now focus on improving relations with China and the Soviet Union, and the United States would no longer have to pour its resources into a war that deeply divided the country.

Two years after the Paris conference, however, North Vietnamese troops launched a final offensive against the remnants of the South Vietnamese army. Although Thieu insisted that Nixon had pledged continued U.S. support in the event of such an offensive, Nixon had resigned under the cloud of the Watergate scandal and President Gerald R. Ford, under great pressure from Congress and public opinion, refused to recommit American resources to Vietnam.[16]

16. This scandal involved illegal activities by the Nixon administration during its 1972 reelection campaign and the elaborate means devised by Nixon to cover up these activities.

Thieu resigned on April 21, 1975, and nine days later Saigon fell to the Vietminh as the last American officials in the city were hurriedly shuttled away by helicopter. South Vietnam then surrendered unconditionally. Twenty-one years after the failed Geneva agreement of 1954, Vietnam was again reunited, its long and painful quest for independence having finally borne fruit.

Congress versus the 'Imperial Presidency'

America's defeat in Vietnam revealed the limitations of its power and raised serious questions about its strategy of containing communism in all corners of the world. At home, the abysmal failure of the Vietnam campaign led lawmakers in Washington to curb presidential power in foreign policy, especially the power of the commander in chief to commit American forces to battle. Under the Constitution, the president holds primary responsibility for the routine conduct of foreign policy, but Congress also shares many of these responsibilities, including the power to declare war. In the 1950s, congressional conservatives had wished to limit presidential authority, because the president was, in their minds, not anticommunist enough, and he might, acting on the advice of the "pro-communists" in the State Department, sell the country down the river. Beginning in the late 1960s, liberals also sought to restrain the president's authority, but for a different reason: in their opinion, the president, the "military-industrial complex," and the Central Intelligence Agency were *too* anticommunist and were intent on involving the country in too many costly adventures abroad.

Conservative or liberal, the remedy for the "imperial" presidency's alleged abuse of its authority and its almost solo determination of foreign policy was the same: to reassert congressional control of the formulation of foreign policy and to restore the constitutional balance that presumably had been upset.[17] Presidents would be restrained so that they could no longer appease America's enemies, thereby pleasing conservatives, or act in an interventionist, warlike manner, thereby pleasing liberals. The abuse of power by Nixon, a conservative president whose anticommunist zeal dated back to the inception of the Cold War, reinforced the liberal sentiment to curb presidential powers and compel a more restrained and moderate policy.

Taking the political offensive, Congress passed in 1973 the War Powers Act to constrain the president and assert its own constitutional

17. See Arthur M. Schlesinger Jr., *The Imperial Presidency* (Boston: Houghton Mifflin, 1989).

authority. Under the act, which was approved over President Nixon's veto, the president was obligated to consult Congress before committing troops overseas and to report to Congress immediately afterward about the need to continue the mission. The president also was obligated to terminate the mission within sixty days unless Congress agreed to extend it, a provision designed to preclude the kind of "mission creep" that occurred in Vietnam. Although rejected by later presidents as unconstitutional and rarely invoked by Congress, the War Powers Act symbolized the national mood that blamed the war on excessive presidential power.[18]

Additional evidence of the new mood was the widespread belief that priority should be given to the nation's domestic problems. These problems became apparent in the 1960s when the "affluent society," as it was called in the 1950s, began to reveal its dark side, such as urban slums, suburban sprawl, air and water pollution, and deteriorating schools and hospitals. Critics of the war wanted to spend money to improve the quality of life for all American citizens. Instead of crusading for democracy abroad, they argued, the United States should start crusading to make *America* safe for democracy. Liberal critics of the war in Vietnam quoted Edmund Burke to the effect that "example is the school of mankind." The example should be one of a democratic society protecting the rights of its citizens as its paramount task.

But such freedom could not be fully enjoyed in a nation whose excessive preoccupation with foreign affairs drained its powers and resources, both human and material. An expansionist foreign policy, it was charged, was unlikely to bring with it any lasting greatness, prestige, and security. Rather, as the founders of the United States had been quick to emphasize centuries earlier, the constant expenditure of energy on adventures abroad would ruin the country's domestic base. The Cold War preoccupation was corrupting American society. An institutional imbalance was eroding constitutional processes, particularly when powerful and energetic presidents, in the name of national security, not only committed the nation to war but also sanctioned plots to assassinate foreign leaders such as Fidel Castro, lied to the American people and Congress about what they were doing or why they were doing it (intervention in Vietnam), acted covertly (bombing Laos and Cambodia, overthrowing elected regimes in Guatemala and Chile), and in various ways violated the constitutional rights of American citizens. Moreover, the

18. "If events have suggested that the goal has not been reached," one scholar observed in 1990, "the [War Powers] resolution still remains as a serious legal attempt to solve an enduring dilemma." See Morris S. Ogul, "The War Powers Resolution: Congress versus the President," in *The Constitution and National Security: A Bicentennial View,* ed. Howard E. Shuman and Walter R. Thomas (Washington, D.C.: National Defense University Press, 1990), 314.

large-scale diversion of the country's resources to its external commitments meant a corresponding neglect of domestic needs.

In short, extensive involvement in the world was tainting the American promise and vision, just as early American leaders had warned. This idea had been at the heart of the old isolationism: America could take care of its own needs, serve as an example for humankind, and remain pure in a morally wicked world only if it avoided or minimized political involvement in it. An active U.S. role internationally would endanger, not protect, American democracy.

Perhaps the most revealing evidence of America's reaction to Vietnam was the reassertion of the deep-seated attitude that the exercise of power internationally was immoral and corrupting. To many, the Vietnam War represented a moral turning point in American foreign policy; the United States was guilty of backing the more repressive and illegitimate side. Fulbright, who had long equated American foreign policy with moral mission, now attacked America's global role as evidence of an "arrogance of power." [19] He did not merely assert that the United States had overextended itself and needed to cut back on its commitments. He stated something far more fundamental: that all great powers felt compelled to demonstrate that they were bigger, better, and stronger than other nations. This sense of hubris was the real cause of international conflict and war.

In brief, it was the exercise of power per se that, regardless of a nation's intentions, made it arrogant. Power itself was corrupting; democracy and power politics were simply incompatible. No idea could have been more characteristically American.

In the United States, the "Vietnam syndrome" lingered until the end of the Cold War in 1989. In terms of its influence on foreign policy, the country became far less willing to commit itself to military intervention abroad. Furthermore, the Vietnam syndrome entailed a growing skepticism and distrust toward the government and its military leadership. It did not help that Richard Nixon's administration was shamed during this period by the Watergate scandal. But even without Watergate, for the first time the United States was confronted with the prospect that its power in the world had peaked. For many Americans, disillusionment with Vietnam led them to believe that their country's reputation as the world's "beacon of democracy" had been tainted, and that during the war their leaders had been guilty of misjudgment, deception, and wanton destruction of human life. The United States, it seemed, had reduced itself to the status of an "ordinary" world power.

19. J. William Fulbright, *The Arrogance of Power* (New York: Vintage Books, 1967).

CHAPTER SIX

Détente and World-Order Politics

Henry Kissinger and President Richard M. Nixon share an informal moment in September 1973 after Kissinger was sworn in as the fifty-sixth U.S. secretary of state. Kissinger, the architect of the détente policy that eased Cold War tensions, had previously served as Nixon's national security adviser.

The United States emerged from the Vietnam War with new doubts about its role in foreign affairs. Having assumed the status of a global superpower for only one generation, America found its traditional antipathy toward world politics quickly reasserting itself. The debacle in Vietnam confirmed many Americans' worst fears about how the United States would behave once it joined the ranks of the great powers. The episode also raised serious doubts about using anticommunism as the basis for the country's foreign policy. Before Vietnam, the United States had readily asserted itself overseas to contain communism at every turn. After Vietnam, American leaders became much more cautious about intervening in regional conflicts.

The U.S. containment policy had been weakened by the growing pluralism of the communist bloc. It was one thing to fight a communism that seemed monolithic, but when the communist states became fragmented globally and divided internally, the appropriate Western response became more difficult to define. Did the United States now have to distinguish among the communist states, determining which posed a true threat? What changes in the distribution of power could America safely allow? And where, if anywhere, and against whom did it still have to draw frontiers? These questions became troublesome in the 1970s because with each case policy makers now faced several policy options—and a situation fraught with intense controversy and bitter debate. In addition, anticommunism would no longer be as useful a means of eliciting popular support, not just because of the Vietnam fiasco but also because the United States might well be supporting one communist state against another.

During this period, the administrations of Richard Nixon and Gerald R. Ford, Nixon's successor after the Watergate scandal, pursued détente—a relaxation of tensions—because of changes in the United States and in the global balance of power. The United States had become, after the Vietnam War, a nation weary of its foreign policy burdens. As noted in Chapter 5, this mood was demonstrated by attacks on the "imperial presidency" and restraints imposed on the White House by a more assertive and watchful Congress.[1] Moreover, America's self-appointed role as the "global police" was widely criticized as emphasis shifted to the nation's own shortcomings and limitations as a world superpower. This sentiment was expressed frequently by Jimmy Carter, who after he became president in 1977 sought to reclaim the moral high ground in American foreign policy.

Fueling the drive for reduced Cold War tensions was a significant shift in the U.S.-Soviet balance of military power. Simply put, the Soviet Union had caught up with the United States. Before 1970, the balance between the two superpowers had long been between the U.S. Strategic Air Command (SAC) and the Red Army. From the 1950s to the late 1960s, American bombers and missiles, increasingly bolstered by the navy's nuclear submarines, deterred the Soviet Union by threatening to destroy its cities. Moscow balanced America's strategic power with its Red Army. These powerful ground forces, it was believed, could overrun Western Europe and quickly defeat North Atlantic Treaty Organization (NATO) forces. Thus the balance of power had been asymmetric: the

1. See Barbara Sinclair, "Congressional Party Leaders in the Foreign Policy and Defense Policy Arena," in *Congress Resurgent: Foreign and Defense Policy on Capitol Hill*, ed. Randall Ripley and James M. Lindsay (Ann Arbor: University of Michigan Press, 1993).

United States held strategic superiority and an intercontinental reach; the Soviet Union maintained conventional superiority and a regional reach. But in 1964, the Soviets began a massive weapons buildup, and by 1970 the Soviet Union's nuclear arsenal had achieved parity with that of the United States. Moreover, the Soviet buildup showed no sign of slowing, not even after reaching the level of mutual assured destruction (MAD) with the United States.

Even during the period of U.S. strategic superiority, Soviet leaders were willing to risk limited challenges, such as in Berlin and Cuba, but they remained cautious during confrontations. When there was resistance, the Kremlin retreated. American power, therefore, set limits as to how far the Soviets felt they could push. But because the strategic balance was now shifting, a continuation of the containment policy by means of nuclear deterrence was becoming riskier. Soviet leaders had gained a new sense of confidence in their power. Indeed, the Soviet Union now belonged to the most exclusive club in the world, and the implications of its membership were clarified when the Soviet foreign minister informed the world that, henceforth, no important issue anywhere could be resolved without the Soviet Union.

At the same time that it was strengthening its nuclear arsenal, the Soviet Union was engaging in a massive conventional buildup. As the Soviet Union's ability to neutralize America's nuclear force grew, its capacity to project its conventional power beyond Eurasia also grew. The Soviet naval buildup, which by the late 1970s had produced a navy that exceeded that of the United States in numbers of combat ships, was not needed for defense. Would the Soviet Union, in these new circumstances, be content to expand its influence only on land and in nearby areas? Or would it, as a result of its new might, gain confidence and act more boldly? By contrast, would the United States, once it lost its strategic superiority, be more reluctant to react?

Henry Kissinger, Nixon's influential national security adviser, compared the Soviet Union's emergence as a world power to Germany's appearance on the world scene in the early twentieth century. In both cases, the challengers were land powers. The symbols of their aspirations and determination to expand were the navies they built. Nothing could have carried greater symbolic weight for Britain and the United States, the two greatest naval powers in their respective times. The United States recognized that Germany's emergence and desire to become a world power had resulted in World War I. In this respect, how could the Soviet Union's newly gained power and its determination to pursue a *Weltpolitik* (global policy) be managed peacefully so as not to threaten American security interests? As a badge of its newly achieved equal status, the Soviet Union, like Germany years earlier, sought overseas clients, revolutionary states that would become members of the Soviet bloc. Although these territories were usually of limited strategic and economic value, they were important as symbols of communism's global advance. Therefore the Soviet Union's military buildup raised questions not just about the military balance and its stability but also about the Soviets' ultimate intentions.

Nations that have seen their power decline relative to that of other states normally adjust by reducing their commitments or by seeking new allies or greater contributions from current allies. They generally also seek to reduce threats to their interests through diplomacy. When it lost its strategic superiority, however, the United States did not curtail its obligations; instead, it sought to preserve them through détente. As a political means of managing the superpowers' adversarial relationship, this strategy was aimed at securing American interests at lower levels of tension and cost than those required by the policy of Cold War confrontation and crisis management. The U.S.-Soviet balance would still be bipolar, but it would be more complex and fluid than in the earlier Cold War era.[2]

Managing the Superpower Rivalry

One crucial question the decline of anticommunism posed for the future conduct of American foreign policy was whether, in the absence of anticommunism, the United States would dirty its hands by conducting diplomacy on the basis of traditional "power politics." When during the early Cold War *Realpolitik,* based on power, was synonymous with *Idealpolitik,* based on ideology, the United States had found it easy to be a leader and to organize various coalitions against the ideological foe. The U.S. government could maintain the balance of power as long as it could disguise from its own people what it was doing and pretend it was engaged in a moral crusade. But could a nation that historically had condemned power politics adapt its outlook and style to a world in which justifying foreign policy in terms of ideological crusades was outmoded? Or would America, no longer believing it had an ideological mission, lapse into its traditional withdrawal from great-power politics?

In 1968 the incoming Nixon administration confronted a novel postwar situation: how to conduct foreign policy in the absence of a domestic consensus. In response to this dilemma the administration turned to a foreign policy based on the traditional logic of the state system. This dramatic shift away from a style that stemmed from the nation's domes-

2. The post–Vietnam War balance of power is best understood as *bipolycentric,* meaning that the two superpowers remained dominant but that other countries, particularly those in Western Europe and East Asia, became stronger and more assertive.

tic values and experiences to a balance-of-power rationale was somewhat surprising because Nixon previously had been virulently anticommunist and possessed by an inflexible moralism that rejected having anything to do with communists. But as president, he and Henry Kissinger, a German-born Jewish immigrant and Harvard professor who became secretary of state in Nixon's second term, rejected the traditional American justification for participating in foreign affairs.[3]

Indeed, the administrations of Nixon and Ford might well be called the Kissinger era. Kissinger developed, articulated, and justified the new American grand strategy, which in many ways ran counter to the country's traditional style of foreign policy. He personally carried out much of its public as well as private diplomacy, and he provided an element of continuity amid the transfer of power in August 1974 from Nixon to Ford. Kissinger so dominated these eight years that one observer described him as the only national security adviser and secretary of state ever served by two presidents.

THE KISSINGER PHILOSOPHY

The philosophy underlying American foreign policy during the Kissinger years (1969–1977) began with the assumption that international politics was not a fight between a "good" side and a "bad" side. All states, communist or noncommunist, had the right to exist and possessed legitimate interests. A nation, therefore, did not launch crusades against an adversary on the assumption that differences of interests represented a conflict of virtue and evil. The better part of wisdom, Kissinger believed, was to learn to live with other states, to defend one's interests if encroached upon, but also to attempt to resolve differences and build on shared interests. International politics was not just conflict but cooperation as well. Differences, admittedly, would not be easily or quickly reconciled; views of national interests usually were deeply held and not easily relinquished. Summit meetings were an important part of the negotiating process, but one summit could not solve all problems, and to raise false hopes that it would was to produce the cynicism and disillusionment that would endanger diplomacy itself. Good personal relations among leaders might smooth this process, but they were not a substitute for hard bargaining, and accords basically reflected the ratio of power between the nations the leaders represented.[4]

3. For a thorough review of Kissinger's life and career, see Walter Isaacson, *Kissinger: A Biography* (New York: Simon and Schuster, 1992). For a more critical appraisal, see Seymour H. Hersh, *The Price of Power: Kissinger in the Nixon White House* (New York: Summit Books, 1983).

4. For an instructive comparison of Kissinger's approach to that of other realists, see

How then should the United States deal with a communist dictatorship whose values and practices it abhorred? The most the United States could expect was to nudge the Soviet Union's international behavior in a responsible direction. American power was too limited to transform another superpower's domestic behavior; American demands would be resisted, which, in turn, would jeopardize accords on international issues that otherwise might have been resolvable. The United States, then, simply had to abandon its habit of crusading to democratize adversaries. Coexistence with a communist regime such as that of the Soviet Union was necessary if peace and security were to be preserved. The key, of course, was the balance of power, and the United States had to try to accommodate the legitimate needs of the principal challenger to that balance. Power neutralizes opposing power, and by satisfying the interests of other great powers the United States would be more likely to produce acceptance of the present international system than by perpetuating their hostility to a system in which they had little vested interest. No state could be completely satisfied, but a state could be relatively satisfied.

Kissinger's view, then, concentrated on the powerful actors in the state system. Although he brought the rhetoric and style of American foreign policy more in line with the operational norms of the international system, a fundamental continuity in policy remained in place. The U.S.-Soviet balance remained the preoccupation; it was still the Soviet Union, as a great power, whose influence needed to be contained and its behavior moderated. This unity of rhetoric and action—the explanation of U.S. policy in terms of power, balances, spheres of influence, national interests, and the limits of American power, as well as the specific rejection of ideological justifications and crusades—represented the socialization of American foreign policy by the state system.

EXPLOITING THE SINO-SOVIET SPLIT

When the Nixon administration entered office in January 1969, the United States had no official relationship with the communist government in China. Leaders in Beijing opposed establishing relations with the United States as long as Washington officially recognized the Nationalist regime in Taiwan. But Nixon recognized the changing strategic circumstances and considered it vital to bring mainland China, still led by

Michael Joseph Smith, *Realist Thought from Weber to Kissinger* (Baton Rouge: Louisiana State University Press, 1986). For an application of Kissinger's worldview to his actions as a policy maker, see Stephen G. Walker, "The Interface between Beliefs and Behavior: Henry Kissinger's Operational Code and the Vietnam War," *Journal of Conflict Resolution* (March 1977): 129–168.

Mao Zedong, into the diplomatic constellation. By calling the regime by its chosen name, the People's Republic of China (PRC), ending regular patrols of the Taiwan Strait by the Seventh Fleet, and lifting trade and visitation restrictions against the PRC, Nixon opened the way for a personal visit to China in February 1972. For the American public and Congress, long hostile to dealing with Beijing, this visit symbolized a dramatic shift in American policy. By playing the "China card," Nixon and Kissinger began clearing away mutual hostilities and exploring areas of mutual cooperation.

In executing this strategy, Nixon was able to exploit the rivalry between the Soviet Union and China; relations between the two former allies had become deeply embittered. As the capital of the first communist-controlled state, Moscow had monopolized the international communist movement and dictated its policies since the early 1920s. Moreover, after World War II it had established control over the states of Eastern Europe. Of these states, only Yugoslavia was controlled by its indigenous Communist Party and not by Moscow. When Yugoslavia resisted Joseph Stalin's efforts to impose absolute control, it was ejected from Stalin's empire. The birth of communist China—another state controlled by a homegrown, independent party—thus represented a serious problem for the Soviets. The Chinese leadership, while communist, was like that of Yugoslavia—highly nationalistic and therefore not likely to subordinate itself to the Kremlin. The potential for a schism, then, was built into the Sino-Soviet relationship.[5] A falling-out was therefore inevitable, despite the treaty of friendship signed by the two countries in 1950.

By the late 1960s, both countries had allowed their treaty to lapse, leaving the Sino-Soviet split clearly visible to Western leaders. In public statements, the Soviets compared Mao to Adolf Hitler and the Chinese to the Mongol hordes who overran Russia a millennium earlier. The Chinese, meanwhile, described the "Soviet revisionist clique" as a "dictatorship of the German fascist type." The incoming Nixon administration thus had a grand opportunity to exploit these tensions and end a twenty-year period of hostile relations with China that had been strategically harmful to the United States. Most important, the Sino-Soviet split gave the United States leverage to play the two communist giants against each other and gain the upper hand in the triangular balance of power.

In the Shanghai communiqué released at the end of Nixon's historic visit to China in 1972, the United States and China declared their oppo-

5. Historical distrust between the Russian and Chinese peoples, based largely on territorial claims, preceded the Cold War and further aggravated relations between the communist states.

sition to the hegemony of *any* power in Asia—but they clearly were referring to the Soviet Union. Thus Sino-American relations were established on a firm foundation of mutual self-interest. As for the United States, the eagerness to attract China into an anti-Soviet coalition was reflected in America's declaration that it would gradually remove all its forces and installations from Taiwan and would not interfere in a "peaceful settlement" between the communists and the Nationalists. The agreement ended once and for all the irrationality of a situation in which the United States for almost a quarter-century had ignored the existence of the world's most populous country, a nation with great potential power and long-standing animosity toward Moscow. Sino-Soviet quarrels reflected entrenched conflicts of interest more profound than the apparent bond of communist ideology.

On January 1, 1979, the People's Republic of China and the United States exchanged diplomatic recognition and ambassadors. This exchange was followed by an official visit to Washington by China's future leader, Deputy Premier Deng Xiaoping, who had succeeded Mao as chairman of the Communist Party two years after Mao's death in September 1976.

With mutual recognition came new opportunities for trade. China looked to the West to help it modernize everything from its hotel and steel industries to exploitation of its enormous oil reserves. By the 1990s, China had emerged as one of the major trading partners of the United States; its importance to Washington was revealed annually when the U.S. government extended China most-favored-nation status despite the continuation of communist rule and political repression. For the United States, access to China's vast markets proved irresistible, a fact not lost on Chinese leaders who continued to reject American calls for political reforms and moderation.

Arms Control and the Linkage Strategy

Even though the opening of diplomatic relations with China drove the wedge deeper between Beijing and Moscow, the détente strategy adopted by Nixon and Kissinger called for closer contact with the Soviet Union on a variety of issues. In the world of *Realpolitik* that Kissinger imported to American foreign policy, even proclaimed adversaries could cooperate when their interests converged. In this respect, both sides stood to benefit from the lowering of tensions and the creation of a stable working relationship. Indeed, the interstate system as a whole would gain much-needed relief from the superpower rivalry, which inflamed domestic politics in many nations and provoked regional conflicts that sometimes escalated into head-on collisions.

One area of potential U.S.-Soviet cooperation was strategic arms control, which over the years had assumed greater importance. The arms race was an expression of the deep political differences between the United States and the Soviet Union. The danger was that the arms race, fueled by continuing conflict, would at some point spill over into a nuclear war. To avoid such a cataclysmic outcome, each side built up its nuclear forces and created new ways to deliver the deadly missiles from all distances. After establishing a strong lead in nuclear systems, the United States maintained a status quo nuclear deterrent during Nixon's first term (see Figure 6-1). The Soviet Union, meanwhile, caught up to the United States in submarine-launched ballistic missiles (SLBMs) and exceeded U.S. totals of ground-launched intercontinental ballistic missiles (ICBMs). Because nuclear weapons were unlikely to be abolished, both sides recognized that the next best tactic was to manage the nuclear balance through arms control agreements.[6]

The Strategic Arms Limitation Talks (SALT), one of Nixon's major achievements, stood at the center of détente. The talks, which involved high-level U.S. and Soviet officials, had four objectives. The first was to make the arms race more predictable by establishing, documenting, and reporting the number of strategic weapons possessed by each side. The second was to ensure parity. The assumption was that if the two sides had about the same number of nuclear warheads (the explosives attached to ballistic missiles and bombs), neither side could launch a crippling strike against the other. In the absence of nuclear superiority, the United States and the Soviet Union would each retain a sufficient second-strike capability to ensure mutual assured destruction. The third purpose of SALT was to reduce threats to each side's deterrent forces. The development of a new defensive weapon was a concern. The Soviets had deployed antiballistic missiles (ABMs) around Moscow and were thought to be working on a second-generation ABM for possible nationwide deployment. If ABMs could shoot down American ICBMs and reduce the destruction inflicted on the Soviet Union to an "acceptable" level of casualties, the ABMs would undermine U.S. deterrence, which depended on its capacity to impose "assured destruction."[7] Finally, SALT was crucial for détente. The failure to arrive at an agreement or at least to continue the SALT dialogue was bound to have a debilitating effect on the overall U.S.-Soviet political relationship. Yet only a relaxation of tensions would enable the two nuclear giants to

6. This effort was frequently at odds with the U.S. government's traditional approach to foreign affairs, as outlined elsewhere in this volume. See Colin S. Gray, *Nuclear Strategy and National Style* (Lanham, Md.: Hamilton Press, 1986).

7. See Robert E. Osgood, *The Nuclear Dilemma in American Strategic Thought* (Boulder, Colo.: Westview Press, 1988), 48–55.

FIGURE 6-1 U.S.-Soviet Nuclear Balance, 1967–1973

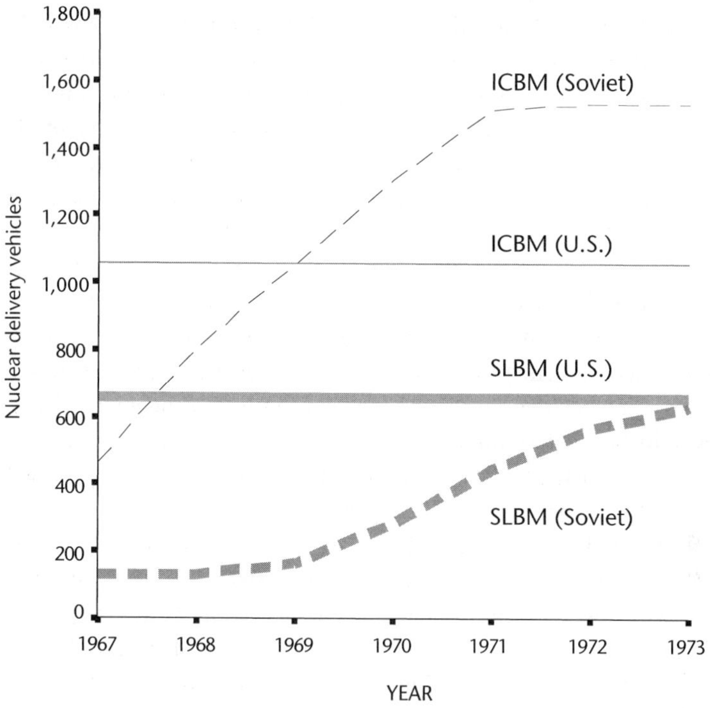

Note: ICBM = intercontinental ballistic missile; SLBM = submarine-launched ballistic missile.
Source: International Institute for Strategic Studies (IISS), *The Military Balance, 1973–1974,* No. 2 (London: IISS, 1973), 71, 1141.

arrive at an arms agreement that would leave them feeling more secure. SALT, in short, became a symbol of détente.

Nixon and Soviet leader Leonid Brezhnev signed the first set of agreements, known as SALT I, in May 1972. SALT I, which had taken two and a half years to negotiate, incorporated two agreements. The first limited each country's ABMs to two hundred launchers, later to be reduced to one hundred each. For all practical purposes, by restricting ABMs the two powers acknowledged the dangers of strategic defense and shifted their focus to offensive weapons. Thus the second agreement froze offensive missile batteries at the number each side possessed at the time. Each side retained the right to improve its weapons within the overall quantitative agreement, thus preserving parity. Although no on-site inspection to check for violations was established, both sides pledged not to interfere with each other's reconnaissance or spy satellites, which would be the principal means of checking compliance with both accords.

The follow-up agreement, SALT II, was regarded as critical to a long-term effort to stabilize mutual deterrence. President Ford, after Nixon's resignation, arrived at the guidelines for SALT II at a 1974 meeting with Brezhnev in Vladivostok. It was a complex series of agreements, carefully balancing the varying interests and different force structures of the two superpowers. But the debate over SALT II became moot after the Soviet Union sent troops into Afghanistan in late 1979 to shore up a pro-Soviet military regime. Yet despite the heated rhetoric from both Washington and Moscow, the terms of SALT II were observed into the late 1980s, when efforts to reduce nuclear stockpiles accelerated again under President Ronald Reagan (see Chapter 7).

While arms control provided for mutual gains in the strategic competition, détente opened the doors to other agreements and cooperative measures beneficial to both powers. The key to such arrangements, however, would be *linkage,* directed primarily toward Moscow. If the two countries could achieve understandings on matters such as arms control and trade, the Soviet Union would gain a vested interest in good relations with the United States. Thus the Soviet Union would face, as before, a strong American military, but this "stick" would be supplemented with enough "carrots" to make cooperation more rewarding. Military sanctions against the Soviet Union at a time of strategic parity were becoming riskier for the United States. The linkage strategy, which offered economic rewards for restraint, could achieve the same outcomes with far fewer risks. Progress on one front would be tied to progress on another.

By the time Nixon entered office in 1969, the Soviet economy, always particularly vulnerable, was in serious trouble. After expanding rapidly in the 1950s and early 1960s, the economy saw its 5 percent growth rate fall to 2 percent by the early 1970s. The economic decline was particularly notable in those sectors associated with the "second" industrial revolution: computers, microelectronics, and telecommunications. In short, the Soviet Union was falling further behind the West in those industries that were most important for economic growth. Moreover, the Soviet workplace was plagued by high absenteeism, drunkenness, corruption, and shoddy production. The implications of this decline, which was matched by a stagnant agricultural sector, damaged the Soviet Union's appeal as a socialist state, hampered its ability to compete with the United States, and threatened its superpower status.

The result of this dismal situation was that the Soviet Union was the only industrial society in which the peacetime life expectancy of males was declining and infant mortality was rising. Soviet leader Brezhnev, who came to power in 1964, was well aware that the failure of his predecessor, Nikita Khrushchev, to achieve a higher standard of living had led directly to his downfall. Khrushchev, reeling from his setback in the Cuban missile crisis, had raised popular expectations about economic growth and then failed to meet them. The same thing could happen to Brezhnev, who took over as the Soviet standard of living was slipping both in absolute terms and in comparison to those enjoyed by Western capitalist states.

For Moscow, trade with the United States, with its enormous mass production capabilities, technological advances, and agricultural abundance, was desirable, and it also saw the benefits in broader collaboration. Because the Soviet Union had little to sell the United States, Soviet leaders offered to let Americans develop the huge Soviet deposits of raw materials, especially in Siberia. American capital to help finance this extraction would presumably be repaid in oil, natural gas, and other mineral resources. The Soviets also looked to the United States for surplus agriculture in years of shortages, which were occurring more and more frequently.

The Nixon administration believed these economic problems would give the United States leverage. Trade between the Cold War rivals could be quite profitable for American industry and agriculture, but the main reason for establishing such ties was political. American productivity, it was hoped, would provide powerful material reinforcement for a Soviet foreign policy of restraint and accommodation. According to Kissinger, economic relations could not be separated from the political context. The United States should not be asked to reward hostile conduct with economic benefits. In return for the expansion of trade, it was not unreasonable to require the Soviets to cooperate on important foreign policy issues. In effect, the linkage strategy would give Moscow incentives to practice *self-containment.*

Disillusionment with Détente

Although détente marked a breakthrough in U.S.-Soviet relations, implementing the new strategy proved difficult for Nixon and Ford. Nixon's White House was consumed by its futile search for an "honorable peace" in Vietnam, and later by the Watergate scandal that forced Nixon's resignation on August 9, 1974. Ford, a former congressional leader without any foreign policy experience, devoted his start-up presidency to restoring political stability at home. Furthermore, as a strategy that combined both conflict *and* cooperation, détente was confusing to many Americans. It was easier to explain a relationship that was overtly hostile or friendly, not something in between. The Cold War aroused people; détente relaxed them, as if it were the same thing as *entente,* meaning friendship. But détente meant a reduction of tensions, not an absence of tensions or superpower rivalry. Expectations that it represented a harbinger of harmony were bound to produce frustration.

The concept of détente was bound to pose several problems for the United States, especially in its relationships with its allies. Alliances normally are composed of countries drawn together by common perceptions of an overriding external threat. But what cements the bonds of such relationships when the principal members of the coalition no longer see that threat as great? In Europe, among America's most important allies, that appeared to be the situation in the 1970s and 1980s. Washington now negotiated directly with the Kremlin on key issues as relations with Moscow became, in some respects, more important than those with NATO members. Not surprisingly, the European states also went their own way; West Germany, for example, pursued a policy of *Ostpolitik,* or accommodation, toward its eastern neighbors.

Economic issues proved especially divisive among members of the Western allies. In the immediate postwar era, economic policies such as the Marshall Plan had been consistent with and supported America's containment strategy. But now, economic relations between the United States and the nations of Western Europe, which were rapidly forming a cohesive economic bloc, were complicating the other strands of NATO policy. As the 1970s began, Europe was no longer the weak, divided, and demoralized continent it had been after 1945. Indeed, the emerging Common Market had become an increasingly powerful economic competitor. During the Cold War, the United States had been a leading proponent of European integration; a cohesive Western Europe could make a significant contribution to the U.S.-led struggle against the Soviet Union, and the competitiveness of an economically unified Europe was thought to be worth the risk. In a period of détente and growing tensions between the United States and Europe, however, the united front that had long confronted the Soviet bloc was threatening to fragment.[8]

While the superpowers negotiated the size of their nuclear arsenals in the "spirit of détente," much of the outside world remained torn by internal unrest and regional conflict. Within the developing world, the ideological rivalry of the Cold War had infected many unstable governments, dividing their populations into hostile ideological camps, producing ever greater forms of repression, and undermining their prospects for political stability and economic growth. Among other flashpoints in the developing world, a military coup in Chile and civil war in Angola demonstrated the limitations of détente and fueled disillusionment with the strategy. After the declaration of the Monroe Doc-

8. For a review of Western Europe's progress toward "functional integration" during this period, see Martin Holland, *European Integration: From Community to Union* (London: Pinter, 1994), 22–59.

trine in 1823, the United States regarded South America as within its sphere of influence. Although Washington gradually became more accommodating to the nationalism of its Latin neighbors, it feared the emergence of radical left-wing revolutions and regimes that might bring Soviet influence close to America's shores. When in 1970 Chilean citizens elected the Marxist Salvador Allende to the presidency, the Nixon administration sought first to prevent Allende from becoming president and then, when that failed, to make life difficult for him. Of particular concern to Nixon was Allende's effort to nationalize many of Chile's industries and to displace U.S.-owned copper mines, banks, and utilities, including the International Telegraph and Telephone Company (ITT), whose senior officers pressured the Nixon administration to restore their holdings. Allende's refusal to bend to American pressure led Nixon to remove him from power in 1973 through a military coup d'état that was engineered by the Central Intelligence Agency (CIA) and carried out by disgruntled Chilean military forces.

Chile was then controlled by a four-man junta led by Gen. Augusto Pinochet, who assumed the office of president through force and intimidation. In the years to come, Pinochet emerged as a ruthless leader, but one loyal to the United States and determined to lead a socialist revolution in Chile. In return for Washington's patronage, Pinochet served as a loyal U.S. client in South America through the end of the Cold War.[9] But his reign produced constant criticism that Washington was "coddling" a foreign dictator in the name of containment, a charge that was largely valid. As in other developing countries during the Cold War, the United States allied itself with a military dictatorship in Chile rather than run the risk that the nation would become a beachhead of Marxist revolution. Moral absolutism in these cases gave way to moral relativism. Authoritarian government fell far short of Jeffersonian democracy, but from the American perspective anything was better than a totalitarian Marxist regime.[10]

A second foreign upheaval occurred in 1975 in Angola, a country rich in oil and mineral resources and one that geographically divided the white-ruled states of Africa—Rhodesia and South Africa—from black Africa. As a Portuguese colony, Angola had helped to protect the two racist states from black liberation movements. But as Portuguese colonialism came to an end, Angola's interim government, which was composed of three factions based on tribal allegiances, was consumed by a

9. Pinochet remained in power until 1990, when Chilean citizens voted to restore civilian rule.

10. For an elaboration of this view by a former U.S. ambassador to the United Nations, see Jeane J. Kirkpatrick, "Dictatorships and Double Standards," *Commentary* (November 1979): 34–45.

power struggle. This rivalry continued after Angola became independent, and the leftist Popular Movement for the Liberation of Angola attracted Soviet support and thousands of Cuban troops. The administration—including Secretary of State Kissinger—viewed the Cubans as Soviet proxies and their intervention in Angola as a rejection of détente.

The result was the introduction of the great-power rivalry into southern Africa. Rejecting U.S. military intervention (a direct result of the "Vietnam syndrome"), Washington provided covert arms to the faction opposing the Soviet-supported ones. But not only did this effort not match that of the Soviet Union, it also was cut off by the Senate, fearful of another Vietnam in an area that did not constitute a vital American interest. Rejecting the contention that Angola might become another Vietnam, Ford and Kissinger conceded that Angola was not a significant American interest. But they still believed that Soviet intervention could not be ignored. Angola might be far away, but, in their view, it was a test case of the new superpower relationship. Kissinger charged that Angola was far beyond any Soviet sphere of influence and that the Soviet action constituted a military intervention to impose a regime of Soviet choice. The Soviet Union defended its behavior by asserting that support of national liberation movements, including armed intervention, was not incompatible with détente—a view rejected by the United States. In this superpower stalemate, Angola endured a prolonged civil war that left nearly half a million dead and continued long after the cessation of the Cold War.

Carter's Quest for World Order

It was not surprising that views of détente swung from euphoria, as the 1970s began, to growing disillusionment by 1976, Ford's last year in power. Indeed, the United States had always wavered between such opposite and mutually exclusive categories: isolation or intervention, peace or war, diplomacy or force, idealism or realism, harmony or strife, optimism about America's destiny or cynicism about an evil world that resists reform. The promotion of détente reinforced expectations that the superpowers had put their conflicts behind them. But raising people's hopes too high was bound to lead to disappointment and cynicism when events did not live up to expectations.

In such times of national self-doubt Americans often turn to an outsider who appears untarnished by past government actions and who promises a fresh approach to domestic and foreign policy. In the 1976 U.S. presidential campaign, Democrat Jimmy Carter, a peanut farmer and former governor of Georgia, filled this role.[11] Carter seemed to epit-

11. For a detailed account of Carter's rise to power, see Betty Glad, *Jimmy Carter: In Search of the Great White House* (New York: Norton, 1980).

omize the moral virtues Americans found lacking in previous presidents. Drawing on his experience as a Sunday school teacher in his Baptist church, Carter eloquently described the country's need for moral rejuvenation and spiritual rebirth after the traumas of Vietnam and Watergate. His words struck a chord with the American people, who elected him president over Ford in the November election.

A NEW EMPHASIS ON HUMAN RIGHTS

President Carter's worldview differed profoundly from those of Nixon and Kissinger. Rather than emphasizing the Cold War and the East-West conflict, Carter paid more attention to global "interdependence" and the need for closer cooperation between the wealthier, more industrialized countries of the North and the poorer countries of the South. Carter's perspective incorporated several widely perceived trends in world politics, such as greater concern about the environment and global population growth and recognition of the growing importance of economic versus military power. In keeping with these views, he denounced U.S. military interventions abroad that caused death and destruction. Like America's first generation of leaders, he believed such adventures threatened democracy at home and invited tyranny.

Drawing on the idealism of President Woodrow Wilson, Carter identified human rights as the appropriate basis of American foreign policy. In equating the nation's moral principles with universal standards, Carter personified the American style of foreign policy. The new president also offered a way out of what he called the "malaise" within the United States. The best course for the country, he argued, was to reject power politics, seek renewal and purification by concentrating on domestic affairs, and build a fully free and socially just society whose example would radiate throughout the world. In the words of a former chair of the Senate Foreign Relations Committee, J. William Fulbright, America should "serve as an example of democracy to the world" and play its role in the world "not in its capacity as a *power,* but in its capacity as a *society.*"[12] Virtue, not power, would be the hallmark of foreign policy; American influence in the world would derive from the nation's moral standing as a good and just society. Other nations would be attracted to the United States by its principles, not its strength.

History has demonstrated that democratic states cannot conduct foreign policy effectively in the absence of domestic consensus. For most of its history, America had enjoyed such a consensus, which centered

12. J. William Fulbright, *The Arrogance of Power* (New York: Vintage Books, 1967), 256 (emphasis in original).

around the need for detachment from European great-power politics and the primacy of domestic economic and political development. In the absence of an external threat, the United States had wanted only to be left to its own devices. When provoked, however, its citizens had been easily mobilized and united for its foreign policy crusades. In the wake of Vietnam and in the midst of détente, however, no such provocation appeared on the horizon, and the American penchant for withdrawal resurfaced.

The task of re-creating consensus on foreign policy was embraced by Carter, who thought he could find it in America's self-proclaimed historical role as the defender of democracy and individual liberty. Human rights became the platform on which he expected to mobilize popular support. Carter pledged to condition American relations with other countries, rich and poor alike, on their respect for human rights. But he largely directed his quest for "world-order politics" toward the developing world, where the majority of the world's population lived and where standards of living were the worst.[13] Carter felt that the superpowers, by extending their Cold War to all corners of the world, had encouraged military dictators of all ideological stripes, undermined democratic reforms, and retarded economic development. In short, the Cold War had only made the miserable conditions in the developing countries worse.

The United States thus once more stood for something, having reclaimed its democratic heritage and a moral basis for its foreign policy. American flirtations with the Machiavellian world of great-power diplomacy during the "high" Cold War had only confirmed the founders' dire warnings. Indeed, the United States had learned its lesson; it would no longer search for "monsters to destroy." A new foreign policy more consistent with its traditional style would be adopted. Jimmy Carter, the born-again Christian, became the redeemer of American ideals and moral principles.

Recognizing Global Interdependence

By 1976 the nations of the world had become more interdependent, meaning that their fates were more closely connected than ever before. All sides in the Cold War acknowledged that a nuclear war of any kind would affect all corners of the world and possibly render much of the planet uninhabitable. The expansion of the global economy into a single marketplace rewarded governmental cooperation and coordination.

13. See Stanley Hoffmann, *Primacy or World Order: American Foreign Policy since the Cold War* (New York: McGraw-Hill, 1978).

Finally, the effects of pollution and the population explosion collectively made interdependence not just an aspiration but also a reality in world politics. No nation was "an island, entire of itself" any longer.

The attraction of interdependence was its prospect of a more peaceful and harmonious world consistent with American values and an escape from the troublesome world of power politics. It was not surprising that this vision of transnational interdependence strongly influenced Carter, who came to power when the United States was recovering from the Vietnam War. Many of Carter's foreign policy advisers had participated earlier, during the Kennedy-Johnson years, in the decision making about the war. They openly regretted the abuse of American power and the "coddling" of dictators throughout the world. Thus they dismissed Kissinger's balance-of-power approach as obsolete; the world had moved beyond the days when this "European" approach seemed relevant and justified U.S. support for right-wing dictatorships in the name of freedom. As for détente with the Soviet Union, Carter hoped "managing" interdependence rather than superpower rivalry would have the same effect on international stability while upholding the nation's moral principles.

A central concern to Carter was relations between North and South—that is, the wealthy industrialized states of North America, Western Europe, and East Asia, and the largely impoverished developing states of Latin America, Africa, and southern Europe. Prospects for the developing countries grew worse as the Cold War dragged on. With few exceptions, they were still impoverished. The optimism had faded that foreign aid would propel their modernization or, later, that "trade, not aid" would permit them largely to earn their own way and to finance their own development. Food shortages and famines in Africa and southern Asia were stark reminders of what could happen. Thus the expectation of the former colonial states that they would realize their dreams of better and more rewarding lives for their peoples was unfulfilled. Illiteracy, starvation, and disease continued to coexist with dreams of national dignity and material welfare. For a variety of complex reasons, the billions of dollars in annual support from the North had little or no impact in the Southern Hemisphere. Despite the creation of an elaborate development aid "regime," gaps between the world's richest and poorest populations only widened.[14] Carter sought to reverse this trend and to close the North-South gap.

Global economic interdependence also extended to energy supplies. The latest war between Israel and its Arab neighbors in 1973 had led to

14. See Robert E. Wood, *From Marshall Plan to Debt Crisis: Foreign Aid and Development Choices in the World Economy* (Berkeley: University of California Press, 1986).

spiraling gasoline prices. These shocks to the industrialized economies were engineered by the Organization of the Petroleum Exporting Countries (OPEC), which gained control of the supply, and thus the price, of petroleum on world markets. The major oil companies, most of which were based in the United States, exerted substantial control over the countries in which they operated, located largely in the Middle East.[15] The cartel's bid to gain control over the world's oil reserves left no country untouched.[16] In the United States, high oil prices prompted "stagflation" (simultaneous inflation and recession) and a surge in unemployment. The energy crisis of the 1970s did not merely cause occasional inconveniences such as long lines to buy gas or higher prices at the gas pump; it profoundly upset entire economies and changed ways of life, as evidenced by smaller cars and lower speed limits in the United States. Mao Zedong, who once said "power grows out of the barrel of a gun," would have been equally correct had he referred to a barrel of oil.

Is it any wonder, then, that the developing countries were delighted and held high hopes in the wake of the oil shocks of the 1970s? Indeed, OPEC's actions gave rise to three expectations: first, that OPEC would use its leverage to raise the prices of natural resources from the other developing countries; second, that the other commodity producers would follow OPEC's example by organizing their own cartels; and, third, that the OPEC "petrodollars" would flow to the developing world in the form of foreign aid. But to the chagrin of these countries, none of these expectations materialized. The cartel fragmented as its members reverted within a decade to their previous patterns of undercutting the cartel oil prices.[17] Producers of other commodities, driven by their own competition for Northern markets, did not adopt OPEC's example. And finally, OPEC profits were not shared with developing countries in the form of aid. Still, the capacity of the world's oil producers to wreak havoc across the industrialized world had been demonstrated, and a second oil "shock" during the Carter years led to further economic distress in the United States.

Carter's Middle East Breakthrough

For Jimmy Carter, stemming the conflict between Israel and its neighbors in the Middle East was a primary foreign policy goal. Four years

15. See Daniel Yergin, *The Prize: The Epic Quest for Oil, Money, and Power* (New York: Simon and Schuster, 1991).

16. The German word *Schadenfreude* says it best: pleasure received from seeing someone suffer who deserves it.

17. For an elaboration, see Fadhi J. Chalabi, "OPEC: An Obituary," *Foreign Affairs* (winter 1997–1998): 126–140.

before he took office, regional tensions had erupted in warfare that threatened to draw in both superpowers. In 1973 Egypt and Syria attacked Israel on the highest of all Jewish holy days—Yom Kippur, or the Day of Atonement. Egypt entered the conflict because its leader, Anwar Sadat, was frustrated by Israel's refusal to relinquish the Egyptian territory it captured in the Six-Day War in 1967. The Egyptians and their Syrian allies, supported by massive military supplies from the Soviet Union, achieved initial success in restoring the previous status quo. The United States responded with a similar airlift of military supplies to Israel, which drove the Syrians back from the Golan Heights and then attempted to destroy the Egyptian army on the eastern side of the Suez Canal. After the Soviet Union threatened to deploy troops to the region,

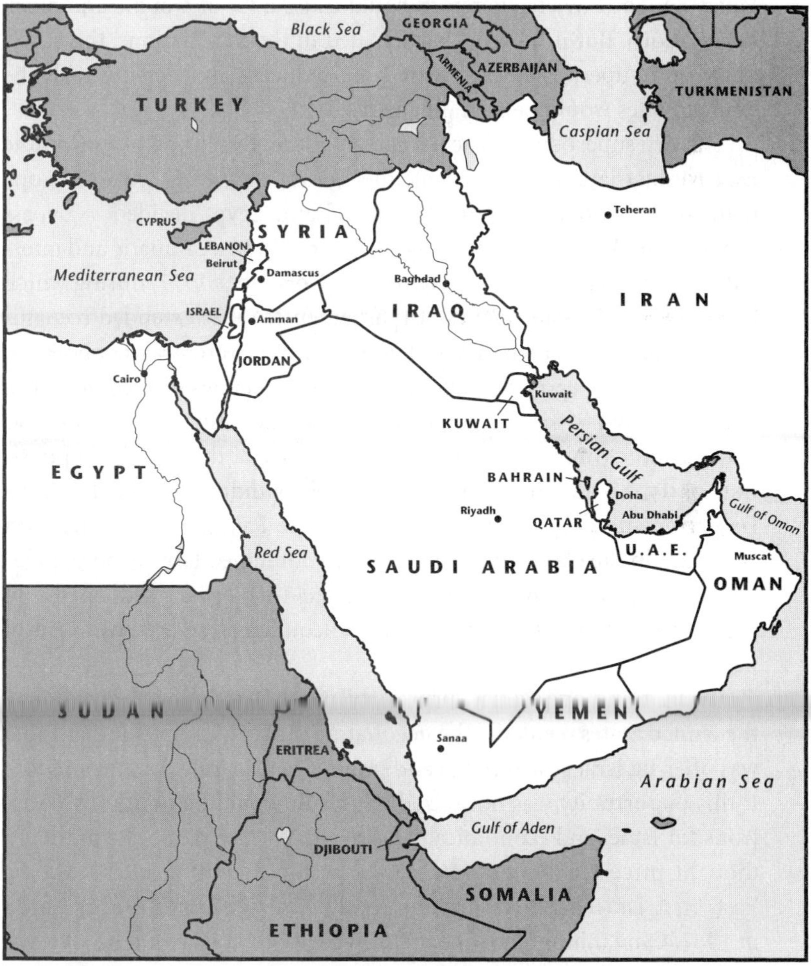

THE MIDDLE EAST

American military forces were placed on a worldwide nuclear alert. Moscow backed off, however, and the United States, also eager to avoid an escalation, pressured Israel to end its military advance. These moves assured a welcome but fragile cease-fire.

In 1977 the incoming Carter administration viewed the volatile Arab-Israeli dispute with alarm. Resentment from the Yom Kippur War remained sharp, with both sides acquiring new and more advanced weapons systems in its aftermath. Carter therefore proposed that all parties resume the negotiations they had begun in Geneva after the 1973 war. Carter decided to approach the Soviets and enlist their cooperation in achieving a peace settlement. Moscow had influence with the more militant Syrians and within the Palestine Liberation Organization (PLO), which had formed to press the cause of renewed statehood for Palestine. The Soviets, therefore, could cause a lot of trouble and block negotiations. But if Moscow participated in the negotiations, the possibility of a superpower clash would be reduced, and détente with the United States would be strengthened.

The two superpowers reached agreement on resolution of the Middle East conflict late in 1977, but neither Jerusalem nor Cairo was happy with the U.S.-Soviet accord. Thus Israel and Egypt decided to bypass Moscow and Washington and negotiate directly. In a dramatic and internationally televised visit to Jerusalem in November 1977, during which he addressed the Israeli Knesset (parliament), Sadat extended recognition to the Arabs' archenemy. The mood afterward was euphoric. A comprehensive peace with all of Israel's Arab enemies seemed near. The mood did not last long, however. Israel's new coalition government was led by Prime Minister Menachem Begin, leader of the principal opposition party, Likud. He proposed an Israeli withdrawal from the Sinai Desert but refused to offer statehood to the Palestinians on the West Bank and in the Gaza Strip, each of which contained large Arab populations. The Israeli government announced that Jewish settlements in these areas would remain, and it even encouraged the establishment of new ones.

When, to no one's great surprise, bilateral negotiations broke down, the United States reentered the negotiating process. Carter felt that Sadat was offering Israel the security and peace it had so long sought, and that if this opportunity was not seized the result would be politically disastrous for Israel and economically disastrous for the West. The president thought three conditions were necessary for a solution in the Middle East. First, Israel had to return most of the Arab territory it had captured in 1967. Only minor adjustments for security reasons could be allowed. Second, the Palestinians had to participate in the peace-making process. Carter himself declared that the Palestinians had a right to a "homeland," a deliberately vague term but one that nevertheless carried great symbolic weight. Third, in return for such Israeli concessions, the Arab states had to commit themselves not only to ending their hostilities with Israel but also to signing a peace treaty.

Begin was at odds with the first two conditions. He was opposed to a Palestinian state, which he—and indeed most Israelis—felt would endanger the existence of Israel. Moreover, he promoted his own plan for Israeli settlements in the occupied lands. Since 1967, however, the United States had consistently opposed these settlements as illegal. The Carter administration repeated this while it watched in disbelief as the Israeli government, in the middle of the peace process, actively encouraged new settlements on the land the Arabs claimed to be theirs. In September 1978, Carter gambled and invited Begin and Sadat to meet with him at Camp David, the presidential retreat in Maryland. The invitation was a gamble because had this summit meeting produced no results, the president's prestige, already low, would have been even more seriously impaired, American mediating attempts would have run their course, and U.S.-Israeli relations would have been set back even further. But the president persisted and after twelve days of patient negotiations emerged with a series of agreements, including a commitment by the two leaders to sign a peace treaty within three months.

Egypt made most of the concessions. Sadat did not gain a commitment to an eventual Israeli withdrawal from the West Bank and Gaza Strip or full Palestinian self-determination. The Israelis, however, promised to recognize "the legitimate rights of the Palestinians," to permit West Bank and Gaza Palestinians to participate in future negotiations on these areas and ratify or reject a final agreement, and to halt temporarily new Israeli settlements on the West Bank. In return, Israel gained a separate peace treaty with the strongest of its Arab neighbors; without Egypt the others could not by themselves take on Israel. Thus for a seemingly small investment Israel had gained the enormous dividend of a real sense of security.

Sadat hoped that a peace agreement would prompt other Arab states to resolve their differences with Israel. But the Arab reaction to the Camp David Accords was negative, with many Arab leaders condemning Sadat. Still, Carter's courageous intervention—including his visits to Egypt and Israel—produced the necessary diplomatic breakthrough and brought peace between these two historic enemies. The United States supported this peace with massive transfers of foreign aid to Israel and Egypt that totaled more than $8 billion annually. To Carter, such expenses would represent a bargain if they bought time for an expansion of the Middle East "peace process" and mutual recognition between Israel and other Arab states in the embattled region.

IMPACT AND INFLUENCE

Anwar Sadat, Jimmy Carter, and Menachem Begin

President Jimmy Carter struggled throughout most of his presidency trying to redirect the course of American foreign policy away from the rigid policy of anticommunist containment and Henry Kissinger's strategy of détente, which was based on amoral calculations of power politics. Although Carter's shift toward "world-order politics" and attempt to highlight human rights were ultimately frustrated by global events, his central role in mediating the Camp David Accords in 1978 made it possible for peaceful relations to be established between Israel and its western neighbor—relations that continue today.

Carter, along with Egyptian president Anwar Sadat and Israeli prime minister Menachem Begin, took enormous risks in launching the Arab-Israeli peace process at the presidential retreat outside Washington, D.C. Failure at Camp David could have prompted yet another war in the region and America's military intervention in behalf of its ally, Israel. As for the two leaders whose willingness to recognize each other's governments exposed them to attacks by their opponents at home, Sadat, a former military officer, had earlier renounced Egypt's friendship treaty with the Soviet Union and was looking to the United States for economic and military assistance. Begin, a veteran of the Polish army in World War II, risked his stature as leader of Israel's Likud Party, which favored a hard line against the Arab states. For his part, Carter promised both Middle Eastern leaders large volumes of American foreign aid if they signed the agreements, and he reassured them that the United States would lead the effort to extend the peace process across the Middle East.

In awarding Sadat and Begin the Nobel Peace Prize in December 1978, the award committee's chair Aase Lionaes captured the importance of the Camp David Accords: "Never has the Peace Prize expressed a greater or more audacious hope—a hope of peace for the people of Egypt, for the people of Israel, and for all the peoples of the strife-torn and war-ravaged Middle East." Although Arab-Israeli tensions have persisted since the accords, Israel and Egypt have remained at peace.

Blowback and the Soviet Power Play

For all of their differences, Richard Nixon and Jimmy Carter were both determined to alter the course of American foreign policy in response to changes in the interstate system and balance of power. The Vietnam War left the United States militarily, economically, and morally exhausted. At the same time, the war bolstered and emboldened the Soviet Union, which could not be displeased with the serial misjudgments by the White House and Pentagon that left the American forces deep in the quagmire of Indochina. The Soviet Union appeared upwardly mobile by comparison and seductive to the teeming, impoverished populations of post-colonial Africa, Latin America, and southern Asia. Through its vast nuclear arsenal and advanced delivery systems, the Kremlin also appeared capable of negating, for an indefinite period of time, American primacy in world politics.

Jimmy Carter's embrace of world-order politics in the mid-1970s coincided with many Americans' "crisis of confidence" in their government. The Watergate scandal tore at the nation's deeply embedded faith in the legitimacy of its political institutions, whose only functional drawbacks seemed related to the inefficiencies built into the separation of powers. Richard Nixon's cover-up, which included bugging the Oval Office and routinely tapping the phones of those on the administration's "enemies' list," aimed to shield the president as he went to extreme lengths, including breaking the law, to advance his political agenda. The scandal compounded the public's cynicism in the wake of the Vietnam War and the distortions of truth that went with it from the start.

The effect of these assaults on the public trust extended far beyond domestic politics. Even though President Carter sought continued détente with the Soviet Union, the term was closely identified with the disgraced Nixon administration. Carter thus rarely used the term and instead diminished the superpower struggle as a diversion from the new realities of world politics. But the East-West struggle was not just an old, bad memory. It was still very much alive, even if the United States insisted that containment was no longer relevant in the face of global interdependence, the diffusion of power in the world, the growing nationalism in developing countries, and the shift from power politics to world-order politics. Many U.S. interventions in countries had embittered their citizens and left Washington vulnerable to "blowback," or acts of vengeance against the United States and its allies.

For their part, the Soviets shared neither the belief that international politics had changed, nor the view that military force had become less relevant in foreign policy. Abroad, the Soviet Union exploited hostility among developing countries toward the North and offered those countries, for emulation, its model of communism and centrally directed industrialization. The internal decay of the Soviet economy, not yet visible to the outside world, was obscured by the heightened capacity of Soviet military power. It would take another decade for the root rot within the nation to be fully revealed.

Whereas Nixon and Kissinger followed realist tradition in charting a new course, Carter's liberal path was more in keeping the American sense of moral mission and manifest destiny. But in acknowledging the nation's past violations of its own principles, and in pledging to uphold human rights and self-determination in deeds as well as words, Carter implicitly encouraged uprisings in foreign countries whose citizens had felt betrayed and victimized by the United States in the past and now mobilized to rectify these wrongs. The upheavals that followed, though a predictable response to Carter's liberal turn in American foreign policy, posed new and unforeseen challenges to the United States. Indeed, after December 1979, when the Soviet Union responded to Carter by staging a military takeover of Afghanistan, both détente and world-order politics were in shambles. A new escalation of the Cold War had begun.

NICARAGUA'S SANDINISTA REVOLUTION

Carter's call for human rights was well received in Central America, where decades of economic distress, military dictatorship, and ideological polarization had spawned a variety of revolutionary movements. These movements often were directed not only against the reigning rulers but also against the United States, whose support for dictators in the name of containing communism engendered widespread resentment throughout Latin America and the Caribbean. The United States, the self-proclaimed protector of the region under the Monroe Doctrine, was viewed by many in the region as more of a menace than a supportive patron. Carter hoped to change this perception by reforming U.S. policy and establishing a new reputation as a truly "good neighbor."

In Nicaragua, Carter opposed the long-standing military dictatorship of Anastasio Somoza, whose family had ruthlessly controlled the country for nearly five decades (after the departure of U.S. Marines from the country). Carter's reversal of American policy was consistent with his overall effort to shift attention from Cold War concerns to internal social and economic problems in poorer countries. Continued U.S. support for right-wing dictatorships, he felt, would certainly doom U.S. interests in the region and throughout the developing world. Popular resentment and anger would eventually lead to the overthrow of such dictatorships, and identification of America with the status quo would only alienate the new rulers. Unlike in Vietnam, the argument went, the United States had to place itself on the "right side of history." Thus Carter favored social and political change and tried to identify U.S. policy with such change rather than oppose it.

The rebellion against Somoza accelerated in the late 1970s, despite the leader's increasingly brutal use of the Nicaraguan National Guard. The government-backed murder in January 1978 of Pedro Joaquin Chamorro, a newspaper publisher and leading opponent of the regime, prompted a general strike and a call for free elections by the Organization of American States. The spiral of violence came home to Americans in June 1979 when Bill Stewart, an ABC News reporter, was executed by government forces on a Managua city street in full view of camera crews. As disgust with Somoza spread far beyond Nicaragua, the regime finally collapsed in July.[18] At first, Carter favored the coalition of anti-Somoza forces led by the Sandinista National Liberation Front (FSLN), which—at least initially—was supported on the domestic front by the Catholic Church, the educated middle class, and the business community. Thus in its first years under the coalition, Nicaragua received allotments of $80 million in foreign aid from the United States and promises for long-term support.

The new regime in Nicaragua, however, did not live up to Carter's expectations. The broad-based anti-Somoza coalition rapidly dissolved as the Sandinistas, led by Daniel Ortega, centralized authority within a five-member "Junta of National Reconstruction." Free elections were delayed, the press was again censored, and other political restrictions were imposed by the new regime, which turned increasingly to Marxist-Leninist models for building a self-sufficient communist state. Ortega tightened his hold and power and declared common cause with Cuba and the Soviet Union. In addition, he offered to aid rebels in neighboring El Salvador, where a similar uprising had begun against its military dictatorship. The Salvadoran dictatorship responded to the uprising by sending "death squads" into the impoverished countryside and murdering suspected insurgents. When their victims included a Catholic archbishop and three American nuns, the Carter administration rescinded U.S. aid to El Salvador and watched as the civil war became bloodier. No immediate reversal of American policy, however well intentioned, was likely to counteract the bitterness and resentment that had developed for so long toward "*yanqui* imperialism."

18. For a more thorough treatment, see Anthony Lake, *Somoza Falling* (Boston: Houghton Mifflin, 1989).

AMERICA 'HELD HOSTAGE' IN IRAN

The depths of anti-American hostility were further illustrated in November 1979 by the storming in the Middle East of the American embassy in Teheran by a mob of protestors. In the melee, militant students seized fifty-two American embassy workers. This event came on the heels of the ouster of Iran's pro-American leader, Shah Mohammed Reza Pahlevi, whose decades of brutal domestic repression were justified—in Teheran and Washington—on the basis of anticommunism. The ousted shah's admission to the United States in October for cancer treatment outraged Iranian nationalists and sparked the hostage crisis.[19] The seizure of American hostages paralyzed Carter, and his subsequent efforts to gain their safe release became high public drama. Nightly U.S. television networks featured images of Iranian crowds chanting anti-American slogans and burning Carter in effigy.

The newly installed revolutionary authorities, hoping to create an Islamic theocracy in Iran, gave the unprecedented hostage-taking their blessing and support. The Ayatollah Ruhollah Khomeini, Iran's chief religious leader and *imam*, or leader, of all Shiite Muslims, called America the "Great Satan." And "Death to America" was the battle cry on the streets of Teheran. Carter, who had stressed human rights in his election campaign, was caught between conflicting views. While the shah's removal from power was consistent with Carter's rhetoric, the president's understanding of Khomeini was superficial. Neither Carter nor other world leaders in that secular age had given serious consideration to the strength of a religious movement and the possibility that it would transform Iran into an Islamic theocracy.

In the 444 days following the hostage-taking, the world watched as the Carter administration tried one means after another to gain the hostages' release. Among other things, the White House appealed to the United Nations and the International Court of Justice and applied a series of economic sanctions. But all was in vain. The holding of the hostages was a symbolic act of defiance and revenge for America's support of the shah, who was portrayed by the new regime as an American puppet who had cruelly exploited Iranians in behalf of U.S. interests. As the administration's patience wore thin, it attempted a rescue mission in the spring of 1980. The mission was called off, however, when three of the eight helicopters malfunctioned in a desert sandstorm. Even worse, one helicopter collided on the ground with the refueling

19. The shah died a few months later in Egypt. For a review of his long and intimate relationship with the United States, see Mark Gasiorowski, *U.S. Foreign Policy and the Shah: Building a Client State in Iran* (Ithaca, N.Y.: Cornell University Press, 1991).

aircraft for the flight out of Iran, killing eight servicemen and injuring five others. To a nation on edge, the failure of the mission dramatically symbolized the apparent helplessness of the United States, as well as the low level of readiness, competence, and reliability of its armed forces. Secretary of State Cyrus Vance resigned in protest of the mission, revealing deepening divisions within the Carter administration over foreign policy.[20]

Two events helped to gain the hostages' release on January 20, 1981, the day Carter left office. The first was the Iraqi attack on Iran in the fall of 1980. The war suddenly made the U.S. economic sanctions, especially the freeze on Iranian money in U.S. banks, painful for Iran, because its military forces were largely American-equipped. The need for spare parts and the cash to buy them and other goods grew as oil production in Iran fell to almost nothing. The second event was the November 1980 victory of Republican Ronald Reagan, the former governor of California, in the U.S. presidential elections. Because he had run on a tough foreign policy platform and had denounced the Iranians as "barbarians" and "kidnappers," the Iranians expected harsher measures from Reagan, including military action. In these circumstances, diplomacy finally proved successful. The fifty-two hostages were released just after Reagan's inauguration in a gesture fraught with symbolism.

THE SOVIET TAKEOVER IN AFGHANISTAN

In the second half of Carter's term the divisions between the adherents of détente—among them, Secretary of State Vance—and the hard-liners, epitomized by National Security Adviser Zbigniew Brzezinski—continued to fester. After Soviet troops and tanks poured into Afghanistan in December 1979 to back up a new pro-Soviet regime, Vance's influence waned and Brzezinski's rose. The administration had overlooked the Soviet-backed coup a year earlier in Afghanistan, but the 85,000 Soviet troops that entered the country were hard to ignore. Among their other concerns, the Soviets feared that the Islamic fundamentalism then sweeping Iran and Pakistan might engulf Afghanistan, which lay between these two countries, creating an insecure situation on the Soviet Union's southern border where approximately fifty million Soviet Muslims lived. In response to the situation, Moscow invoked the Brezhnev Doctrine, which asserted that once a nation had become socialist, it was not to be surrendered to "counterrevolution." Earlier, this doctrine had been invoked only in Eastern Europe—in Hungary in 1956 and Czecho-

20. See Jeral A. Rosati, *The Carter Administration's Quest for Global Community* (Columbia: University of South Carolina Press, 1987), 142–149.

slovakia in 1968. Now the Red Army was to ensure history's progress outside of the Soviet sphere in a developing country.

The Soviets expected Americans to merely condemn their action as deplorable. In fact, believing their vital security interests to be at stake, the Soviets did not give much thought to American reaction and felt they had little to lose. After all, the Soviet Union had received few of the trade, technology, and financial benefits it had expected from détente. Indeed, Moscow had been denied most-favored-nation commercial status, which China had received, despite its own lack of political and social reform. Nevertheless, such a disregard for American reaction, implying contempt for American power, was unprecedented.

For Carter and Vance, who had pinned so much of their hopes for world-order politics on superpower cooperation, the Soviet invasion was a shock. Chagrined, Carter called the Afghanistan invasion the greatest threat to world peace since World War II, saying, "[the Soviet action] made a more dramatic change in my opinion of what the Soviets' ultimate goals are than anything they've done in the previous time I've been in office." With those words, the president demonstrated dramatically his own naiveté. He then became a hard-liner. He stepped up military spending, halted high-technology sales, embargoed grain shipments, and imposed a U.S. boycott on the Olympic Games scheduled for Moscow in the summer of 1980. The Senate, meanwhile, refused to ratify the SALT II treaty. Most important of all, Carter announced his own doctrine: the United States would henceforth consider any threat to the Persian Gulf to be a direct threat to its own vital interests. It would be one of many steps in Carter's anguished transition to a more aggressive, militaristic, and Cold War–oriented foreign policy.

Nixon's détente and Carter's world-order politics thus came to an end in 1980 as superpower relations disintegrated. As noted earlier, the Nixon administration's "linkage" strategy failed to elicit goodwill in Moscow. For his part, Carter's foreign policy was based on the assumption that not all regional conflicts were tests of superpower strength and credibility. In truth, however, few purely regional quarrels existed outside the context of superpower tensions. Efforts to reduce these tensions ultimately collapsed because of a series of regional conflicts that the United States had attempted to isolate from the Soviet-American rivalry—only to find that it could not do so. As Soviet activities in the developing world showed, the Soviet Union did not consider this rivalry over. In fact, quite the opposite was true: it took advantage of America's post-Vietnam reluctance to act and its illusion that problems in developing countries could be separated from the superpower competition. The uprisings in Nicaragua and Iran only fortified the Soviet Union's resolve on such regional issues.

Reagan, who for decades had taken a hard line toward Moscow, benefited from these turbulent developments. Although inflation and rising unemployment may have been important factors in Reagan's election, the fact remained that because of OPEC and the overthrow of the shah the domestic economy was inseparable from American foreign policy. Whereas Carter was forced to acknowledge that the events of 1979 and 1980 had undermined his idealistic worldview, Reagan was able to argue that they had confirmed his expectations. "Historical forces" were not moving in the direction of transnational cooperation, as Carter had claimed. They had never diverted from their consistent path, which was plagued by conflicting interests and tests of strength.

CHAPTER SEVEN

The Revival of Superpower Confrontation

Ronald Reagan, often called the "great communicator," promoted hard-line policies toward communist countries during the early 1980s. He left office in 1989 with the Soviet bloc in disarray.

Just as Jimmy Carter's rise to power reflected the introspective and sullen American mood of the Vietnam-Watergate era, Ronald Reagan's assumption of leadership embodied the more assertive national spirit of the early 1980s. A former movie star and pitchman for General Electric, President Reagan was known neither for his intellect nor for his long hours spent in the Oval Office.[1] The contrast with his predecessor was widely apparent. Whereas Carter's worldview emphasized the complexi-

1. For an informative biography, see Lou Cannon, *Reagan* (New York: Putnam, 1982). For a more recent and controversial treatment, see Edmund Morris, *Dutch: A Memoir of Ronald Reagan* (New York: Random House, 1999).

ties of interdependence, Reagan's was unabashedly one-dimensional. Whereas Carter pored over background reports and anguished over policy choices, Reagan literally dozed through high-level meetings. But he brought to the office two characteristics that were to help transform U.S.-Soviet relations: strong anticommunist instincts and a powerful ability to mobilize public opinion. Both characteristics served him well.

Reagan attempted to restore the country's battered stature and the national pride of Americans by reviving the notion that an active U.S. role in international affairs was essential to world peace. Soviet leaders, he felt, had exploited détente, the Vietnam syndrome, and Carter's attempts to place human rights at the center of American foreign policy. As Reagan's supporters saw it, a clear line could be drawn from Carter's idealism to the Soviet invasion of Afghanistan, the Sandinista revolution in Nicaragua, and the seizure of American hostages in Iran. Believing the United States must match the Soviet nuclear and conventional military buildup of the 1970s, Reagan proposed a massive buildup of U.S. armed forces. A compliant Congress approved his proposals to double American defense spending in his first term and to match recent Soviet deployments of intermediate-range nuclear missiles in Europe with a new generation of North Atlantic Treaty Organization (NATO) missiles.

Reagan often boasted that he was blessed with the luck of the Irish. Indeed, he certainly had the good fortune to take office as the torch was being passed in Moscow from the old guard to a new generation of reformers led by Mikhail Gorbachev. The reduced tensions between the superpowers, so unexpected at the beginning of the decade, often have been attributed to Gorbachev, who took over the Kremlin in 1985, during Reagan's second term in office. The new Soviet leader was said to be the first enlightened ruler since the 1917 revolution. His generation of Soviet elites hailed from urban rather than rural backgrounds and had some exposure to foreign countries. As a result, they were more aware of the failings of the Soviet system and critical of its internal defects. Had Leonid Brezhnev or his two immediate successors survived, Gorbachev's new domestic and foreign policies might not have seen the light of day. Nor is it likely the Cold War would have ended on terms that were as peaceful or as beneficial to the West.

To some, the collapse of the Warsaw Pact and the Soviet Union in 1991 was a fait accompli, a historical inevitability no matter who was the president of the United States in the 1980s. The ossified Soviet system was already in an advanced stage of decline, its internal problems were growing worse daily, and its hold on its clients in Eastern Europe and beyond was becoming increasingly tenuous. Thus Gorbachev—or any leader of the country—had to implement drastic reforms in the Soviet Union's political and economic systems; permit the restive populations in Warsaw, Prague, and East Berlin to express themselves; and adopt a more cooperative posture toward the United States. These measures would, according to those holding this view, only magnify the deficiencies of the Soviet system and hasten its self-destruction.

But this interpretation of events, which minimizes the roles of both Reagan and Gorbachev, does not tell the full story. It fails to recognize the crucial part Reagan played in raising the costs of the superpower competition and in forcing the Soviet Union to reform its system. The U.S. military buildup, which actually began in Carter's last year, required greater Soviet investments in arms at a time when the dwindling resources of the nation were needed for domestic priorities. Moreover, the new NATO missile deployments in Western Europe negated the strategic advantages of recent Soviet installations. The president's proposals for a Strategic Defense Initiative further worried the Soviets because, whether or not it succeeded in creating a missile-proof "shield" over the United States, the research might lead America to a quantum leap in technology at a time when the Soviet Union was struggling with growing economic problems at home. Finally, the Reagan Doctrine of supporting guerrillas against Soviet-backed Marxist regimes further increased the costs of Soviet expansion.

In short, the Brezhnev foreign policy, which at first had appeared so successful, had become counterproductive: it had provoked a strong American reaction, held NATO together, and left the Soviet Union surrounded by enemies (including Japan and China). For his part, Reagan had increased the strains on the Soviet Union so much that it could no longer muddle through. Reagan eliminated any flexibility that Gorbachev might have had and forced him to retrench abroad, cut military spending, and subordinate foreign policy to domestic affairs. Initially thought to be reckless and widely condemned as a cowboy (especially in Europe) because he appeared trigger-happy, the president left office in January 1989 with the superpower relationship on its best terms since 1945. Thus, despite some setbacks, Reagan left office with a favorable conclusion to the Cold War within America's grasp.

Reagan's Rhetorical Offensive

When Reagan came into office, the national disillusionment with détente was widespread. The president's longtime hostility toward communism in general and the Soviet Union specifically fit the new post-détente mood. Soviet leaders would "lie, steal, cheat, and do anything else to advance their goals," warned Reagan.[2] Opposition to the Soviet

2. *New York Times,* January 30, 1981.

Union was, therefore, a religious as well as a political imperative. Reagan also spoke of the march of freedom and democracy that would leave "Marxism-Leninism on the ash heap of history." Of Eastern Europe he said, "Regimes planted by bayonets do not take root"—that is, the communist regimes had no legitimacy. The United States could not accept the "permanent subjugation of the people of Eastern Europe." [3] In making the point that democracy and freedom were the waves of the future, the president was not just giving the Soviets a dose of their own medicine, for the Soviets regularly denounced the United States and forecast the "inevitable end" of Western capitalism. More important, he was questioning the legitimacy and longevity of communism as a social and political system in Eastern Europe and the Soviet Union.

Many American critics dismissed Reagan's predictions about communism being swept aside by the tide of democracy as empty rhetoric. By the end of his second term, however, as many repressive noncommunist states were being transformed along democratic lines and communist regimes were being exposed to greater demands for liberties from within, Reagan's prediction looked less like right-wing ranting than accurate insight into historical development. While far from being a political theorist, Reagan was a spirited polemicist whose expectation of communism's demise in Europe materialized on his watch.

Reagan's harsh denunciations of the Soviet Union also served two tactical purposes. First, the war of words was intended to remobilize American public opinion after the years of détente. Reagan, to whom détente had all along been an illusion based on the unwarranted belief that the Soviets would change their character, sought to arouse American opinion for the longer term. Second, the president's public statements were intended to send the Soviet leaders a message, one that probably was heeded all the more because the Soviet leadership was in the throes of a geriatric crisis. Three Soviet leaders died in three years: Leonid Brezhnev in late 1982, Yuri Andropov in early 1984, and Konstantin Chernenko, in ill health when he took over, in 1985. Gorbachev, who had risen rapidly to the top of the Communist Party hierarchy, now became the Soviet Union's fourth leader since Reagan had assumed office. At age fifty-four, he was the youngest man to take charge of the nation since Joseph Stalin.

Reagan bluntly informed the new Soviet leaders that the Vietnam syndrome was a thing of the past. America's will to resist Soviet expansion was back. Reagan wanted to make sure the Soviet Union would not act, as it had during the 1970s, in the belief that America would not

3. Address to members of the British Parliament, June 8, 1982, in Strobe Talbott, *Russians and Reagan* (New York: Vintage Books, 1984), 89–104.

respond to its provocations. Minor U.S. military actions against Soviet proxies such as Libya and Grenada—which the United States could not lose and were not costly—were intended to drive this message home. In that sense, the tough words were essentially a substitute for riskier deeds.

The early Reagan years may have been characterized by rhetorical confrontations, but there were no direct encounters or crises. Despite his reputation for machismo, the president was operationally cautious. Indeed, to the extent the Soviets saw him as a leader spoiling for a fight, they were no doubt strengthened in their conviction that they needed to act with restraint. Reagan's foreign policy was basically a return to the containment policy of the immediate post–World War II years. The primary emphasis was on East-West relations, on the Soviet Union as a communist expansionist state, and on the need to contain that expansion—by force if necessary.

Expanding U.S. Military Forces

The late 1970s in the United States was rife with antimilitary sentiment and cries for a renewed emphasis on domestic priorities and reductions in the defense budget. Indeed, those years witnessed "the most substantial reduction in American military capabilities relative to those of the Soviet Union in the entire postwar period."[4] American defense expenditures had fallen to the 1950 (pre–Korean War) low of 5 percent of the nation's gross national product (GNP) at a time when the Soviet Union, despite having an economy only half the size of the U.S. economy, was spending substantially more than the United States on defense. By 1981 any president would have been concerned about Soviet intentions and capabilities.

After a decade and a half of Soviet efforts to exploit America's Vietnam-induced malaise and a weakened presidency, the Soviet Union possessed the strategic and conventional forces needed to project its power beyond Eurasia. It was in the context of their perceptions of a changing "correlation of forces" that the Soviets had exploited unstable situations in poorer countries to increase their influence. This task was undertaken by military advisers and arms, proxies such as the Vietnamese in Cambodia and the Cubans in Africa, and, of course, their own troops in Afghanistan. The Reagan administration was especially worried about the state of U.S. nuclear forces and warned that a "window of vulnerability" had opened that could leave the United States vulnerable to Soviet nuclear blackmail.

4. John Lewis Gaddis, *Strategies of Containment: A Critical Appraisal of Postwar American National Security Policy* (New York: Oxford University Press, 1982), 320–322.

FIGURE 7-1 U.S. Military Spending, 1976–1988

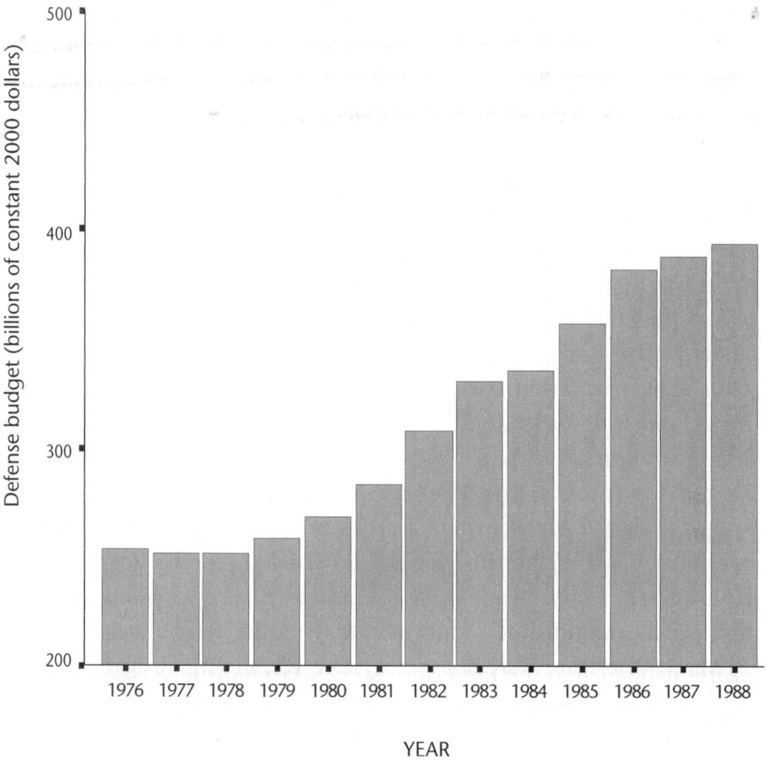

Source: White House, Office of Management and Budget, http://www.whitehouse.gov/omb/budget/fy2005/pdf/hist.pdf (accessed April 21, 2006).

Yet Reagan's promise to revive U.S. military power alarmed many Americans, who feared the onset of a global nuclear war. Even more disturbing was Secretary of State Alexander Haig's talk of nuclear warning shots, "protracted" nuclear war, nuclear "war-fighting," and "prevailing" in a nuclear war. Thus the administration's five-year, $1 trillion defense program (which actually totaled almost $3 trillion over Reagan's two terms in constant 2000 dollars) sparked an enormous controversy (see Figure 7-1). The sharp rise in spending conveyed the impression that by relying too much on military strength Reagan was flirting with disaster, and it revived charges that the United States was largely responsible for the arms race. The momentum of the Soviet Union's arms program since the mid-1960s and its impact on the balance of forces were forgotten in the uproar over the administration's rearmament program.

OPPOSITION TO ARMS CONTROL

This uproar was intensified by Reagan's strong opposition to arms control, the centerpiece of both Nixon's and Carter's policies toward the Soviet Union. Rejection of the SALT process reflected the Reagan administration's strong distrust of the Soviets and its conviction that past arms control efforts had led to America's relative decline. Reagan announced that he would postpone any arms negotiations until the United States could "negotiate from strength." But postponing new arms control talks proved difficult, because public opinion equated arms control with a sincere search for peace. The pressure on the administration therefore grew. When negotiations finally began in 1982, the administration claimed it was shifting the emphasis from arms limitation—setting ceilings on missile launchers and warheads—to drastic reductions in both categories. Thus Reagan changed the name of the process from SALT (Strategic Arms Limitation Talks) to START (Strategic Arms Reduction Talks). The administration's real motive for this change, however, was to make its approach politically appealing at home, to deflect domestic criticism, and to weaken the newborn nuclear freeze movement while the buildup continued. The initial arms control proposals from the Reagan White House were clearly meant to be rejected by Moscow, thereby winning time for the administration to win over the American public.

Many Americans were not fooled, however, and the Reagan administration's efforts provoked a widespread peace movement in the early 1980s. Its adherents ranged from academics to religious leaders, especially many Catholic and Methodist bishops, who in 1983 questioned the morality of nuclear deterrence, a policy based on the threat to use nuclear weapons in order to prevent their use. The bishops condemned not only the use of nuclear weapons, but also their very presence in the arsenals and military doctrines of both superpowers.[5] Yet if such weapons could not be used even in retaliation, how could deterrence be made credible? Was the goal of peace moral but the means of preserving it immoral? In the meantime, antinuclear books and films became popular, climaxing in an ABC-TV movie entitled *The Day After* that depicted the nuclear devastation of an average American city.

In addition to decrying the immorality of nuclear deterrence, the peace movement asserted that nuclear war would mean the end of civilization, the "last epidemic" as a medical association phrased it. This theme was supported strongly by new scientific evidence that the smoke produced by the many fires caused by nuclear attacks would shut out

5. National Conference of Catholic Bishops, *Challenge and Peace: God's Promise and Our Response* (Washington, D.C.: United States Catholic Conference, 1983).

sunlight, plunging the world into darkness for several months and causing a prolonged freeze, or "nuclear winter," leading to the extinction of most plant and animal life. Regardless of who "won" a nuclear war, climatic catastrophe would follow and spread over the globe.[6]

Although the antinuclear movement confused the issue of threatening nuclear force to bolster deterrence with its actual use, that confusion did not stop the movement from gaining enormous momentum by 1982. The danger of nuclear war appeared to be the nation's first concern. In New York City, three-quarters of a million people turned out for the largest political gathering in American history. For those demonstrators and the others marching, meeting, and debating the nuclear issue across the country, the ultimate goal was to eliminate nuclear weapons, but the immediate goal was to achieve a nuclear freeze. Proposals for a freeze on the testing, production, and deployment of nuclear weapons to stop the arms race were passed (or almost passed) by many town-hall meetings and by voters in ten of the eleven states on whose ballots the proposals appeared in the midterm 1982 election. Congress, especially the Democratic House, reflected this antinuclear mood, and, after coming within two votes of endorsing a nuclear freeze in 1982, it endorsed a modified version of the freeze in 1983. In 1984 all Democratic presidential candidates but one came out in favor of a freeze on building new nuclear weapons.

THE STRATEGIC DEFENSE INITIATIVE

Reagan introduced his Strategic Defense Initiative (SDI) in the midst of this controversy about arms control. The proposal was quickly dubbed "Star Wars" by its critics because of its reliance on sophisticated space-based technologies glimpsed only in movies, such as lasers and particle beams. SDI was intended to render nuclear missiles "impotent and obsolete," presumably protecting America's population. According to official descriptions, SDI would be a "layered" defense using different technologies to destroy approaching missiles during each phase of the ballistic trajectory. Mutual assured survival would replace mutual assured destruction. Was it not better to save lives on both sides, the president asked, than to kill the population of the aggressor in revenge for a first strike?

For the president, the SDI plan served three primary purposes, the first of which was domestic and political. Criticized for increasing the defense budget while cutting social services and assailed for being a

6. See Carl Sagan, "Nuclear Winter and Climatic Catastrophe: Some Policy Implications," *Foreign Affairs* (winter 1983–1984): 257–292.

warmonger, Reagan was able to seize the initiative with SDI. He would pose as a man of vision who would end the threat of missile attacks and ensure that the populations of the United States, the Soviet Union, and, indeed, the world would survive. He did arms control advocates one better, not merely by stabilizing the balance of offensive missiles but by seeking to banish their life-threatening potential. Reagan became an abolitionist who spoke of a world devoid of nuclear weapons as his ultimate goal. The president clearly was uncomfortable with the deterrent strategy to which all of his predecessors had been committed, and he condoned the addition of new nuclear stockpiles only as a means to hasten arms control efforts. Indeed, at the Reykjavík (Iceland) summit in 1986 Reagan came close to agreeing with Gorbachev to the total elimination of all nuclear weapons within a ten-year period.[7]

Second, SDI's utopian side was matched by a more pragmatic consideration. If it worked, Americans would gain the upper hand on the Soviets, whose superpower status was based in large measure on their arsenal of intercontinental ballistic missiles (ICBMs). The planned missile shield threatened the value of this Soviet investment and Moscow's claims to equality with the United States. What would be the point of a Soviet attack if its missiles would be destroyed before reaching the United States?

Third, although defense of the population and elimination of all ICBMs were presumably the long-term goals of SDI, the system could potentially defend U.S. land-based ICBMs in the future. A defense against Soviet-launched missiles would relieve the American fear that its ICBMs were vulnerable and increase Soviet uncertainty that they could launch a successful first strike. Such a strike would, therefore, be very reckless, rendering the U.S. nuclear deterrent more credible.

The SDI plan was denounced by critics for many reasons: it would be enormously expensive; it would accelerate the arms race; it would have to work perfectly the first time it was needed; it would tempt a Soviet first strike if the Soviets felt they were on the verge of becoming "nuclear hostages" to an unassailable United States. In short, SDI would only lead to new arms races, offensive and defensive, in which the defensive technologies, even if they gained the upper hand, would do so only temporarily. Moreover, the system would be so expensive that it would threaten U.S. budgets for other strategic and conventional forces, not to mention domestic priorities. Therefore, it was doubtful that the United States or the Soviet Union would be any more secure. The reduction of arms through bilateral negotiations was the better course.

7. Ironically, it was Reagan's refusal to postpone research on SDI that undermined that agreement.

But if the critics were correct, why did the Soviets denounce Reagan's "arms race in space"? Why, after previously walking out of all arms control negotiations, were the Soviets so eager to resume talks? Clearly SDI worried them; they were as fearful of an American first strike as the Americans had been of a Soviet first strike since the early 1970s. The Soviets perceived SDI to be part of an offensive, not defensive, strategy, a prelude to an American strike that would be launched once the U.S. population could be protected. They also were aware that SDI research and development would result in American technology taking a huge step forward at a time when Soviet technology already was behind. With its domestic economy deteriorating rapidly, the Soviets could not afford to accelerate the arms race on so great a scale.

'Rollback' in Developing Countries

Although President Reagan refocused the attention of American foreign policy on the East-West struggle, the developing countries remained a matter of concern. Among Reagan's top priorities on taking office was a reversal of what he saw as Soviet gains during the 1970s in, among other places, Afghanistan, Angola, Cambodia, Ethiopia, and Yemen after the Vietnam War. The Soviets and their allies had been using force to make inroads in these areas—direct force in Afghanistan, indirect force through proxies elsewhere. And in Central America the Marxist Sandinista government in Nicaragua was seeking to extend its influence to neighboring countries, especially El Salvador.

Past administrations, committed to containment, had not hesitated to intervene to save a friendly regime from being attacked from outside or from within by the Soviet Union or its friends. Yet, except for episodic efforts such as President Harry Truman's attempt to "liberate" North Korea and President John Kennedy's Bay of Pigs operation in Cuba, the official policy of the U.S. government had never been to unseat Soviet-supported regimes. Dwight Eisenhower's administration had spoken of the "liberation" of Eastern Europe and the global "rollback" of communism but had never acted on those words; containment remained a fundamentally defensive doctrine. The new Reagan policy, however, was offensive.

Dubbed the "Reagan Doctrine," the policy aimed to reverse Soviet gains. Afghanistan, Angola, and Nicaragua had established Marxist governments that had not yet fully consolidated their power, and all faced resistance movements. The Soviets had justified their expansion in the developing world with the doctrine of "national liberation" and then asserted that communism was irreversible once a society had become Marxist. Reagan now adopted his own national liberation strategy against governments that had not come to power by means of democratic processes. In his eyes, such regimes lacked legitimacy. Moscow had placed them in power, and, unlike his predecessors (with the partial exception of Jimmy Carter in Afghanistan, where a U.S. program of largely covert assistance for resistance fighters was already in place), he refused to accept Moscow's claim that the civil wars were over once governments were in place. As he saw it, the domestic conflicts were not over until popular governments, acceptable to the people (and presumably to Washington), were in power. In short, the Reagan Doctrine set out to disprove the claim of the Brezhnev Doctrine that once a nation had become part of the Soviet bloc it could never leave.

The rollback strategy was based on certain assumptions: that the Soviet Union had become overextended in the 1970s; that the global balance of military power was increasingly favoring the United States; that the Soviet Union's most critical problems were domestic; that, except for Afghanistan, only peripheral Soviet interests were involved; that the Soviet Union would not want to risk a confrontation with the United States; and that a democratic tide was sweeping across the developing world. In practice, the Reagan Doctrine amounted to little more than bleeding the targeted governments and especially Moscow. The anti-communist forces were not strong enough to overthrow the Marxist regimes, but with American help they could keep the wars going.

As noted, the Reagan administration turned Marxist ideology on its head by arguing that "historical forces" were on the side of Western democracy and capitalism, not communism. For evidence, the administration pointed to Latin America, where during the Reagan years (1981–1989) Argentina, Bolivia, Brazil, Guatemala, Honduras, Peru, and Uruguay had become, at least nominally, democratic, in addition to El Salvador, Grenada, and Haiti. Whatever the reason for this phenomenon, the administration claimed it was part of an irreversible process. The Soviet bloc, by denying human freedom and dignity to its citizens, was running against the tide of history.

Drawing on the traditional hemispheric preoccupation of the Monroe Doctrine, Reagan identified Central America, South America, and the Caribbean as vital U.S. interests and vowed to turn back any outside (that is, Soviet) incursions into America's backyard. To demonstrate his resolve, Reagan intervened directly on the tiny Caribbean island of Grenada, where a military coup had led to the installation of a Marxist regime in 1983. The U.S. military operation, which ostensibly was designed to liberate American medical students from the island, took longer than expected because of logistical problems and a considerable amount of bungling by U.S. Army, Navy, and Marine forces. But the mission achieved its main objective of eliminating the Marxist regime.

The U.S. invasion of Grenada was intended to raise the risks and the costs for the Soviets and Cubans should they continue to try to extend their political and military control in the Western Hemisphere—or elsewhere. Asserting that it had intervened to prevent Grenada from becoming a "Soviet-Cuban colony," the administration called Grenada a "warning shot" that actually was targeting the Sandinista regime in Nicaragua. The administration was convinced that the Sandinistas, led by Daniel Ortega, harbored ideologically motivated ambitions beyond their own frontiers (see Chapter 6).[8] Because they also accepted support from Havana and Moscow, they were, in Washington's eyes, a continuing source of instability and tension for the vulnerable states in the region. The Sandinistas' pledge to confine themselves to Nicaragua was regarded with skepticism by those who recalled Ortega's earlier pledges to promote political pluralism, a mixed economy, and a nonaligned foreign policy.

What the Reagan administration sought in Nicaragua was to undo the Sandinistas' growing monopolization of power and return the country to its immediate post-1979 state, when the popular anti-Somoza revolution had produced a new coalition government composed of the major factions—religious groups, entrepreneurs, and large segments of the middle and working classes—that had helped to overthrow the dictator. Once in power, however, the Sandinistas began to consolidate their hold on government, gradually suppressing the voices of criticism. They postponed general elections, censored the news media while building an army larger than that of dictator Anastasio Somoza, restricted activities by opposition political parties, extended control over worker and peasant organizations, and strengthened their police and security apparatus. They also turned toward Cuba and the Soviet Union for diplomatic support and economic assistance. But the question was not how *Marxist* the regime would become as it turned against the Catholic Church, the business community, professional organizations, trade unions, and student groups that had helped it to depose Somoza. The question was how *dictatorial* it would become and how closely it would align with Havana and Moscow.

The United States, which initially supported the new regime in Nicaragua with foreign aid, was increasingly distressed by the regime's consolidation of power and militaristic behavior. Thus after Reagan took office, he authorized the formation of an anti-Sandinista army known as the "contras." Trained by U.S. military advisers in neighboring

8. The Sandinistas derived their name from Cesar Angusto Sandino, the Nicaraguan nationalist who led the resistance against the U.S. occupation of the country in the early 1930s. Sandino was killed by the U.S.-trained Nicaraguan National Guard in 1934.

Honduras, the soldiers staged a series of military offenses against the Sandinista regime. Honduras received increased U.S. military assistance for these purposes, even though Reagan encouraged the public to view the contras as an indigenous, independent army of "freedom fighters."

The Reagan administration also placed the Central American country of El Salvador, a country the size of New Jersey with a population of six million, within the context of the superpower conflict. Adapting the Eisenhower administration's "domino theory" of communist expansion to Latin America, Reagan expressed concerns that the Sandinista revolution in Nicaragua would spread to El Salvador, and ultimately the rest of Central America. Furthermore, the threat was defined as applying to the wider U.S. position throughout the world. "If Central America were to fall," the president asked, "what would the consequences be for our position in Asia, Europe, and for alliances such as NATO? If the United States cannot respond to a threat near our own border, why should Europeans or Asians believe that we are seriously concerned about threats to them?"[9] Specifically, Reagan alleged that the Nicaraguan government was shipping weapons to rebels in El Salvador, and he proposed increasing the U.S. arms transfers to El Salvador to match the reported Sandinista arms transfers.

Whether El Salvador was the right place to take a stand against Soviet communism and its proxies or whether the revolution should be allowed to follow its natural course were open questions in view of the U.S. government's past experience. Critics of the administration's plans argued that the appalling domestic social and economic conditions and political repression were the principal cause of the civil war in El Salvador, not the Nicaraguan arms. The United States should not support the privileged few who had long exploited the poor. Social justice demanded nonintervention; so perhaps did self-interest if the United States wished to avoid being identified with the losers, as it had been so many times before. The Vietnam War served as a reminder of the dangers of supporting the wrong side—an unpopular political elite whose vested interest lay in preservation of the status quo. In any event, no purely military solution was possible.

In the developing countries, the United States often had appeared trapped between reactionary forces, whose rigid commitment to the status quo only intensified revolutionary sentiment, and radical forces, which tended to be Marxist and to look to Havana and Moscow. The administration was saved from this trap in El Salvador by Napoléon Duarte, who was in power for most of the Reagan years and sought to

9. Ronald Reagan, "Central America: Defending Our Vital Interests," *Current Policy* (U.S. Department of State), April 27, 1983.

pursue democratic reforms while preventing the radical left from capturing power. Duarte strengthened the Reagan case for assistance to El Salvador, because Reagan could rightfully claim that the United States was not supporting the right wing as an alternative to the radical left.

The Salvadoran precedent of support for a democratic center was widely recognized after the events of 1986 in the Philippines, where the United States had long supported the dictator Ferdinand Marcos. But his despotism, economic mismanagement, transparent corruption, and the military's abuses had fueled public discontent and a rebirth of the communist guerrilla force called the Nationalist People's Army. In the absence of basic reforms, it appeared that the guerrillas might defeat the poorly trained and badly led Philippine army. Nevertheless, Marcos refused to heed suggestions for reform and, to prove his legitimacy, called for snap elections. The opposition candidate, Corazon Cojuangco Aquino, was the widow of the popular opposition leader Benigno Aquino, who in 1983 had been assassinated upon returning from exile in the United States. After her husband's assassination, Corazon Aquino became both a symbol of democracy and a rallying point for the opposition. When it became obvious that he would not win the election, Marcos tried to alter the results with widespread fraud, but his attempts were clearly visible to international observers. Thus Marcos lost his legitimacy even while "winning" another term. The United States encouraged him to step down. When top army commanders defected, Marcos fled to Hawaii and Corazon Aquino became president.

Also in 1986 the Reagan administration helped the Haitian people oust Jean-Claude "Baby Doc" Duvalier, who had succeeded his father as dictator of the Western Hemisphere's poorest state. The United States first advised Duvalier not to use force against protesting crowds and then furnished him with an airplane to flee to France. Previously, the U.S. government had backed the military juntas in Haiti in the name of communist containment and often had looked the other way as vicious dictators tortured, killed, and otherwise silenced their enemies, real or imagined. The Reagan administration now declared its new policy: "The American people believe in human rights and oppose tyranny in whatever form, whether of the left or the right."[10] Under this variation of Carter's human rights policy, the United States would support those struggling for democracy and oppose not just radical Marxist regimes but also pro-American military dictatorships.

And it did so. In 1987, after considerable turmoil that had flared on and off for years, the military government of South Korea was persuaded to promise free presidential elections. Administration pressure

10. "President Reagan's March 14 Message to Congress," *New York Times*, March 15, 1986.

on South Korea, a key U.S. ally and beneficiary of U.S. aid, had been instrumental in the long-awaited transition. Similar pressure on Chile resulted in an election that displaced its military leader, Gen. Augusto Pinochet, and opened the way for the establishment of democratic rule.

EVALUATING THE REAGAN DOCTRINE

Although the Reagan administration invoked its claim of a global pro-democratic tide to support resistance movements in Afghanistan, Angola, and Nicaragua, the insurgencies it supported in the name of spreading freedom often fell considerably short of that virtue. Indeed, the administration's emphasis on human rights was compromised in many instances by the absence of moderate factions that had any chance of taking power. For Reagan, it became a matter of identifying and supporting the lesser of evils; "authoritarian" regimes that supported Washington were preferable to Soviet-backed "totalitarian" regimes.[11] In Afghanistan, the opponents of Soviet rule were Islamic fundamentalists, who, if they won, were more likely to establish an Iranian-style theocracy than a democracy and to fragment the Muslim world further. And in Nicaragua some of the principal contra commanders were former members of Somoza's detested National Guard. Although Reagan was initially critical of his predecessors' double standards, he later adopted many of them.

Lack of congressional and public support for the Nicaraguan contras left Reagan with only one option when the presidents of Costa Rica, El Salvador, Guatemala, Honduras, and Nicaragua agreed to a regional peace plan in 1987. Reagan had to support the Contadora initiative because if the plan failed and its failure could be clearly attributed to the Sandinistas' unwillingness to open Nicaragua to genuine democratization as stipulated by the peace plan, he might regain support for further financial assistance of the contras. But the Democratic-controlled Congress remained disenchanted with the contras, whose ties to the U.S. government were obvious despite administration denials, and used the peace plan as a reason not to fund any more military aid. Such assistance, it was claimed, would only thwart efforts to bring peace to Nicaragua and the region. Thus the administration's plan to overthrow the Sandinistas seemed doomed to failure. This failure appeared even more certain after the five Central American presidents, over the protests of the United States, called for disbanding the contras and for general elections in Nicaragua.

11. This distinction was earlier made by Jeane J. Kirkpatrick, Reagan's ambassador to the United Nations, in a journal article entitled "Dictatorships and Double Standards," *Commentary* (November 1979): 34–45.

Under continuing international pressure, Ortega finally agreed to hold multiparty elections in 1990. He and his military aides were confident about the outcome. They had gradually consolidated power during their ten years in office despite the contras' challenge and expected to exploit their control of the government, including the police and army, to ensure an electoral victory that would give them international legitimacy and eliminate any possible rationale for further U.S. interference. Like Marcos in the Philippines, the Sandinistas were confident they would not lose the general election and have to relinquish their power. But lose they did. Despite Sandinista control of the government and efforts to intimidate opposition candidates and rallies, as well as the holdup of congressionally approved funds from the U.S. for the opposition, Ortega lost to Violeta Chamorro, widow of the anti-Somoza newspaper editor whose assassination had rallied the Sandinista-led revolution that brought down the dictator Somoza.

It was unclear who should have received the credit for the defeat of the Sandinistas: the five Central American presidents led by Costa Rica's Oscar Arias, the Nicaraguan people who had the courage to vote against an oppressive regime, or the Sandinistas themselves for believing they could survive an unpopular draft and a mismanaged economy in a relatively free election. But there was no doubt of the consequences. For the Salvadoran guerrillas, the loss of Nicaraguan political support and military assistance constituted a serious setback to their campaign to overthrow the government or negotiate a favorable settlement that would give them a share of the power. For Fidel Castro, who had served as an idol for the Sandinistas and a source of help and support, it meant further isolation now that he was the only remaining revolutionary in Latin America. As for Nicaragua, the solid defeat of the Sandinistas gave that country a second opportunity to build a democracy, to reintegrate the contras into Nicaraguan society, to reconcile political opponents, and to reestablish cordial relations with the United States.

As Reagan prepared to leave office in 1988, many of the regional conflicts in which the United States and the Soviet Union were engaged came to an end. In Afghanistan, Gorbachev, realizing that the war was an unending drain and a political embarrassment, withdrew Soviet forces. In Angola, after years of fruitless negotiations, the Cubans agreed to pull out their forces; meanwhile, South Africa agreed to grant independence to neighboring Namibia, which they had governed since World War I. These arrangements were followed by a settlement of the Angolan civil war and a largely effective effort by the United Nations to hasten the region's democratic transition. The reality was clear: Gorbachev had to resolve the Soviet Union's regional quarrels, because he needed to conserve his resources for investment in the stagnating Soviet economy. Still, Moscow did not suffer a set of total defeats, nor did the United States achieve a series of unqualified triumphs. Marxist ideology retained power and influence in many countries even as the Soviet economy and government fell into critical condition.

ABUSES OF THE REAGAN DOCTRINE: THE IRAN-CONTRA SCANDAL

In executing the Reagan Doctrine in Nicaragua, the Reagan administration managed to tarnish the president's reputation. In 1987 Reagan's competence, integrity, and sense of judgment were laid open to question when it was revealed that profits from secret arms sales to Iran, now an anti-American Islamic theocracy, had been used to fund the Nicaraguan contras from late 1984 to 1986 in defiance of a congressional ban on the use of U.S. funds for this purpose. In fact, in an effort to elude Congress the administration had shifted the conduct of the contra war from the Central Intelligence Agency (CIA) to the National Security Council (NSC) staff. Both operations were reputedly run by CIA director William Casey and his point man in the NSC, Oliver North, a marine lieutenant colonel.[12]

Labeled the only "five-star" lieutenant colonel in the U.S. military, North supervised the arms sales made to Iran in the hope that U.S. hostages, seized in Lebanon by pro-Iranian terrorists in the mid-1980s, would be released. He also directed an effort to raise private funds for the contras from tax-exempt organizations and from wealthy U.S. citizens and foreign governments. In addition, North commanded a vast network of arms dealers, ships, and airplanes to supply the contras, for whom he also provided tactical intelligence and advice on how to conduct the war. Under his guidance, then, the NSC became a "shadow government" that organized a secret campaign to direct and fund the contra war effort. NSC staff not only kept any knowledge of what they were doing from Congress, but also lied to Congress. When the "off-the-shelf" operation was finally discovered, the NSC attempted to cover up its involvement and to minimize the president's role in affair—even resorting to shredding relevant documents or smuggling them out of NSC offices. To make matters worse, when the story broke the president first denied knowledge of many of the details of the Iran-contra activities, making it appear as if his deputies had taken American foreign policy into their own hands.

12. For a detailed account of this scandal by its chief investigator in the U.S. government, see Lawrence E. Walsh, *Firewall: The Iran-Contra Conspiracy and Cover-Up* (New York: Norton, 1997).

IMPACT AND INFLUENCE

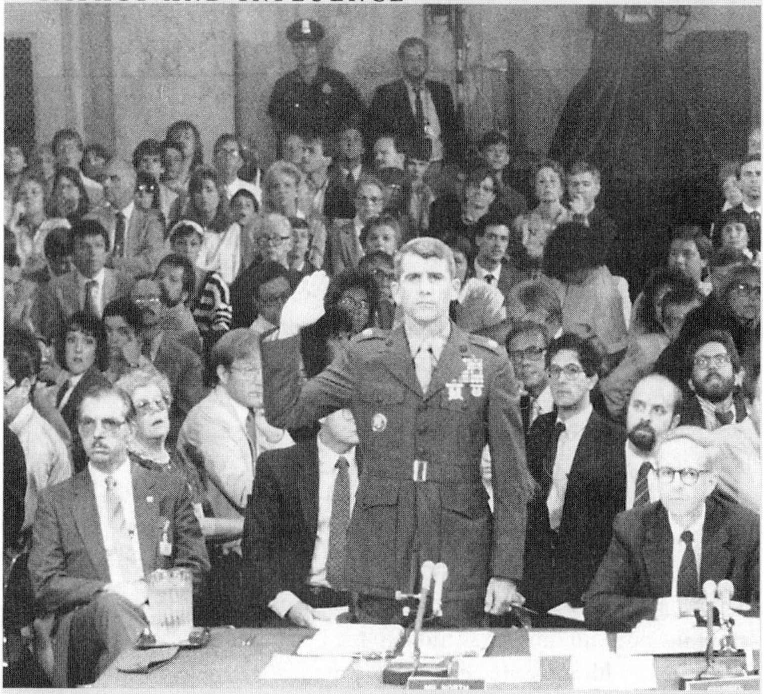

OLIVER NORTH

The Iran-contra scandal of 1986 revealed the extreme lengths to which the Reagan administration had gone in order to reverse communist gains in the developing world. As information about the scandal became known, so did the central role played by Lt. Col. Oliver North. A military aide to the National Security Council, North personally negotiated secret arms sales to Iran and used the profits to supply the U.S.-backed "contra" rebels in Nicaragua who were attempting to overthrow that country's communist government.

In testimony to a special congressional committee in 1987, North (pictured here being sworn in) defended his actions and said he was following the orders of senior Reagan administration officials. Two years later, he was tried and convicted of destroying government documents vital to the investigation, but his conviction was later overturned on the grounds that he had previously testified on the same charges under a grant of immunity. In the 1990s, North remained a highly visible public figure, espousing his conservative views on radio and television talk shows and even making a run (unsuccessful) for the U.S. Senate.

Public opinion polls showed that most Americans thought Reagan was lying, and the hearings Congress held to look into the matter revealed plainly he was actively involved and informed, especially on the contras. In response, the president suddenly reversed direction and claimed he knew about everything except the diversion of funds, but he argued that the congressional restrictions did not apply to him or his staff. The secrecy with which the Iran and contra operations were carried out, however, suggested that the administration knew very well it was breaking the law even though when Congress had first forbidden military assistance, the administration had claimed repeatedly it was obeying the law. All the participants, once they were caught, asserted they were acting only out of patriotic motives. In several cases, however, their patriotism seemed well greased by private gain.

Reagan was badly damaged by the scandal. He was, after all, the presidential candidate who had accused his opponent, Jimmy Carter, of weakness in dealing with the Iranian hostage situation. Under his own leadership, Reagan had vowed, the United States would "never negotiate with terrorists," let alone sell them weapons. He had consistently projected an image of toughness and confidence, and he had claimed that the nation could "stand tall" again. Many Americans shared this new sense of patriotism and regarded the president as the man who would make them proud again and who could—and did—stand up to the Soviets. Even President Reagan's admirers and supporters were puzzled. They knew that if congressional investigators had been able to find a "smoking gun" linking the scandal to the Oval Office, Reagan might, like Nixon before him, have faced impeachment for his violation of federal laws. As it was, he survived the crisis and left office with a clouded reputation. The Iran-contra scandal also haunted the administration of Reagan's successor, George H. W. Bush.[13]

Alliance Politics in the Late Cold War

The Reagan administration's early attacks on détente, its preoccupation with rearmament, its reluctance to engage in arms control negotiations, and its vigorous pursuit of the Reagan Doctrine exerted great pressure on the Soviet Union throughout the 1980s. This pressure exacerbated the already strong tensions within the Warsaw Pact countries, where long years of political repression and economic stagnation had left people increasingly frustrated and restive.

Along the way, the renewed Cold War also strained the Western alliance and provoked public demonstrations from Washington to Bonn. Old questions resurfaced about the status of Western Europe as a potential superpower battleground, about the dominant role of the United States in NATO, and about the freedom of each member of NATO to

13. The U.S. government's misunderstanding of Central American politics in general, and Nicaragua in particular, ensured that such foreign policy miscues would continue. See Robert A. Pastor, *Condemned to Repetition: The United States and Nicaragua* (Princeton, N.J.: Princeton University Press, 1987).

pursue its own foreign policy. But the most important confrontation came over the issue of new Soviet missile deployments, which compelled the United States to propose its own series of new installations of intermediate-range missiles in Europe. With both the NATO and Warsaw Pact alliances wavering, the outcome of the most recent standoff in Europe was very much in doubt: Would NATO disintegrate because of its members' internal differences? Or would the Warsaw Pact succumb to its own deficiencies and to the mounting pressure from the West?

As these and other questions loomed, Reagan's policies produced great volatility on both sides of the iron curtain. What few people anticipated, however, was that this latest round of alliance posturing and self-doubt was a prelude to resolution of the post–World War II division of Europe. The curtain was falling rapidly on the Cold War.

POLAND AND THE RISE OF SOLIDARITY

The first crack in the Soviet empire came in Poland, where in 1980 a labor union, asserting first its economic rights and then its political demands, led the Soviet-backed communist government to impose martial law. This crackdown, reminiscent of past actions in Eastern Europe, further inflamed Cold War tensions.

It was ironic that it was in Poland, a so-called people's democracy and a communist state that purported to represent and protect the interests of the working class, that a truly spontaneous workers' revolution against their exploiters occurred and threatened the Communist Party's monopoly of power and control. Stimulated by a failing economy—the result of poor political leadership, inefficient bureaucratic planning, and mismanagement—Polish workers demanded the right to form their own independent trade union that would have the right to strike. Even though such a demand was unheard of in a communist country where the party claimed to embody the workers' aspirations, the Polish workers, and their leader, Lech Walesa, rejected this notion and challenged the party's legitimacy.

After strikes brought down the government, the new political leadership recognized the right of the workers to form their own union, called Solidarity.[14] In effect, this development eliminated the party's monopoly of power. Solidarity then began to issue demands that were not only economic but also political. As the party-controlled government retreated before each demand, the demands increased and the party withdrew further in the face of threatened strikes. With each success, Solidarity grew more militant, publicly asserting that it was "the authentic voice of

14. See Lawrence Goodwyn, *Breaking the Barrier: The Rise of Solidarity in Poland* (New York: Oxford University Press, 1991).

the working class" and announcing support for other East European workers who also might wish to form independent unions. Domestically, the union demanded free elections, free speech, and a voice in government policy, including running the economy.

Although the Soviets accused Solidarity of provocative behavior, they refrained from invading Poland. This restraint contrasted sharply with earlier Soviet behavior in Hungary (1956) and Czechoslovakia (1968). In those countries, the Soviet army had intervened when the Communist Party's monopoly of power was threatened. Yet Poland, where the Soviets had not intervened, was far more critical geographically than either country. It was the nation through which every Western invader of Russia had marched and through which the Soviet Union had projected its power into the center of Europe after World War II.

Nevertheless, the risks and costs of direct Soviet intervention were great. The Soviets recognized that Solidarity was not just a trade union seeking better working conditions; it also represented a well-organized mass movement. In suppressing Solidarity, the Soviets faced the real possibility of a clash with units of the Polish army, the costs of occupation, and the difficulties of pacifying the population. In addition, the cost of paying off Poland's $27 billion debt to the West would be a drain at a time when the Soviet economy was in trouble, and any chance of establishing better relations with the United States would be jeopardized. No less important, Reagan could exploit a Soviet invasion of Poland to rally the NATO allies. Thus for more than a year Moscow demonstrated remarkable restraint. When the move against Solidarity finally came in December 1981, it was the Polish military and police who arrested the union leaders and imposed martial law in Poland.

Whether Moscow ordered the intervention or the Polish government acted on its own, there can be little doubt of increasing Soviet pressure to crack down on what the Soviets called "counterrevolutionary" elements. Solidarity, by winning the sympathies of almost ten million members, about one-third of the population, was a living refutation of the party's claim of representation; it symbolized the bankruptcy of communism. Unable either to produce a decent standard of living or to tolerate a minimal degree of freedom, communism in Poland had forfeited its legitimacy. The lesson was not lost on other parts of Eastern Europe, where the struggle by Solidarity served as an inspiration and a precursor of greater challenges to come.

THE MISSILE DEBATE IN EUROPE

In Western Europe, one almost heard a collective sigh of relief that the Red Army had not invaded Poland. The Polish army's crackdown was considered a domestic affair, not a matter over which détente would be sacrificed. This reaction reflected anxieties in the region about the growing hostilities between East and West, with Western Europeans finding themselves trapped in the middle. Indeed, it had become apparent in the early 1980s that Western Europeans wanted to pursue an independent foreign policy while still counting on the United States for their defense. They wanted to "uncouple" themselves politically from Washington but to remain "coupled" militarily. But even the military relationship was called into question when public opinion in Western Europe turned against a decision, collectively agreed to by the United States and its NATO allies, to meet the threat of new intermediate-range Soviet missiles (SS-20s) with a new generation of NATO missiles to be deployed in the region.

The intermediate-range nuclear force (INF) deployments were supposed to reassure the allies, who were troubled by the Soviet SS-20s. Instead of being strengthened by new American resolve, however, the NATO "marriage," in the words of the French foreign minister, came close to a divorce. Huge crowds in many countries demonstrated for months against the proposed deployment of the new missiles, with the greatest opposition in West Germany. There, the Protestant churches, universities, Social Democratic opposition party, and a new political movement, the pro-peace and proenvironment Green Party, were all opposed to the deployment. Moscow was not considered the chief threat. Washington, which had defended Western Europe since 1949 and had not yet deployed a single Pershing II missile, was charged with being the bigger menace to peace.

Reagan felt compelled to respond to the demonstrations in Europe and to the Soviet initiative. He proposed a "zero-zero option" whereby the United States would not deploy any of its Pershings and cruise missiles if the Soviets dismantled all of their intermediate-range missiles, which had a maximum range of 1,500 miles. It sounded good; all such missiles were to be eliminated. What could be more beneficial for peace and more moral than doing away with a whole class of dangerous weapons? The United States, however, did not expect Moscow to accept this offer. The zero-zero option was a public relations move; by turning it down, the Soviets would enable the U.S. deployment to go ahead as a clearly necessary and defensive move; the street demonstrations would decline; and the blame for the American missile buildup in Europe would be placed at the Kremlin's door.

The intra-NATO "missile crisis," however, had by then done considerable damage to the alliance. For many Europeans, the protests against INF deployment expressed their concern about Reagan's foreign policy and, more generally, their desire to reduce the risk of war. For many

Americans, the protests were a reminder that Europeans did not appear ready to take the measures necessary for their own defense. Although their combined population and industrial output exceeded that of the Soviet Union, America's European allies were still unwilling to increase the size of their conventional forces. They wanted to continue relying on the American strategic deterrent at a time when the superpowers strategically neutralized one another. The U.S. government, consequently, faced a no-win situation; both action and inaction provoked bitter criticism from Europe.

In the United States, demands began for the withdrawal of some or all American forces from Europe over a period of several years. Most of the American defense budget allocated for hardware and maintenance was not spent on nuclear forces; half went for the upkeep of the more expensive conventional forces whose primary mission was the defense of Europe. When the NATO alliance had been formed, the European nations still vividly remembered their attempts to appease a totalitarian regime, the defeats and suffering of World War II, their postwar collapse, and their need for American protection against the new threat from the East. By the 1970s and 1980s, these memories were fading. Protected by the United States, that generation had little awareness of a central facet of international politics: good intentions in the absence of countervailing military power against a determined adversary could not assure a lasting peace.

For a time, the missile crisis faded as the deployment continued. Then in a complete turnabout, Gorbachev accepted the earlier Reagan proposal for the complete elimination of intermediate-range missiles for both powers. The Soviet leader needed a relaxation of international tensions in order to give priority to domestic affairs and rebuilding the Soviet economy. The administration's determination had paid off. It had not abandoned the deployment, nor, when the Soviets responded by walking out of all arms control negotiations, had it delayed deployment, despite widespread calls to do so. Unable to achieve Soviet goals with threats, Moscow capitulated.

The zero-zero solution was a significant achievement that meant trading about fourteen hundred Soviet warheads for just over three hundred U.S. warheads. This move eliminated an entire class of weapons rather than placing limits on their deployment—as in SALT I and SALT II. Moscow also accepted intrusive verification procedures to monitor the agreement. In retrospect, the Soviet turnabout was the first sign that the Soviet Union needed a cease-fire in the Cold War. Resolution by the United States had paid off.

It was clear, however, that Europeans' confidence in the United States had weakened severely since Vietnam. During the Nixon-Ford détente years, Europeans had complained about possible U.S.-Soviet deals at Europe's expense; during the Carter years, of vacillation and weakness; and during the Reagan years, of too much machismo or "Ramboism." Europe's fear of war also had risen. Not Soviet behavior, but the arms race itself, was seen as the critical danger, as was "provocative" American behavior in remote regions that could ignite a head-on clash in Europe. These attitudes translated into public doubts about the value of NATO and growing worries about American hegemony in Western Europe.

From Confrontation to Conciliation

The tensions of the 1980s may have ruptured the cohesion of both alliances, but, in the end, as Reagan left office in January 1989 U.S.-Soviet relations were better than they had been since the two countries had been allies against Nazi Germany during World War II. How could that be? How, in a few years, could such a profound transformation of superpower relations have occurred?

The rapidity of the change was astounding. The Cold War had spanned more than four decades, exceeding the time that had elapsed from the beginning of World War I (1914) to the end of World War II (1945). Moreover, the 1970s had been a period of great confusion and self-doubt for the United States. Having withdrawn from Vietnam without victory, the nation was shaken further by the Watergate scandal. Meanwhile, the U.S. economy and that of other Western nations had suffered twice from oil shocks during the decade. Some of the most ominous events occurred in 1979: the Somoza government fell to the Sandinistas in Nicaragua; the Iranians seized the U.S. embassy and fifty-two American hostages; and the Soviets took control of Afghanistan. In general, the 1970s deflated American confidence like no other decade in the twentieth century. By contrast, the Soviet Union appeared confident and optimistic about the future course of the balance of power.

The apparent successes of the Soviet Union were deceptive, however, for two reasons. The first was the failure of the Soviet economy. Its economic growth rate, 5 percent in the 1960s and only 2 percent by the early 1970s, had stagnated by 1980. It was capable of producing only a plentiful supply of weapons and no longer able to supply basic goods and public services. After harvests failed repeatedly in the 1970s, grains and produce had to be imported from the United States and other countries. By the late 1980s, the Soviets were importing many necessities. and basic foodstuffs were being rationed. The centralized Soviet economy was nearing a breakdown. Gorbachev, who when first appointed general secretary in 1985 had believed that economic growth could be stimulated by more discipline in the workplace, less worker absenteeism and drunkenness, and higher productivity, by 1987 realized the severity of the crisis he faced. The second reason for the Soviet turnabout was the cost of Brezhnev's foreign policy. With a gross domestic product (GDP) that was half that of the United States and a military budget that the CIA estimated at 16 percent of GDP (compared with 6 percent for the United States and 3 percent for Western Europe), the civilian economy was starved.

Outside the Soviet Union, Moscow's unrelenting arms buildup and expansionist activities in developing countries had produced fear and suspicion of Soviet intentions. The result was the very encirclement Soviet leaders had long feared. In Asia, the growing Soviet threat allowed the United States to play divide-and-conquer, attracting China to the Western coalition in a decisive shift of power. Thus the Soviet Union, like Germany at the turn of the century, had created its own worst nightmare and increased its sense of vulnerability.

The United States played no small role in this scenario. American-supplied weapons had raised the price of the Afghanistan intervention, placing victory out of reach, and prolonged the civil war in Angola. Although the administration did not succeed in overthrowing the Sandinistas in Nicaragua, the Soviet effort to sustain that revolutionary faction was the only bargain in an otherwise unending financial drain. The imperial outposts that had looked so promising only ten years earlier had now lost their luster, and support for proxies such as Cuba, Ethiopia, and Vietnam had become prohibitively expensive. Gorbachev had no choice but to appreciate what Marxists always had prided themselves on recognizing: objective reality. The Soviet Union—hampered by a structurally unsound economy, looking at a resurgent U.S. economy (despite its rapidly increasing federal and trade deficits), and surrounded by a strengthened Western alliance—was forced to recognize the need for conciliation with the United States.

The Soviet weakness and consequent desire to end the Cold War first became apparent in 1987, when the Soviet delegates walked back into the INF talks and accepted virtually all U.S. demands. Even more significant, Gorbachev and his supporters contradicted long-held Soviet doctrine and positions by stating that (1) the "all-human value of peace" would now take precedence over the class struggle; (2) Soviet (and American) security could not be achieved unless there was "common security"; (3) security could best be achieved not by threats of force but by political negotiation and compromise; (4) "reasonable sufficiency" would be the new standard by which the Soviet Union would judge the military strength it needed; (5) Soviet forces would be reorganized in a "nonoffensive" manner so that NATO would be reassured; and (6) superpower negotiations would seek to reduce disparities in all classes of weapons, thereby assuring a balance of forces and further assuring cooperation.

In the developing countries, Moscow de-emphasized the revolutionary struggle for national liberation and muted its rhetoric about the future of socialism. In addition, by withdrawing from Afghanistan and helping to resolve several other regional conflicts, Gorbachev reduced Soviet foreign policy costs and diminished the likelihood of new conflicts with the United States and the chance that current ones would undermine the emerging improvement in U.S.-Soviet relations. More broadly, Gorbachev sought to deprive the American-led coalition encircling the Soviet bloc of an enemy. His "charm offensive," including visits abroad, was very effective in Europe, especially in West Germany, where "Gorby" rated far higher as a statesman and peacemaker than either Reagan or his vice president and successor, George Bush.

Gorbachev changed priorities and launched his program of *glasnost* (openness) and *perestroika* (restructuring) to revitalize Soviet society and the economy. He realized that the two were intimately related: without more openness in Soviet society, without a harnessing of the energies of the Soviet people, long used to suppression and obedience, the Soviet economy would not recover from its stagnation. Gorbachev advocated strengthening civil liberties—more freedom in the press, arts, literature, scholarship, and even in the reexamination of the darker side of Soviet history, long kept secret. He also called for decentralizing the economy, cutting back on the pervasive role of the Moscow-based central planning bureaucracy, and permitting the profit motive and market forces a greater role in stimulating production, including a degree of private ownership and entrepreneurship. And he urged the removal of the Communist Party from the daily management of the economy and other sectors of Soviet life, permitted real but limited competition in party and legislative elections, and allowed the Soviet parliament to assert itself, plus a host of other reforms.

The shift from competition to conciliation was further propelled by the amicable personal relationship between Gorbachev and Reagan. Both leaders came to power with deeply entrenched ideological differences and suspicions regarding the other superpower. Although no prospect existed for resolving the ideological rivalry, the two leaders came to respect one another through the process of summit diplomacy. Their recognition of shared interests and opportunities for mutually beneficial agreements emerged gradually from these recurring face-to-face contacts. As a result, "the overwhelming suspicion characteristic of the Cold War was gradually replaced by trust—not blind trust, but trust supported and reinforced by proof that promises were kept." [15]

15. Jack F. Matlock Jr., *Reagan and Gorbachev: How the Cold War Ended* (New York: Random House, 2004), 319.

Gorbachev's reform efforts were not embraced by all Soviets, however. He faced strong resistance from Communist Party officials and government bureaucrats, who had a vested interest in the status quo. Change threatened their jobs, status, and privileges. Opposition to Gorbachev was further fueled by the fear that any loosening of central controls would be harmful, if not fatal, politically. It was the ethnic Russians who in the Soviet Union, as in czarist Russia, controlled the levers of power and feared that such a devolution of power away from Moscow might result in calls for political power among the dozens of non-Russian nationalities. Economic decentralization would then spill over into political chaos. In other words, the fundamental structural reforms required by the Soviet Union might threaten not only the party's sole control of power but also Moscow's imperial control over its own vast frontier. The ongoing unrest in the Baltic republics (Estonia, Latvia, and Lithuania) and similar agitation in the central Asian republics were in this respect very worrisome. This uneasiness was compounded by the mounting efforts of Eastern European governments to throw off their communist yokes. Quite contrary to Marxist analysis, the political system determined the fate of the economy rather than the other way around. The Soviet political system had become the greatest obstacle to economic modernization. That was why Gorbachev, besieged by internal problems and challenges, had to end the Cold War.

CHAPTER EIGHT

The End of the Cold War

German citizens celebrate the opening of the Berlin Wall in November 1989. The wall, erected during the height of the Cold War, symbolized the division of Europe into two blocs, one controlled by the Soviet Union and the other within the American sphere of influence. In opening the wall, these German citizens effectively demonstrated that the Cold War was over.

The implosion of the Soviet bloc had already begun by the time George H. W. Bush became president in January 1989. Mikhail Gorbachev's reforms were rapidly undermining the Communist Party's hold in Moscow, the Baltic states were demanding independence, and the first streams of Eastern Europeans were making their way across the iron curtain with the reluctant assent of their crippled political leaders. Some analysts (including George Kennan, father of the containment policy) proclaimed the Cold War effectively over. Others suggested more cautiously that it was coming to a close, perhaps.

President Bush was a lifelong politician who lacked Ronald Reagan's flamboyance and his convictions. But his experience as director of the Central Intelligence Agency (CIA), ambassador to China, and U.S. representative to the United Nations left little doubt that he was competent in foreign affairs. When he became president, Bush said he would not use the term *Cold War* to characterize America's latest relationship with the Soviet Union. He referred instead to a period of U.S.-Soviet relations "beyond containment" in which the principal task would be to integrate the Soviet Union into the "community of nations." In 1990, however, after citing the "Revolution of '89" in his State of the Union address, Bush said the changes in Eastern Europe had been so striking and momentous that they marked "the beginning of a new era in the world's affairs." This proclamation proved to be an understatement.

In truth, very few observers, including the most experienced and perceptive analysts of international relations, anticipated the sudden collapse of the Soviet system. Most predicted either a prolonged stalemate between the superpowers, a gradual convergence of the capitalist and communist systems, or, more gloomily, an apocalyptic military showdown. The suggestion that one of the two superpowers would simply disappear from the world map without a shot being fired and virtually without preconditions would have been rejected as sheer fantasy. Napoleonic France, imperial Japan, and Nazi Germany did not just vanish. They had to be defeated on the battlefield, at horrendous cost.

For Bush, the principal task of American foreign policy would be to manage this historic transition as smoothly as possible. The president sought to ensure that the demise of the Warsaw Pact and, later, of the Soviet Union, would not be followed by new crises in world politics. Bush looked forward to a harmonious new era in which the benefits of the Western political and economic system would be extended into the former communist bloc and provide the basis for global stability and prosperity.

Bush's Management of the Soviet Collapse

At first, the Bush administration was not sure what to believe about the Cold War and its apparent end. In the context of more than forty years of strained relations and of previously dashed hopes that the Cold War was over, the administration—and especially the president—tended to be cautious. If Gorbachev were to fall and be replaced by a hard-line conservative, the United States did not want to be caught off guard. Nevertheless, Secretary of State James A. Baker III, a holdover from the Reagan team, acknowledged that the "new thinking" in Soviet foreign and defense policies created opportunities for East-West cooperation that were unimaginable a few years earlier.[1] Uncertainty about Soviet reforms was all the more reason to seize the opportunities represented by Gorbachev. Thus after a period of hesitation, the Bush administration followed President Reagan's lead and embraced Gorbachev, whose continuation in power was deemed good for the United States.

Events, already moving rapidly, accelerated both within the Soviet Union and beyond as the 1980s ended. In these circumstances, predicting what lay ahead for the Soviet Union was risky business, because the changes had come so quickly and had been so unexpected. The year 1990 witnessed growing upheaval in Moscow as the communist system, seventy-three years after its inception, began to crack. It became apparent that the Soviet Union was operating from a position of grave weakness and that Gorbachev's foreign policy amounted to a diplomacy of retreat and damage control. The result was that regardless of who held power in Moscow, the United States had a golden opportunity to exploit the shifting balance of power. Any leader of the Soviet Union would face severe domestic constraints on the conduct of foreign policy.

As the victorious power in the Cold War, the United States had to give thought to its terms of peace. What kind of post–Cold War world did the United States wish to see? Washington, in short, had to define its goals. Even if Gorbachev did not survive, the United States needed to take advantage of the time he was in office to ensure that Soviet concessions would be irreversible. Granted, America's influence on Soviet internal affairs was limited, and the ultimate success of the Gorbachev policy of *perestroika* (restructuring) depended on events within the Soviet Union. But if the United States were responsive to Gorbachev's policies and proposals, it could assist the process of domestic reform and bolster his position in the Kremlin. Washington's principal recourse, therefore, was to lend its support to the peaceful reform of the Soviet state.

The Soviet Union's negotiating position was very weak—a problem that was to worsen as Eastern Europe defected, ethnic nationalism grew, and communism as a political and economic system was directly challenged inside the Kremlin. Yet Gorbachev would not surrender unconditionally. Thus American leaders could not simply impose their terms

1. See James A. Baker III, with Thomas M. DeFrank, *The Politics of Diplomacy: Revolution, War, and Peace, 1989–1992* (New York: Putnam, 1995), chap. 5.

on Moscow. Moreover, a victory that humiliated the loser would result in a peace built on sand. World War I had ended with a victor's peace imposed on Germany, but it had lasted only as long as Germany remained weak. After World War II, both Germany and Japan were treated in a more conciliatory fashion. Neither, therefore, had been bent on revenge. For a durable peace, the Soviet Union also had to find the emerging international order hospitable. The two powers therefore embarked upon complex negotiations about the terms on which the Cold War would end, as well as about the construction and shape of the new balance of power.

The final resolution of the Cold War depended basically on the fulfillment of three conditions: (1) dismantling Joseph Stalin's empire in Central and Eastern Europe, (2) detaching Leonid Brezhnev's outposts in developing countries, and (3) reducing arms and achieving a stable nuclear balance. When these conditions were fulfilled, Bush was thrust into the tenuous position of managing the disintegration of the Soviet Union and directing the transition of U.S. bilateral relations toward the largest successor state, Boris Yeltsin's Russia.

DISMANTLING STALIN'S EMPIRE

Events in China during the summer of 1989 served as a prelude to the autumn uprisings in Eastern Europe and suggested that the erosion of communism's appeal and legitimacy had extended to the world's most populous communist state. As in Moscow, dissidents in Beijing had been granted greater freedom to express their grievances in public and to exercise some degree of political freedom. After they erected a miniature Statue of Liberty in Beijing's Tiananmen Square, however, the communist government moved in with tanks and brutally quashed the growing rebellion. The worldwide television audience that witnessed these events was understandably horrified. China's decrepit regime dismissed the condemnation of foreign governments and intensified its crackdown on pro-democracy activists. When their time came, Eastern Europeans were inspired by the Chinese example to accelerate their own anticommunist revolution and guarantee that it could not be turned back.

One important sign of Soviet willingness to end the Cold War was its acceptance of Eastern Europe's rapid moves away from Communist Party control. The Soviet Union's conquest and Stalinization of Eastern Europe, together with the division of Germany, had split the continent after World War II. This division was at the heart of the Cold War, and only self-determination for Poland, Hungary, Czechoslovakia, and the other Eastern European states could end it. Events in Central Europe also were critical because each of the major wars of the twentieth century had broken out there. The disintegration of the Austro-Hungarian Empire had led to the eruption of successive Balkan wars and World War I; Germany's absorption of Austria and Czechoslovakia and its invasion of Poland had sparked World War II; and the de facto Soviet annexation of Eastern Europe had led to the Cold War.

American foreign policy during World War II had been sensitive to Soviet security concerns in Eastern Europe, but the United States also had been committed to national self-determination. President Franklin Roosevelt had presumed that after the war Soviet security and need for a protective boundary of sympathetic nations could be made compatible with democratic freedom in Eastern Europe. His thinking reflected that of a traditional great power: small nations living within a superior power's sphere of influence do not have to have governments that reflect the latter's ideological and political values. They must, however, be willing to make virtues out of necessities: to make the best of their geographic situation, to be aware of their constrained freedom and maneuverability, and to acquiesce to the wishes of the regionally dominant power.

But Soviet ideology defined security in Marxist terms: the communist regime could be secure only if potential class enemies—even those who frowned on relations with capitalist states—were kept out of power. As for the Soviet troops stationed throughout Eastern Europe, they were intended not merely to protect these states from perceived Western threats, but also to assure that these states adhered to Soviet control.

Could Moscow in the late 1980s separate its ideology from its definition of security? The initial answer came in 1989 in Poland. The Communist Party there was unable to form a government after its disastrous showing in the free June elections in which the Solidarity labor movement had claimed overwhelming popular support. Because the communists had been repudiated, Solidarity, which had in effect received a mandate to govern, was asked to organize the government. Poland thus formed its first noncommunist—indeed anticommunist—government in the post–World War II era. However, Lech Walesa, Solidarity's leader and spokesman, announced that Poland would remain a member of the Warsaw Pact—just the kind of political sensitivity that Roosevelt had in mind.

Gorbachev was willing to accept a noncommunist Poland and a more traditional sphere of influence in Eastern Europe for several reasons. One was his preoccupation with worsening domestic matters. Another was that Eastern Europe had not proved to be a security belt. Instead, the region had added to Soviet *insecurity*. Its people were sullen and resentful of the Soviet-imposed regimes, and they had not forgotten that earlier efforts to rid themselves of these regimes had been suppressed by brute force. Gorbachev did not want to be confronted with an explosive situation that, among other things, would be a major, if not fatal, setback to the reemerging détente with the West. The installation of more acceptable and legitimate governments would avoid this confrontation and thus enhance Soviet security. Furthermore, because of the strains on the Soviet economy, he could not afford continued subsidies to Poland and the rest of Eastern Europe to prop up their troubled economies. It made eminent sense, therefore, to unburden his floundering economy. Finally, by accepting a more modest sphere of influence, he could resolve a principal issue that had precipitated and prolonged the Cold War.

The dominoes fell throughout 1989. In Hungary, the parliament dropped the word "People" from the country's formal name, and the Communist Party renamed itself the Democratic Socialist Party in order to survive a Polish-style disaster in the upcoming multiparty elections. (Even so, the party kept only 30,000 of its original 720,000 members.) Similarly, Czechoslovakia dropped "Socialist" from its name, and the East German Communist Party also sought to shed its Stalinist skin to better compete in the 1990 elections. In a decision of critical importance, the Hungarian foreign minister opened his country's borders with Austria on September 10, 1989. A free fall then ensued when 200,000 East Germans, mostly young, skilled workers vital to that nation's industry, fled their country—via Czechoslovakia, Hungary, and Austria—for West Germany. These events collectively foreshadowed the "terminal crisis of Communism." [2]

To make the best of the situation, Gorbachev announced that socialist countries had no right to intervene in each other's affairs; each country was responsible for its own destiny. The clear implication was that the Brezhnev Doctrine was dead. To make the point clearly, in late 1989 Gorbachev paid a symbolic visit to Finland, a country that always had been sensitive to Soviet security interests and yet had maintained a relatively autonomous democracy. He presented Finland as a model of a relationship between a big and little country that were neighbors but had different social systems. Gorbachev also visited East Germany to observe its fortieth anniversary as a communist state. There, by stating the new doctrine of nonintervention, he further propelled the demise of the Warsaw Pact. The process gained even more momentum after Moscow and its four Warsaw Pact allies that had jointly invaded Czechoslovakia in 1968 condemned that invasion as "illegal" and pledged a strict policy of noninterference in each other's affairs. Moscow issued its own declaration of repentance.

Gorbachev's actions were most keenly felt in East Germany, where the exodus of its youth threatened to depopulate the country of sixteen mil-

2. Zbigniew Brzezinski, *The Grand Failure: The Birth and Death of Communism in the Twentieth Century* (New York: Scribner's, 1989).

lion and undermine its hopes for the future. Mass demonstrations finally led to the removal of its despotic communist leader, Erich Honecker, in December 1989. In what was a genuine people's revolution, Soviet troops stood by instead of propping up the regime, and the new party leader promised radical changes, including free elections in May 1990. Among the first reforms, all restrictions on travel and emigration were lifted, inciting hundreds of thousands of East Germans to scale the Berlin Wall in the hours after that announcement. Altogether, 1.5 million East Germans poured across the wall that first weekend. As for the wall itself, entire sections were leveled with sledgehammers, and fragments were taken home as souvenirs. From its construction in 1961, the wall had been the embodiment of what the Cold War was all about—tyranny versus freedom. Its collapse on November 9, 1989, exactly fifty-one years after Adolf Hitler unleashed his storm troopers against German Jews, symbolized more than any other event the end of the Cold War.

After the fall of the Berlin Wall, the winds of change swept over Czechoslovakia. What happened there also had great symbolic importance, although it was not widely noted at the time because of the tumult elsewhere. The great powers had inflicted tremendous injustices on Czechoslovakia, the only central European democracy before World War II. The country had been betrayed by France and England in their efforts to appease Hitler in 1938. A decade later, it had been violently transformed into a communist nation by the Soviets. Efforts to introduce a more democratic form of communism during the Prague Spring of 1968 had been crushed by Soviet tanks. The collapse of the communist regime in Prague, therefore, also was a sign of the times.

Everywhere in Eastern Europe—in what Ronald Reagan had once called the "evil empire"—people were saying openly just how evil that empire had been. They demanded not just the reform of communist parties but their removal from office, ending what many saw as nearly a half-century of foreign occupation. They also called for free elections and interim governments composed mainly of noncommunists. Only in Bulgaria and Romania did the local communist parties manage to run under new names, promising that they had reformed, and easily win the first free elections after the collapse of the Soviet-supported governments.

The United States responded by expressing support for the new governments of Eastern Europe, and President Bush provided a visible show of support by visiting Poland and Hungary in 1989. Beyond this effort, however, Bush did not want to arouse Soviet security concerns. In fact, Gorbachev, with these concerns in mind, sought a tacit understanding with Bush. The Soviet leader would continue to support, if not encourage, the transformations in Eastern Europe, and he would not resist the changes even if they went further down the road to "decommunization" than he preferred. In return, the United States would not exploit the geopolitical transformation then under way in the Soviet empire, nor would it jeopardize Soviet security or add to the humiliation Moscow already was suffering from the popular rejection of communism by its Warsaw Pact allies. Because it was in Washington's interest to manage the changes in the Soviet Union and Eastern Europe peacefully, the Gorbachev-Bush bargain held.

The path of nonviolent transformation was chosen not only by the Eastern European rulers but also by the masses, even though they had been exploited and oppressed by Soviet-imposed regimes for forty years. Only Romania fell into violence as its dictator, Nicolae Ceausescu, sought in vain to buck the trend in the rest of Eastern Europe and stay in power. But he failed; army units defected to the opposition and fought his security forces. Captured as they attempted to flee, Ceausescu and his wife, Elena, were executed on Christmas Day 1989 after a hasty trial. With that single exception, nonviolence prevailed. Czechoslovakia's new president, the playwright Vaclav Havel, set the tone by calling on his fellow citizens to act with dignity, honesty, and honor. The slogan of the demonstrators massed in the streets of Prague was "We are not like them."

Another important issue involved the rebirth of the "German problem." For more than forty years East and West had lived with a divided Germany. Each side preferred a partitioned Germany, because such an arrangement ensured that Germany would not initiate another war. The "terminal crisis" of communism in Eastern Europe, however, ended this division. Thousands of East Germans poured into West Germany every month, further crippling the East German state, its economy, and its social cohesion. Moreover, as the authority of the East German government waned, the calls in East Germany for unification grew stronger. To everyone's surprise, the East German election held in March 1990 (earlier than planned because of the mounting crisis) was won by the followers of West German chancellor Helmut Kohl, thereby ensuring reunification. The large votes for the Christian Democrats and the Social Democrats, both tied to their West German counterparts, amounted to a death sentence for the German Democratic Republic and an endorsement of a "buyout" by the richer and more powerful West Germans.

But a reunited Germany, even a democratic one, posed all sorts of problems and potential instabilities. In fact, the collapse of the Warsaw Pact and the inevitable, increasingly imminent, reunification of Germany meant constructing a new European balance of power. Western officials insisted that the reunited Germany be a member of the North Atlantic Treaty Organization (NATO). They did, however, offer Moscow several reassurances. First, no Western armies, including German troops assigned to NATO, would be stationed on former East German territory.

in view of Moscow's certain opposition to the presence of NATO troops on the Polish border. Second, during a three- to four-year transition period, the 380,000 Soviet troops already in East Germany would remain there. Germany also would guarantee its neighbors' borders, renew West Germany's pledge that it would not seek to acquire nuclear weapons, and agree to limit its armed forces to 370,000, below West Germany's 474,000 in 1990 and well below the 667,000 level of the two Germanies.

Gorbachev's initial opposition was based on memories of the German defeat of czarist Russia in World War I and of the twenty million Soviet lives lost repelling German invasion in World War II. He insisted that a reunited Germany be a neutral, disarmed state. But this condition was unacceptable to virtually everyone else, and probably even Moscow did not think it was the best solution. The real question was whether a united but neutralized Germany would become once more a nationalistic, dangerously destabilizing force on the continent. Pushed even by his former allies to accept a reunited Germany restrained by the NATO alliance, Gorbachev proposed that Germany be a member of both the Warsaw Pact and NATO. But this condition, too, was rejected as merely another formula for neutrality.

Nevertheless, Gorbachev, weak or not, continued to resist the Western solution. He realized that when it came, the collapse of East Germany would spell the end of a major Soviet Cold War goal: hegemony over Europe based on neutralizing West Germany. Even more humiliating, a reunited Germany would likely emerge as the financial and economic center of Europe, the dominant power in Eastern Europe, and the principal source of capital and machinery for the Soviet Union.

In July 1990, however, only four months after declaring that German membership in NATO was "absolutely out of the question," Gorbachev bowed to the inevitable and accepted a reunited Germany in NATO. His acceptance was made easier by the promise of $8 billion in German credits to help the failing Soviet economy. Nevertheless, like his acceptance of a larger number of U.S. troops than Soviet troops in the new Europe, Gorbachev's acquiescence to German membership in NATO was tantamount to Soviet surrender. This event had none of the drama of VE Day or VJ Day, which in 1945 marked the end of the war in Europe and in the Pacific, respectively. Yet history will note July 16, 1990, as the day the Soviet Union gave up, effectively ending the Cold War. Indeed, the American insistence on Soviet acceptance of Germany's admission to NATO appeared in large part driven by the need to clarify this issue.

An all-German election of an all-German parliament was set for December 2, 1990. The new year would therefore start with the convocation of the new parliament and the formation of the new government. As for the future, the reunited Germany would assume the role of

Europe's most powerful economic actor and, like Japan, the other country vanquished in World War II, would quickly become a principal actor in the post–Cold War multipolar international system. The world hoped, however, that Germany's preponderant size, population, and economic power would be directed not toward fulfilling selfish interests but toward serving as a catalyst for political stability and economic growth throughout Europe and, indeed, within the Soviet Union.

DETACHING BREZHNEV'S OUTPOSTS

The second condition for ending the Cold War was Soviet cooperation in resolving regional conflicts in the developing world. As noted earlier, Soviet support for Marxist regimes and insurgencies had hindered U.S.-Soviet relations for decades. But now the Soviet Union's desire to avoid trouble with the United States was likely to prevent further challenges.

Gorbachev's reversal of his country's expansionism was dramatic. The Soviets withdrew from Afghanistan and later admitted that the invasion had been a mistake, a result of their foreign policy's overreliance on force. In Angola, after prolonged negotiations failed to achieve the exit of fifty thousand Cuban troops from that country in return for South Africa's withdrawal from Namibia, a deal was struck under which the Cubans would withdraw in return for the independence of Namibia.[3] In Southeast Asia, with Soviet encouragement, Vietnam withdrew from Cambodia. And in the Middle East, Moscow moved initially toward rapprochement with Israel—it had broken diplomatic relations in 1967—and later toward the reestablishment of relations. It also supported the U.S. objective of an Israeli-Palestinian treaty and raised the possibility of increased Jewish emigration from the Soviet Union to Israel.

But in Central America, the Soviets continued to supply arms to revolutionary forces despite soothing words about seeking peaceful settlements. Soviet arms shipments to the Nicaraguan government, although reduced, continued; shipments from Cuba made up the difference. Soviet-made weapons also reached the communist rebels in El Salvador, who launched attacks on the capital city of San Salvador in 1989. Bush strongly protested these policies of support as "Cold War relics," calling these countries "Brezhnevite clients" during the informal summit meeting that Gorbachev and Bush held in December 1989 off the Mediterranean island of Malta. Gorbachev denied sending weapons to Central America, but Bush would have none of it. Cuba and Nicaragua were Soviet clients. Washington clearly expected Moscow, which elsewhere

3. South African troops had frequently attacked Angola in pursuit of guerrilla forces operating in Namibia, one of the last African colonies to gain independence.

had pressured its proxies to resolve their internal and regional differences, to do the same in the Western Hemisphere.

The more critical issue was the February 1990 election in Nicaragua, which, as noted in Chapter 7, held out the promise of easing regional tensions in Central America. Gorbachev prevailed on the Sandinistas to permit free elections like those held in Eastern Europe. When the Sandinistas lost the elections, which were closely monitored by the United Nations and the Organization of American States, the Soviet Union lost yet another overseas client. National reconciliation, disbanding the contras, rebuilding the economy, ensuring a democratic and more just society, and reestablishing good relations with the United States were to be the central tasks of Nicaragua's new government.

The only remaining source of real friction between Washington and Moscow was Cuba. Castro swore that socialism would continue to be practiced on his island even if that ideology had been "betrayed" by Gorbachev and even if it were abandoned virtually everywhere else. In 1991 Moscow discontinued its massive annual subsidies to Cuba, which were largely in the form of petroleum and other necessities, announcing that future economic relations between Cuba and the Soviet Union would be on a trade-only basis. The Soviet military training brigade also would be withdrawn. The Soviet Union, itself seeking economic help from the West, was responding to the Bush administration's insistence that it would not consider providing such assistance while Moscow continued to provide Castro with the equivalent of $5 billion annually. Thus the Soviet retreat from the developing world continued.

REDUCING ARMS AND STABILIZING THE NUCLEAR BALANCE

The third condition for ending the Cold War was a reduction in superpower arms and a stable nuclear balance—a consistent U.S. goal in the evolving new superpower relationship. More specifically, U.S. policy had three objectives. The first, especially in view of Gorbachev's uncertain tenure, was to reach agreements to reduce strategic and conventional arms; once achieved, such arms reductions would be politically and economically difficult to reverse. The second objective was to reduce the likelihood of surprise attack, a goal that was pursued by both sides through a variety of confidence-building measures. And the third objective was to reduce the burden of defense spending and to realize a "peace dividend" to be spent on domestic needs.[4]

4. For Gorbachev, this financial benefit was probably the driving force behind all his arms proposals. As the U.S. budget deficit grew, Bush also wanted to see a reduction in defense spending.

From the beginning of the Strategic Arms Limitations Talks (SALT) process, the long-term objective was to cut drastically the strategic arsenals of both powers. Renamed START (Strategic Arms Reduction Talks) by the Reagan administration to emphasize more ambitious reductions—a 50 percent cut—the treaty was aimed at eliminating Soviet land-based missiles, which, with their multiple and accurate warheads, were the principal threat to the survival of American intercontinental ballistic missiles (ICBMs). In short, reductions per se were not the objective; the aim was to *stabilize* reductions. By the time Reagan left office, the START negotiations were substantially completed. Each side had agreed to a ceiling of 1,600 delivery vehicles, an aggregate of 6,000 strategic weapons, and a ballistic missile warhead limit of 4,900. Although the overall reduction in strategic forces was closer to 30 percent, the most destabilizing forces—ballistic missiles with multiple warheads—were reduced by 50 percent.

The chief obstacle from the very beginning was the Strategic Defense Initiative (SDI), or the American plan to defend its territory from incoming nuclear missiles (see Chapter 7). The Soviets insisted that they would not reduce their ICBM force until they knew whether they would have to cope with American strategic defenses. But Reagan clung to his vision of SDI, and therefore the Soviets refused to sign the START treaty. To break the deadlock, Moscow announced in 1989 its willingness to sign the treaty on the condition that the United States abide by the 1972 Antiballistic Missile Treaty.

As for conventional forces, after 1987 Gorbachev had talked repeatedly about a shift from an offensive to a defensive military doctrine, as well as sizable military budget cuts as the Soviet Union scaled its forces back to "reasonable sufficiency." He promised and carried out unilateral reductions in Soviet forces, including the withdrawal of troops and tanks facing NATO. For Warsaw Pact forces to shift to a strategy that could repel an attack but not launch a massive surprise attack on NATO was obviously very much in the West's interest. Such a shift would greatly relieve Western fears stemming from the Soviet Union's sizable forces and Soviet military doctrine, and it would be a tangible sign that Soviet intentions had fundamentally changed.

The Conventional Forces in Europe (CFE) negotiations sought to reduce Soviet forces in Eastern Europe and American forces in Western Europe to 275,000 each. The talks also sought equal numbers of tanks, armored personnel carriers, artillery pieces, and combat aircraft for the two military alliances. But events in Eastern Europe were moving so fast that in January 1990 President Bush called for a further U.S.-Soviet troop reduction in Central Europe to less than 200,000. Surprisingly,

Gorbachev accepted the U.S. proposal even though it would leave the United States with more troops in Europe than the Soviet Union, a first since World War II. Militarily, this was unimportant, but politically and psychologically it provided further evidence of Soviet disintegration. The drawdown of U.S. troops was unlikely to be the last because of the strong domestic pressure in the United States to cut U.S. forces well below 100,000.

Such reductions were possible because by 1990 the Soviet-led alliance, organized to protect the Soviet-imposed socialist systems, had little to defend as Eastern Europe defected from the Warsaw Pact. In these circumstances, Moscow could no longer count on, if it ever could, the armies of Bulgaria, Czechoslovakia, East Germany, Hungary, Poland, and Romania for any joint military action against the West. And so in 1990, Moscow agreed to withdraw its forces from Czechoslovakia, Hungary, and Poland by the end of 1992. But this pledge became irrelevant as the Warsaw Pact self-destructed first and was formally buried in 1991.

Would NATO also disappear? That was unlikely, at least in the short run, because the alliance still had several functions. One was to continue to guard the West against the possibility of a renewed Soviet (or, later, Russian) threat. There remained widespread concern that the old communist guard might overthrow Gorbachev and then reimpose Soviet hegemony in Eastern Europe.[5] Another function of NATO, not spoken of openly for diplomatic reasons, was to restrain the new Germany. After twice calling on American power to defeat it, Europeans were unsure that they alone could manage a reunified Germany. Retaining NATO would keep American power in Europe. Finally, the United States wanted the NATO alliance to serve as an institutional link through which it could influence the shape of the emerging new order in Europe as the European Community moved toward greater economic and political integration (see Chapter 11).

Bush's arms control initiatives continued even after the Soviet Union itself dissolved in late 1991; he carried on START II negotiations with Russian president Boris Yeltsin. At their June 1992 summit meeting, the two sides agreed to even deeper cuts in nuclear arms, among them the most destabilizing multiple-warhead missiles that had become a headache to strategic planners in Moscow and Washington. The agreement called for both sides to reduce their arsenals to about three thousand missiles by the year 2003, or sooner if the United States could assist the financially strapped Russians in dismantling their weapons.

5. Even after the attempted coup in August 1991 against Gorbachev, which led to the Soviet Union's own demise, Russia, the successor state, retained significant military power.

Chapter Eight

Endgame: The Collapse of the Core

Between 1989 and 1991, the Soviet Union itself underwent a rapid and profound transformation. With the disintegration of its economy, the political regime lost its legitimacy and was further weakened by internal conflicts between Moscow and some of the Soviet republics. Demands for autonomy, if not independence, erupted in many areas, and ancient ethnic feuds reemerged. These events threatened the integrity of the Soviet state and compelled the regime to move Soviet tactical nuclear warheads out of the Baltics and the volatile southern republics to parts of Russia considered more secure.

In addition, the Communist Party, showing growing signs of disintegration, was losing its authority to impose decisions on the nation. In the Baltics, Soviet communists were faced with the defection of the Lithuanian Communist Party, which identified itself with Lithuania's demand for independence. In Azerbaijan, the Soviet army had to be deployed not only to restore order between the Azerbaijanis and Armenians, but also to prevent the communist government from falling into the hands of the Azerbaijani popular front—much as communist regimes in Eastern Europe had fallen to opposition groups. In several cities and regions, party officials had to resign because of popular outrage over their corruption and privileges. Indeed, in Moscow, Leningrad, and other cities the emerging democratic political opposition inflicted embarrassing defeats on the communists by winning majorities in local elections.

Gorbachev, alert to popular disenchantment with the party, gradually shifted his base of power from the Communist Party, whose members continued to resist his reforms, to the elected Supreme Soviet and the presidency, a post he held in addition to that of general secretary of the party. A new Congress of People's Deputies was established to promote a more democratic government; elections to this body in May 1989 gave the Russian people their first taste of democracy. Gorbachev went even further by calling on the Communist Party to give up its seventy-year constitutional monopoly of power, although he clearly considered the party to be the most capable of guiding the nation through its turmoil. For the party to remain the political vanguard, however, it would have to earn the Soviet people's trust, and to do this, it would have to restructure itself. Gorbachev even suggested the establishment of rival political parties. His radical call was persuasive: in February 1990 the party's Central Committee opened the door to opposition parties. The political landscape of the Soviet Union was irreversibly transformed in this "February Revolution."

Gorbachev's strongest challenger for power was Boris Yeltsin, a former Communist Party leader who in May 1990 was elected president of

IMPACT AND INFLUENCE

MIKHAIL GORBACHEV AND BORIS YELTSIN

Amid the collapse of the Soviet Union, the peaceful transfer of power from Mikhail Gorbachev (left) to Boris Yeltsin (right) proved to be an extraordinary achievement. Indeed, Yeltsin's defense of the Soviet leader during the failed coup attempt by communist hard-liners in August 1991 preserved their generally cordial relations even as the Soviet Union crumbled around them.

Gorbachev, the last leader of the Soviet Union, could not prevent his democratic reforms from weakening the Communist Party's hold over Eastern Europe and, later, the Soviet Union itself. Once out of power, Gorbachev formed a private foundation and continued to advocate "democratic socialism." Meanwhile, Yeltsin remained president of Russia throughout the 1990s, defending his political and economic reforms against challenges from neocommunists and militant nationalists. But Russia suffered under his watch, and economic stagnation, political corruption, and a failed effort to quell a secessionist revolt in Chechnya were largely to blame. Ailing and frustrated, Yeltsin abruptly resigned on the final day of 1999 and yielded power to Prime Minister Vladimir Putin, who was elected to a full term as Russia's president in March 2000.

the Russian republic. Russia occupied two thirds of the territory of the former Soviet Union and had almost half of its population and most of its oil, natural gas reserves, and coal. Yeltsin was quick to sense the popular disaffection with the power and privileges of the Communist Party. Once Gorbachev's protégé, Yeltsin became his fiercest critic and archrival; the Soviet leader had not, in Yeltsin's judgment, moved quickly enough to change the system.

On the day after his election by the Russian parliament, Yeltsin challenged the system by proposing Russia's economic autonomy and a radical decentralization in which republic law took precedence over Soviet law and the president of the Soviet Union would have no greater authority than the presidents of the fifteen republics. Indeed, not only would Russia claim sovereignty and determine the prices of its natural resources, it also would make its own agreements with the other members of the Soviet Union. And just to make his challenge clear, Yeltsin made the Russian presidency a popularly elected office, which he won overwhelmingly. As elected president of the Soviet Union's largest republic, Yeltsin acquired a legitimacy Gorbachev never had.

A few weeks later, Yeltsin, together with the reformist mayors of Moscow and Leningrad, resigned from the Communist Party. Their resignations were symptomatic of growing national disenchantment with the party and Gorbachev's declining popularity. Next, Ukraine, the Soviet Union's second largest republic and its "breadbasket," with a population of more than fifty million, declared its sovereignty and announced that its laws would supercede those of the Soviet Union. Ukraine also claimed an independent foreign policy role by stating it would be a neutral state, it would not participate in military blocs, and it would ban the production and deployment of nuclear weapons on its territory. These actions were followed by a similar declaration from Belarus, a small but geographically vital republic located between Ukraine and the Baltic states. Eventually, all of the Soviet Union's fifteen republics issued sovereignty declarations, asserting either outright independence or more cautious assertions of their rights. Gorbachev's Soviet Union was crumbling around him, piece by piece.

By late 1990, Gorbachev had become more and more irrelevant in domestic affairs. Yeltsin was setting the pace and scope of change by supporting the drive for independence of the Baltic republics and by proposing a plan for transforming the Russian economy into a market economy within five hundred days. Gorbachev found himself maneuvering between the increasingly radical forces on the left and the forces of reaction on the right, represented by the traditional instruments of Soviet power—the military, secret police, and Communist Party bureaucracy—which had survived all his attempts at reform. They were the elite and therefore had a strong vested interest in the status quo. In the meantime, Gorbachev had his hands full just trying to hold the union together and stem the republics' nationalism. Thus he shifted his original direction and aligned himself with the forces of "law and order." He dismissed many of his former liberal allies in the struggle for *glasnost* and *perestroika,* began cracking down on the Baltic republics, and reimposed censorship.

Gorbachev's new allies, however, tried to limit his power and enhance their own, because they felt he was leading the country to chaos and anarchy. Moreover, they despised him, because he had retreated from

Eastern Europe and had given up the Soviet Union's World War II gains. In response, Gorbachev swung back to ally himself once more with the reformers. He made his peace with the republics and promised the presidents of the nine republics who agreed to stay within the union, including Yeltsin, to turn the Soviet Union into a new voluntary federation that all republics would have the right to join or not join. They also would be free to choose their own form of government and exercise most of the power over their natural resources, industry, foreign trade, and taxes. He promised a new constitution and a newly elected central government.

But just as the new All-Union Treaty was about to be signed, the hardliners struck. Fearing that their power was waning and that it soon would be too late to do anything about it, they launched a coup in August 1991, arresting Gorbachev while he was on vacation. But the coup plotters failed to understand the effects of the six years of Gorbachev's policies. Led by the popularly elected Yeltsin, who showed enormous courage in condemning the coup, the people of Moscow rallied behind Gorbachev, resisting those who would reimpose the old dictatorship. When units of the military and secret police opposed the coup, it quickly collapsed. This event struck the death blow to the Soviet Union.

All the republics now wanted their independence from Moscow and central authority. The three Baltic republics were let go, and their independence was recognized by Moscow. At this point, seven of the twelve remaining republics, including Russia, planned to stay together in a loose confederation. They were still economically interdependent, although the agriculturally and industrially important Ukraine would not commit itself to creating a "common economic space" and a single currency, the foundation of a free-market economy.

What was absolutely clear in these times of uncertainty was that the old regime had disgraced itself by the coup attempt. Statues of Stalin and Lenin were toppled and unceremoniously removed from public squares. The old imperial flag designed by Peter the Great once again flew over the Russian parliament, the center of the resistance to the coup. Leningrad was renamed St. Petersburg, its pre-revolutionary name, in accordance with the wishes of its citizens. Many said it also was time to remove Lenin's body from the mausoleum in Red Square (a step that was not taken). For all practical purposes, the Communist Party as a governing body was dead. It could no longer block the path to democracy and radical economic reform. The revolution of 1917 had been undone in a stunning sequence of events.

The republics, however, were still grappling with their future. At the moment of decision, the seven republics that had endorsed the new union would not commit themselves, leaving its fate in the hands of their national parliaments. When Ukraine voted on December 1, 1991, for independence and instantly became Europe's fourth largest country, it became clear that nothing could stop the process of Soviet disintegration. With even a weak confederation now dead, Russia was left as the successor state to the Soviet Union. This status had become overwhelmingly clear earlier, when in November 1991 the central government of the Soviet Union had declared bankruptcy and Russia assumed its debts and promised to fund what remained of the central government's ministries. In capitalist language, this act constituted a leveraged buyout of the former Soviet Union. Russia also claimed the Soviet Union's permanent seat on the UN Security Council.

The Soviet Union's demise became official on December 8, 1991. In an act of desperation to stop the complete disintegration of the nation, the presidents of the three Slavic republics—Russia, Ukraine, and Belarus—established a commonwealth and invited other republics to join. The new Commonwealth of Independent States (CIS) was to assume all the international obligations of the Soviet Union, including control over its nuclear arsenal. Coordinating bodies would be established to decide on cooperative policies in foreign affairs, defense, and economics.[6] Later, the commonwealth agreement was signed by eleven of the remaining twelve Soviet republics after the defection of the three Baltic states; the twelfth republic, Georgia, was consumed by civil war. On December 25, 1991, the red hammer-and-sickle flag that had flown over the Kremlin was lowered for the last time. Seventy-four years after the Bolshevik revolution, the Soviet Union literally disappeared from the world map.

Reasons for the Soviet Collapse

Throughout his presidency, George Bush was dogged by the accusation that he lacked a coherent vision of the future of world politics. Furthermore, he was criticized for what seemed to be an overly cautious approach to U.S.-Soviet relations, for his continuing embrace of Gorbachev after the Soviet leader lost legitimacy, and for his resistance to immediate deep cuts in American defense spending. Bush, the lifelong government bureaucrat, manager, and caretaker, presumably lacked the panache to seize such a profound historic opportunity.

Twenty-first-century historians probably will be kinder to Bush. A careful review of his performance reveals how skillfully he manipulated one of the crucial turning points in history, not only to the advantage of the United States but also in the interests of global stability. The three-

6. Internal tensions greatly limited the actual role of the CIS in the 1990s, although the commonwealth remained officially intact into the twenty-first century.

year free fall of the Soviet system was by no means a certainty when Bush arrived in office, and its peaceful demise was without precedent. In assisting Gorbachev when he urgently needed outside support, in insisting on German unification on Western terms, and in exploiting the opportunity for drastic nuclear disarmament, Bush successfully navigated the United States and its allies through a complicated phase of international relations toward their ultimate victory in a protracted conflict of global proportions. Bush was chastised for adhering to the most "prudent" approach to world politics. But history may suggest that prudence was precisely the approach the world required.[7]

THE CONTENDING ARGUMENTS IN PERSPECTIVE

Immediately after the Cold War ended, the question was raised whether the United States had "won" the war and whether its containment policy had been successful. Or was it more accurate to say that the Soviet Union, plagued by internal problems of its own making, had "lost" the Cold War? These questions—two sides of the same coin and not conducive to definitive answers—sparked a contentious debate among scholars, journalists, and policy makers.[8] But it was not merely an academic exercise, for the answers to these questions would reveal the central lessons of the Cold War, which in turn would figure in the establishment of guidelines for future American foreign policy.

Advocates of the view that the United States had "won" the Cold War claimed that the Western system of political, economic, and military organization simply had been more durable than that of the Soviet Union and its allies. Furthermore, the U.S.-led containment policy had successfully combined pressure and patience to overwhelm Soviet capabilities.[9] In other words, containment had worked much as George Kennan predicted it would nearly fifty years earlier, preventing Soviet expansion through the selective application of Western resistance.

Conversely, those believing that the Soviet Union had "lost" the war diminished the role of the containment policy. If the United States had "won," it was merely because the Soviet Union's flawed system had made its demise inevitable. Its excessive centralization of power, bureaucratic planning, and supervision of every detail of Soviet life,

7. A more thorough review of Bush's performance is provided by Michael Beschloss and Strobe Talbott in *At the Highest Levels: The Inside Story of the End of the Cold War* (Boston: Little, Brown, 1993).

8. For a review of these arguments, see *The End of the Cold War: Its Meanings and Implications,* ed. Michael J. Hogan (New York: Cambridge University Press, 1992).

9. See John Lewis Gaddis, *The United States and the End of the Cold War* (New York: Oxford University Press, 1992), 193.

economic and otherwise, as well as its command economy and ideological oppression, had contributed to its undoing.[10] Furthermore, for some neo-Marxists the demise of the Soviet Union reflected its failed application of Marxist ideals and principles, not the bankruptcy of the political theory.

Both views call for a closer look at the Soviet experience in converting the aspirations of the 1917 Russian Revolution into practice. Seventy years after the revolution, the Soviet standard of living was so low that even Eastern Europe, with its own economic problems, appeared affluent by contrast. The former Soviet Union's own statistics reveal that about 40 percent of its population and almost 80 percent of its elderly citizens lived in poverty. One-third of its households had no running water. Indeed, the Soviet Union was the only industrialized society in which infant mortality had risen and male life expectancy had *declined* in the late twentieth century. In Zbigniew Brzezinski's words, "Perhaps never before in history has such a gifted people, in control of such abundant resources, labored so hard for so long to produce so little." [11]

The Soviet economy, which was supposed to have demonstrated the superiority of socialism, sputtered for decades and then collapsed. Deliberately isolating itself from the global capitalist economy, the Soviet Union had intended to build an economy that was self-sufficient and productive, assuring a bountiful life for the workers and peasants who had been deprived for so long. Instead, the centralized command economy meant no domestic competition among firms, and its self-exclusion from the international economy ensured that it remained unchallenged by foreign competition. The Soviet economy thus became a textbook example of what free traders have long argued results from state control: inefficiency, lack of productivity, unresponsiveness to consumer needs, and technological stagnation. There was little in the writings of Karl Marx, which had more to do with revolution than communist governance, that provided a solution to this central problem.

Soviet communism was efficient only in producing military hardware. But this efficiency, ironically, also contributed to its defeat. As a state with few natural protective barriers, frequently invaded throughout its history, first Russia and then the Soviet Union kept sizable standing forces for its defense. Its twentieth-century experiences with Germany did nothing to relieve the longtime Russian sense of insecurity,

10. See Walter Laquer, *The Dream That Failed: Reflections on the Soviet Union* (New York: Oxford University Press, 1994), 50–76. Also see Charles W. Kegley Jr., "How Did the Cold War Die? Principles for an Autopsy," *Mershon International Studies Review* (summer 1994): 11–41.

11. Zbigniew Brzezinski, *Game Plan: A Geostrategic Framework for the Conduct of the U.S.-Soviet Contest* (Boston: Atlantic Monthly Press, 1986), 123. Also see Brzezinski, *Grand Failure.*

fueled by the Marxist conception of politics as a constant struggle and its perception that enemies were everywhere. But whether Soviet expansionism stemmed from a defensive preoccupation with security or from an offensive ideological goal of aggrandizement, Moscow's drive for absolute security left other states feeling absolutely insecure. It is no wonder, then, that such insecurity drove all of the Soviet Union's great-power neighbors (Western Europe, on one side; Turkey, Iran, China, Japan, and South Korea, on the other sides) to accelerate their own defense spending. Furthermore, many Soviet accomplishments, such as its inroads in developing countries, considered at the time as setbacks for the United States, were actually setbacks for Moscow. Cuba in the 1960s, Angola and Ethiopia in the 1970s, and Afghanistan in the 1980s gave the Soviet system a bad case of indigestion.

Strobe Talbott, *Time* magazine's Soviet expert and later a deputy secretary of state in the Clinton administration, asserted that the Soviet threat was a "grotesque exaggeration" and claimed in retrospect, "The doves in the great debate of the past 40 years were right all along."[12] The Soviet "meltdown" in the Cold War was self-inflicted and "not because of anything the outside world has done or not done or threatened to do." Thus American and Western policies had little to do with the Soviet defeat in the Cold War because its cause was purely internal. Characteristic of the revisionist view that has followed every major American war, Talbott pointed out that there really had been no major danger to this country; the nation's long, intense, and dangerous involvement in the post–World War II world had not been necessary; and the U.S. containment policy, instead of playing a key role in the defeat of America's adversary, had merely prolonged the Cold War. Thus it would have been better to have avoided the "grand obsession" with the "Red Menace."

Soviet communism, a far cry from the worker's utopia envisioned by Karl Marx, surely deserves much of the credit it has been given for abetting its own collapse. But to conclude from this that the containment policy was not necessary, or, if necessary, was not a key ingredient in the Soviet Union's demise, is to differ from the conclusions drawn by its potential victims. As the United States attempted to withdraw from Europe after World War II, countries such as Iran and Turkey, followed by those in Western Europe, pleaded with American leaders to help them. The collapse of the former great powers of Western Europe left the Soviet Union as the potential hegemon throughout Eurasia. All countries saw their independence and national integrity at stake; America's continued presence was their only protection. Had the United States detached itself from great-power politics as it did after World War I, the

12. Strobe Talbott, "Rethinking the Red Menace," *Time,* January 1, 1990, 66–71.

countries on the periphery of the Soviet Union would have been vulnerable to the same assertion of Soviet power being felt east of the iron curtain.

Western Europe remained the pivotal strategic stake throughout the Cold War. The Soviets repeatedly tried to intimidate these nations, to divide them (especially West Germany from the United States), and to drive the United States back to its shores. But the containment policy made Moscow cautious about expanding its power. From this perspective, the ancient rule of states is a prudent one: power must be met by countervailing power. A balance among states is the only guarantee that they will retain their independence and preserve their way of life. Without containment, the inefficiencies of the Soviet system might not have mattered as much; the Soviet Union would not have had to engage in a costly arms race.

Containment, however, was not directed just at blocking Soviet domination of Western Europe and the rest of Eurasia. It also was intended to win time for the Soviet leadership to reexamine its goals and moderate its ambitions. Thus the American strategy in the Cold War rested largely and correctly on a tactical assumption of Soviet behavior. As George Kennan had explained years earlier, the United States had "it in its power to increase enormously the strains under which Soviet policy must operate . . . and in this way *to promote tendencies which must eventually find their outlet in either the breakup or the gradual mellowing of Soviet power.*"[13]

In retrospect, these words were prophetic. The Cold War experience demonstrated the virtue of patience in foreign policy. While interpreting the Soviet threat as the country's paramount concern, Kennan foresaw no quick fixes and recommended no immediate solutions to the problem. To the contrary, he anticipated a prolonged, low-intensity struggle across several distant frontiers. The conflict would be settled most effectively—and most peacefully—through the gradual exposure of contradictions within Soviet society. Soviet communism, in his view, would ultimately *self-destruct* under the weight of these contradictions. In the meantime, the United States would have to pursue a "long-term, patient, but firm and vigilant containment of Russian expansive tendencies." From Truman to Bush, that is just what U.S. presidents did.

The importance of the containment policy becomes even more evident when it is contrasted to the preceding period of American foreign policy. By failing to take a firm stand against Soviet policy during World War II, after it had become evident that it was impossible to accommo-

13. George Kennan, *American Diplomacy, 1900–1950* (Chicago: University of Chicago Press, 1951), 127–128 (emphasis added).

date Soviet interests in Eastern Europe and Asia, the United States had to accept some of the blame for the Cold War that followed. This is not to say that the United States passively accepted Soviet expansionism, but only that it did not oppose Stalin early enough, that it continued to cling to its hope for postwar amity with the Soviet Union despite Soviet behavior in the late stages of the war, and that after hostilities had ceased, it dissipated its strength immediately in a helter-skelter demobilization. Not until after the war did the United States act and draw the lines beyond which Soviet expansion would not be tolerated.

The American containment policy, then, played a critical role in the defeat of the Soviet Union. If the United States had not resisted Soviet expansion, Moscow, believing that communism represented the wave of the future, would likely have become even more assertive and aggressive; perceived weakness always invited efforts to expand. For example, when Nikita Khrushchev claimed that the balance of power had turned in favor of the Soviet Union, he precipitated a series of crises in West Berlin and Cuba that stretched from 1957 to 1962. And later, when Brezhnev's Soviet Union attained nuclear parity while also fielding a sizable army and building a growing navy, it exploited America's "Vietnam syndrome," using its own forces and sponsoring clients in Southeast Asia, Africa, Latin America, and Afghanistan.

American policy compelled Soviet caution and moderation. If the United States and its allies, especially NATO, had not opposed Soviet expansion in the wake of Vietnam, there would have been no need for Gorbachev to reassess his predecessors' policy and seek an accommodation with the West. It was obvious when he assumed power that the Soviet Union was "losing the capacity to generate the resources necessary to the leadership's three central objectives: a minimally acceptable standard of living; traditional foreign policy goals; and sufficient investment to ensure future growth." [14]

EXCESSES OF THE CONTAINMENT POLICY

Containment was by no means a flawless policy. Once the Cold War began, U.S. misperceptions, like those of Soviet leaders, fed the superpower conflict. For example, Washington frequently exaggerated Soviet military capabilities. Fears of Soviet superiority—the bomber gap in the 1950s, the missile gaps in the 1960s, and "the window of vulnerability" in the early 1980s—added momentum to the arms race already well under

14. James W. Davis and William C. Wohlforth, "German Unification," in *Ending the Cold War: Interpretations, Causation, and the Study of International Relations,* ed. Richard K. Herrmann and Richard Ned Lebow (New York: Palgrave Macmillan, 2004), 134.

way. In addition, the U.S. government's fixation with ideology and the bipolar balance of power rendered American policy blind to the national identities of new states. As a result, the Middle East Treaty Organization (METO) and Southeast Asia Treaty Organization (SEATO) proved unfit for the task of containing communism. To the contrary, the alliances did little more than alienate important states such as Egypt and India, both of which shifted allegiance toward the Soviet Union, and align the United States with discredited regimes such as Nationalist China, the Philippines, and the shah's Iran. For a variety of reasons, American leaders saw no democratic alternatives to the regimes it backed other than left-wing pro-Soviet or pro-Chinese ones, which were unacceptable.

The U.S. government also consistently exaggerated the monolithic nature of international communism. The fall of Nationalist China, the Korean War, and the communist Chinese intervention in that war transformed the containment policy—which originally was limited to responding to Soviet moves in the eastern Mediterranean and Western Europe—into global anticommunism. The events of 1949 and 1950 led to virulent anticommunism in the United States, with the Republicans (notably Sen. Joseph McCarthy) accusing the Democrats of being "soft on communism" and engaging in paranoid witch-hunts. Future Democratic administrations therefore would not be able to exploit the growing differences between the Soviet Union and China.

The American penchant for crusading, already demonstrated vividly in two "hot" wars, was not to be denied in the Cold War. America's failure to distinguish between vital and secondary interests—or to discriminate between different communist regimes—resulted in a war the United States could not win, dividing the country deeply and undermining the domestic consensus that had been the basis of the Cold War. Ironically, Vietnam destroyed the aggressive mode of American anticommunism, and U.S. policy shifted back toward a more passive containment of Soviet power—but this time in a de facto "alliance" with China. Finally, as detailed in Chapter 7, the overzealous pursuit of the Reagan Doctrine resulted in the Iran-contra scandal, which raised new doubts about the extent to which the U.S. government would go to fulfill its mission of defeating communism.

A Final Appraisal

Its shortcomings aside, the American containment policy must be pronounced, on the whole, a success. The expansion of American power and influence in the world has, despite the excesses of the Cold War, been associated with the promotion of democracy. America's World War II enemies, once dictatorial, are today stable, free, and prosperous societies. And its allies, particularly in Western Europe, have benefited from the opportunity to integrate their economies and pursue cooperative foreign relations. If one looks at the societies "liberated" by the Soviet Union during World War II, the contrast is striking. No East European country, until Gorbachev, was granted self-determination by the Kremlin; earlier attempts by Czechoslovakia, East Germany, Hungary, and Poland to move toward greater freedom were crushed by Soviet forces or their proxies. East Germany had to build a wall across Berlin and a barbed-wire fence along its entire border with West Germany to prevent its citizens from escaping.

Over the four decades of the Cold War, the United States acquired many authoritarian allies, mostly in developing countries, which weakened Washington's moral standing and laid open its foreign policy to the charge of hypocrisy. It would have been preferable, of course, to have democratic allies, but that was not always possible in a world in which most developing countries had never been democratic in the Western sense of the term. Security, both internally and globally, was bound to conflict with democratic development, just as today the values of economic growth and human rights frequently clash. Which value was to be given priority presented a difficult, often agonizing, choice both for American leaders and for the leaders of developing countries.

The basic fact remains, however, that the principal thrust of American foreign policy after World War II, as before the war, was to preserve a balance of power that would safeguard democratic values in the United States and other like-minded states. Indeed, this had been a consistent policy since World War I, whether the threat had come from the right or the left. American policy makers in the twentieth century opposed fascism and communism because they threatened not just U.S. security but, more broadly, the international environment in which democratic values could prosper. Communism, especially as reflected in the Soviet Union that Gorbachev inherited, was antithetical to individual freedoms, whether of speech or religion, to multiparty competition and genuine political choice, and to a distinction between state and society. It was America's power, not simply its democratic ideals, that protected these values.

Indeed, the end of the Cold War was witness not only to the end of the Soviet challenge but also to the defeat of the second totalitarian challenge to Western-style democracy in this century. The Nazis will forever be identified with the concentration camps of Auschwitz, Bergen-Belsen, and Treblinka, where they systematically murdered millions of people, including six million Jews, and with the unleashing of World War II, which, before it was over, cost the lives of seventeen million soldiers and thirty-four million civilians. Just as the Nazi system was epitomized by

Hitler, the Soviet system remains identified with Stalin and his cruel collectivization of the Soviet peasantry, the deliberate starvation of the Ukrainian peasants in the early 1930s, and the purges and other crimes that claimed the lives, conservatively estimated, of twenty million people and imprisoned and deported twenty million more. Stalin, like Hitler, was an infamous mass murderer. His ability to impose overwhelming control over such a massive territory had no historical precedent. The defeat of Stalin's successors, therefore, had global significance.

Although the U.S. victory in the Cold War coincided with America's own economic woes, the country still had reason to be proud of its overall record. There had been no nuclear conflict during the nearly half-century of Cold War in which the United States had led the Western coalition. Soviet expansionist ambitions had been checked. Democracy had emerged in a steadily growing number of countries. And after winning the Cold War, the U.S. government refused to gloat, seeking instead to attract the former Soviet bloc as a partner in the process of economic and political reform. Although this process would be as complex, difficult, and potentially dangerous as that of containing communism, it would gradually extend the domain of European cooperation and produce a degree of stability not seen before in the twentieth century.

CHAPTER NINE

America's 'Unipolar Moment'

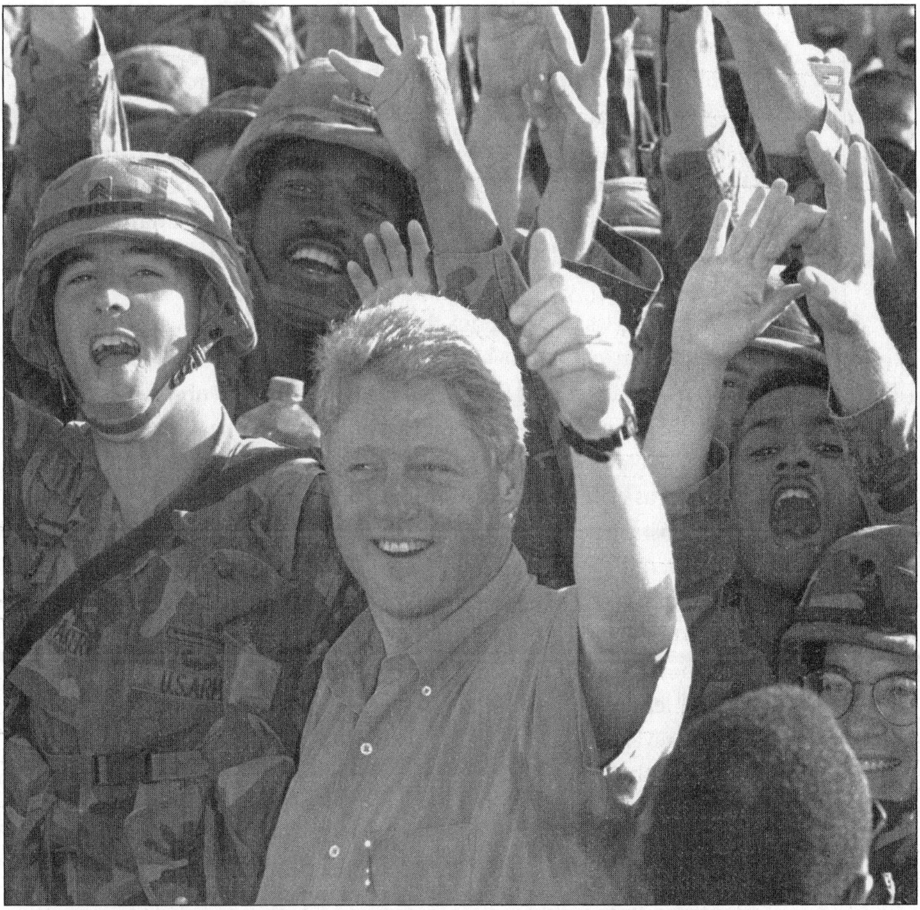

President Bill Clinton rallies U.S. forces stationed in Kuwait in October 1994. The collapse of the Soviet Union three years earlier left the United States with unprecedented military power along with immense economic wealth and political influence.

The abrupt collapse of the Cold War in the late twentieth century caught most world leaders by surprise and produced new uncertainties about world politics. Despite its perils, the rivalry between the Soviet Union and the United States had become a familiar reality that guided the foreign policies of all countries, large and small. In its absence, once-clear distinctions between friends and foes became blurred. Old alignments were either no longer necessary or, in many cases, no longer advisable. Consequently, future alignments and the source and intensity of new fault lines were hard to distinguish.

A central question during this transition revolved around the new balance of power. As noted, global stability traditionally has relied on a stable balance, or equilibrium, among the world's strongest powers and their allies. During the early nineteenth century, the Concert of Europe established a *multipolar* balance of power that produced a "long peace" among the great powers. The dissolution of this balance, beginning with the unification of Germany in 1870, set the stage for two world wars. During the Cold War, the *bipolar* balance between the American and Soviet blocs, which was bolstered by nuclear weapons and threats of "mutual assured destruction," prevented an even more cataclysmic world war.

One thing was clear about the post–Cold War balance of power: the disintegration of the Soviet Union had brought an end to the bipolar order that had persisted since the late 1940s. To many observers, the international system had again become multipolar. The Western European states had retained their previous status, and the European Union was taking shape as a single entity. Russia remained a force to be reckoned with. And a host of newly industrialized countries—primarily in East Asia—were emerging as formidable players on the global stage. The United States, in this view, was one of many countries of comparable strength and capabilities. Its foreign policy would have to adapt accordingly.

A more convincing argument was made by those who recognized that, at least for the immediate period, a *unipolar* balance of power would prevail. The United States held a variety of advantages that, when taken together and compared with the aggregate resources of any other single power, marked the arrival of America's "unipolar moment." According to the columnist Charles Krauthammer, who coined the term, "American preeminence is based on the fact that it is the only country with the military, diplomatic and economic assets to be a decisive player in any conflict in whatever part of the world it chooses to involve itself." [1]

The economic statistics spoke for themselves. In 1991—the last year of the Cold War—American firms produced $5.6 trillion in goods and services, or 26 percent of the world's output. Japan ranked second worldwide in gross domestic product (GDP), yet its output of $3.4 trillion was just three-fifths of the U.S. total. As for Europe, America's GDP

1. Charles Krauthammer, "The Unipolar Moment," *Foreign Affairs* (winter 1990–1991): 24.

exceeded the combined totals of France, Germany, Italy, and the United Kingdom. In all three areas of economic output—manufacturing, agriculture, and services—the U.S. economy set the pace for its competitors. Although foreign commerce contributed only about 10 percent to its GDP, the United States also served as an engine of growth overseas by importing far more goods—worth $506 billion in 1991 alone—than any other country. All of this was especially noteworthy in view of the fact that the United States was home to less than 5 percent of the world's population.[2]

In terms of military capabilities, America's preponderance was even greater. The United States maintained its global presence, with military forces deployed across the Western Hemisphere, Europe, the Middle East, and East Asia. The U.S. Navy patrolled most of the vital sea-lanes, and the U.S. Air Force maintained uncontested supremacy of the skies. American military spending of $280 billion in 1991 represented 27 percent of the worldwide total and a much larger sum than the combined totals of its potential adversaries.[3] Although the Soviet Union possessed a vast nuclear arsenal and came close to the United States in defense spending, the Central Intelligence Agency (CIA) had consistently overstated its role as a viable military competitor. Between 1989 and 1991, its military strength plummeted as the Soviet bloc slowly dissolved, and those forces left were plagued by outdated equipment and sagging morale. Most other countries that maintained large and modern defense forces were longtime allies of the United States. Thus they effectively added to U.S. military power. When the technical superiority of U.S. conventional and nuclear forces was factored into the equation, the United States enjoyed an unprecedented degree of global military might.

Finally, the United States emerged from the Cold War with a stable political system that, despite occasional controversies and scandals, had endured for more than two hundred years. Citizens of other nations who had known only oppression and dictatorial rule eagerly sought the democratic freedoms offered by the United States. America's vast network of colleges and universities attracted thousands of students from overseas. And its popular culture—expressed in fashion, music, publishing, movies, and television—appealed to a worldwide audience. In this increasingly important area of "soft power," including the less tangible aspects of cultural and political influence, the United States held a sizable advantage.[4]

2. World Bank, *World Development Report 1993* (New York: Oxford University Press, 1993), 239–265.

3. U.S. Arms Control and Disarmament Agency, *World Military Expenditures and Arms Transfers, 1991–1992* (Washington, D.C.: Government Printing Office, 1994), 47–87.

4. Joseph Nye Jr., *Bound to Lead: The Changing Nature of American Power* (New York: Basic Books, 1990), chap. 6.

All of this did not suggest that the unipolar world would necessarily be a stable one, or one of long duration. Simply put, the modern nation-state system had never witnessed such a concentration of power in a single state. There was no comparable past experience from which to draw informed predictions. The few standard cases for comparison—including the Roman, Ottoman, Spanish, French, British, and Russo-Soviet empires—were hardly global in scope, nor did they possess the many reinforcing elements of "hard" and "soft" power that yielded U.S. predominance in the 1990s. The European empires had, however, imposed a tighter grip over their domains, whereas U.S. influence was generally less direct, taking the form of political and cultural role modeling or military hegemony rather than conquest and formal occupation. But this difference only worked to further America's advantage. History had proven repeatedly that heavy-handed rulers who ignored the interests of their citizens ultimately became victims of their own tyranny.

Unipolarity also did not mean the United States would face no immediate challenges to its efforts to prevent its domestic base from eroding or to preserve its lead role in world politics. To the contrary, American leaders in the 1990s faced a bewildering array of problems at home and overseas during the first post–Cold War decade. The central point, however, is that the United States confronted these challenges with a superior range of resources. Thus the most compelling question was: How effectively would America bring its predominance to bear in the aftermath of the Cold War?

The remainder of this book seeks to answer this vital question. This chapter explores the domestic transition that occurred within the United States, particularly the intellectual debates, policy innovations, and institutional struggles that unfolded as the post–Cold War dawned. Chapters 10 and 11 then examine the regional issues and conflicts that confronted American leaders in the developing areas and in Europe, respectively. The final chapters review the U.S. government's response to the September 2001 terrorist attacks, the shifts in foreign policy related to the Bush Doctrine, the ongoing wars in Afghanistan and Iraq, and the array of other global challenges currently facing the United States.

Great Expectations after the Cold War

The end of the Cold War not only elevated the stature of the United States, but also gave rise to a new sense of euphoria throughout the West. The world seemed on the verge of a profoundly new era of peace, prosperity, and individual freedom. This hope was based in part on the collapse of the Soviet Union and the anticipated replacement of Cold War rivalry with U.S.-Russian cooperation. The very forces that historically had fueled international tensions were themselves being transformed. As one scholar declared, "What we may be witnessing is not just the end of the Cold War, or the passing of a particular period of history, but the end of history as such: that is, the end point of mankind's ideological evolution and the universalization of Western liberal democracy as the final form of human government." [5]

Two forces would presumably characterize this "post-historical" world: democracy and free-market capitalism. Both had already taken hold in many parts of the developing world and were expected in the 1990s to spread across Eastern Europe and the former Soviet Union. To adherents of this view, the expansion of democracy would benefit average citizens while enhancing the prospects for global stability. After all, democracies, while frequently engaging in armed struggles against nondemocratic states, traditionally had engaged in peaceful behavior toward other democratic states. The "democratic peace" they had established with like-minded foreign governments allowed for multiparty elections, observed the rule of law, and respected human rights.[6] In the economic sphere, a market-based world economy would presumably tie nations together in a cooperative search for prosperity. Not only would military conflicts become less frequent, but the powerful nations of the world also would be able to confront global problems such as environmental decay, weapons proliferation, population growth, and widespread poverty. Furthermore, economic "globalization" would lift the poorest regions of the world from poverty, thereby reducing the economic disparities that had grown ever wider during the Cold War as political leaders engaged in polarized, ideologically driven quarrels over the most effective means to provide for social welfare.

Another part of this equation was the nature of military power in the post–Cold War era. Nuclear weapons, it was widely believed, had rendered warfare among the great powers suicidal and thus prohibitive. Large-scale military conflict was destined to become obsolete, just as dueling, once widely accepted, became viewed as "contemptible and stupid" in the nineteenth century.[7] Because of the climbing costs of conventional warfare and the tangible rewards that could be expected from growing economic cooperation, war also might become obsolete among developing countries, where most violent conflicts were occurring.

5. Francis Fukuyama, "The End of History?" *National Interest* (summer 1989): 4.

6. See Bruce Russett, *Grasping the Democratic Peace: Principles for a Post–Cold War World* (Princeton, N.J.: Princeton University Press, 1993); and Michael W. Doyle, "Liberalism and World Politics," *American Political Science Review* (December 1986): 1151–1169. For a critique, see Joanne Gowa, *Ballots and Bullets: The Elusive Democratic Peace* (Princeton, N.J.: Princeton University Press, 1999).

7. John Mueller, *Retreat from Doomsday: The Obsolescence of Major War* (New York: Basic Books, 1989), 10.

George H. W. Bush, the first U.S. president to serve in the aftermath of the Cold War, took all of these factors into account and proclaimed to a joint session of Congress in March 1991, "We can see a new world coming into view, a world in which there is the very real prospect of a new world order, a world where the United Nations—freed from Cold War stalemate—is poised to fulfill the historic vision of its founders; a world in which freedom and respect for human rights find a home among all nations." [8]

For a president who had long been associated with a pragmatic if not a conservative approach to foreign policy, Bush's exaltations seemed out of character. But his vision was very much in keeping with the country's traditional idealism and emphasis on moral principles. In predicting the global spread of democracy, Bush recalled the optimism of Thomas Jefferson. In expressing faith in multilateral organizations to uphold widely accepted norms of international behavior, Bush echoed Woodrow Wilson. And in placing the United States at the center of such a reformed world, Bush restated themes advanced by Franklin Roosevelt and John Kennedy. His outlook, then, fit neatly into a mold that was well established by past U.S. presidents. The only difference: for Bush, this long-awaited future had arrived.

Later, President Bush would be taken to task as events demonstrated how *disorderly* the post–Cold War era would actually be. In 1991, however, his heralding of a transformed world seemed appropriate. The Cold War was over; the Soviet Union had disappeared; Germany was finally reunited. Democracies and market economies were taking shape far from the fallen iron curtain, extending to populations that long had been trapped by colonial domination and superpower rivalry. In short, it was a world American leaders had yearned for since the country's founding more than two centuries earlier.

Revived Debates about America's World Role

Even as Bush announced the arrival of the "new world order," debates began about the future role of the United States. One question raised frequently was whether American foreign policy after the Cold War would resemble that of 1918, when the United States retreated into its hemispheric shell after World War I, or that of 1945, when it assumed a strong internationalist posture after World War II. Of central concern

8. Quoted in Stanley R. Sloan, "The U.S. Role in a New World Order: Prospects for George Bush's Global Vision," Congressional Research Service Report to Congress, March 28, 1991, 19.

was how much attention and how many resources should be devoted to foreign policy when, for all practical purposes, the nation no longer confronted any formidable military threats.

In Washington and around the country, many people also questioned whether the United States needed a "grand strategy" in the wake of the Cold War. After all, the U.S.-Soviet rivalry and the bipolar balance of power had been unique in history. Communism had represented a stark challenge to American principles, political institutions, and physical security. In a clear response to that challenge, the United States had implemented George Kennan's containment strategy. But it was now also clear that the United States could not pursue a coherent post–Cold War foreign policy in the dark. No great power can survive in the absence of an explicit statement of purpose. Vital interests must be recognized and articulated. Priorities must be established, budgets prepared, and resources deployed in a systematic fashion. Furthermore, allies must be reassured and potential adversaries put on notice by a government speaking with one voice. Otherwise, policy vacillates and drifts, government agencies move in separate directions, and public support is impossible to sustain. Most troubling, challengers to the status quo inevitably exploit the void that results when a great power leads by improvisation.

To address these concerns, policy analysts inside and outside the U.S. government devised an array of possible strategies that clustered around four basic models: (1) a retreat from global leadership, (2) a campaign of liberal internationalism, (3) an effort to maintain U.S. economic and military primacy, and (4) an ad hoc policy of "selective engagement." [9] The first two positions reflected long-held but divergent feelings about America's role in world politics. As noted throughout this book, the country's foreign policy traditionally had lurched between periods of detachment from great-power politics and periods of moral crusading. The third and fourth positions were specific to the post–Cold War era and suggested a subtle yet significant evolution in the country's approach to world politics that reflected its experience as a great power.

Although America had over the years sought to distance itself from the intrigues and frequent conflicts of the major powers and thereby remain untainted by power politics, isolationism, the first strategy, had never meant that the United States would not intervene in "its" area of influence in the Western Hemisphere. Nor did it mean that the United States would not be an aggressive player in the world economy. What isolationism did mean was that the nation would distance itself politi-

9. For an elaboration on these strategies, see Barry R. Posen and Andrew Ross, "Competing Visions for U.S. Grand Strategy," *International Security* (winter 1996–1997): 5–53.

cally, diplomatically, and militarily from the affairs of the great powers in Europe and Asia. The nation would lead by example instead. In the wake of the Cold War, a large segment of the general public supported this withdrawal from what, for most of the twentieth century, had been a demanding and exceedingly troublesome world beyond the Western Hemisphere.[10]

The appeal of isolationism was strong, and particularly so in light of the nation's traditional fears of open-ended commitments and "entangling alliances." But most policy makers and analysts in the 1990s recognized that the United States, with its absolute and relative strengths in so many categories of power, would find it difficult, if not impossible, to maintain a purely defensive position. After all, a new era of intensifying global economic competition had dawned, computer technologies were uniting the far reaches of the globe, ecological problems were growing more severe, and weapons of mass destruction were falling into unknown hands. For all these reasons, and in view of the risk that a rival power might again unleash havoc if the United States let down its guard, policy makers concluded that a revival of American isolationism was out of the question.

An alternative approach, liberal internationalism, was closely related to America's self-image as the "city on a hill." As noted earlier, many Americans believed their nation to be an exceptional one whose foreign policy must pursue a moral course, even if other nations did not. Because of the human and economic sacrifices borne by the United States during its rise as a great power, America should exploit its hard-fought victory by supporting democracy and improving social welfare throughout the world. Liberal internationalists believed the time was right for a constructive and activist U.S. role in world politics. The United States was uniquely capable of putting its moral principles into practice. The "peace dividend" stemming from the collapse of the Cold War could be used to ensure the continued spread of democratic institutions, to solve transnational problems such as pollution and the AIDS epidemic, and to hasten the economic growth of developing countries. No other country had this ability to harness global energies for the betterment of humankind.

The third strategy also called for the United States to play an active role in world politics, but one that sought to preserve the gains of the Cold War primarily through the assertion of U.S. power. This so-called "primacy" school presumed that an American withdrawal into an isola-

10. For an elaboration of this view, see Patrick J. Buchanan, "America First—and Second, and Third," *National Interest* (spring 1990): 77–82. The isolationist view was more fully articulated by Eric A. Nordlinger in *Isolationism Reconfigured: American Foreign Policy for a New Century* (Princeton, N.J.: Princeton University Press, 1995).

tionist mode, or an open-ended campaign of global altruism, would tempt potential enemies to challenge America's status as the world's lone superpower. The best hope—for both U.S. security and global stability—was for the United States to prolong its "unipolar moment" by exploiting its military predominance, imposing itself in regional power struggles, and aggressively containing potential challengers. In short, only through a *pax Americana* could the anarchic world be saved from itself. "A world without U.S. primacy," wrote the political scientist Samuel Huntington, "will be a world with more violence and disorder and less democracy and economic growth than a world where the United States continues to have more influence than any other country in shaping global affairs." [11]

The fourth option called for the United States to pursue a middle course in which American leaders would confront and react to international problems on a case-by-case basis.[12] This course became attractive to many in light of the country's experience as a world power during the twentieth century. The attempted escape of the United States from great-power politics after World War I only encouraged the fascist challengers to the status quo, who then ignited the Second World War. By contrast, America's escalation of the Cold War from a geopolitical struggle against the Soviet Union into a global anticommunist crusade produced its own calamities.

As noted, the first two strategies represented well-worn aspects of America's traditional approach to foreign policy. The third and fourth strategies, by contrast, were more consistent with the realist tradition that Americans had long rejected as a vestige of the Old World. By the 1990s, however, realism had become appealing to many Americans, because it seemed to eschew moral crusading and frequent interventions in regional disputes of little consequence to the United States. In short, realism restrained America's crusading impulse and shifted attention to more mundane considerations common to all states such as self-defense, international stability, and economic growth. The pursuit of these interests did not require American foreign policy to abandon the country's ideals and moral values. They would simply have to be reconciled with the reality of a world of smoldering civil and regional conflicts that could easily reignite in the absence of bipolarity.

Each of these strategies for American foreign policy competed for favor in the early 1990s. But, beyond a recognition that some new grand strategy was needed, few policy makers agreed on exactly what that

11. Samuel Huntington, "Why International Primacy Matters," *International Security* (spring 1993): 83.

12. See Stephen Van Evera, "Why Europe Matters, Why the Third World Doesn't: American Grand Strategy after the Cold War," *Journal of Strategic Studies* (June 1990): 1–51.

strategy should be. Furthermore, as foreign policy analysts and political leaders quarreled over the proper course, the general public seemed largely indifferent. With the country at peace and facing no serious threats from overseas, the public wondered, why worry about foreign policy at all?

Into this void came the closely contested presidential campaign of 1992. Bush's public approval ratings were generally positive as he managed the fall of communism, negotiated German unification, and organized a multilateral effort to reverse Iraq's invasion of Kuwait (see Chapter 10). At the same time, however, the U.S. economy had fallen into a recession that produced high unemployment and accelerating trade and budget deficits. These concerns opened the door for Arkansas governor Bill Clinton, a previously little-known Democrat who promised to concentrate on domestic problems rather than foreign policy. Capitalizing on the broad public support for his domestic platform, Clinton defeated Bush and the independent candidate, H. Ross Perot.

Upon taking office, President Clinton assessed the basic tenets that had guided American foreign policy in the past. He knew the American people longed to be free of the great-power conflicts that frequently had dragged the United States into regional conflicts and close to a cataclysmic showdown with the Soviet Union. Yet Clinton also recognized that the United States had enormous stakes in the rapidly changing international system, particularly in the outcome of political and economic reforms adopted around the world. Thus the president concluded that the United States must play a role in world politics that was commensurate with its stature and resources.

Three other significant assertions by Clinton also shaped his foreign policy. First, the country's primary goal in the mid-1990s would be achievement of strong economic growth, and, more than ever, this growth would depend on a robust global economy. Second, many of the problems neglected during the Cold War—ecological decay, rapid population growth, and political repression (in capitalist as well as communist states), among others—must receive attention at once. Finally, international institutions such as the United Nations and World Bank should play a meaningful role in achieving the nation's goals. In his view, these institutions discouraged self-serving behavior among states and encouraged cooperative solutions to problems that crossed political borders. Thus a U.S. policy of "assertive multilateralism" would best serve both the United States and global interests.

Clinton charted a course for American foreign policy that was, by and large, consistent with the spirit of Bush's "new world order" and most closely paralleled the strategy of liberal internationalism. The United States not only would refuse to lapse into isolationism, but also would exploit and extend the advantages that derived from its privileged position in the unipolar world. In so doing, American leaders would look beyond the country's immediate self-interests and collaborate actively with like-minded governments and transnational institutions. By behaving cooperatively and in a nonthreatening manner, the United States would engender trust among the second-tier powers and forestall challenges to its post–Cold War primacy.

Clinton's Embrace of 'Geoeconomics'

The future of the U.S. economy figured prominently in the foreign policy of President Clinton, who was keenly aware of the deep national anxieties about the country's economic outlook. This sense of unease, reflected consistently in public opinion polls, was truly remarkable. One might have expected the American people to feel jubilant after the country's victory in the Cold War. After all, "the Soviet Union wasn't just beaten on points, it was dismembered. Communism wasn't just relegated to second place—it was utterly delegitimized. And all with remarkably little bloodshed."[13]

Many Americans, however, were preoccupied with the country's internal health. Smokestack industries had fallen to foreign competition, and the high-technology sector had faltered in the 1980s. It was not hard to understand the implications: the loss of America's historic economic vitality meant a decline in the country's status and power in the world. The simultaneous rise of many industrializing states, particularly China, meant a loss of jobs and opportunities to improve America's wage structure and standard of living. As never before, the country had become aware of its dependence on exports for employment and economic growth. Thus with these concerns in mind, Clinton had made the U.S. economy the centerpiece of his bid for the presidency. He laid out a program of domestic reforms and emphasized that without a strong and growing economy accompanied by declining budget and trade deficits, the United States could not afford to play an influential role in world politics.

As Clinton and others acknowledged during this period, the "decline" of the U.S. economy during the Cold War was in many respects inevitable.[14] The overwhelming strength of the U.S. economy just after World War II, when it accounted for half of global production, stemmed

13. Owen Harries, "My So-Called Foreign Policy," *New Republic*, October 10, 1994, 24.

14. Concern over national decline, unusual for a great power but typically American, was reflected in the strong response to Paul M. Kennedy's *The Rise and Fall of the Great Powers: Economic Change and Military Conflict from 1500 to 2000* (New York: Random House, 1987). It suggested that the United States was on the verge of "imperial overstretch."

from the wreckage of the Western European and Pacific economies. That strength, however, lasted only until these economies recovered; by the early 1990s the U.S. share of global production was about the same as just before World War I. Thus the country's economic predominance after World War II was a historical aberration. Its *relative* economic decline was not a harbinger of economic collapse. On an absolute basis, the U.S. economy continued to grow.

From this perspective, the deep-seated fears of many Americans about the economy were unfounded. Nevertheless, the United States faced many daunting economic problems, some of which were self-inflicted. Many U.S. corporations had become complacent and were unprepared for the sudden burst of overseas competition. In the public sector, the U.S. government had built a military superior to any other and had funded growing social and entitlement programs, but it had refused to approve tax increases to pay for the new programs. Enormous budget deficits, which surpassed $100 billion in the early 1980s and reached $290 billion by 1992, were the result. Because almost every part of American society bore some responsibility for the problems confronting the U.S. economy, the president argued that resolution of the problems would require an aggressive national effort. In focusing on domestic problems that went beyond fiscal matters—to include social divisions, deteriorating schools and hospitals, and widespread public cynicism toward government—Clinton confronted a series of issues that had deep historical roots and would thus be difficult to overcome.

THE COURSE OF AMERICA'S ECONOMIC TROUBLES

In the aftermath of World War II, American leaders rarely raised the issue of affordability when responding to a foreign threat or a regional crisis that was of "vital interest" to the United States. Few asked whether the United States could afford a Marshall Plan or expanded military programs. In the words of President John Kennedy, America could "bear any burden" thought necessary. The nation was wealthy enough, citizens assumed, to support a high standard of living at home and an activist presence abroad.

The 1950s and 1960s were decades of unprecedented economic growth in the United States. Wages rose rapidly as trade unions grew powerful and negotiated sizable annual raises paid by industries that apparently could afford them while still earning handsome profits. In Washington, first John Kennedy and then Lyndon Johnson vastly expanded the welfare state in the 1960s in their effort to build a "Great Society." They established new entitlement programs and hiked spending on older programs such as Social Security. Some newer programs, such as Medicare and Medicaid, started small but grew rapidly as their clientele and services multiplied.

The bubble burst in the early 1970s. The enormous expense of the Vietnam War combined with the dramatic rise in oil prices produced soaring inflation, interest rates, and unemployment. "Stagflation" set in as economic growth slowed. Meanwhile, the war-ravaged industrial economies of Western Europe had recovered and new competitors in East Asia were entering the global marketplace. In the United States, it had become obvious that the country no longer could afford an unlimited supply of both guns and butter. It had to make choices. Richard Nixon first responded in 1971 by suspending the gold standard and ending the U.S. dollar's role as the basis of the world's monetary system. He also extricated the United States from Vietnam, lowered tensions with Moscow, and transformed China from an adversary to an ally, thereby reducing the cost of foreign policy.

In the late 1970s, Jimmy Carter tried to revive the economy by further reducing military spending and keeping taxes in line with growing entitlement programs. But a second oil shock in 1978–1979 produced a new round of inflation, punctuated by double-digit interest rates and unemployment. The resurgence of Soviet expansionism and anti-American revolutions in Iran and Nicaragua then forced Carter to reverse his military cutbacks. His successor in office, Ronald Reagan, accelerated expansion of the military in the early 1980s and simultaneously cut taxes, thereby fulfilling two campaign promises. Yet despite his efforts to reduce domestic spending on social programs and to crack down on "waste, fraud, and mismanagement," government expenditures continued to mount.

Free spending is usually followed by a free fall. The long-term expectation of Reagan's "supply-side" economics was that the U.S. economy, stimulated by lower taxes, would grow as rapidly in the 1980s as it had during the 1950s and 1960s. But the American economy had changed greatly since the 1960s. Although American agriculture was the most bountiful in the world, by the mid-1980s its overseas markets were shrinking. Other industrialized countries and many developing states such as India, China, Thailand, and Indonesia had become food exporters. More important, traditional American industries such as steel and automobile manufacturing were caught off guard as the newly industrialized countries (NICs) produced superior goods at less cost and thereby increased their shares of export markets. A string of trade deficits plagued the U.S. economy in addition to the growing budget deficits recorded in Washington. The annual trade deficits with Japan and China alone averaged $80 billion by the mid-1990s.

The reasons for the twin deficits of the eighties and early nineties were similar to those for the overall deterioration of American industry: low capital investments in nonmilitary research and development; the preoccupation of corporate leaders with quarterly profits and dividends to the detriment of long-term growth; and the decline of the American labor force, a by-product of lower educational standards. In addition, there was a lack of corporate enterprise. During the 1980s, capital investment and modernization took second place to merger mania and hostile takeovers. Although this shuffling of paper was profitable financially for a small group of investment bankers and lawyers, it added little to economic growth. As for American consumers, despite the stagnation of their disposable incomes they continued to spend freely, often with credit cards, thereby draining the economy of an essential pool of national savings.

But not all of the blame for America's economic lethargy could be directed inward. The economies of East Asia and Western Europe were expanding rapidly, and those of Eastern Europe and Latin America also were heating up. As more countries enacted economic reforms based on private enterprise and open markets, they joined the fast-paced competition in export markets and attracted record volumes of private investment. Leading economists heralded the arrival of economic globalization, meaning that a single, integrated worldwide market had replaced national and regional markets. Increasingly, commerce would have no political boundaries; firms would compete not only with others within their country but also with those based overseas. A typical corporation in the "globalized" economy would have its headquarters in the "home" country but engage in research and development, production, marketing, and sales all over the world. "There is coming to be no such thing as an American corporation or an American industry," wrote the economist Robert B. Reich, who became secretary of labor in the Clinton administration. "The American economy is but a region of the global economy." [15]

Some observers argued that economic globalization would gradually weaken the authority, if not the sovereignty, of nation-states. Even though early U.S. leaders had longed for a world dominated by economic rather than political competition, many contemporary Americans worried that the United States would lose control of its own destiny if global economic forces were truly allowed to dominate. Suddenly, the social and economic protections afforded by the U.S. government seemed at risk, along with the country's political clout. As a result, many Americans looked to Washington for relief from the transformed world the United States had played a major role in creating.

15. Robert B. Reich, *The Work of Nations: Preparing Ourselves for 21st Century Capitalism* (New York: Knopf, 1991), 243.

RESPONSES BY THE CLINTON ADMINISTRATION

The superior production capacity of the United States underwrote its victory in World War II and its successful Cold War campaign against the Soviet Union. But economic stagnation in the 1980s and early 1990s raised the critical question of whether the economy could still support a foreign policy that maintained 300,000 U.S. soldiers in Western Europe, defended Japan and South Korea, policed the Persian Gulf and the Middle East, and retained the traditional sphere of influence in Latin America. Could the United States do all this while supporting ever-growing domestic programs and keeping up with interest payments on the national debt, the fastest-growing area of federal spending?

Upon taking office, Clinton declared that for the United States to compete more effectively with the outside world the federal government would have to "reinvest" in its domestic base—that is, to reform the national health care system, improve the quality of American schools, and restore the country's basic infrastructure such as roads and bridges. Furthermore, he sought to ease the long-standing antagonism between the federal government and many large industries. Toward this end, the president met in 1993 with leaders from the U.S. automobile industry and proclaimed a "new partnership" between the federal government and automakers. These two groups would act as allies rather than adversaries in promoting economic growth, much as their counterparts had done in Japan. In promoting his own version of "industrial policy," Clinton was prepared to play by many of the same rules as his international competitors.

The president also was determined to see U.S. economic relations assume the same institutional prominence as its diplomatic and military relations. Clinton elevated the status of the U.S. trade representative and gave his secretaries of the Treasury (Lloyd M. Bentsen Jr.), commerce (Ron Brown), and labor (Robert Reich) unprecedented power to shape the nation's foreign policy. He also created the National Economic Council to coordinate economic relations and to serve as a counterpart to the National Security Council (NSC). Even the NSC, established early in the Cold War, was expanded to include economic advisers.

Among Clinton's other priorities in foreign economic policy was expanding the U.S. role in regional trading blocs. The early 1990s witnessed a wave of regional economic integration, much of it based on the success of the European Union, which had linked its member states into a single economic market (see Chapter 11). By removing barriers to trade and investment within the bloc, by encouraging the movement of workers and services across national borders, and by unifying health and safety regulations, these states hoped to increase economic efficiency and raise overall levels of production.

The first such achievement for the United States was the passage in 1993 of the North American Free Trade Agreement (NAFTA). Conceived and negotiated by the Bush administration, NAFTA was aimed at reducing or eliminating the tariffs that had limited trade among the United States, Canada, and Mexico. American critics of NAFTA charged that it would encourage U.S. manufacturers to relocate their factories in Mexico, where labor was far cheaper, thereby crippling American firms and their surrounding communities. Others claimed NAFTA would reward Mexico's one-party government for its longtime neglect of its impoverished population. NAFTA supporters countered that in Mexico the treaty would stimulate economic growth, relieve poverty, and move the country toward democracy, all while creating new markets for American goods. They further argued that trade with Canada, the largest export market for the United States, had been severely limited by cross-border restrictions. Finally, they proclaimed NAFTA to be consistent with the laissez-faire principles of free markets that the United States had long espoused. In the end, the pro-NAFTA forces prevailed; the treaty passed narrowly in Congress and went into effect on the first day of 1994.

The United States also became actively involved in a second, but more loosely knit, regional organization known as Asia-Pacific Economic Cooperation (APEC). The Pacific market had emerged as the most dynamic area of economic exchange for the United States; it was growing faster and producing more jobs than Europe. According to the president, Asian export markets had become the "lifeblood" of U.S. economic growth. Political divisions ran deep among APEC members, however, thereby limiting progress on economic reforms. Nevertheless, the organization provided potential avenues for political as well as economic reforms, and, significantly, leaders of the Pacific region's most powerful states—including the United States, Japan, China, and Russia—became enthusiastic supporters of APEC.[16]

Overall, this move toward regional integration in global trade relations both resulted from and contributed to the market-driven world economy sought by the United States throughout its history. A further step in this direction was taken late in 1994 when Congress ratified the latest General Agreement on Tariffs and Trade (GATT), approved by most other member states earlier that year. The agreement reduced tar-

16. Economic integration already had moved forward among Asian states in 1992, when Brunei, Indonesia, Malaysia, the Philippines, Singapore, and Thailand—all members of the Association of Southeast Asian Nations (ASEAN)—committed themselves to creating a free trade area by 2003. In addition, several countries in South America formed an economic alliance known as Mercosur that sought to rival the European, North American, and Asian blocs.

iffs on most products sold by member states overseas and was hailed by Clinton as the "largest tax cut in world history." Passage of GATT, which had seemed assured, was briefly placed in doubt after several members of Congress criticized its provisions for a World Trade Organization (WTO) to monitor trade practices and enforce compliance. The criticisms were silenced, however, after Clinton assured Congress that the United States would not surrender its sovereign authority to the WTO. In fact, the United States would be in a strong position to use the WTO as a vehicle to promote its own economic agenda. After Clinton's Republican rivals finally endorsed the agreement, the latest GATT accord was ratified easily and the WTO became a fixture of world politics.

EAST ASIA'S ECONOMIC 'MIRACLE'

Major challengers of the United States in the rapidly integrating global economy were the countries of East Asia. Led by Japan and the "four tigers"—Hong Kong, Singapore, South Korea, and Taiwan—these NICs enjoyed the world's most rapid rates of economic growth in the 1980s and early 1990s. Unlike the developing countries in Latin America and Africa that had sought to insulate themselves from the capitalist "core" in the United States and Western Europe, the NICs plunged into global trading markets, welcomed foreign investments, and aggressively located their own manufacturing firms in Western countries. Between 1965 and 1990, Japan and the four tigers increased their share of world trade from 7 percent to 16 percent, nearly reaching the share of global trade attained by all the other developing countries combined.[17] In addition, East Asia attracted nearly all of the private investments that were flowing from industrialized states to developing regions.

The East Asian states became more competitive in large measure by violating the terms of the "liberal international economic order" promoted by the United States under the Bretton Woods regime (see Chapter 3). Japan, in particular, was widely viewed as a culprit because of its status as a role model and "engine of growth" for the other NICs, many of which hoped to repeat Japan's success story. Since the 1950s, the Japanese government had actively supported the expansion of its key industries, particularly automobiles and consumer electronics, by providing them with generous tax breaks, research funding, and protection from foreign competitors. The Japanese Ministry for International Trade and Industry (MITI), which included a small group of top government and corporate leaders, epitomized this collusion between

17. World Bank, *The East Asian Miracle: Economic Growth and Public Policy* (New York: Oxford University Press, 1993), 38.

Japan's public and private sectors.[18] Within MITI, this small group decided which manufactured goods Japan would mass-produce for export, where the exports would be targeted, and how Japanese industries could be protected from foreign competition. These practices incited charges of *neomercantilism* from the United States, Japan's primary export market, which was unable to sell its products in Tokyo at competitive prices. Relations between the two countries suffered as a result, especially after the Cold War when Japan's strategic role as an East Asian bulwark of containment had lapsed. As Japan annually recorded trade surpluses over the United States in excess of $40 billion, and as the United States struggled with chronic trade deficits and a soaring national debt, many Americans demanded an end to Tokyo's days as a "free rider."

The East Asian version of industrial policy was troubling to American leaders and workers, who feared that the combination of lower wages, government subsidies, and import restrictions would damage American industries. These critics, however, conveniently overlooked the fact that the U.S. government had engaged in many of the same practices during its rise as a regional and then global economic power. Indeed, such a strategy was openly advocated in the country's earliest years by Alexander Hamilton, the first secretary of the Treasury, who believed America's "infant industries" should be carefully protected through government controls. The critics also forgot that the United States had condoned the protectionist practices of many East Asian governments during the Cold War because those governments served as essential agents of the U.S. containment strategy. And this permissive attitude in Washington had been accompanied by large volumes of foreign aid, which further hastened Tokyo's economic resurgence.

To those who felt threatened by the East Asian economic "miracle" in the aftermath of the Cold War, all of this was beside the point. Not only did the policies of the East Asian governments violate the sacrosanct American creed of free markets, they also were widely seen as taking jobs away from American workers and threatening the country's economic prosperity. The critics' complaints demonstrated that the new era of geoeconomics often would depart from the "harmony of interests" envisioned by the eighteenth-century Scottish economist Adam Smith. Territorial disputes, ideological conflicts, and political power struggles remained facts of life in a world still dominated by nation-states. Thus American leaders, with the Cold War winding down, stepped up their

18. See Chalmers Johnson, *MITI and the Japanese Miracle: The Growth of Industrial Policy, 1925–1975* (Palo Alto, Calif.: Stanford University Press, 1982). Also see Jeffrey A. Hart, *Rival Capitalists: International Competitiveness in the United States, Japan, and Western Europe* (Ithaca, N.Y.: Cornell University Press, 1992), chap. 2.

efforts to retaliate against unfair competitors, primarily those in East Asia. Under the 1988 Omnibus Trade and Competitiveness Act, the president was required to identify the most flagrant violators and provide means for retaliation. Although the United States rarely employed the act and instead settled for a system of "managed trade" with Japan, the legislation conveyed a strong message that America's patience was wearing thin.

These economic tensions also extended to U.S. relations with China, one of the world's fastest-growing economies. Under Deng Xiaoping, who had replaced Mao Zedong in 1978, China's government remained firmly in the grip of the Communist Party. Deng, however, had departed from Mao's command economy. First, he opened Chinese agriculture to private farms that could earn profits from surplus production. Second, Deng allowed private industries, funded largely by foreign investment, to flourish in the numerous "enterprise zones" created along China's coastline. Taking advantage of the country's massive labor pool, he oversaw a rapid economic expansion in which China's gross national product grew at an average rate of nearly 10 percent in the 1980s and early 1990s.

The contrast between Deng's reforms and those of Mikhail Gorbachev in the Soviet Union during the 1980s was revealing. Gorbachev had sought to reform the ossified Soviet political system through *glasnost* and *perestroika,* but he had kept the country's command economy largely intact. Deng, by contrast, opened and greatly expanded the Chinese economy while refusing to consider meaningful political reforms. In the end, Gorbachev's politically based strategy proved suicidal, while Deng's economic strategy left its communist government with ample power to prevent "counter-revolution." The implications were clear: whereas effective economic reforms could improve living conditions in the absence of democratic rule, political reforms combined with economic stagnation invited popular backlash and jeopardized the state's very existence.

Even after Richard Nixon's recognition of the communist government in Beijing, the United States frequently condemned China's repressive system of rule and systematic violations of human rights, particularly the crackdown on pro-democracy activists during and after the 1989 Tiananmen Square uprising. American leaders after the Nixon years tried to link China's most-favored-nation (MFN) trade status, which provided it with open access to American consumers, to its progress in respecting human rights. But officials in Beijing insisted that their domestic behavior would not be tailored to satisfy Americans. Their defiance only grew stronger as the Chinese economy boomed in the early 1990s. Clinton, who was well aware of the economic value of U.S.-Chinese trade, was trapped by American policy.

When push finally came to shove, Clinton backed down on his political demands and announced in 1994 that human rights no longer would be linked directly to China's MFN status. The carrot of continuing trade would better elicit reforms in China than the stick of trade sanctions, asserted Clinton. But China's treatment of its political dissidents became even harsher after Clinton's "engagement" policy (described in the next section) was announced. The policy remained a sore point for congressional critics, human rights groups, and even the State Department, which through its annual survey of human rights kept up a steady barrage of criticism toward China. But neither these criticisms nor the continuing trade imbalances that favored China deterred Clinton from maintaining close economic ties with Beijing.

Promoting Democracy and Sustainable Development

By the time the Cold War collapsed, urgent global problems such as environmental decay, rapid population growth, and the growing gap between rich and poor were demanding immediate attention. Attempts to address these problems and the effort to consolidate global democratic reforms became part of a distinct post–Cold War global agenda. Clinton, who as a presidential candidate called for greater attention to global problems along with a heightened emphasis on economic issues, seized on these aspects of "low politics" once in office. His variant of liberal internationalism recalled John Kennedy's Alliance for Progress and Jimmy Carter's world-order politics, both of which emphasized cooperative North-South relations, human rights, and the interdependence of all countries in the modern world. Now, though, this approach would be applied for the first time in the absence of superpower tensions.

A Grand Strategy of Democratic 'Enlargement'

Long before Clinton took office, the United States had sought to promote the expansion of democratic rule overseas. The roots of this longtime American quest can be traced to Thomas Jefferson's "empire of liberty," to the widespread presumption of America's "manifest destiny," and to Woodrow Wilson's pledge to make the U.S. role in World War I a mission "for democracy, for the right of those who submit to authority to have a voice in their own government, for the rights and liberties of small nations . . . and to make the world itself free." The renewal of this democratic crusade after the collapse of the Soviet Union was, then, merely the continuation of an existing practice. "No national security

FIGURE 9-1 Democratization around the World, 1979–1999

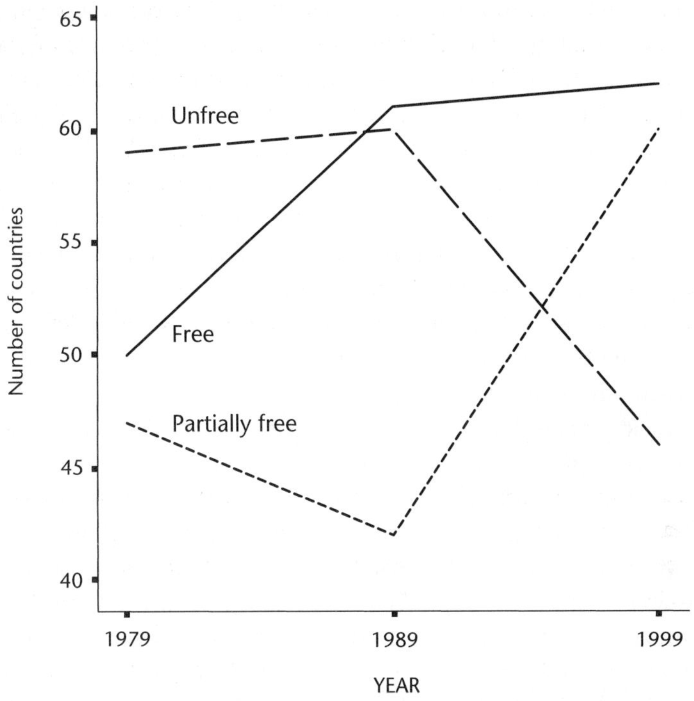

Source: Freedom House, "Freedom in the World Country Rating 1972–2004," http://www.freedomhouse.org/template.cfm?page=1 (accessed April 24, 2006).

issue is more urgent, nowhere is our country's imperative more clear," candidate Clinton declared in 1992. "I believe it is time for America to lead a global alliance for democracy as united and steadfast as the global alliance that defeated communism." [19]

The Clinton administration's pledge to emphasize political reforms not only extended a long national tradition of promoting democracy, but also recognized undeniable political trends that had been under way for a decade. By the time of Clinton's election, more countries than ever had adopted representative governments, permitted the formation of multiple political parties, established the rule of law, and allowed basic political and civil rights. Competitive elections were held for the first time across Latin America during the Reagan and Bush years and throughout Eastern Europe after the Cold War. Although most African

19. Bill Clinton, "A Strategy for Foreign Policy," *Vital Speeches of the Day,* May 1, 1992, 421, http://www.votd.com/ (accessed April 24, 2006).

governments remained under autocratic control, South Africa took a giant step toward democracy by dismantling its racist system of apartheid and permitting free elections in April 1994. The rise to power of Nelson Mandela, who had spent much of his life in South African prisons, was just one more symbol of the global reach of democracy.

It was in this environment that the Clinton administration sought to make the promotion of democracy the centerpiece of its foreign policy. Echoing George Kennan, the intellectual founder of containment, Clinton national security adviser Anthony Lake asserted in 1993: "The successor to a doctrine of containment must be a strategy of enlargement—enlargement of the world's free community. . . . We must counter the aggression—and support the liberalization—of states hostile to democracy. . . . The United States will seek to isolate [non-democratic states] diplomatically, militarily, economically and technologically." [20]

Secretary of State Warren Christopher cited U.S. involvement in Eastern Europe, southern Africa, the Middle East, and Latin America as evidence of the administration's determination to match its words with deeds. Commitments of Western aid to Russia and its neighbors—at a time when public support for U.S. foreign aid had descended to record lows—were viewed as a critical component of this effort. Administration officials also pointed out that the United States, which had always portrayed itself as the world's "beacon of democracy," could not stand by while countries sought to consolidate democratic institutions in the face of internal upheaval. Driven by this logic, the Clinton White House proceeded to identify "rogue states"—including Cuba, Iran, Iraq, Libya, and North Korea—which it felt threatened the foundations of democratic rule, and then sought to punish them through economic sanctions, diplomatic exclusion, and occasional military coercion. America's allies were expected to follow suit.

The Clinton administration faced an uphill battle, however, in arousing public and congressional support for its democratization campaign. Many Americans questioned whether the effort was actually vital to U.S. security and economic interests. Furthermore, the targets of the democratization strategy were scattered throughout the world, often in remote areas with little or no tradition of representative government. Already, internal revolts had upended democratic regimes in many countries, which then succumbed to ethnic rivalries and military rule. In most of the countries that maintained authoritarian rule through their armed forces, elections were largely for show. Finally, in several Eastern European countries many former communists were being elected to leader-

20. Anthony Lake, "From Containment to Enlargement," *Dispatch* (Department of State), September 27, 1993, 658–664.

ship positions, demonstrating that the ballot box was no guarantee that leaders favorable to the United States would come to power.

Clinton also confronted charges by human rights activists that the United States was observing double standards in its most recent campaign of democratization. Violations of human rights by the Chinese government were subordinated to the primary goal of expanded economic ties. Meanwhile, Saudi Arabia and Egypt, loyal friends of the United States—one the source of oil, the other a strong supporter of Arab-Israeli peace—were ruled by repressive governments. And Turkey, which was engaged in a brutal crackdown of its Kurdish minority, continued to receive generous allotments of U.S. military aid, not to mention full partnership in the North Atlantic Treaty Organization (NATO). But the United States would not be denied its self-appointed democratic mission. After all, it had succeeded in defeating fascism during World War II and the world's most powerful communist state in the Cold War—campaigns not undertaken merely to resurrect a stable balance of power but also to liberate world politics from the scourge of tyranny. In this context, obstacles to democratization in the more benign setting of the 1990s did not appear insurmountable, and occasional exceptions by the United States would not significantly undercut the general policy of democratic enlargement.

SUPPORT FOR SUSTAINABLE DEVELOPMENT

Beyond his policy to support democracy, Clinton embraced the global effort to promote "sustainable development" in developing countries. Sustainable development was a loose-knit concept that combined political reforms, environmental protection, population control, and market-based economic growth. Chronic problems in developing countries, where most of the world's people lived and where population growth was most rapid, could no longer be ignored by the industrialized nations. Their problems were becoming transnational in scope, spilling into neighboring countries and threatening global security. Solving these problems, Clinton proclaimed, would require cooperative action and sacrifice on an equally universal scale—and strong leadership by the United States.

Like the democratization policy, plans to promote sustainable development preceded Clinton's arrival in office, and they originated from many sources outside the United States. The impetus for sustainable development had emerged in June 1992 during the UN Conference on Environment and Development, at the time the largest single gathering of world leaders in history. *Agenda 21,* the concluding statement of the "Earth Summit," constituted a call to arms to pursue this goal. The eight-hundred-page manifesto recommended annual spending of more than $125 billion in dozens of areas such as pollution control, education, health care, poverty relief, technology transfer, and the empowerment of women. According to the preamble to *Agenda 21,* "peace, development, and environmental protection are interdependent and indivisible."[21]

President Bush had rejected many of these provisions. More concerned in the summer of 1992 about his fading reelection prospects, he virtually had to be dragged to the Earth Summit in Rio de Janeiro, Brazil. Once there, Bush provoked worldwide criticism by refusing to sign the Biodiversity Convention, designed to protect woodlands and habitat that were hard-hit by accelerating development. He believed the treaty unfairly restricted the access of American companies to the tropical forests of Latin America and Asia and imposed excessive demands (more than $200 million initially) on wealthy countries to aid equatorial states that would lose revenue if development halted in these sensitive areas. The United States stood alone in opposing the treaty, which was approved by 153 other governments. Bush's defiance of the Earth Summit and the estrangement of the United States from the revived environmental movement provided strong ammunition for Clinton, who made the unpopular U.S. stance one of the few foreign policy issues of his campaign.

Once elected, Clinton adopted *Agenda 21* as a prototype for his environmental proposals of 1993 and 1994. Vice President Al Gore, a self-proclaimed environmentalist, was designated to oversee the effort.[22] In the State Department, a new position was created—under secretary of state for global affairs—symbolizing the administration's concern for these issues. Clinton also signed the Biodiversity Convention and restored funding for the UN Population Fund, which had been suspended by Bush and Reagan.

Clinton's foreign policy goals were brought together in the Peace, Prosperity, and Democracy Act of 1994, a wide-ranging bill supported by the president and a Congress then dominated by the Democratic Party. For a brief time, it appeared that Clinton's "pragmatic neo-Wilsonian" foreign policy, as it was described by Anthony Lake, would come to pass. But this was not to be. Clinton's window of opportunity slammed shut in November 1994 after midterm congressional elections reversed the political tide and brought an entirely different agenda to Washington.

21. UN Conference on Environment and Development, *Agenda 21* (New York: United Nations, 1992).

22. Gore outlined his environmental views in *Earth in the Balance: Ecology and the Human Spirit* (New York: Plume, 1993).

Domestic Challenges to Clinton's Foreign Policy

It was not upheavals abroad that provoked the challenge to Clinton's foreign policy in his first term. The backlash began at home, within the U.S. government, for reasons only marginally related to foreign policy. Despite the administration's progress in reducing the federal deficit and stimulating economic growth, public opinion polls suggested widespread distrust of the federal government. The extremism of regional militia groups served as a potent expression of growing public disenchantment with "business as usual" in Washington.

This widespread distrust was accompanied by the revival of the Republican Party in many state governments, particularly in the South, where a historic realignment in state legislatures had been under way for more than a decade. Although many political observers expected Republican Party gains in the national midterm elections, few predicted that the elections of 1994 would produce a historic resurgence of the Republican Party—its first claim to majority status in both houses of Congress since 1954. The Republicans, who had held just 176 of the 435 House seats before the elections, won 231 seats to capture majority control. On the Senate side, the Republican Party increased its share from 43 to 52 of the 100 seats—a solid, if not veto-proof, majority. Thus the remainder of Clinton's first term would feature a reversal of the pattern of divided government experienced by Reagan and Bush: now a *Republican* Congress would offset a *Democratic* White House.

Republican leaders in Congress favored a foreign policy that departed from Clinton's in several respects. In general, they sought a more modest role for the United States, because the Soviet threat had disappeared and because no other power comparable to the Soviet Union had emerged in its absence. American policy should be based on tangible self-interests rather than ambiguous global concerns and on strong military defenses rather than on foreign aid and a reliance on international organizations. Congressional Republicans followed the lead of North Carolina senator Jesse Helms, an outspoken critic of Clinton's foreign policy who became chair of the powerful Senate Foreign Relations Committee in January 1995. Within five months, Helms had introduced legislation for a "new" State Department that included major cutbacks in foreign affairs spending, particularly foreign aid, which Helms charged was being poured down a "rathole" overseas. Helms and his Republican allies proposed increased spending on the U.S. military as a more appropriate means of achieving the country's goals in the post–Cold War world.

By the end of 1995, Helms was holding much of U.S. foreign policy hostage, including nearly four hundred foreign service promotions,

IMPACT AND INFLUENCE

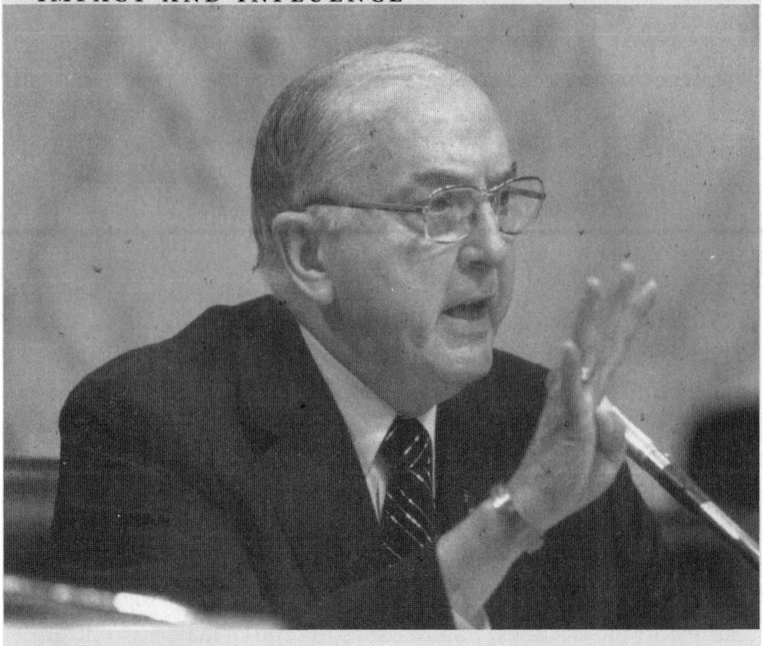

JESSE HELMS

The conventional wisdom "politics stops at the water's edge" certainly did not apply to American foreign policy after November 1994, when the Republican Party captured control of Congress. The new congressional leaders quickly challenged President Bill Clinton, a Democrat, on many aspects of his foreign policy, leading to bitter policy debates and reversals.

Sen. Jesse Helms, chair of the Senate Foreign Relations Committee, aggressively opposed Clinton's foreign policy of liberal internationalism. A staunch conservative from North Carolina, Helms demanded a lower American profile in world politics. He then used his personal clout—along with Congress's many constitutional powers—to oversee deep cuts in the U.S. foreign aid budget, curb U.S. involvement in the United Nations, impose new sanctions against Cuba, and advocate the rejection of several arms control treaties. Meanwhile, Helms demanded increases in military spending and an assertive stance toward Russia, China, and other foreign powers. His self-proclaimed "hard-ball" political tactics deepened the divisions between Congress and the White House that prevented the United States from facing the post–Cold War world with a united front.

thirty ambassadorial nominations, more than a dozen treaties and international agreements, and many daily functions of the State Department. Moreover, as Helms made clear, until Clinton agreed to the Republicans' demands to restructure the State Department, the Foreign Relations Committee would remain recessed indefinitely and many routine operations of U.S. foreign policy would cease. As a result, the State Department had to furlough many of its Washington-based staffers and temporarily halt processing the nearly thirty thousand visa applications received daily. The U.S. government stopped paying utility bills at many foreign embassies, and the funding needed to operate the State Department's computer and cable services was suspended. "The day-to-day foreign policy business on Capitol Hill has ground to a halt," reported the *New York Times* in September 1995.[23]

Shaken by the Republican victories of November 1994, Clinton placed his "neo-Wilsonian" foreign policy on the back burner. What little fervor he had demonstrated previously—most of the real passion for enlargement and sustainable development had come from his subordinates—was all but extinguished after the elections. Thus when the Republican Congress demanded the ouster of UN Secretary General Boutros Boutros-Ghali of Egypt, Clinton complied. When Congress expressed doubts about the 1993 Chemical Weapons Convention, which had been signed by dozens of other governments, Clinton removed the treaty from the table. And when Congress demanded a larger defense budget than was requested by the Joint Chiefs of Staff, along with deep cuts in foreign aid that greatly reduced the U.S. contribution to sustainable development, Clinton again conceded. Rarely in American history had a president so passively relinquished his control over American foreign policy.

The growing schism between Clinton and Congress revealed that the debate over America's role in the post–Cold War world was far from resolved. Both aspects of the American style of foreign policy—detachment from the "outside world" and moral crusading—found expression in the debate and in the country's actions throughout the world. Meanwhile, the military doctrine of global primacy remained in place as U.S. armed forces were repeatedly, but selectively, sent into battle to support the country's declared goals. Taken together, these actions suggested that, of the four competing grand strategies summarized earlier in this chapter—renewed isolationism, liberal internationalism, global primacy, and selective engagement—a peculiar course was ultimately adopted: all of the above. It was not surprising, then, that the United States became widely viewed as an erratic and unpredictable power in the heyday of its "unipolar moment."

23. Elaine Sciolino, "Awaiting Call, Helms Puts Foreign Policy on Hold," *New York Times*, September 24, 1995, 1A.

CHAPTER TEN

Old Tensions in a New Order

A Somali woman runs across a field as U.S. Army helicopters land outside the town of Afgoi, where armed bandits had prevented the delivery of food aid. The U.S. mission in Somalia, aimed at restoring political order, was later abandoned after U.S. and UN troops were killed in fighting between rival militias.

The mid-1990s in the United States saw the euphoria surrounding the end of the Cold War quickly succumb to partisan bickering and a congressional assault on President Bill Clinton. Overseas, an outbreak of conflicts raised doubts about the president's global ambitions. Ethnic and religious disputes sparked violence across the developing world, challenging ruling elites and threatening regional power balances. Meanwhile, the jockeying continued among the great powers for power and strategic advantage. Western leaders expressed concern about the sluggish reform movement in Russia, lest the country slip back into its old dictatorial ways and expansionism. They also grew increasingly anxious about China's growing military strength and assertiveness after the Sino-American partnership, which in large measure was directed against the Soviet Union, became null and void after the Cold War.

Taken together, these problems demanded a coherent response by the United States, whose historical vision of a more democratic and peaceful world faced new challenges. But such a response became less likely amid the political war being waged between Clinton and Congress. Their struggle, which culminated in Clinton's impeachment by the House of Representatives in December 1998 for a sex scandal, boosted the level of public cynicism to record levels, infuriated U.S. allies who looked to Washington for leadership, and tempted potential adversaries to exploit America's internal divisions.

As conflicts erupted in many parts of the developing world and in Europe, where renewed fighting broke out in the Balkan peninsula and Russia's reforms faced unending challenges (see Chapter 11), U.S. leaders were forced to make difficult choices about their ability—and willingness—to intervene in the regional disputes, many of which dated back centuries. Their decisions played a vital role in the outcome of many conflicts. More generally, the responses by the United States signaled to the rest of the world how America would handle its responsibilities as the world's preeminent power.

Sources of Global Fragmentation

Among those who felt the "end of history" was at hand after the Cold War, the defining trend in world politics was the technological revolution that was rapidly drawing the far reaches of the world closer together. This process of global *integration* was welcomed for several reasons: world leaders would increasingly recognize and solve problems that crossed national boundaries; integration would discourage self-serving and nationalistic behavior; nongovernmental organizations would mobilize global public opinion and highlight human rights and environmental concerns; economic globalization would increase prosperity; and the spread of democratic rule would reduce the likelihood of war.

It was not long, however, before the equal but opposite forces of global *fragmentation* raised doubts about these rosy scenarios. The reason: the shift in the global balance of power had produced a volatile and violent international order.[1] Bipolarity had been relatively stable because of its very simplicity. Watching each other constantly, the superpowers maintained the balance, always aware of the danger of nuclear war and its suicidal potential. Consequently, there was no third world war; after the 1962 Cuban missile crisis there were no comparable crises between

1. See Benjamin Barber, *Jihad vs. McWorld: How Globalism and Tribalism Are Reshaping the World* (New York: Times Books, 1995), chaps. 10–14.

the superpowers; and despite tensions, Europe experienced the longest period of peace in the twentieth century. But all of this changed with the collapse of the Soviet Union, leading some analysts to express nostalgia for the Cold War.[2]

The breakdown of bipolarity wrought instability and encouraged fragmentation in three distinct ways. First, the retreat of the Soviet Union revived the nationalist, ethnic, and religious tensions that had accompanied the breakup of the Austro-Hungarian, Russian, and Ottoman (Turkish) empires after World War I but that were kept largely in check during the Cold War. The breakup of the Soviet Union into fifteen republics produced armed clashes between Armenia and Azerbaijan, a war of secession in the Russian province of Chechnya, civil war in Tajikistan, and new tensions between Russia and its formidable neighbors China and India. The end of communist rule in Yugoslavia sparked a new and ghastly round of religious warfare. In fact, the reemergence of the fault lines separating ethnic and religious groups in many parts of the world suggested that a "clash of civilizations" was imminent.[3]

A second consequence was that aspirants to regional hegemony felt free to pursue their aggressive designs. It was no longer true that each superpower, dominant in its own sphere of influence, could restrain its clients and prevent local conflicts. Expansionist middle powers were now free to fill the void left by the superpowers. Iraq's invasion of Kuwait in 1990, described later in this chapter, was unthinkable so long as the Soviet Union remained a key regional player that wished to avoid a confrontation with the United States. Similarly, the resurgence of ethnic conflict across Africa and the escalation of tensions between India and Pakistan coincided with the withdrawal of the great powers.

Finally, the fragmented world order tested the resilience of U.S. alliances. Organized to counter the power of the Soviet Union and China, these alliances gave priority to common interests in collective security. With the Cold War over, the mission of the North Atlantic Treaty Organization (NATO) became unclear as other security arrangements were devised for the European Union. The fears of U.S. leaders that NATO would become obsolete explained much of their enthusiasm for its eastward expansion. Meanwhile, the web of multilateral alliances created by the United States across the Pacific Ocean had long ceased to exist in any meaningful sense, and the durability of its bilateral ties to several nations in East Asia was thrown into question. The United States reaffirmed its regional presence by extending its security pact with Japan

2. See John Mearsheimer, "Why We Will Soon Miss the Cold War," *Atlantic Monthly*, August 1990, 33–50.

3. Samuel Huntington, "The Clash of Civilizations?" *Foreign Affairs* (summer 1993): 22–49.

in 1996 and keeping its troops in South Korea. But it was doubtful that the emerging powers of the Pacific Rim would indefinitely accept their status as de facto protectorates of the United States.

The contradictory forces of global integration and fragmentation had far deeper roots than the Cold War and its aftermath.[4] Advances in transportation and communication had been making the world "smaller" for centuries. By the same token, the outbreak of civil wars was a logical result of the spread of democracy and its calls for self-determination, which first became a strong political force during the Enlightenment era of the eighteenth century. The end of the Cold War, however, ruptured the geopolitical basis for world order and allowed both forces to find full expression.

For James Woolsey, Clinton's first director of central intelligence, all of this boiled down to a simple metaphor: although the Soviet "dragon" had been slain, America now existed in a "jungle filled with a bewildering variety of poisonous snakes."[5] This newer environment was potentially menacing to the United States in several ways. The "snakes" were just as deadly, and they were more numerous and difficult to identity. In practical terms, then, the United States had to concern itself not only with other major powers, but also with the terrorist groups, drug cartels, organized crime syndicates, and black market weapons dealers who threatened the world of the early 1990s. The nation would have to guard itself against threats that could take several forms and come from any direction.

War and Peace in the Middle East

The first trouble spot to disrupt the "new world order" was the Middle East. Ample and inexpensive oil from the Persian Gulf had powered the twentieth century's Industrial Revolution. But after the Arab members of the Organization of the Petroleum-Exporting Countries (OPEC) embargoed oil shipments to the United States in 1973 and provoked a second oil shock in 1978, the West recognized all too well its dependence on Middle East oil and its vulnerability to future disruptions of oil flows. In the 1990s, the absence of a superpower rivalry left a power vacuum in the Middle East that one regional leader, Iraq's Saddam Hussein, attempted to fill. Saddam's bid for hegemony produced the first world crisis of the post–Cold War era. Meanwhile, the peace process between Israel and its Arab neighbors inched forward between spasms of violence and political crisis.

4. See John Lewis Gaddis, "Toward the Post–Cold War World," *Foreign Affairs* (spring 1991): 102–122.

5. Quoted in Loch Johnson, "Reinventing the CIA," in *U.S. Foreign Policy after the Cold War,* ed. Randall B. Ripley and James M. Lindsay (Pittsburgh: University of Pittsburgh Press, 1997), 135.

IRAQ'S CHALLENGE IN THE PERSIAN GULF

The year 1990 found Saddam Hussein at least $80 billion in debt from his eight-year war (1980–1988) with Iran that had left more than one million dead or injured on each side. On August 2, Saddam ordered his battle-tested army to invade his oil-rich neighbor, the emirate of Kuwait. The Iraqi army quickly overran the largely undefended Kuwaiti capital, Kuwait City. With his troops poised on the border of Saudi Arabia and many Arab neighbors afraid of him, Saddam then sought to intimidate the Persian Gulf oil kingdoms and assert his dominance over the entire region.

At the time, there was no one in the Middle East to oppose Saddam's bid for power. Egypt, traditionally the leader of the Arab states, had lost that status when it made peace with Israel. Moreover, in an era in which "petrodollars" produced political and military power, Egypt, without oil reserves, was weaker than the Persian Gulf states. Syria, another frequent rival for Arab leadership, was left isolated with the disappearance of its patron in Moscow. Saddam reasoned that by establishing Iraq as the dominant power in the region, he could launch his campaign for regional hegemony against the moderate Persian Gulf oil kingdoms and rival Arab states.

Saddam expected little resistance from the United States. After being ejected from Iran in 1979, Washington sought vengeance against Tehran and a new U.S. support base in the Persian Gulf. Toward both ends, President Ronald Reagan provided Saddam with intelligence, military equipment, and agriculture credits worth billions, many of which Saddam bartered for military supplies.[6] The Reagan administration also removed Iraq from the U.S. list of state sponsors of terrorism despite evidence that the nation still maintained ties to Palestinian terrorists. Meanwhile, export licenses allowed Saddam to buy "dual-use" technology that could be used to produce biological and chemical weapons, and he repeatedly used these weapons against Iranian targets. Saddam also launched such weapons of mass destruction (WMD) against Kurdish citizens in his own country, who opposed his regime. A single gas attack on the Kurdish city of Halabja in March 1988 left an estimated five thousand dead and ten thousand injured.

In return for Washington's support, Saddam pledged to keep the Persian Gulf free of communist influence, a role previously played by Iran, and to provide America with a modest discount on Iraqi oil. This marriage of convenience ended with the conclusion of the Iran-Iraq war.

6. See Bruce W. Jentleson, *With Friends Like These: Reagan, Bush, and Saddam, 1982–1990* (New York: Norton, 1994).

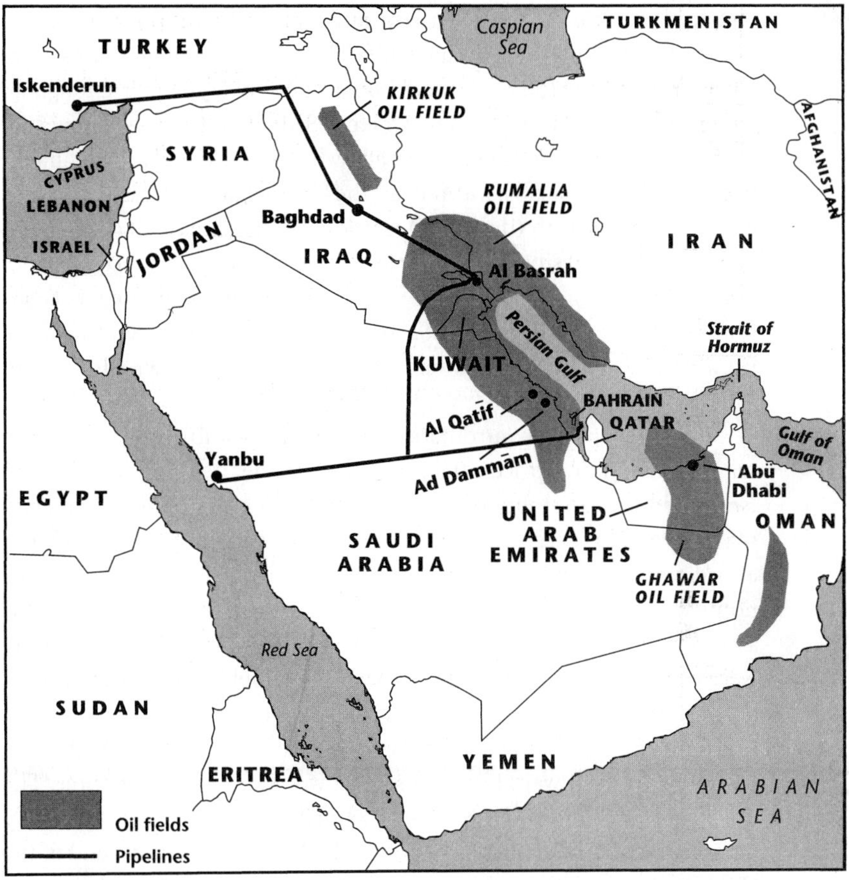

THE PERSIAN GULF, WITH KEY OIL FIELDS AND PIPELINES

Concerned about Iraq's WMD program, Congress threatened the Iraq leader with economic sanctions. But Saddam still received positive signals from the White House and expected U.S. leaders to look the other way when he set his sights on Kuwait in 1990. This proved to be a fateful miscalculation.[7] President George H. W. Bush, heir to Reagan's hands-off policy toward Saddam, abruptly reversed course and announced that Iraq's blatant aggression "would not stand."

As Iraqi forces massed near Saudi Arabia's border, the possibility that Saddam might soon control 40 percent of the world's oil reserves and dictate the terms of OPEC production forced an aggressive response. Japan and the Western powers froze Iraqi assets in their countries and those of the deposed government of Kuwait. This measure was accompanied by an

7. Rick Francona, *Ally to Adversary: An Eyewitness Account of Iraq's Fall from Grace* (Annapolis, Md.: U.S. Naval Institute Press, 1999), 5–6.

embargo on Iraqi oil and other economic sanctions, to be enforced by a naval blockade of the Persian Gulf. The two central questions were whether Iraq's customers would honor the embargo long enough to bankrupt the Iraqi economy and whether Saddam ultimately would succumb to the economic sanctions or allow his people to suffer indefinitely, like Fidel Castro in Cuba. Meanwhile, the United States proceeded with its largest troop buildup (dubbed Operation Desert Shield) since the Vietnam War; 250,000 troops were deployed to deter an Iraqi attack on Saudi Arabia. American officials hoped the prospect of war with the UN coalition—composed mainly of U.S., British, and French forces and those from several Arab states—would persuade Saddam to withdraw from Kuwait.

The stakes in this confrontation were clear: possible Iraqi control of oil production and prices, the stability of moderate Arab regimes and Israel, and the durability of the post–Cold War balance of power. Having rhetorically accepted the challenge, the United States could not afford to back down. If it did, it would endanger its security, its economic growth as well as that of its major trading partners, and its status as the world's lone remaining superpower. If its Arab allies and Israel were neglected in their moment of peril, they might not trust the United States again. The stage was set for a showdown.

The United Nations gave Saddam a deadline of January 15, 1991, to withdraw from Kuwait. If he refused, he would be ejected by force. The unanimity within the UN Security Council was remarkable and clearly demonstrated how great-power politics had changed with the end of the Cold War. Previously, the council's five permanent members—the United States, the Soviet Union, Britain, France, and China—had agreed on virtually nothing and the two superpowers had vetoed any call for collective action. But with Mikhail Gorbachev clinging to power in the Soviet Union and seeking accommodation with the West, the great powers were for once able to cooperate. Saddam, hoping to disrupt this marriage of the great powers, instead provided a rationale for the UN to test its long-dormant system of collective security. As his tactics became more ruthless, they infuriated world opinion and stiffened the resolve of the UN coalition.

The unprecedented UN solidarity was not matched within Congress, however, which insisted that President Bush gain its assent before he used force. Many members, still haunted by memories of Vietnam, argued that economic sanctions would be sufficient to dislodge Iraq. Their arguments were shared by thousands of peace activists, who held candlelight vigils and public demonstrations to denounce the impending war. With the UN deadline nearing and the U.S. troop deployment increasing to nearly 500,000, Congress held a historic debate about the

Iraqi challenge and narrowly approved the military operation. When the January 15 deadline passed with Iraqi forces still in Kuwait, the United States and coalition partners transformed Operation Desert Shield into Operation Desert Storm.

The massive air assault that began on January 17 sent Saddam's forces fleeing for cover. Allied air forces flew more than 100,000 sorties, devastating Iraqi targets from the front lines to Baghdad. In the first phase, they took out Iraqi command-and-control posts, airfields, communications centers, and other military installations. In the second phase, they destroyed the bridges and roads being used to supply the Iraqi forces in Kuwait. Cut off, those forces were then subjected to constant pounding. Their poorly concealed tanks and armored personnel carriers were destroyed by laser-guided U.S. missiles, which either killed the Iraqi soldiers or left them stranded in the desert. Not until February 24 did the coalition's tank forces launch their ground attack across the Saudi border.

The results of this military response exceeded the expectations of the most optimistic military planners. Within one hundred hours, the ground forces had surrounded the Iraqis, most of whom surrendered quickly. Once feared as the world's fourth largest fighting force, these troops were only too glad to throw down their arms in return for food and water. Facing almost no opposition, coalition convoys rolled toward Kuwait City, past oil fields set ablaze by Iraq's retreating forces. When the first wave of liberation forces, mostly from Arab countries, reached the Kuwaiti capital, they were greeted and embraced by cheering mobs. The Gulf War had lasted forty-three days. More than 100,000 Iraqi soldiers were killed in the blitzkrieg; coalition casualties were less than two hundred. In the end, Saddam was forced to revoke his annexation of Kuwait and withdraw what was left of his occupation force.

The war, however, did not result in Saddam's removal from power; that had never been the goal of the UN. Indeed, had the tank columns rolled on to Baghdad, the coalition likely would have come apart. The Arabs wanted to ensure that Saddam would no longer pose a threat, but they were against his overthrow. And Washington wanted no part in governing a nation in civil war, which appeared likely in the wake of Saddam's defeat. Iraq's Kurds and Shiite Muslims, constituting the majority of the country's population, rebelled in separate regions against Saddam, a Sunni Muslim. But they were not strong enough to defeat the remnants of Saddam's Republican Guard, many of whom were saved at the last moment by the abrupt cease-fire.

Despite Saddam's undisguised brutality toward his own people, the United States and its allies, as noted, did not want to see Iraq disintegrate. They expected the country to maintain its pivotal role in the Middle East balance of power, a role not possible if it were partitioned. More important, they did not want the surrounding countries, especially Iran and Syria, to carve up the country in their own bids for regional dominance. Iraqi Kurds and Shiites charged the United States with encouraging them to revolt against Saddam and then ignoring them once they were engaged in battle and ultimately defeated. But the realities of the regional power balance overrode those criticisms.

After the war, Saddam defied a series of international demands, making it clear that despite the coalition's victory he would remain a threat. In late 1994, he displayed his capacity to menace the Persian Gulf region at will when he again massed troops on the Kuwaiti border, this time to protest continuing UN sanctions against Iraq. The United States, now led by President Bill Clinton, responded by mobilizing its remaining forces in the Persian Gulf and deploying thousands of additional troops to the region. Saddam then backed down and ordered his Republican Guards to return to their bases. Two years later, he sponsored attacks against the Kurdish population of northern Iraq, a region declared off-limits by the UN and occupied by a U.S.-led relief force. After the United States responded with air strikes against Iraqi military installations, Saddam withdrew once more.

Despite the coalition's spectacular success in routing Iraq from Kuwait in 1991, Saddam remained firmly in power and demonstrated repeatedly his ability to create havoc. He recognized Iraq's importance to the strategic interests of the Western powers. And he openly exploited his freedom to inflame the region at the time and place of his choosing. As he did so, Saddam wore down the UN coalition. Two factors aided his divide-and-conquer strategy. First, the United States was steadily losing support within the UN Security Council. Among the permanent members, Russia and China were growing more supportive of Iraq—less because of their affinity for Saddam than because of their desire to curb U.S. influence. They were joined in their defiance by France, which used any opportunity to display its independence from Washington. Only Britain, led by Prime Minister Tony Blair, remained loyal to the United States in the Security Council.

Saddam also was aware of Clinton's faltering domestic support, particularly within the Republican-controlled Congress. Even within the Clinton administration, splits were widely reported among Secretary of State Madeleine Albright, Secretary of Defense William Cohen, and National Security Adviser Sandy Berger. The president's ability to lead was further impaired by the deepening White House scandals that ultimately triggered a congressional effort to remove him from office. Although Saddam remained secluded and his whereabouts were unknown, he obviously kept up with current events in Washington. The

Iraqi leader's repeated provocations were timed to coincide with the crisis points in the president's political struggles at home.

In 1997 Saddam directed his wrath toward the United Nations Special Commission (UNSCOM), which had been given the difficult task of ensuring that Iraq dismantled its chemical, biological, and nuclear weapons programs. The role of UNSCOM was vital, because Iraq had used biological weapons against Iran and its own Kurdish population. There also was evidence that since the 1980s Iraq had filled missile warheads with botulism, anthrax, and other deadly biological agents. The fears that Iraq was secretly storing such weapons and would use them if given the opportunity were therefore justified. Saddam had agreed to the creation of UNSCOM, but he soon resisted inspections of Iraqi military installations, which frequently were conducted without warning. A cat-and-mouse game quickly ensued, with UNSCOM agents arriving at suspected Iraqi weapons facilities only to find they had been recently vacated. Saddam turned up the heat late in 1997 by expelling the U.S. members of UNSCOM, whom he accused of dominating the inspections and conspiring with the U.S. Central Intelligence Agency to overthrow him. A second expulsion in February 1998 led Clinton to threaten a punitive military strike, averted at the last moment by UN Secretary General Kofi Annan. Annan, flying to Baghdad, received Saddam's assurances that Iraq would allow UNSCOM inspections. Saddam then reneged on this pledge, and the UN inspectors returned home.

Clinton was clearly losing this standoff with Iraq. His lack of political support at home and overseas left him with little room to maneuver. More than anything, Clinton feared he would be condemned for launching a military attack on Iraq at a time when Saddam was widely viewed as seeking reconciliation. Political concerns took precedence over military strategy, and in the political sphere Clinton's hand was growing weaker every day. His concessions to Iraq only stiffened Saddam's resolve and energized the anti-American coalition in the UN. When Clinton resorted to force, as in the December 1998 aerial bombardments code-named Operation Desert Fox, he was accused of trying to distract attention from domestic problems. Clinton remained trapped in a no-win Iraq policy with Iraq for the rest of his presidency.

OBSTACLES TO AN ARAB-ISRAELI PEACE

In the wake of Operation Desert Storm, the United States judged the time right for a new effort to gain a comprehensive peace between Israel and its neighbors. The oil kingdoms owed Washington a favor for saving them from Saddam Hussein. Syria, deprived of Soviet patronage and protection, also seemed ready for a settlement. Moreover, shortly after the Gulf War Israel's hard-line Likud government, which had a cool relationship with the United States, was replaced by a more accommodating Labor Party government headed by Yitzhak Rabin.

The unexpected breakthrough came in September 1993 when the Palestine Liberation Organization (PLO) and Israel agreed to mutual recognition. In the historic Oslo Declaration of Principles, which was facilitated by the Norwegian government, the PLO abandoned its call for the destruction of Israel and renounced terrorism. In return, Israel would withdraw from the Gaza Strip and the West Bank town of Jericho and allow the Palestinians to govern themselves. It was assumed that, over time, Palestinian control over education, health, social services, taxation, and tourism would be extended over the West Bank except in the areas settled by the Israelis. It also was assumed that the Palestinians would keep order, police themselves, and, in particular, end the *intifada* (uprising) against Israel and its supporters. If these expectations were realized, the two sides eventually would hold "final-status" talks about whether the Palestinians would be allowed to establish a state of their own.

Why did these two deadly enemies finally decide to negotiate their differences? For one thing, the end of the Cold War deprived the PLO of a strong political supporter—the Soviet Union. For another, the Gulf War had left the organization almost broke; PLO leader Yasir Arafat had made the disastrous decision to support Iraq against the oil kingdoms that had provided the PLO with most of its funds. Even earlier, however, the spontaneous outburst of the *intifada* among West Bank Palestinians, frustrated by the continued Israeli occupation and Arafat's inability to solve their problems, had demonstrated his declining influence. In response, Arafat had established a "Palestinian authority" in the occupied areas, thereby suggesting a two-state solution instead of Israel's elimination. For their part, the Israelis were tired of the conflict and the costs—physical, economic, and human—of the six-year-old *intifada.* But more than that, they were worried about the growing support among Palestinians for extremists. If Israel could achieve a stable peace, the country's economy would prosper, especially with the large influx of skilled Russian immigrants who were fleeing the anti-Semitism that was flourishing once more in their homeland. Talks with the PLO had therefore become inevitable, and the hope was that these would lead to a comprehensive peace agreement.

Over the opposition of extremists in Israel, the Middle East peace process edged further forward in 1994 when Israel resolved its major differences with Jordan. Under the terms of this second agreement, both countries acknowledged the right of the other to exist, bringing their de facto state of war to an end. In addition, Jordan's King Hussein and Israel's Yitzhak Rabin agreed on the boundaries between the two states

IMPACT AND INFLUENCE

YASIR ARAFAT

For most of his life, Yasir Arafat personified the struggle among Palestinians to gain statehood in territories granted to Israel upon its creation in 1948. Arafat was born in Egypt in 1929, but he spent much of his childhood in Jerusalem. Even though he returned to Egypt to study civil engineering, his interests shifted toward political and military activism. From Cairo, Arafat established a network to smuggle arms to Palestinians resisting the creation of Israel and, later, to support Palestinian efforts to destroy the Jewish state. He fought briefly for the Egyptian army, but once he received his engineering degree in 1956, he moved to Kuwait to begin work as a building contractor. Arafat continued, however, to be committed to the Palestinian cause, and in 1957 he helped to found Al-Fatah, an underground network of activists engaged in armed struggle against Israel. Al-Fatah became the primary faction within the Palestine Liberation Organization (PLO), created in 1964, and Arafat rose to become the PLO's leader in 1969. He spent the next two decades seeking international support for the PLO and organizing its ongoing low-intensity war against Israel, along with terrorist attacks on Israeli targets in other areas. Arafat maintained the status of an influential and colorful world leader during this period, visiting foreign capitals and, in 1988, speaking before the UN General Assembly in his military fatigues and familiar Arab headdress.

In the early 1990s, prospects for peace brightened between the Israelis and Palestinians—both sides were exhausted by the endless political violence. The Oslo accords of 1993, described in this chapter, raised hopes for a "two-state solution" that would one day bring peace to the embattled region. But Arafat later proved unable, or unwilling, to restrain his own deputies from sponsoring terrorist attacks on Israelis. His refusal to compromise on key issues in the final-status talks in 2000 left him politically isolated and under virtual house arrest by Israeli forces in his Ramallah compound. American leaders, who had struggled since the days of the Camp David Accords to mediate an end to the conflict, looked to other Palestinian leaders for a lasting peace. Arafat died in 2004 with the Arab-Israeli peace process far from complete.

and divided control over underground water reservoirs and other natural resources; they also established the basis for bilateral trade and tourism. As part of the treaty, the United States agreed to forgive its portion of Jordan's foreign debt, which had soared after years of economic stagnation.

Syria was another story. The United States had hoped that Israel and Syria would agree on a peace accord that would incorporate Syria and Lebanon, Syria's satellite, and produce peace on the northern border of Israel. Since the 1967 Six-Day War, Israeli troops had occupied the Golan Heights region connecting the three countries as well as a strip of southern Lebanon. But despite news reports that Israel's prime minister Rabin and Syria's president Hafez al-Assad both privately endorsed the principle of a return of the Golan Heights to Syria in return for Syria's recognition of Israel, no such agreement was concluded.

Suddenly, just as in the past, the progress toward Arab-Israeli peace was shattered by violence and tragedy. On November 4, 1995, a Jewish extremist assassinated Rabin in order to halt the peace process. In the spring of 1996, Palestinian terrorists staged four suicide bombings in nine days, killing fifty-nine Israelis and wounding more than two hundred. Israelis, now doubtful about the peace process, showed their misgivings at the polls. The conservative Likud Party was restored to power with the election of its leader, Benjamin Netanyahu, to the office of prime minister. Netanyahu pledged to bring "peace with security" to Israel, meaning he would not support further concessions to the Arabs without explicit guarantees that Israel's security would be protected on all fronts.

When these guarantees were not forthcoming, Netanyahu delayed the withdrawal of Israeli troops from the West Bank and from Hebron, a city in the heart of the occupied territories. As each side accused the other of trying to scuttle the agreements, a new round of bloody attacks occurred in the spring and summer of 1996. Each massacre and the inevitable counterattacks that followed diminished the prospects for a Middle East settlement. With the peace process on the verge of collapse, Israel, under great pressure from the United States and other countries, agreed in January 1997 to withdraw from Hebron, a concession that at least temporarily restored the lost momentum. But Netanyahu's insistence on building new Jewish settlements in East Jerusalem, home to many Palestinians, led to another round of violence. Despite the best efforts of the United States, a resolution of the Arab-Israeli conflict remained elusive.

The Plight of 'Failed States'

Among the most notable trends in world politics after World War II was the steady rise in the number of nation-states—from fifty-five in 1946 to nearly two hundred by the turn of the millennium. Most of the new

LEBANON
GOLAN HEIGHTS AREA: Occupied by Israel in 1967. Unilaterally annexed by Israel in 1981.
WEST BANK AREA: Unilaterally annexed by Jordan in 1950. Occupied by Israel in 1967. Currently portions under Palestinian control.
GAZA STRIP: Occupied by Israel in 1967. Currently under Palestinian control.
SINAI PENINSULA: Returned to Egypt by Israel in 1982.
GOLAN HEIGHTS
SYRIA
Haifa
Sea of Galilee
Nazareth
Jordan River
Tel Aviv
WEST BANK
Amman
Jericho
Mediterranean Sea
Jerusalem
Gaza
GAZA STRIP
Hebron
Dead Sea
Beersheba
ISRAEL
EGYPT
SINAI PENINSULA
JORDAN
NEGEV
Gulf of Aqaba

ISRAEL AND DISPUTED TERRITORIES

countries were created from former European colonies in Africa and southern Asia. Others, such as the Czech Republic and Slovakia, emerged after the Cold War in Eastern Europe. Still others were carved out of the former Soviet Union. This proliferation of nation-states dramatically changed the face of world politics during the late twentieth century. The new countries, often located in the world's poorest areas, received large volumes of foreign aid from wealthier nations and accepted their help in the complicated task of "nation building." Yet despite some progress in their living conditions, these developing countries remained generally hostile to the industrialized North. In the UN, the new states united with other developing countries to form a majority in the General Assembly, which served as a forum to express their grievances against the United States and other industrialized nations.

This resentment steadily intensified during the Cold War, when many developing countries became battlegrounds for the superpower conflict, illustrating the aphorism that "when two elephants fight, the grass suffers." The ideological nature of these conflicts polarized the developing countries and often pitted neo-Marxist revolutionaries against right-wing military juntas, which became ever more repressive when challenged for power. Neither a middle class nor a moderate political center was possible under these circumstances. Frequently, extremists on both sides received modern weaponry from the superpowers or their allies, which further inflamed the conflicts.

In this respect, the end of the Cold War was welcomed by the most impoverished nations, which were still reeling from the punishing economic distress of the 1980s, widely labeled the "lost decade" of development. By the late 1990s, however, the social and economic problems plaguing many poor countries had only worsened. Contrary to widespread expectations, the accommodation between Washington and Moscow had produced lower levels of foreign aid to the world's poor; indeed, the United States had all but eliminated aid to "non-strategic allies." Instead, U.S. policy makers called on developing countries to seek private investments to boost their economies. But such investment was unlikely where poverty and political unrest prevailed. In contrast to the flood of foreign investment that flowed to the newly industrialized countries of East Asia, the poorest states received barely a trickle.

Some observers suggested dismantling what was left of the most desperate developing countries and putting them under UN trusteeship. Such a response was highly unlikely, but it revealed the depths to which many of these countries had fallen. Indeed, in many areas the post–Cold War era witnessed the emergence of the "failed state": "From Haiti in the Western Hemisphere to the remnants of Yugoslavia in Europe, from Somalia, Sudan, and Liberia in Africa to Cambodia in Southeast Asia, a disturbing new phenomenon is emerging: the failed nation-state, utterly incapable of sustaining itself as a member of the international community. . . . [T]hose states descend into violence and anarchy—imperiling their own citizens and threatening their neighbors through refugee flows, political instability, and random warfare."[8]

These crises raised questions about the arrangements that had created these countries in the first place, particularly those in Africa whose ethnic groups overlapped state boundaries drawn by colonial rulers. For the United States, which had sought support from these impoverished states to counter Soviet influence in the region, their plight was suddenly remote to its strategic self-interests. Americans, however, could not escape the scenes of warfare and starvation appearing on their televisions daily and crying out for action by the world's richest and most powerful country. Yet what form, if any, this help should take remained unclear.

SOMALIA AND CENTRAL AFRICA

One of the first states to arouse international attention was the impoverished country of Somalia, located along the Horn of Africa at the entrance to the Red Sea (see the map "Africa Today" in Chapter 4). During the Cold War, the Soviets had supported the government of Somalia because its larger neighbor to the north, Ethiopia, was aligned with the United States. But when a pro-Soviet military regime came into power in Ethiopia, Somalia's ruler switched sides as well. Gen. Muhammad Siad Barre became a loyal client of the United States despite his ruthless oppression of the Somali people. All of this perversely made sense in the context of Cold War rivalry. But when the Cold War ended and Barre was overthrown, Somalia became embroiled in a war of succession among rival factions. The government ceased to function and chaos prevailed. Widespread starvation followed when the rival militias prevented farmers from planting, disrupted the activities of nomadic traders, and killed most of the nation's livestock. An estimated 300,000 Somalis died of starvation; another two million were in immediate danger.

For months, the world looked the other way. Media attention finally compelled a Western response through the United Nations. More than 27,000 troops, at first mainly American, were dispatched in late 1992 to provide order and food. After they had accomplished the mission of Operation Restore Hope, the U.S. forces were to be withdrawn and replaced by

8. Gerald B. Helman and Steven R. Ratner, "Saving Failed States," *Foreign Policy* (winter 1992–1993): 3. Also see *Collapsed States: The Disintegration and Restoration of Legitimate Authority,* ed. I. William Zartman (Boulder, Colo.: Lynne Rienner, 1995).

a temporary contingent of UN forces. Saved by the foreign intervention, a "restored" Somalia would then be able to chart its own course.

Unfortunately, the reality in Somalia was not so simple. It soon became clear that, once the outside forces were withdrawn, the Somali warlords would resume their struggle for power, leading to renewed killing and hunger. Thus in 1993 the UN changed its mission from one of humanitarian relief to one of rebuilding Somalia's political and economic structures. But the country's principal warlord, Gen. Mohammed Farah Aidid, who controlled Somalia's capital, Mogadishu, resisted the enlarged UN mission, because it called for his own removal and disarmament. In the fighting that followed, twenty-four Pakistani peacekeepers were ambushed and killed. Later, more UN troops were killed, including U.S. soldiers who were deployed to capture the elusive general. As the number of U.S. casualties mounted—and after a slain U.S. soldier was dragged through the streets of Mogadishu before cheering crowds and television cameras—demands began for the withdrawal of U.S. troops. Clinton responded by accelerating their departure, and the United Nations suspended the mission in the spring of 1995.

How did the Somali operation go so tragically wrong? The international peacekeepers, initially dispatched for the humanitarian purpose of feeding the people, ignored the political situation that had created the hunger in the first place. Food shortages had not stemmed from a natural disaster; they were man-made. Indeed, it should have been clear from the beginning that resolving the anarchic political situation was a prerequisite to resolving the humanitarian crisis. What was originally thought to be a short mission ended up taking two and a half years, underlining the fact that there was no such thing as an apolitical, purely humanitarian intervention. A lasting solution to the Somali conflict was possible only through internal reconciliation undertaken by the Somalis themselves. Thus a worthy, moral effort to help Somalia turned into an open-ended, futile commitment, after which Somalia remained in the grip of civil war for the rest of the decade.

In the waning days of the Somalia debacle, the world was confronted with an even more grotesque humanitarian nightmare in the African state of Rwanda. In 1994, over a period of less than three months, violence between the Hutus, who dominated the government, and the minority Tutsi population had resulted in more than 800,000 casualties, mainly Tutsi. This death toll far exceeded that in Bosnia, where the killing of about 200,000 Muslims by the Serbs had been labeled genocide (see Chapter 11). Because the multilateral response had proved unworkable in Somalia, a concerted peacekeeping effort in Rwanda was out of the question. For this reason, the UN was largely silent in the face of the Rwandan tragedy.

The responsibility for outside intervention fell to the French government, which considered francophone Africa within its sphere of influence even after its colonial control had ended.[9] But by the time French troops intervened in Rwanda, it was too late. Corpses choked Rwanda's rivers, many horribly hacked with machetes. The subsequent victory of the Tutsi army and the establishment of a Tutsi-led government then provoked one of the world's greatest human migrations. Fearing vengeance, the Hutus virtually emptied Rwanda—half a million fled to Burundi, another half-million to Tanzania, and a million to Zaire. This relentless flow of refugees overwhelmed local and international efforts to help and led to widespread deaths from starvation, cholera, dehydration, and exhaustion.

Personal apologies by President Clinton in 1998 for the lack of a U.S. response did nothing to relieve the suffering of the Rwandans. Nor did the UN's admission in December 1999 that it made "serious mistakes" in failing to prevent the catastrophe.[10] But for all of their admissions of guilt and pledges to act more decisively in the future, the United States and the UN could not escape the central reality: Rwanda had been deemed irrelevant by most non-African countries and unworthy of their sacrifice. Under the spell of the "Somalia syndrome," Clinton had signed a presidential directive in May 1994 that had placed strict conditions on U.S. support for UN peacekeeping. These conditions included a clear threat to U.S. security, substantial public support for intervention, participation by other countries under UN supervision, and an assurance that long-term "nation building" would not be necessary. Because of these restrictions, a repeat of the Rwandan episode would likely elicit the same nonresponse by the United States.

The regional conflicts in Africa widened in the late 1990s with no end in sight. Violent attacks and reprisals between the Tutsi-led government of Burundi and the majority Hutu population raised the prospect of another Rwandan-style bloodbath. The fighting there provoked yet another exodus of refugees, mostly to eastern Zaire, where the corrupt regime of the ailing dictator Mobutu Sese Seko battled its own insurgency. Thousands of Hutu refugees were trapped in the crossfire between rebel forces, led by Laurent Kabila, and Mobutu's army. Mobutu had virtually no support among Zaire's civilian population, and, unlike during the Cold War, he could not count on military assistance from the United States, which declared during the rebellion that "the era of

9. Although Rwanda was a Belgian colony, it had been incorporated into France's sphere of influence after its independence.

10. See United Nations, *Independent Inquiry into the Actions of the United Nations during the 1994 Genocide in Rwanda* (New York: United Nations, 1999).

Mobutuism is over." The rapid advance and victory of Kabila's forces in May 1997 were therefore unstoppable.

Upon seizing control of the capital of Kinshasa, Kabila restored the country's original name—Democratic Republic of the Congo—and sought international recognition. His new regime, however, proved to be no more democratic or effective in improving living conditions than Mobutu's dictatorship. To the contrary, Kabila presided over Africa's newest failed state. His country was overrun by ethnic conflict that produced thousands of new casualties, ghastly human rights abuses, and intervention by half a dozen neighboring countries. Described by Secretary of State Madeleine Albright as "Africa's first world war," the conflict raged well into 2000 despite the proclamation of a cease-fire.

These events in Africa proved how difficult the process of political and economic development would be in countries recovering from colonial rule and intervention by the Cold War superpowers. The conflicts also revealed the inability of outside actors—whether governments or relief organizations—to prevent atrocities and humanitarian nightmares. In fact, many critics charged that foreign aid programs were designed to promote the self-interests of the donors themselves, not to relieve suffering in developing countries, and that relief agencies like CARE, UNICEF, and the U.S. Agency for International Development were most concerned with enhancing their own stature.[11] By the end of the 1990s, more people were dying in sub-Saharan Africa's wars than in the rest of the world combined. But the region still reverted to its pre–Cold War status—off the radar screen of American foreign policy.

HAITI

The Clinton administration was confronted with yet another crisis in the failed state of Haiti, the poorest country in the Western Hemisphere. Ruled by the U.S.-backed Duvalier dictatorship until 1986, the Haitian people had their first democratic elections in 1990 when they elected the Reverend Jean-Bertrand Aristide to the country's presidency. But Aristide's proposed reforms, including his plans to demilitarize the country and redistribute wealth, resulted in his overthrow six months later by the military. With Aristide in exile in the United States, Haiti's military leaders, led by Gen. Raoul Cédras, launched a campaign of terror across the island, killing, torturing, and imprisoning those who had fought for reforms and who continued to resist the new rulers. In response, thousands of Haitians constructed makeshift boats and fled to the United

11. Michael Maren, *The Road to Hell: The Ravaging Effects of Foreign Aid and International Charity* (New York: Free Press, 1997).

States. In his final months in office, President Bush announced that the United States was unprepared to accommodate these "boat people" and ordered the U.S. Coast Guard to turn them back. His decision angered many human rights groups, as well as candidate Bill Clinton, who declared that as president he would allow the Haitians to seek asylum in the United States.

But just as in other areas of foreign policy, Clinton's position on Haiti changed once he took office. Suddenly, he shared Bush's reservations about absorbing the mass emigration of Haitians. Such a policy would surely anger residents of Florida, who were as vital to Clinton's electoral fortunes as they had been to those of President Bush. While continuing to demand Aristide's return to Haiti and denouncing the military rulers, Clinton announced he would not allow Haitian refugees to enter the United States. Instead, a UN-sponsored economic embargo was imposed on Haiti, but it had little effect on the political and social crisis. In July 1993, Clinton and the Haitian leadership reached an agreement that would have brought about Aristide's return to power in exchange for amnesty for Cédras and other military leaders. When the 270 U.S. and Canadian peacekeepers arrived in Haiti on the U.S.S. *Harlan County* to oversee the transition back to civilian rule, they were greeted by armed demonstrators. The ship then beat an ignominious retreat. An angry and disappointed Aristide publicly condemned the Clinton administration's reversal and was joined by many liberals on Capitol Hill, including members of the Congressional Black Caucus, who saw a racial bias in Clinton's acceptance of Cuban refugees, whereas Haitians, of African origin, were turned back in open waters.

The tentative American response to disorder in Haiti became a symbol of the Clinton administration's general lack of resolve in foreign policy. The *New York Times*, which supported most of Clinton's domestic initiatives, expressed dismay at his reversals in handling the deepening crisis in Haiti: "After months of vacillating from one policy to another, America faces the troubling prospect that Mr. Clinton is drifting into using troops in Haiti because he wants to compensate for other policy embarrassments and does not have a better idea."[12] Clinton also was condemned by conservatives, aghast at his retreat at the first sign of opposition by a weak and corrupt military regime and at the squandering of U.S. prestige.

The turmoil in Haiti continued into the fall of 1994 even while Haitian refugees were being diverted to an overcrowded settlement camp on the Guantánamo naval base in Cuba, then to temporary facilities as far away as Panama City. Clinton finally concluded that the Haitian prob-

12. "Which Haiti Policy?" (editorial), *New York Times*, July 7, 1994, A18.

lem could only be resolved by U.S. military intervention, and he issued a public ultimatum to the Cédras junta. His threat of war was widely denounced in the United States, where congressional opponents demanded time to debate and vote on the impending invasion, but Clinton had gone beyond the point of no return. As American warplanes were preparing to leave for the capital Port-au-Prince, Clinton dispatched a high-level mission, headed by former president Jimmy Carter, to confront Cédras, offer him a final opportunity to leave peacefully, and prevent a military clash. Cédras accepted the offer, but only after being notified that the invasion was imminent.

The military assault on Haiti was then transformed into a "semipermissive occupation" by twenty thousand U.S. troops that extended well into 1995. As in Somalia, the United States was thrust into the role of nation builder. Aristide was returned to power, and he was succeeded peacefully the next year by René Préval. The elections, although closely monitored, were widely boycotted by Haiti's political parties and its largely illiterate citizens. Stability on the island depended on the presence of U.S. troops, a steady stream of Western foreign aid, and the deployment in March 1996 of six thousand UN peacekeepers. By the end of 1999, any hopes that Haiti could be converted into a stable and democratic country had vanished. The country's unemployment rate hovered at around 60 percent and almost all foreign investment had been withdrawn. Haiti's government was so paralyzed that it could not pass the minimal legislation needed to permit $500 million in aid to be sent to the island. Faced with an impossible task, U.S. troops abandoned Haiti, followed closely by UN officials and private relief groups. The warring factions were left to their own devices.

Nuclear Brinkmanship in South Asia

Growing regional tensions and the absence of superpower-induced restraint also afflicted South Asia in the decade after the Cold War. The problem reached especially alarming proportions when India and Pakistan conducted underground nuclear tests in May 1998. In doing so, both governments incurred worldwide wrath, diplomatic isolation, and economic sanctions. But this was a price they were willing to pay in return for their entry into the "nuclear club."

The roots of this conflict extended deep into the historical animosities between Muslims and Hindus in the region. These differences exploded into violence after India, once the "crown jewel" of the British empire, was granted independence in 1947. Rather than exist as a minority within a Hindu-dominated India, members of the rival Muslim League sought their own state. The creation of Pakistan in 1947

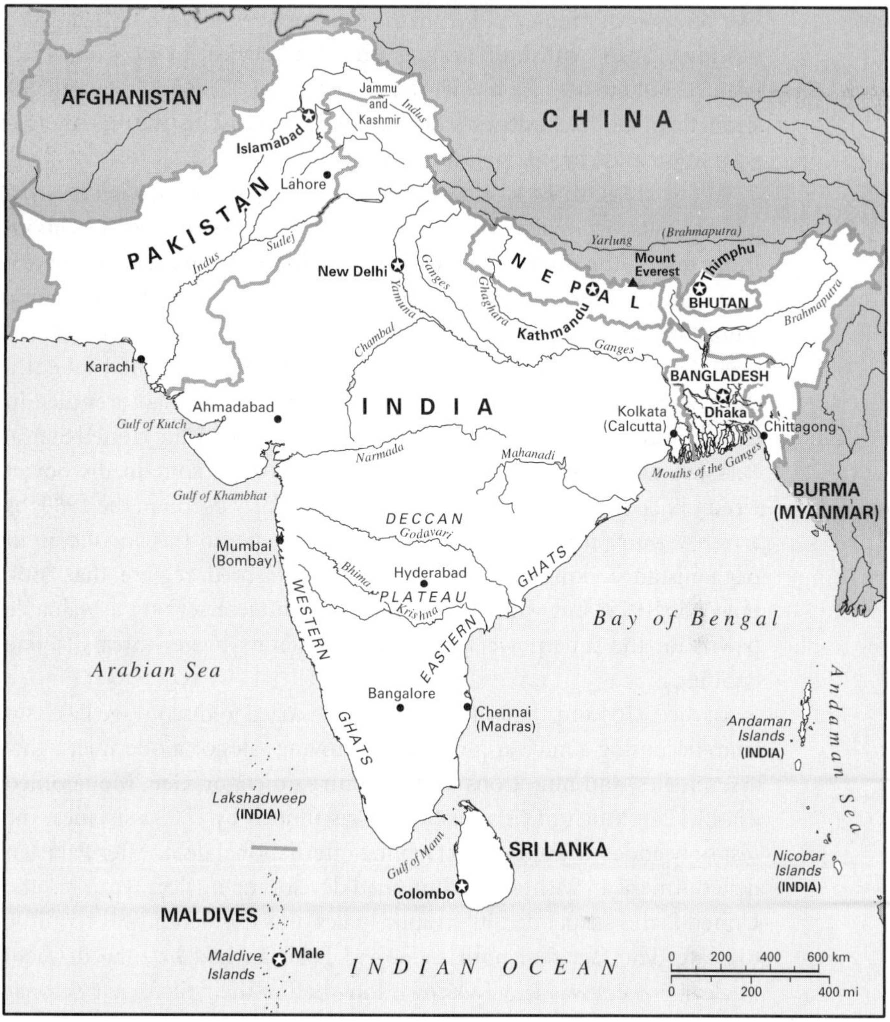

SOUTH ASIA

came with immense bloodshed as nearly one million people were killed and another twelve million were displaced from their homes. The mutual distrust between India and Pakistan sparked two more wars and constant border skirmishes, particularly in the Kashmir region of northern India, whose majority Islamic population was claimed by Pakistan.

Greatly complicating matters, both countries had become entangled in the Cold War—Pakistan as a U.S. ally, India on the side of the Soviet Union.[13] In return for their allegiance, both governments received mas-

13. The India case was noteworthy because the Indian government, under the leadership of Jawaharlal Nehru, had declared itself a leader of the "nonaligned movement" in the 1950s.

sive volumes of military aid from the superpowers. A regional arms race quickly ensued, with India testing a nuclear "device" in 1974 and Pakistan rushing to acquire its own nuclear weapons. The growing military strength of both countries stood in stark contrast to their economic stagnation and chronic political unrest.

In few areas of the world did the power politics of the Cold War so contaminate regional relations as in South Asia. For the Soviet Union, India served the dual function of blunting the U.S. presence in South Asia and countering China, which had sought to restrain Moscow's ambitions in the region. Since independence, India's government had been mired in a chronic border dispute with China and had fought a short war against Mao Zedong's forces in 1962. China had prevailed in that struggle, but the border tensions remained. As for the United States, Pakistan played a central role in the U.S. effort to contain the Soviet Union in South Asia. Pakistan became particularly useful in the 1980s as a transit point for covert U.S. military shipments to the *mujahadin* in Afghanistan seeking to oust the Soviet-sponsored regime that took power in 1979. But while India and Pakistan were serving as valuable pawns for the superpowers, they were becoming bigger threats to one another.

In the 1970s and 1980s, the United States tried to discourage Pakistan from becoming a nuclear power by approving sales of modern jet fighters, missiles, and munitions to the country's dictator, Gen. Mohammed Zia ul-Haq. Much of this weaponry was funded by U.S. assistance; the rest only added to Pakistan's crippling international debt. After Pakistan defied American wishes and continued developing nuclear weapons, the United States suspended its weapons sales. But this action was too little too late. The fact that both India and Pakistan had become de facto nuclear powers was widely known long before their tit-for-tat detonations in the spring of 1998.

The end of the Cold War deprived India and Pakistan of any leverage they had to expand their military arsenals. Both countries, already armed to the teeth, looked to other arms exporters to provide them with additional weaponry. The only question was how they would employ their military might at a time when their citizens remained in poverty. Domestic politics thus played a key role in fueling tensions as leaders on both sides of the hotly contested border deliberately inflamed nationalist passions in order to enhance their popularity. Indian prime minister Atal Bihari Vajpayee, elected in March 1998, became a hero among Hindu nationalists for his nuclear show of force. "The nuclear tests have given the government an aura of credibility and decisiveness," one Indian scholar observed. "It is difficult to think of any decision in India's recent history that has had such overwhelming public support."[14] The Indian tests also played into the hands of Pakistan's autocratic premier, Nawaz Sharif, who resisted international pleas for restraint. In ordering the Pakistani tests, Sharif declared a state of emergency that enabled him to clamp down even more harshly on his political opponents at home.

The nuclear tests raised the stakes of South Asia's power struggle. They also imperiled global efforts to prevent the spread of nuclear weapons. In particular, the addition of India and Pakistan to the nuclear club greatly weakened the nuclear Non-Proliferation Treaty (NPT), which had been extended indefinitely by 168 governments in 1995. Although the two South Asian states had refused to sign the NPT, it was hoped they would eventually succumb to international pressure. But the result was just the opposite. The nuclear tests by India and Pakistan raised anxieties elsewhere and tempted potential proliferators to cross the nuclear threshold.

The world, then, had to adjust to the new reality of seven self-proclaimed nuclear powers.[15] Far from backing down in the face of global pressure and sanctions, India's National Security Council announced in August 1999 a military doctrine of "minimum credible deterrence," complete with a triad of ground-, sea-, and land-based nuclear missiles. Indian officials then approved a 28 percent increase in military spending early in 2000, the largest single-year increase in the nation's history. And in Pakistan, Sharif's campaign of political repression backfired as he was driven from power in October 1999 in a military coup. The new military regime, however, was in no mood to disarm the country's nuclear program at a time when India was flaunting its arsenal and promising new deployments. Efforts by President Clinton to defuse the regional arms race—including an extended trip to both countries in March 2000—did not produce concessions by either side.

Lessons from the Regional Crises

The regional conflicts just described collectively deflated the euphoria that followed the end of the Cold War. Many members of Congress—including Clinton's allies in the Democratic Party—openly doubted that the United States had vital interests in the failed states. But they generally supported the humanitarian interventions in the early 1990s, which appealed to the nation's historical sense of mission and moral responsi-

14. Pratap Bhanu Mehta, "Exploding Myths," *New Republic,* June 8, 1998, 18.

15. Israel also maintained a nuclear capability, making it the eighth nuclear power, but this well-known fact was not confirmed by the Israeli government. It also was believed that North Korea maintained a small nuclear arsenal after its weapons program was "frozen" in 1994. (See Chapter 14.)

bility. Support for U.S. involvement quickly evaporated, however, when it became clear the United States could not resolve the underlying problems in these countries—or when U.S. interventions clashed with domestic priorities. As for India and Pakistan, it is doubtful that the United States could have prevented the two bitter rivals from raising the stakes of their dispute, and their nuclear tests compounded the rising sense of global disorder felt by Congress, administration officials, and the general public.[16] For many Americans, a retreat from the chaotic struggles overseas became more appealing. They could then enjoy the unprecedented prosperity that had overtaken the country.

Although at this time the restraints on U.S. intervention were fewer than ever, it became clear that Washington could not solve the many problems in developing countries that were sparking widespread violence after the Cold War. America's vast military arsenal was of little or no use in most trouble spots; constructive, long-term solutions were required. Moreover, most of the conflicts were civil wars, not disputes between states—a fact that reinforced the lesson that homegrown solutions, not ones imposed by other states, were needed. This stubborn reality challenged the long-held view among many Americans that, once the United States committed its military forces to battle, their overwhelming strength would subdue any foe. The Vietnam trauma had previously thrown this presumption into doubt. But this time, many people assumed, the righteousness and selflessness of the American cause were irrefutable, and the country had never been more capable of asserting itself throughout the world.

The failed military intervention in Somalia reminded American leaders that they must pay attention to the interests at stake in any conflict—as well as the cost, level of public support, likelihood of success, and existence of a coherent exit strategy. These preconditions became part of the so-called "Powell Doctrine," named after Gen. Colin L. Powell, chairman of the Joint Chiefs of Staff under Presidents Bush and Clinton. In the early days of the Persian Gulf crisis, Powell had urged Bush to extend the economic sanctions against Saddam Hussein rather than unleash Operation Desert Storm. But once Bush ordered military action, Powell sought to defeat Iraq quickly with overwhelming force and then withdraw American forces from the region just as quickly. As for Somalia, Powell had warned that it would be a reckless operation with predictable consequences. But Bush and Clinton dismissed his warnings. They were convinced that good intentions coupled with superior military force could solve virtually any problem overseas—a view deeply embedded in

16. For an elaboration, see Stanley Hoffmann, *World Disorders: Troubled Peace in the Post–Cold War Era* (Lanham, Md.: Rowman and Littlefield, 1998).

the country's traditional approach to foreign affairs. The failure of the Somali mission quickly exposed their delusions.

The regional conflicts also demonstrated the limits of multilateral intervention and peacekeeping. As in the early 1930s, when the League of Nations failed to resist Japan's invasion of Manchuria, pledges by UN members to act collectively in the 1990s turned out to be hollow. The reasons for such reneging were eerily similar to the League of Nations precedent: the primacy of national self-interests over transnational concerns; unresolved disputes among the great powers; and doubts about the world body's political and military leadership. While hardly alone, the United States was the most conspicuous in turning away from the UN. "Assertive multilateralism" had been a cornerstone of Clinton's early foreign policy, and the UN had been embraced as a bulwark against aggression in the post–Cold War era (see Chapter 9). After the honeymoon, however, the marriage became strained. Congressional leaders, who controlled the country's purse strings, viewed the UN with suspicion—if not contempt—and refused to meet U.S. financial obligations to that organization.[17]

While the lessons from the regional conflicts prescribed a healthy dose of moderation for U.S. military policy, in other respects the wrong lessons were learned. The failure of the humanitarian interventions, combined with more general misgivings about Clinton's foreign policy, provoked a general backlash against U.S. activism in developing areas. As the pendulum swung toward the other extreme—global *disengagement*—Congress cut deeply into the State Department's budget and closed dozens of foreign embassies, consulates, and missions. Many foreign aid programs to the poorest countries of Africa, southern Asia, and Latin America were eliminated.[18] As a result, the United States deprived itself of a key resource with which to address the underlying problems in the poor countries and contribute to constructive, peaceful, and long-term change. The fact that the world's most prosperous country scaled back its foreign service and virtually dismantled its foreign aid program—at a time when its defense budget was returning to Cold War levels even without a serious foreign threat—sent a clear but troubling message about Washington's future intentions.

17. In late 1999, the United States began to pay off its overdue financial commitment to the UN, which amounted to more than $1 billion, but only after being faced with the loss of its vote in the General Assembly.

18. As a percentage of economic output, U.S. foreign aid spending was by 1995 lower than that of all other industrialized countries. Michael O'Hanlon and Carol Graham, *A Half Penny on the Dollar: The Future of Development Aid* (Washington, D.C.: Brookings, 1997), 25.

CHAPTER ELEVEN

The Shifting European Landscape

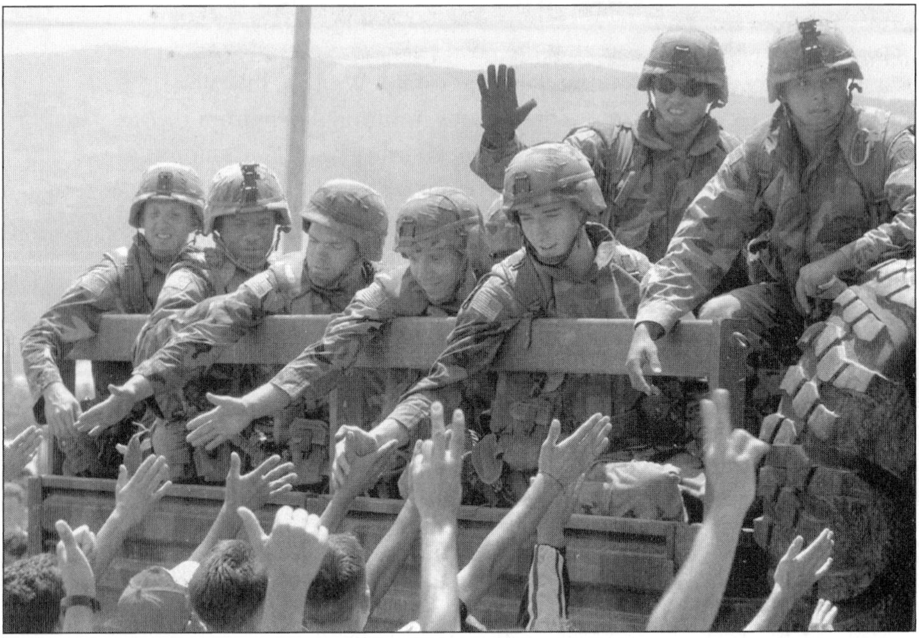

American troops and others from the North Atlantic Treaty Organization (NATO) greet Kosovar refugees after NATO's liberation of the Yugoslav territory in June 1999. The U.S.-led NATO mission in Kosovo was one of many that tested American foreign policy in the turbulent post–Cold War decade.

After the Cold War, the United States continued to maintain a visible presence on the European continent, hoping to exploit the gains stemming from the collapse of the Soviet Union and to prevent the emergence of new fault lines. The U.S. effort, however, yielded contradictory results. As Europeans became stronger and more unified, they also grew wary of their American caretaker and sought to become more self-sufficient. Above all, they hoped to regain their place among the great powers after being trapped for nearly a half-century in the middle of the East-West struggle.

America's preoccupation with Europe was, of course, nothing new. It always had viewed a stable Europe as essential to its security. Specifically, a *balance* among the European powers was required to prevent a single country from dominating the continent and, in turn, threatening the United States. Throughout the nineteenth century, this geopolitical concern had led U.S. leaders to avoid alliances with the European powers, a strategy clearly laid out in President George Washington's Farewell Address (1796) and in the Monroe Doctrine (1823). American detachment from the great powers of Europe was further justified on moral terms: the European monarchs had brazenly denied their citizens fundamental political rights and routinely placed them in harm's way in their deadly game of power politics. The United States, by contrast, would remain true to its democratic principles by refusing to play this game. This strategy worked so long as the Concert of Europe maintained a balance of power and the British navy protected the Atlantic sea-lanes. But American fears that one country would try to dominate the European continent were affirmed in the two world wars, which forced the United States to abandon its policy of "splendid isolation" once and for all.

As the Cold War set in, American foreign policy makers faced a dilemma in contemplating future relations with Europe. With the United States the strongest world power in 1945 and with the Soviet Union quickly emerging as its chief rival, U.S. isolation from Europe *even in peacetime* was no longer conceivable. This dilemma led the United States to prolong its presence in Western Europe, where it sought to enmesh those states in a variety of international organizations that would reward regional cooperation, suppress nationalism, and discourage self-serving economic and security policies.

This strategy of European "institutionalism" served the vital function of strengthening Western Europeans against the Soviet Union, but it also contained a logic that extended beyond the Cold War. Having Europeans cooperate rather than fight one another would mark a historic break for the region and a relief for the United States. It was not surprising, then, that Presidents George H. W. Bush and Bill Clinton adhered to this strategy throughout the 1990s amid rapidly changing circumstances in Europe. As this chapter describes, the Western European states edged closer toward a confederation by creating in 1992 the European Union (EU), which eventually adopted a common currency. Meanwhile, their neighbors in Eastern Europe were rebuilding their political institutions and economies largely along the lines of the EU states. They also were taking a keen interest in the North Atlantic Treaty Organization (NATO), which, far from dissolving along with the Soviet Union, expanded into Eastern Europe and became embroiled in "out-of-area" conflicts. All the while, the Russian government lurched from crisis to crisis, thereby keeping tensions high all across Europe.

First Bush and then Clinton tried to play a stabilizing role as Europe adjusted to the new strategic landscape. Both presidents knew that a democratic Europe that embraced free markets not only would benefit Europeans, but also would make the United States more secure. Yet the United States could not prevent conflicts from breaking out in the Balkan Peninsula and within the former Soviet Union. Nor could it prevent its European allies from erecting new military structures and devising new strategies that would, if fully implemented, amount to a declaration of independence from Washington. "The EU is no longer merely a client of the United States and now often takes the lead on major issues in international gatherings," wrote an official in the European Parliament. "This can have advantages or disadvantages for U.S. policy, but whatever the outcome, it is a new fact of political life that Washington must now consider." [1]

Western Europe: From Community to Union

The integration of Western Europe into a more cohesive European Union brought those states closer and provided them with a forum in which to resolve their long-standing political differences. In 1992 the twelve members of the European Commission ratified the Maastricht Treaty, which created the European Union and moved the alliance beyond economic integration to include goals such as a unified legal code and a common foreign policy.[2] In 1995 three previously neutral countries—Austria, Finland, and Sweden—joined the European Union, bringing its full membership to fifteen.[3] With the EU growing in both numbers and responsibilities, a system of "dual sovereignty" emerged. Although member states retained ultimate political control over their territories and citizens, they transferred an ever-growing share of their authority to the EU's central government in Brussels. By 2000 it appeared that the historical vision of a "United States of Europe," long dismissed by skeptics, might actually come to pass.

From the standpoint of Washington, Europe's gradual move toward confederation was both welcome and potentially troubling. As noted,

1. Christopher Piening, *Global Europe: The European Union in World Affairs* (Boulder, Colo.: Lynne Rienner, 1997), 102.

2. The twelve countries were Belgium, Denmark, France, Germany, Greece, Ireland, Italy, Luxembourg, the Netherlands, Portugal, Spain, and the United Kingdom.

3. Another thirteen countries had formally applied for EU membership by 2000. Of these, ten were cleared for membership in 2004: Cyprus, Czech Republic, Estonia, Hungary, Latvia, Lithuania, Malta, Poland, Slovakia, and Slovenia. Bulgaria and Romania were previously approved to join the EU in 2007. Turkey, left out of the most recent round of expansion, was invited to restart membership talks in 2004, and Croatia is also under review for membership.

THE EUROPEAN UNION

American leaders had long encouraged regional integration as a means of defusing the bitter rivalries among the European powers. The Truman administration explicitly made regional cooperation a condition for Marshall Plan funding and military aid. But a revitalized Europe could very well seek to chart an independent course, even if this meant alienating the United States.

TABLE 11-1 **United States and European Union: A Comparison of Basic Indicators, 2000**

	United States	European Union
Population (millions)	282	377
GDP (trillions of constant 2000 U.S. dollars)	$9.8	$7.9
Per capita GDP (constant 2000 U.S. dollars)	$34,599	$22,756
Imports of goods and services (billions of constant 2000 U.S. dollars)	$1,476	$279
Export of goods and services (billions of constant 2000 U.S. dollars)	$1,096	$284
Military expenditure (billions of current U.S. dollars)	$302	$209

Source: World Bank, *World Development Indicators* (Washington, D.C.: World Bank, 2005).
Note: EU figures exclude trade among member states.

Changes in the European landscape also produced a changing of the political guard. The new generation of leaders that took power in the 1990s sought to put the Cold War behind them and enter the new millennium with a clean slate. These leaders included Prime Minister Tony Blair of Britain, President Jacques Chirac of France, and Chancellor Gerhard Schroeder of Germany. All three supported the continued push toward European integration, and they used their political advantages within the EU to pressure the smaller states. The leaders of the "big three" European governments had something else in common: they were appalled by the disabling conflict between Bill Clinton and the U.S. Congress, irritated by the resulting stalemate in U.S. foreign policy, and determined to pursue their own interests with or without the United States.

The greatest leap forward in European integration came in January 1999 with the introduction of a common currency, the euro.[4] Because a national currency represents one of the central pillars of sovereignty, it always has been closely guarded by political leaders, especially in Europe, where the nation-state system evolved during the seventeenth century. But the presence of many national currencies, all with different and

4. Four EU members did not immediately adopt the common currency. The governments of the United Kingdom and Denmark chose not to participate, and Sweden and Greece initially did not meet the economic requirements for entry. (Greece has since met these requirements and adopted the euro; Sweden retains its own currency.) For the eleven other member states of the EU, the euro became the basis of foreign exchange in 1999 and began circulation in January 2002.

wildly fluctuating values, became a nuisance after the Europeans created a single internal market. A common currency would be the most efficient way to do business.

The euro, however, came at a hefty price: each government was forced to relinquish its fiscal and monetary authority and rein in public spending, reduce debts, and lower inflation. Welfare programs were scaled back and government subsidies reduced in all eleven participating countries. In the past, external pressures to undertake such reforms had incited charges of imperialism, and austerity measures often had sparked demonstrations or riots when spending cuts increased unemployment or reduced popular social services. But European leaders and their constituencies willingly accepted these curbs on their autonomy in exchange for the promise of greater prosperity.

Internal harmony among the European economies did not mean their chronic trade disputes with the United States suddenly vanished. Quite the contrary, these disputes became even more contentious, only this time U.S. trade negotiators faced a united front instead of separate foreign ministries. In 1999 the growing strains between Washington and the EU led to a "banana war" in which the United States imposed 100 percent tariffs on many European goods in retaliation for the EU's refusal to import bananas from U.S.-based corporations. A second dispute over the sale of aircraft engines prompted U.S. officials to ban Europe's supersonic Concorde from landing in the United States. Meanwhile, European investors ignored the U.S.-led economic embargo against Cuba and other sanctions that targeted Cuban leader Fidel Castro's trading partners. Taken together, these problems made it clear that a united Europe whose population and economic output exceeded that of the United States could become a formidable rival in the intensifying competition for world markets.

The EU's pursuit of a "common foreign and security policy," mandated in the Maastricht Treaty, was even more ambitious than its adoption of a common currency. By pledging to pool their diplomat corps and military forces, EU members seemed prepared to surrender the last and most vital element of their national sovereignty. But large, familiar hurdles to an all-European foreign policy remained. The nationality of the armed forces would become irrelevant, but that of the military leadership would not. Which of the major powers would lead the all-European forces? What roles would the other EU members play in the command structure?[5] Furthermore, it was never clearly established how the

5. France and Germany had already sparked a political crisis by clashing at the last minute over the leadership of the European Central Bank. The German-backed candidate, Willem Duisenberg, was finally appointed in May 1998, but only after agreeing to "retire" halfway through his eight-year term and to be replaced by the French candidate.

Europeans would pay for such a military force, or, more fundamentally, what the substance of a "common" foreign policy would actually be.

These ambiguities had had little effect so long as the United States ran things from Washington—and from NATO headquarters in Brussels. The alliance had not only spared Europeans a perilous decision over military leadership, but also had allowed them to skimp on military spending, thus freeing up funds for the more generous social programs favored by European citizens. In the wake of the Cold War, however, a growing number of Europeans, particularly the French, associated NATO with American hegemony. Thus France moved forward on a joint defense force with Germany that would bring the common foreign policy to life. Its efforts, if successful, threatened to make the United States a victim of its own success. "Where the mark, the franc, the lira, and the guilder are headed, armies, fleets, and air squadrons will eventually follow," one scholar observed. "A Europe moving toward real economic integration may be a less reliable and less predictable partner for the United States—or perhaps not even a partner at all."[6]

Jump-Starting Democracy in Eastern Europe

The fate of the "transition" countries of Eastern Europe also was of great importance to the United States. Long viewed as a fulcrum in the power balance between East and West, Eastern Europe had twice been turned into a bloodbath by the Russian and German armies. The same nations then served as Soviet pawns in the Cold War, enduring decades of political repression and economic decay under communist rule. For all the major powers, then, the fate of the wide-ranging reforms undertaken in the early 1990s in Eastern Europe had implications that extended well beyond that region.

Because most Eastern European governments lacked historical experience with either democratic rule or market economics, they faced enormous difficulties in instituting reforms. But the demise of the Cold War suggested that better times lay ahead. Francis Fukuyama's vision of the "end of history," outlined in Chapter 9, was therefore welcomed by most Eastern Europeans, whose histories had consisted largely of foreign conquest and domination.

The newly liberated Eastern European states quickly put into place the variety of institutional components required of democratic governments. They wrote and approved constitutions that provided for basic political and civil rights, and they established modern legal codes and

6. Ronald Steel, "Eurotrash," *New Republic*, June 1, 1998, 12.

court systems to assure that the rule of law prevailed. They also created legislatures in which elected leaders from competing political parties could debate and enact the new laws. By and large, their efforts to build the structural foundations of democracy, mostly from scratch, were fruitful. But the success of these political reforms depended on the progress of the simultaneous economic reforms that sought to replace the centrally planned economies of the Soviet era with those based on private enterprise. This task proved quite difficult in many parts of Eastern Europe and threatened the region's move toward democratic rule.

The difficulties stemmed from several sources. First, the cost of rebuilding these economies was far greater than expected. Economic conditions after the Cold War were dismal throughout Eastern Europe. Decaying factories, crumbling roads, outdated utilities, and widespread environmental damage blighted the landscape. School systems had fallen into disrepair, course materials were out of date, and teachers were paid barely enough to survive. It soon became clear that educating and training the productive workforce required for long-term economic growth would take many years, possibly more than a generation.[7]

Second, many citizens of Eastern Europe were demoralized by the half-century of communist rule that had deprived them of the political power and prosperity enjoyed in the West. They had little experience in forming independent trade unions, rival political parties, and other democratic movements—and no experience at all in campaigning for elected positions of their own. As a result, they often were unprepared to manage the demands of political leadership that came with their freedom from Soviet rule. The widespread layoffs and cutbacks in social services that followed from the "structural adjustments" produced mass protests against national leaders, many of whom had been exalted as saviors during Eastern Europe's rise against communism.

Further hampering the recovery, most Eastern European countries were not immediately attractive to large-scale foreign investment, which at the time was flowing primarily to the United States, Western Europe, and the newly industrialized countries of East Asia. Private investors and multinational corporations generally adopted a wait-and-see attitude toward the former communist countries. Only Poland, Hungary, and—to a lesser extent—the Czech Republic received large volumes of foreign investment. Thus it was not surprising that by 2000 each had emerged as a market economy that could compete with its counterparts in Western Europe. Poland, with by far the largest level of economic output in Eastern Europe, had introduced reforms quickly, through "shock therapy."

7. These problems persisted despite a massive inflow of aid funds from the EU to Eastern Europe. See Karen E. Smith, *The Making of EU Foreign Policy: The Case of Eastern Europe* (New York: St. Martin's Press, 1999).

After several sluggish years, its economy grew in the late 1990s at an annual rate of more than 5 percent, and inflation and unemployment rates fell steadily. In Hungary, more than $17 billion in foreign investments fueled a similar resurgence. It was no coincidence that these countries quickly rose to the top of the EU's list of candidates and were welcomed into NATO (described in the next section).

Elsewhere, what little private capital was invested was quickly withdrawn at the first sign of trouble. The smaller economies in Eastern Europe were especially vulnerable. Economic output in Bulgaria and Romania declined throughout the 1990s, forcing their leaders to rely on emergency aid from the International Monetary Fund (IMF) to prevent economic collapse. Meanwhile, government corruption and organized crime undermined public confidence in reform efforts. Many became nostalgic for the communist regimes of the Cold War era, which at least assured them of jobs and a minimal level of income. Thus in 1994 the Bulgarian Socialist Party gained control of that nation's legislature. In Romania, the National Salvation Front, led by high-ranking members of the former Communist Party, became the most popular political party.

All of this was tied in to the fourth problem affecting reform—a problem that became evident long after the transitions had begun. Throughout Eastern Europe, the most powerful government officials often were former communists who had, at least rhetorically, rejected communism and embraced free markets. In practice, however, these former members of the communist *nomenklatura* exploited their status and connections to ensure for themselves a sizable share of the public enterprises that were placed in private hands. But once they obtained control, the former communist technocrats were no better able to stimulate productivity and economic growth than they had been during the Cold War. "Crony capitalism" prolonged the economic stagnation of many Eastern European economies and failed to improve living standards.

NATO's Search for a New Mission

Beyond the economic realm, the future of European military security remained uncertain after the Cold War. Of central concern was the status of NATO, which had accomplished its stated mission of protecting the Western European states from possible Soviet aggression. In view of this achievement, many felt the alliance should be disbanded. But to others, including Presidents Bush and Clinton, NATO remained useful in confronting potential new threats to its members on both sides of the Atlantic Ocean.

Confusion over NATO's future reflected widespread misunderstandings about its past. Contrary to official proclamations, containing the

Soviet bloc was not the only purpose served by NATO during the Cold War (see Chapter 3). Lord Hastings Ismay, its first secretary general, aptly summarized its broader functions when he pointed out that NATO was needed "to keep the Americans in, the Russians out, and the Germans down." Only the second function was directly related to the Cold War; the first and third had deeper roots. These functions, combined with nagging doubts about Russia in the 1990s, propelled the alliance into a new and ambiguous future.

The military "umbrella" offered by the United States was critical to NATO's founding and eagerly welcomed by Western European leaders at the time. Not only did the U.S. presence in NATO fortify the front lines of the Cold War, it also stifled the chronic *internal* rivalries that had twice led to world war. Protected by the alliance, Western Europeans were able to focus their energies on economic recovery and political cooperation. In this sense, the United States provided "a sense of reassurance to the Europeans that they would not otherwise have and thereby helped make security relations, and also political and economic relations, within Western Europe more stable than they would otherwise be." [8]

Germany also figured prominently in the NATO equation. Through NATO, German leaders rejoined the Western European community without provoking new fears of expansionism. In so doing, German chancellors from Konrad Adenauer to Gerhard Schroeder also sought to strengthen Germany's fragile democracy and ensure its success in a country with a dictatorial history. The alliance, in effect, adopted a policy of "double containment" of Germany and Russia. But, like America's role as a regional caretaker, the need to keep Germany "down" was rarely mentioned publicly.

NATO, then, provided for the collective *defense* of Western Europe against foreign attack and for the region's collective *security* against its own self-destructive tendencies. Both roles, as it turned out, remained valid after the Cold War. Developments in Russia, described later in this chapter, were hardly reassuring to the other European states. Nor was Germany's emergence as the EU's economic powerhouse. NATO was thus seen as a guarantor against another German-Russian collision (like that before World War I) or further collusion (like that before World War II). The alliance also could soothe tensions between other members. For example, disputes between Greece and Turkey over Cyprus and other matters simmered during and after the Cold War. These and other points of contention required a continued and pervasive U.S. presence in Europe.

8. Robert J. Art, "Why Western Europe Needs the United States and NATO," *Political Science Quarterly* (spring 1998): 12.

An immediate rationale for NATO's continued survival was found in the desire of former Soviet bloc states to become part of the "West." Thus the question quickly became not whether the alliance should disband, but whether it should *expand.* The timing for "enlargement" (the term favored by military planners) seemed right because of the new power vacuum in Eastern Europe created by the abolition of the Warsaw Pact. Unless NATO stepped in to fill this vacuum, countries such as Poland and Hungary would have to build independent military forces. They also might be tempted to create another regional bloc. Neither scenario was appealing to NATO members, nor to Eastern Europeans themselves who saw NATO as a stepping-stone to EU membership.

The decision to expand NATO beyond its sixteen members was complicated by Russia, whose leaders had always feared encirclement by hostile neighbors. Thus any move to add the Eastern European states to NATO threatened to inflame Russian nationalism and to isolate Russian moderates. This development would, in turn, introduce pressures for Russia to rearm and divert resources badly needed to ensure the success of its political and economic reforms. Clinton and other NATO leaders arrived at a compromise solution in October 1993. Under the rubric of a "Partnership for Peace," the former Warsaw Pact members and Soviet republics were invited to become junior partners of NATO. In this capacity, they would participate in some NATO deliberations and training exercises. But they would not receive the security guarantees of full members. If the "partnerships" proved successful, these auxiliary states would be considered for full membership.[9]

Russian president Boris Yeltsin first rejected the partnership concept, but he soon recognized the futility of his position. He then insisted, also in vain, that Russia receive preferential treatment because of its military strength and permanent membership in the UN Security Council. Yeltsin further protested NATO's plans to invite Poland, Hungary, and the Czech Republic to join the alliance as its first new full members. Exploiting the tensions within NATO, the Russian president warned all Europeans about subjecting themselves to continued U.S. military control. He declared that a "cold peace" was setting in between Moscow and Washington and suggested that it would thaw only after suspension of the proposed eastward expansion of NATO.

The United States and its NATO allies dismissed Yeltsin's thinly veiled threats, which were attributed to his need to appease nationalists at a

9. Twenty-seven countries had agreed to join the partnership by 2003: Albania, Armenia, Austria, Azerbaijan, Belarus, Bulgaria, Croatia, Estonia, Finland, Georgia, Ireland, Kazakhstan, Kyrghyzstan (the Kyrghyz Republic), Latvia, Lithuania, (the former Yugoslav Republic of) Macedonia, Moldova, Romania, Russia, Slovakia, Slovenia, Sweden, Switzerland, Tajikistan, Turkmenistan, Ukraine, and Uzbekistan.

time when his hold on power was tenuous. They moved forward on their plan to add the three Eastern European countries to NATO membership by 1999, the alliance's fiftieth anniversary, and to leave the door open for other new members. Faced with the inevitable, Yeltsin again softened his stance. Instead of blocking NATO expansion, he successfully negotiated a separate treaty that would prevent the placement of foreign troops or nuclear weapons in Eastern Europe. The Russian-NATO Founding Act of 1997 called for military cooperation rather than competition between the former Cold War adversaries. Under the agreement, Russia would be given a "voice, but not a veto" over NATO policy.

Yeltsin's surrender on NATO expansion revealed the depths to which his country had fallen. One need only consider how Washington would have reacted if the Soviet Union had won the Cold War and then invited Mexico and other Latin American countries to join the Warsaw Pact. In reality, NATO's offer not to place nuclear weapons in the Eastern European states was hollow, because the offer could be quickly withdrawn in a crisis. Yet Russia still accepted the face-saving agreement and reaped the rewards: billions of dollars in continued economic aid from the West. Having attained Russia's compliance, NATO welcomed Poland, Hungary, and the Czech Republic into its fold in March 1999. The expansion was quickly approved by all the European states and Canada. In the United States, even the Senate, which had opposed Clinton on nearly every foreign policy issue, approved the expansion by a vote of 80–19. To Secretary of State Madeleine Albright, Europe had taken a giant step toward becoming "whole and free."

But what was to be the mission of the enlarged NATO? Its new "Strategic Concept" omitted the previous objective—to preserve a "strategic balance in Europe"—yet it failed to outline a coherent future role. If, as the document proclaimed, the meaning of regional security would be broadened beyond military concerns, how would the alliance solve the vast array of political and social problems it would then confront? And how exactly would the alliance conduct a global crackdown against weapons of mass destruction, as Albright had proposed? No clear answers were forthcoming for the uncomfortable reason just noted: the real driving forces behind NATO's endurance—restraining Russia and Germany while preserving a dominant U.S. military presence in Europe—were too politically sensitive to acknowledge openly.

Yet another question raised during the expansion debate—whether NATO would intervene in conflicts beyond the borders of its member states—was answered by NATO jet fighters. At the very time of the anniversary celebration, they were bombing Yugoslavia in southeastern Europe. This was the second round of NATO assaults on the former communist country, which had become embroiled in a brutal civil war. The protracted conflict in the Balkan Peninsula, long known as the "tinderbox of Europe," put NATO and its hazy new mission to the ultimate test.

'Ethnic Cleansing' in the Balkans

The violent disintegration of Yugoslavia in the 1990s served as a frightening example of how the removal of Cold War restraints could unleash nationalistic rivalries. Yugoslavia, created in the aftermath of World War I, was a diverse federation of ethnic and religious groups—mainly Serbs (Eastern Orthodox), Slovenes and Croats (Catholic), and Bosnians and Albanians (Muslim). During the Cold War, the country was held together under Marshall Josip Tito, who had relied on Marxist ideology and a monopoly of political power to suppress any divisions. But Tito's makeshift arrangements began crumbling soon after his death in 1980. They collapsed altogether in 1989 along with the communist regimes in other Eastern European states. Ancient religious hatreds quickly returned to the surface, and Yugoslavia's descent into a spiral of violence soon followed.[10]

The dominant Serbs, who still controlled the capital of Belgrade and the country's formidable armed forces, opposed Yugoslavia's disintegration and sought instead to create a Greater Serbia that would include territories occupied primarily by non-Serbs. After the provinces of Slovenia and Croatia declared independence in 1991 and were immediately recognized by the European Community, the Yugoslav army intervened in both territories. Serbian troops inflicted great damage but were unable to prevent the secession of the two new states, both of which were promptly admitted to the United Nations. The Serbs then directed their military campaign to the heart of Bosnia and Herzegovina (referred to as Bosnia here), the most multinational of the Yugoslav provinces, which also had declared its independence from Belgrade. There, the Bosnian Serbs launched a self-described campaign of "ethnic cleansing" that consisted of driving Muslims from their communities in order to expand Serbian territory. Masked paramilitary forces burned and looted villages, tortured and starved non-Serbs in concentration camps, raped Islamic women, and besieged the Bosnian capital, Sarajevo, for three years, depriving its citizens of food, water, and electricity.

These actions appalled outside observers and drew widespread condemnation. Many Americans, including presidential candidate Bill Clin-

10. For an account by the former U.S. ambassador to Yugoslavia, see Warren Zimmerman, *Origins of a Catastrophe: Yugoslavia and Its Destroyers—America's Last Ambassador Tells What Happened and Why* (New York: Times Books, 1996). For another historical perspective, see Robert D. Kaplan, *Balkan Ghosts: A Journey through History* (New York: Vintage Books, 1993).

THE FORMER YUGOSLAVIA

**The last remaining provinces of the former Yugoslavia, Serbia and Montenegro, became separate nation-states following Montenegro's declaration of independence in June 2006.*

ton, called in 1992 for military intervention. Horrified onlookers charged that the systematic expulsion of Muslims constituted genocide, which was explicitly prohibited by the UN Charter, and they called on all countries to intervene and prevent the mass slaughter, which was based on ethnic or religious differences. But charges of widespread war crimes went both ways, because Croat and Muslim forces also committed atrocities against the Serbs—a familiar pattern in the region's history.

Opponents of intervention argued that this was a civil conflict, not an international war, despite the establishment of new states recognized by the European Community and United Nations. The Pentagon asserted that any military intervention to separate the combatants and restore order would entail a massive commitment of between 200,000 and 400,000 troops, heavy fighting, and extensive casualties. Moreover, the foreign troops probably would have to remain in the treacherous mountain territory for many years, and no coherent "exit strategy" was evident. Most important, the conflict appeared to be contained within the Balkan Peninsula, posing little threat to the great powers, especially the United States. The Bush administration generally adopted this cautious view and pursued a negotiated outcome. Likewise, once elected, Clinton soon retracted his earlier calls for outside intervention and pressed for a diplomatic solution, preferably mediated by the newly reorganized European Union. Later, he would be gravely disappointed when the EU member states, preoccupied with regional integration and plagued by conflicting allegiances in the Balkans, failed to take a united stand.

An international arms embargo imposed on Yugoslavia in the early days of the conflict favored the Serbs, because the Yugoslav army—well equipped from its years of association with a communist dictatorship—supplied the Bosnian Serbs with weapons from its arsenal. The Muslims, by contrast, could not acquire sufficient arms to protect themselves. Nevertheless, European leaders opposed lifting the embargo, arguing it would only broaden the violence and endanger their own peacekeeping forces, which were protecting so-called "safe havens" in the remaining Muslim-held areas. The arms embargo continued into 1995, along with an economic boycott against the Serbian regime in Belgrade.

When Clinton occasionally advanced proposals for multilateral military action and for lifting the arms embargo against Bosnia, he was opposed by most Western European governments and many influential members of the United Nations, including Russia, a traditional ally of the Slavic Serbs. Most experts in the Defense Department also opposed a military response, because, in their view, air strikes would have little effect without the massive deployment of U.S. ground forces. Within Congress and among the general public, domestic issues were of greater concern than the seemingly intractable problems in the Balkans. In short, many Americans asked the same question: if the Europeans did not feel sufficiently threatened by events in Bosnia to intervene, why should the United States?

For all these reasons, Clinton was unwilling to assert himself and demand action as Bush had done in Kuwait. Instead, he wavered, sometimes threatening to intervene with air power and to lift the arms embargo, at other times retracting these positions, citing allied reluc-

IMPACT AND INFLUENCE

MADELEINE ALBRIGHT

Among the most forceful proponents of an activist U.S. world role after the Cold War was Secretary of State Madeleine Albright, the first woman to hold the post and the highest-ranking woman in the U.S. government. As the world's "indispensable nation," she argued, the United States was duty bound to promote democratic freedoms far from its borders, even through the use of military force.

Albright's personal history profoundly shaped her worldview. Her family fled Czechoslovakia in 1939 after Adolf Hitler's takeover of the country, and three of her Jewish grandparents died in German concentration camps. Upon Hitler's defeat, Albright's family returned home, but soon became refugees again when the Soviet Union seized control of the government in a 1948 communist coup. The daughter of a Czech diplomat, Albright served during Clinton's first term as U.S. ambassador to the United Nations. Her calls for U.S. participation in several UN peacekeeping missions resulted in frequent clashes with Republican leaders in Congress. Yet she remained well respected on Capitol Hill and was easily confirmed as secretary of state in 1997.

tance as his reason for inaction. Clinton knew that if the United States intervened unilaterally, the war would soon become "America's war." Like President Lyndon Johnson in Vietnam, he might become stuck in military quicksand, jeopardizing his domestic priorities, stimulating a peace movement, and endangering his chances for reelection in 1996.

Meanwhile, the United Nations pressed forward with a plan to partition Bosnia along ethnic lines, but the Serbs continued shelling Muslim enclaves that the UN had promised to protect. UN peacekeepers provided the besieged Muslims with medicine and food, but only the threat of air strikes against Serbian positions in the mountains surrounding Sarajevo temporarily brought relief to that city and other safe havens. Serbian defiance resumed, however, when the few air strikes authorized by the UN and undertaken by NATO revealed that the foreign powers did not have the will to stop the Serbian aggression. To deter future air attacks, the Serbs seized hundreds of UN peacekeepers and placed them around bombing targets as human shields. The Serbs thus accomplished their goal of displacing the Muslims from their homes throughout

Bosnia and succeeded in humiliating the UN by demonstrating that its peacekeeping forces never had a peace to keep. In a final turn of the screw, the Serbs overran the Muslim safe havens of Srebrenica and Zepa in July 1995. While UN peacekeepers watched helplessly—under orders to use force only in self-defense—the Serbs separated Muslim families and herded thousands of men and boys into concentration camps, where they were later executed and buried in mass graves.

THE DAYTON ACCORDS

Suddenly in late 1995, a shift in the regional balance of power transformed this situation. The Croatian army, showing surprising strength, launched a successful ground attack against the Serbs, depriving them of many of their earlier territorial gains. Muslim forces joined the counteroffensive, which produced a new flood of refugees, this time Serbs fleeing the Croats and Muslims. Recognizing the shifting power balance and outraged by the most recent Serbian atrocities, NATO launched a sustained bombing campaign against Serbian munitions dumps, bridges, and air defenses that further weakened the Serbs. By this time, the multilateral economic sanctions against Belgrade had begun taking their toll and forced Serbian president Slobodan Milosevic to assert his authority over the Bosnian Serbs.

In this improved climate, American leaders seized their opportunity to negotiate a deal among the Balkan rivals. Despite the violence and the deepening mutual hatreds, each of the factions had strong reasons to end the fighting: for the Serbs, to consolidate the Bosnian Serb gains before they were lost or reversed and to end the economic sanctions; for the Croats, to secure their independent state and the safety of their nationals in other areas; and for the Muslims, to relieve the suffering of their people and to create a Bosnian state with strong Muslim representation. Forced to negotiate face-to-face at a U.S. Air Force base in Dayton, Ohio, leaders of the three factions signed a complex agreement in November 1995 that led to a cease-fire in 1996. Under the Dayton Accords, nearly sixty thousand NATO troops were deployed to the region as part of Operation Joint Endeavor. Once in place, they separated the armed factions, protected civilian populations, and delivered economic assistance to the war-ravaged Bosnian communities. Bosnian leaders then created a new government led by a three-member presidency, one from each ethnic group, to be chosen by the Bosnian people in national elections.

Shortly after his reelection in November 1996, Clinton extended the NATO mission in Bosnia through June 1998, a move that surprised no one and was followed by longer extensions of the foreign presence. Clinton argued that the troops were still needed to buy time for the new civilian-led government to take full control. Thus NATO troops, accompanied by Russian peacekeepers, would continue to separate and disarm the combatants in three zones supervised by the United States, Britain, and France, respectively. The United States and Western European governments formally put the Bosnians on notice: continue the peace process or face new economic sanctions and the withdrawal of the peacekeeping force.

The Bosnian war revealed critical shortcomings in the system of collective security that was supposed to guarantee peace in the post–Cold War era. The United Nations was incapable of harnessing a united response to aggression, much less ending and punishing "ethnic cleansing." This failure of the UN reflected the failure of the Western great powers, which, until forced into action, were deeply divided by the crisis. The European Union, which at the same time was trying to create a "common foreign and security policy," proved especially impotent. Because of all these shortcomings, it was doubtful that the externally imposed peace would provide a basis for long-term reconciliation.

THE KOSOVO SHOWDOWN

Tragically, the Balkan wars did not end in Bosnia. As many feared, Milosevic simply redirected his military machine against another Yugoslav province, Kosovo. The province held great symbolic value to Belgrade despite its chronic poverty and small Serbian population, for it was there that Serbian armies had made their last stand against the Ottoman Turks in the 1389 Battle of Kosovo. After the Serbian defeat, most Kosovars converted to Islam. The remaining Serbs adhered to Christianity and submitted to five centuries of repressive rule by the Ottoman Empire, all the while plotting their revenge. They received their first chance when Kosovo was folded into the new federation of Yugoslavia after World War I. The Serb-dominated government immediately sought to settle the score, ejecting the majority population of ethnic Albanians from Kosovo and repopulating their villages with Serbs. But this early round of ethnic cleansing was cut short by the Second World War, as the region again became a battleground for the great powers.

Tito allowed the conflict in Kosovo to smolder during the early stages of the Cold War and even permitted the region's autonomy under the new Yugoslav constitution of 1974. But Milosevic had other ideas once he assumed power fifteen years later. He quickly rescinded the constitution, nullified the rights of Kosovar Albanians, and installed Serbs in key provincial offices. Yet Serbs, because of their mass exodus from Kosovo over a period of centuries, made up only about 10 percent of the province's population; ethnic Albanians made up the other 90 percent. In this respect, the crackdown that began in 1989 was doomed from the start. The Kosovars responded by declaring independence and organizing a defense force that became known as the Kosovo Liberation Army (KLA). Their appeals for statehood, however, were drowned out—first by the jubilation that attended the collapse of the Soviet Union, and then by the eruption of violence elsewhere in Yugoslavia.

To Milosevic, revenge in Kosovo was the only way to overcome his humiliating defeats in Slovenia, Croatia, and Bosnia. His paramilitary troops forced Albanian families from their homes, seized their possessions, and then set entire villages on fire. The KLA responded by conducting raids against the small population of Serbs, primarily police and government officials. In February 1999, attempting to prevent a full-scale war, the United States and several European powers brought the rival factions together in Rambouillet, France. The deal proposed by the mediators—the retreat of Serbian forces from Kosovo, the introduction of a NATO-led peacekeeping force, and renewed autonomy (but not independence) for Kosovo—appealed to neither the Serbs nor the Kosovars. Under intense pressure from U.S. and European leaders, the Kosovar delegation agreed to the deal anyway, but only because Milosevic's rejection of the accords was a foregone conclusion.

With the Rambouillet Accords in tatters, NATO faced little choice but to act on its threats to respond with military force. Withholding military intervention would have revealed the threats as empty. Furthermore, in doing nothing NATO ran the risk of undermining the alliance at the very time it was seeking new life—and new members. The threatened NATO bombardment, code-named Operation Allied Force, began in late March. President Clinton, under pressure from domestic critics and many anxious European leaders, publicly ruled out a ground offensive.[11] In gaining support for the intervention by minimizing the risk of NATO casualties, however, Clinton and his NATO counterparts provided cover for Milosevic to create the very cataclysm NATO sought to avoid: widespread destruction in Kosovo and the displacement of more than one million citizens.

The events were ghastly, but familiar. Thousands of Muslim men were rounded up, tortured, and murdered. Serbian troops raped Muslim women, often in front of their children. Homes and businesses were pillaged and burned. Entire cities such as Pec and Djakovica, and even Kosovo's capital, Pristina, were reduced to ashes. Those who escaped the

11. The German government, in particular, insisted that ground forces be avoided. The mere prospect of introducing ground troops to Kosovo was certain to incite a backlash against Chancellor Gerhard Schroeder's new administration.

onslaught were stripped of their identification papers and sent wandering into the mine-filled mountain passes out of Kosovo. Many elderly refugees fell to their deaths along the way, their bodies compounding the horror of the survivors. Other refugees were separated from their families, stuffed into locked trains, and shuttled to refugee camps in Albania and Macedonia that could not adequately feed or house them, nor provide them with medical care. Although seemingly random and spontaneous, and contrary to Serbian claims that the exodus was caused by NATO bombing, the campaign of terror had been "meticulously organized and aimed, from the outset, at expelling huge numbers of people." [12]

Clinton soon confronted the consequences of NATO's decision to adopt a bombing campaign based on gradual escalation rather than an immediate and overwhelming destructive force that would have inflicted real pain on the civilian population. Based on the successful experience in Bosnia, the president had wrongly assumed that a modest show of NATO muscle—lasting just two or three days—would again drive Milosevic to the bargaining table. But this time the pinprick attacks on Serbian artillery and command centers only accelerated the gutting of Kosovo. Clinton therefore had only one option: to intensify the bombing campaign by directing NATO air strikes against the heart of Serbia. Early on, however, a series of targeting errors by NATO bombers, including the destruction of passenger trains and of the Chinese embassy in downtown Belgrade, left scores of civilians dead and prompted widespread condemnation. Such mistakes were to be expected, however, because pilots were prevented from flying below fifteen thousand feet, within the reach of Serbian antiaircraft missiles. Meanwhile, by this point the NATO barrage and its commitment to a final victory were irreversible.

After lengthy internal negotiations, the NATO states finally acknowledged in May that ground forces might be required to support the air campaign. The alliance also assented to a renewed ground campaign by KLA forces that would flush Serbian forces from their concealed positions in Kosovo and expose them to a crippling round of NATO attacks. As in Bosnia, where aerial attacks had been bolstered by the Croat-Muslim counteroffensive, the military campaign in Kosovo finally produced results. Repeated attacks on Belgrade's electrical grid, which literally "turned off the lights" in the Yugoslav capital, were especially helpful in demonstrating NATO's heightened resolve. Faced with another defeat and under pressure by Russian officials to end the war, Milosevic

12. John Kifner, "How Serb Forces Purged One Million Albanians," *New York Times*, May 29, 1999, 1A.

agreed in June to withdraw the Serbian forces and allow the displaced Kosovars to return to the remnants of their communities.

This latest round of the latest Balkan ordeal achieved the general objectives of NATO. Serbia's ten-year campaign of terror and intimidation was finally brought to an end, and fears of a widened conflict beyond Yugoslavia were dispelled. In gaining Milosevic's final surrender, Western leaders had delivered their message that ethnic cleansing in Europe was a thing of the past. In defeating Serbia without a single NATO casualty, Clinton and his European counterparts had prevented their domestic opponents from mobilizing against the war, challenging their leadership, and threatening the future of the alliance.

In other respects, the NATO victory was partial and highly qualified. Kosovo was "liberated," but it would remain—at least in name—a part of Yugoslavia. Milosevic and his top military aides still held the reins of power, even after being indicted by a UN court for crimes against humanity. As for the European governments, the Kosovo intervention clearly showed them how far they had to go to attain any semblance of a common foreign policy. In tactical terms, it was significant that U.S. aircraft had carried out most of the estimated six thousand bombing missions, and that nearly every target had been identified by U.S. intelligence sources. The European states, by contrast, had had little to offer in the way of skilled manpower and weapons systems. "The Kosovo war was mainly an experience of Europe's own insufficiency and weakness," German foreign minister Joschka Fischer observed. "We as Europeans never could have coped with the Balkan wars that were caused by Milosevic without the help of the United States. The sad truth is that Kosovo showed Europe is still not able to solve its own problems." [13]

U.S.-Russian Relations under Stress

One of the most bizarre episodes of the war in Kosovo occurred after the fighting had ended and the peace treaty had been signed. Before dawn on June 12, 1999, an armored column of Russian troops entered the smoldering ruins of Pristina, the capital city. The city's remaining Serbs cheered the soldiers as they rolled toward the airport, where they took up their position as an occupying force.

But there was a problem: the Russians were not supposed to be in Pristina; they were supposed to be at their peacekeeping posts in Bosnia. Their surprise arrival several hours ahead of the NATO contingent—including British, French, Italian, and U.S. troops—stole the spotlight

13. Quoted in Ivo H. Daalder and Michael E. O'Hanlon, "Unlearning the Lessons of Kosovo," *Foreign Policy* (fall 1999): 137.

from the very forces whose military campaign had brought about Milosevic's surrender of Kosovo. Russian leaders, who considered the Slavic people of Serbia to be allies, had consistently *opposed* the bombing campaign and promised to veto any UN effort to prevent the ethnic cleansing of Kosovar Albanians. The Russian "liberation" of Pristina was, therefore, a farce. But it offered the Russian troops and their leaders in Moscow a brief moment of glory, along with a barely concealed sense of satisfaction that they had beaten the NATO powers to their prize.

This misplaced show of force illustrated just how decrepit Russia had become during its torturous period of transition after the Cold War. Eight years of political and economic crises had produced almost daily political struggles in Moscow, a declining economic output, and a string of military challenges inside and beyond Russia's borders. Were it not for a steady supply of economic aid from Western countries, Boris Yeltsin's faltering regime—and his democratic reforms—would likely have collapsed long before the Kosovo conflict and its surreal aftermath. Yet Yeltsin somehow had managed to remain in power until after the Balkan wars, and his country retained the one source of power that could not be denied: a massive nuclear stockpile. As a result, Russia continued to preoccupy American leaders into the new millennium.

INTERNAL CHALLENGES TO REFORM

The collapse of communist rule exposed deep fault lines within the former Soviet Union. Just as the breakup of the Ottoman and Austro-Hungarian empires contributed to the onset of World War I, and just as the dismantling of the European colonial empires after 1945 set off violence between and within many new states, new possibilities for conflict appeared after the Soviet Union fractured into fifteen republics, all claiming sovereignty. The Baltic states of Estonia, Latvia, and Lithuania reclaimed their pre–World War II independence. Because the Russians had long controlled both the czarist and communist states, ethnic Russians were left scattered throughout the Commonwealth of Independent States (CIS), the loose-knit group of twelve non-Baltic republics formed after the fall of the Soviet Union. In addition to the Russians, dozens of other ethnic groups inhabited its vast frontiers.

This intermingling of ethnic groups inflamed the hatreds between the Russians and the peoples they had long dominated, particularly Muslims living in the southern tier of CIS states. In Russia, the revival of ethnic tensions gave xenophobic nationalists and former communists bent on destroying the liberal state and market economy the reformers were trying to create a strong emotional issue with which to bring down Yeltsin's centrist regime. Moldova and Georgia (a non-CIS state) imme-

COMMONWEALTH OF INDEPENDENT STATES

diately faced secessionist movements. Ukraine was internally divided between its own ethnic group and a sizable Russian population. Belarus, Turkmenistan, and Uzbekistan came under dictatorial rule. Tajikistan was engulfed in civil war. And Armenia and Azerbaijan fought a costly war over an enclave—Nagorno-Karabakh—each claiming it as a rightful possession.

But despite all of these conflicts, Russia remained a potentially formidable military power with the ability to destroy the fragile political arrangements that were emerging in the 1990s. The Russian government continued to command an army of more than one million soldiers, two hundred thousand of whom remained outside its borders within the CIS. Yeltsin instituted ambitious political and economic reforms, but they proved difficult to impose on a society that had never been exposed to democracy or the free market. Prominent communists, elected under the old Soviet constitution, still dominated the legislature and state bureaucracy, and they blocked the Russian president's reform efforts. Also opposed to Yeltsin's efforts were Russian nationalists, who shared the communists' resentment at the loss of empire and status, and a powerful "mafia" that exploited the vast black market in Russia's largest cities.

Boris Yeltsin was caught in the middle of a political cyclone.[14] In September 1993, the Russian president dissolved the Russian parliament, whose members were elected under the Soviet system and opposed many of his political and economic reforms. The dissidents then called for armed insurrection against Yeltsin and barricaded themselves within the "White House," as the building that housed the parliament was known. Yeltsin, faced with growing unrest on the streets of Moscow, responded by declaring a state of emergency and ordering Russian troops to shell the White House, which had served as a symbol of democracy and resistance to the communist regime prior to the collapse of the Soviet Union. More than one hundred people were killed in the assault, and the leading political opponents were arrested. Yeltsin then quickly introduced a new constitution that greatly enhanced his powers and called for elections to a new bicameral federal assembly. These actions, he argued, were necessary to ensure the success of Russia's experiment with democracy.

The elections in December, however, only made matters worse. Extremists from both the right and the left dominated the new federal assembly. The most outspoken nationalist, Vladimir Zhirinovsky, pledged to restore the old Russian empire, even suggesting he would gain the return of Alaska. As conditions worsened across the country, many Russians welcomed his appeals and longed openly for the more "orderly" system under Lenin, Stalin, and Brezhnev.

In the United States and Western Europe, questions were raised about the continuing flow of Western aid to Russia. Should the new Russia be left to wallow in its economic misery, perhaps to emerge some day as a resentful state—like Germany after World War I? Or should Russia's former adversaries furnish the support Russia needed to grow economically and become politically stable—in much the same way the United States helped Germany after World War II? The Western powers adopted the latter course and agreed that Russia should receive economic assistance, but only so long as the money was used effectively. They demanded that Yeltsin's political reforms move forward and that Russian leaders hold

14. On the debilitating effect of Russia's internal politics, see Lilia Shevtsova, *Yeltsin's Russia: Myths and Reality* (Washington, D.C.: Carnegie Endowment for International Peace, 1999). Also see Dimitri K. Simes, *After the Collapse: Russia Seeks Its Place as a Great Power* (New York: Simon and Schuster, 1999).

inflation in check and stop subsidizing inefficient or Mafia-controlled industries. Even though they were faced with their own economic problems, Western leaders, led by the German government, promised Russia more than $30 billion in aid. Meanwhile, the International Monetary Fund approved an additional $10 billion in low-interest loans.

Despite Yeltsin's reelection in 1995, the Russian president could not prevent his nation's continued slide into disarray. Economic output finally increased by 1997, but then it plunged again in 1998 amid a collapse of the ruble, renewed inflation, and Russia's default on its foreign debt. Much of the Russian economy had been reduced to barter transactions. Tax collection was sporadic and selective, and government regulators routinely supplemented their meager incomes by demanding bribes. The "crony capitalism" that was sweeping across Eastern Europe became an art form in Russia, where former communists gobbled up huge public industries such as the Gazprom energy consortium and kept the profits for themselves. Meanwhile, Yeltsin's behavior became ever more erratic as he battled not only his domestic enemies but also a series of health problems that left him frail and often incapacitated.

UNREST IN THE 'NEAR ABROAD'

Yeltsin's problems were further aggravated by turmoil in the "near abroad" region of central Asia, home to the largely Islamic states of the CIS whose people had struggled against Russian domination ever since the Cossacks first entered the Caucasus Mountains in the sixteenth century. The sparse and impoverished Muslim population had succumbed to the brute strength of czarist Russia, and during the Cold War it had suffered even worse repression as a captive member of the Soviet Union. Because of this history, it is no wonder that the liberated republics of central Asia welcomed the collapse of the Soviet Union and seized their opportunity to be finally free of Moscow's control.

Moscow worried that other Islamic powers in the region, including Iran and Turkey, would exploit the vacuum created by the Soviet Union's demise and attempt to impose their own hegemonic designs on the region. All of central Asia seemed up for grabs in the 1990s as militant Islamic groups seized control of Afghanistan and civil wars raged in neighboring CIS republics. In the meantime, the United States and European powers quietly pursued their own interests in the rich oil fields of the Caspian Sea and sought to construct pipelines out of the area that would not be subject to Russian control.

The threat of Islamic movements within Russia itself quickly became real in the territory of Chechnya, which had long struggled against

Moscow's hegemony.[15] After Chechen leaders declared "our independence is forever" in 1994, Yeltsin sent Russian troops to the Chechen capital, Grozny, and the Russian air force bombed residential neighborhoods. But his poorly organized and underequipped troops faltered against the more determined Chechens, who drew support from neighboring Islamic states and continued to press their case for independence into the late 1990s.

Such independence would set a dangerous precedent for other dissatisfied ethnic groups. Yet nothing the Russian troops did was sufficient to overcome the Chechen fighters, whose defiance in the face of a stronger enemy was reminiscent of the Afghan *mujahadin.* The Chechens stood firm, held elections in January 1997, and then issued an even more explicit declaration of independence. Humiliated, Yeltsin unleashed another attack in 1999. The military campaign served as the only rallying point for the Russian people, who were otherwise demoralized and destitute after years of stalled economic reforms.

The United States clung to Yeltsin throughout this ordeal, viewing the Russian leader as the best and perhaps only hope for the country's peaceful reform. Although Clinton and Yeltsin bickered over issues such as NATO expansion and Yugoslavia, they agreed on the basic designs of the new Russia. And they knew that Russia would need continued infusions of aid—accompanied by exceptional patience—from the West in order to prevent a catastrophe. From the standpoint of U.S. leaders, only Yeltsin could keep bilateral arms control talks from coming apart and prevent Russia's nuclear technology from being sold to the highest bidders. The latter was especially important to the United States. It had spent nearly $3 billion between 1992 and 1999 to "denuclearize" Belarus, Kazakhstan, and Ukraine and to remove other weapons of mass destruction from across the former Soviet Union. But more work was needed to prevent the sale of nuclear technology, which had become an attractive prospect to the cash-starved economies of the region. Clinton was therefore restrained in criticizing Yeltsin. After first condemning the crackdown in Chechnya, Clinton defended the Russian leader's sovereign right to keep the province and only asked that Yeltsin avoid excessive force.

Clinton's hands-off stance could not disguise Russia's military humiliation or the futility of its effort to defeat the Chechen nationalists. Facing mounting domestic problems, and seizing his chance to shape his own succession, Yeltsin abruptly resigned on the last day of 1999 and transferred power to his latest prime minister, Vladimir Putin. The former KGB officer had become a hero for leading the most recent crackdown in Chechnya, despite the mission's tactical failures that were not

15. See Anatol Lieven, *Chechnya: Tombstone of Russian Power* (New Haven, Conn.: Yale University Press, 1998).

reported in the Russian press. Putin also had just consolidated his political power in parliamentary elections, giving him a distinct advantage in the March 2000 presidential elections, which he won easily after pledging to revive Russia's economy at home and in world markets, root out corruption, and strengthen the military forces.

While such a brazen power play would have been widely condemned in the United States, Yeltsin's timely resignation received little fanfare within or outside Russia. The mere fact that power had been transferred peacefully was considered a major achievement—and a source of relief. Nevertheless, the prospects for Russia in the post–Yeltsin era were highly uncertain. The aging Russian leader had kept his tenuous hold on power only by resorting to many of the same autocratic measures that had sustained his predecessors. But none of this would work for Russia in the future, under Putin or any other Russian leader, because, as one historian aptly noted, "at the end of the twentieth century international power rests not on the extent of territory a state controls but on its level of economic and technological developments. Politically, economically, and morally the age of territorial empires is over: crossing frontiers with armies is no longer a permissible road to national aggrandizement. . . . Thus Russia, no matter how organized politically, must first become rich if she wishes again to be powerful; and getting rich, with the handicap of a Soviet legacy, will take no small length of time." [16]

Faced with this stubborn reality, the United States remained patient with Russia into the twenty-first century. It was simply too large, too well stocked with nuclear weapons, and too politically volatile to be ignored. Put more positively, a democratic Russia with a vibrant economy would be a force for global stability. For different reasons, U.S. leaders also had no choice but to maintain their close contacts with the Eastern European governments, which still claimed allegiance to the democratic values long espoused by the United States even as their economic reforms came under fire. America's vision of democratic governance and market economics had finally been given its chance on the dividing line between East and West. This was no time for the United States to retreat into its hemispheric shell.

16. Martin Malia, *Russia under Western Eyes: From the Bronze Horseman to the Lenin Mausoleum* (Cambridge, Mass.: Belknap Press, 1999), 417.

America under Fire

The north tower of the World Trade Center collapses after being struck by a highjacked jet on September 11, 2001. The terrorist attacks on New York City and Washington, D.C., prompted a swift response by the Bush administration and a new era in American foreign policy.

The "unipolar moment" proclaimed at the Cold War's end was not a moment at all. If anything, the global primacy of the United States *increased* during the decade that followed the Soviet Union's collapse. The U.S. economy grew steadily in the 1990s, fueled by greater worker productivity, soaring foreign investment, and an end to federal budget deficits. Wall Street enjoyed a decade-long bull market, while American firms enjoyed the largest market share of the computer industry and other high-technology sectors. The United States also extended its lead in military power, spending more on defense in 1997 than the next six countries combined.[1] American military supremacy was especially pronounced in the area of weapons technology, which allowed the nation to enhance the firepower and precision of its vast arsenal while reducing the size of its armed forces. In addition, the influence of America's democratic values and the cultural impact of its civil society demonstrated its enduring "soft power."

Global developments accentuated these advantages. Russia's government floundered in the 1990s amid economic stagnation, political corruption, and the endless civil war in Chechnya. The European Union (EU) suffered through the growing pains of monetary union and the launch of a common currency, the euro. Despite the EU's call for a "common foreign and security policy," its members could not form a united front even as ethnic warfare raged across Yugoslavia.

Economic troubles in East Asia, meanwhile, extended the gap in global production between the United States and other industrial powers. Japan, the long-time regional "locomotive," was battered by economic scandals and overheated capital markets, and its rupture quickly spread far beyond East Asia (see Chapter 14). Only the People's Republic of China emerged from the 1990s with greater world power. Military spending in China grew steadily during the decade, with much of this expansion directed toward high-technology weapons systems and enhanced "3CI" (command, control, communications, and intelligence). Beijing's ability to project this power, however, was constrained by its repressive political system and its crushing domestic burdens. Although China's economy was booming—it grew at an annual rate of nearly 10 percent between 1980 and 2000—the daily task of feeding more than 1.3 billion citizens (more than four times the U.S. population) remained the government's primary focus. For the time being, Chinese leaders were content with economic and military modernization, and with lending an appearance of political moderation. They knew the time was not right, not yet anyway, for challenging American interests in the Taiwan Straits, the Korean peninsula, or other regional hot spots.

The unipolar balance of world power, therefore, had become an entrenched fact of geopolitical life. To many analysts, it was a force for global stability. Because of the wide lead of the United States in so many categories of national power, rational second-tier states would "bandwagon" with Washington rather than challenge it, either alone or by creating rival blocs. As one scholar put it, "The raw power advantage of the

1. U.S. Arms Control and Disarmament Agency, *World Military Expenditures and Arms Transfers* (Washington, D.C.: USACDA, 1998), 40. Four of these six countries—France, Japan, Britain, and Germany (listed in order of spending amounts)—were allies of the United States during this period. China and Russia were second and third on the list, respectively.

United States means that an important source of conflict in previous systems is absent: hegemonic rivalry over leadership of the international system. No other major power is in a position to follow any policy that depends for its success on prevailing against the United States in a war or an extended rivalry. None is likely to take any step that might invite the focused enmity of the United States." [2]

In the popular imagination, the United States was more immune than ever from the perils of the outside world and more capable of fulfilling its self-appointed mission to lead the world toward freedom, peace, and prosperity. The experience of the 1990s led many, inside and outside of government, to believe this mission could be accomplished with little effort or sacrifice. Opinion polls consistently found that most Americans, while believing the nation should play a leadership role abroad, were more concerned about domestic problems than foreign policy. News organizations closed overseas news bureaus and cut back on world news. Congress cut foreign aid. Despite President Bill Clinton's adoption of an ambitious foreign policy agenda based on global "engagement" and democratic "enlargement," the State Department's budget in 1997 fell to its lowest level in twenty years.[3]

Such a casual approach to global leadership seemed reasonable in view of the resounding victory of the United States in the Cold War, its swift success in the Persian Gulf War, and its halting of ethnic violence in Bosnia and Kosovo with few American casualties. Clinton, stung politically by the abrupt U.S. withdrawal from Somalia (see Chapter 10) and aware that the public would not accept casualties in other humanitarian interventions, had refused to place U.S. troops in harm's way in the Balkans (see Chapter 11). Yet he had achieved his goal of ending both conflicts, largely through the use of high-altitude bombing raids that reinforced the sense that wars could be won painlessly, at least for the United States. In other cases, such as the 1998 terrorist attacks on American embassies in Kenya and Tanzania, a few long-range cruise missiles delivered to enemy targets were deemed sufficient to keep the peace.

The United States, it appeared, could enjoy an unprecedented degree of global dominance while taking or leaving the burdens of leadership as it saw fit. All this seemed natural for a nation whose political, economic, and social systems were widely believed to be superior to others. As a rising power, the United States had lurched between periods of activism and detachment. Global hegemony, it seemed, allowed American foreign policy makers to have it both ways.

2. William Wohlforth, "The Stability of a Unipolar World," *International Security* 24 (summer 1999): 7.

3. See Steven W. Hook, "Domestic Obstacles to International Affairs: The State Department under Fire at Home," *PS: Political Science and Politics* (January 2003): 23–29.

Strains in the Unipolar Order

The relative calm of the late 1990s affirmed Americans' long-standing belief that peace, not war, is the natural state of global affairs, and that the spread of democracy and free markets would suppress violent conflict. But beneath this veneer of commitment and solidarity, antagonism was setting in between the United States and the international community. American preeminence provoked resentment—and a certain measure of envy—within states and societies with fewer resources and less clout. Much of the discontent was directed toward the agents of American soft power, the multinational corporations and media outlets whose promotion of consumer culture threatened traditional customs and forms of expression in many societies. But critics also denounced American foreign policy, particularly the government's selective adherence to free trade, its antagonism toward the United Nations, its cornering of the global arms market, the enormous gap between its defense and foreign aid spending, and its opposition to international agreements favored by most other countries. Above all, critics perceived American officials to be overly moralistic—not because the government's proclaimed democratic values were misplaced, but because U.S. actions often contradicted them.

These controversies tarnished America's image at the peak of its world power. Americans traditionally viewed the nation as an exceptional "city on the hill," but foreign governments and citizens saw a Washington arrogant with power and indifferent to problems such as global warming, mass starvation in Africa, the AIDS epidemic, and weapons proliferation. Some analysts in the United States warned of "blowback," a term used by the Central Intelligence Agency (CIA) to describe retaliation against the nation by vindictive foreign governments and groups.[4] Whatever the outcome, it was clear that the unipolar order was far from a harmony of interests, let alone a universal embrace of American leadership.

THE GLOBALIZATION BACKLASH

The Clinton presidency will long be associated with globalization, or the linking of national and regional markets into an integrated world economy. Toward that end, the World Trade Organization (WTO) held particular allure for Clinton. He had argued that the WTO, with 135 members in 1999, would bolster a world economy based on private enterprise

4. For an application of this concept, see Chalmers Johnson, *Blowback: The Costs and Consequences of American Empire* (Boston: Little, Brown, 2000).

and free trade. Trade disputes would be resolved in an orderly fashion, agreements would be reached on regulating global financial transfers, and new standards would be adopted to protect workers and preserve the environment. Most important, the WTO would mesh with other international organizations, ensuring political stability and harmony worldwide.

Directly challenging this logic was a vast network of local, national, and transnational interest groups. Widely dispersed but closely connected through the Internet, these groups had little in common except their shared disdain for the WTO. Environmental activists viewed the organization as an agent of global warming and deforestation. Labor unions saw their jobs being shipped away by WTO bureaucrats. Human rights advocates accused the WTO of tolerating sweatshop labor. And self-styled anarchists alleged that the WTO represented a stepping-stone toward an oppressive world government. To critics, globalization threatened cultural diversity and prevented local and national leaders from controlling their own political, economic, and cultural development. Multinational corporations would be given free rein, and the world would effectively be made safe for McDonald's, Wal-Mart, Coca-Cola, and General Motors.

Distracted by domestic upheavals and regional conflicts, Clinton failed to recognize this rising tide of dissent. He had assumed that the growing networks of nongovernmental organizations (NGOs) would *advance*, not oppose, the globalist cause. Nor did Clinton appreciate the deep divisions between rich and poor countries over issues such as labor standards and the costs of environmental protection, or the strained trade relations between the United States and European Union that were engulfing the WTO. The president also disregarded the lesson from the East Asian economic crisis that unfettered foreign investments, especially short-term stock and bond purchases, often cause more problems than they solve. His apparent obliviousness to these points came back to haunt him, however, after he made the fateful decision to host the annual meeting of the WTO in Seattle, Washington.

The December 1999 conference was a fiasco from start to finish. First, Clinton aides waited until the last minute to invite foreign leaders. Thus by the time the aides tried to arrange a "Millennium Round" of trade negotiations, most heads of government had other plans. Second, Clinton failed to achieve even a minimal consensus on the agenda, which ensured that the conference would also lack any sense of focus. Third, by the time the meeting began, widespread protests were overwhelming the Seattle police, who had ignored the problems at the most recent WTO summit in Geneva and failed to take the necessary precautions against civil disobedience. Storefronts were smashed and looted, police were pelted by rocks, and hundreds of protesters were injured or arrested. Many WTO delegates, including Secretary of State Madeleine Albright and UN Secretary General Kofi Annan, were confined to their hotels for much of the conference, unable to pass through the chaos.

Disillusionment also set in at the International Monetary Fund (IMF), whose actions before and during the economic crisis in East Asia in the late 1990s (described in Chapter 14) were widely criticized. In encouraging the tidal wave of private investments in East Asia, which then proved unable to absorb the funds, the IMF helped to spark the economic wildfire. And in providing vast sums of aid after the bottom fell out, the IMF rewarded the same state bureaucrats and foreign investors whose reckless behavior had produced the crisis. Under the terms of its aid, the IMF was ensured of eventual repayment; the East Asian countries were left to pick up the pieces. The painful readjustments fell most heavily on the laborers, property owners, and small merchants who had nothing to do with creating the economic meltdown. This experience was similar to that in Russia and many parts of Eastern Europe, where IMF funds effectively rewarded government corruption and ineptitude.

The turmoil within the IMF and WTO provided ample evidence that the honeymoon for globalization was over. If for every action there is an equal and opposite reaction, it should not have been surprising that globalization sparked opposition. Ironically, the same forces that propelled the trend—computer technologies, multinational corporations, massive cash flows across borders, and transnational interest groups—also were vital to the backlash. Globalization came to be negatively identified with the United States, which had long anticipated a single world marketplace as the realization of the country's historical vision.

RETREAT FROM MULTILATERALISM

In addition to the unrest over globalization, a second source of tension confronted American foreign policy makers after the Cold War: the growing rift between Washington and the array of international institutions the United States had actively supported since World War II. In turning against these multilateral institutions (involving three or more governments) and the agreements they produced, American leaders seemed to be turning their backs on the more democratic world order that, like globalization, also represented a long-standing American dream.

This unilateral turn in American foreign policy occurred despite Clinton's continued calls for engagement with the international community. But the president could not overcome pressure from Congress, still controlled by the Republican Party, to scale back the nation's non-military commitments. In fact, Clinton, who was generally more concerned with domestic policy, did not strongly resist this pressure and effectively surrendered his grand strategy to legislators. Even then, Clinton's relations with Congress grew worse with time. The Monica Lewinsky scandal, which led in 1998 to the president's impeachment by the Senate for not being open about his extramarital affair, left Clinton humiliated and politically wounded for the remainder of his presidency.[5]

The depth of Clinton's downfall in foreign policy was demonstrated by the Senate's October 1999 rejection of the Comprehensive Test Ban Treaty (CTBT), which Clinton had praised three years earlier as "the longest-sought, hardest-fought prize in the history of arms control." More than 150 foreign governments had pledged to support the treaty, which was based on the premise that a ban on testing would prevent potential proliferators from building weapons in the first place. Critics predicted that hostile nations would exploit American restraint and threaten the United States when its guard was down. But the primary motive of Clinton's Republican opponents was political: the treaty gave them a golden opportunity to humiliate the president on the world stage. The Senate defeat of the CTBT marked its first repudiation of a major treaty in eighty years and its first-ever rejection of a nuclear treaty. The refusal of the world's foremost nuclear superpower to join the moratorium on nuclear testing sent a strong signal to would-be nuclear powers: if the United States reserved the right to test these weapons, why shouldn't others?

The United States also found itself an outcast on a wide variety of other international agreements. Under pressure from the Pentagon, Clinton refused to sign the Ottawa Convention calling for a worldwide ban on land mines, whose primary victims were civilians in war-torn developing countries. The U.S. government's opposition was ironic—an American citizen, Jody Williams, won the Nobel Peace Prize in 1997 for organizing the public campaign that garnered support for the treaty from more than 120 other countries.[6] However, the Department of Defense opposed the land mines treaty on the grounds that "anti-personnel" mines were vital to preventing a North Korean invasion of South Korea.

5. Clinton maintained broad public approval during this period despite the scandal, and public surveys found most Americans believing the Senate's impeachment was politically motivated and unjustified. See Nancy Gibbs and Michael Duffy, "The Great Disconnect," *Time*, January 25, 1999. The president was not convicted by the House of Representatives and thus completed his second term in January 2001.

6. The treaty entered into force in March 1999 and was ratified by 148 governments by 2006. For the most recent figures, see the Web site of the International Campaign to Ban Landmines, http://www.icbl.org.

Washington's retreat from multilateralism gained momentum when Republican George W. Bush became president in January 2001. The governor of Texas and the son of Clinton's predecessor in office, Bush was in no mood to mend fences with the "international community," a term his national security adviser, Condoleezza Rice, had dismissed during the campaign as an illusion.[7] In her view, the multilateral cooperation and institution building embraced by the United States since the end of World War II had not brought the rest of the world in line with the nation's democratic values. Instead, they had produced open-ended commitments and mounting obligations that threatened U.S. sovereignty while empowering countries hostile to the United States. The second Bush administration, therefore, would be selective in observing such commitments and making new ones. Rather than working through formal organizations such as the United Nations or North Atlantic Treaty Organization (NATO), the United States would form "coalitions of the willing" on a case-by-case basis and dismantle them when their missions were accomplished. When help from other nations was not deemed necessary or was not forthcoming, the United States would go its own way.

Bush, with a Republican majority in Congress, eagerly joined the legislative attacks on multilateral commitment that had begun in 1995. Claiming that American chemical companies would face intrusive visits by international inspectors, the president blocked new measures to strengthen the 1972 Biological Weapons Convention. He also opposed a global treaty that restricted the trafficking of small arms, and he nullified a prior U.S. commitment to the International Criminal Court Treaty on the grounds that U.S. troops on peacekeeping missions would be unfairly singled out for prosecution. As noted in Chapter 1, Bush was supported in these actions by "neoconservatives" in Washington who had spoken out harshly against Clinton's engagement strategy and gained high-level positions in the Bush administration. The only dissenter in the new president's inner circle was Secretary of State Colin Powell, who adopted the conventional view that diplomatic agreements establishing standards of appropriate behavior in world politics served both U.S. national interests and the greater cause of international stability.

Of greatest concern to the new president was the 1972 Antiballistic Missile Treaty (ABM Treaty) with Russia, signed along with other nuclear arms control agreements by Richard Nixon and Leonid Brezhnev. The Bush administration concluded that the treaty, based on deter-

7. Condoleezza Rice, "Promoting the National Interest," *Foreign Affairs* 79 (January–February 2000): 45–62.

rence and mutual assured destruction (see Chapter 3), was obsolete in the new era of "rogue states" and freelancing terrorists with appetites for weapons of mass destruction. Thus Bush withdrew from the ABM Treaty, despite protests by Russian leaders and warnings by strategic analysts of a new global arms race, this time in antimissile technologies. The Department of Defense promptly stepped up its testing of missile defenses and planned for the deployment of a National Missile Defense system in Alaska and California by 2004.

Two events in the spring of 2001 dramatized the deepening isolation of the United States. In March, Bush renounced the Kyoto Protocol to the UN Framework Convention on Climate Change, which had been signed by Vice President Al Gore in 1997 but never submitted to the Senate for ratification.[8] The treaty, approved by eighty-three other governments, required industrialized countries to reduce their greenhouse gas emissions. The Clinton administration had agreed to reduce U.S. emissions by 7 percent of their 1990 levels by 2012. In rejecting the treaty, Bush refuted the scientific evidence linking greenhouses gases to global warming.[9] He charged instead that the protocol would merely slow U.S. economic growth and unfairly burden the United States while exempting developing nations, including China. The president also claimed that verifying compliance and enforcing the mandatory emission cutbacks would be impossible. No treaty at all, he argued, was better than a flawed one.

The president's dismissal of the Kyoto Protocol and his failure to propose a more rigorous alternative despite earlier pledges to do so incited widespread criticism from abroad. The United States was producing about one-quarter of the world's greenhouse gases—by far the largest share. Indeed, at the very time America renounced the Kyoto Protocol, U.S. highways were filled with gas-guzzling minivans and sport-utility vehicles (SUVs) that, because of the political muscle of domestic automakers, were exempt from federal fuel efficiency standards. This spectacle was especially offensive to government leaders and environmental groups in Europe, where conservation and the use of alternative energy sources had become a way of life.

The second revealing episode occurred in May 2001, when the UN Human Rights Commission denied the United States a seat on the panel for the first time since its creation in 1947 under the leadership of Eleanor Roosevelt. The move was clearly political payback for Washington's refusal

8. Clinton knew that the Senate most likely would reject the treaty, and for this reason did not submit it for ratification. See http://www.unfccc.int for a full text of the Kyoto Protocol (accessed May 1, 2006).

9. See, for example, the Intergovernmental Panel on Climate Change, "Climate Change 2001: Impacts, Adaptation, and Vulnerability" (New York: United Nations, February 2001).

to pay past UN dues, for its effort to force the resignation of the previous secretary general in 1996, and for its opposition to international agreements, most of which had nothing to do with human rights. The fact that repressive states such as Sudan and Syria were voted onto the commission made it clear that human rights were not a primary concern to the governments that denied the United States its customary seat. The incident further convinced Bush that the policy of "assertive multilateralism" so favored by his predecessor was a dead-end street.

John Bolton's appointment as undersecretary of state for arms control and international security in 2001 further underscored Bush's mistrust of global commitments. A prominent critic of agreements that restricted Washington's freedom of action, Bolton spent most of his time at the State Department blocking, weakening, and withdrawing from them. This approach was in direct contrast to the actions of previous undersecretaries, who had pursued *closer* ties and formal agreements with other governments. Bolton's adversarial approach often clashed with that of his boss, Colin Powell. But Bolton's appointment to his position in the State Department, and his temporary appointment in 2005 as ambassador to the United Nations, was very much in keeping with the unilateral turn in American foreign policy.

The Growing Threat of 'Sacred Terror'

As we have seen, after the Cold War many Americans believed the nation's primary threat stemmed from attempts by the United Nations and other global institutions to stifle American sovereignty in the name of "global governance." Such concerns, however, merely distracted the United States from another transnational force. Adherents of militant Islam, based in the Middle East but extending in disillusioned pockets across the Muslim world, had for years expressed ill will toward the West on several counts. For one thing, they resented the role of earlier Western leaders in redrawing the map of the Middle East after the downfall of the Ottoman Empire and after the two world wars of the twentieth century. Similarly, they strongly opposed the UN's creation of the state of Israel in 1948 and the support given by Western leaders, again primarily those in Washington, to the Jewish state.

Islamic militants also charged the industrialized countries, primarily the United States, with exploiting the Middle East's vast petroleum reserves, often with the approval of autocratic monarchs and military dictators who enriched themselves at their people's expense. Living standards in the former empire stagnated for decades despite the accelerating extraction of this oil wealth, which literally fueled the West's industrial boom and rapid economic growth.

Finally, the militants believed that Western cultural influence was corrupting their societies with its materialism, permissive lifestyles, and political freedoms that violated the strictures of the Koran, the Islamic sacred text. As these dissidents and their spiritual mentors in the Islamic mosques and *madrassas* (religious schools) saw it, the Western states and societies were preventing Muslims everywhere from recapturing the Ottoman Empire's promises and creating a new and enduring caliphate, or sphere of Islamic rule.

American leaders were aware of these antagonistic feelings, which had surfaced earlier with the Iranian revolution of 1979 and then the siege of the U.S. embassy in Teheran. But the rise of militant Islam was only of secondary concern to foreign policy makers, whose focus during the Cold War remained on containing Soviet communism. More generally, the threat posed by advocates of *jihad,* or holy war, was not given much priority in Washington because American leaders thought of the balance of world power in terms of nation-states. From this perspective, no country in the Middle East, or anywhere else for that matter, came close to presenting a clear and present danger to the United States. And certainly no private organization, however vengeful, could hope to contend with American power.

EARLY WARNINGS AND RESPONSES

The euphoria surrounding the end of the Cold War further discouraged American leaders from confronting the threat of militant Islam, whose tactic of choice—terrorist attacks—was not readily understood by a defense establishment hard-wired for conventional war. Indeed, the United States, a secular state despite its cultural attachment to Christian principles, was especially ill-equipped to anticipate the onslaught of "sacred terror" on its own territory.[10]

But developments at home exposed Americans to the mounting danger of international terrorism (see Table 12-1). A series of attacks in 1993, including an attempt to topple New York City's World Trade Center by means of underground explosives and a shooting spree outside CIA headquarters in Langley, Virginia, forced Clinton to confront the problem. By June 1995, he was sufficiently alarmed to issue a Presidential Decision Directive (PDD-39) calling for greater coordination among federal agencies in anticipating future attacks and responding effectively should they occur. "The United States," Clinton's directive stated, "regards all such terrorism as a potential threat to national security

10. Daniel Benjamin and Steven Simon, *The Age of Sacred Terror* (New York: Random House, 2002).

TABLE 12-1 **Major Transnational Terrorist Attacks against U.S. Targets, 1983–2001**

Year	Terrorist incident	Chief suspect or claimant of responsibility
1983	*(April)* Car bomb destroys U.S. embassy in Beirut, Lebanon, killing seventeen Americans, including CIA's Middle East director.	Hezbollah (Lebanon)
	(October) Suicide bombing of U.S. military compound in Beirut, Lebanon, kills 241 marines.	Hezbollah (Lebanon)
1984	*(March)* CIA agent William Buckley kidnapped, tortured, and killed in Beirut.	Islamic Jihad (Syria)
	(September) Twenty-four workers at U.S. embassy in Beirut killed by bomb blast.	Hezbollah (Lebanon)
1985	*(October)* Italian cruise ship *Achille Lauro* hijacked off Egyptian coast; wheelchair-bound American tourist Leon Klinghoffer killed.	Palestinian Liberation Front
1986	*(April)* Bomb attack on discotheque in West Berlin kills one U.S. serviceman and injures forty-four others.	Libyan government
1988	*(December)* Passenger jet destroyed in midair bomb attack over Lockerbie, Scotland; death toll of 270 includes 189 Americans.	Libyan government
1993	*(January)* Two CIA employees shot to death outside CIA headquarters in Langley, Virginia.	Pakistani militant
	(February) Bomb attack damages World Trade Center in New York City; sixty-three killed and 1,049 injured.	Followers of Egyptian Sheik Omar Abdel-Rahman
	(April) Former president George H. W. Bush is target of assassination attempt during visit to Kuwait.	Iraqi government
1995	*(March)* Two U.S. diplomats killed in U.S. consulate in Karachi, Pakistan.	Unknown

as well as a criminal act and will apply all appropriate means to combat it."[11] In May 1998, Clinton issued another directive that created the position of national coordinator for security, infrastructure protection, and counterterrorism, a move designed in part to demonstrate the president's resolve in fighting terrorism.

These measures aside, the White House had a difficult time persuading members of Congress that the threat was urgent. According to the first "counterterrorism czar," Richard A. Clarke, his position was accom-

11. White House, Presidential Decision Directive 39, "U.S. Policy on Counterterrorism," June 21, 1995, http://www.fas.org/irp/offdocs/pdd39.htm (accessed May 1, 2006).

TABLE 12-1 Major Transnational Terrorist Attacks against U.S. Targets *(continued)*

Year	Terrorist incident	Chief suspect or claimant of responsibility
1996	*(June)* Car bomb near U.S. Army compound in Al Khobar, Saudi Arabia, kills or wounds more than 250 U.S. military personnel.	Saudi Hezbollah, Iranian government
1997	*(February)* Tourists at Empire State Building in New York City are target of machine gun attacks; one visitor killed and several others wounded.	Palestinian militant
1998	*(August)* U.S. embassies in Dar es Salaam, Tanzania, and Nairobi, Kenya, attacked in nearly simultaneous bombings. Death toll of nearly three hundred includes twelve Americans; more than five thousand are wounded.	al Qaeda (Afghanistan)
1999	*(February)* Three American human rights activists in Venezuela kidnapped and then killed.	Revolutionary Armed Forces of Colombia
2000	*(October)* USS *Cole* bombed while refueling in Aden, Yemen; seventeen sailors killed and thirty-nine others injured.	al Qaeda (Afghanistan)
2001	*(September)* Suicide aircraft attacks on World Trade Center and Pentagon kill more than three thousand and injure thousands more.	al Qaeda (Afghanistan)

Sources: U.S. State Department, "Significant Terrorist Incidents, 1961–2001: A Chronology," http://www.state.gov/r/pa/ho/pubs/fs/5902.htm (accessed May 5, 2006); Center for Defense Information, "Chronology of Major Terrorist Attacks Against U.S. Targets," http://www.cdi.org/terrorism/chronology.html (accessed May 6, 2006); and Public Broadcasting Service, "Target America: Terrorist Attacks on Americans, 1979–1988," *Frontline,* http://www.pbs.org/wgbh/pages/frontline/shows/target/ (accessed May 6, 2006).

Note: Although the countries most closely linked to Hezbollah, Islamic Jihad, and al Qaeda at the time of attacks are noted in parentheses, the state sponsors of these groups vary over time and in connection with different attacks.

panied by "no budget, only a dozen staff, and no ability to direct actions by the departments or agencies."[12] After a high-level task force warned of impending terrorist strikes in 2000, legislators expressed alarm but approved no major initiatives or funding measures to fortify U.S. counterterrorism programs.[13] Meanwhile, emergency responders received little or no training in handling terrorist attacks. Depending almost

12. Testimony of Richard A. Clarke before the National Commission on Terrorist Attacks upon the United States, March 24, 2004, http://www.9-11commission.gov/hearings/hearing8/clarke_statement.pdf (accessed May 1, 2006).

13. National Commission on Terrorism, *Countering the Changing Threat of International Terrorism* (Washington, D.C.: National Commission on Terrorism, June 2000).

entirely on scarce local funds, these units maintained tight budgets largely designed for routine matters such as house fires and automobile accidents.

Basic statistics will help to explain this complacent attitude. Although international terrorists occasionally targeted Americans in the 1980s and 1990s, the 666 deaths from these attacks were modest compared with the battle deaths resulting from World War II (291,557) and the wars in Korea (33,651) and Vietnam (47,378).[14] Indeed, the victims of terrorism during these two decades were vastly outnumbered by the deaths caused by highway accidents, which averaged about 40,000 annually. The deadliest single act of terrorism, the bombing of the U.S. Marine barracks in Beirut in 1983, killed 241 Americans, but it was overshadowed the next day by the U.S. invasion of Grenada. Public and political reaction was also muted because the Beirut attack, like the later bombings of the Khobar Towers in Saudi Arabia in 1996 and the USS *Cole* off the Yemen coast in 2000, occurred far from the United States. Still, it is significant that the death toll from terrorist attacks between 1980 and 2000 greatly exceeded the combined casualties that resulted from U.S. military actions in Grenada, Haiti, Kuwait, Panama, Somalia, and the former Yugoslavia.

It is well known that open societies are by their nature highly vulnerable to terrorism. This certainly applied to the United States before the terrorist attacks of September 11, 2001. America's borders with Canada and Mexico were lightly guarded, as were its coastlines and airports. Foreign citizens traveled to and from the United States with little scrutiny, attaining work permits, student visas, and even American citizenship with relative ease. Furthermore, the U.S. economy was highly dependent on overseas markets, particularly on oil. Any disruption of economic activity in these markets would jeopardize American prosperity. The global reach of the U.S. government—its worldwide web of embassies, consulates, diplomatic missions, and military bases—provided terrorists with a multitude of potential targets. The same could be said of private American citizens, who traveled the world in numbers that greatly exceeded those from any other country.

Other factors placing the United States at risk of terrorist attacks stemmed, paradoxically, from its democratic political system. The openness of American government—most congressional proceedings and records were open to the public—provided potential enemies with ample information. The *Congressional Record* and C-Span revealed daily the bitter divisions within the federal government, and commercial

14. Paul R. Pillar, *Terrorism and U.S. Foreign Policy* (Washington, D.C.: Brookings, 2001), 18–19.

media sources fueled debilitating political scandals with nonstop coverage. Government agencies, of course, were expected to operate within the law and according to standard operating procedures. But none of these constraints, so vital to the preservation of democracy, applied to terrorist groups, whose deliberations and movements were hidden and whose members operated without regard to legal restrictions. Furthermore, terrorist groups adapted quickly to changing circumstances in stark contrast to the notoriously risk-averse agencies of the U.S. federal government.

THE AL QAEDA CONNECTION

American investigators discovered a common link to many of the acts of Islamic terrorism in the 1990s: the terrorist group al Qaeda, based in Afghanistan. Like other militant Islamic groups, al Qaeda rejected Western cultural, social, and economic values and openly declared its intention to destroy Western political institutions, military forces, and economic assets.[15] Initially composed largely of veterans of the Soviet resistance, al Qaeda expanded in the 1990s, opening training camps in Sudan, Yemen, and other countries with large, impoverished, and embittered Muslim populations. At least sixty al Qaeda cells existed worldwide in 2001 and formed their own coalitions of the willing with like-minded groups in Bosnia, Chechnya, Somalia, and other hotbeds of Islamic unrest. The group was linked to the anti-American resistance in Somalia in 1993, the bombing of the World Trade Center in the same year, the 1998 bombings of American embassies in Kenya and Tanzania, and the 2000 bombing of the USS *Cole* off the coast of Yemen.[16] The attacks of September 11 served as a natural extension of al Qaeda's mounting aggression.

The campaign to bring al Qaeda to justice soon took on a human dimension. Osama bin Laden, the group's leader, grew up in a wealthy Saudi Arabian family and was well known to the U.S. government since the days when he organized the *mujahadin,* or "holy warriors," against the Soviet occupation of Afghanistan in the 1980s. The CIA secretly provided logistical and financial support to the *mujahadin,* which helped

15. See Gilles Kepel, *Jihad: The Trail of Political Islam* (Cambridge, Mass.: Belknap Press, 2002), chap. 13.

16. Terrorists linked to al Qaeda were involved in the 1993 bombing of the World Trade Center in New York City. The person convicted of the attack, Ramzi Yusef, had also planned with other al Qaeda members to bomb the Lincoln and Holland Tunnels and the United Nations headquarters in New York City. The al Qaeda cell in the city was led by Sheik Omar Abdel-Rahman, a spiritual leader who had developed a working relationship with al Qaeda leader Osama bin Laden during the "blind sheik's" years as a member of Egyptian Islamic Jihad. Richard A. Clarke, *Against All Enemies: Inside America's War on Terror* (New York: Free Press, 2004), 78–79.

them to overcome the larger and more technologically advanced Soviet forces.

This marriage of convenience ended, however, after the Soviet Union's defeat in 1989. Bin Laden returned to Saudi Arabia, where he spoke out against the monarchy's secular form of government and close ties to the United States. His criticism so angered Saudi officials that they ejected him from the kingdom in 1991. Undeterred, bin Laden moved to the North African country of Sudan, whose government, dominated by the National Islamic Front, was engaged in a genocidal crackdown against its black population who followed Christian and other non-Islamic religious traditions. Safe in Sudan, bin Laden had ample freedom and resources to organize al Qaeda, whose English translation "the base" neatly captured the organization's intended role as a foundation for Islamic *jihad* (holy war). Al Qaeda soon created cells in other countries, including Egypt, Russia, and the former Yugoslavia, providing soldiers, weaponry, and other forms of assistance to Muslim insurgents seeking to gain political power by force. Al Qaeda also established a presence in European cities, including London, Milan, and Vienna, funding "charitable organizations" that served as fronts for al Qaeda operations. In Afghanistan, years of civil war after the war against the Soviet Union led to the rise of the Taliban, whose leaders welcomed bin Laden's return in 1996 after he was forced by international pressure to leave Sudan (see Chapter 13). With his globalized network of al Qaeda cells now fully mobilized, bin Laden used his sanctuary in Afghanistan to begin planning his frontal assault on the American infidels.

Terror in the Morning Sky

Despite the diplomatic tensions that accompanied Washington's rejection of multilateral engagement, the first months of George W. Bush's presidency were relatively quiet ones. The nation remained focused on domestic problems, particularly an economic slowdown after a decade of rapid growth. Although foreign leaders scoffed at the unilateral turn in American foreign policy, they continued to support Washington on most issues. An extended period of global stability, albeit one of occasional discord, was widely expected.

All this changed on September 11, 2001, when nineteen terrorists turned four hijacked airliners into weapons of mass destruction. Their assaults on New York City and Washington, D.C., shattered America's sense of invulnerability. Not only was the United States attacked with devastating effect; the strikes targeted its commercial and political centers. The fact that an invisible adversary—lacking national sovereignty, formal armies, or territory—committed the attacks exposed the limits of

IMPACT AND INFLUENCE

OSAMA BIN LADEN

Not long after the September 11, 2001, attacks on New York City and Washington, D.C., American leaders became aware of their source: the terrorist group al Qaeda and its leader, Osama bin Laden. Born the seventeenth of fifty-two children to the wealthiest construction magnate in Saudi Arabia, bin Laden enjoyed a childhood of privilege. He received a college degree in civil engineering in 1980 and then moved to Afghanistan to help the Islamic mujahadin *wage war against Soviet invaders. It was there that bin Laden first put his university training to use, along with the machinery and financial assets of his father's construction empire. By 1986, he was leading his own band of guerrilla forces from Syria and Egypt in combat operations that ultimately forced the Soviet Union's retreat from Afghanistan.*

Having overcome one Cold War superpower, bin Laden set his sights on the other. He condemned U.S. support for Israel, its close ties to secular Arab regimes, and its military presence in the oil-rich Persian Gulf. Creating al Qaeda, he instructed Muslims in all countries "to kill the Americans and plunder their money wherever and whenever they find it." Efforts by the United States to apprehend bin Laden failed as the scale of his attacks steadily escalated, culminating in the events of September 11. He remained at large long after the United States ousted the Taliban from Afghanistan and offered large rewards for his capture, "dead or alive."

America's ability to defend itself despite its overwhelming power and influence.

The four airliners used in the attacks took off within a two-hour period—two from Boston, a third from Washington, and the fourth from Newark, New Jersey. All were bound for California and were loaded with fuel. In each case, the terrorists hijacked the jets shortly after takeoff, using box cutters to subdue the flight crews, enter the cockpits, and take the controls. The first jet left Boston for Los Angeles but suddenly changed course toward New York City before flying into the north tower of the World Trade Center at 8:48 a.m. Initial news reports suggested the collision was accidental. But fears of a terrorist attack were confirmed eighteen minutes later, when a second jetliner crashed into the south tower. Half an hour later, a third jet plunged into the Pentagon. The fourth jet, hijacked over Ohio and set on a course toward Washington, crash-landed at 10:10 a.m. in rural Pennsylvania. Passengers on the plane tried to overpower the hijackers, and although they could not save themselves, they likely spared the U.S. Capitol or the White House. In all, 266 people died in the four planes.

Images of the crippled World Trade Center, the workplace of some fifty thousand people, transfixed the nation and the world. Thousands of rescue workers descended on the area and hundreds raced up the stairways toward the fires, hoping somehow to reach the office workers trapped above the flames. But as the burning jet fuel melted the towers' steel supports the twin skyscrapers gave way. The upper floors simply fell onto the floors beneath, causing a downward chain reaction that extended to the basements of both towers. The south tower was the first to go, at 10:05 a.m. After the north tower followed at 10:28, a cloud of smoke and debris enveloped Manhattan for the rest of the day.

President Bush was in Florida at the time of the attacks, reading to schoolchildren as part of a campaign to promote his education reforms. Amid the confusion, he was flown secretly to Air Force bases in Louisiana and Nebraska before it was considered safe for him to return to Washington. Vice President Dick Cheney, working in the White House, was rushed to an underground bunker. Cabinet members were moved to various locations around the capital to ensure that they all would not be in one place in the event of another strike. The attacks paralyzed routine activities across the nation. All 4,546 airplanes aloft at the time were ordered to land immediately. The Mexican and Canadian borders were closed, along with federal offices, foreign embassies, and highly visible landmarks such as the Golden Gate Bridge, the Sears Tower, and Disney World. The New York Stock Exchange, located blocks away from "ground zero," suspended trading indefinitely. Schools and private businesses across the country closed early as the gravity of the terrorist attacks set in.

The United States received immediate global support. The French newspaper *Le Monde* featured a banner headline on September 12 that declared, "We Are All Americans." The United Nations condemned the attacks and called for swift and concerted retaliation. For the first time in its history, the North Atlantic Council, the executive body of NATO, invoked Article 5 of its charter that declared an attack on any NATO member to be an attack on the entire alliance. Congress also responded quickly, passing a joint resolution that authorized Bush to use "all necessary and appropriate force" against the terrorists.

Bush declared the terrorist attacks an act of war. In a televised address on the night of the attacks, the president vowed to wage war against terrorism, not simply against those who were behind the assaults on New York City and Washington. Bush then widened the scope of the U.S. response by announcing that he would "make no distinction between the terrorists who committed these acts and those who harbor them." Thus state sponsors of terrorism would also be targeted by the United States. "Every nation, in every region, now has a decision to make," Bush declared to a joint session of Congress on September 20. "Either you are with us, or you are with the terrorists." With these words, Bush set the course of an American counteroffensive that would take many forms against many adversaries throughout much of the world.

For all of their horrible consequences, the attacks of September 11 ended the decade-long drift in American foreign policy. No longer could this period in history be regarded vaguely as the "post–Cold War era," a term that related to the past rather than the present. No longer could the U.S. public turn its back on threats from overseas previously thought unimportant. And no longer could the U.S. government veer from one grand strategy to another. Henceforth, the war against terrorism would consume the government's attention, providing the basis for foreign policy and many aspects of domestic policy.

Elements of Counterterrorism

The prospect of an imminent war against terrorism raised questions about how such a war would differ from the conventional wars previously fought by the United States. As noted earlier, the distinctive style of American foreign policy traditionally viewed warfare as an exception to the general rule of peaceful coexistence among states and societies. The war on terrorism declared by Bush would depart from this tradition in several ways, including the open-ended nature of the conflict. Fighting "terror" as opposed to a definitive enemy would commit the United States to an extended struggle in any number of areas. Indeed, the remote prospect of vanquishing terrorism altogether made it likely that the struggle would never be fully "won" or "lost" and instead would continue indefinitely.

Definitions of terrorism vary widely, based in large part on disagreements over what constitutes a "terrorist" as opposed to a "freedom fighter" or the like.[17] American officials formally defined the term as "premeditated, politically motivated violence perpetrated against noncombatant targets by subnational groups or clandestine agents, usually intended to influence an audience."[18] According to this definition, acts of terrorism share the following elements: the involvement of private individuals and groups as opposed to government agents, extensive prior planning, an intention to change government policy, the willful use of violence, and the targeting of civilians or off-duty military personnel.

Beyond these elements, three other aspects of terrorist activity also must be considered. First, neglected in the U.S. government's definition is the importance of symbolism in many acts of terrorism. The World Trade Center towers were not only New York City's tallest buildings, but also a symbol of American-led global commerce. The Pentagon was the ultimate symbol of U.S. military power. Their destruction was meant to symbolize, in turn, the failings of American values and the limits of American power. To terrorist groups that lack the resources to challenge a superpower directly, such statements are invaluable. Second, the psychological impact of terrorism is vital. Terrorists aim to incite mass anxiety, or in some cases panic, as a means of disrupting government policy and creating doubts about the ability of political leaders to protect their citizens. The fact that civilians, not military personnel, were killed *en masse* on September 11 had enormous appeal to the terrorists, because from that day on Americans would feel a little less secure as they went about their normal daily routines. Such mass anxiety could not have been achieved had military forces rather than civilians been targeted. As one author describes it:

> The distinction between the fair fight of an open military confrontation and the unfair one of a terrorist attack comes into play. Ask the average American if the life of a soldier who dies in battle is worth the same as the life of a countryman who has died from terrorism, and the answer will be yes. But ask after each type of event how much shock and revulsion that American is feeling, and the reaction will be stronger after the terrorist incident. . . . [H]owever much one might try to talk down the subject, some of the special shock of a terrorist attack will always be there; it is in the nature of the event.[19]

Finally, the messianic nature of the Islamic *jihad* cannot be ignored. Angry, disgruntled groups of many kinds have resorted to terrorism in modern history to achieve a variety of goals—for example, secession from a nation-state or changes in government policies.[20] By contrast, al

17. For an elaboration, see Walter Laqueur, *The New Terrorism: Fanaticism and the Arms of Mass Destruction* (New York: Oxford University Press, 1999); and Bruce Hoffman, *Inside Terrorism* (New York: Columbia University Press, 1998).

18. *U.S. Code,* 22 (2000), § 2656f (d).

19. Pillar, *Terrorism and U.S. Foreign Policy,* 24.

20. See Andrew Sinclair, *The Anatomy of Terror: A History of Terrorism* (New York: Macmillan, 2003).

Qaeda's motivation for the September 11 attacks "was neither political calculation, strategic advantage, nor wanton bloodshed," wrote two former National Security Council (NSC) analysts. "It was to humiliate and slaughter those who defied the hegemony of God. . . . It was an act of cosmic war."[21] To the United States, which had long equated its own global ambitions with "manifest destiny," the Islamists' presumption of divine guidance was not entirely unfamiliar.

No one doubted that the United States maintained overwhelming military superiority, vast economic wealth, and close political ties with other powerful governments. With these advantages, the United States could not be defeated in a conventional war. An alternative battle plan was needed. Just like those waging guerrilla warfare (see Chapter 6), the challenger would have to exploit the element of surprise, appeals to popular opinion, and knowledge of the local terrain. Unlike the large armies deployed by the superior power, which could easily bog down in a protracted conflict, the terrorists could afford to be patient. In the parlance of military strategists, the war against al Qaeda would be an *asymmetric* war in which calculations based on standard ratios of power would not apply. "In its basic form, asymmetrical warfare utilizes one side's comparative advantage against its enemy's relative weakness. Successful asymmetrical warfare exploits vulnerabilities—which are easy to determine—by using weapons and tactics that are unplanned or unexpected."[22]

Unlike Clinton, Bush did not have the luxury of taking pot shots at the terrorists and relegating counterterrorism to the back burner. The war on terrorism would be Bush's primary concern for the remainder of his presidency. But the White House would need both the public's support and its understanding because of the likelihood of military setbacks and additional terrorist attacks—not to mention the high cost of such an undertaking. Maintaining this support would not be easy, because the United States could not hope to destroy the enemy in one blow. Instead, it would have to fight a war of attrition over an extended period of time.[23] In summary, the war against al Qaeda forced the United States to abandon its traditional approach to warfare based on the use of overwhelming force against a discernible enemy in a clearly defined location. Beyond the need of the United States to gain public support and patience, three other factors would determine its success or failure in the coming struggle: intelligence, diplomacy, and homeland security.

21. Benjamin and Simon, *The Age of Sacred Terror,* 357–360.

22. Rob de Wijk, "The Limits of Military Power," *Washington Quarterly* 25 (winter 2002): 79.

23. See Barry R. Posen, "The Struggle against Terrorism: Grand Strategy, Strategy, and Tactics," *International Security* 26 (winter 2001/2002): 39–55.

INTELLIGENCE

Among the first questions raised after September 11 was how the most vital centers of American government and commerce could have been attacked so decisively and unexpectedly. Press reports shortly after the attacks revealed that the CIA knew of al Qaeda's threats to U.S. territory and of its heightened activities in the summer of 2001.[24] Other reports disclosed that the Federal Bureau of Investigation (FBI) and local and state law enforcement agencies also were aware of growing terrorist activity during this period. The failure of these organizations, and of the federal government as a whole, to "connect the dots" not only demonstrated the fragmentation of the U.S. intelligence community but also unquestionably contributed to the success of the terrorist attacks.

The obstacles to prompt reform, however, were daunting. Fourteen federal agencies were engaged in different aspects of intelligence gathering and analysis—and none was eager to compare notes with the others. The CIA and FBI rigidly adhered to separate missions, as did the intelligence units of the four armed services. The chronic failure of federal, state, and local law enforcement agencies to coordinate their efforts further widened the intelligence gap. A joint House-Senate congressional investigation reported in 2002 a "breakdown in communication" that resulted from "a number of factors, including differences in agencies' missions, legal authorities, and cultures. Information was not sufficiently shared, not only between Intelligence Community agencies, but also within agencies, and between the intelligence and law-enforcement agencies."[25]

Despite these obstacles, sound intelligence was essential for the United States to meet the threat posed by terrorist groups. High-altitude satellite imagery, intercepted communications, and other forms of technical surveillance were of limited utility; the groups themselves had to be penetrated directly. Only "human intelligence," or face-to-face contacts with the enemy, would produce real results. A flood of new agents with expertise and experience in the Arab world, militant Islam, and counterterrorism were required. The work of undercover agents and informants would be difficult, costly, and extremely dangerous. The United States would also have to cooperate with foreign intelligence agencies. Pakistan's Inter-Services Intelligence (ISI), for example, main-

24. James Risen, "In Hindsight, C.I.A. Sees Flaws That Hindered Effects on Terror," *New York Times,* October 7, 2001, A1, B2.

25. U.S. Congress, Senate Select Committee on Intelligence, and U.S. House Permanent Select Committee on Intelligence, *Joint Inquiry into Intelligence Community Activities before and after the Terrorist Attacks of September 11, 2001,* 107th Cong., 2d sess., December 2002, xvii.

tained close ties with informants on both sides of the Afghan border, a crucial region for U.S. counterterrorist operations.

But even if the U.S. intelligence "community" connected all the dots, there were still no guarantees they would foil future terrorist attacks on the United States or its allies. Secretary of Defense Donald H. Rumsfeld frequently observed that, with regard to foreign threats, there were "knowns, known unknowns, and unknown unknowns." As for the latter, "We don't even know we don't know them." [26] CIA director George Tenet also pointed out that U.S. intelligence analysts suffered from such a bad case of "threat fatigue" that they could not be sure which of the thousands of warning signs that appeared daily should be acted upon. Thus it was not surprising that when the CIA's August 6, 2001, "President's Daily Brief" featured the headline "Bin Laden Determined to Strike in U.S.," it prompted little decisive action by the president.[27]

DIPLOMACY

Bush also faced an uphill battle gaining the political cooperation he needed from other governments in the war on terrorism. The United States simply did not have the option of going it alone in this struggle. Dozens of other countries were needed to provide intelligence, military assets such as base rights, and political support for the United States in international organizations. Because militant Islamists were threatening not only the United States but also the West in general and "infidels" within many Islamic societies, it initially appeared that more than just rhetorical support would be forthcoming. But it was one thing for foreign leaders to declare common cause in the war on terrorism; it was quite another for them to commit resources or risk the lives of their citizens. Too close a connection to the United States exposed these leaders to political challenges by anti-American groups or even to terrorist attacks within their borders. This was especially true after the U.S. government retreated from many international agreements and increasingly chose unilateral solutions to foreign policy problems.

Nevertheless, the war on terrorism did provide opportunities for foreign leaders to align their own agendas with the American-led war on terrorism. In Russia, President Vladimir Putin welcomed the chance to portray his ongoing struggle against Chechen rebels as a struggle against terrorism. So did Chinese leaders, who faced challenges from Muslim separatists on their western frontier. By identifying their respective

26. Quoted in Jeffrey Goldberg, "The Unknown," *New Yorker,* February 10, 2003, 42–43.
27. For a full text, see "Text: President's Daily Brief on August 6, 2001," *Washington Post,* April 10, 2004, www.washingtonpost.com/ac2/wp-dyn/A2285-2004Apr10?language=printer (accessed May 1, 2006).

enemies as terrorists, the Indian and Pakistani governments each sought support from the United States in their decades-long struggle over Kashmir. The same could be said for the leaders of Israel, Peru, the Philippines, Turkey, and other countries with long histories of security cooperation with the United States. The more these governments could identify themselves as partners in America's war on terrorism, the more material support they could expect to receive from Washington. But "checkbook diplomacy" would not be enough in this conflict. The United States needed real allies, not simply clients whose allegiance would end when the last check was cashed.

HOMELAND SECURITY

The third key factor in fighting the war on terrorism was the home front. Unlike the Japanese attack on the U.S. naval base at Pearl Harbor in Hawaii in 1941, the attacks of September 11 targeted the continental United States. Civilians rather than military personnel were the primary victims, and the terrorists themselves had been openly engaged in American society prior to their deadly assaults. In this context, strict new measures were clearly needed to protect airports, coastlines, electrical utilities, communication networks, and government buildings from future attacks. Domestic law enforcement agencies had to identify potential terrorists in their communities and share their leads with federal authorities. Local first responders had to devise new methods to handle terrorist attacks, some of which may involve chemical, biological, or even nuclear weapons. And the American public had to prepare for possible new attacks.

The scale of this effort would be immense. Few areas of American society would not be affected, and often the routine conveniences to which Americans had long been accustomed would have to be eliminated. Indeed, the U.S. government was forced to adopt many measures, such as intrusive searches at airports and the "profiling" of minority groups associated with terrorism, that were common in other countries. The White House placed new limits on public information, expanded the scope of domestic surveillance, and curbed the legal protections of suspected terrorists. These measures, stemming from the USA PATRIOT Act passed shortly after the attacks, provoked charges that civil liberties had become an additional casualty of the war on terrorism.[28] It was also unclear how the new Department of Homeland Security, whose creation

28. The formal name of the act was the Uniting and Strengthening America by Providing Appropriate Tools Required to Intercept and Obstruct Terrorism (USA PATRIOT) Act of 2001 (see Chapter 14).

involved the largest reorganization of the federal government since the early days of the Cold War, would make Americans safer. The most visible early actions of Homeland Security Secretary Tom Ridge—he devised color-coded terrorist alerts and urged Americans to buy duct tape and other necessities in preparation for extended stays in shelters—simply heightened public apprehensions.

The worst fears of domestic terrorism were realized in October 2001 when dozens of Americans were exposed to anthrax. The deadly bacteria were sent through the mail; the first exposure occurred at a newspaper office in Florida, killing one employee and disabling two others. Within weeks, powdery traces of anthrax were found in envelopes addressed to the NBC and CBS news studios, the Microsoft Corporation, and the office of New York governor George Pataki. The opening of an anthrax-laced envelope in the office of Senate majority leader Tom Daschle led to mass evacuations and the almost otherworldly spectacle of FBI agents in biohazard suits swarming into congressional offices. Traces of anthrax were later found in the mailrooms of the Supreme Court, the State Department, and the CIA. Two postal workers in Washington, D.C., died from inhaling the bacteria, and others were afflicted at sorting facilities in New Jersey and New York.

Still reeling from the trauma of September 11, Americans faced the immediate risk of bioterrorism in their own homes. No one felt secure as news of the anthrax attacks dominated the headlines. The Bush administration, caught off guard by the wave of terrorism, issued a series of public alerts that only reinforced public fears. The first warning referred to a "credible" but unspecified threat; subsequent alerts identified suspension bridges and nuclear power plants as possible targets. In a satellite speech to eastern Europeans, Bush warned of a potential threat "to civilization itself." As for the terrorists, the high anxiety this speech produced around the world represented a victory of its own kind.

Meanwhile, American military strategists devised a war plan that would unfold in several stages, first against the Taliban regime in Afghanistan, then in other parts of the world where al Qaeda cells were believed to be organized. Both the terrorists and their state sponsors would be targeted. Large numbers of U.S. troops would be required in some of these missions. In others, smaller special forces would take the lead, often in tactical alliances with indigenous forces. As in the case of guerilla warfare (see Chapter 5), the line between civilians and military forces would always be blurry because the terrorists were embedded in civilian areas and were, in the strictest sense of the word, civilians themselves. "Collateral damage," military jargon for civilian casualties, would be inevitable, possibly on a large scale.

Chapter Twelve

A Grand Strategy of Primacy and Preemption

As noted previously, even before the terrorists struck, President Bush had changed the direction of American foreign policy. As a presidential candidate in 2000, he had rejected the "assertive multilateralism" of the Clinton-Gore years and called instead for unilateral action based on U.S. self-interests. Later, President Bush, Vice President Cheney, and other members of the Bush foreign policy team complained that the deck was stacked against the United States in international organizations, which provided hostile governments with a forum to gang up on Washington. These adversaries were located not only in less developed countries, which held a majority in most intergovernmental bodies, but also in wealthy nations such as France that openly assailed the American "hyperpower." Bush's message upon taking office in January 2001 was clear: the United States would be concerned primarily with its own interests and would go it alone to secure these interests whenever necessary. Realism, not idealism, would guide American foreign policy on his watch. Still, Bush did not initially proclaim a new foreign policy "doctrine" that provided a clear basis for action.

The terrorist attacks provided just this opportunity, lending credence to the dark vision of mounting global threats the president and his advisers had long maintained. When these threats came to life and death on September 11, few doubts remained that a new grand strategy, a new statement of the ends and means of American foreign policy, was required. A new grand strategy, however, presented Bush with two grand dilemmas. First, although the president's pessimistic worldview was affirmed on September 11, his previous elevation of U.S. self-interests over global concerns had alienated foreign leaders whose support the United States needed. Among many other ironies of the new era, the United States could not succeed in the war against terrorism without help from the same international community that Bush had derided, to great effect, during his campaign for office.

The second dilemma was more deeply rooted. Bush's embrace of minimal realism, of coldly calculated national interests and the means to achieve them, contradicted America's long-standing sense of universal moral purpose. The American people had always viewed the United States as an exceptional nation that stood for more than just maintaining its own territorial integrity. World politics from the American perspective ultimately involved a struggle over values, not raw power. America's core values of political liberty, spiritual tolerance, and economic opportunity were meant for export. Their adoption overseas represented the fulfillment of America's historic mission, not the "second-order effect" identified by Bush's national security adviser, Condoleezza Rice.[29] The new grand strategy, therefore, had to appeal to a wider community than the United States. And it had to exalt values and principles that transcended American self-interests.

Fortunately for Bush, the resolution of the twin dilemmas could be found in the hated ideology of Osama bin Laden, in the Taliban torture chambers, and, most of all, in the mass murder committed by the terrorists on September 11. As in the past, where American principles were rejected, tyranny and carnage reigned. The United States again confronted a foreign movement—this time in the form of a religious faction—that rejected the values and lifestyles of American citizens and the political principles, institutions, and actions of the U.S. government. The disciples of militant Islam had declared holy war not only against Americans, but also against all others who did not subscribe to the dictates of their radical ideology.

The very nature of this latest challenge allowed Bush to meld his realist instincts with traditional American idealism, thereby forming a new basis for American foreign policy. The United States, Bush proclaimed, was thrust into yet another struggle between good and evil. "Freedom and fear, justice and cruelty, have always been at war, and we know that God is not neutral between them," Bush declared to Congress nine days after the terrorist attacks. In his January 2002 State of the Union address, Bush proclaimed that the United States confronted an "axis of evil" linking the governments of Iran, Iraq, and North Korea, along with terrorist groups, in a global conspiracy to destroy the United States. The task before the nation, Bush argued, went far beyond simply capturing Osama bin Laden and putting al Qaeda out of business. A global fight against terrorism and the evil it represented had to be mounted on all fronts. In making these claims, Bush echoed Ronald Reagan's earlier charges of an "evil empire" led by the Soviet Union. Bush also revived memories of the Truman Doctrine, proclaimed fifty-five years earlier, which envisioned two clashing global systems, one founded on freedom and the other on hatred and persecution.

These statements formed the pretext of a grand strategy that was formally unveiled in September 2002.[30] The strategy, which amounted to a Bush Doctrine, covered all aspects of foreign policy and affected relations with every country and international organization. Two pillars—the virtues of American primacy and the nation's right to wage preemptive war against perceived threats—captured the essential ends and means, respectively, of the new strategy.

29. Rice, "Promoting the National Interest," 47.

30. White House, "The National Security Strategy of the United States of America," September 2002. For the full text, see http://www.whitehouse.gov/nsc/nss.html (accessed May 1, 2006).

The first of these pillars, American primacy, viewed the unipolar balance of power as the defining aspect of world politics after the Cold War and into the new millennium. As Bush noted in his introduction to the grand strategy, U.S. victories against fascism and communism left the world with "a single sustainable model for national success—freedom, democracy, and free enterprise." The U.S. government, the champion and embodiment of this model, would not exploit its advantages to dominate the world in a tyrannical fashion, as did empires of the past, but would serve these universal interests by shaping a "balance of power that favors human freedom." Competing against the United States in a unipolar world would be self-defeating and would divert the resources of would-be challengers from constructive purposes. "Our forces will be strong enough to dissuade potential adversaries from pursuing a military build-up in hopes of surpassing, or equaling, the power of the United States." [31]

The second pillar of the Bush Doctrine called for preemptive war, or striking first against enemies determined to inflict imminent harm on the United States. To the administration, the rise of private terrorist groups and their state sponsors changed the calculus of world politics to such an extent that conventional instruments of coercive statecraft no longer applied. In particular, nuclear deterrence and containment had been rendered null and void in a world of suicide bombers and proliferating weapons of mass destruction.[32] What would work in this perilous new world? Only taking the offensive: "The United States has long maintained the option of preemptive action to counter a sufficient threat to our national security. The greater the threat, the greater the risk of inaction—and the more compelling the case for taking anticipatory action to defend ourselves, even if uncertainty remains as to the time and place of the enemy's attack. To prevent or forestall such hostile acts by our adversaries, the United States will, if necessary, act preemptively." [33]

In justifying preemptive war, the Bush Doctrine challenged a central tenet of international law that required nation-states to identify an imminent danger before they could legitimately resort to military force. But such clarity is not possible, the Bush Doctrine argued, because weapons of mass destruction can be easily concealed and delivered suddenly with catastrophic results. The call for preemptive war also called into question the concept of national sovereignty, which had formed a centerpiece of the nation-state system for more than three centuries. As

31. Ibid., 30.

32. For an analysis of suicide terrorism, the most common tactic used in recent years, see Robert Pape, "The Strategic Logic of Suicide Terrorism," *American Political Science Review* 97 (August 2003): 343–361.

33. White House, "The National Security Strategy of the United States," 15.

Richard Haass, director of policy planning for the State Department, observed earlier, "Sovereignty entails obligations. One is not to massacre your own people. Another is not to support terrorism in any way. If a government fails to meet these obligations, then it forfeits some of the normal advantages of sovereignty, including the right to be left alone in your own territory."[34]

Although few Americans were aware of it, this was not the first time a strategy founded on U.S. primacy and preemption had been proposed. A decade earlier, officials in the first Bush administration devised a similar formula. "Our strategy must now refocus on precluding the emergence of any future global competitor," wrote Paul Wolfowitz, the undersecretary of defense for policy who became Defense Secretary Rumsfeld's deputy in 2001. American leaders "must establish and protect a new order that holds the promise of convincing potential competitors that they need not aspire to a greater role."[35] Although favored by then–secretary of defense Cheney, the "defense guidance" was replaced by a softer version after it was leaked to the press and sparked public charges that the elder Bush was seeking world domination.[36] With much the same cast reassembled for the second Bush administration, and with the terrorist attacks providing a compelling pretext, the time for this new grand strategy had finally come.

In effect, the Bush Doctrine called for an American protectorate of the interstate system for an indefinite period of time, possibly on a permanent basis. The proclaimed goal of this grand strategy—U.S. primacy—would presumably be welcomed by leaders overseas, who could then turn their defense needs over to the global police force in Washington. American primacy would, in this respect, globalize America's security "umbrella" that earlier had relieved the NATO states and Japan of the burdens of national defense. And the same allies who shared Washington's view that a strictly defensive posture in the age of terror was a prescription for suicide would presumably embrace the means of the new strategy—preemptive war against those who threatened this world order. Foreign governments would face few risks in coming to this conclusion, because the United States would handle the dirty work.

No other document in American diplomatic history, including the Monroe Doctrine, had ever made such bold assumptions or advanced such ambitious claims. Indeed, the scope of the new grand strategy was

34. Quoted in Nicholas Lemann, "The Next World Order: The Bush Administration May Have a Brand-New Doctrine of Power," *New Yorker,* April 1, 2002, 45.

35. "Excerpts from Pentagon's Plan: Prevent the Re-emergence of a New Rival," *New York Times,* March 8, 1992, A14.

36. See David Armstrong, "Dick Cheney's Song of America: Drafting a Plan for Global Dominance," *Harper's,* October 2002, 76–82.

unprecedented in world history. The fact that it was accepted with little debate or fanfare in Congress, by the press, and among the public provides stark evidence of the hubris, or unbridled zeal, that was felt across the United States even after the September 11 attacks.

The Bush Doctrine, however, came into being as global uncertainties mounted and fears of a growing spiral of violence grew more acute. The war on terrorism, while taking several high-profile prisoners, failed to break the back of al Qaeda or prevent calamitous terrorist attacks in many parts of the world. At the same time, a deepening slump in the world economy, combined with widening gaps between the world's rich and poor, further dampened the prospects for stability. The new grand strategy, which was designed to stabilize the international system by asserting the benevolent intentions of its most powerful state, initially appeared to have the opposite effect. Global anxieties would intensify further as the U.S. counteroffensive extended beyond Afghanistan to Iraq, the subject of the next chapter.

CHAPTER T

Hot
Afghanistan an

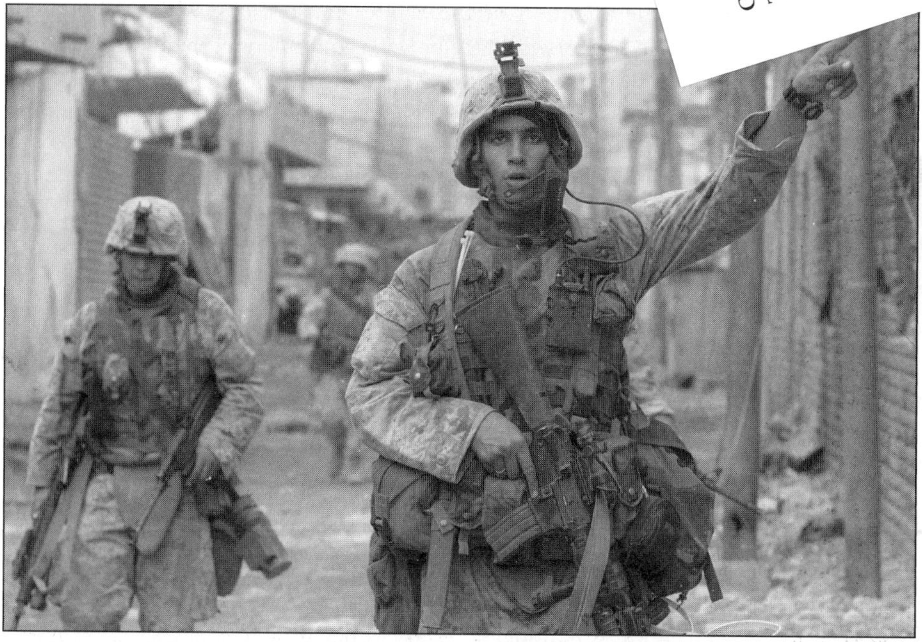

A U.S. Marine leads his unit toward the center of Fallujah, Iraq, during a November 2004 assault on the city. Fallujah, a stronghold of Sunni Muslims who were aligned with Saddam Hussein's regime, was virtually destroyed by the U.S. siege and protracted urban warfare between coalition forces and insurgents.

The Bush Doctrine laid out an ambitious future for American foreign policy, including plans to extend the nation's primacy long into the twenty-first century. The path ahead, however, was uncertain and treacherous. By its very nature, the war on terrorism would be virtually impossible to win decisively, dimming the prospects for the return to "normalcy" that Americans expected. Counterterrorism would likely become a permanent feature of American foreign relations and of public life at home, fundamentally altering the nation's traditional sense of security and its conception of military conflict as an exception to the general rule of peaceful coexistence. The Bush Doctrine's implicit security guarantees to compliant states, many of which confronted their own domestic and regional tensions, further assured the onset of perpetual war.

The president did not wait to proclaim his new doctrine before taking action after the September 11 attacks. The U.S. invasion of Afghanistan in November 2001 targeted the planners of those attacks, who had to be subdued if Bush's vision of benevolent global hegemony would ever be realized. In the Middle East, however, Saddam Hussein's Iraq soon became the true test of the doctrine, including its call for preemptive war. The U.S. war in Iraq, which started in March 2003, would consume the attention of the White House, along with an immense share of the nation's military power, economic wealth, and diplomatic clout. Invading Iraq without the UN Security Council's blessing would leave the United States isolated beyond a meager and largely symbolic "coalition of the willing." Most ominously, battling an unforeseen and deeply entrenched insurgency in Iraq would limit Washington's capacity to manage other trouble spots such as North Korea and Iran.

Although the U.S. invasions of Afghanistan and Iraq pursued separate short-term goals—destroying al Qaeda's sanctuary in the first instance, removing Saddam Hussein's weapons of mass destruction (WMD) in the second—their long-term objectives were aligned. In short, Afghanistan and Iraq, home to two of the world's most repressive governments, had to be made safe for democracy. The Muslim belt from North Africa across the Middle East and southwest Asia had resisted the trend of democratic reform that had swept across other developing regions in the late twentieth century. By 2002, when nearly 70 percent of all national governments were maintaining electoral democracies, such a system applied to less than a quarter of states in the Muslim belt.[1] Douglas J. Feith, Bush's under secretary of defense for policy, saw no "inherent incompatibility" between Islam and Western-style democracy. An Iraq ruled by and for its newly empowered citizens "might be inspirational for people throughout the Middle East to try to increase the amount of freedom that they have." [2]

The domino theory, first adopted by President Dwight Eisenhower and applied to the spread of communism (see Chapter 5), found new life in the war on terrorism. But this time the dominoes would presumably fall in favor of American interests and moral mission. From the White House's vantage point, the spread of democracy to Afghanistan and Iraq, even at the point of an M-16 automatic rifle, would inspire democratic revolutions in other Islamic states. Not only would they establish friendly and mutually beneficial relations toward one another, but, in accordance with democratic peace theory, they would make amends

1. Freedom House, *Freedom in the World: The Annual Survey of Political Rights and Civil Liberties, 2001–2002* (New Brunswick, N.J.: Transaction Publishers, 2002), 10.

2. Quoted in Nicholas Lemann, "After Iraq: The Plan to Remake the Middle East," *New Yorker,* February 17, 2003, 71–72.

with Western powers, including the United States. Thus a crucial piece of unfinished business after the Cold War—simmering tensions in and around the oil-rich Middle East—could yet be completed.

The Afghanistan Campaign

The U.S. military response to the September 11 attacks first targeted the government of Afghanistan, whose overthrow was deemed essential if the al Qaeda terrorists based in the country were to be captured. Bush's initial demands to the Afghan leaders—that they "hand over the terrorists" or "share their fate"—quickly yielded to a more aggressive strategy based on the regime's ejection from power. For better or worse, American forces would soon be thrust into the same mountainous terrain and impenetrable tribal societies that earlier had denied the imperial ambitions of Britain and the Soviet Union.

Afghanistan entered the twenty-first century utterly exhausted by two decades of warfare, first against the Soviet occupiers and then against internal warlords and rivals for power. Most of the country's infrastructure—roads, bridges, electrical utilities, communication systems, schools, and hospitals—had been damaged or destroyed in the conflicts. Meanwhile, the Afghan people had one of the world's shortest life expectancies (forty-three years), a literacy rate of less than 40 percent, and per capita incomes of less than $1,000. Hundreds of thousands of Afghans died in the civil wars of the 1990s; millions more fled the nation as refugees. But time would not allow for national recovery at the dawn of the new millennium, because Afghanistan became the prime target in America's war on terrorism.

Benign Neglect after the Cold War

From the Carter administration through the Reagan years, U.S. leaders refused to accept the Soviet Union's 1979 invasion of Afghanistan, which was prompted by the demise of the pro-Soviet regime in Kabul. The covert operation undertaken in Afghanistan by the U.S. Central Intelligence Agency (CIA) during the 1980s on behalf of the Afghan *mujahadin,* or "freedom fighters" as they were then known in Washington, was crucial in reversing the Soviet attempt to expand its sphere of influence. William Casey, Reagan's CIA director, was an impassioned anti-communist who saw the Soviet intervention for what it was: a monumental blunder and a golden opportunity for the United States to gain the strategic advantage in South Asia. Not only did Afghanistan become the Soviet Union's Vietnam, but the economic and military costs of the occupation also sapped what little was left of the Kremlin's strength.

Thus for American leaders, the few billions of dollars required to support the *mujahadin* were well spent, even if some of the money went to shadowy figures with uncertain political ambitions, including Osama bin Laden.

The American government's clarity of purpose dissolved, however, once the Soviet tanks left Afghanistan in 1989 and the Soviet Union's downward spiral began. In South Asia, like elsewhere in the world, the end of the Cold War reshaped American interests. While the State Department was opening diplomatic posts in the new post–Soviet states such as Kazakhstan, foreign policy makers were reexamining ties with existing states. President George H. W. Bush, preoccupied with the democratic transitions in Eastern Europe, had little interest in Afghanistan after the Soviet withdrawal. In his view, the U.S. mission there had been accomplished; what happened later was up to the Afghans.[3]

This policy of benign neglect, typical of the United States in the aftermath of major conflicts, would come back to haunt American leaders. Even before the last Soviet troops had departed, the regional warlords across Afghanistan who had fought together against their common Soviet enemy turned on each other. From the Pashtuns in the southern plains to the ethnic Uzbeks and Tajiks in the north, well-armed militias, including the so-called Northern Alliance, sought to protect their territorial enclaves and, wherever possible, to carve out larger spheres of influence. Controlling the central government in Kabul, which was reduced to rubble after a decade of Soviet occupation and armed struggle, was of secondary interest.

Afghanistan remained in the hands of the crumbling Marxist regime during this period. Its overthrow came in February 1992, when northern rebels led by Ahmed Shah Massoud shot their way into the presidential palace. Although Massoud preached the gospel of national unity, he lacked support across Afghanistan's splintered society and so succumbed to civil war and lawlessness. Heroin and opium became the nation's chief exports, along with the huge stockpiles of Soviet and American weapons that were no longer needed in the post-occupation era. Still, plenty of those weapons remained in the hands of Afghan outlaws who filled the void in government control. In 1993 the anarchy spread across Afghanistan, as vividly described by journalist Steven Coll:

> Trucking mafias that reaped huge profits from the heroin trade and other smuggling rackets propped up local warlords. Any group of young Pashtun fighters with a few Kalashnikovs [Russian rifles] and rocket-propelled grenade launchers could set up a checkpoint and extort payments on the

3. James A. Baker III, Bush's secretary of state, made only two references to Afghanistan in his 672-page memoir, *The Politics of Diplomacy: Revolution, War and Peace, 1989–1992,* written with Thomas M. DeFrank (New York: Putnam, 1995).

> highways. By 1994 the main road from Quetta in Pakistan through Kandahar and on toward Herat and Iran was choked by hundreds of extralegal roadblocks. So was the road from Kandahar to Kabul. Shopkeepers in the ramshackle markets . . . battled ruthless extortion and robbery gangs. Reports of unchecked rape and abduction, including child rape, fueled a local atmosphere of fear and smoldering danger.[4]

The turmoil continued until September 1996, when a well-organized political and religious movement known as the Taliban seized power in Kabul and gradually, but viciously, established order across Afghanistan. The Taliban ("religious students" in English) also imposed a strict doctrine of Islamic law, or *Sharia,* which became the basis of government policy. Women were forbidden to attend schools, pursue occupations, or leave their homes without a male relative. Men were forced to wear beards and maintain them at a certain length. "Frivolous" activities such as flying kites and playing cards were banned, along with watching television, playing music, or using the Internet. The Taliban enforced these laws by means of public floggings, amputations, and mass executions held in soccer stadiums. Meanwhile, the government crushed religious movements that did not follow the *Sharia* code and expelled dozens of international aid agencies from Afghanistan.

In Washington, President Bill Clinton watched these developments unfold and, lacking moderate contacts in Afghanistan, initially sought friendly relations with the Taliban. From Clinton's perspective, the new rulers at least seemed able to maintain order in the country and possibly to shut down its flourishing narcotics trade. The Sunni Muslims who led the Taliban, though supported by Pakistan and Saudi Arabia, expressed contempt for the Shiite clerics who ruled Iran, so the emergence of a monolithic Islamic theocracy across central Asia was unlikely. Perhaps the United States, which would undoubtedly be a sworn enemy of such a regime, could find common cause with the religious zealots in Kabul.

Clinton's chief regional concern at the time centered on Osama bin Laden and his al Qaeda followers, whose pursuit of Islamic "purification" through violent means had found a receptive home in Afghanistan. The president, who had linked al Qaeda to a growing wave of anti-American terrorist attacks, proposed a deal to the Taliban. American political and economic support in return for bin Laden's surrender. But only the most naïve members of Clinton's National Security Council expected the offer to be accepted. Mullah Mohammad Omar, the Taliban's spiritual and political leader, denied having a close relationship with bin Laden. His assurances were contradicted by the growing

4. Steven Coll, *Ghost Wars: The Secret History of the CIA, Afghanistan, and Bin Laden, from the Soviet Invasion to September 10, 2001* (New York: Penguin, 2004), 282–283.

presence of al Qaeda, which had opened training camps for aspiring *jihadists* from across the Islamic world.

As noted in Chapter 12, the president's domestic troubles, particularly the Monica Lewinsky sex scandal during his second term, denied him the political support he needed to act forcefully against the Taliban and al Qaeda. Members of Congress, still dominated by the rival Republican Party, ridiculed Clinton's Pentagon for missing its al Qaeda targets in the August 1998 cruise missile strikes after the terrorist attacks on the U.S. embassies in Kenya and Tanzania. Clinton was also preoccupied with other foreign policy concerns such as Kosovo, funding for the United Nations, and the nuclear test ban treaty. The effect of all these distractions was to diminish in the minds of top decision makers the threat posed by al Qaeda.

When President George W. Bush came to power in January 2001, his foreign policy priorities included recasting China as a "strategic competitor" and launching a national missile defense system. Bush considered Islamic terrorism a major but not an urgent concern, and he adopted a strategy of pursuing al Qaeda with the help of Massoud's rebel armies in Afghanistan along with a hefty infusion of CIA funding. But this strategy was nullified on September 9, 2001, when al Qaeda agents posing as sympathetic Arab journalists murdered Massoud in his bungalow. His assassination left the United States without influential friends in Afghanistan or any hope of restraining bin Laden's wildest ambitions.

PHASE 1: DISLODGING THE TALIBAN

The September 11 attacks were traced immediately to Afghanistan, making a large-scale U.S. invasion of the country inevitable. The counterattack would unfold in two stages. First, American forces would help antigovernment Afghan militias overthrow the Taliban and round up the al Qaeda terrorists responsible for the September 11 attacks. Second, the U.S. government would lead an effort, presumably with the United Nations, to create a new, democratic regime that would not threaten its neighbors or serve as a sanctuary for Islamic terrorists. The military commanders' goal in the first phase was to apply enough muscle to topple the Taliban, but not so much force that neighboring Islamic countries would feel threatened. Under the plan for Operation Enduring Freedom, U.S. ground forces would be limited to special operations, such as identifying targets for aerial attacks. The ground offensive would be conducted by home-grown forces, including the Northern Alliance and a second flank of southern Pashtun forces. The combination of U.S. bombing raids and pressure on the ground would send the enemy fleeing for refuge to Pakistan, where they would be captured and turned over to the United States.

Pakistan's cooperation, therefore, was essential to the American military campaign, and it was achieved at considerable expense: more than $1 billion in foreign aid along with the lifting of the economic sanctions imposed after Pakistan became a nuclear power in 1998. Gen. Pervez Musharraf, Pakistan's leader who came to power in a 1999 military coup, took a substantial risk by siding with the United States. Pakistan and Afghanistan shared not only a 1,500-mile border, but overlapping pockets of Islamic militants, or Islamists. It was not surprising, then, that supporters of al Qaeda denounced Musharraf's cooperative relationship with Washington and called for his overthrow. The threat of assassination became a daily part of the Pakistani leader's life, and he looked to Washington for personal as well as national security.

Musharraf's attitude toward the United States had its roots in the 1980s, when Pakistan received large volumes of U.S. aid in return for its help in turning back the Soviet occupation of Afghanistan. The American financial offers were simply too generous for the cash-starved Pakistani government to turn down. In addition, Musharraf viewed America's war on terrorism as an extension of his own struggle against Islamists in Pakistan. In addition to threatening his hold on power, the Islamists tempted war against India by staging unauthorized attacks against Indian forces in the disputed territory of Kashmir. Because of the bitter animosities between India and Pakistan, such a war could very quickly escalate to a nuclear exchange and unspeakable devastation. Musharraf's only hope was to cling to his American benefactors and try to keep a lid on the Islamists.

The American-led offensive against Afghanistan's Taliban regime began on September 22, 2001, less than two weeks after the September 11 terrorist attacks, when members of the Northern Alliance initiated attacks on government positions. The bombing raids on Afghanistan, conducted by American and British air forces, began in early October. The first wave of bombings disabled the Taliban's transportation and communication networks in the urban centers around Kandahar and Kabul. Troops from the Northern Alliance then swept into Kalafghan and Mazar-e-Sharif, capturing both strategic cities with little resistance. Kabul, the capital city, fell on November 12, and Afghanistan was freed from the grip of the Taliban regime.

Several factors led to the Taliban's surprisingly prompt surrender. American and British air forces flew more than twenty thousand bombing sorties in this first phase of the conflict, exceeding the number of strikes against Serbian targets in Bosnia in 1995 and Kosovo in 1999 combined. Laser-guided "bunker busters" destroyed many of the

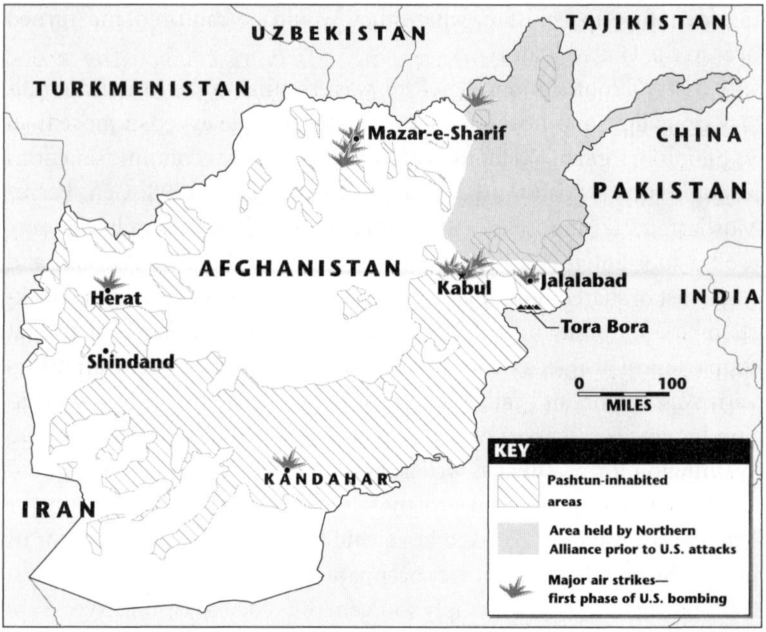

THE WAR IN AFGHANISTAN, AUTUMN 2001

underground caves that sheltered the regime, while 15,000-pound "daisy cutters," the biggest conventional bombs in the U.S. arsenal, decimated the ground forces. The bombing campaign was aided by a new innovation in military technology, unmanned intelligence drones that hovered above targets and provided precise coordinates to American and British pilots. And in a technological feat without historical precedent, other drones dropped guided missiles on enemy targets, including al Qaeda commanders. Bin Laden, however, remained at large.

The indigenous ground forces outside of Kabul proved remarkably effective in routing the Taliban. It was widely believed before the offensive that only a massive deployment of U.S. ground troops could accomplish this task. But the relatively modest Northern Alliance and Pashtun troops, supported by the U.S.-led air strikes, quickly dislodged the Taliban from their positions. An estimated fifteen thousand enemy forces died in the fighting, and about seven thousand others were sent to a makeshift prison camp at the U.S. military base in Guantánamo Bay, Cuba. The death toll among American troops in the first phase of the war was far smaller—about fifty.[5]

5. Michael E. O'Hanlon, "A Flawed Masterpiece," *Foreign Affairs* (May–June 2002): 47–63.

The central task of bringing the al Qaeda leaders to justice still lay ahead, and this proved far more difficult than the combat. The second phase of the military campaign, Operation Anaconda, was designed to round up the terrorists, including bin Laden, as they fled from their headquarters and training centers. But the mission failed. In the climactic battle at Tora Bora, U.S. special forces were overmatched by bin Laden's armed supporters in the rugged mountain peaks. Meanwhile, the supposedly pro-American militias did not stop members of al Qaeda from crossing into Pakistan. Thus bin Laden, who was believed to be pinned down in the area, escaped. Even a U.S. reward of $5 million for his capture proved inadequate in a region where bin Laden retained widespread support. So, rather than seeing news footage of the al Qaeda leader's arrest, the U.S. public watched videotapes of bin Laden boasting about the September 11 attacks and vowing that Americans "will never dream of security [until] the infidel armies leave the land of Muhammad."

PHASE 2: NATION BUILDING IN RUGGED TERRAIN

Even if American forces had captured bin Laden, the United States still had to put Afghanistan back together. A common Western expression, taken from the sign at a pottery barn and repeated occasionally by Secretary of State Colin Powell, seemed apt: "You break it, you own it." Thus whatever came of the al Qaeda search-and-destroy mission, a new regime was needed in Kabul to run the government while assuming the role of a cooperative international "citizen." As American leaders saw it, Afghanistan must be converted into a Western-style democracy, complete with a constitution, elected leaders, and a legal system that protected human rights. By helping to create a democratic Afghanistan that was presumably friendlier toward with the West, the United States and its allies would also gain a higher measure of security.

The Bonn Accords, sponsored by the UN and approved by regional leaders in December 2001, called for a "gender-sensitive, multi-ethnic, and fully representative" Afghan government that would cooperate with "the international community in the fight against terrorism, drugs, and organized crime." [6] The agreement called for an interim government that would keep the state functioning until elections could be held for a president and parliament. Mohammed Zahir Shah, the former king of Afghanistan, gave the Bonn Accords his blessing and, at age eighty-eight, was granted the ceremonial title of "Father of the Country." The task of

6. United Nations, "Agreement on Provisional Arrangements in Afghanistan Pending the Re-establishment of Permanent Government Institutions," December 5, 2001.

overseeing the electoral process fell to Hamid Karzai, a Pashtun tribal leader whose friendly relations with the West and appeals for national reconciliation made him a natural choice by American and UN officials to lead the interim government.

The very concept of *national* elections was unfamiliar to most Afghans, who identified more closely with regional or local politics. But to the architects of Afghanistan's political future, truly representative government meant holding "free and fair" national elections open to all citizens. And that is exactly what transpired, as a majority of Afghans elected Karzai to be president in October 2004 and as voters returned to the polls in September 2005 to elect members of parliament. The newly elected legislators, a quarter of whom had to be women under strict election rules, admitted they did "not know even the basics of democracy, in particular how a Western-devised Parliament works." [7] They were willing to learn, however—and that alone was cause for hope among Western nation builders.

These political reforms left open the question of military control of Afghanistan, which remained deeply divided by power struggles among regional factions, primarily the southern Pashtuns and members of the Northern Alliance. There was also the question of the Taliban, whose leaders had fled rather than be captured by the American invaders. Like the *mujahadin* during the Soviet occupation, the Taliban leaders in Afghanistan retreated to the surrounding mountains and valleys, where they regrouped and plotted their return to power. It was clear, then, that Karzai's authority extended barely past the city limits of Kabul. It was also clear that no central government could survive for long under such circumstances.

American and British forces, therefore, faced an extended mission to keep the new Afghan government from succumbing to internal pressures. In 2003 the two allies turned for help to the North Atlantic Treaty Organization (NATO), whose gradual deployments to Afghanistan marked the first "out-of-area" ones in the alliance's history. The NATO contingent was initially limited to Kabul and the northwestern areas of Afghanistan, with American forces patrolling the treacherous southern region and the Pakistani border. Under a plan devised in 2005, NATO's International Security Assistance Force would assume responsibility for all of Afghanistan by 2007. For the United States, the presence of NATO forces added credibility to its nation-building mission in Afghanistan. Moreover, the reinforcements allowed the Pentagon to redirect its energies and resources elsewhere.

7. Carlotta Gall, "Afghan Legislators Get Crash Course in Ways of Democracy," *New York Times*, December 19, 2005, A11.

Still unclear was how just fifteen thousand NATO troops could be expected to control Afghanistan, a territory the size of Texas with immensely more rugged terrain. Indeed, escalating attacks by the Taliban in 2006 clearly demonstrated its staying power. Another source of concern was how long NATO forces could maintain support from Pakistan, whose government was either unwilling or unable to stop the displaced Taliban leaders and al Qaeda terrorists from using its territory as a staging area for attacks on the new regime. By 2006 Pakistani rebels were engaged in an escalating civil war against Musharraf's regime, and American efforts to "decapitate" the rebels on both sides of the border were proving fruitless. But the uneasy alliance between the United States and Pakistan remained intact, which allowed the process of democratic nation building in Afghanistan to continue.

Although history offered little cause for optimism, the American strategy of stabilizing Afghanistan through democratic reform and Western military support seemed to be working well enough. By voting in large numbers, the Afghan people expressed their willingness to give democracy a chance. All the alternatives—renewed civil war, the restoration of Taliban rule, or the takeover of Afghanistan by al Qaeda terrorists—were far more ominous for the nation's future. As for the United States, the fragile peace that emerged in Afghanistan and the transition to NATO-led military control permitted foreign policy makers to turn their attention to the second front in the war on terrorism—Iraq.

Renewed Hostilities against Iraq

As described in Chapter 12, preemptive war was a central component of the George W. Bush administration's new military doctrine. But this position was controversial because, under international law, nations are prohibited from attacking other nations unless they are attacked first or face the near certainty of imminent attack. Just-war doctrine, which dates back to the Middle Ages and remains a common point of reference, forbids the use of force unless all peaceful alternatives have been exhausted. From Bush's standpoint, waiting to be attacked in the age of terrorism and WMD merely invited aggression, a lesson learned with terrible effect on September 11, 2001.

The doctrine of preemptive war was tailor-made to fight Iraq.[8] Saddam Hussein remained firmly in control of the country despite the

8. Although the Bush administration freely applied the doctrine of preemptive war to Iraq, the 2003 invasion would actually constitute *preventive*—not preemptive—war. Preemptive war is launched against a foreign power that is clearly on the verge of attacking one's own territory—that is, its forces are about to storm the gates. Saddam's forces did not pose that kind of immediate threat to the United States. He would thus be overthrown to *prevent* Iraq from menacing the United States and its coalition partners in the longer term.

IMPACT AND INFLUENCE

SADDAM HUSSEIN

For all of its advantages as the world's "lone superpower" after the Cold War, the United States could not prevent hostile foreign leaders from sparking regional conflicts and prompting intervention by U.S. military forces. Among these leaders, Iraqi president Saddam Hussein caused the first post–Cold War crisis by invading Kuwait in 1990 and threatening to seize control of the Persian Gulf's vast oil supplies.

Saddam originally achieved prominence as a leader of the Ba'ath Party, an Arab nationalist movement. After taking power in Iraq in 1979, he quickly prepared its army to invade neighboring Iran and topple its newly installed Islamic government, which he viewed as a threat. The ensuing Iran-Iraq War produced hundreds of thousands of casualties. It was soon followed by another conflict, this time arising from Iraq's invasion of Kuwait, which was reversed by a UN coalition led by the United States. After his defeat, Saddam remained firmly in power despite harsh UN economic sanctions against Iraq and repeated efforts by the United States and its allies to destroy Iraq's military arsenal. After the terrorist attacks of September 2001, President George W. Bush called for Saddam's overthrow and mounted a new military effort to remove him from power.

virtual collapse of its military forces and of its economy from years of UN sanctions. Although American and British air forces kept Iraq bottled up by rigidly enforcing no-fly zones across most of the country, the U.S. strategy of containing Saddam did not weaken his resolve. To the contrary, the Iraqi leader became more deeply entrenched, more brutal in suppressing internal dissent, and more contemptuous of the United States and other Western powers.

After Saddam ejected UN weapons inspectors in 1998, it was impossible for outside observers to know whether Iraq was reassembling the WMD stockpiles that UN crews had previously found and removed. It was also unclear what had happened to the large quantities of hazardous materials that could be used to develop biological and chemical weapons. Past experience, the absolute secrecy of the Iraqi government, and Saddam's defiant posture all suggested that he still possessed such weapons and would freely use them, as he had in the past. This unsettling prospect after the September 11 attacks raised the specter of technology transfers from Iraq to terrorist groups such as al Qaeda that shared its hostility toward the United States.

President Clinton spent his entire presidency in a frustrating and ultimately futile effort to manage Saddam, the Sunni-led Ba'ath Party that represented his power base, and the tangle of UN sanctions imposed on Iraq. Clinton's containment policy, much like George Kennan's strategy for the Soviet Union, presumed that, in time, external isolation would ultimate suffocate the enemy. But, in this case, it was the United States that wore down. Saddam remained secure by comparison, and he even devised a variety of schemes to reap a personal financial windfall from the UN-sponsored Oil for Food Program.[9] His defiance and later ejection of the weapons inspectors prompted new demands by neoconservatives for regime change. In February 1998, a private group, including Donald Rumsfeld, Paul Wolfowitz, and John Bolton, sent an open letter to Clinton demanding "a comprehensive political and military strategy for bringing down Saddam and his regime."[10]

Under congressional pressure in October 1998, Clinton signed the Iraq Liberation Act, which declared regime change an American policy goal and authorized nearly $100 million for anti-Ba'athist rebels and civil society groups. The president authorized as well a new round of aerial bombardments. Operation Desert Fox, which also involved the British air force, destroyed suspected WMD facilities across Iraq. But nothing Clinton did could shake Saddam from power, and the president left office in January 2001 with Iraq's fate just as uncertain as it was eight years earlier.

The appeal of invading Iraq was so strong to some U.S. officials after the attacks of September 11 that they called for such action to take place *before* the Afghanistan campaign. Deputy Secretary of Defense Paul

9. The Oil for Food Program (OFP), which ran from December 1996 until the invasion of Iraq in March 2003, allowed Saddam Hussein to purchase $38 billion in food, medicine, and other "humanitarian goods" for his citizens. Although the program reduced malnutrition in Iraq and provided for mass polio vaccinations, Saddam reportedly embezzled $4.4 billion in OFP oil revenues between 1997 and 2002 and raised an additional $5.7 billion in profits from illegal oil sales. See Joseph A. Christoff, "United Nations: Observations on the Oil for Food Program," U.S. General Accountability Office, April 7, 2004, http://www.gao.gov/new.items/d04651t.pdf (accessed May 8, 2006).

10. The authors, all of whom later assumed top positions in the Bush administration, wrote on behalf of the Committee for Peace and Security in the Gulf. See http://www.iraqwatch.org/perspectives/rumsfeld-openletter.htm (accessed May 3, 2006) for a copy of the letter.

Wolfowitz reportedly made this case to the Bush war cabinet on September 15, 2001. "He worried about 100,000 American troops bogged down in mountain fighting in Afghanistan six months from then," journalist Bob Woodward reported. "In contrast, Iraq was a brittle, oppressive regime that might break easily. It was doable." [11] Although Afghanistan did come first, the White House quickly turned its attention to Iraq. "Simply stated, there is no doubt that Saddam Hussein now has weapons of mass destruction," Vice President Dick Cheney told war veterans on August 26, 2002. "There is no doubt he is amassing them to use against our friends, against our allies, and against us." [12]

Advocates of regime change believed overthrowing Saddam would produce other benefits beyond putting to rest fears of Iraq's arsenal and ties to al Qaeda. First, military action would send a clear signal to other "rogue states" that the United States had taken the offensive. Second, a takeover of Iraq would give U.S. military forces a forward staging area in the heart of the Middle East from which it could conduct other antiterrorism operations. Third, with the birth of a new regime the Iraqi people would be spared further dictatorial rule, economic privation, and human rights abuses—a moral victory of its own. Finally, as noted earlier, a democratic transition in Iraq would serve as a role model for other autocratic societies in the region.

In calling attention to Iraq's abuses of human rights, American leaders echoed the claims of the UN and private human rights groups. In April 2002, the UN Commission on Human Rights condemned the "all-pervasive repression and suppression" of Iraqi citizens that was "sustained by broad-based discrimination and widespread terror." [13] Private groups such as Amnesty International provided lurid details of torture, including electric shocks, the extraction of fingernails, forced suspension by the limbs, and severe beatings with cables. Scores of female prisoners were reportedly raped or beheaded in front of their relatives. Other prisoners were "subjected to mock execution." [14]

Finally, the potential economic benefits of Saddam's removal were considerable. The low level of Iraqi oil production—down nearly half from its peak before the Gulf War—was inflating petroleum costs on world markets at a time of slowing economic growth. Even if the UN sanctions were lifted and Saddam resumed full production, exports

11. Bob Woodward, *Bush at War* (New York: Simon and Schuster, 2002), 83.

12. White House, "Vice President Speaks at VFW 103rd National Convention," August 26, 2002, http://www.whitehouse.gov/news/releases/2002/08/20020826.html (accessed May 3, 2006).

13. UN Commission on Human Rights, "Resolution: Situation of Human Rights in Iraq," April 11, 2002, http://www.iraqcp.org/framse1/002426UNHCR-1.htm (accessed May 8, 2006).

14. Amnesty International, *Report 2002* (Oxford, UK: Alden Press, 2002), 132.

would profit Iraq's oppressive rulers and be subject to constant manipulation. Although advocates of military action against Iraq dismissed claims that such action was motivated by a desire to seize Iraq's oil reserves, they did concede that a stable world supply was a vital collective interest worth fighting for. Less openly stated was the potential windfall to U.S. firms that would receive contracts for rebuilding Iraq's oil fields, refining the crude oil, and delivering it to consumers.[15]

The presumed benefits of a second war against Iraq in 2003 were offset, however, by an array of strategic, tactical, and political problems. Skeptics questioned many of the assumptions made by "hawks" in the Bush administration. The primary strategic concern was that military action in Iraq would divert the attention and resources of the U.S. government from the war on terrorism. Saddam was obsessed with consolidating his power base at home; promoting Islamic causes elsewhere did not capture his interest. As Brent Scowcroft, U.S. national security adviser in the first Bush administration, observed in August 2002: "Saddam's goals have little in common with the terrorists who threaten us, and there is little incentive for him to make common cause with them. He is unlikely to risk his investment in weapons of mass destruction, much less his country, by handing such weapons to terrorists who would use them for their own purposes and leave Baghdad as the return address."[16]

Tactical obstacles to regime change also existed. If Saddam possessed weapons of mass destruction and felt his capture to be imminent, he might be tempted to use those weapons against American forces, their allies' forces, or an allied country such as Israel. A U.S.-led invasion also might provoke new terrorist attacks. Even if the invasion succeeded without much resistance, it was unclear how long the postwar occupation would last, how much it would cost, and who would foot the bill. Diplomatic problems raised further doubts. As noted earlier, the United States was a "lonely superpower" by the time Bush entered the White House, and his rejection of many multilateral organizations and treaties further isolated the United States on many issues. Moderate Arab states refused to endorse a U.S.-led invasion of Iraq at a time when Washington was doing little to prevent Israel from cracking down on Palestinians. Even U.S. allies in Western Europe were skeptical of the call to arms,

15. Close links between these firms and the Bush administration raised ethical questions about postwar reconstruction deals. The U.S. Army Corps of Engineers disclosed in April 2003 that a subsidiary of Halliburton Co., a firm led by Vice President Cheney from 1995 to 2000, received a contract in December 2001 worth up to $7 billion to restore Iraqi oil wells in the aftermath of a successful invasion by the United States. Citing national security concerns, U.S. officials did not solicit competitive bids for this and other contracts. See http://news.findlaw.com/wp/docs/halliburton/ace408034rsp.pdf (accessed May 3, 2006).

16. Brent Scowcroft, "Don't Attack Saddam," *Wall Street Journal,* August 15, 2002, A12.

and opposition from Canada threatened the goodwill that normally prevailed between the two North American neighbors. Among the major regional powers, only British prime minister Tony Blair supported the White House. But Blair's pledge in behalf of Britain's "special relationship" with Washington greatly weakened him politically.

MAKING THE CASE FOR WAR

None of these concerns stopped the Bush administration from pressing forward with its plan for regime change in Iraq. From its perspective, continued containment was doomed to failure because of the eroding grip of economic sanctions and mounting international pressure to ease or lift them altogether. Bush also rejected deterrence because of Saddam's past erratic behavior and the possibility that he might share his WMD arsenal with terrorists. A covert operation by Iraqi dissidents to stage a coup was dismissed as an option, because Saddam maintained iron-fisted control over his internal enemies. For lack of better choices, preemptive war was the "least bad" alternative to the White House.[17]

Although Bush remained determined to oust Saddam, he initially bowed to pressure for a multilateral approach to the situation. Secretary of State Powell, echoing the stated concerns of most foreign leaders, insisted that the United States gain the UN Security Council's endorsement of military action against Iraq. A U.S. invasion without such an endorsement, Powell argued, would lack legitimacy and turn much of the world against the presumed "liberators" of Baghdad. Bush reluctantly agreed and supported a UN resolution that gave Saddam another, and presumably final, chance to disarm. In a speech to the General Assembly on September 12, 2002, the president issued a direct challenge: "All the world faces a test, and the United Nations a difficult and defining moment. Are Security Council resolutions to be honored and enforced, or cast aside without consequence? Will the United Nations serve the purposes of its founding, or will it be irrelevant?"[18]

Persuading the UN to follow his lead on Iraq was one of two political challenges facing the president. The other was Congress, which had stood on the sidelines while Bush elevated Iraq to the top of his foreign policy agenda. Legislators strongly supported the war on terrorism, but they were less enthusiastic about waging a second and simultaneous war against Saddam Hussein. Members of Congress had to be convinced that

17. For a detailed assessment of these options, see Kenneth M. Pollack, *The Threatening Storm: The Case for Invading Iraq* (New York: Random House, 2002).

18. See George W. Bush, "President's Remarks at the United Nations General Assembly," September 12, 2002, http://www.whitehouse.gov/news/releases/2002/09/20020912-1.html (accessed May 3, 2006).

war with Iraq was a necessity, not a choice. Bush's foreign policy team had to make that case to Congress.

The strength of the White House's case depended, in turn, on the latest intelligence about the threat posed by Saddam. Pentagon officials doubted the inconclusive findings of the CIA and even the Defense Intelligence Agency. Thus in September 2002 they opened their own unit, the Office of Special Plans, whose probe extended beyond conventional sources to include Iraqi exiles who had long advocated Saddam's overthrow. Ahmed Chalabi, the most prominent of these exiles, met frequently with U.S. officials, including President Bush. Educated in the United States and long an advocate of a democratic and secular Iraqi state, Chalabi was widely viewed in the White House as Saddam's ideal successor.[19] The information provided by Iraqi exiles became part of a National Intelligence Estimate (NIE), issued in October, whose opening lines summarized the case against Saddam:

> Iraq has continued its weapons of mass destruction (WMD) programs in defiance of UN resolutions and restrictions. Baghdad has chemical and biological weapons as well as missiles with ranges in excess of UN restrictions; if left unchecked, it probably will have a nuclear weapon during this decade. Baghdad hides large portions of Iraq's WMD efforts. Revelations after the Gulf War starkly demonstrate the extensive efforts undertaken by Iraq to deny information. Since inspections ended in 1998, Iraq has maintained its chemical weapons effort, energized its missile program, and invested heavily in biological weapons; most analysts assess Iraq is reconstituting its nuclear weapons program.[20]

The political calendar was also on Bush's side as he pressed for war against Iraq. Midterm elections were scheduled for November 5, and members of Congress knew that opposing a popular president in wartime was political suicide. Bush appealed directly to voters on October 7. "America must not ignore the threat against us," he told an audience in Cincinnati. "Facing clear evidence of peril, we cannot wait for the final proof—the smoking gun—that could come in the form of a mushroom cloud." Within days, both houses of Congress approved a joint resolution calling for military action against Iraq with or without the UN's blessing. Republican candidates swept most races in November, securing control of both chambers and ensuring a united front against Iraq.

Bush's electoral triumph led to his success in the UN Security Council on November 8. Without the prospect of dividing and conquering the

19. George Packer, *The Assassin's Gate: America in Iraq* (New York: Farrar, Straus and Giroux, 2005), 105–109.

20. Director of Central Intelligence, "Iraq's Weapons of Mass Destruction Programs," October 2002, http://www.cia.gov/cia/reports/iraq_wmd/Iraq_Oct_2002.pdf (accessed May 8, 2006).

U.S. government, the Security Council fell into line with Washington. Resolution 1441 declared Iraq in "material breach" of past UN resolutions and required Saddam to provide "immediate, unconditional, and unrestricted" access to government offices, military installations, factories, and the dozens of presidential palaces previously off limits to the UN. Iraq faced "serious consequences" if it failed to cooperate with the inspectors. Although these consequences were not identified, there was little doubt what form they would take: a full-scale attack by the United States and any countries that chose to follow its lead into Baghdad.

The UN resolution prompted Saddam to adopt a diplomatic strategy that ultimately cost him control of his country. According to information gathered after the U.S. invasion, Saddam secretly informed his military commanders in December 2002 that Iraq's WMD stockpiles had been destroyed in order to deprive the United States of a legitimate *casus belli,* or rationale for war. Saddam ordered his commanders, who were not consulted on most high-level decisions, to rule out WMD attacks as an option in the upcoming conflict. He further ordered them to "scrub the country so that the U.N. inspectors did not discover any vestiges of old WMD." [21] Still, Saddam remained evasive in his contacts with weapons inspectors, and he purposefully sent mixed signals in providing them with documents and access to suspected WMD sites. His reason for adopting this stance was revealing: Saddam hoped to maintain leverage in his rivalry with neighboring Iran, which, fourteen years after the Iran-Iraq War, he still considered his nation's primary foreign threat. By leaving some doubt about his alleged WMD arsenal, Saddam felt better protected against a second war with Iran. In so doing, however, he opened the door to the U.S. invasion and his own overthrow.

Unaware of Saddam's secret meetings, Bush was confident that the UN inspectors, who visited three hundred sites without notice in December 2002 and January 2003, would confirm his allegations of an Iraqi WMD arsenal. But the president also played his military card. He ordered nearly 200,000 U.S. troops to the Persian Gulf in a mobilization that included four army divisions, five aircraft-carrier battle groups, six hundred strike aircraft, and thirty ships from which cruise missiles could be launched. The British government moved thirty thousand troops and scores of additional bombers to the Persian Gulf as well. The combined forces, Bush said, provided the muscle to back up the UN ultimatum. The advance deployments were also necessary because military action in the winter and spring would be preferable to fighting in the stifling heat of an Iraqi summer.

21. Michael R. Gordon and Gen. Bernard E. Trainor, *Cobra II: The Inside Story of the Invasion and Occupation of Iraq* (New York: Pantheon, 2006), 119. On Iran, see ibid., 64–65.

In keeping with Saddam's secret strategy, the eagerly awaited interim report of the UN weapons inspectors did not provide clear evidence one way or another. Hans Blix, head of the inspection team, told the Security Council on January 27 that he had found no WMD stockpiles in Iraq that would justify a military response. This did not mean that Saddam fully cooperated with the inspectors or resolved all doubts about his weapons arsenal. To the contrary, Blix accused the Iraqi leader of hindering inspections, not fully accounting for suspected caches of chemical and biological agents, and preventing Blix's team from interviewing scientists without government "minders" present. Mohamed ElBaradei, chief inspector of the International Atomic Energy Agency, also reported mixed results. His team of inspectors had found no trace of an Iraqi nuclear weapons program. Like Blix, he appealed for more time and more inspections.

The White House, however, rejected these calls and declared that further delays would only prolong the cat-and-mouse game Saddam had mastered in the 1990s. But the president faced stiff opposition in the UN Security Council. French president Jacques Chirac vowed to use his veto power to defeat a war resolution, and German leaders also refused to support war without further evidence of Iraqi violations. Secretary of Defense Donald Rumsfeld then poured salt in the diplomatic wounds by dismissing France and Germany as remnants of the "old Europe" and likening Germany's behavior to that of Libya and Cuba. His comments were clearly designed to isolate the two European powers from their neighbors—particularly the Eastern European states that supported Bush's call to arms.

The rift quickly spread to NATO. France, Germany, and Belgium blocked the transfer of NATO military equipment to Turkey, an alliance member that found itself a front-line state in the Iraq crisis. The three governments, which opposed the invasion of Iraq without the UN's endorsement, refused to send weapons or other military hardware that could be used in the invasion. Although most of these weapons were eventually shipped to Turkey—for its "defensive purposes" only—the strains within the Atlantic alliance were open for all to see even as NATO approved, in November 2002, a new round of eastward expansion.[22] In the end, the dispute over Iraq created long-lasting ill will between most member states and the alliance's dominant power.

Back in the UN Security Council, French resistance to the Iraq invasion was joined with that of China and Russia, two other veto-wielding members. All three countries maintained political and economic contacts with Saddam, and all three feared the outbreak of terrorist attacks within their borders that might follow such an invasion. More generally,

22. The new NATO members inducted in 2004 were the Baltic states of Estonia, Latvia, and Lithuania, along with Bulgaria, Romania, Slovakia, and Slovenia.

they opposed any violation of sovereignty by the world's dominant power. The task of convincing the Security Council fell to Secretary of State Powell, who addressed the council on February 5. Powell described U.S. intelligence reports of Saddam "disbursing rocket launchers and warheads containing biological warfare agents," of WMD laboratories in railroad cars, and of shipments of aluminum tubes to Iraq for the production of nuclear fuel. "Leaving Saddam in possession of weapons of mass destruction for a few more months or years is not an option, not in a post–September 11 world," Powell concluded.[23] But his words failed to convince the Security Council that Iraq could not be contained by expanded UN inspections and "smarter" sanctions.[24]

The United States was clearly losing the battle over world public opinion. Massive antiwar rallies were held across Europe on February 15, a peculiar spectacle given that war had not yet broken out. Nearly one million protesters turned out in London, while 600,000 filled the streets of Rome and 500,000 rallied in Berlin. A central concern of would-be allies was that their own citizens would rise up if their governments supported preventive war against Iraq. Turkish legislators so feared allying with the United States that they refused to offer their territory to stage a northern front against Iraq. In the Philippines, where the Pentagon had deployed seventeen hundred troops to help government forces repel domestic terrorists, a public outcry prompted leaders in Manila to disavow their need for U.S. reinforcements.

Large demonstrations also took place across the United States. More than one hundred city councils, including those of Chicago, Detroit, Los Angeles, and Philadelphia, approved resolutions opposing action against Iraq without UN endorsement. Although most public opinion polls found Americans supportive of regime change, those polled generally preferred a war sanctioned by the UN and supported by America's key allies. As the Iraqi endgame approached, many questions were left unanswered: Would Saddam's removal create the very power vacuum and risk of civil war that discouraged Bush's father from toppling the Iraqi leader in 1991? How much would the war cost at a time of revived U.S. budget deficits? And how would the United States create democracy in a country that lacked a democratic tradition and was torn by intense ethnic and political divisions?

23. White House, "U.S. Secretary of State Colin Powell Addresses the UN Security Council," February 5, 2003, http://www.whitehouse.gov/news/releases/2003/02/20030205-1.html (accessed May 3, 2006).

24. Although this critique had always been prevalent among liberals, many realists—who normally favored the assertion of U.S. power—also did not believe Iraq posed an imminent threat to the United States. See John J. Mearsheimer and Stephen M. Walt, "Iraq: An Unnecessary War," *Foreign Policy* (January–February 2003): 50–59.

Bush, who had always been critical of nation building, offered only vague details about Iraq's postwar rehabilitation. Earlier, he had approved a State Department effort, the Future of Iraq Project, which collected information on topics such as postwar political reform, public finance, rebuilding utilities, and improving Iraq's educational system. The group's final report, comprising thirteen volumes and 2,500 pages, cautioned against invading Iraq without assurances that the reconstruction would be completed swiftly. The report warned that delays in restoring order and public services would spark challenges to the foreign occupation. But the Pentagon found these warnings too pessimistic and urged Bush to disregard them. After Secretary of Defense Rumsfeld relayed his concerns to the White House, the project's director, Thomas Warrick, was relieved of his duties and his report was no longer considered by war planners.[25]

Disputes *within* the Pentagon also erupted into public view in February. The army's chief of staff, Gen. Eric Shinseki, told the Senate Armed Services Committee on February 25 that "several hundred thousand" troops were required to topple Saddam, maintain order, and provide security long enough for a functioning new government to be elected and assume sovereign authority. Two days later, Deputy Defense Secretary Wolfowitz contradicted the army chief, calling his estimates "wildly off the mark." In the end, the invasion force included fewer than 200,000 troops, which was less than half the level of forces used to eject Iraq from Kuwait in 1991. For the United States to maintain the same ratio of troops to population that existed in the 1999 Kosovo intervention, it would have had to deploy 480,000 troops to Iraq.

In early March, American and British diplomats tried, but failed, to convince the other members of the UN Security Council to set a March 17 deadline for Saddam's "full compliance" with the weapons inspectors. But the deployment of coalition forces to the Persian Gulf created its own impetus for a military solution sooner rather than later. Average temperatures in Iraq were rising daily, as was the cost of the huge deployment. The return of these troops at this point, without resolution of the standoff, would bring humiliation to the United States. Thus the invasion of Iraq was a foregone conclusion even as the political quarrels wore on.

OPERATION IRAQI FREEDOM

The invasion of Iraq, dubbed Operation Iraqi Freedom, began early on March 20, 2003, with a U.S. attempt to decapitate Iraq. Intelligence

25. See James Fallows, "Blind into Baghdad," *Atlantic Monthly*, January–February 2004, 53–74.

reports had indicated that Saddam and his two sons, Qusay and Uday, were meeting at the Dora Farms military compound outside of Baghdad. President Bush approved a sneak attack on the compound with 2,000-pound "bunker busters" and other cruise missiles. Although the bombs did reach their targets, it later became clear that the intelligence reports were faulty; Saddam and his sons were not at the compound. Even without reaching their targets, however, the attacks provided a thunderous signal that the invasion of Iraq had begun.

A sustained bombing campaign, dubbed "shock and awe" by U.S. military commanders, followed on March 21 and coincided with a massive ground offensive by coalition forces on a trajectory from Kuwait through the desert to Baghdad. As American tanks from the Third Infantry Division rolled toward Baghdad on April 6, British forces took control of Basra, Iraq's second largest city located near the Persian Gulf. Early resistance by Iraqi forces soon withered and cleared the path to the Iraqi capital, where U.S. Marines toppled a statue of Saddam on April 9. Saddam's whereabouts remained unknown, and no one was certain whether he was dead or alive, but his reign of terror was over. Two days later, Kurdish forces in the north ejected Iraqi government forces from the city of Kirkuk, cementing the military victory.

The success of Operation Iraqi Freedom, with its relatively few casualties, demonstrated once again the supremacy of U.S. military power. The simultaneous air and ground attacks, a departure from the 1991 war plan, permitted coalition forces to capture Iraqi oil fields before they could be destroyed by retreating Iraqi forces. Even without the tactical advantage of a sizable northern front, the synchronized ground advances by army and marine divisions swiftly overran Iraqi defenses outside of Baghdad. All of Iraq's major cities were under allied control by the end of April. On May 1, President Bush, dressed in a flight suit, made a dramatic landing on an aircraft carrier off the coast of California to celebrate the overthrow of Saddam's regime. Under a banner proclaiming "Mission Accomplished," Bush then announced that "major combat operations in Iraq have ended."

But the routing of Saddam's regime did not settle matters. Allied forces could not simply declare victory and return home as they had done twelve years earlier. The troops had to restore order to and ultimately rebuild the cities, which erupted not only in celebration but also in widespread looting, violent reprisals against Saddam loyalists, and attacks on U.S. soldiers. Armed Iraqis ransacked stores, government ministries, hospitals, military installations, and the National Museum of Iraq. Attacks on media outlets and electrical utilities left Baghdad literally in the dark and lacking a telephone system or other means of internal communication. The chaos in Baghdad and other cities revealed a darker reality for the occupation forces, most of whom were not "greeted as liberators" as Vice President Cheney had predicted on NBC's *Meet the Press* three days before the invasion.

The White House's postinvasion plan called for a short period of U.S. military occupation, followed by the drafting of a constitution and national elections. Rather than turning this process over to the State Department, which traditionally has managed postconflict recovery efforts, Bush ordered the Pentagon to assume this responsibility. But the agency created for this purpose, the Office of Reconstruction and Humanitarian Assistance, was quickly overwhelmed by the demands of governing Iraq. Jay Garner, a retired lieutenant general appointed to oversee the office, only lasted one month in the post. His replacement, L. Paul Bremer, created the Coalition Provisional Authority (CPA) on April 21 to manage the reconstruction efforts and in July formed the Iraq Governing Council, composed largely of regional leaders who shared a common hatred for Saddam. Although the council provided the appearance of power sharing, Bremer alone made the critical decisions regarding Iraq's future. Clad in a pinstriped suit even in the scorching heat of the Iraqi desert, he assumed the image of a colonial viceroy.

The American occupation quickly faced new problems, however. Contrary to the Bush administration's assurances that, in the words of CIA director George J. Tenet, uncovering evidence of WMDs in Iraq was a "slam dunk," weapons inspectors failed to find any stockpiles in the weeks and months following the invasion. The absence of WMD shattered the White House's rationale for invading Iraq. At the end of 2003, with no such weapons found, chief weapons inspector David Kay testified to Congress that the prewar intelligence was "almost all wrong." The White House then quickly shifted its rationale for the war to democratic nation building, a goal that was part of the original war justification but secondary to WMD concerns and Saddam's alleged links to the September 11 terrorists.

But even nation building soon proved impossible for coalition forces and the civilian contractors hired to rebuild Iraq. Well-armed insurgents launched virtually constant attacks on the troops and contractors, largely in the form of suicide attacks and the detonation of "improvised explosive devices" (IEDs). The insurgents bombed the UN headquarters in August and the International Red Cross headquarters in October, both located in Baghdad. By attacking recruitment stations for military and police officers, the insurgents sent a separate message to Iraqis: cooperate with the foreign invaders and you will be killed. The December 13 capture of Saddam, who was hiding in an underground bunker near his hometown of Tikrit, provided a temporary source of relief. But news of failed WMD searches, a growing insurgency, and mounting casualties—nearly five hundred by the end of the year—indicated that the Iraqi mission had veered perilously off course.

Who were the insurgents? Many were identified as members of Saddam's ousted government, the Ba'ath Party, and the Republican Guard. These Sunni Muslims, who represented just 20 percent of Iraq's population, had for decades dominated Iraq from their territorial base in the central region (see map of Iraq). They had the most to lose from Saddam's overthrow and the most to gain from preventing the creation of a democratic government that would leave them with little political power. Many of these insurgents were part of the Iraqi leader's *Fedayeen* ("Men of Sacrifice"), a paramilitary unit that was disbursed throughout the country after the U.S.-led invasion to stage attacks on the foreign troops and to punish defectors from Iraq's regular army. Other insurgents fought on behalf of the Shiite cleric Moqtada Sadr, and still others were aligned with Kurdish militants in northern Iraq. All of these groups welcomed assistance from outside Iraq's borders, although the number of these foreign insurgents and their ties to Iraqi groups are difficult to ascertain.

Taken together, the insurgents frustrated the attempts by coalition forces to maintain control of Iraq after Saddam's overthrow. As Lieut. Gen. William Scott Wallace later acknowledged, "This was not the enemy we war-gamed against." Indeed, the U.S. strategy, code-named Cobra II after the Allied land offensive against Germany in World War II, focused almost entirely on the capture of Baghdad. Relatively little attention was paid to occupying and rebuilding the country, which was expected to be handled primarily by Iraqi forces and civil servants.

Two fateful decisions by American leaders added fuel to the insurgency. First, the small size of the invading force deployed by Secretary of Defense Rumsfeld did not include enough troops to control Iraq's external borders. This decision literally opened the door to Saddam's foreign supporters, Islamists, and soldiers of fortune, who seized their golden opportunity to thwart the U.S.-led occupation. Thus if Iraq was not a "nest of terrorists" before Operation Iraqi Freedom, it became one soon afterward. Second, the insurgency attracted a horde of indigenous recruits in May 2003 after Bremer abruptly disbanded Iraq's military and police forces. Intending to start from scratch with entirely new security forces, Bremer left more than 300,000 Iraqis suddenly unemployed and deeply resentful. They retained their weapons, however, along with their experience and contacts within Iraqi society, all of which could now be turned against the United States and other foreign troops.

As coalition forces struggled to overcome the insurgency for a year after the invasion, often through bloody urban warfare, a new scandal compounded the damage. In April 2004, photographs of the widespread abuse of Iraqis by U.S. troops stationed at Abu Ghraib prison outside of Baghdad filled newspapers and Internet sites. The photographs depicted

ETHNIC AND RELIGIOUS GROUPS IN IRAQ

bound Iraqi prisoners being taunted by attack dogs, forced to lie naked on bare floors, and exposed to electric shock, often in the company of American military police who smiled for the cameras and displayed the "thumbs-up" sign.[26] The graphic images, which directly contradicted the U.S. government's claims to be introducing civility and the rule of law to Iraq, inflamed anti-American passions worldwide. Bush condemned the mistreatment of Iraqi prisoners and later renounced torture. He argued, however, that the Geneva Convention and other protections did not apply to "unlawful combatants," a term the Pentagon adopted to differentiate suspected insurgents and terrorists from conventional prisoners of war.

As the president ran for reelection in the summer and fall of 2004, he insisted that American forces were gaining the upper hand against the Iraqi insurgents. Bush criticized his opponent in the fall election, Sen. John Kerry of Massachusetts, for questioning the war effort while American forces remained in harm's way. As polls showed Kerry leading in the final week of the campaign, President Bush received a boost from the most unlikely of sources: Osama bin Laden. The al Qaeda leader appeared on videotape three days before the election ridiculing his

26. Seymour Hersh, "Torture in Iraq," *New Yorker,* May 10, 2004.

American enemies and predicting victory in the war on terrorism. Bush, who was perceived by many as tougher than Kerry in the war effort, gained just enough popular support to win a second term and another four years to achieve his military goals.

A RACE AGAINST TIME

The Bush administration began its second term in a race against time in Iraq. American troops continued to struggle in the face of insurgent attacks, and most large cities remained chaotic and largely ungovernable. At the same time, Iraq formally regained its sovereignty in June 2004; a prime minister—Ayad Allawi—was appointed by the interim government, and the timetable for popular elections remained intact. The first round of legislative elections, held on January 30, 2005, brought more than eight million Iraqis to the polls to select a 275-member assembly. The purple-ink-stained fingers of voters, which verified their participation in the election, instantly became a symbol of political freedom in Iraq. The voter turnout was almost 60 percent, higher than that for most American national elections since World War II.

But the outcome of the election presented more troubling news for those seeking a peaceful transition of power. More than 70 percent of the seats in the assembly were won by Shiite candidates, most of whom favored a government that closely followed Islamic law and customs, thereby mirroring the theocratic regime that had ruled Iran since its 1979 revolution. Another quarter of the seats went to ethnic Kurds in the north, whose vision of an Iraqi state granted them almost complete autonomy. Conspicuously absent were votes from Sunnis and members of Saddam's ousted Ba'ath Party, who largely boycotted the election. Taken together, the results did not bode well for Washington's model of a moderate, secular state that would unify the Iraqi people. Indeed, the results seemed to codify Iraq's fragmentation.

By the time the election was held, more than twelve hundred American soldiers had died and thousands more had been wounded in Iraq. Although the death toll among insurgents was unknown, a study by the Oxford Research Group found that nearly 25,000 Iraqi civilians were killed in the first two years of the war. Almost half died in Baghdad; the second largest death toll was recorded in Fallujah, a rebel stronghold west of the capital that fell to U.S. forces after months of armed struggle.[27] By the end of the war's third year, in March 2006, more than 2,300

27. Hamit Dardagan, John Sloboda, Kay Williams, and Peter Bagnall, "Iraq Body Count: A Dossier of Civilian Casualties, 2003–2005," Oxford Research Group, July 2005, http://reports.iraqbodycount.org (accessed May 3, 2006).

FIGURE 13-1 Iraq War Casualties, March 2003–March 2006

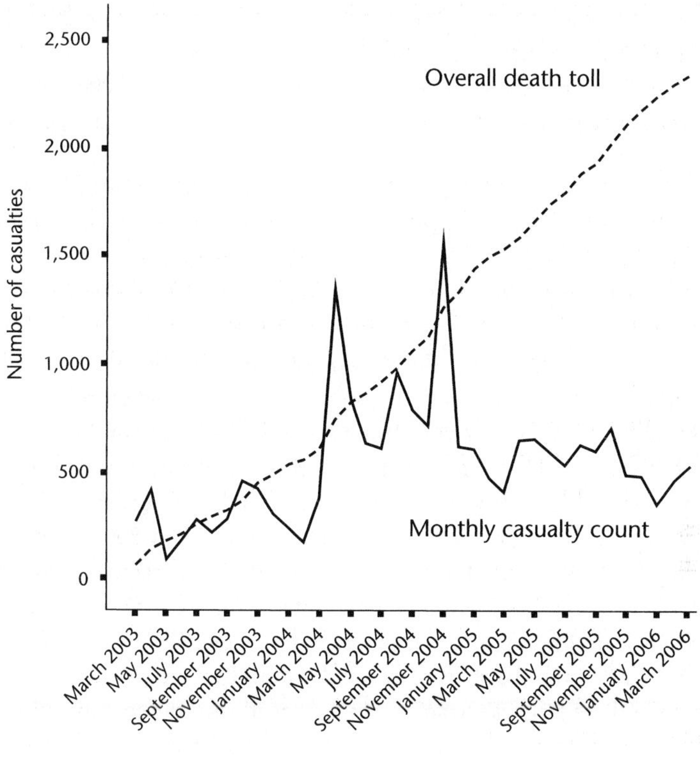

Source: Iraq Coalition Casualty Count, http://icasualties.org/oif/ (accessed May 8, 2006).

Note: Casualties include both dead and wounded.

Americans had died in Iraq, and more than 16,000 others had been wounded (see Figure 13-1). The economic costs of the two wars were astronomical: more than $250 billion since the war began and an estimated $6 billion per *month* as the conflicts in Iraq and Afghanistan continued into 2006.[28] The overall U.S. defense budget, including the operations in Afghanistan and Iraq, was likely to exceed half a *trillion* dollars beginning in fiscal year 2007, or about $2,000 for every American citizen.

These numbers were damaging to President Bush, whose public approval fell below 40 percent in 2005 and below 30 percent in 2006. A majority of Americans reported in surveys that they felt going to war in

28. Amy Belasco, "The Cost of Iraq, Afghanistan, and Other War on Terror Operations Since 9/11," Congressional Research Service, April 24, 2006, http://www.fas.org/sgp/crs/natsec/RL33110.pdf (accessed May 8, 2006).

Iraq was a mistake, a sentiment that grew with the death toll. For the first time, most survey respondents expressed doubts about Bush's honesty in leading the nation to war. Members of Congress also tired of the U.S. presence in Iraq. Senators passed a resolution on November 15, 2005, calling for faster progress toward "full Iraqi sovereignty" in 2006. And in the House of Representatives, Rep. John Murtha of Pennsylvania, a decorated war veteran and advocate of strong defense, concluded that the Iraq war "is not going as advertised. It is a flawed policy wrapped in illusion." Murtha demanded a prompt U.S. withdrawal from Iraq and the handing over of military control to Iraqi forces, which at the time had only one of 126 battalions capable of fighting effectively without American support.[29]

Adding to the difficulties, Bush's war coalition was shrinking. Several countries withdrew their forces in 2004. Among the most prominent of these defections was Spain, where multiple terrorist attacks on March 11, 2004, killed nearly two hundred citizens. Elections held three days later brought the antiwar Socialist Party to power and the subsequent removal of Spanish troops from Iraq. The exodus continued in 2005 with the departure of troops from Italy, New Zealand, the Netherlands, Portugal, Thailand, and Ukraine, among other countries. A series of July 2005 terrorist attacks in London left British citizens on edge, but Prime Minister Tony Blair refused to back away from his commitment to the war.

Despite these setbacks, Iraq's formal steps toward democratic governance continued. Iraqi voters approved a national constitution in October 2005 that provided the blueprint for a "democratic, federal, representative republic." An elected parliament would pass legislation and approve by majority vote the selection of presidents and prime ministers. More important, the constitution granted sweeping powers to regional authorities, including control over oil deposits and revenues. The weak central state, clearly designed to prevent the return of "Saddamism," also ensured that the coalition of Kurds and Shiites would call the shots. Desperate for a voice in Iraq's new government, many Sunnis voted in the December 2005 legislative elections that ended the transitional period, but they won only 44 of the 275 seats; most were awarded to Shiites and Kurds. The election's outcome provided further evidence that democracy in Iraq, if it materialized at all, would only perpetuate the nation's ethnic and sectarian divisions.

Continuing problems with Iraq's reconstruction further suggested the United States was losing its race against time. A January 2006 U.S. gov-

29. Kenneth Katzman, "Iraq: U.S. Regime Change Efforts and Post-Saddam Governance," Congressional Research Service, November 21, 2005, http://fpc.state.gov/documents/organization/58276.pdf (accessed May 3, 2006).

ernment report found that many projects were behind schedule or had been cancelled entirely. Only 49 of 136 water projects would ever be completed; of 425 electrical projects, 125 had to be scrapped. The high cost of fighting Iraqi insurgents was blamed for the "reconstruction gap." [30] The effort was also plagued by widespread corruption, with funds for some projects being diverted to insurgents and others paid to American contractors without services being rendered. In most areas, from electrical generation to sewage treatment and road maintenance, public services by 2006 had yet to reach their prewar levels. Meanwhile, insurgent attacks continued at a rate of more than three hundred per week. Larry Diamond, an expert on democratic reforms who had served in Baghdad as a senior adviser to the Coalition Provisional Authority, concluded that "America's quest to stabilize and democratize Iraq seemed to be becoming one of the major overseas blunders in U.S. history." [31]

Back to Vietnam?

The American experience in Iraq invites comparison to the Vietnam War, described in Chapter 5. The two conflicts, which produced the longest large-scale deployments of American forces since World War II, are alike in many ways. These similarities, and the shared lessons that can be derived from both conflicts, are worth considering as the struggle in Iraq, as well as those in Afghanistan and on other fronts in the war on terrorism, continue.

This discussion will begin, however, by identifying some basic *differences* between the conflicts in Iraq and Vietnam. First, before the U.S. intervention in Vietnam the nation was little known to most Americans and of little geopolitical interest to the United States. The opposite could be said of Iraq, whose regime led by Saddam Hussein was very familiar to Americans and whose vast oil deposits made Iraq a vital American interest, whether as a friend or foe. A second difference relates to the demographic features of the two countries. Vietnam's population was ethnically homogeneous and thus maintained a keen sense of national identity even under centuries of colonial rule. Iraq's people, by contrast, were divided between Arabs and Kurds. Even the Arab population, divided between the two Islamic sects, lacked a common identity.

The circumstances of each U.S. intervention also differed in important respects. Whereas the Vietnamese opposition produced a unifying

30. Special Inspector General for Iraq Reconstruction, "Quarterly and Semiannual Report to Congress," January 30, 2006, http://www.sigir.mil/reports/QuarterlyReports/Jan06/pdf/Report_Complete_-_January_2006.pdf (accessed May 8, 2006).

31. Larry Diamond. *Squandered Victory: The American Occupation and the Bungled Effort to Bring Democracy to Iraq* (New York: Times Books, 2005), 279.

figure—Ho Chi Minh—no such leader emerged in Iraq after Saddam's overthrow. Instead, the disparate insurgents were led by a variety of figures with very different goals for Iraq, from the restoration of "Saddamism" to the creation of an Iranian-style theocracy or Afghan-style Taliban. Before his death at the hands of American forces in June 2006, Abu Musab al-Zarqawi, leader of al Qaeda in Iraq, rallied many insurgents behind his terrorist attacks, but their targets were frequently Iraqi Shiites, the nation's majority population. And whereas in Vietnam the United States intervened in behalf of a pro-American regime that was beset by domestic rivals (the Viet Cong), in Iraq the United States overthrew a hostile regime whose departure, and the power vacuum that resulted, sparked a previously dormant insurgency.

These differences posed distinct problems for the United States in Vietnam and Iraq. The strong sense of Vietnamese nationalism undercut American efforts to win the population's "hearts and minds," whereas the ethnic and sectarian divisions among Iraqis prevented them from rallying behind a central leader or creating a united central government. But it is the similarities in the two cases that are more troublesome, because the many presumed lessons of the Vietnam War were neglected to varying degrees in the conflict with Iraq.

Five similarities can be identified. First, American foreign policy makers cast both regional conflicts in the context of a global dispute—the Cold War in the case of Vietnam, the war on terrorism in Iraq's case. By framing the conflicts in this way, policy makers ignored the unique historical, cultural, and political dynamics at work in each society. The depths of Vietnamese nationalism surprised American leaders, who blithely assumed the conflict was all about ideology. Likewise, the confrontation with Iraq was considered meaningful only as a front in the U.S. war on terrorism. In both conflicts, Americans' cross-cultural blinders led them to place excessive faith in military solutions to problems that were far more complex and resistant to foreign intervention than they believed.

Second, in both cases decision makers suffered from an apparent case of "groupthink," or a tendency to limit outside advice to those who already supported the administration's viewpoint and policy preferences. Irving L. Janis, the psychologist who coined the term, found that a small "in-group" within the administration of Lyndon Johnson dominated policy toward Vietnam and excluded skeptics in the "out-group" from influencing the president.[32] The same pattern was evident in the Bush White House, which, like that of Johnson and Nixon in the Vietnam years, was more receptive to guidance from military advisers than

32. Irving L. Janis, *Groupthink,* 2d rev. ed. (Boston: Houghton Mifflin, 1973), Ch. 5.

from those in the State Department. Lawrence B. Wilkerson, Secretary of State Colin Powell's chief of staff, found that key decisions about Iraq were made by a "secretive, little-known cabal" that left experienced regional experts from the State Department out of the loop.[33] Also like its predecessors, the Bush administration cited intelligence reports on Iraq selectively in order to bolster its arguments for military intervention, as demonstrated by Powell's presentation to the UN Security Council.

The nature of the military opposition represents a third similarity in the Vietnam and Iraq conflicts. In both, American forces were better prepared for conventional wars than for the asymmetric wars that followed, in which enemy forces used their relatively small size, lack of formal military organization, and grassroots bases of support as a tactical advantage. In Vietnam, guerrilla warriors melted in with sympathetic civilian populations, took advantage of familiar terrain, and staged hit-and-run attacks on American forces rather than large-scale offensives. For their part, the Iraqi insurgents adopted even more evasive military tactics, killing American troops with remote-controlled IEDs and recruiting suicide bombers to destroy high-value military and civilian targets. The U.S. military's failure to anticipate and manage this unconventional form of warfare in Iraq further suggests that the lessons of Vietnam failed to take hold in the minds of Pentagon strategists.

Fourth, the scale and timing of military deployments in Vietnam and Iraq worked to the advantage of insurgents. As noted earlier, American troops were sent to Vietnam in a piecemeal fashion, buying time for Vietminh forces to mobilize and plan their attacks. That experience prompted the Weinberger and Powell doctrines of the post–Vietnam era that called for nothing less than overwhelming force in future American interventions.[34] But soon after the invasion of Iraq, it became clear that the deployment of fewer than two hundred thousand troops was inadequate to bring order to the nation and allow for a peaceful political transition and long-term reconstruction. The Pentagon's dominant voice, Rumsfeld believed future American wars would be fought with the lighter, more mobile forces that were central to his "transformation" of U.S. defense. Although such forces captured Baghdad with remarkable speed, they were inadequate to secure the nation's external borders or provide sufficient internal order.

Finally, the outcome of American actions in each case was precisely what the United States had sought to avoid. In Vietnam, a communist regime took power—albeit one that did not start the dominos falling as American leaders had predicted. In Iraq, a despotic but strong state that

33. Lawrence B. Wilkerson, "The White House Cabal," *Los Angeles Times,* October 25, 2005, B11.

34. Caspar Weinberger was secretary of defense in the Reagan administration.

had previously suppressed Islamist terrorism was replaced by a state so feeble that it virtually invited Islamists to gain political control, whether by force or, perversely, by the electoral procedures put into place by the occupying power. These developments further clouded the prospects for an exit strategy in Iraq that would achieve the U.S. government's political as well as military objectives.

To this list of historical parallels one might add yet another—the start of each conflict under false pretenses. Congress authorized President Lyndon Johnson to "take all necessary measures" to protect U.S. forces in Vietnam in the Gulf of Tonkin Resolution—an authorization based on Pentagon reports of attacks on an American patrol boat that later proved to be misleading.[35] Similarly, much of the Bush administration's case about Iraq's WMD programs—claims about nuclear deals in Africa, intercepted aluminum tubes, mobile germ warfare laboratories, and Iraqi–al Qaeda contacts—were refuted after hostilities had begun.[36] Although evidence may yet emerge that the Bush administration acted prudently in the face of uncertainty and Saddam's mixed signals, more critical judgments are bolstered by White House miscalculations of expected costs, troop commitments, and the ease of "stability operations."

Fully informed assessments of the wars in Afghanistan and Iraq will require greater time and accumulation of evidence. At minimum, however, American leaders exhibited a remarkable degree of naïveté in planning both wars that was in keeping with the nation's traditional style of foreign policy. From Washington's vantage point, the wartime goals of the United States would be achieved simply because they represented universal moral values such as human freedom, democracy, and legal equality. In the words of the administration's 2006 National Security Strategy, "The United States must defend liberty and justice because these principles are right and true for all people everywhere." [37] Success was further assured by the paradoxical fruits of American exceptionalism: the world's most productive economy combined with the world's most destructive military forces. With these assets in hand, along with their providential blessings, why worry about such mundane matters as power generation and sewage treatment? These details would take care of themselves. And why try to understand the foreign culture or society when the American intervention offered a superior model that could be readily adopted overseas?

35. Stanley Karnow, *Vietnam: A History* (New York: Viking, 1983), 366–373.

36. See James Risen, *State of War: The Secret History of the CIA and the Bush Administration* (New York: Free Press, 2006), ch. 5.

37. White House, National Security Council, "National Security Strategy of the United States," March 2006, 2. http://www.whitehouse.gov/nsc/nss/2006/nss2006.pdf

Such self-confidence and optimism, however, contrasted sharply with events on the ground. The constant threat of attacks left U.S. troops confined to the "green zones" of Baghdad and Kabul or to heavily fortified fortresses in remote provinces. In Iraq especially, daily patrols and routine public interactions tempted sudden death—a lesson learned by foreign investors, civil servants, and missionaries, who had long since moved on to safer destinations. Meanwhile, the isolation and demoralization of American forces contradicted the nation's messianic self-image and ingrained sense of manifest destiny. With each passing day, and with each car bombing, sniper shot, or raid on a police station, the uphill battle facing American nation builders grew steeper.

As the final chapter describes, concerns about preserving democracy at home, which sparked mass protests during the Vietnam era, were also raised during the Iraq conflict and the broader war on terrorism. Indeed, the nation's own moral principles and democratic values were put to the test, along with its traditional assumptions of peaceful coexistence as the norm rather than exception in world politics. At the same time, the United States confronted other foreign policy challenges, including antiglobalization movements in South America, nuclear proliferation in North Korea and Iran, and new obstacles to peace between Israel and its neighbors. All of these challenges further threatened the Bush Doctrine's vision of U.S. primacy, the creation of a world of American-style democracies, and a new, enduring era of world peace.

CHAPTER FOURTEEN

A World of Trouble

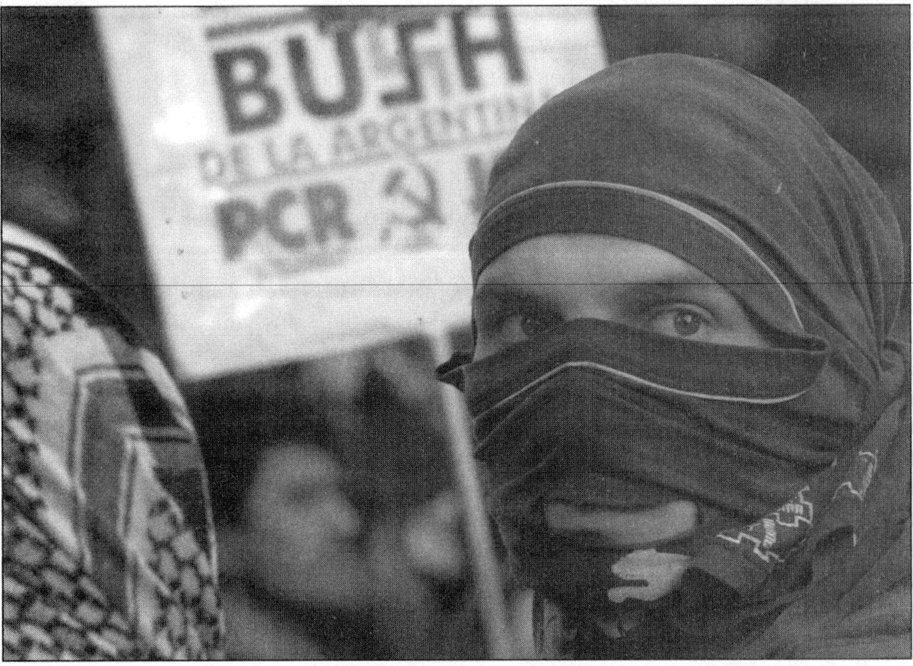

Anti-American protesters march in Mar del Plata, Argentina, where President Bush and other world leaders convened in November 2005 for the Fourth Summit of the Americas. The demonstrators spoke out against many aspects of American foreign policy, including the wars in Iraq and Afghanistan and the U.S.-backed Free Trade Area of the Americas.

As the previous five chapters described, the volatile international system of the post–Cold War era did not wait for the United States to clarify its foreign policy goals. Upheavals in several regions shattered the widely anticipated new world order. Rather than heralding the arrival of a Kantian "perpetual peace," the demise of the Soviet Union sparked a Hobbesian wildfire of military conflicts that had been suppressed earlier only by the standoff of two nuclear superpowers.[1] Iraq's invasion of

1. See Michael W. Doyle, *Ways of War and Peace: Realism, Liberalism, and Socialism* (New York: Norton, 1997), chaps. 3 and 8.

Kuwait in 1990 and the subsequent outbreak of civil wars in Yugoslavia and Somalia revealed dangerous fault lines. Bloodbaths in Rwanda, the former Zaire, the Russian province of Chechnya, and Indonesia followed, along with a campaign of genocide in Sudan. The terrorist attacks on the United States in 2001 and the wars in Afghanistan and Iraq confirmed that the United States, which still maintained the largest concentration of state power in history, faced a world of trouble.

To President George W. Bush, the unraveling threads of the global order did not threaten only U.S. interests. Also at risk was his vision of a democratic and prosperous world order whose stability would be underwritten by U.S. military might. The Bush Doctrine, based on a fusion of American power and principle, was also based on the belief that the national interest was synonymous with global justice, peace, and prosperity. The doctrine's general effect, however, was to alarm the very governments it was meant to reassure. Bush's pledge that U.S. primacy would bring not oppression but "a balance of power that favors human freedom" most often fell on deaf ears. Instead of eliciting goodwill toward Washington, the prospect of world domination by any single government, whatever its declared motives or intentions, troubled large and small countries alike.

Bush should have expected nothing less. He had come to power sending a very different message: U.S. interests trumped global concerns, the "international community" was a myth, and most problems overseas should be allowed to run their course without U.S. intervention. In jettisoning the liberal internationalism of the post–World War II era, he struck a chord with a longer tradition in American foreign policy that distrusted global activism. The prevailing fear was that "foreign entanglements" would only bring the United States closer to the Old World's corrupt and autocratic governments. America's democratic values, its primary asset and gift to the world, would be sullied if the nation went out "in search of monsters to destroy," as Secretary of State John Quincy Adams warned nearly two centuries earlier.

But when modern-day foreign entanglements came to America's shores on September 11, 2001, retreat from an activist world role became impossible. The United States was at war, as were other countries that shared its values, democratic institutions, and stakes in a market-based world economy. Whereas Bush's initial worldview frustrated foreign leaders by threatening withdrawal of U.S. leadership, the new grand strategy troubled them by reducing their nations to pawns in the latest game of power politics.

The contrast between Bush's earlier rejection of the international community and his later bid to liberate the world through the

IMPACT AND INFLUENCE

CONDOLEEZZA RICE

No member of the George W. Bush administration carried more responsibility during the president's two terms than Condoleezza Rice, who served as national security adviser from 2001 until 2005, and then as secretary of state. Rice, born in 1954, grew up in Birmingham, Alabama, where, as an African American, she experienced the social upheaval that came with racial desegregation. She excelled in school and graduated at age nineteen from the University of Denver with a degree in political science. In 1981 Rice earned a doctorate degree in international studies from the same university, and then joined the faculty at Stanford University, where she served as a professor and then as provost from 1993 until 1999. Having served earlier on the first Bush administration's National Security Council (NSC), Rice was well known to George W. Bush when he took office in 2001 and appointed her to the position of national security adviser.

Rice's academic work concentrated on the Soviet Union and Central Europe in the final stages of the Cold War. Her interest in the field of international relations was stimulated in graduate school by the Czech refugee Josef Korbel, father of President Bill Clinton's second secretary of state, Madeleine Albright. As an analyst for the NSC between 1989 and 1991, Rice adopted a skeptical stance toward Soviet leader Mikhail Gorbachev's reforms and urged the White House to maintain economic and military pressure on the Soviet leader. After she returned to the White House in 2001, Rice at first espoused a modest foreign policy and cautioned against nation building overseas. But after the terrorist attacks of September 11, 2001, Rice, like Bush, was quickly transformed into a foreign policy activist. She was a primary author of Bush's 2002 National Security Strategy, which called for preserving American primacy in global politics and resorting to overwhelming military force, even preemptive war, when and where U.S. interests were threatened.

unabashed assertion of U.S. power could not have been greater. Indeed, the president epitomized America's schizophrenic style of foreign policy—a style that has persisted for more than two centuries despite profound changes in the nation's role in the world. American foreign policy continued its historic pattern of pendulum-like swings between two contradictory impulses: morally inspired activism to save the world and detachment from a sinful world. Both impulses derived from the nation's self-image as an exceptional world power. As Hans Morgenthau, a prominent realist of the Cold War, observed in 1969, "While the two positions are obviously identified with utterly different foreign policies—indiscriminate involvement here, indiscriminate abstention there—it is important to note that they share the same assumptions about the nature of the political world and the same negative attitudes toward foreign policy correctly understood. They are equally hostile to that middle ground of subtle distinctions, complex choices, and precarious manipulations which is the proper sphere of foreign policy."[2]

Bush's midcourse correction was most vividly demonstrated by his determination to invade Iraq. His pledge to take preventive action against Iraqi dictator Saddam Hussein sparked widespread protests overseas and fractured U.S. relations with the United Nations and alliance partners. The subsequent setbacks in Iraq—the widespread looting and disorder, the absence of weapons of mass destruction (WMD), the scandal at Abu Ghraib prison, the steadily growing insurgency, and the sluggish efforts to provide basic services and rebuild infrastructure—made other governments relieved that they had stayed home. Meanwhile, the two other members of Bush's "axis of evil," North Korea and Iran, inched closer to becoming nuclear powers. Economic problems from East Asia to Latin America produced a worldwide recession. And in the United States, political controversies left many citizens questioning their own democratic system of government.

Individually, these developments did not threaten American security. But taken together, they sapped the nation's capacity to sustain the global primacy it had achieved in the twentieth century. Which tradition would the United States draw upon to solve these problems—detachment or moral crusading? Or would foreign policy makers hold true to form and try to have it both ways?

New Threats of Nuclear Proliferation

The crisis in Iraq produced troubling spillover effects elsewhere in the world. With Washington's attention riveted on Baghdad, and to a lesser

2. Hans Morgenthau, *A New Foreign Policy for the United States* (New York: Praeger, 1969), 15.

extent on Kabul, other U.S. adversaries sought to enhance their military power and reinforce their defenses against possible American attacks. A prudent reading of the Bush Doctrine, along with remarks by U.S. officials about their intentions in a post–Saddam world, convinced hostile governments to prepare for the worst. This approach applied especially to the other members of the "axis of evil" for whom nuclear weapons emerged as an appealing means to deter American attempts to change their own regimes. The government of North Korea was the first to seek to parlay nuclear threats into economic concessions and security guarantees from its neighbors and the United States. And then Iran, which maintained links to Islamic militants and considered the United States and Israel sworn enemies, announced it had begun producing enriched uranium, the essential ingredient of nuclear weapons. Bush's explicit inclusion of the two countries in the "axis of evil," far from subduing the two regimes, emboldened them instead.

BREAKOUT IN NORTH KOREA

If the Bush Doctrine's call for preemptive war was made to order for Iraq, it also seemed well suited to North Korea. Its Stalinist dictator, Kim Jong Il, chose the Iraqi crisis as an opportune time to provoke a nuclear crisis in northeast Asia. Late in 2002, Kim renounced his earlier pledge to "freeze" North Korea's nuclear program, ejected international weapons inspectors, and prepared to restart North Korea's nuclear reprocessing plant at Yongbyon. The nation had enough fissionable material to build several nuclear bombs at the time of the freeze. Its breakout from the agreement would allow it to build several more bombs each year afterward.

This move by North Korea was timed to gain new concessions from Washington. In 1994 President Bill Clinton had yielded to the nuclear blackmail of Kim's father, Kim Il Sung. The ransom paid was incredible: $4 billion for the construction of two light-water nuclear power generators that would not yield weapons-grade plutonium, a free supply of oil for eight to ten years, and diplomatic relations with the United States and Japan. What did the United States receive in return? Only promises that North Korea would allow weapons inspections within eight years and would shut down the reprocessing plant—a promise it had made years earlier and then violated. Its nuclear program remained intact, only frozen, allowing it to keep the handful of weapons it already had while buying time to build more if its leaders decided later to up the ante. That time had now come.

To Kim, more nuclear warheads would deter a preemptive U.S. invasion and increase North Korea's regional leverage. In the meantime,

North Korea could sell its surplus nuclear materials to the highest bidder. The nation's communist regime, like that of the defunct Soviet Union, was adept at building military hardware for export even as its civilian economy floundered. A famine during the 1990s had left more than two million dead and spurred a worldwide relief effort.[3] Yet North Korean engineers still developed and launched a three-stage missile over Japan in 1998—not an inexpensive endeavor. Adding nuclear materials to its weapons inventory would enhance Pyongyang's share of the global market for ballistic missiles.

This new regional crisis forced George W. Bush to confront the limits of his grand strategy. North Korea's nuclear breakout, and its declared intention to produce more bombs than were essential for its self-defense, had implications for regional and global security that were at least as ominous as Iraq's alleged stockpile of weapons of mass destruction (WMD). But taking on two "rogue states" simultaneously was impossible at a time when the United States was also waging an open-ended war against terrorism. In addition, Bush was bound by his earlier decision to suspend diplomatic relations with North Korea, one of his first acts as president. He refused to negotiate with Kim, whom he had once called a "pygmy," until the North Korean leader refroze his nuclear program and rejoined the Nuclear Non-Proliferation Treaty. Both concessions were unlikely, because Kim felt personally threatened by the U.S. campaign of regime change in Baghdad.

Having ruled out direct talks, the United States turned to North Korea's neighbors to do its bidding. But the headaches only grew worse for the White House. South Korea's new leader, Roh Moo Hyun, pledged to continue his country's "sunshine policy" of engagement with North Korea and encouraged the United States to follow his lead. China and Russia, upset with U.S. actions in Iraq, advised Bush to handle his own diplomacy. Kim stoked the flames further in March 2003 by intercepting a U.S. reconnaissance plane within North Korean airspace, which prompted Bush to deploy twenty-four U.S. bombers to the western Pacific. Kim responded by testing a new generation of intermediate-range missiles. The fact that North Korea's thirteen thousand artillery launchers could reduce Seoul to rubble in minutes, killing thousands of U.S. soldiers in the process, provided protection enough for North Korea's leader. The prospect of nuclear breakout further excited Kim, who relished the global attention he gained from standing up to the United States.

Bush's insistence on a multilateral approach to the North Korea crisis stood in stark contrast to the unilateral course he had adopted

3. For more on the causes of this crisis and faltering relief efforts, see Andrew W. Natsios, *The Great North Korean Famine* (Washington, D.C.: U.S. Institute of Peace, 2001).

in the showdown with Iraq. Eventually, he was joined in that approach by other governments seeking a way out of the North Korean impasse. But while carrying out that approach, the United States saw all of the liabilities of multilateral diplomacy come into play. Aside from the United States, four other countries would have to negotiate with Kim: South Korea, Russia, China, and Japan. These governments would first have to agree among themselves what terms would be offered to gain Kim's "denuclearization" and who would pay those costs. The only question would be how large a ransom North Korea would demand.

Fortunately, the Bush administration's diplomatic partners shared its desire for a prompt resolution of the crisis. Like the Clinton bargain, which was roundly criticized by Bush's foreign policy advisers at the time, the offer included a generous mix of economic assistance, security guarantees, and the means to generate nuclear energy for civilian uses. North Korea's agreement to those terms in September 2005 briefly eased tensions, but the deal quickly broke down. Kim insisted that his power plant, with a light-water nuclear reactor, be built before the dismantling of his nuclear program. The United States and its partners rejected this demand, which would effectively reward Kim's bad behavior.

With the talks again in a stalemate, Kim cancelled the meetings scheduled for early in 2006, and the United States reverted to its earlier name-calling strategy by declaring North Korea a "criminal regime." Kim's newest demand, that the United States lift recently imposed economic sanctions against his country, were predictably shrugged off by the White House. Meanwhile, living conditions in North Korea remained destitute, with much of the country lacking even the most basic public services needed to sustain modern life. As the uneasy status dragged on, a new threat of nuclear proliferation emerged in the Middle East.

IRAN'S QUEST FOR 'NUCLEAR RIGHTS'

The government of Iran also seized the moment to develop nuclear power, and possibly weapons. Its leaders had observed the developments in North Korea and learned two important lessons. First, playing the game of nuclear brinkmanship could be a highly lucrative venture, both politically and economically. And, second, the would-be proliferators held all the trump cards. What worked for Kim on the Korean peninsula would no doubt work for the mullahs in Iran as well.

Although Iran's addition to the nuclear club would not produce the first "Islamic bomb"—Pakistan had already claimed that status—a nuclear Iran would greatly complicate the global strategic balance and further inflame tensions in the Middle East. Other Islamic states in the region, including Egypt and Saudi Arabia, would be tempted to follow suit because of their own ill will toward Iran. A nuclear Iran would also directly threaten Israel, its sworn enemy, which for years had been plagued by Iranian-backed terrorist groups such as Hezbollah. Thus any prospect for a nuclear-free Middle East, a longtime goal of Israel's Arab neighbors, would likely give way to a nuclear arms race in the region.

Iran and the United States had remained at odds ever since the ejection of the U.S.-backed shah and the Islamic revolution in 1979. After the terrorist attacks of September 2001, however, there were new incentives to cooperate. Iran shared the U.S. government's hostility toward the Taliban regime in Afghanistan, albeit for different reasons. Whereas Washington's hostility stemmed from the Taliban's harboring of al Qaeda, Iran's enmity had ethnic and sectarian roots: most Iranians were ethnically Persian and followers of Shiism; most Afghans were Pashtuns and Sunnis. These differences overrode the strict fundamentalism and repressive rule of the two regimes. From the perspective of Teheran, the Taliban were more of a threat to Iran than a soulmate, especially after Osama bin Laden and his army of Sunni *jihadists* were granted safe haven in Afghanistan.

For American foreign policy makers, however, the old adage "the enemy of my enemy is my friend" did not apply to Iran. The wounds of recent history, including the humiliating hostage crisis of 1979 and charges of America as the "great Satan," were, for U.S. leaders, too deep to heal. Still, Iranian leaders continued to look for a "strategic opening" to Washington.[4] Mohammad Khatami, Iran's president since 1997, pursued a more moderate path in foreign policy than the anti-Western clerics who had dominated the government. He also tried to dampen the popular unrest produced by the political and social restrictions imposed by the Council of Guardians.

Khatami's reform movement and attempts at Iranian-style détente ended in June 2005 with his retirement from power and the election of the conservative mayor of Teheran to Iran's presidency. Mahmoud Ahmadinejad, an overwhelming favorite of Iranian clerics, vowed to reverse Khatami's secular reforms and crack down on those who sought greater political freedoms and contact with the West. The new president rejected his predecessor's moderate foreign policies, including his solicitous posture toward the United States. Ahmadinejad's most intense wrath was directed toward Israel, which must be "wiped off the map," he declared in October 2005. The Jewish holocaust in World War II was a "myth," he said

4. Flynt Leverett, "The Gulf between Us," *New York Times*, January 24, 2006, A21.

The new leader's other priority was nuclear power. He insisted that Iran develop "peaceful" nuclear energy to serve as an alternative to oil. His goal to diversify Iran's energy sources, however peculiar for such an oil-rich nation, struck a chord among many Iranians for whom "nuclear rights" became a popular rallying cry. Thus Iran, a signatory of the Nuclear Non-Proliferation Treaty, resumed the process of uranium enrichment, a vital step in the production of nuclear fuel. In February 2006, the International Atomic Energy Agency (IAEA) declared that its efforts to restrain Iranian nuclear ambitions had proven futile. Ahmadinejad announced in April that Iran had enriched a small amount of uranium, a stepping-stone on the way to nuclear weapons. At this rate, and with a determined government effort, the Islamic republic would have a modest stockpile of "deliverable" nuclear warheads by 2015.

The United States found itself in a bind as its nuclear showdown with Iran unfolded; none of the four policy options was attractive. The first one, an array of U.S. economic sanctions, imposed years earlier after the State Department designated Iran a sponsor of terrorism, had merely provided fodder for anti-American rallies in Teheran and other cities. A second option, large-scale U.S. military action and "regime change," were out of the question because of the ongoing drain on U.S. forces in Iraq and Afghanistan. Even limited military strikes against Iranian nuclear facilities faced widespread opposition in the United States and among its allies. Deploying weapons inspectors from the UN or IAEA would only revisit bad memories of Iraq in the 1990s. And the fourth option, taking diplomatic action against Iran through the UN Security Council, faced the same resistance that confronted Bush in the early stages of the Iraq crisis. The cast of characters and their roles were familiar. The United States, Britain, and France pushed for strict demands for denuclearization and sanctions against Teheran. With their Security Council vetoes in hand, Russia and China preferred softer language and longer negotiations. The net result: inaction.

Not only were Bush's hands tied by his military commitments elsewhere, but he also lacked cordial relations with many U.S. allies because of previous breakdowns over foreign policy. With no better choices, the Bush administration publicly stuck to its policy to "isolate Iran, promote a diplomatic solution to Iran's nuclear ambitions, expose and oppose the regime's support for terrorism, and advance the cause of democracy and human rights within Iran itself." [5] Less clear, however, was whether the White House was secretly planning preemptive military action. Accord-

5. This policy was summed up by Under Secretary of State Nicholas Burns on November 30, 2005, and quoted in Kenneth Katzman, "Iran: U.S. Concerns and Policy Responses," CRS Report for Congress, April 6, 2006, 24, http://fpc.state.gov/documents/organization/64413.pdf (accessed May 9, 2006).

ing to journalist Seymour M. Hersh, Pentagon officials had proposed a large-scale bombing attack against Iran's nuclear sites, possibly with U.S. tactical nuclear weapons. American troops and intelligence agents had already begun "clandestine activities" inside Iran to make way for the coming attack, Hersh further reported.[6] As U.S. officials denied these claims, new tensions in the Arab-Israeli conflict compounded the nuclear deadlock.

An Israeli-Palestinian Stalemate

For the United States, no breakthrough in the Middle East would have had a greater impact than a "final-status" peace treaty between Israel and the Palestinians. There had been little hope for a breakthrough since July 2000, when President Clinton came close but ultimately failed to broker a treaty that would have effectively created a Palestinian state. Israel's prime minister, Ehud Barak, had agreed to the plan, but neither he nor U.S. mediators could elicit compromises from Yasir Arafat, the Palestinian leader. The months after the breakdown of negotiations saw a wave of suicide bombings by Palestinian terrorists, along with a violent crackdown on Palestinian communities by Israeli forces. In Israel, the coming to power in February 2001 of Ariel Sharon, a former military leader and head of the conservative Likud Party, brought a harder line against the Palestinians.

After September 11, Bush's preoccupation with his own war on terrorism removed the United States from what little remained of the peace process. Instead, the president stood by while Sharon built new Jewish settlements in disputed areas as well as a wall across Jerusalem that, both literally and figuratively, cemented the divisions between Israelis and Palestinians. The death of Palestine Liberation Organization (PLO) leader Yassir Arafat in October 2004 altered the balance of political power in the occupied territories, providing opportunities for control to extend beyond Arafat's Fatah Party. His successor, Mahmoud Abbas, tried to continue Arafat's hold on the Palestinian Authority. But decades of resentment against Arafat, rampant government corruption, and depressed economic conditions sparked a popular uprising on the Palestinian "street."

This uprising gained momentum in 2005 and led in January 2006 to electoral victories by Hamas, an Islamist party with a long history of terrorism that had only recently entered the political process. Hamas, which gained control of the Legislative Council in the elections, refused to denounce its calls for Israel's destruction and the use of terrorism. Making matters worse, Israel's government was at the time on automatic

6. Seymour M. Hersh, "The Iran Plans," *New Yorker,* April 17, 2006, 30.

pilot, because Prime Minister Sharon remained in a coma after suffering a stroke three weeks earlier. Sharon was eventually replaced by Ehud Olmert, a more moderate figure whose first order of business was creating a coalition government in Israel. Taking on Hamas and the emboldened Palestinian Authority would come later, along with any other steps forward in the battered Arab-Israeli peace process.

The rise of Hamas to political power represented a rude awakening for the Bush administration. In keeping with his predecessors and with American political tradition, Bush viewed "free and fair" elections as visible proof of democracy in action, illustrated vividly by the purple fingers of Iraqi voters. Such faith, however, was contradicted by the Palestinian elections, which, far from producing a more tolerant and pacific government, led to greater repression of domestic opponents and belligerence toward the voters' sworn enemies.[7] In a sense, electoral democracy "worked" in Palestine, but only by providing political legitimacy to a movement fueled by vengeance. As the Palestinians' plight worsened in response to the shutdown in the flow of foreign aid, their half-century struggle against Israel reached a new boiling point.

Still, Washington's response to this latest crisis in Arab-Israeli relations was muted, perhaps because such strains had become the norm, suggesting that the regional and historic hatreds between Israelis and their neighbors were beyond the point of no return. Another factor was that U.S. support for Israel, the largest recipient of U.S. economic and military aid for decades, had become such an accepted fact of life in American foreign policy, critics were considered anti-Semitic. A prominent critique early in 2006, which attributed the U.S. government's close ties to Jerusalem to the "Israel Lobby" in Washington, provoked such charges.[8] Yet regardless of the sources of amity between the two countries, another fact of life remained: no peace in the Middle East would ever be possible, nor would an end to U.S. disputes in the Persian Gulf or global struggles against Islamist terrorism, in the absence of Israeli reconciliation with its neighbors. This was the true tipping point in American foreign policy.

Economic Strains and Challenges

Despite its military problems and a worldwide recession early in the new millennium, the United States maintained its status as the foremost eco-

7. Further evidence of "illiberal democracy" could be found in Vladimir Putin's Russia, where elections and reelections were followed by crackdowns on the press and widespread government corruption. See Fareed Zakaria, "The Rise of Illiberal Democracy," *Foreign Affairs* (November–December 1997), 23.

8. John J. Mearsheimer and Stephen M. Walt, "The Israel Lobby," *London Review of Books*, March 23, 2006, http://www.lrb.co.uk/v28/n06/mear01_.html (accessed May 10, 2006).

nomic power. American firms produced $11.7 trillion in goods and services in 2004, nearly 30 percent of the $41 trillion gross domestic product (GDP) recorded by all countries. The annual per capita income of Americans also rose to more than $41,000 in 2004, making the United States the third most affluent country after Norway and Switzerland. Together, U.S. firms were by far the world's biggest traders, and the country continued to lead in agricultural production, software, and other major industries. All of this was quite remarkable for a nation whose population of 294 million represented less than 5 percent of the world total.[9]

But in other ways, the United States was losing ground. Its $413 billion budget deficit in fiscal year 2004 was the largest in its history, as was its national debt, which had grown to more than $8 trillion by 2006. Even though the size of the U.S. economy grew steadily in the first years of the twenty-first century, blue-collar workers and minority groups suffered a net decline in real wages.[10] On another economic front, the U.S. trade balance deteriorated as Americans spent far more on goods and services produced overseas than they sold to foreign customers (see Figure 14-1). The $726 billion U.S. trade deficit was larger than all of Russia's economic output in 2005—or that of Mexico and India, for that matter. Globally, after years of dynamic growth most regions of the world suffered an economic downturn after 2000 and projected continued declines for the rest of the decade.

Such struggles were hard to imagine in the boom years of the 1990s, when industrialized and developing countries alike adhered to the "Washington consensus" that embraced markets, not states, as the primary engines of economic growth and prosperity. According to this consensus, economic growth required a combination of pro-business government policies, including restraints on public spending, low tax rates, privatized and deregulated industries, and openness to trade and foreign investment.[11] But by the end of the century, this formula for success was under attack, because the reforms put into place by many developing countries failed to produce the expected economic growth or to relieve the endemic poverty of their citizens. At the same time, the

9. World Bank, *World Development Report 2006: Equity and Development* (New York: Oxford University Press, 2006), 292–299.

10. According to the Federal Reserve Board, the richest 10 percent of Americans enjoyed rising incomes and an average net worth of $3.1 million in 2004, but those in the bottom 25 percent fell so far behind that their average net worth was a *negative* $1,400. Brian K. Bucks, Arthur B. Kennickell, and Kevin B. Moore, "Recent Changes in U.S. Family Finances: Evidence from the 2001 and 2004 Survey of Consumer Finances," *Federal Reserve Bulletin* (February 2006): A1–A38, http://www.federalreserve.gov/PUBS/oss/oss2/2004/bull0206.pdf (accessed May 6, 2006).

11. See John Williamson, *Latin American Adjustment: How Much Has Happened?* (Washington, D.C.: Institute for International Economics, 1990).

FIGURE 14-1 U.S. Trade Balance, 1996–2004

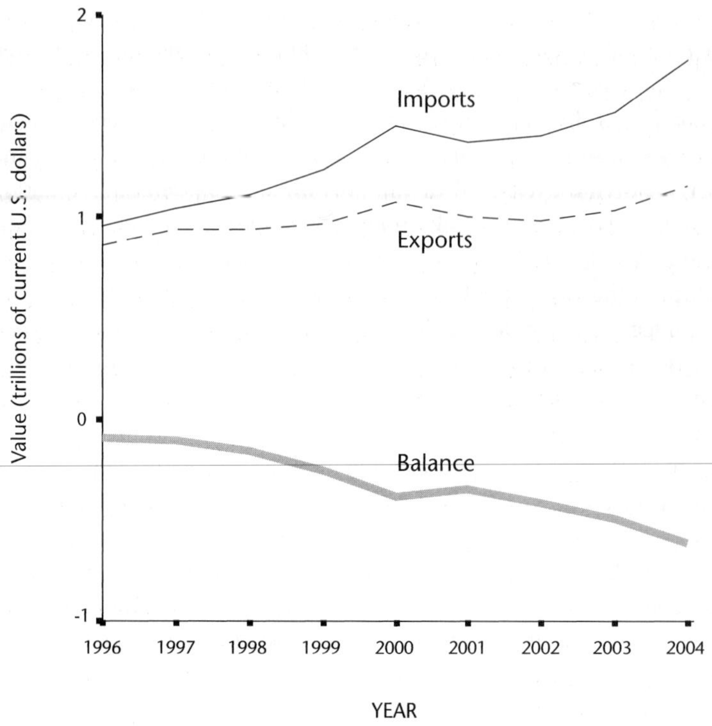

Source: U.S. Census Bureau, http://www.census.gov/foreign-trade/statistics/historical/gands.txt (accessed May 6, 2006).

economic "miracle" in East Asia proved to be an illusion; governments in the region found themselves plagued by widespread corruption and the mismanagement of assets. These developments left citizens disillusioned in many parts of the world and ready to experiment with other economic models that did not rely on the good graces of Adam Smith's "invisible hand."

EAST ASIA'S REVERSAL OF FORTUNE

The global economic recession of the late 1990s began in the same place the global boom began—Japan, South Korea, and other East Asian states. A decade earlier these states had become role models for other newly industrialized countries (NICs) by plunging into global trade markets (see Chapter 9). The region's civil societies had long been valued for their emphases on education, discipline, and family values. East

Asian governments were acclaimed in financial circles for maintaining fiscal discipline, encouraging high rates of savings, and protecting private property. This record contrasted sharply with those of other developing regions, where state intervention and isolation from trade and capital markets had become the standard, albeit ineffective, means of achieving economic growth.

In 1997 the East Asian miracle gave way to a crisis that threatened to slow or reverse worldwide economic growth. Problems were first reported in Japan, which faced falling demand for its exports, rising debts, and an unstable currency. Thailand's government devalued its currency, prompting the rampant withdrawal of capital from the country. South Korea and Indonesia caught the "Asian flu" in 1998 as banks recalled outstanding debts, many of which could not be repaid. Then the Russian economy, already in disarray, suffered from a series of currency devaluations and delayed debt payments. As the crisis spread, economic globalization assumed a new and darker form. The high level of interdependence among the world's market economies, once thought to be a blessing, turned out to be a curse as well.

The crisis originated from two closely related sources. The first involved structural problems within the East Asian countries themselves, which were ill equipped to handle the rapid economic growth and inflows of foreign capital. Inflated expectations of even greater prosperity produced a building boom that quickly exceeded the level of demand. Making matters worse, a small group of government bureaucrats, bankers, and industrialists practiced the same "crony capitalism" that had become commonplace in Russia and Eastern Europe since the fall of communism.

These internal problems set the stage for disaster when combined with the second source of trouble: the massive and largely uncontrollable flow of private capital into East Asia. More than $200 billion poured into the region in the mid-1990s as private investors, bond traders, and currency speculators sought to share in the economic boom. But at the first signs of stress, these same investors just as quickly pulled their money out. Large-scale capital flight compounded the economic calamity and forced Western governments, along with the International Monetary Fund (IMF), World Bank, and Asian Development Bank, to provide more than $100 billion in emergency relief to Thailand, South Korea, and Indonesia. The relief efforts were required to prevent an even worse "contagion" effect in other areas.

The United States was hardly an innocent bystander in this crisis. President Clinton's efforts to permit the free flow of capital across national borders helped to trigger the influx—and subsequent exodus—of foreign capital. In 1996 alone, foreign investors pumped $93 billion into just five countries: Indonesia, Malaysia, the Philippines, South Korea, and Thailand. It was no coincidence that these countries became the primary victims of the regional economic crisis, and the first to line up for relief. Without outside help, their economies would have been set back for decades. Even with the aid, East Asia had lost its luster.

These economic strains coincided with rising tensions between the United States and China, whose communist government sustained rapid economic growth by embracing capitalism. China's future course became uncertain after the February 1997 death of Deng Xiaoping, the reformist leader who had succeeded Mao Zedong two decades earlier. Deng's successor, Jiang Zemin, followed the same formula of economic reform that had proven so effective in the past, while continuing to crush political dissent and violate human rights. Jiang dispelled any doubts about his iron rule by cracking down on pro-democracy activists and arresting followers of a popular spiritual movement, Falun Gong. State visits between Jiang and Russian leaders produced tirades against U.S. imperialism reminiscent of the Cold War.

These developments led to predictions in the United States of a "coming conflict with China." [12] According to this view, as China became stronger economically and militarily and as its leaders appealed to nationalism as a substitute for communism, they would assert China's rightful place as Asia's dominant power. Throughout his presidency, Clinton had maintained the more optimistic view that "engaging" China would produce greater domestic freedoms there and more cooperation with the United States. Clinton adhered to this view so strongly that in 2000 he persuaded Congress to normalize U.S.-Sino trade relations. The move was widely supported by U.S. firms that sought greater access to China's massive domestic market and ultimately resulted in China's membership in the World Trade Organization (WTO) in 2001. Yet despite this breakthrough, Beijing continued its repressive domestic policies and resistance to U.S. foreign policies.

As noted previously, China was the only country to emerge from the first post–Cold War decade as a potential rival of the United States. When George W. Bush entered the White House in January 2001, he adopted a hard line toward Beijing, which he considered a strategic "competitor" rather than a "partner." Bush openly criticized Chinese leaders for imposing rigid population control measures that included mass abortions and the forced sterilization of women. And he accused the same leaders of exporting sophisticated weapons to repressive and unstable countries such as Iran. The terrorist attacks of September 11,

12. Richard Bernstein and Ross H. Munro, *The Coming Conflict with China* (New York: Viking, 1997).

2001, however, prompted the United States and China to find common ground in the war on terrorism. Bush looked to Jiang and his successor, Hu Jintao, for help in capturing terrorists and preventing their state sponsors from acquiring ballistic missiles or weapons of mass destruction.[13] In return for its assistance, the Chinese government secured pledges by the White House to restrain from criticizing its domestic policies and even to support Beijing's bid to host the 2008 Olympics.

Underlying this warming of relations were the deepening economic ties between the two countries. Both sides knew well that their global objectives depended on business as usual, at least for the moment. Hu's visit to Washington in April 2006 elicited the usual pledges of security cooperation and greater bilateral trade. Such goodwill, however, did not mask the many potential conflicts of interest between the two superpowers.

RISING DISCONTENT IN LATIN AMERICA

East Asia's economic slowdown soon spread to all parts of the world. Especially hard-hit were the developing countries that chronically lagged behind the industrialized world and had barely tasted the fruits of prosperity even during boom years. In Africa, living standards remained the world's lowest as the AIDS epidemic and ethnic warfare left a trail of death and suffering across the continent. The nations of South Asia, also mired in poverty, fell victim to the escalating violence in the Middle East and the nuclear rivalry between India and Pakistan, which precluded any cooperation on regional economic development.

Continuing economic distress in these regions not only contradicted the forecasts of the World Bank and other financial institutions, but also heightened public demands for new economic policies that would produce material equality as well economic liberty. To leaders in some developing countries, Japan's "neo-mercantile" model of tariffs and collusion between state and corporate managers was appealing even after the bursting of the East Asian bubble. Others were drawn to socialist alternatives that called for higher taxes on the wealthy, nationalized industries, and greater welfare spending.

Economic discontent was particularly acute in Latin America, which had experienced robust economic growth in the 1990s.[14] Heightened prosperity was attributed to several factors, including the booming U.S. economy and the insatiable appetite of Americans for foreign goods.

13. Hu rose to the presidency in 2003 and continued his predecessor's general policies of economic modernization and rigid control over China's government and society.

14. By 2000, annual per capita incomes stood at just over $6,000 in South America and $4,000 in Central America. World Bank, *World Development Indicators 2002,* http://www.worldbank.org/data/wdi2002 (accessed May 6, 2006).

Also credited for the economic boom in Latin America was the adoption of pro-business policies by many governments that had embraced the Washington consensus. The benefits from this economic growth, however, were unevenly distributed. Only a minority of citizens enjoyed higher living standards; most continued to suffer from inadequate housing, high infant mortality, hunger, illiteracy, and lack of economic opportunities. The widening gap between rich and poor created new strains between the large but disenfranchised lower classes and the small but powerful elite—the bankers and industrialists who were more closely tied to their counterparts in the industrialized states than to their fellow citizens.

As the new millennium began, many political leaders in Latin America had little to show for their faith in "the magic of the market." But, in reality, they had little choice but to embrace the Washington consensus. Facing large foreign debts, devalued currencies, and deteriorating living standards, these governments turned for relief to the International Monetary Fund, which imposed spending cutbacks and required countries to open their domestic markets to foreign goods and services. The reforms theoretically improved prospects for long-term economic growth, but in the short term they worsened many citizens' living conditions. Deep spending cuts balanced government budgets but left schools and hospitals in disrepair. The opening of domestic markets brought foreign goods and services to Latin America, but forced domestic firms out of business. This region thus became especially vulnerable to global economic shocks, particularly the crisis in East Asia. Such vulnerability to ruptures in the world economy was precisely what the "new international economic order" of the 1970s had sought to prevent.

These problems led to a populist backlash and political turmoil in South America. In Venezuela, Hugo Chávez came to power in 1998 after promising to turn the country's vast oil wealth over to the poor. In Ecuador, army colonel Lucio Gutierrez was elected president in November 2002 on a platform to wipe out the "corrupt oligarchy" that had previously ruled the country. Meanwhile, Brazilian voters elected Luiz Inácio Lula da Silva, a former union leader and outspoken advocate of socialism, as their president. Like Chávez and Gutierrez, "Lula" opposed the U.S.-led plan for a Free Trade Area of the Americas (FTAA) that would extend the North American Free Trade Agreement (NAFTA) across the Western Hemisphere. His threats to stop repaying Brazil's $260 billion in foreign debt alarmed American leaders, who already had committed billions to rescue Argentina from default.

President Bush had pledged to make Latin America a foreign policy priority when he took office, and he symbolized that priority by holding his first state meeting with Mexican president Vicente Fox. But then other foreign policy problems captured the White House's attention, such as the September 11, 2001, terrorist attacks and the wars in Afghanistan and Iraq that followed. Although these conflicts were not directly related to Latin America, the economic rupture that followed September 11 was devastating to the region. Even so, Bush met rarely with Mexico's president, and what discussions they did have centered on border controls rather than economic cooperation. Beyond their own homeland security, only the threat posed by "narco-terrorists" in South America concerned American foreign policy makers.

Latin America's new era of discontent continued into Bush's second term. With incomes sagging across the region, "free trade" became synonymous with American domination. Only the United States could flood the entire hemisphere with its agricultural surplus, which resulted in part from government subsidies to farmers. The low commodity prices that resulted from oversupply hurt Latin America's farmers, who at the same time were denied entry to the U.S. market for many of their goods. If there were any doubts about the FTAA's unpopularity, they were laid to rest in Argentina, where thirty-four heads of state from across the Western Hemisphere met in November 2005. Rioters smashed storefronts on the streets of Mar del Plata, and while Bush and other leaders huddled in a secluded resort, Hugo Chávez taunted the U.S. president and eulogized the trade pact before 25,000 supporters at a nearby soccer stadium. "FTAA is dead, and we, the people of the Americas, are the ones who buried it," he declared. The summit's final communiqué, issued the next day, simply noted that "conditions do not exist" to bring the free-trade zone to life.[15]

By this point in Bush's presidency, two key principles of American foreign policy were coming under assault. The first principle—that free elections necessarily produce moderate and amicable leaders—was refuted by voters across Latin America as well as in Iran and the Palestinian territories. The second principle—that free trade produces "win-win" outcomes for sellers and buyers alike—was rejected by developing countries that could not compete with the more advanced economies. But abandoning these principles, the roots of which ran deeply through American history and across its society, was unthinkable for the United States. The nation's very identity was based on such principles and their respective models of government and commerce rather than on a common ethnic background, religion, or language. It was no surprise, then,

15. The United States and Central American governments had agreed to form a free trade area in the region earlier in 2005, although the scale of this compact was far more modest than the proposed FTAA.

that American leaders stuck to their guns, and to their traditional style of foreign policy.

Threats to Democracy at Home

As detailed in Chapter 13, U.S. military forces encountered constant tactical problems in their nation-building missions in Afghanistan and Iraq. The insurgents, unseen but able to strike at the time and place of their choosing, proved adept at asymmetric warfare. A weak sense of national unity in both countries frustrated American attempts to train new security forces. The challenges facing the United States were not confined to the battlefield, however, as the war on terrorism unfolded. A series of legal and ethnical controversies stemming from the war further clouded the prospects for success. These problems, which struck at the core of America's righteous self-image, were particularly troubling in view of its stated mission to bring democratic government, tolerance, and protections of human rights to the war zones overseas.

A primary concern of many Americans was the USA PATRIOT Act, a wide-ranging measure approved by Congress and signed by the president within weeks of the September 11 attacks. The act eased government restrictions on domestic surveillance and intelligence gathering within the United States, allowing federal agents to gain access more readily to citizens' phone and medical records, business transactions, and e-mail messages. The act also allowed for more "sneak-and-peak" searches of private property without the owners' knowledge and prohibited those who divulged personal information, including doctors and librarians, from disclosing the searches to anyone. The act, which reinforced other new curbs on immigration, travel, and public access to government documents, also made it easier for federal agents to detain and deport foreign citizens suspected of either being or supporting terrorists. Despite its complexity and enormous scope, the act passed both houses of Congress without the lengthy committee hearings and deliberations that normally occur in the legislative process. Bush signed the legislation on October 26, less than seven weeks after the terrorist attacks.

Although it was defended as an essential step toward protecting the United States from another terrorist attack, the PATRIOT Act alarmed many citizens and groups. Seven state legislatures and 396 local governments, including those of New York City, Los Angeles, and Chicago, passed resolutions declaring the act a violation of civil liberties. The city council of Arcata, California, passed an ordinance in April 2003 that made voluntary compliance with the act *illegal.* Critics charged that the act violated the U.S. Constitution's Fourth Amendment, which prohibits the government from violating "[t]he right of the people to be secure in their persons, houses, papers, and effects, against unreasonable searches and seizures." Some of the PATRIOT Act's provisions were scheduled to expire in 2005, but after two extensions Congress renewed the act in March 2006 with minor changes.

Fears of a "police state" were raised further in December 2005, when it was revealed that the National Security Agency (NSA) had eavesdropped on thousands of the international phone calls and e-mails of Americans since 2002 without permission from the courts.[16] The highly secretive NSA, located near Baltimore, had long been engaged in electronic surveillance overseas. But domestic spying was much more controversial because of the great importance Americans attached to privacy and freedom from "big brother." When federal officials were found to be spying on civil rights advocates and Vietnam War protesters decades earlier, Congress had passed the Federal Intelligence Surveillance Act of 1978, which required investigators to seek warrants from a new secret court.

The domestic spying was revealed by government agents who were concerned they were being asked to break the law. The Bush administration argued that most "monitored" phone calls and e-mail messages involved suspected al Qaeda members or supporters and that gaining warrants in each case would burden investigators. Attorney General Alberto R. Gonzales further claimed that Congress had effectively approved domestic spying in the joint resolution it passed after September 11 authorizing the president to "use all necessary and appropriate force against those nations, organizations, and persons he determines planned, authorized, committed, or aided in the attacks." Gonzales also argued that the president had authority, as commander in chief, to protect the United States as he saw fit. Although critics rejected the claim that the war on terrorism allowed for such a broad extension of presidential power, they were unable to prevent the NSA from continuing its program of domestic surveillance.

Questions were also raised about the U.S. government's treatment of captives in the war on terrorism. In November 2001, Bush determined that captured enemy forces would not be considered "prisoners of war," because most did not formally serve foreign governments but were instead linked, however loosely, to al Qaeda or other private terrorist groups. As "unlawful combatants," these captives would not be granted the protections reserved for prisoners of war under the 1949 Geneva

16. James Risen and Eric Lichtblau, "Bush Secretly Lifted Some Limits on Spying in U.S. After 9/11, Officials Say," *New York Times,* December 15, 2005, A1. The White House had asked the *Times* not to run the story, fearing it would jeopardize intelligence operations, but the newspaper published the report after a year of "additional reporting."

Conventions to which the United States was a party.[17] Instead, the "detainees" would be considered ongoing risks to U.S. national security and thus would be subject to indefinite detention without being charged or granted legal representation. The president's military order provided few details about where those detainees would be held or how they would be interrogated.

A partial answer to the first question came in January 2002, when the Pentagon opened a detention center at Guantánamo Bay, Cuba. About five hundred suspected terrorists were transported to the facility, located near a U.S. naval station operated in Cuba since 1898.[18] The "high-value" detainees, presumably linked to al Qaeda, had been hooded, chained to their seats, and transported the eight thousand miles from Afghanistan, and later from Iran. The extent of the interrogations that followed was unknown, although U.S. officials acknowledged that "coercive" techniques were occasionally used to gain information from the captives. Anticipating legal challenges to these techniques, the Justice Department interpreted the 1994 Convention on Torture, which defined the practice, as "any act by which severe pain or suffering, whether physical or mental, is intentionally inflicted on a person . . . [by] a public official or other person acting in an official capacity." To the Justice Department, the U.S. government's treatment of captives did not reach the threshold of "severe" pain: "Where the pain is physical, it must be of an intensity akin to that which accompanies serious physical injury such as death or organ failure. . . . [T]here is a significant range of acts that, though they might constitute cruel, inhuman, or degrading treatment or punishment, fail to rise to the level of torture." [19]

The revelations in May 2004 of abuses at Iraq's Abu Ghraib prison suggested that the Bush administration had put its restrictive definition of torture into practice. The White House insisted the military prison guards would be punished in cases of flagrant abuse, but that the United States would continue to use coercive techniques to extract information.

17. The United States had also ratified the International Covenant on Civil and Political Rights, and in 1948 was a founding signatory of the Universal Declaration of Human Rights, which declared in Article 5, "No one shall be subjected to torture, or to cruel, inhuman, or degrading treatment or punishment."

18. The whereabouts of other detention centers was less clear, although American officials later confirmed that several prisons were operating secretly in Eastern Europe as well as in Afghanistan and Thailand. Dana Priest, "CIA Holds Terror Suspects in Secret Prisons," *Washington Post,* November 2, 2005, A1.

19. Jay S. Bybee, "Memorandum for Alberto R. Gonzales, Counsel to the President," U.S. Department of Justice, August 1, 2002, http://files.findlaw.com/news.findlaw.com/nytimes/docs/doj/bybee80102mem.pdf (accessed May 6, 2006), 46. The memorandum further concluded that "under the circumstances of the war against al Qaeda and its allies," the restrictions on the president in handling prisoners "may be unconstitutional," and that even if clear violations of the act occurred, "necessity or self-defense could provide justification that would eliminate criminal liability."

In February 2006, the UN Commission on Human Rights found that the evidence of abuse at Guantánamo Bay warranted closing the facility and requiring the prisoners there to be either formally charged and tried or released. Unsurprisingly, Bush rejected the UN findings.

This was not the first time the military's efforts on behalf of democracy overseas were accompanied by domestic threats to democracy. During World War II, 126,000 Japanese Americans—more than half of them born in the United States—were forced into internment camps. The Vietnam War, as noted earlier, gave birth to sweeping restrictions on press freedoms and widespread domestic surveillance. Nor was the United States unique among democracies in holding suspected terrorists for extended periods without charges or trials; such practices also had been adopted in Britain, India, and South Africa. Still, the latest revelations were acutely problematic because of the White House's emphasis on democratic freedoms and human rights. "The United States, as the sole superpower, has a special responsibility for shaping the world in the twenty-first century," observed Richard Goldstone, chief war crimes prosecutor in Yugoslavia and Rwanda. "It can only hope to establish an international rule of law and to encourage democratic forms of government if it sets a good example at home." [20]

Global Orders and American Power

The many dilemmas facing American foreign policy today reflect the uneasy relationship between the anarchic international system and the peculiar cultural and political traditions of the United States. Tensions between these systemic and domestic pressures are visible daily as foreign policy makers confront an international system undergoing constant changes in its structure, power relations, and the behavior of its governing units, nation-states. The relationship between this system and the United States, which has always been marked by tensions and contradictions, is a reciprocal one. Although the system creates the boundaries of choice for American foreign policy makers, the United States shapes the international system in profound ways as well, and it has especially done so during the period covered in this book—the post–World War II era in which the United States has been the world's preeminent power.

Four types of international order have existed in modern history: imperial, Westphalian, constitutional, and hegemonic. Each order has its

20. Richard Goldstone, "Combating Terrorism and Protecting Civil Liberties," *Human Rights in the 'War on Terror,'* ed. Richard A. Wilson (New York: Cambridge University Press, 2005), 165–166.

own design for regulating political behavior and commerce within its domain, and each has a distinctive design for maintaining peace among states. The United States has experienced all four, which have coexisted in various combinations since the American colonies launched their drive for independence from Britain.

In an *imperial* order, a rising power establishes territorial and political control beyond its own borders.[21] The subjugated territories thus lose their claims to sovereignty, the defining element of statehood, both in terms of their internal decision-making authority and in terms of their external relations with foreign governments. Such an order, which previously had been established only at the regional level, achieves peace through a combination of the imperial ruler's unquestioned predominance, the compliance of the ruler's subjects, and the absence of a competing empire or other challenger to its dominion. The American colonies experienced and ultimately overcame this type of order as subjects of the British Empire.

The *Westphalian* order, built from the wreckage of the Thirty Years' War, established a system of nation-states and endowed them with the internal and external powers of sovereignty just noted. This order, based on the 1648 Treaty of Westphalia, originated on a regional scale in central Europe, but later it assumed global proportions and still provides the organizing framework of the state system. War among these states is always possible; peace arises from a balance of power, or equilibrium, among the most powerful nation-states comprising the system. It is commonly believed that a multipolar balance of power contributed to the European "long peace" that extended for a century after the Napoleonic Wars. The United States benefited from the stalemate among the European powers and their retreat from North America, which allowed U.S. leaders to focus on internal development and western expansion. A bipolar balance of power during the Cold War, fortified by nuclear weapons, prevented a direct clash between the United States and the Soviet Union.

The *constitutional* order emerged after World War I, but it took full form after World War II. Built on the structural features of the Westphalian order, the new order sought to mitigate the old order's primary defect: anarchy, or the lack of centralized political authority at the global level. American leaders after World War II took the lead in creating a constitutional order, which established rules of behavior to be promoted by international institutions such as the UN and the World Bank. By using its vast resources to create such a system, the U.S. government "locked in" its advantages while enlisting more partners in its pursuit of

21. See Michael W. Doyle, *Empires* (Ithaca, N.Y.: Cornell University Press, 1986).

a globalized state system of democracies and free markets. This order encourages peace because "the power capabilities of relevant states are highly constrained by interlocking institutions and binding agreements." [22] The prospects for peace are further enhanced by the tendency of democratic states—by their nature drawn toward such an international order—not to wage war against one another. A constitutional order also improves the prospects for solving collective problems, such as global warming, as well as responding to humanitarian disasters, such as the Asian tsunamis and the genocide of black Africans in the Darfur region of Sudan.[23]

Finally, a *hegemonic* order possesses the same coercive elements as an imperial order, but it allows weaker states to retain their legal sovereignty and control over domestic affairs. The weaker states become part of the hegemon's "sphere of influence." Peaceful relations within the sphere are encouraged, and the hegemon protects its nations from attack or intimidation by other great powers. These weaker states "despair of modifying the status quo, and yet the hegemonic state does not try to absorb the units reduced to impotence. It does not abuse hegemony, it respects the external forms of state independence, it does not aspire to empire." [24] Without explicitly using the term, the Bush Doctrine called for a hegemonic world order with the United States at its hub.

Hegemonic control is not new to the United States, which has maintained a sphere of influence over Latin America and the Caribbean since the proclamation of the Monroe Doctrine in 1823. The relative stability within these regions for nearly two centuries, the freedom of its states from invasion or renewed colonization, and their general adherence to U.S. foreign policy goals are all products of regional U.S. hegemony. In seeking to globalize the scope of U.S. hegemony, Bush's concern was not the feudal lords of Europe and Asia—the adversaries to whom the Monroe Doctrine had spoken—rather, it was the terrorist groups and "rogue states" that threatened American interests and those of its allies. The U.S. government's bid for a hegemonic order was also motivated by its view that intergovernmental organizations, which played such a vital role in the constitutional order, were ganging up on America's global ambitions.

22. G. John Ikenberry, *After Victory: Institutions, Strategic Restraint, and the Rebuilding of Order after Major Wars* (Princeton, N.J.: Princeton University Press, 2001), 36.

23. While the U.S. government considered the deaths of more than 200,000 Sudanese citizens at the hands of government militias beginning in February 2003 to be genocide, Bush did not push for UN military intervention without the support of Sudan's Islamist government. The African Union, a newly created regional organization, proved unable to enforce a cease-fire in Darfur.

24. Raymond Aron, *Peace and War: A Theory of International Relations* (New York: Praeger, 1966), 151.

To its proponents, a U.S.-led hegemonic order would overcome the shortcomings of the other three. An imperial order was unattainable on a global scale without provoking a cataclysmic world war. The turbulence associated with Westphalian anarchy could be held in check only by the overwhelming power of the United States. Finally, globalized U.S. hegemony would improve on the constitutional order by preserving the nation's sovereignty even as it freed Washington of the potential persecution of voting majorities in intergovernmental organizations. Unlike its European counterparts, which were comfortable with the notion of "pooling" sovereignty, the U.S. government strongly resisted efforts to limit its political authority and freedom to maneuver.

The post–September 11 grand strategy of primacy and preemption called for a U.S.-led hegemonic order, although not by name. Perhaps this omission stemmed from hegemony's abstract nature and from advocates' concern that the concept would be unfamiliar to the Bush Doctrine's mass audience. More likely, however, proponents did not wish to convey the message that the United States would exploit its subordinates as other dominant states had done. The doctrine instead offered weaker states shelter in a community of nations with shared ideals and interests. The United States would provide collective goods, such as military security and the tools for economic growth, while upholding the political rights of the citizens under its control. In short, this was to be a "benevolent global hegemony" intended to inspire faith, not fear.[25]

To these four international orders a fifth may be added—*federation*—with the significant caveat that it has never existed and is unlikely to in the future. Still, such an order is worth considering, because it may be viewed as a logical extension, or even the culmination, of the constitutional order that persists today even after being shaken by the U.S. bid for global hegemony. A federal order would resolve the problem of systemic anarchy by creating a single government that would replace those of nation-states. It would presumably build upon the framework of the UN and other intergovernmental bodies, extending their legal control and ultimately permitting them to supercede the sovereignty of all states.

Such an encroachment on state sovereignty was precisely the outcome foreseen and resisted by American leaders as they blocked efforts to create an International Criminal Court, opposed international bans on land mines and nuclear testing, and renounced the Kyoto Protocol. They feared that American officials would be subject to civil and crimi-

25. This term "benevolent global hegemony" was coined midway through the Clinton years by two prominent neoconservatives who later enjoyed strong influence in the Bush administration. See William Kristol and Robert Kagan, "Toward a Neo-Reaganite Foreign Policy," *Foreign Affairs* (July–August 1996): 18–32.

nal prosecution if they signed on to such agreements but later failed to live up to them. Paradoxically, the Bush Doctrine's hegemonic ambitions stemmed in part from the threats to sovereignty posed by the same institutions that were, in large measure, created by the United States after World War II.[26] The UN, the Bretton Woods agencies, and other global institutions would not exist today were it not for American leadership more than a half-century ago. Now these institutions had matured, spawned new institutions, and reached deeper into the affairs of nations, including the United States.

The shape of tomorrow's global order will be determined in large measure by the manner in which American leaders wield their power today. Historical experience suggests that the conduct of any dominant state dictates the extent to which lesser powers either "bandwagon" with that state or "balance" against it. When the most powerful state is "unalterably aggressive," Stephen M. Walt observes, "other states are unlikely to bandwagon." [27]

At present, no country is capable of challenging the United States alone. Russia remains in disarray, with economic output of less than 4 percent of the U.S. level and a government, under Vladimir Putin's tightening control, that is dismantling whatever is left of its postcommunist civil society. China, despite its arms buildup and dynamic economy, has more immediate priorities related to managing domestic demands. Historic tensions between these two countries, combined with the continued inability of the European Union to devise a "common" foreign policy, discourage collective efforts to counter the United States.[28] Thus, although recent actions by the United States have provoked considerable dismay around the world, most nations remain on the American bandwagon.

The continued flaunting of American power, however, is likely to produce defiance rather than compliance with the nation's global objectives. Power plays by any state, no matter how benevolent, inevitably produce backlash even from those who claim to share the hegemon's values. Such is the logic of the international system, whose members have been taught through historical experience to resist a concentration of political power regardless of its source. Indeed, such was the instinct of American leaders during the nation's rise as a great power. For the

26. This is a central argument of Steven W. Hook in *U.S. Foreign Policy: The Paradox of World Power* (Washington, D.C.: CQ Press, 2005).

27. Stephen M. Walt, *The Origins of Alliances* (Ithaca, N.Y.: Cornell University Press, 1987), 26.

28. As a percentage of economic output, the defense spending of most EU countries has steadily fallen in recent years, hardly the sign of a rising hegemon. Keir A. Leiber and Gerard Alexander, "Waiting for Balancing: Why the World Is Not Pushing Back," *International Security* (summer 2005): 120.

United States to expect others to accept a unipolar world indefinitely is, at best, an exercise in naïveté and, at worst, a sign of arrogance.

Amid all of this turbulence, American foreign policy continues to reveal the persistence of a distinctive national style. The "promised land" that aspires to lead by example is also the "crusader state" that seeks, often aggressively, to remake other states in its image.[29] Despite their contradictions, both impulses stem from a sense of national exceptionalism that views the United States, in the language of the Monroe Doctrine, as "essentially different" from other countries. With much of the world poised anxiously on the brink of war or peace, poverty or prosperity, the choices made by the United States will be crucial not only for the realization of its global ambitions but also for the fate of all nations.

29. Walter McDougall, *Promised Land, Crusader State: The American Encounter with the World since 1776* (Boston: Mariner Books, 1997). Also see Walter Russell Mead, *Special Providence: American Foreign Policy and How It Changed the World* (New York: Knopf, 2001).

APPENDIX A

U.S. Administrations since World War II

President	*Secretary of State*	*Secretary of Defense*	*National Security Adviser*
Harry Truman 1945–1953	Edward Stettinius James Byrnes George Marshall Dean Acheson	James Forrestal Louis Johnson George Marshall Robert Lovett	
Dwight Eisenhower 1953–1961	John Dulles Christian Herter	Charles Wilson Neil McElroy Thomas Gates	Robert Cutler Dillon Anderson Robert Cutler Gordon Gray
John Kennedy 1961–1963	Dean Rusk	Robert McNamara	McGeorge Bundy
Lyndon Johnson 1963–1969	Dean Rusk	Robert McNamara Clark Clifford	McGeorge Bundy Walt Rostow
Richard Nixon 1969–1974	William Rogers Henry Kissinger	Melvin Laird Elliot Richardson James Schlesinger	Henry Kissinger
Gerald Ford 1974–1977	Henry Kissinger	James Schlesinger Donald Rumsfeld	Henry Kissinger Brent Scowcroft
Jimmy Carter 1977–1981	Cyrus Vance Edmund Muskie	Harold Brown	Zbigniew Brzezinski
Ronald Reagan 1981–1989	Alexander Haig George Shultz	Caspar Weinberger Frank Carlucci	Richard Allen William Clark Robert McFarlane John Poindexter Frank Carlucci Colin Powell
George Bush 1989–1993	James Baker Lawrence Eagleburger	Richard Cheney	Brent Scowcroft
Bill Clinton 1993–2001	Warren Christopher Madeleine Albright	Les Aspin William Perry William Cohen	Anthony Lake Samuel Berger
George W. Bush 2001–	Colin Powell Condoleezza Rice	Donald Rumsfeld	Condoleezza Rice Stephen Hadley

Appendix B
Chronology of Significant Events

1945 Yalta Conference seeks to organize postwar world.
World War II with Germany ends.
World War II with Japan ends after two atomic bombs are dropped on Japan.
President Franklin D. Roosevelt dies; vice president Harry S. Truman succeeds him.
United Nations is established.
Soviet military forces occupy Poland, Romania, Bulgaria, Hungary, and Czechoslovakia.

1946 United States confronts the Soviet Union over Iran; Moscow withdraws its troops.
Winston Churchill, Britain's wartime prime minister, delivers "iron curtain" speech at Fulton, Missouri, warning of Soviet threat.
George F. Kennan, a U.S. Foreign Service officer, provides the government with the analysis that becomes the basis of the containment policy of the Soviet Union.

1947 Truman Doctrine commits the United States to assisting Greece and Turkey.
Secretary of State George Marshall, formerly U.S. Army chief of staff and architect of victory during World War II, devises plan for the economic recovery of Western Europe.
India becomes independent from British colonial rule.

1948 Soviet coup d'état takes place in Czechoslovakia.
Soviets blockade all ground traffic from West Germany to West Berlin; the Western airlift starts.
Vandenberg resolution in U.S. Senate commits American support to the Brussels Pact of self-defense.
U.S. Congress passes Marshall Plan.
North and South Korea are established.
State of Israel is established and receives immediate U.S. recognition.
Truman wins upset election.
Stalin expels Yugoslavia's Josip Tito from communist bloc.

1949 North Atlantic Treaty Organization (NATO) is formed.
Soviet Union ends Berlin blockade.
East and West Germany are established.
Soviet Union explodes atomic bomb.
Nationalist China collapses and People's Republic of China (PRC) is established.
U.S. troops are withdrawn from South Korea.
Truman announces Point Four foreign aid program for developing countries.

1950 Soviet Union and communist China sign thirty-year treaty of mutual assistance.
North Korea crosses the thirty-eighth parallel and attacks South Korea.
United States intervenes on behalf of South Korea.
Communist China intervenes after U.S. forces advance into North Korea toward China's frontier.
Sen. Joseph McCarthy begins his attacks on the government for treason and "coddling communism."

1951 Gen. Dwight D. Eisenhower is appointed supreme allied commander in Europe; Truman sends U.S. forces to Europe.

U.S.-Japanese mutual security pact is signed.
Truman fires Gen. Douglas MacArthur in Korea for proposing that the United States attack communist China.
European Coal and Steel Community (ECSC) is formed.

1952 Eisenhower is elected president.
Greece and Turkey join NATO.
Britain tests its first atomic weapon.

1953 Joseph Stalin dies.
Armistice negotiated along thirty-eighth parallel in Korea.
Soviet Union intervenes in East Germany to quell revolt.

1954 United States explodes first hydrogen bomb.
France is defeated at Dien Bien Phu in Indochina.
United States threatens to intervene in Indochina.
At the Geneva Conference, Vietnam is partitioned at the seventeenth parallel.
Southeast Asia Treaty Organization (SEATO) is formed.
U.S.-Korean pact is signed to prevent a renewal of the war.
U.S.–Nationalist China defense treaty is signed.
U.S. Central Intelligence Agency (CIA) overthrows Guatemala's left-wing government.

1955 Communist China shells the Nationalist Chinese (Taiwanese) islands of Quemoy and Matsu.
Formosa resolution authorizes Eisenhower to use force, if necessary, to protect Taiwan against a possible communist Chinese invasion.
Middle East Treaty Organization (Baghdad Pact) is formed.
West Germany joins NATO, and Soviets establish "their NATO," called the Warsaw Treaty Organization.

1956 United States withdraws offer to help finance Egypt's Aswan High Dam.
Egypt nationalizes the Suez Canal.
Suez War breaks out after Israel attacks Egypt; France and Britain intervene.
UN forces are sent to Egypt to keep the peace between Israel and Egypt.
Soviets suppress Hungarian revolt and almost intervene in Poland.
Soviet leader Nikita Khrushchev attacks Stalin at twentieth Communist Party Congress.

1957 Soviet Union tests intercontinental ballistic missile (ICBM).
Soviets launch two <I>Sputniks,</I> or satellites, into space.
British test hydrogen bomb.
Eisenhower Doctrine commits the United States to assisting Middle East countries that resist communist aggression or states closely tied to the Soviet Union, such as Egypt.

1958 United States lands marines in Lebanon, and Britain lands paratroopers in Jordan after Iraqi revolution.
Soviet Union declares it will end the four-power occupation of Berlin and turn West Berlin into a "free city."
European Economic Community (Common Market) is established.
First of several Berlin crises erupts.
Communist China shells Quemoy and Matsu again.

1959 Khrushchev and Eisenhower meet at Camp David over Berlin issue.
Fidel Castro seizes power in Cuba.
Central Treaty Organization (CENTO) replaces the Baghdad Pact.

1960 Soviets shoot down U.S. U-2 spy plane over the Soviet Union.
Paris summit conference collapses over the incident.
The Congo becomes independent from Belgium, causing the first superpower crisis in sub-Saharan Africa.
UN forces sent to the Congo to help resolve the crisis.
France becomes an atomic power.
John F. Kennedy wins presidential election.

1961 Kennedy launches abortive Bay of Pigs invasion of Cuba.
Kennedy proposes Alliance for Progress for Latin America.
Soviets send Yuri Gagarin into orbital spaceflight.
Kennedy holds summit conference with Khrushchev in Vienna.
Kennedy sends first military advisers to South Vietnam.
Soviets build Berlin Wall.

1962 United States sends John Glenn into orbital spaceflight.
In Cuban missile crisis, the United States blockades Cuba to compel the Soviets to withdraw their missiles.
Chinese-Indian frontier conflict erupts.

1963 French president Charles de Gaulle vetoes Britain's entry into the Common Market.
"Hot line" established between the White House and the Kremlin for direct emergency communications.
Atomic test ban treaty is signed.
President Kennedy is assassinated; vice president Lyndon B. Johnson succeeds him.

1964 Congress passes Gulf of Tonkin resolution, raising the U.S. commitment to the defense of South Vietnam.
Khrushchev falls from power and is replaced by Prime Minister Aleksei Kosygin and Communist Party Secretary Leonid Brezhnev.

1965 United States starts bombing North Vietnam and sends American land forces into South Vietnam.
Antiwar protests start.
United States intervenes in the Dominican Republic.
War erupts between Pakistan and India.

1966 People's Republic of China becomes a nuclear power.
France withdraws its forces from NATO's integrated command structure but remains a member of the alliance.

1967 Six-Day War takes place between Israel and its Arab neighbors.
Greek colonels seize power in Greece.

1968 Tet offensive in South Vietnam escalates demand for U.S. withdrawal from Vietnam.
Johnson withdraws from presidential race.
Richard Nixon elected president.
Vietnamese peace talks begin in Paris.

Nuclear Non-Proliferation Treaty (NPT) is negotiated.
Soviet Union intervenes in Czechoslovakia to quell revolt.

1969 Brezhnev Doctrine is proclaimed, asserting the right of Soviet Union to intervene in Soviet sphere to suppress "counterrevolution."
U.S. Senate narrowly approves antiballistic missile (ABM) deployment.
United States tests multiple independently targeted reentry vehicle (MIRV).
Strategic Arms Limitation Talks (SALT) begin.
"Vietnamization" program starts. South Vietnamese are to do more of the fighting while the United States begins troop withdrawal.
North Vietnamese leader Ho Chi Minh dies.
United States lands men on the moon.
Lt. William Calley Jr. stands trial for My Lai massacre of civilians in South Vietnam by U.S. troops.
First of several Sino-Soviet border clashes occurs.

1970 West Germany, East Germany, the Soviet Union, and Poland conclude treaties recognizing Poland's western border and acknowledging Germany's division into East and West Germany.
U.S. Senate repeals Gulf of Tonkin resolution.
U.S. invasion of Cambodia causes widespread student protests, which escalate after National Guard kills four students at Kent State University.
Chile elects Salvador Allende, a Marxist, president.

1971 India and Pakistan go to war over the Bangladesh (East Pakistan) secession effort.
People's Republic of China joins UN.
Four-power Berlin settlement is reached, ensuring Western access to Berlin.

1972 Nixon visits communist China, beginning a process of normalizing relations after two decades of hostility.
North Vietnam invades South Vietnam.
Nixon retaliates by expanding air war against North Vietnam and blockading the harbor of Haiphong.
Nixon visits Moscow for summit conference with Soviet leaders; signs SALT I and ABM Treaty.
Watergate affair starts when police arrest five men who had broken into Democratic Party headquarters.
Soviets buy enormous quantities of U.S. grain, raising domestic prices in the United States.
Paris peace talks, close to success, break down; the United States bombs North Vietnam heavily during Christmas season.
Nixon reelected president in a landslide that carried every state but Massachusetts

1973 Henry Kissinger is appointed secretary of state while remaining the president's national security adviser.
Vietnamese peace agreement is signed.
United States and China establish liaison offices, or informal embassies, in Washington and Beijing.
Yom Kippur War breaks out in Middle East.
Arab members of the Organization of Petroleum Exporting Countries (OPEC) embargo oil to the United States because of U.S. support for Israel.
Britain, Denmark, and Republic of Ireland join Common Market, increasing membership to nine countries.

OPEC quadruples oil prices.
U.S.-Soviet Mutual and Balanced Force Reductions talks start in Europe.
West and East Germany exchange recognition and ambassadors, acknowledging Germany's division into two countries.
U.S. Congress passes the War Powers Resolution over Nixon's veto.
Vice President Spiro T. Agnew resigns; U.S. House leader Gerald R. Ford succeeds him.
Allende is overthrown by military in Chile.

1974 India detonates "peaceful" nuclear device.
U.S. Congress asserts right to veto large arms sales to other nations.
Annual Nixon-Brezhnev summit conference further reduces small numbers of ABMs the United States and Soviet Union are allowed by SALT I.
Kissinger negotiates first agreements between Israel and Egypt and Syria as part of his "step-by-step" diplomacy intended to achieve a comprehensive regional peace.
Nixon visits Egypt, Syria, and Israel.
Nixon, upon threat of impeachment, resigns, and Ford becomes unelected president. New York governor Nelson A. Rockefeller becomes vice president.
Ford and Brezhnev set Vladivostok guidelines for SALT II negotiations.

1975 Soviet Union rejects U.S.-Soviet trade agreement because of the Jackson-Vanik amendment.
South Vietnam collapses; a unified communist Vietnam is established.
Cambodia falls to Cambodian communists.
Cambodians seize U.S. merchant ship *Mayaguez*; the United States reacts forcefully to free crew and ship.
SEATO dissolves itself.
Helsinki agreements, including Western recognition of Europe's division (and Soviet domination in Eastern Europe), arrived at by Western and Eastern states.
In Angola, three major factions struggle for control as Portugal grants independence.

1976 Soviet-Cuban forces in Angola win victory for Marxist-led faction over pro-Western factions.
Communist Chinese leader Mao Zedong dies.
Jimmy Carter elected president.

1977 Carter announces U.S. withdrawal from South Korea (to be reversed later).
Soviets denounce Carter's human rights campaign as violation of Soviet sovereignty.
Carter submits new SALT II plan to Soviet Union, which quickly rejects it because it is not based on Vladivostok guidelines.
United States and Panama sign Panama Canal treaties.
Menachem Begin is elected prime minister in Israel.
Egyptian president Anwar Sadat pays historic visit to Israel, offering peace and friendship. He is denounced by other Arab states.

1978 Soviet-Cuban military intervention in Ethiopia's war against Somalia forces Somalian troops out of Ogaden.
Soviet-inspired coup occurs in Afghanistan.
At Camp David, representatives of the United States, Israel, and Egypt arrive at "framework for peace" between Israel and Egypt. Other Arab states denounce framework because it does not provide for a Palestine solution.
U.S. Senate approves Panama Canal treaties.

1979 Shah Mohammad Reza Pahlavi leaves Iran.

United States officially recognizes the People's Republic of China; it then suspends formal relations with Taiwan government and ends mutual defense treaty.

China invades Vietnam to punish it for the invasion of Cambodia.

Shah's regime in Iran is replaced by Islamic republic led by Ayatollah Ruhollah Khomeini.

U.S. embassy in Tehran is seized and employees are held hostage by militant Islamic students after shah is hospitalized in United States for cancer treatment.

United States freezes Iran's financial assets in United States and boycotts Iranian oil.

Oil prices shoot upward as Iranian oil production drops and world supplies tighten.

SALT II treaty signed by Brezhnev and Carter at Vienna summit conference.

Soviets send eighty thousand troops into Afghanistan to ensure survival of pro-Soviet regime.

NATO decides to deploy 572 theater nuclear weapons to counter Soviet "Eurostrategic" missile buildup.

1980 U.S. mission to rescue hostages in Tehran ends in disaster before it reaches embassy.

SALT II "temporarily" withdrawn from Senate by Carter after Soviet invasion of Afghanistan.

Carter embargoes shipments of feed grain and high technology to Soviet Union; declares United States will boycott Summer Olympic Games in Moscow.

Carter Doctrine commits United States to security of Persian Gulf oil-producing states if they are externally threatened.

United States organizes rapid deployment force to back up the Carter Doctrine.

Iraq attacks Iran, sparking an eight-year war of attrition between the two nations.

Ronald Reagan elected president.

1981 U.S. hostages released moments after Reagan assumes presidency.

Reagan declares United States will not allow Saudi Arabia to become "another Iran."

Begin reelected in Israel.

Sadat assassinated in Egypt.

Reagan decides on large program to rebuild U.S. military power, including 100 MX missiles and 100 B-1 bombers.

Polish government imposes martial law.

United States imposes economic sanctions on Poland and on Soviet Union, believed to be behind Polish crackdown.

1982 Reagan announces economic assistance plan for Caribbean Basin (the Caribbean and Central America) as he supports El Salvador's government against rebel forces and attempts to isolate the Sandinistas in Nicaragua despite congressional criticism.

Israel invades Lebanon, attempting to destroy the Palestine Liberation Organization (PLO).

U.S. Marines are sent into Beirut as part of a multinational peacekeeping force to supervise the PLO's departure.

China and the United States sign agreement on the reduction of U.S. arms sales to Taiwan.

Brezhnev dies and is succeeded by Yuri Andropov, former head of the Soviet secret police.

Argentina invades the British Falkland Islands, long claimed by Argentina. Britain reconquers the islands.

1983 Reagan denounces the Soviet Union as an "evil empire."

Bipartisan Scowcroft Commission recommends deployment of 100 MX missiles and the eventual replacement of missiles equipped with MIRVs with mobile, smaller missiles with single warheads. Congress accepts these recommendations.

Catholic bishops in pastoral letter decry nuclear deterrence for its immorality. French bishops endorse deterrence as "service to peace."

Two hundred and forty-one marines are killed in truck-bomb suicide attack on their barracks in Beirut.

Soviet Union shoots down Korean 747 jetliner with 269 passengers aboard after it strays into Soviet airspace.

U.S. forces, together with troops from six Caribbean states, invade the island of Grenada. They depose the Marxist government, return Cuban worker-soldiers to Cuba, and withdraw.

United States begins deployment of Pershing II and ground-launched cruise missiles in Europe. Soviet Union responds by breaking off all arms control talks.

1984 Bipartisan Kissinger Commission recommends extensive economic and military assistance to Central America to combat domestic poverty and Soviet-Cuban intervention. Congress is critical of administration policy.

Andropov dies; Brezhnev's confidant, Konstantin Chernenko, succeeds him.

Reagan is reelected.

United States pulls marines out of Lebanon.

Napoléon Duarte wins Salvadoran presidency, defeating right-wing candidate.

Congress cuts off all military assistance to the contras in Nicaragua.

United States declares Iran a supporter of international terrorism.

1985 Chernenko dies and is succeeded by Mikhail Gorbachev.

Africa, especially Ethiopia, which is engaged in a civil war, suffers from widespread starvation.

Christian Democratic Party, led by Duarte, wins majority in Salvadoran National Assembly.

Various terrorist groups hijack a TWA plane flying from Athens to Rome, seize an Italian cruise ship, and attack Israel's El Al passengers at the Vienna and Rome airports.

Reagan orders limited economic sanctions against South Africa; Congress imposes harsher sanctions in 1986.

Reagan and Gorbachev hold their first summit conference in Geneva, Switzerland.

1986 Ferdinand Marcos in the Philippines and Jean-Claude Duvalier in Haiti are forced to flee their respective countries; the Reagan administration proclaims its new human rights policy, opposing dictatorships of the left and right.

United States attacks Libya for terrorist acts.

World's worst nuclear accident takes place at Chernobyl in Ukraine. Sweden breaks news of radioactivity coming from the Soviet Union.

Reagan and Gorbachev meet in Iceland; Reagan refuses to trade limitations in Strategic Defense Initiative (SDI) research for deep cuts of Soviet strategic missiles and a mutual elimination of all intermediate-range missiles in Europe.

United States exceeds SALT II limits and declares that the unratified 1979 treaty is no longer "operational."

Iran-contra scandal breaks.
OPEC's oil price falls to $9–$10 a barrel, but then stabilizes at $18 a barrel.
Spain and Portugal join the European Economic Community (EEC).

1987 Congressional hearings into Iran-contra scandal raise doubts about Reagan's effectiveness for the remainder of his term.
United States and Soviet Union agree to a worldwide ban on short- and intermediate-range missiles (double zero option), ending years of tension over Soviet SS-20 missile deployment.
United States reflags Kuwaiti oil tankers in the Persian Gulf and escorts them with U.S. warships to protect them from Iranian attacks.
Five Central American presidents devise a plan for peace in their region. The contras and Sandinistas are to negotiate an end to the civil war; the Sandinista government commits itself to hold a general election by spring 1990.
Palestinians begin the *intifada,* or uprising, protesting the continued Israeli occupation of the West Bank, opposition to a Palestinian state, and the PLO failure to seek a diplomatic solution.
Gorbachev denounces Stalin's historical legacy and defends his own program of *perestroika* at the seventieth anniversary celebration of the Bolshevik revolution.

1988 George H. W. Bush is elected president.
Gorbachev proposes democratic reforms of Soviet government.
U.S. Navy shoots down Iranian commercial jetliner with 290 people aboard over Persian Gulf.
Iran and Iraq agree to a cease-fire in their eight-year war.
Panama's strongman, Gen. Manuel Noriega, is indicted for drug running by two Florida grand juries.
PLO and Yasir Arafat declare the right of all states in the region to live in peace with secure boundaries, proclaim a Palestinian state in the West Bank and the Gaza Strip, recognize Israel, and reject terrorism.
Soviet Baltic republics assert their desire for autonomy, if not independence; ethnic clashes in the southern Soviet Union between Azerbaijanis and Armenians lead to increasing violence.
Gorbachev announces unilateral military reductions.

1989 Gorbachev elected president of the Soviet Union.
Free elections in Poland result in repudiation of the Polish Communist Party.
Hungary allows emigration to the West. Mass demonstrations in East Germany protest a regime celebrating its fortieth year; cabinet resigns. Hard-line Communist Party leaders are replaced.
Czechoslovakia and Bulgaria follow the reformist path of Poland, Hungary, and East Germany. Only in Romania does the government resist and use force, but its leader, Nicolae Ceausescu, is overthrown and executed nevertheless.
Soviet Union withdraws its troops from Afghanistan.
Speaking from neutral Finland, Gorbachev states that the Soviet Union has no moral or political right to interfere in the affairs of its neighbors.
Ayatollah Khomeini dies in Iran.
Huge pro-democracy demonstrations in Beijing are violently suppressed by the communist leadership.
Berlin Wall is opened, beginning process of German reunification.
Panamanian general Noriega voids result of national election. United States overthrows Noriega and brings him to the United States for trial on narcotics-trafficking charges.

1990 Lithuanian Communist Party breaks from the Soviet party and speaks for independent Lithuania.

Gorbachev sends in the Soviet army to Azerbaijan to restore order and keep the Communist Party in power.

Gorbachev renounces the communist monopoly of power in the Soviet Union and declares his support for a multiparty system and private enterprise.

Eastern European free elections in the spring produce noncommunist governments, except in Romania and Bulgaria, where the communists, under a new name, win by large majorities.

Iraqi troops invade neighboring Kuwait, provoking condemnation and economic sanctions by UN.

East and West Germany reunify. New government remains part of NATO.

Soviet Union's two largest republics, Russia and Ukraine, declare their sovereignty and assert that their laws are superior to those of the Soviet Union. Other republics follow.

Nicaraguan government agrees to free election and loses to rival coalition. The contras disband.

1991 Iraq, refusing to withdraw from Kuwait, is forced out in forty-three days by a U.S.-led UN coalition.

United States and Soviet Union sign a Strategic Arms Reduction Talks (START) agreement, reducing strategic weapons by 30 percent.

Warsaw Treaty Organization is formally dissolved. Soviet troops leave Hungary and Czechoslovakia.

Boris Yeltsin, Gorbachev's rival, becomes the first elected leader of the thousand-year-old Russian republic.

Gorbachev's political opponents launch coup. Yeltsin defies the coup attempt and it fails. Gorbachev survives, but his authority declines further as Yeltsin establishes his primacy versus Soviet leaders.

Estonia, Latvia, and Lithuania are granted independence. After efforts to establish a confederation fail, Russia, Belarus, and Ukraine declare the Soviet Union dead and form the Commonwealth of Independent States. Other republics are invited to join.

European Free Trade Association, consisting of Austria, Finland, Liechtenstein, Sweden, and Switzerland (neutrals during the Cold War), and Norway and Iceland (NATO members), establishes a common free trade area with the European Community (EC).

Soviet Union dissolves. Gorbachev resigns and cedes the Kremlin to Yeltsin.

Slovenia and Croatia secede from Yugoslavia. Serb-dominated Yugoslav army resists secessions with force.

1992 Government of El Salvador reaches accord with Farabundo Marti Liberation Front (FMLN), ending decade of civil war.

U.S. government begins forcible repatriation of Haitian refugees. Joint military force for Commonwealth of Independent States established.

UN peacekeeping troops intervene in Balkans. Voters in Bosnia-Herzegovina approve independence by referendum. EC and United States recognize Bosnia-Herzegovina along with independent Croatia and Slovenia. UN offers membership to all three countries; Yugoslavia expelled by General Assembly.

Members of the EC ratify the Maastricht Treaty, designed to move the now-named European Union (EU) beyond economic integration toward creation of a common foreign and security policy.

U.S. Senate and Russian Supreme Soviet ratify START agreement.

U.S. and German governments announce plan by the industrialized powers (known as the G-7) to provide Russia with $24 billion in economic aid.

NATO announces final removal of all ground-based tactical nuclear weapons from Europe.

Asia-Pacific Economic Cooperation (APEC) group announces program of liberalized and expanded trade within region.

Philippine government gains control of Subic Bay Naval Base from United States, ending century of American presence in country.

Bill Clinton elected president on platform of domestic reform.

1993 EU initiates single market.

United States and Russia approve new START treaty calling for deeper cuts in strategic arms.

Terrorist bomb damages World Trade Center, killing six people and forcing the evacuation of fifty thousand.

North Korean government announces withdrawal from Nuclear Non-Proliferation Treaty.

United States pledges to accelerate efforts to restore deposed Haitian leader Jean-Bertrand Aristide to power. UN Security Council imposes economic sanctions against Haitian military regime.

United States endorses Vance-Owen plan to partition the former Yugoslavia along ethnic lines. United States airdrops relief supplies to besieged Bosnian Muslims.

Twelve American soldiers are killed in Mogadishu, Somalia. Clinton orders reinforcements and sets timetable for U.S. withdrawal.

Israel and PLO sign peace treaty.

U.S. Congress ratifies North American Free Trade Agreement (NAFTA).

South African government approves new constitution, abolishing apartheid and setting agenda for national elections.

1994 United States and Japan reach agreement on future bilateral trade. United States suspends linkage between bilateral trade and China's behavior in human rights.

Assassination of Rwandan president sparks genocide as Hutu militias rampage across Rwanda and Burundi, killing nearly one million Tutsi citizens.

North Korean leader Kim Il-Sung dies and is replaced by his son, Kim Jong-Il. North Korea agrees to freeze its nuclear weapons program in exchange for economic and technological assistance from the United States and other countries.

The Uruguay Round of the General Agreement on Tariffs and Trade (GATT) yields multilateral trade pact.

Cuban refugees launch new boatlift to Florida coast. U.S. and Cuban governments reach agreement on future emigration levels.

Scandinavian states (except Norway) agree to join EU.

United States begins "semi-permissive" occupation of Haiti.

Iraqi armed forces amass along Kuwaiti border. U.S. forces are deployed to Persian Gulf to deter invasion.

UN announces plans to withdraw from Somalia by March 1995; it cites continuing clan warfare as reason for suspension of efforts.

Midterm elections bring collapse of Democratic majority in U.S. Congress.

1995 Russian troops reclaim control of Grozny, Chechnya's capital, after secession attempt.

United States provides $10 billion in loan guarantees to prevent collapse of Mexican economy.

NATO launches air strikes against Serbian forces after Serbs seize "safe havens" in Srebenica and Zepa and attack civilians in Sarajevo.

Massacre of Israeli citizens by Islamic terrorists threatens to undermine peace accord between Israel and PLO. Israeli prime minister Yitzhak Rabin is assassinated and is succeeded by Benjamin Netanyahu of rival Likud Party.

Muslim and Croatian forces launch successful offensive against Serbs, changing balance of power in region. All sides convene in Dayton, Ohio, and agree to cease-fire, temporary NATO occupation, and formation of new Bosnian government.

United States threatens trade war against China over Beijing's alleged violations of international copyright laws.

1996 U.S. Congress ratifies START II accord with Russia.

United States deploys naval forces to region in response to Chinese military provocations in Taiwan Straits.

Control over peacekeeping mission in Haiti is transferred from United States to UN.

United States deploys naval forces to free foreign nationals trapped in Liberia.

President Clinton and Russian president Boris Yeltsin meet in Moscow with leaders of Western industrial democracies.

Boris Yeltsin is reelected president of Russia.

Iraq intervenes in Kurdish-held territories considered off-limits by Western powers. United States responds with aerial attacks on Iraqi military installations.

Clinton signs Comprehensive Test Ban Treaty and encourages other states to enter the agreement, which prevents nuclear testing.

Ethnic violence spreads from Rwanda and Burundi to other parts of Central Africa. Massive refugee population threatens political stability in region.

Clinton is elected to second term, defeating former senator Bob Dole.

U.S. government leads effort to replace UN secretary-general Boutros Boutros-Ghali with Ghana's Kofi Annan.

1997 Chinese leader Deng Xiaoping dies, leading to uncertain period of political transition.

United States rejects authority of World Trade Organization (WTO) over threatened U.S. economic sanctions against Cuba.

Clinton and Boris Yeltsin meet in Helsinki, Finland, and agree to new round of nuclear weapons reductions, labeled START III.

Israel announces plans for new Jewish settlements in East Jerusalem, setting off violent demonstrations by Palestinians and new threats to peace process.

British Labour Party leader Tony Blair replaces Conservative John Major as prime minister.

Devaluation of Thailand's currency sparks East Asian economic crisis. which soon spreads to Russia and the West.

Congress ratifies Chemical Weapons Convention, already signed by most other governments.

Czech Republic, Hungary, and Poland are invited to join NATO. Russian government approves security charter with NATO that calls for consultations and limited security cooperation.

Chinese government assumes control of Hong Kong, a former British colony.

1998 Pope John Paul II, visiting Cuba for the first time, criticizes Fidel Castro's communist government and the ongoing U.S. economic sanctions against Cuba.

Attacks by the Kosovo Liberation Army against Serbian police prompt a military crackdown in the Yugoslav province of Kosovo.

President Clinton visits six African countries and denounces past U.S. support for dictatorships on the continent.

With assistance from U.S. mediators, a landmark peace settlement is reached in Northern Ireland that paves the way for greater self-government in the British-held territory.

Eleven Western European countries agree to adopt a common currency, the euro, which will become the basis of foreign exchange in 1999.

Underground nuclear tests conducted by India and Pakistan provoke worldwide condemnation.

Suharto, Indonesia's long-reigning military dictator, relinquishes power after thirty-two years.

Clinton visits China. He vows to maintain close economic ties between the two countries but presses Beijing to improve its human rights record.

Iraqi leaders suspend cooperation with UN weapons inspectors.

U.S. embassies in Kenya and Tanzania are bombed in terrorist attacks. The United States retaliates by bombing suspected terrorist bases in Sudan and Afghanistan.

North Korea fires a three-stage ballistic missile over Japan as a demonstration of its military capabilities.

Gen. Augusto Pinochet, the former Chilean dictator, is arrested in London at the request of a Spanish judge who hopes to try Pinochet on charges of crimes against humanity.

Israeli and Palestinian leaders meet at Wye River Plantation in Maryland to begin "final-status" negotiations on possible Palestinian statehood.

American bombers strike Iraqi military headquarters, intelligence agencies, and weapons plants in response to Saddam Hussein's defiance of UN weapons inspections.

U.S. House of Representatives votes to impeach President Clinton for his role in a White House sex scandal, but he remains in office after the U.S. Senate fails to convict him on charges of perjury and obstruction of justice.

1999 On its fiftieth anniversary, NATO expands to include the Czech Republic, Hungary, and Poland.

NATO bombers conduct aerial assaults against hundreds of targets in Serbia. Yugoslav president Slobodan Milosevic responds by expelling more than one million ethnic Albanians from Kosovo. Continued NATO bombings force Milosevic to allow refugees to return and place Kosovo under the supervision of UN and NATO peacekeepers.

Ehud Barak, leader of Israel's Labor Party, is elected prime minister and pledges to seek a "true, lasting peace" between Israel and its neighbors.

Nelson Mandela completes five-year term as president of South Africa and is replaced by Thabo Mbeki of the African National Congress.

Residents of East Timor vote overwhelmingly to secede from Indonesia. An attempt by the Indonesian government to prevent secession with military force prompts the UN to deploy peacekeepers to East Timor.

Russian troops escalate their crackdown against separatists in Chechnya.

U.S. Senate rejects the Comprehensive Test Ban Treaty signed by Clinton in 1996 and by the leaders of more than 150 foreign governments.

Protesters disrupt annual meetings of the WTO in Seattle.

U.S. troops, along with human rights monitors from the UN and Organization of American States, abandon peacekeeping mission in Haiti.

Yeltsin resigns as Russian president and names Prime Minister Vladimir Putin as his successor.

2000 Voters in Taiwan elect secessionist candidate Chen Shui-bian president.

Leaders of North Korea and South Korea agree to hold the first-ever summit meeting between the two countries.

Seven African presidents seek help from UN in halting civil war in the Democratic Republic of the Congo. Turmoil in Sierra Leone also requires intervention by UN peacekeepers.

U.S. government pledges more than $1 billion to support Colombia's efforts to stem the flow of illegal narcotics.

Russian legislators ratify START II and the Comprehensive Test Ban Treaty, but threaten to abrogate both treaties if the United States builds an antiballistic missile system.

EU endorses Chinese entry into WTO. U.S. Congress votes to establish permanent normal trade relations with China.

Israeli troops withdraw from buffer zone in southern Lebanon, which they had occupied since 1978.

United States signs trade accord with Vietnam.

Terrorist attack on USS *Cole* kills seventeen and wounds thirty-seven American sailors.

World leaders attending UN's Millennium Summit approve sweeping measures to reduce global poverty by 2015.

George W. Bush is declared winner of closely contested presidential election.

2001 Scottish court convicts Libya's Baset al-Megrahi of 1988 terrorist bombing of Pan Am Flight 103 over Lockerbie, Scotland.

Ariel Sharon, a former military leader and head of the right-wing Likud Party, is elected Israel's prime minister.

U.S. nuclear submarine accidentally strikes Japanese fishing boat during training exercise, killing ten fishermen.

Bush announces he will not seek Senate ratification of the Kyoto Protocol.

U.S. Navy plane makes a forced landing in China after colliding with Chinese jet during surveillance mission. The American crew is detained in China for nearly two weeks.

United States is denied a seat on UN Human Rights Commission.

Former Yugoslav president Slobodan Milosevic is extradited to The Hague for trial on charges of war crimes by international tribunal.

Russian and Chinese leaders sign friendship and cooperation agreement.

U.S. and Israeli delegations walk out of the UN-sponsored World Conference Against Racism in protest of attempts by other delegates to equate Zionism with racism.

On September 11, Islamic terrorists hijack four U.S. passenger jets and use them to destroy the World Trade Center in New York City and to damage the Pentagon near Washington, D.C. The fourth jet crash-lands in Pennsylvania. The attacks kill thousands and spark a U.S. war on terrorism.

Letters laced with anthrax spores are mailed to several federal offices, media outlets, and other locations. Five people are killed.

Bush signs USA PATRIOT Act, a wide-ranging measure designed to strengthen domestic security.

United States invades Afghanistan, routing the Taliban regime from power and disrupting al Qaeda, the terrorist group linked to the September 11 attacks.

Suicide bombings by Palestinian terrorists prompt Israeli leaders to escalate military offensive against Palestinian Authority.

Bush announces U.S. intent to withdraw from 1972 ABM Treaty with Russia.

2002 U.S. Special Forces deployed to Philippines to assist in government crackdown against Islamic terrorists linked to al Qaeda.

In State of the Union address, Bush declares Iran, Iraq, and North Korea to be part of an "axis of evil" that also includes private terrorist groups.

Muslims in India set fire to train filled with Hindu nationalists, killing fifty-seven and injuring hundreds more.
U.S. forces launch Operation Anaconda in eastern Afghanistan but fail to apprehend Osama bin Laden, leader of al Qaeda.
Bush orders higher tariffs on foreign steel to protect domestic producers.
Venezuelan populist Hugo Chavez resigns amid national uprising, but returns to power after interim government fails. Ensuing general strike cripples oil industry.
United States and Russia agree to deeper cuts in their nuclear arsenals over next ten years.
Hamid Karzai is elected to two-year term as president of interim government in Afghanistan.
U.S. Congress approves resolution that calls for the disarmament of Iraq, by force if necessary.
Terrorists linked to al Qaeda bomb two nightclubs in Bali, Indonesia, killing nearly two hundred.
UN Security Council votes 15–0 to require Iraqi government to disarm and submit to a new round of weapons inspections. Resolution 1441 threatens "serious consequences" if Iraq does not comply.

2003 North Korea withdraws from Nuclear Non-Proliferation Treaty.
UN weapons inspectors report that Iraq is not fully complying with Resolution 1441.
Ariel Sharon is returned to power in Israeli elections.
Space shuttle *Columbia* breaks up while reentering atmosphere. All seven astronauts are killed.
Secretary of State Colin Powell makes case to UN Security Council for a possible war against Iraq. Most other council members remain opposed to military action.
Hu Jintao becomes president of China, replacing Jiang Zemin.
United States and Britain lead invasion of Iraq and overthrow Saddam Hussein. Iraq placed under U.S. military control amid widespread looting and a growing insurgency.
First Palestinian prime minister, Mahmoud Abbas, takes office.
United States, along with EU, Russia, and UN, propose "roadmap" for peace between Israel and Palestinians.
Iran is found to be developing materials that could be used for nuclear weapons.
NATO assumes control of peacekeeping force in Afghanistan.
Terrorist attacks in Istanbul, Turkey, kill more than fifty and injure hundreds.
Bush suspends higher tariffs on foreign steel in response to pressure from WTO.
U.S. troops in Iraq capture Saddam Hussein.
Earthquake in Iran kills an estimated 40,000 people.

2004 Inspectors in Iraq conclude no weapons of mass destruction (WMDs) are present.
Bomb attacks on commuter trains in Madrid, Spain, kill more than two hundred. Subsequent elections bring Socialist Party to power and withdrawal from Iraq coalition.
NATO admits seven new members: Bulgaria, Estonia, Latvia, Lithuania, Romania, Slovakia, and Slovenia.
U.S. forces lay siege to Fallujah, an insurgent stronghold in Iraq, and eventually take control of the city.
Photographs of U.S. prisoner abuses at Abu Ghraib prison in Iraq provoke anti-American protests.

EU grows to twenty-five member states with addition of Cyprus, Czech Republic, Estonia, Hungary, Poland, Latvia, Lithuania, Malta, Slovakia, and Slovenia.

U.S. government transfers control of Iraq to interim government.

Senate Intelligence Committee finds prewar estimates of Iraqi WMDs were "overstated."

U.S. commission faults government response to September 11 terrorist attacks.

UN Security Council orders Sudanese government to end massacres against civilians. Secretary of State Colin Powell declares government actions genocide.

Armed militants seize school in Russia and hold more than twelve hundred hostages. Attempted rescue by Russian forces leaves most hostages dead or wounded.

Bush eases trade restrictions on Libya.

Bush defeats Democratic senator John Kerry in November presidential elections.

Palestinian leader Yasir Arafat dies in Paris.

Presidential elections in Ukraine are marred by charges of fraud.

Powerful earthquake beneath Indian Ocean triggers tsunami that kills more than 220,000 and destroys coastal communities across southern Asia and Oceania.

2005 More than eight million Iraqi citizens vote in parliamentary elections amid widespread violence.

Israeli and Palestinian officials declare truce.

Syria linked to assassination of former Lebanese prime minister Rafik Hariri.

Kyoto Protocol on global warming goes into effect without U.S. participation.

Paul D. Wolfowitz, former deputy defense secretary, becomes president of World Bank.

Pope John Paul II dies and is succeeded by Cardinal Joseph Ratzinger (Pope Benedict XVI).

John Negroponte is confirmed as first U.S. director of national intelligence.

Voters in France and the Netherlands reject proposed EU constitution, leading to suspension of ratification process.

Terrorist attacks in London kill fifty-six commuters and injure more than seven hundred.

United States and India reach agreement on development of India's nuclear energy program without renunciation of its nuclear weapons.

Bush approves "recess appointment" of John Bolton as U.S. ambassador to UN.

Hurricane Katrina, the most destructive natural disaster in U.S. history, ravages the Gulf Coast and leaves much of New Orleans under water.

Massive earthquake near Pakistan-India border kills more than eighty thousand and leaves more than three million homeless.

Special prosecutor indicts I. Lewis "Scooter" Libby, chief of staff to Vice President Dick Cheney, for leaking identity of undercover CIA agent to news media.

Summit meeting of Western Hemisphere leaders fails to produce agreement on Free Trade Area of the Americas.

Rioting among French immigrants prompts government to declare state of emergency.

Voters in Iraq approve constitution and elect permanent National Assembly as death toll among U.S. forces surpasses two thousand.

2006 Israeli prime minister Ariel Sharon suffers severe stroke and, while in a coma, is replaced by acting prime minister Ehud Olmert.

Hamas, a Palestinian political party with a long history of terrorist attacks, wins parliamentary elections and assumes control of Palestinian Authority.

UN Human Rights Commission calls for closing U.S. detention center at Guantánamo Bay, Cuba, citing widespread reports of torture of suspected terrorists.

U.S. government renews USA PATRIOT Act with modest changes.

Congress rejects sale of six U.S. port facilities to company based in Dubai.

Iranian government announces it has enriched enough uranium to fuel nuclear power plants.

State visit to Washington by Chinese president Hu Jintao produces pledges of mutual security and economic cooperation.

Bush suggests that U.S. forces will remain in Iraq beyond his presidency.

Russian leaders reject Vice President Dick Cheney's criticism of their human rights record.

U.S. National Security Agency (NSA) acknowledges monitoring millions of domestic phone calls while tapping international phone conversations of suspected al Qaeda supporters.

United States fortifies Mexican border to restrict illegal immigration.

Abu Musab al-Zarqawi, leader of al Qaeda in Iraq, is killed by American airstrikes.

Select Bibliography

The following bibliographic entries are books. Readers who wish to keep up with the journal literature on American foreign policy will find the articles in *Foreign Affairs*, *Foreign Policy*, *World Politics*, *International Organization*, and *International Security* useful and relevant.

AMERICAN SOCIETY AND STYLE IN FOREIGN POLICY

Almond, Gabriel A. *The American People and Foreign Policy.* New York: Praeger, 1960.

Bacevich, Andrew J. *The New American Militarism.* New York: Oxford University Press, 2005.

Boorstin, Daniel J. *The Genius of American Politics.* Chicago: Phoenix Books, 1953.

Boot, Max. *The Savage Wars of Peace.* New York: Basic Books, 2002.

Brands, H. W. *What America Owes the World.* New York: Cambridge University Press, 1998.

Dallek, Robert. *The American Style of Foreign Policy.* New York: Knopf, 1983.

Hartz, Louis. *The Liberal Tradition in America.* New York: Harvest Books, 1955.

Hofstadter, Richard. *The Paranoid Style in American Politics.* New York: Vintage Books, 1967.

Holsti, Ole R. *Public Opinion and American Foreign Policy.* Ann Arbor: University of Michigan Press, 1996.

Hunt, Michael H. *Ideology and U.S. Foreign Policy.* New Haven, Conn.: Yale University Press, 1987.

Huntington, Samuel P. *Who Are We? The Challenges to America's Identity.* New York: Simon and Schuster, 2004.

Ignatieff, Michael, ed. *American Exceptionalism and Human Rights.* Princeton, N.J.: Princeton University Press, 2005.

Kaplan, Amy. *The Anarchy of Empire in the Making of U.S. Culture.* Cambridge, Mass.: Harvard University Press, 2003.

Kaplan, Robert D. *Imperial Grunts.* New York: Random House, 2005.

Kennan, George F. *American Diplomacy, 1900–1950.* Chicago: University of Chicago Press, 1951.

Lieven, Anatol. *America Right or Wrong.* New York: Oxford University Press, 2004.

Lippmann, Walter. *U.S. Foreign Policy: Shield of the Republic.* Boston: Little, Brown, 1943.

Lipset, Seymour Martin. *American Exceptionalism.* New York: Norton, 1996.

McDougall, Walter A. *Promised Land, Crusader State.* Boston: Houghton Mifflin, 1997.

McElroy, Robert W. *Morality and American Foreign Policy.* Princeton, N.J.: Princeton University Press, 1992.

Mead, Walter Russell. *Special Providence.* New York: Knopf, 2001.

Merry, Robert W. *Sands of Empire.* New York: Simon and Schuster, 2005.

Michlethwait, John, and Adrian Wooldridge. *The Right Nation.* New York: Penguin Press, 2004.

Morgenthau, Hans J. *In Defense of the National Interest.* New York: Knopf, 1951.

Osgood, Robert. *Ideals and Self-Interest in America's Foreign Relations.* Chicago: University of Chicago Press, 1953.

Perlmutter, Amos. *Making the World Safe for Democracy.* Chapel Hill: University of North Carolina Press, 1997.

Potter, David M. *The People of Plenty.* Chicago: Phoenix Books, 1954.

Smith, Tony. *America's Mission.* Princeton, N.J.: Princeton University Press, 1994.

Trubowitz, Peter. *Defining the National Interest.* Chicago: University of Chicago Press, 1998.

Tucker, Robert W. *The Purposes of American Power.* New York: Praeger, 1981.

Walzer, Michael. *Arguing about War.* New Haven, Conn.: Yale University Press, 2004.
Weigel, George. *American Interests, American Purpose.* New York: Praeger, 1989.

AMERICAN FOREIGN POLICY DURING THE COLD WAR

Aron, Raymond. *The Imperial Republic.* Cambridge, Mass.: Winthrop, 1974.
Bearden, Milt, and James Risen. *The Main Enemy.* New York: Random House, 2003.
Bell, Coral. *The Diplomacy of Detente.* New York: St. Martin's Press, 1977.
Brzezinski, Zbigniew. *Game Plan.* Boston: Atlantic Monthly Press, 1986.
Dukes, Paul. *The Last Great Game.* New York: St. Martin's Press, 1989.
Ehrman, John. *The Eighties.* New Haven, Conn.: Yale University Press, 2005.
Fulbright, J. William. *The Arrogance of Power.* New York: Vintage Books, 1967.
___. *The Crippled Giant.* New York: Vintage Books, 1972.
___. *Old Myths and New Realities.* New York: Vintage Books, 1964.
Gaddis, John Lewis. *The Long Peace.* New York: Oxford University Press, 1987.
___. *Russia, the Soviet Union and the United States.* New York: Wiley, 1978.
___. *Strategies of Containment.* New York: Oxford University Press, 1982.
___. *The United States and the Origins of the Cold War, 1941–1947.* New York: Columbia University Press, 1972.
___. *We Now Know: Rethinking Cold War History.* New York: Oxford University Press, 1997.
Grossman, Andrew D. *Neither Dead nor Red.* New York: Routledge, 2001.
Halle, Louis J. *The Cold War as History.* New York: Harper and Row, 1967.
Hoffmann, Stanley. *Gulliver's Troubles, or the Setting of American Foreign Policy.* New York: McGraw-Hill, 1968.
Kissinger, Henry. *Crisis: The Anatomy of Two Major Foreign Policy Crises.* New York: Simon and Schuster, 2003.
Larson, Deborah Welch. *Origins of Containment.* Princeton, N.J.: Princeton University Press, 1985.
Leffler, Melvyn P. *A Preponderance of Power.* Stanford, Calif.: Stanford University Press, 1992.
Mandelbaum, Richard, and Strobe Talbott. *Reagan and Gorbachev.* New York: Vintage Books, 1987.
Matlock, Jack F., Jr. *Reagan and Gorbachev: How the Cold War Ended.* New York: Random House, 2004.
Moskin, Robert J. *Mr. Truman's War.* New York: Random House, 1996.
Muravchik, Joshua. *The Uncertain Crusade.* New York: Hamilton Press, 1985.
Schlesinger, Arthur, Jr. *The Imperial Presidency.* Boston: Houghton Mifflin, 1973.
Schulzinger, Robert D. *The Wise Men of Foreign Affairs.* New York: Columbia University Press, 1985.
Steel, Ronald. *Pax Americana.* New York: Viking Press, 1967.
Taubman, Philip. *Secret Empire.* New York: Simon and Schuster, 2003.
Yergin, Daniel. *Shattered Peace.* Boston: Houghton Mifflin, 1977.

AMERICAN FOREIGN POLICY AFTER THE COLD WAR

Allman, T. D. *Rogue State: America at War with the World.* New York: Nation Books, 2004.
Anonymous. *Imperial Hubris: Why the West Is Losing the War on Terror.* Washington, D.C.: Brassey's, 2004.
Brawley, Mark R. *Afterglow or Adjustment?* New York: Columbia University Press, 1999.
Caraley, Demetrios J., ed. *The New American Interventionism.* New York: Columbia University Press, 1999.
Chace, James. *The Consequences of the Peace.* New York: Oxford University Press, 1992.

Select Bibliography

Chase, Robert, et al., eds. *The Pivotal States.* New York: Norton, 1999.

Clark, Ian. *The Post–Cold War Order.* New York: Oxford University Press, 2001.

Cox, Michael. *U.S. Foreign Policy after the Cold War.* London: Pinter, 1995.

Cyr, Arthur I. *After the Cold War.* New York: New York University Press, 1997.

Daalder, Ivo H., and James M. Lindsay. *America Unbound.* Washington, D.C.: Brookings, 2003.

De Blij, Harm J. *Why Geography Matters: Three Challenges Facing America.* New York: Oxford University Press, 2005.

Ferguson, Niall. *Colossus: The Price of America's Empire.* New York: Penguin, 2004.

Fukuyama, Francis. *America at the Crossroads.* New Haven, Conn.: Yale University Press, 2006.

Gaddis, John Lewis. *The United States and the End of the Cold War.* New York: Oxford University Press, 1992.

Garten, Jeffrey E. *A Cold Peace.* New York: Times Books, 1992.

Garthoff, Raymond. *The Great Transition.* Washington, D.C.: Brookings, 1994.

Gray, Colin. *War, Peace, and Victory.* New York: Simon and Schuster, 1990.

Haass, Richard N. *The Opportunity: America's Moment to Alter History's Course.* New York: Public Affairs, 2005.

Halberstam, David. *War in a Time of Peace.* New York: Scribner, 2001.

Hirsh, Michael. *At War with Ourselves.* New York: Oxford University Press, 2003.

Hoffmann, Stanley. *World Disorders.* Lanham, Md.: Rowman and Littlefield, 1998.

Hogan, Michael J., ed. *The End of the Cold War.* New York: Cambridge University Press, 1992.

Honey, Martha, and Tom Barry, eds. *Global Focus: U.S. Foreign Policy at the Turn of the Millennium.* New York: St. Martin's Press, 2000.

Hyland, William G. *Clinton's World.* Westport, Conn.: Praeger, 1999.

Ikenberry, G. John, ed. *America Unrivaled.* Ithaca, N.Y.: Cornell University Press, 2002.

Kanter, Arnold, and Linton F. Brooks, eds. *U.S. Intervention Policy for the Post–Cold War World.* New York: Norton, 1995.

Kapstein, Ethan B., and Michael Mastanduno, eds. *Unipolar Politics: Realism and State Strategies after the Cold War.* New York: Columbia University Press, 1999.

Kissinger, Henry. *Does America Need a Foreign Policy?* New York: Simon and Schuster, 2001.

Kitfield, James. *War and Destiny.* Washington, D.C.: Potomac Books, 2005.

Kupchan, Charles A. *The End of the American Era.* New York: Knopf, 2002.

Legro, Jeffrey W. *Rethinking the World: Great Power Strategies and International Order.* Ithaca, N.Y.: Cornell University Press, 2005.

Lieber, Robert J. *The American Era.* New York: Cambridge University Press, 2005.

___, ed. *Eagle Adrift: American Foreign Policy at the End of the Century.* New York: Longman, 1997.

___, ed. *Eagle Rules? Foreign Policy and American Primacy in the Twenty-First Century.* Upper Saddle River, N.J.: Prentice Hall, 2002.

Mahbubani, Kishore. *Beyond the Age of Innocence.* New York: Public Affairs, 2005.

Mandelbaum, Michael. *The Case for Goliath.* New York: Public Affairs, 2005.

Mann, Michael. *Incoherent Empire.* London: Verso, 2003.

Mead, Walter Russell. *Power, Terror, Peace, and War: America's Grand Strategy in a World at Risk.* New York: Knopf, 2004.

Muravchik, Joshua. *The Imperative of American Leadership: A Challenge to Neo-Isolationism.* Washington, D.C.: American Enterprise Institute, 1996.

Nordlinger, Eric A. *Isolationism Reconfigured.* Princeton, N.J.: Princeton University Press, 1994.

Nye, Joseph S., Jr. *Bound to Lead.* New York: Basic Books, 1990.

___. *The Paradox of American Power.* New York: Oxford University Press, 2002.

Oberdorfer, Don. *From the Cold War to a New Era.* Baltimore: Johns Hopkins University Press, 1998.

Odom, William E., and Robert Dujarric. *America's Inadvertent Empire.* New Haven, Conn.: Yale University Press, 2004.

Prestowitz, Clyde. *Rogue Nation.* New York: Basic Books, 2003.

Prybyla, Lan S. *The American Way of Peace.* Columbia: University of Missouri Press, 2005.

Ripley, Randall B., and James M. Lindsay, eds. *U.S. Foreign Policy after the Cold War.* Pittsburgh: University of Pittsburgh Press, 1997.

Rubenstein, Alvin Z., et al., eds. *The Clinton Foreign Policy Reader.* Armonk, N.Y.: Sharpe, 2000.

Ruggie, John Gerard. *Winning the Peace.* New York: Columbia University Press, 1996.

Ruland, Jurgen, Theodor Hanf, and Eva Manske. *U.S. Foreign Policy toward the Third World: A Post–Cold War Assessment.* Armonk, N.Y.: M. E. Sharpe, 2006.

Russett, Bruce M., and John R. Oneal. *Triangulating Peace.* New York: Norton, 2001.

Scott, James M., ed. *After the End.* Durham, N.C.: Duke University Press, 1998.

Steel, Ronald. *Temptations of a Superpower.* Cambridge, Mass.: Harvard University Press, 1995.

Tucker, Robert W., and David C. Hendrickson. *The Imperial Temptation.* New York: Council on Foreign Relations, 1992.

Von Hippel, Karin. *Democracy by Force.* New York: Cambridge University Press, 2000.

Walt, Stephen M. *Taming American Power.* New York: Norton, 2005.

Wiarda, Howard J. *Cracks in the Consensus.* Westport, Conn.: Praeger, 1997.

DIPLOMATIC HISTORIES

Ambrose, Stephen E. *Rise to Globalism: American Foreign Policy since 1938.* 7th ed. rev. New York: Penguin, 1993.

Anderson, Fred, and Andrew Cayton. *The Dominion of War.* New York: Viking, 2005.

Bagby, Wesley M. *America's International Relations since World War I.* New York: Oxford University Press, 1999.

Bailey, Thomas. *A Diplomatic History of the American People.* 10th ed. Englewood Cliffs, N.J.: Prentice Hall, 1980.

Bemis, Samuel. *A Diplomatic History of the United States.* 4th ed. New York: Holt, 1955.

Clarfield, Gerard. *U.S. Diplomatic History.* 2 vols. Englewood Cliffs, N.J.: Prentice Hall, 1992.

Fleming, D. F. *The Cold War and Its Origins, 1917–1960.* 2 vols. Garden City, N.Y.: Doubleday, 1961.

Gaddis, John Lewis. *The Cold War: A New History.* New York: Penguin Press, 2005.

———. *Surprise, Security, and the American Experience.* Cambridge, Mass.: Harvard University Press, 2004.

Hannigan, Robert E. *The New World Power.* Philadelphia: University of Pennsylvania Press, 2003.

Hogan, Michael J., ed. *Paths to Power.* New York: Cambridge University Press, 2000.

Jentleson, Bruce W., and Thomas G. Paterson, eds. *The Encyclopedia of U.S. Foreign Relations.* 4 vols. New York: Oxford University Press, 1997.

Jones, Howard. *Crucible of Power: A History of American Foreign Relations from 1897.* Wilmington, Del.: Scholarly Resources, 2001.

Kissinger, Henry. *Diplomacy.* New York: Simon and Schuster, 1994.

Kunz, Diane B., ed. *The Diplomacy of the Crucial Decade.* New York: Columbia University Press, 1994.

McCormick, Thomas J. *America's Half-Century.* 2d ed. Baltimore: Johns Hopkins University Press, 1995.

McMahon, Robert J. *The Cold War: A Very Short Introduction.* New York: Oxford University Press, 2003.

Melanson, Richard A. *American Foreign Policy since the Vietnam War.* 3d ed. Armonk, N.Y.: M. E. Sharpe, 2000.

Offner, Arnold A. *Another Such Victory: President Truman and the Cold War, 1945–1953.* Stanford, Calif.: Stanford University Press, 2002.
Paterson, Thomas G. *Meeting the Communist Threat.* New York: Oxford University Press, 1989.
Rappaport, Armin. *A History of American Diplomacy.* New York: Macmillan, 1975.
Schulzinger, Robert D. *U.S. Diplomacy Since 1900.* 5th ed. New York: Oxford University Press, 2002.
Stueck, William. *Rethinking the Korean War.* Princeton, N.J.: Princeton University Press, 2004.
Winkler, Allan A. *The Cold War: A History in Documents.* 2d ed. New York: Oxford University Press, 2003.

REVISIONIST INTERPRETATIONS AND DEBATES

Alperovitz, Gar. *Atomic Diplomacy.* New York: Vintage Books, 1967.
Barnet, Richard. *Roots of War.* New York: Atheneum, 1972.
Campbell, David. *United States Foreign Policy and the Politics of Identity.* Minneapolis: University of Minnesota Press, 1992.
___. *Writing Security.* Rev. ed. Minneapolis: University of Minnesota Press, 1998.
Chomsky, Noam. *9–11.* New York: Seven Stories Press, 2002.
Gardner, Lloyd. *Architects of Illusion.* Chicago: Quadrangle Books, 1970.
Johnson, Chalmers A. *Blowback: The Costs and Consequences of American Empire.* New York: Metropolitan, 2000.
___. *The Sorrows of Empire: Militarism, Secrecy, and the End of the Republic.* New York: Metropolitan, 2004.
Johnson, Robert H. *Improbable Dangers.* New York: St. Martin's Press, 1994.
Kolko, Gabriel. *The Roots of American Foreign Policy.* Boston: Beacon Press, 1969.
Kolko, Gabriel, and Joyce Kolko. *The Limits of Power.* New York: Harper and Row, 1972.
Kwitny, Jonathan. *Endless Enemies.* New York: Penguin, 1984.
LaFeber, Walter. *The New Empire.* Ithaca, N.Y.: Cornell University Press, 1963.
Maddox, Robert J. *The New Left and the Origins of the Cold War.* Princeton, N.J.: Princeton University Press, 1973.
Melanson, Richard A. *Writing History and Making Policy.* Lanham, Md.: University Press of America, 1983.
Nieto, Clara. *Masters of War: Latin America and United States Aggression from the Cuban Revolution through the Clinton Years.* New York: Seven Stories Press, 2003.
Parenti, Michael. *Against Empire.* San Francisco: City Lights Books, 1995.
Paterson, Thomas G. *On Every Front.* New York: Norton, 1979.
Sanders, Jerry W. *Peddlers of Crisis.* Boston: South End Press, 1983.
Schrecker, Ellen, ed. *Cold War Triumphalism: The Misuse of History after the Fall of Communism.* New York: New Press, 2004.
Tucker, Robert W. *The Radical Left and American Foreign Policy.* Baltimore: Johns Hopkins University Press, 1971.
Weldes, Jutta. *Constructing National Interests.* Minneapolis: University of Minnesota Press, 1999.
Williams, William Appleman. *The Tragedy of American Diplomacy.* New York: Norton, 1988.

AMERICAN MILITARY STRATEGY

Benjamin, Daniel, and Steven Simon. *The Age of Sacred Terror.* New York: Random House, 2002.
___. *The Next Attack.* New York: Times Books, 2005.
Bloom, Mia. *Dying to Kill: The Allure of Suicide Terror.* New York: Columbia University Press, 2005.
Callahan, David. *Unwinnable Wars.* New York: Hill and Wang, 1997.

Carter, Ashton B., and William J. Perry. *Preventive Defense.* Washington, D.C.: Brookings, 1999.
Feaver, Peter D., and Richard H. Kohn, eds. *Soldiers and Civilians.* Cambridge, Mass.: MIT Press, 2001.
Freedman, Lawrence. *Deterrence.* Cambridge, UK: Polity Press, 2004.
___. *The Evolution of Nuclear Strategy.* 3d ed. New York: Palgrave Macmillan, 2003.
Gaddis, John Lewis, et al., eds. *Cold War Statesmen Confront the Bomb.* New York: Oxford University Press, 1999.
George, Alexander L., and Richard Smoke. *Deterrence in American Foreign Policy.* New York: Columbia University Press, 1974.
Hersh, Seymour M. *Chain of Command: The Road from 9/11 to Abu Ghraib.* New York: HarperCollins, 2004.
Jervis, Robert. *The Illogic of American National Strategy.* Ithaca, N.Y.: Cornell University Press, 1984.
Joes, Anthony J. *America and Guerrilla Warfare.* Lexington: University of Kentucky Press, 2000.
Johnson, Dominic D. P. *Overconfidence and War.* Cambridge, Mass.: Harvard University Press, 2004.
Kaplan, Fred. *The Wizards of Armageddon.* New York: Simon and Schuster, 1983.
Kissinger, Henry A. *Nuclear Weapons and Foreign Policy.* New York: Harper and Brothers, 1957.
Luttwak, Edward N. *The Pentagon and the Art of War.* New York: Simon and Schuster, 1985.
Naftali, Timothy J. *Blind Spot: The Secret History of American Counterterrorism.* New York: Basic Books, 2005.
O'Hanlon, Michael E. *Defense Policy Choices for the Bush Administration, 2001–05.* Washington, D.C.: Brookings, 2001.
___. *Defense Strategy for the Post-Saddam Era.* Washington, D.C.: Brookings, 2005.
Owen, Robert C., ed. *Deliberate Force.* Maxwell Air Force Base: Air University Press, 2000.
Phares, Walid. *Future Jihad.* New York: Palgrave Macmillan, 2005.
Pillar, Paul R. *Terrorism and U.S. Foreign Policy.* Washington, D.C.: Brookings, 2001.
Powell, Robert. *Nuclear Deterrence Theory.* New York: Cambridge University Press, 1990.
Power, Samantha. *"A Problem From Hell": America and the Age of Genocide.* New York: Basic Books, 2002.
Sagan, Scott D., and Kenneth N. Waltz. *The Spread of Nuclear Weapons.* New York: Norton, 1995.
Sarkesian, Sam C., et al. *U.S. National Security.* 3d ed. Boulder, Colo.: Lynne Rienner, 2002.
Schwartz, William A., and Charles Derber. *The Nuclear Seduction.* Berkeley: University of California Press, 1990.
Steinbruner, John. *Principles of Global Security.* Washington, D.C.: Brookings, 2000.
Talbott, Strobe. *Deadly Gambits.* New York: Knopf, 1984.
Taliaferro, Jeffrey W. *Balancing Risks: Great Power Intervention in the Periphery.* Ithaca, N.Y.: Cornell University Press, 2004.
Viotti, Paul R. *American Foreign Policy and National Security: A Documentary Record.* Upper Saddle River, N.J.: Pearson/Prentice Hall, 2005.
Williams, Cindy, ed. *Holding the Line: U.S. Defense Alternatives for the Early 21st Century.* Cambridge, Mass.: MIT Press, 2001.
Wilson, George C. *This War Really Matters: Inside the Fight for Defense Dollars.* Washington, D.C.: CQ Press, 2000.
Wirtz, James J., and Jeffrey A. Larsen, eds. *Rockets' Red Glare.* Boulder, Colo.: Westview Press, 2001.
Woodward, Bob. *Bush at War.* New York: Simon and Schuster, 2002.
___. *The Commanders.* New York: Simon and Schuster, 1991.
___. *Plan of Attack.* New York: Simon and Schuster, 2004.

Select Bibliography

AMERICAN POLICY IN EUROPE AND THE FORMER SOVIET UNION

Ash, Timothy Garton. *Free World: America, Europe, and the Surprising Future of the West.* New York: Random House, 2004.

Asmus, Ronald D. *Opening NATO's Door.* New York: Columbia University Press, 2002.

Balis, Christina V., and Simon Serfaty, eds. *Visions of America and Europe.* Washington, D.C.: CSIS Press, 2004.

Blaney, John W., ed. *The Successor States to the USSR.* Washington, D.C.: CQ Press, 1995.

Brenner, Michael, and Guillaume Parmentier. *Reconcilable Differences: U.S.-French Relations in the New Era.* Washington, D.C.: Brookings, 2002.

Bugajski, Janusz. *Cold Peace: Russia's New Imperialism.* Westport, Conn.: Praeger, 2004.

Cohen-Tanugi, Laurent. *An Alliance at Risk.* Baltimore: Johns Hopkins University Press, 2003.

Dawisha, Karen, and Bruce Parrott. *Russia and the New States of Eurasia.* New York: Cambridge University Press, 1994.

Dean, Jonathan. *Ending Europe's Wars.* New York: Twentieth Century Fund, 1994.

Dunlop, John B. *The Rise of Russia and the Fall of the Soviet Empire.* Princeton, N.J.: Princeton University Press, 1993.

Evangelista, Matthew, and Vittorio Emanuele Parsi, eds. *Partners or Rivals?* Milan, Italy: V&P, 2005.

Fromkin, David. *Kosovo Crossing.* New York: Free Press, 1999.

Goldgeier, James M. *Not Whether but When: The U.S. Decision to Enlarge NATO.* Washington, D.C.: Brookings, 1999.

Goldgeier, James M., and Michael McFaul. *Power and Purpose: U.S. Policy toward Russia after the Cold War.* Washington, D.C.: Brookings, 2003.

Goodby, James E. *Europe Undivided.* Washington, D.C.: U.S. Institute of Peace Press, 1998.

Gordon, Philip, and Jeremy Shapiro. *Allies at War.* New York: McGraw-Hill, 2004.

Hunter, Robert E. *The European Security and Defense Policy: NATO's Companion or Competitor.* Santa Monica, Calif.: RAND, 2002.

Jack, Andrew. *Inside Putin's Russia.* New York: Oxford University Press, 2004.

Judah, Tim. *Kosovo: War and Revenge.* New Haven, Conn.: Yale University Press, 2000.

Kagan, Robert. *Of Paradise and Power.* New York: Knopf, 2003.

Kaplan, Lawrence S. *The Long Entanglement: NATO's First Fifty Years.* Westport, Conn.: Praeger, 1999.

Kaplan, Robert D. *Balkan Ghosts.* New York: St. Martin's Press, 1993.

Keep, John. *Last of the Empires.* New York: Oxford University Press, 1996.

Laquer, Walter. *The Dream that Failed.* New York: Oxford University Press, 1994.

Lindberg, Tod, ed. *Beyond Paradise and Power.* New York: Routledge, 2005.

Lundestad, Geir. *Empire by Integration, 1945–1997.* New York: Oxford University Press, 1998.

Malia, Martin E. *Russia under Western Eyes.* Cambridge, Mass.: Belknap Press, 1999.

Mandelbaum, Michael. *The Dawn of Peace in Europe.* New York: Twentieth Century Fund, 1996.

Mayers, David A. *The Ambassadors and America's Soviet Policy.* New York: Oxford University Press, 1995.

Miller, John J., and Mark Molesky. *Our Oldest Enemy: A History of America's Disastrous Relationship with France.* New York: Doubleday, 2004.

Norris, John. *Collision Course: NATO, Russia, and Kosovo.* Westport, Conn.: Praeger, 2005.

Rieff, David. *Slaughterhouse.* New York: Simon and Schuster, 1995.

Rifkin, Jeremy. *The European Dream.* New York: Penguin, 2004.

Satter, David. *Age of Delirium.* New York: Knopf, 1996.

Shleifer, Andrei. *A Normal Country: Russia after Communism.* Cambridge, Mass.: Harvard University Press, 2005.

Simes, Dimitri K. *After the Collapse.* New York: Simon and Schuster, 1999.

Stokes, Gale. *The Walls Came Tumbling Down.* New York: Oxford University Press, 1993.
Wedel, Janine R. *Collision and Collusion.* New York: St. Martin's Press, 1998.
Wilson, Andrew. *Virtual Politics: Faking Democracy in the Post-Soviet World.* New Haven, Conn.: Yale University Press, 2005.
Yost, David. *NATO Transformed.* Washington, D.C.: U.S. Institute of Peace Press, 1998.
Zimmerman, Warren. *Origins of a Catastrophe.* New York: Times Books, 1996.
Zoellick, Robert B., and Philip D. Zelikow, eds. *America and Russia: Memos to a President.* New York: Norton, 2000.

AMERICAN POLICY IN EAST ASIA

Becker, Jasper. *Rogue Regime: Kim Jong Il and the Looming Threat of North Korea.* New York: Oxford University Press, 2005.
Bernstein, Richard, and Ross H. Munro. *The Coming Conflict with China.* New York: Knopf, 1997.
Cossa, Ralph A. *Restructuring the U.S.–Japan Alliance.* Washington, D.C.: CSIS Press, 1997.
Cumings, Bruce. *Korea's Place in the Sun.* New York: Norton, 1997.
DiLeo, David L. *George Ball, Vietnam, and the Rethinking of Containment.* Chapel Hill: University of North Carolina Press, 1991.
Fishman, Ted C. *China, Inc.* New York: Scribner, 2005.
Gardner, Lloyd C., and Ted Gittinger, eds. *Vietnam: The Early Decisions.* Austin: University of Texas Press, 1997.
Gelb, Leslie, and Richard K. Betts. *The Irony of Vietnam.* Washington, D.C.: Brookings, 1979.
Gelb, Leslie, et al. *The Pentagon Papers.* New York: Bantam Books, 1971.
Green, Michael J., and Patrick M. Cronin, eds. *The U.S.–Japan Alliance.* New York: Council on Foreign Relations Press, 1999.
Halberstam, David. *The Best and the Brightest.* New York: Random House, 1969.
Harrison, Selig S. *Korean Endgame.* Princeton, N.J.: Princeton University Press, 2002.
Hunt, Michael H. *Lyndon Johnson's War.* New York: Hill and Wang, 1996.
Karnow, Stanley C. *Vietnam.* New York: Viking Press, 1983.
Kattenburg, Paul. *The Vietnam Trauma in American Foreign Policy, 1945–1975.* New Brunswick, N.J.: Transaction Books, 1980.
Khalilzad, Zalmay, et al. *The United States and Asia.* Santa Monica,Calif.: RAND, 2001.
Kimball, Jeffrey P. *The Vietnam War Files.* Lawrence: University Press of Kansas, 2004.
Kissinger, Henry. *Ending the Vietnam War.* New York: Simon and Schuster, 2003.
Lind, Michael. *Vietnam, the Necessary War.* New York: Free Press, 1999.
Logevall, Frederik. *Choosing War.* Berkeley: University of California Press, 1999.
McMahon, Robert J., ed. *Major Problems in the History of the Vietnam War: Documents and Essays.* 3d ed. Boston: Houghton Mifflin, 2003.
Metzger, Thomas A., and Ramon H. Myers, eds. *Greater China and U.S. Foreign Policy.* Stanford, Calif.: Hoover Institution Press, 1996.
Sheehan, Neil. *A Bright Shining Lie.* New York: Random House, 1988.
Spanier, John W. *The Truman-MacArthur Controversy and the Korean War.* Rev. ed. New York: Norton, 1965.
Stokes, Mark A. *China's Strategic Modernization.* Carlisle, Pa.: U.S. Army War College, 1999.
Tucker, Nancy B., ed. *China Confidential.* New York: Columbia University Press, 2001.
___. *Dangerous Strait: The U.S.-Taiwan-China Crisis.* New York: Columbia University Press, 2005.
Wainstock, Dennis D. *Truman, MacArthur, and the Korean War.* Westport, Conn.: Greenwood Press, 1999.
Windrow, Martin. *The Last Valley: Dien Bien Phu and the French Defeat in Vietnam.* London: Weidenfeld and Nicolson, 2004.

AMERICAN POLICY IN THE MIDDLE EAST AND SOUTH ASIA

Ahrari, M. Ehsan. *Jihadi Groups, Nuclear Pakistan, and the New Great Game.* Carlisle, Pa.: U.S. Army War College, 2001.

Bensahel, Nora, and Daneil L.Byman, eds. *The Future Security Environment in the Middle East.* Santa Monica, Calif.: RAND, 2004.

Bertsch, Gary K., et al., eds. *Engaging India.* New York: Routledge, 1999.

Bill, James A. *The Eagle and the Lion.* New Haven, Conn.: Yale University Press, 1988.

Carothers, Thomas, and Marina Ottaway, eds. *Uncharted Journey: Promoting Democracy in the Middle East.* Washington, D.C.: Carnegie Endowment for International Peace, 2005.

Coll, Steve. *Ghost Wars.* New York: Penguin, 2004.

Cordesman, Anthony H. *Perilous Prospects.* Boulder, Colo.: Westview Press, 1996.

Diamond, Larry. *Squandered Victory.* New York: Times Books, 2005.

Feldman, Noah. *What We Owe Iraq.* Princeton, N.J.: Princeton University Press, 2004.

Friedman, Thomas L. *From Beirut to Jerusalem.* New York: Anchor Books, 1989.

Gasiorowski, Mark J. *U.S. Foreign Policy and the Shah.* Ithaca, N.Y.: Cornell University Press, 1991.

Gerges, Fawaz A. *America and Political Islam.* New York: Cambridge University Press, 1999.

Graham-Brown, Sarah. *Sanctioning Saddam.* New York: St. Martin's Press, 1999.

Hadar, Leon T. *Sandstorm: Policy Failure in the Middle East.* New York: Palgrave Macmillan, 2005.

Hanson, Victor David. *Between War and Peace: Lessons from Afghanistan to Iraq.* New York: Random House, 2004.

Hiro, Dilip. *Secrets and Lies: Operation "Iraqi Freedom" and After.* New York: Nation Books, 2004.

Hunter, Shireen T. *The Future of Islam and the West.* Westport, Conn.: Praeger, 1998.

Jentleson, Bruce W. *With Friends Like These.* New York: Norton, 1994.

Keegan, John. *The Iraq War.* New York: Knopf, 2004.

Kepel, Gilles. *Jihad: The Trail of Political Islam.* Cambridge, Mass.: Belknap Press, 2002.

Kux, Dennis. *India and the United States.* Washington, D.C.: National Defense University Press, 1993.

Lenczowski, George. *American Presidents and the Middle East.* Durham, N.C.: Duke University Press, 1990.

Lewis, Bernard. *What Went Wrong? Western Impact and Middle Eastern Response.* New York: Oxford University Press, 2002.

Little, Douglas. *American Orientalism: The United States and the Middle East since 1945.* Chapel Hill: University of North Carolina Press, 2002.

Mackey, Sandra. *The Reckoning: Iraq and the Legacy of Saddam Hussein.* New York: Norton, 2002.

McMahon, Robert J. *The Cold War on the Periphery.* New York: Columbia University Press, 1994.

Murray, Williamson, and Robert H. Scales Jr. *The Iraq War: A Military History.* Cambridge, Mass.: Belknap Press, 2003.

Ovendale, Ritchie. *The Origins of the Arab-Israeli Wars.* New York: Pearson Longman, 2004.

Packer, George. *The Assassins' Gate: America in Iraq.* New York: Farrar, Straus, and Giroux, 2005.

Phillips, David L. *Losing Iraq.* Boulder, Colo.: Westview Press, 2005.

Pipes, Daniel. *Militant Islam Reaches America.* New York: Norton, 2002.

Pollack, Kenneth M. *The Persian Puzzle.* New York: Random House, 2004.

Randal, Jonathan. *Osama: the Making of a Terrorist.* New York: Knopf, 2004.

Quandt, William. *Peace Process.* Washington, D.C.: Brookings, 1993.

Rashid, Ahmed. *Jihad: The Rise of Militant Islam in Central Asia.* New Haven, N.J.: Yale University Press, 2002.

___. *Taliban: Militant Islam, Oil and Fundamentalism in Central Asia.* New Haven, Conn.: Yale University Press, 2000.

Safran, Nadav. *Intifada.* New York: Simon and Schuster, 1989.

___. *Israel: The Embattled Ally.* Cambridge, Mass.: Harvard University Press, 1978.

Said, Edward W. *From Oslo to Iraq and the Road Map.* New York: Pantheon, 2004.

Sick, Gary. *All Fall Down.* New York: Penguin Books, 1986.

Sifry, Micah L., and Christopher Cerf, eds. *The Gulf War Reader.* New York: Random House, 1991.

Telhami, Shibley. *The Stakes: America and the Middle East.* Boulder, Colo.: Westview Press, 2002.

AMERICAN POLICY IN AFRICA

Anstee, Margaret Joan. *Orphan of the Cold War.* New York: St. Martin's Press, 1996.

Bowden, Mark. *Black Hawk Down.* New York: Atlantic Monthly Press, 1999.

Clarke, Walter, and Jeffrey Herbst, eds. *Learning from Somalia.* Boulder, Colo.: Westview Press, 1997.

Cohen, Herman J. *Intervening in Africa.* New York: St. Martin's Press, 2000.

Dickson, David A. *United States Foreign Policy toward Sub-Saharan Africa.* Lanham, Md.: University Press of America, 1985.

Giliomee, Hermann, and Lawrence Schlemmer. *From Apartheid to Nation Building.* New York: Oxford University Press, 1990.

Kelly, Sean. *America's Tyrant.* Washington, D.C.: American University Press, 1993.

Layachi, Azzedine. *The United States and North Africa.* New York: Praeger, 1990.

Lyman, Princeton N. *Partner to History: The U.S. Role in South Africa's Transition to Democracy.* Washington, D.C.: U.S. Institute of Peace Press, 2002.

Packenham, Robert A. *Liberal America and the Third World.* Princeton, N.J.: Princeton University Press, 1973.

Schraeder, Peter J. *United States Foreign Policy toward Africa.* New York: Cambridge University Press, 1994.

Stevenson, Jonathan. *Losing Mogadishu.* Annapolis, Md.: Naval Institute Press, 1995.

AMERICAN POLICY IN LATIN AMERICA

Bowden, Mark. *Killing Pablo.* New York: Atlantic Monthly Press, 2001.

Carpenter, Ted Galen. *Bad Neighbor Policy.* New York: Palgrave Macmillan, 2003.

Crandall, Russell. *Driven by Drugs.* Boulder, Colo.: Lynne Rienner, 2002.

Dinges, John. *Our Man in Panama.* New York: Random House, 1990.

Dominguez, Jorge I., and Rafael Fernandez de Castro. *The United States and Mexico.* New York: Routledge, 2001.

Draper, Theodore. *The Dominican Revolt.* New York: Commentary, 1968.

Gutman, Roy. *Banana Diplomacy.* New York: Simon and Schuster, 1988.

Hirst, Monica. *The United States and Brazil.* New York: Routledge, 2005.

Holden, Robert H., and Eric Zolov. *Latin America and the United States: A Documentary History.* New York: Oxford University Press, 2000.

Hufbauer, Gary Clyde, and Jeffrey J. Schott. *Western Hemisphere Economic Integration.* Washington, D.C.: Institute for International Economics, 1994.

Immerman, Robert H. *The CIA in Guatemala.* Austin: University of Texas Press, 1982.

Kelly de Escobar, Janet, and Carlos A. Romero. *The United States and Venezuela.* New York: Routledge, 2002.

LaFeber, Walter. *Inevitable Revolutions.* New York: Norton, 1983.

Lake, Anthony. *Somoza Falling.* Boston: Houghton Mifflin, 1989.

LeoGrande, William M. *Our Own Backyard.* Chapel Hill: University of North Carolina Press, 1998.

Mares, David R., and Francisco Rojas Aravena. *The United States and Chile: Coming in from the Cold War.* New York: Routledge, 2001.

McPherson, Alan. *Yankee No! Anti-Americanism in U.S.–Latin American Relations.* Cambridge, Mass.: Harvard University Press, 2003.

Pastor, Robert A. *Condemned to Repetition.* Princeton, N.J.: Princeton University Press, 1987.

___. *Whirlpool.* Princeton, N.J.: Princeton University Press, 1993.

Rabe, Stephen G. *Eisenhower and Latin America.* Chapel Hill: University of North Carolina Press, 1988.

Schlesinger, Stephen, and Stephen Kinzer. *Bitter Fruit.* Garden City, N.Y.: Anchor Books, 1982.

Schoultz, Lars. *Beneath the United States.* Cambridge, Mass.: Harvard University Press, 1998.

Schulz, Donald E. *The United States and Latin America.* Carlisle, Pa.: U.S. Army War College, 2000.

Shafer, Michael D. *Deadly Paradigms.* Princeton, N.J.: Princeton University Press, 1988.

Sigmund, Paul. *The Overthrow of Allende and the Politics of Chile.* Pittsburgh: University of Pittsburgh Press, 1977.

Smith, Peter H. *Talons of the Eagle.* 2d ed. New York: Oxford University Press, 2000.

Weintraub, Sidney. *Development and Democracy in the Southern Cone: Imperatives for U.S. Policy in South America.* Washington, D.C.: Center for Strategic and International Studies Press, 2000.

Youngers, Coletta A., and Eileen Rosin, eds. *Drugs and Democracy in Latin America: The Impact of U.S. Policy.* Boulder, Colo.: Lynne Rienner, 2005.

AMERICA AND THE INTERNATIONAL POLITICAL ECONOMY

Baldwin, David A. *Economic Statecraft.* Princeton, N.J.: Princeton University Press, 1985.

Bergsten, C. Fred, ed. *The United States and the World Economy.* Washington, D.C.: Institute for International Economics, 2005.

Cohen, Edward S. *The Politics of Globalization in the United States.* Washington, D.C.: Georgetown University Press, 2001.

Dam, Kenneth W. *The Rules of the Global Game.* Chicago: University of Chicago Press, 2001.

DeSouza, Patrick J., ed. *Economic Strategy and National Security.* Boulder, Colo.: Westview Press, 2000.

Destler, I. M. *American Trade Politics.* 2d ed. Washington, D.C.: Twentieth Century Fund, 1992.

___. *American Trade Politics.* 4th ed. Washington, D.C.: Institute for International Economics, 2005.

Gilpin, Robert. *The Challenge of Global Capitalism.* Princeton, N.J.: Princeton University Press, 2000.

Haass, Richard, ed. *Economic Sanctions and American Diplomacy.* New York: Council on Foreign Relations Press, 1998.

Haass, Richard, and Meghan L. O'Sullivan, eds. *Honey and Vinegar: Incentives, Sanctions, and Foreign Policy.* Washington, D.C.: Brookings, 2000.

Hook, Steven W. *National Interest and Foreign Aid.* Boulder, Colo.: Lynne Rienner, 1995.

Kalicki, Jan H., and David L. Goldwyn, eds. *Energy and Security.* Baltimore: Johns Hopkins University Press, 2005.

Kapstein, Ethan B. *Governing the Global Economy.* Cambridge, Mass.: Harvard University Press, 1994.

Kugler, Richard L., and Ellen L. Frost, eds. *The Global Century.* Washington, D.C.: National Defense University Press, 2001.

Kunz, Diane B. *Butter and Guns.* New York: Free Press, 1997.

Luttwak, Edward. *Turbo-Capitalism.* New York: HarperCollins, 1999.
Maren, Michael. *The Road to Hell.* New York: Free Press, 1997.
Markusen, Ann R., and Sean S. Costigan, eds. *Arming the Future.* New York: Council on Foreign Relations Press, 1999.
Pollard, Robert A. *Economic Security and the Origins of the Cold War, 1945–1950.* New York: Columbia University Press, 1985.
Prestowitz, Clyde. *Three Billion New Capitalists: The Great Shift of Wealth and Power to the East.* New York: Basic Books, 2005.
Rodman, Kenneth A. *Sanctions beyond Borders.* Lanham, Md.: Rowman and Littlefield, 2001.
Sachs, Jeffrey. *The End of Poverty.* New York: Penguin, 2005.
Shoch, James. *Trading Blows: Party Competition and U.S. Trade Policy in a Globalizing Era.* Chapel Hill: University of North Carolina Press, 2001.
Stiglitz, Joseph E. *Globalization and Its Discontents.* New York: Norton, 2002.
Stokes, Bruce, and Pat Choate. *Democratizing U.S. Trade Policy.* New York: Council on Foreign Relations Press, 2001.
Wolf, Martin. *Why Globalization Works.* New Haven, Conn.: Yale University Press, 2004.
Zakaria, Fareed. *From Wealth to Power.* Princeton, N.J.: Princeton University Press, 1998.
Zeng, Ka. *Trade Threats, Trade Wars.* Ann Arbor: University of Michigan Press, 2004.

AMERICA AND INTERNATIONAL ORGANIZATIONS

Barnett, Michael, and Martha Finnemore. *Rules for the World: International Organizations in World Politics.* Ithaca, N.Y.: Cornell University Press, 2004.
Bennis, Phyllis. *Calling the Shots.* Brooklyn, N.Y.: Olive Branch Press, 2000.
Byers, Michael, and Georg Nolte. *United States Hegemony and the Foundations of International Law.* New York: Cambridge University Press, 2003.
Frye, Alton. *Toward an International Criminal Court?* New York: Council on Foreign Relations, 1999.
Fukuyama, Francis. *State-Building.* Ithaca, N.Y.: Cornell University Press, 2004.
Holsti, K. J. *Taming the Sovereigns.* New York: Cambridge University Press, 2004.
Ikenberry, G. John. *After Victory.* Princeton, N.J.: Princeton University Press, 2001.
Keck, Margaret, and Kathryn Sikkink. *Activists beyond Borders.* Ithaca, N.Y.: Cornell University Press, 1998.
Luck, Edward C. *Mixed Messages: American Politics and International Organization, 1919–1999.* Washington, D.C.: Brookings, 1999.
Maynes, Charles William, and Richard Williamson, eds. *U.S. Foreign Policy and the United Nations.* New York: Norton, 1996.
Nye, Joseph S., Jr. *Soft Power.* New York: Public Affairs, 2004.
Patrick, Stewart, and Shepard Forman, eds. *Multilateralism and U.S. Foreign Policy.* Boulder, Colo.: Lynne Rienner, 2002.
Ruggie, John G., ed. *Multilateralism Matters.* New York: Columbia University Press, 1993.
Slaughter, Anne-Marie. *A New World Order.* Princeton, N.J.: Princeton University Press, 2004.

DOMESTIC POLITICS AND AMERICAN FOREIGN POLICY

Allison, Graham T., and Philip Zelikow. *Essence of Decision.* 2d ed. New York: Longman, 1999.
Alterman, Eric. *Who Speaks for America?* Ithaca, N.Y.: Cornell University Press, 1998.
Bamford, James. *Body of Secrets: Anatomy of the Ultra-Secret National Security Agency.* New York: Doubleday, 2001.
___. *A Pretext for War: 9/11, Iraq, and the Abuse of America's Intelligence Agencies.* New York: Doubleday, 2004.
Berkowitz, Bruce D., and Allan E. Goodman. *Best Truth: Intelligence and Security in the Information Age.* New Haven, Conn.: Yale University Press, 2000.

Select Bibliography

Bonds, John B. *Bipartisan Strategy: Selling the Marshall Plan.* Westport, Conn.: Praeger, 2002.

Crabb, Cecil V., Jr., and Pat M. Holt. *Invitation to Struggle.* 4th ed. Washington, D.C.: CQ Press, 1992.

Crabb, Cecil V., Jr., et al. *Congress and the Foreign Policy Process.* Baton Rouge: Louisiana State University Press, 2000.

Destler, I. M., Leslie H. Gelb, and Anthony Lake. *Our Own Worst Enemy.* New York: Simon and Schuster, 1984.

Dizard, Wilson P. *Digital Diplomacy.* Westport, Conn.: Praeger, 2001.

Dorrien, Gary. *Imperial Designs: Neoconservatism and the New Pax Americana.* New York: Routledge, 2004.

Foyle, Douglas C. *Counting the Public In.* New York: Columbia University Press, 1999.

Friedberg, Aaron L. *In the Shadow of the Garrison State.* Princeton, N.J.: Princeton University Press, 2000.

Halper, Stefan, and Jonathan Clarke. *America Alone.* New York: Cambridge University Press, 2004.

Halperin, Morton H. *Bureaucratic Politics and Foreign Policy.* Washington, D.C.: Brookings, 1974.

Haney, Patrick J. *Organizing for Foreign Policy Crises.* Ann Arbor: University of Michigan Press, 1997.

Henkin, Louis. *Foreign Affairs and the U.S. Constitution.* 2d ed. Oxford, UK: Clarendon Press, 1996.

Hersman, Rebecca K. C. *Friends and Foes.* Washington, D.C.: Brookings, 2000.

Herspring, Dale R. *The Pentagon and the Presidency.* Lawrence: University Press of Kansas, 2005.

Hertzke, Allern D. *Freeing God's Children: The Unlikely Alliance for Global Human Rights.* Lanham, Md.: Rowman and Littlefield, 2004.

Hess, Gary R. *Presidential Decisions for War.* Baltimore: Johns Hopkins University Press, 2001.

Hinckley, Barbara. *Less than Meets the Eye.* Chicago: University of Chicago Press, 1994.

Janis, Irving L. *Groupthink.* 2d ed. Boston: Houghton Mifflin, 1983.

Jeffreys-Jones, Rhodri. *The CIA and American Diplomacy.* New Haven, Conn.: Yale University Press, 1989.

Johnson, Loch K. *America's Secret Power.* New York: Oxford University Press, 1989.

Kull, Steven, and I. M. Destler. *Misreading the Public.* Washington, D.C.: Brookings, 1999.

Lindsay, James M. *Congress and the Politics of U.S. Foreign Policy.* Baltimore: Johns Hopkins University Press, 1994.

Lowenthal, Mark M. *Intelligence: From Secrets to Policy.* 3d ed. Washington, D.C.: CQ Press, 2006.

Mann, James. *Rise of the Vulcans.* New York: Viking, 2004.

Nathan, James A., and James K. Oliver. *Foreign Policy Making and the American Political System.* 2d ed. Boston: Little, Brown, 1987.

Nutter, John J. *The CIA's Black Ops.* Amherst, N.Y.: Prometheus Books, 2000.

Odom, William E. *Fixing Intelligence.* New Haven, Conn.: Yale University Press, 2003.

Preston, Thomas. *The President and His Inner Circle.* New York: Columbia University Press, 2001.

Ripley, Randall B., and James Lindsay. *Congress Resurgent.* Ann Arbor: University of Michigan Press, 1993.

Risen, James. *State of War: The Secret History of the CIA and the Bush Administration.* New York: Free Press, 2006.

Rothkopf, David J. *Running the World: The Inside Story of the National Security Council and the Architects of American Power.* New York: Public Affairs, 2005.

Shuman, Howard E., and Walter R. Thomas. *The Constitution and National Security.* Washington, D.C.: National Defense University Press, 1990.

Silverstein, Gordon. *Imbalance of Powers.* New York: Oxford University Press, 1997.
Snyder, Richard C., et al. *Foreign Policy Decision-Making.* Rev. ed. New York: Palgrave Macmillan, 2002.
Sobel, Richard. *The Impact of Public Opinion on U.S. Foreign Policy since Vietnam.* New York: Oxford University Press, 2001.
Stearns, Monteagle. *Talking to Strangers.* Princeton, N.J.: Princeton University Press, 1996.
Sutter, Robert G. *U.S. Policy toward China: An Introduction to the Role of Interest Groups.* Lanham, Md.: Rowman and Littlefield, 1998.
Treverton, Gregory F. *Reshaping National Intelligence in an Age of Information.* New York: Cambridge University Press, 2001.
Yetiv, Steve A. *Explaining Foreign Policy: U.S. Decision-Making and the Persian Gulf War.* Baltimore: Johns Hopkins University Press, 2004.
Zegart, Amy B. *Flawed by Design: The Evolution of the CIA, JCS, and NSC.* Stanford, Calif.: Stanford University Press, 1999.

MEMOIRS AND BIOGRAPHIES OF AMERICAN LEADERS

Acheson, Dean. *Present at the Creation.* New York: Norton, 1969.
Baker, James A., III. *The Politics of Diplomacy.* New York: Putnam, 1995.
Bill, James A. *George Ball.* New Haven, Conn.: Yale University Press, 1997.
Bird, Kai, and Martin J. Sherwin. *American Prometheus: The Triumph and Tragedy of J. Robert Oppenheimer.* New York: Knopf, 2005.
Blackman, Ann. *Seasons of Her Life: A Biography of Madeleine Korbel Albright.* New York: Scribner's, 1998.
Blix, Hans. *Disarming Iraq.* New York: Pantheon, 2004.
Bremer, L. Paul. *My Year in Iraq.* New York: Simon and Schuster, 2006.
Brinkley, Douglas, ed. *Dean Acheson and the Making of U.S. Foreign Policy.* New York: St. Martin's Press, 1993.
Brown, Harold. *Thinking about National Security.* Boulder, Colo.: Westview Press, 1983.
Brzezinski, Zbigniew. *Power and Principle.* New York: Farrar, Straus and Giroux, 1983.
Bundy, McGeorge. *Danger and Survival.* New York: Random House, 1988.
Bush, George H. W., and Brent Scowcroft. *A World Transformed.* New York: Knopf, 1998.
Carter, Jimmy. *Keeping Faith.* New York: Bantam Books, 1982.
Chace, James. *Acheson.* New York: Simon and Schuster, 1998.
Christopher, Warren. *Chances of a Lifetime.* New York: Scribner, 2001.
___. *In the Stream of History.* Stanford, Calif.: Stanford University Press, 1998.
Clarke, Richard A. *Against All Enemies: Inside America's War on Terror.* New York: Free Press, 2004.
Dallek, Robert. *Franklin D. Roosevelt and American Foreign Policy, 1932–1945.* New York: Oxford University Press, 1979.
Eisenhower, Dwight D. *Mandate for Change.* New York: New American Library, 1965.
___. *Waging Peace.* New York: Doubleday, 1965.
Endres, Anthony M. *Great Architects of International Finance.* New York: Routledge, 2005.
Feis, Herbert. *Churchill, Roosevelt, Stalin.* Princeton, N.J.: Princeton University Press, 1957.
Franks, Tommy, with Malcolm McConnell. *American Soldier.* New York: Regan Books, 2004.
Garthoff, Raymond L. *A Journey through the Cold War: A Memoir of Containment and Coexistence.* Washington, D.C.: Brookings, 2001.
Gates, Robert M. *From the Shadows.* New York: Simon and Schuster, 1996.
Guhin, Michael. *John Foster Dulles.* New York: Columbia University Press, 1972.
Hanhimaki, Jussi M. *The Flawed Architect: Henry Kissinger and American Foreign Policy.* New York: Oxford University Press, 2004.

Holbrooke, Richard C. *To End a War.* New York: Random House, 1998.
Immerman, Richard H. *John Foster Dulles and the Diplomacy of the Cold War.* Princeton, N.J.: Princeton University Press, 1990.
Isaacson, Walter. *Kissinger.* New York: Simon and Schuster, 1992.
Isaacson, Walter, and Evan Thomas. *The Wise Men.* New York: Simon and Schuster, 1986.
Johnson, Lyndon B. *The Vantage Point.* New York: Popular Library, 1971.
Kalb, Marvin, and Bernard Kalb. *Kissinger.* Boston: Little, Brown, 1974.
Kearns, Doris. *Lyndon Johnson and the American Dream.* New York: Harper and Row, 1976.
Kennan, George F. *Memoirs.* Boston: Little, Brown, 1967.
Kennedy, Robert F. *Thirteen Days.* New York: Norton, 1971.
Kissinger, Henry A. *The White House Years.* Boston: Little, Brown, 1979.
___. *Years of Upheaval.* Boston: Little, Brown, 1982.
Knock, Thomas J. *To End All Wars: Woodrow Wilson and the Quest for a New World Order.* New York: Oxford University Press, 1992.
Lippmann, Thomas W. *Madeleine Albright and the New American Diplomacy.* Boulder, Colo.: Westview Press, 2000.
Maraniss, David. *First in His Class: A Biography of Bill Clinton.* New York: Simon and Schuster, 1995.
McCullough, David. *Truman.* New York: Simon and Schuster, 1992.
McFarlane, Robert C., with Zofia Smardz. *Special Trust.* New York: Cadell and Davies, 1994.
McNamara, Robert S. *In Retrospect: The Tragedy and Lessons of Vietnam.* New York: Vintage, 1996.
Miscamble, Wilson D. *George F. Kennan and the Making of American Foreign Policy, 1947–1950.* Princeton, N.J.: Princeton University Press, 1992.
Morris, Edmund. *Dutch: A Memoir of Ronald Reagan.* New York: Random House, 1999.
Nixon, Richard. *RN.* New York: Grosset and Dunlap, 1978.
Parmet, Herbert S. *Eisenhower and the American Crusades.* New York: Macmillan, 1972.
Pogue, Forrest C. *George C. Marshall.* New York: Viking Press, 1987.
Powell, Colin L. *My American Journey.* New York: Random House, 1995.
Ross, Dennis. *The Missing Peace: The Inside Story of the Fight for Middle East Peace.* New York: Farrar, Straus, and Giroux, 2004.
Rubin, Robert E., and Jacob Weisberg. *In an Uncertain World: Tough Choices from Wall Street to Washington.* New York: Random House, 2003.
Schulzinger, Robert D. *Henry Kissinger.* New York: Columbia University Press, 1989.
Sherwood, Robert E. *Roosevelt and Hopkins.* New York: Harper, 1948.
Smith, Gaddis. *Dean Acheson.* New York: Cooper Square Publishers, 1972.
Sorensen, Theodore C. *Kennedy.* New York: Bantam Books, 1966.
Talbott, Strobe. *The Russia Hand.* New York: Random House, 2002.
Truman, Harry S. *Memoirs.* 2 vols. New York: New American Library, 1965.
Vance, Cyrus. *Hard Choices.* New York: Simon and Schuster, 1982.
Weinberger, Caspar W. *Fighting for Peace.* New York: Warner, 1990.

Select Web Sites

The following Web sites may be useful to students of American foreign policy—either as supplements to this text or as resources for research projects. This list is by no means exhaustive. It can, however, provide a gateway to related sites and sources of information. Each URL should be preceded by http://.

U.S. GOVERNMENT: EXECUTIVE BRANCH

White House (www.whitehouse.gov)
Department of Commerce (www.commerce.gov)
Department of Defense (www.defenselink.mil)
- Defense Intelligence Agency (www.dia.mil)
- Joint Chiefs of Staff (www.dtic.mil/jcs)
- North Atlantic Treaty Organization (www.nato.int)
- U.S. Air Force (www.af.mil)
- U.S. Army (www.army.mil)
- U.S. Marine Corps (www.usmc.mil)
- U.S. Navy (www.navy.mil)

Department of Homeland Security (www.dhs.gov)
- Transportation Security Administration (www.tsa.gov)

Department of State (www.state.gov)
- U.S. Agency for International Development (www.usaid.gov)

Federal Bureau of Investigation (www.fbi.gov)
Millennium Challenge Corporation (mca.gov)
National Security Agency (www.nsa.gov)
National Security Council (www.whitehouse.gov/nsc)
Office of the Director of National Intelligence (www.dni.gov)
- Central Intelligence Agency (www.cia.gov)

U.S. Mission to the United Nations (www.un.int/usa)
U.S. Trade Representative (www.ustr.gov)

U.S. GOVERNMENT: LEGISLATIVE BRANCH

Congressional Budget Office (www.cbo.gov)
Library of Congress (www.loc.gov)
- Congressional Research Service (www.loc.gov/crsinfo/)

U.S. House of Representatives (www.house.gov)
- Armed Services Committee (www.house.gov/hasc)
- International Relations Committee (www.house.gov/international_relations)

U.S. Senate (www.senate.gov)
- Armed Services Committee (www.senate.gov/~armed_services)
- Foreign Relations Committee (www.senate.gov/~foreign)

U.S. GOVERNMENT: JUDICIAL BRANCH

U.S. Court of International Trade (www.cit.uscourts.gov)
U.S. Federal Courts (www.uscourts.gov)

INTERNATIONAL GOVERNMENTAL ORGANIZATIONS

Asia-Pacific Economic Cooperation (www.apecsec.org.sg)
Association of South East Asian Nations (www.aseansec.org)
European Union (www.europa.eu.int)
International Court of Justice (www.icj-cij.org)
International Criminal Court (www.icc-cpi.int)

Select Web Sites

International Finance Corporation (www.ifc.org)
International Labor Organization (www.ilo.org)
International Monetary Fund (www.imf.org)
Organisation for Economic Co-operation and Development (www.oecd.org)
Organization of American States (www.oas.org)
Organization of Petroleum Exporting Countries (www.opec.org)
United Nations (www.un.org)
World Bank (www.worldbank.org)
World Trade Organization (www.wto.org)

INTERNATIONAL NONGOVERNMENTAL ORGANIZATIONS

AFL–CIO (www.aflcio.org)
American Israel Public Affairs Committee (www.aipac.org)
Amnesty International (www.amnesty.org)
Corporate Watch (www.corpwatch.org)
Freedom House (www.freedomhouse.org)
GreenNet (www.gn.apc.org)
Greenpeace (www.greenpeace.org)
Human Rights Watch (www.hrw.org)
International Chamber of Commerce (www.iccwbo.org)
International Committee of the Red Cross (www.icrc.org)
MoveOn.org (moveon.org)
Program on International Policy Attitudes (www.pipa.org)
Progressive Policy Institute (www.ppionline.org)
Public Citizen (www.citizen.org)
Sierra Club (www.sierraclub.org)
Stockholm International Peace Research Institute (www.sipri.org)
World Wildlife Fund (www.wwf.org)

THINK TANKS AND FOUNDATIONS

American Enterprise Institute (www.aei.org)
Brookings Institution (www.brookings.org)
Carnegie Endowment for International Peace (carnegieendowment.org)
Cato Institute (www.cato.org)
Center for Defense Information (www.cdi.org)
Council on Foreign Relations (www.cfr.org)
Economic Policy Institute (www.epinet.org)
Federation of American Scientists (www.fas.org)
Foreign Policy in Focus (www.foreignpolicy-infocus.org)
Global Policy Forum (www.globalpolicy.org)
Heritage Foundation (www.heritage.org)
National Science Foundation (www.nsf.gov)
Project for a New American Century (www.newamericancentury.org)
RAND (www.rand.org)
United States Institute of Peace (www.usip.org)

Index

Note: Page numbers followed by *f, t, p, m,* or *n* indicate figures, tables, photos, maps, and notes, respectively.

Photo Credits

Page 1	Roger L. Wollenberg/UPI/Landov
9	Courtesy of the National Archives
23	Courtesy of the National Archives
41	AP/Wide World Photos
50	Courtesy of the National Archives
66	AP/Wide World
80	Corbis/Bettmann
104	AP/Wide World
110	Courtesy of the National Archives
125	LBJ Library Collection
136	AP/Wide World
158	White House
166	Reagan Presidential Library
183	AP/Wide World Photos
193	AP/Wide World Photos
207	Reuters
246	Reuters
257	AP/Wide World
272	Reuters
287	Scott J. Ferrell, Congressional Quarterly
299	Jeff Christensen/Reuters
315	UPI Photo Service
329	AP/Wide World Photos
340	Stringer/Iraq/Reuters (left); AP/Wide World (right)
362	AP Wide World Photos
364	Dennis Brack/Landov

About the Authors

Steven W. Hook is associate professor of political science at Kent State University. He is the author of *U.S. Foreign Policy: The Paradox of World Power* (2005) and *National Interest and Foreign Aid* (1995) as well as editor of *Comparative Foreign Policy: Adaptation Strategies of the Great and Emerging Powers* (2002) and *Foreign Aid Toward the Millennium* (1996). He is a past president of the Foreign Policy Analysis sections of the American Political Science Association and the International Studies Association.

John Spanier received a PhD from Yale University. Since joining the faculty of the University of Florida in 1957, Spanier has lectured at the U.S. State Department's Foreign Service Institute, the Naval War College, military service academies, and several universities. Among his many other books is *Games Nations Play* (1996).